AP

ASSOCIATED PRESS STYLEBOOK

2012

EDITED BY

Darrell Christian
Sally Jacobsen
David Minthorn

www.apstylebook.com

Published by
THE ASSOCIATED PRESS
450 W. 33rd St.
New York, NY 10001

Library of Congress Catalog Card Number: **91-070484**
ISBN: **978-0-917360-56-5**

Design and content management by Satchmo Publishing Inc.
Printed in the United States of America
Printed by WorkflowOne
Cover design by Tina Antonion
Product management by Colleen Newvine

First Edition, August 1977
47th Edition, 2012

CONTENTS

FOREWORD

The first Associated Press Stylebook came out in 1953. It was 60 pages, stapled together, distilled from a thousand suggestions and ideas, a stack of newspapers and a big dictionary.

It proclaimed itself the "most definitive and inclusive work ever undertaken by a group of newspapers," and yet it proved to be just the start of a work that is constantly in progress.

There were major revisions in 1977 and 1986 and complete annual updates since 2008.

Far more than just a collection of rules, the book became part dictionary, part encyclopedia, part textbook — an eclectic source of information for writers and editors of any publication.

Today, the 21st-century Associated Press has become the essential global news network. And the AP Stylebook has become the essential tool for anyone who cares about good writing.

The Stylebook also is now available electronically. It continues to add entries that reflect the language of our fast-changing world. Truly, it is a tool now for wired editors as well as wire editors.

But just as the AP remains dedicated to its fundamental journalistic principles, the AP Stylebook remains committed to its original concept: to provide a uniform presentation of the printed word, to make a story written anywhere understandable everywhere.

Our thanks and appreciation go to those who have helped enrich this book by their questions and suggestions. Many entries reflect contributions by the AP staff, the AP's members and subscribers, journalism teachers and students, and specialists in a host of fields. There also have been countless contributions from everyday readers of the news who share with us a distinct pride in the clarity and precision of language.

Tom Curley

TOM CURLEY
President and
Chief Executive Officer

WHAT'S NEW

In this edition of the AP Stylebook

New sections were added on Fashion Guidelines and Broadcast Guidelines, and the Social Media Guidelines and Interactives/Graphics sections were expanded, to include AP policies and practices, plus style and terms specific to those areas.

Fashion Guidelines includes 185 entries, from A-line to Giorgio Armani, bodysuit to pantsuit to zoot suit.

Broadcast Guidelines provides a primer on differences in style and writing between print stories and radio and television stories, and adds 29 terms, including actuality, b-roll, incue/inq/in-point, live shot, lockout, LSR, MOS, sigout, voice-over, voice track and voicer.

Social Media Guidelines expands in focus as well as size (seven pages to 29). It serves as a how-to handbook on setting up accounts in social media services, and the proper use of social media for newsgathering and source-building, illustrated with practical examples from AP staffers. Section topics include digital security for journalists and how to protect privacy; searching for people and their photos and video; and the complete social media guidelines for AP employees. The Key Terms and Definitions section includes new entries on cloud, direct message and modified tweet. Other terms were modified or updated to reflect the fast-evolving world of social media.

Briefing on Media Law added sections titled Publishing on the Internet and Social Media and Material Posted To Your Site(s) by Others.

A summary of The Associated Press Statement of News Values and Principles was replaced with the complete text.

Separate conference affiliations for major college basketball and football were added to Sports Guidelines, which was updated from A to Z.

Other changes and updates include: ages, hopefully, Ku Klux Klan, PAC, peninsula, privacy, pushup/pullup/situp, race, and in Sports Guidelines: Olympics.

New entries include: Achilles tendon, concentration camps, Godspeed, fracking, hydraulic fracturing, Hells Angels, hideout, Hodgkin lymphoma, Holy Land, Huffington Post, illegitimate, individual retirement account, Islamist, Marcellus Shale, menorah, Nativity scene, OB-GYN, sexually transmitted diseases, shoutout, Sudan, underwater and year-round.

QUICK REFERENCE GUIDE

STYLEBOOK KEY

This updated and revised version of The Associated Press Stylebook has been organized like a dictionary. Need the acronym for a government agency? Look under the agency's name. Should you capitalize a word? Check the word itself or the **capitalization** entry. What's the format for baseball boxes? See **baseball**.

Following is a key to the entries:

airport Capitalize as part of a proper name: *LaGuardia Airport, O'Hare International Airport.*

The first name of an individual and the word *international* may be deleted from a formal airport name while the remainder is capitalized: *John F. Kennedy International Airport, Kennedy International Airport* or *Kennedy Airport.* Use whichever is appropriate in the context.

Do not make up names, however. There is no *Boston Airport,* for example. The *Boston airport* (lowercase *airport*) would be acceptable if for some reason the proper name, *Logan International Airport,* were not used.

Entry words, in alphabetical order, are in **boldface**. They represent the accepted word forms unless otherwise indicated.

Text explains usage.

Examples of correct and incorrect usage are in italics. AP doesn't use italics in news stories.

airstrike

airtight

air traffic controller No hyphen.

Many entries simply give the correct spelling, hyphenation and/or capitalization.

airways The system of routes that the federal government has established for airplane traffic.

See the **airline, airlines** entry for its use in carriers' names.

Related topics are in **boldface**.

aka Abbreviation for *also known as.* No spacing is an exception to Webster's New World College Dictionary.

Abbreviate indicates the correct abbreviation of a word.

Alabama Abbreviate *Ala.* in datelines or stories. Postal code: *AL*
See **state names**.

Other abbreviations used in the Stylebook:
n.: noun	**adj.:** adjective
v.: verb	**adv.:** adverb

a- The rules of **prefixes** apply, but in general no hyphen. Some examples:

achromatic   atonal

AAA Formerly the American Automobilc Association.

Headquarters is in Heathrow, Fla.

a, an Use the article *a* before consonant sounds: *a historic event, a one-year term* (sounds as if it begins with a *w*), *a united stand* (sounds like *you*).

Use the article *an* before vowel sounds: *an energy crisis, an honorable man* (the *h* is silent), *an homage* (the *h* is silent), *an NBA record* (sounds like it begins with the letter *e*), *an 1890s celebration.*

A&P Acceptable in all references for *Great Atlantic & Pacific Tea Co. Inc.* Headquarters is in Montvale, N.J.

AARP Use only the initials for the organization formerly known as the American Association of Retired Persons.

abbreviations and acronyms

A few universally recognized abbreviations are required in some circumstances. Some others are acceptable depending on the context. But in general, avoid alphabet soup. Do not use abbreviations or acronyms that the reader would not quickly recognize.

Guidance on how to use a particular abbreviation or acronym is provided in entries alphabetized according to the sequence of letters in the word or phrase.

An *acronym* is a word formed from the first letter or letters of a series of words: *laser* (light amplification by stimulated emission of radiation). An *abbreviation* is not an *acronym.*

Some general principles:

BEFORE A NAME: Abbreviate titles when used before a full name: *Dr., Gov., Lt. Gov., Mr., Mrs., Rep., the Rev., Sen.* and certain military designations listed in the **military titles** entry.

For guidelines on how to use titles, see **courtesy titles; legislative titles; military titles; religious titles;** and the entries for the most commonly used titles.

AFTER A NAME: Abbreviate *junior* or *senior* after an individual's name. Abbreviate *company, corporation, incorporated* and *limited* when used after the name of a corporate entity. See entries under these words and **company names.**

In some cases, an academic degree may be abbreviated after an individual's name. See **academic degrees.**

WITH DATES OR NUMERALS: Use the abbreviations *A.D., B.C., a.m., p.m., No.,* and abbreviate certain months when used with the day of the month.

Right: *In 450 B.C.; at 9:30 a.m.; in room No. 6; on Sept. 16.*

Wrong: *Early this a.m. he asked for the No. of your room.* The abbreviations are correct only with figures.

Right: *Early this morning he asked for the number of your room.*

See **months** and individual entries for these other terms:

IN NUMBERED ADDRESSES: Abbreviate *avenue, boulevard* and *street* in numbered addresses: *He lives on Pennsylvania Avenue. He lives at 1600 Pennsylvania Ave.*

See **addresses**.

STATES: The names of certain states and the *United States* are abbreviated with periods in some circumstances.

See **state names; datelines;** and individual entries.

ACCEPTABLE BUT NOT REQUIRED: Some organizations and government agencies are widely recognized by their initials: *CIA, FBI, GOP.*

If the entry for such an organization notes that an abbreviation is acceptable in all references or on second reference, that does not mean that its use should be automatic. Let the context determine, for example, whether to use *Federal Bureau of Investigation* or *FBI.*

See **second reference**.

AVOID AWKWARD CONSTRUCTIONS: Do not follow an organization's full name with an abbreviation or acronym in parentheses or set off by dashes. If an abbreviation or acronym would not be clear on second reference without this arrangement, do not use it.

Names not commonly before the public should not be reduced to acronyms solely to save a few words.

SPECIAL CASES: Many abbreviations are desirable in tabulations and certain types of technical writing. See individual entries.

CAPS, PERIODS: Use capital letters and periods according to the listings in this book. For words not in this book, use the first-listed abbreviation in Webster's New World College Dictionary. Generally, omit periods in acronyms unless the result would spell an unrelated word. But use periods in most two-letter abbreviations: *U.S., U.N., U.K., B.A., B.C.* (*AP*, a trademark, is an exception. Also, no periods in *GI* and *EU.*) In headlines, do not use periods in abbreviations, unless required for clarity.

Use all caps, but no periods, in longer abbreviations when the individual letters are pronounced: *ABC, CIA, FBI.*

Use only an initial cap and then lowercase for acronyms of more than six letters, unless listed otherwise in this Stylebook or Webster's New World College Dictionary.

ABC Acceptable in all references for *American Broadcasting Cos.* (the plural is part of the corporate name).

Owned by The Walt Disney Co. Divisions are *ABC News, ABC Radio* and *ABC-TV.*

ABCs

able-bodied

ABM, ABMs Acceptable in all references for *anti-ballistic missile(s)*, but the term should be defined in the story. (The hyphen is an exception to Webster's New World College Dictionary.)

Avoid the redundant phrase *ABM missiles.*

Aborigine Capitalize when referring to Australian indigenous people.

abortion Use *anti-abortion* instead of *pro-life* and *pro-abortion rights* instead of *pro-abortion* or *pro-choice*. Avoid *abortionist*, which connotes a person who performs clandestine abortions.

aboveboard

absent-minded

Abu Sayyaf Muslim separatist group based in the southern islands of the Philippines. The name is Arabic for *father of the sword*.

academic degrees If mention of degrees is necessary to establish someone's credentials, the preferred form is to avoid an abbreviation and use instead a phrase such as: *John Jones, who has a doctorate in psychology.*

Use an apostrophe in *bachelor's degree, a master's*, etc., but there is no possessive in *Bachelor of Arts* or *Master of Science*.

Also: an *associate degree* (no possessive).

Use such abbreviations as *B.A., M.A., LL.D.* and *Ph.D.* only when the need to identify many individuals by degree on first reference would make the preferred form cumbersome. Use these abbreviations only after a full name — never after just a last name.

When used after a name, an academic abbreviation is set off by commas: *John Snow, Ph.D., spoke.*

Do not precede a name with a courtesy title for an academic degree and follow it with the abbreviation for the degree in the same reference.

See **doctor, Master of Arts, Master of Science, Master of Business Administration**.

academic departments Use lowercase except for words that are proper nouns or adjectives: *the department of history, the history department, the department of English, the* *English department*, or when *department* is part of the official and formal name: *University of Connecticut Department of Economics*.

academic titles Capitalize and spell out formal titles such as *chancellor, chairman*, etc., when they precede a name. Lowercase elsewhere.

Lowercase modifiers such as *department* in *department Chairman Jerome Wiesner*.

See **doctor** and **titles**.

academy See **military academies**.

Academy Awards Presented annually by the Academy of Motion Picture Arts and Sciences. Also known as the *Oscars*. (Both *Academy Awards* and *Oscars* are trademarks.)

Lowercase *the academy* and *the awards* whenever they stand alone.

accent marks Do not use any diacritical or accent marks because they cause garble for some users.

accept, except *Accept* means to receive.
Except means to exclude.

accommodate

accounts payable Current liabilities or debts of a business which must be paid in the near future (within one year).

accounts receivable Amounts due to a company for merchandise or services sold on credit. These are short-term assets.

accused A person is *accused of*, not *with*, a crime.

To avoid any suggestion that an individual is being judged before a trial, do not use a phrase such as *accused slayer John Jones;* use *John Jones, accused of the slaying.*

For guidelines on related words, see **allege**; **arrest**; and **indict**.

Ace A trademark for a brand of elastic bandage. *Elastic bandage* is preferred in all references.

Achilles tendon No apostrophe for the tendon connecting the back of the heel to the calf muscles. But it's *Achilles' heel*, with an apostrophe, for a vulnerable spot.

acknowledgment

acquisition The process of buying or acquiring some asset. The term can refer to the purchase of a block of stock or, more often, to the acquisition of an entire company.

acre Equal to 43,560 square feet or 4,840 square yards. The metric equivalent is 0.4 (two-fifths) of a hectare or 4,047 square meters.

One square mile is 640 acres.

To convert to hectares, multiply by 0.4 (5 acres x 0.4 equals 2 hectares).

See **hectare**.

acronyms See **abbreviations and acronyms**.

act Capitalize when part of the name for pending or implemented legislation: *the Taft-Hartley Act.*

ACT Use only the initials in referring to the previously designated *American College Testing*.

acting Always lowercase, but capitalize any formal title that may follow before a name: *acting Mayor Peter Barry*.

See **titles**.

act numbers Use Arabic figures and capitalize *act*: *Act 1*; *Act 2, Scene 2*. But: *the first act, the second act.*

actor (man) **actress** (woman) It is acceptable to use *actor* for a woman if she prefers it.

Actors' Equity Association
Headquarters is in New York.

A.D. Acceptable in all references for *anno Domini*: in the year of the Lord.

Because the full phrase would read *in the year of the Lord 96*, the abbreviation *A.D.* goes before the figure for the year: *A.D. 96.*

Do not write: *The fourth century A.D. The fourth century* is sufficient. If *A.D.* is not specified with a year, the year is presumed to be A.D.

See **B.C.**

addresses Use the abbreviations *Ave., Blvd.* and *St.* only with a numbered address: *1600 Pennsylvania Ave.* Spell them out and capitalize when part of a formal street name without a number: *Pennsylvania Avenue*. Lowercase and spell out when used alone or with more than one street name: *Massachusetts and Pennsylvania avenues.*

All similar words (*alley, drive, road, terrace,* etc.) always are spelled out. Capitalize them when part of a formal name without a number; lowercase when used alone or with two or more names.

Always use figures for an address number: *9 Morningside Circle.*

Spell out and capitalize *First* through *Ninth* when used as street names; use figures for *10th* and above: *7 Fifth Ave., 100 21st St.*

Abbreviate compass points used to indicate directional ends of a street or quadrants of a city in a numbered address: *222 E. 42nd St., 562 W. 43rd St., 600 K St. NW.* Do not abbreviate if the number is omitted: *East 42nd Street, West 43rd Street, K Street Northwest.* No periods in quadrant abbreviations — NW, SE — un-

less customary locally.
See **highway designations**.
Use periods in the abbreviation
P.O. for P.O. Box numbers.

adjectives The abbreviation
adj. is used in this book to identify
the spelling of the adjectival forms
of words that frequently are misspelled.

The **comma** entry provides guidance on punctuating a series of adjectives.

The **hyphen** entry provides guidance on handling compound modifiers used before a noun.

adjustable-rate mortgage A
mortgage that has a fixed interest
rate for a short period of time and
then resets, usually yearly, over the
life of the loan, based on an index
tied to changes in market interest
rates. *ARM* should be used only in
direct quotes.

ad-lib

administration Lowercase: *the
administration, the president's administration, the governor's administration, the Bush administration.*

See **government, junta, regime**
for distinctions that apply in using
these terms and *administration*.

administrative law judge This
is the federal title for the position
formerly known as *hearing examiner*.
Capitalize it when used as a formal
title before a name.

To avoid the long title, seek a
construction that sets the title off
by commas: *The administrative law
judge, John Williams, disagreed.*

administrator Never abbreviate. Capitalize when used as a formal title before a name.
See **titles**.

admiral See **military titles**.

admissible

admit, admitted These words
may in some contexts give the erroneous connotation of wrongdoing.

A person who acknowledges
that he is a recovering alcoholic, for
example, is not *admitting* it. *Said* is
usually sufficient.

ad nauseam

adopt, approve, enact, pass
Amendments, ordinances, resolu-
tions and rules are *adopted* or *ap-
proved*.
Bills are *passed*.
Laws are *enacted*.

adoption The adoptive status of a child or his or her parents
should be mentioned only when its
relevance is made clear in the story.
Use the term *biological parents* to
refer to the birth mother and father.
Preferred phrasing: *A child is placed
for adoption*, rather than *given up for
adoption*.

Adrenalin A trademark for the
synthetic or chemically extracted
forms of epinephrine, a substance
produced by the adrenal glands.

The nonproprietary terms are
epinephrine hydrochloride or *adrena-
line*.

adult A person who has reached
18. See **privacy**.

Advance Publications Inc. Privately held company whose holdings
include Condé Nast Publications,
Parade Publications and newspapers
in more than 20 U.S. cities, including The Star-Ledger of Newark, N.J.,
and The Oregonian of Portland, Ore.
Headquarters is in Staten Island,
N.Y.

Adventist See **Seventh-day Adventist Church**.

adverbs The abbreviation *adv.* is used in this book to identify the spelling of adverbial forms of words frequently misspelled.

See the **hyphen** entry in the **Punctuation** chapter for guidelines on when an adverb should be followed by a hyphen in constructing a compound modifier.

adverse, averse *Adverse* means unfavorable: *He predicted adverse weather.*

Averse means reluctant, opposed: *She is averse to change.*

adviser Not *advisor.*

advisory

Aer Lingus Headquarters of this airline is in Dublin, Ireland.

Aeroflot Headquarters of this airline is in Moscow.

Aeromexico Headquarters of this airline is in Mexico City.

aesthetic

affect, effect *Affect*, as a verb, means to influence: *The game will affect the standings.*

Affect, as a noun, is best avoided. It occasionally is used in psychology to describe an emotion, but there is no need for it in everyday language.

Effect, as a verb, means to cause: *He will effect many changes in the company.*

Effect, as a noun, means result: *The effect was overwhelming. He miscalculated the effect of his actions. It was a law of little effect.*

Afghan The term for the people and culture of Afghanistan. *Afghani* is the *Afghan* unit of currency.

AFL-CIO Acceptable in all references for the *American Federation of Labor and Congress of Industrial Organizations.*

A-frame

African Of or pertaining to Africa, or any of its peoples or languages.

In some countries of Africa, *colored* is used to describe those of mixed white and black ancestry. In other societies *colored* is considered a derogatory word.

Because of the ambiguity, avoid the term in favor of a phrase such as *mixed racial ancestry.* If the word cannot be avoided, place it in quotation marks and provide its meaning. See **colored**.

African-American Acceptable for an American black person of African descent. Also acceptable is *black*. The terms are not necessarily interchangeable. People from Caribbean nations, for example, generally refer to themselves as *Caribbean-American*. Follow a person's preference. See **nationalities and races** and **race**.

African Union The African Union, established in 2002 to succeed the Organization of African Unity, has the following members:

Algeria, Angola, Benin, Botswana, Burkina Faso, Burundi, Cameroon, Cape Verde, Central African Republic, Chad, Comoros, Congo, Djibouti, Egypt, Equatorial Guinea, Eritrea, Ethiopia, Gabon, Gambia, Ghana, Guinea Bissau, Guinea, Ivory Coast, Kenya, Lesotho, Liberia, Libya, Madagascar, Malawi, Mali, Mauritania, Mauritius, Mozambique, Namibia, Niger, Nigeria, Republic of Congo, Rwanda, Sao Tome and Principe, Senegal, Seychelles, Sierra Leone, Somalia, South Africa, Sudan,

Swaziland, Tanzania, Togo, Tunisia, Uganda, Western Sahara, Zambia, Zimbabwe.

after- No hyphen after this prefix when it is used to form a noun:

aftereffect   afterthought

Follow *after* with a hyphen when it is used to form compound modifiers:

after-dinner drink   after-theater snack

afterward Not *afterwards*.

Agence France-Presse A global news agency with headquarters in Paris. *AFP* acceptable on second reference.

agenda A list. It takes singular verbs and pronouns: *The agenda has run its course.*

The plural is *agendas*.

agent Lowercase unless it is a formal title used before a name.

In the FBI, the formal title is *special agent*. Use *Special Agent William Smith* if appropriate in a special context. Otherwise, make it *agent William Smith* or *FBI agent William Smith*.

See **titles**.

ages Use when deemed relevant to the situation. If someone is quoted as saying, *I'm too old to get another job*, the age is relevant. Generally, use ages for profiles, obituaries, significant career milestones and achievements unusual for the age. Do not use ages for sources commenting or providing information in an official capacity. Appropriate background, such as a *mother of two young children* or a *World War II veteran*, may suffice instead of the actual age.

Always use figures. *The girl is 15 years old; the law is 8 years old; the 101-year-old house.* When the context does not require *years* or *years old*,

the figure is presumed to be *years*.

Use hyphens for ages expressed as adjectives before a noun or as substitutes for a noun.

Examples: *A 5-year-old boy*, but *the boy is 5 years old. The boy, 7, has a sister, 10. The woman, 26, has a daughter 2 months old. The race is for 3-year-olds. The woman is in her 30s* (no apostrophe).

See also **boy**; **girl**; **infant**; **youth** and **numerals**.

See **comma** in punctuation guidelines.

ages of history See **historical periods and events**.

agnostic, atheist An *agnostic* is a person who believes it is impossible to know whether there is a God.

An *atheist* is a person who believes there is no God.

aid, aide *Aid* is assistance.

An *aide* is a person who serves as an assistant.

aide-de-camp, aides-de-camp A military officer who serves as assistant and confidential secretary to a superior.

AIDS Acceptable in all references for *acquired immune deficiency syndrome*, sometimes called *acquired immunodeficiency syndrome*.

AIDS is a disease that weakens the immune system, gradually destroying the body's ability to fight infections and certain cancers. It is caused by *human immunodeficiency virus*, or *HIV*. (*HIV virus* is redundant.)

HIV is spread most often through sexual contact; contaminated needles or syringes shared by drug abusers; infected blood or blood products; and from infected women to their babies at birth or through breast-feeding.

Several types of tests are available for *HIV*. One is a blood test that looks for antibodies the body has made to defend against *HIV*. Other tests look for parts of the virus itself in blood. Avoid using *HIV/AIDS* construction. People can be infected with the virus and not have *AIDS*; they do not have *AIDS* until they develop serious symptoms. Many remain infected but apparently healthy for years.

ain't A dialectical or nonstandard contraction. Use it only in quoted matter or special contexts.

air bag Two words.

air base Two words. Follow the practice of the U.S. Air Force, which uses *air force base* as part of the proper name for its bases in the United States and *air base* for its installations abroad.

On second reference: *the Air Force base, the air base,* or *the base.*

Do not abbreviate, even in datelines:

LACKLAND AIR FORCE BASE, Texas (AP) —

Air Canada Headquarters of this airline is in Saint-Laurent, Canada.

Air China Headquarters of this airline is in Beijing.

air-condition, air-conditioned (v. and adj.) The nouns are: *air conditioner, air conditioning.*

aircraft names Use a hyphen when changing from letters to figures; no hyphen when adding a letter after figures.

Some examples of aircraft: *B-1, C-5A, FH-227, F-15 Eagle, F-16 Falcon, MiG-29, Tu-154, Il-96, Boeing 737-800, 747, 747B. Airbus A380, A380F* (no hyphen) is an exception.

This hyphenation principle is the one used most frequently by manufacturers and users. Apply it in all cases for consistency. For other elements of a name, use the form adopted by the manufacturer or user. If in doubt, consult Jane's All the World's Aircraft.

NO QUOTES: Do not use quotation marks for aircraft with names: *Air Force One, the Spirit of St. Louis.*

AVOID PROMOTIONAL NAMES: *Boeing 787,* not Dreamliner.

PLURALS: *747s.* But: *747B's.* (As noted in plurals, the apostrophe is used in forming the plural of a single letter.)

SEQUENCE: Use Arabic figures to establish the sequence of aircraft, spacecraft and missiles: *Apollo 10.* Do not use hyphens.

aircraft terms Use *engine,* not *motor,* for the units that propel aircraft: a *twin-engine* plane (not *twin engined*).

Use *jet plane* or *jetliner* to describe only those aircraft driven solely by jet engines. Use *turboprop* to describe an aircraft on which the jet engine is geared to a propeller. Turboprops sometimes are called *propjets.*

See **engine, motor**.

airfare One word.

air force Capitalize when referring to U.S. forces: *the U.S. Air Force, the Air Force, Air Force regulations.* Do not use the abbreviation *USAF.*

Congress established the Army Air Forces (note the *s*) in 1941. Prior to that, the air arm was known as the U.S. Army Air Corps. The U.S. Air Force (no *s*) was created as a separate service in 1947.

Use lowercase for the forces of other nations: *the Israeli air force.*

This approach has been adopted for consistency, because many foreign nations do not use *air force* as the proper name.

See **military academies** and **military titles**.

air force base See **air base**.

Air Force One The Air Force applies this name to any of its aircraft the president of the United States may be using.

In ordinary usage, however, *Air Force One* is the name of the Air Force plane normally reserved for the president's use.

Air France Corporate name is *Air France-KLM*. Headquarters of this airline is in Roissy, France.

Air India Headquarters of this airline is in Mumbai, India.

airline, airlines Capitalize *airlines*, *air lines* and *airways* when used as part of a proper airline name.

Companies that use *Airlines* in the title include American, Continental, Hawaiian, Japan, Southwest and United.

Companies that use *Airways* include British, JetBlue, Qantas and US.

Delta uses *Air Lines*.

Companies that use none of these include Aer Lingus, Aeromexico, Air Canada, Air France, Air India, Alitalia, Emirates and Iberia.

On second reference, use just the proper name (*Delta*), an abbreviation if applicable, or the airline. Acceptable abbreviations are *ANA* for *All Nippon Airways*, *BA* for *British Airways* and *JAL* for *Japan Airlines*. Use airlines when referring to more than one line.

Do not use *air line*, *air lines* or *airways* in generic references to an airline.

Major U.S. airlines are, with ticker symbol and headquarters:

Alaska Air Group Inc. (ALK) Seattle

Allegiant Air, owned by Allegiant Travel Co. (ALGT), Las Vegas

AMR Corp., parent of American Airlines (AMR) Fort Worth, Texas

Continental Airlines Inc. A unit of United Continental Holdings Inc., Chicago.

Delta Air Lines Inc. (DAL) Atlanta

Frontier Airlines Holdings Inc. (FRNT) Denver (now owned by Republic Airways)

JetBlue Airways Corp. (JBLU) New York

Mesa Air Group Inc. (MESA) Phoenix

Republic Airways Holdings Inc. (RJET) Indianapolis

SkyWest Inc. (SKYW) St. George, Utah

Southwest Airlines Co. (LUV) Dallas

Spirit Airlines Inc. (SAVE) Miramar, Fla.

United Continental Holdings Inc. (UAL) Chicago

US Airways Group Inc. (LCC) Tempe, Ariz.

Virgin America, Burlingame, Calif.

Major international airlines are, with U.S. ticker symbol where applicable and headquarters:

Air Canada, Saint-Laurent, Canada

Air China Ltd., Beijing

Air France-KLM, Roissy, France

Alitalia, Rome

All Nippon Airways Co. Ltd., Tokyo

British Airways PLC, Owned by holding company International Consolidated Airlines Group SA, Hounslow, England.

Cathay Pacific Airways Ltd., Hong Kong

China Eastern Airlines Corp. LTD (CEA), Shanghai

China Southern Airlines Co. Ltd. (ZNH), Guangzhou, China

Deutsche Lufthansa AG, Frankfurt, Germany

Emirates, Owned by The Emirates Group, Dubai, United Arab Emirates

Iberia, Owned by holding company International Consolidated Airlines Group SA, Hounslow, England.

Japan Airlines Corp., Tokyo

Korean Airlines Co. Ltd., Seoul, Korea

Malaysia Airlines System Berhad, Subang, Malaysia

Qantas Airways Ltd., Mascot, Australia

Ryanair Holdings PLC (RYAAY), Dublin

Singapore Airlines, Singapore

Thai Airways International PLC, Bangkok

Virgin Atlantic Airways Ltd., Crawley, England

airmail

airman See **military titles**.

Air National Guard

airport Capitalize as part of a proper name: *LaGuardia Airport, O'Hare International Airport.*

The first name of an individual and the word *international* may be deleted from a formal airport name while the remainder is capitalized: *John F. Kennedy International Airport, Kennedy International Airport,* or *Kennedy Airport.* Use whichever is appropriate in the context.

Do not make up names, however. There is no *Boston Airport,* for example. The *Boston airport* (lowercase *airport*) would be acceptable if for some reason the proper name, *Logan International Airport,* were not used.

airstrike

airtight

air traffic controller No hyphen.

airways The system of routes that the federal government has established for airplane traffic.

See the **airline, airlines** entry for its use in carriers' names.

aka Abbreviation for *also known as.* No spacing is an exception to Webster's New World College Dictionary.

Alabama Abbreviate *Ala.* in datelines or stories. Postal code: *AL*
See **state names**.

Al-Aqsa The mosque completed in the 8th century atop the Haram al-Sharif, or *Noble Sanctuary*, in the old city of Jerusalem; Arabs also use *Al-Aqsa* to refer to the whole area, which houses the Dome of the Rock shrine, too. To Jews the area is known as the *Temple Mount*, the site of the ancient Jewish temples.

Alaska Do not abbreviate in datelines or stories. Largest land area of the 50 states. Postal code: *AK*
See **state names**.

Alaska Air Group Inc. Headquarters of this airline is in Seattle. *Alaska Airlines* is subsidiary.

Alaska Standard Time The time zone used in all of Alaska, except the western Aleutian Islands and St. Lawrence Island, which are on *Hawaii-Aleutian Standard Time.*

There is also an *Alaska Daylight Time.*
See **time zones**.

Alberta A province of western Canada. Do not abbreviate.
See **datelines**.

albino, albinos

Alcoa Inc. *Alcoa* is acceptable in all references to the formerly named Aluminum Company of America.

Alcoa also is a city in Tennessee.

alcoholic Use *recovering*, not *reformed*, in referring to those who have the disease of alcoholism.

Alcoholics Anonymous *AA* is acceptable on second reference. Except for legal or official references, in accordance with the organization's policy use only first names and first initials of last names when identifying members in stories. *Joe S.* or *Jane D.*

alderman Do not abbreviate. See **legislative titles**.

alert See **weather terms**.

A-list

Alitalia Airlines Headquarters of this airline is in Rome.

Al-Jazeera Pan-Arab satellite television news network based in Doha, Qatar.

all- Use a hyphen:

all-around (not all-round)   all-out
all-clear   all-star

See **all right** and the **all time, all-time** entries.

Allah The Arabic word for God. The word *God* should be used, unless the Arabic name is used in a quote written or spoken in English.

Allahu akbar The Arabic phrase for *God is great*.

allege The word must be used with great care.

Some guidelines:

—Avoid any suggestion that the writer is making an allegation.

—Specify the source of an allegation. In a criminal case, it should

be an arrest record, an indictment or the statement of a public official connected with the case.

—Use *alleged bribe* or similar phrase when necessary to make it clear that an unproved action is not being treated as fact. Be sure that the source of the charge is specified elsewhere in the story.

—Avoid redundant uses of *alleged*. It is proper to say: *The district attorney alleged that she took a bribe.* Or: *The district attorney accused her of taking a bribe.* But not: *The district attorney accused her of allegedly taking a bribe.*

—Do not use *alleged* to describe an event that is known to have occurred, when the dispute is over who participated in it. Do not say: *He attended the alleged meeting* when what you mean is: *He allegedly attended the meeting.*

—Do not use *alleged* as a routine qualifier. Instead, use a word such as *apparent*, *ostensible* or *reputed*.

For guidelines on related words, see **accused**; **arrest**; and **indict**.

Allegheny Mountains Or simply: *the Alleghenies*.

Allegiant Air Airline is owned by Allegiant Travel Co. Headquarters is in Las Vegas.

alley Do not abbreviate. See **addresses**.

allies, allied Capitalize *allies* or *allied* only when referring to the combination of the United States and its Allies during World War I or World War II: *The Allies defeated Germany. He was in the Allied invasion of France.*

All Nippon Airways Headquarters of this airline is in Tokyo.

all right (adv.) Never *alright*. Hyphenate only if used colloquially as a compound modifier: *He is an all-right guy.*

all-terrain vehicle *ATV* is acceptable on second reference.

all time, all-time An *all-time high,* but *the greatest runner of all time.*

Avoid the redundant phrase *all-time record.*

allude, refer To *allude* to something is to speak of it without specifically mentioning it.

To *refer* is to mention it directly.

allusion, illusion *Allusion* means an indirect reference: *The allusion was to his opponent's war record.*

Illusion means an unreal or false impression: *The scenic director created the illusion of choppy seas.*

alma mater

almost never Do not use the phrase. Instead use *seldom* or *hardly ever.*

al-Qaida Headed by Osama bin Laden until his death by U.S. forces in Pakistan in May 2011.

Al-Quds The Arabic name for Jerusalem; it means *the holy.*

al-Shabab The preferred spelling for the Somali militant group.

also-ran (n.)

altar, alter An *altar* is a tablelike platform used in a religious service. To *alter* is to change.

Altria Group Inc. Headquarters is in Richmond, Va.

alumnus, alumni, alumna, alumnae Use *alumnus* (*alumni* in the plural) when referring to a man who has attended a school.

Use *alumna* (*alumnae* in the plural) for similar references to a woman.

Use *alumni* when referring to a group of men and women.

Alzheimer's disease A progressive, irreversible neurological disorder. Most victims are older than 65, but Alzheimer's can strike in the 40s or 50s.

Symptoms include gradual memory loss, impairment of judgment, disorientation, personality change, difficulty in learning and loss of language skills.

No cure is known.

AM Acceptable in all references to the *amplitude modulation* system of radio transmission.

Amalgamated Transit Union Use this full name on first reference. Headquarters is in Washington.

ambassador Use for both men and women. Capitalize as a formal title before a name.

See **titles**.

Amber Alert A procedure for rapidly publicizing the disappearance of a child.

amendments to the Constitution Use *First Amendment, 10th Amendment,* etc.

Colloquial references to the Fifth Amendment's protection against self-incrimination are best avoided, but where appropriate: *He took the Fifth seven times.*

American An acceptable description for a citizen of the United States.

American Airlines Headquarters is in Fort Worth, Texas. Parent company is AMR Corp.

American Baptist Association
See **Baptist churches**.

American Baptist Churches in the U.S.A. See **Baptist churches**.

American Bar Association
ABA is acceptable on second reference. Also: *the bar association, the association.*
Headquarters is in Chicago.

American Broadcasting Cos.
See **ABC**.

American Civil Liberties Union ACLU is acceptable on second reference.
Headquarters is in New York.

American depositary receipt
A negotiable certificate representing a foreign company's equity or debt. ADR is acceptable on second reference.

American depositary share A security issued by a foreign company representing an ownership interest in that company. It can represent a fixed number of securities on deposit, or a fraction of them. ADS is acceptable on second reference.

American Express Co. Headquarters is in New York.

American Federation of Government Employees Use this full name on first reference to prevent confusion with other unions that represent government workers. AFGE is acceptable on second reference.
Headquarters is in Washington.

American Federation of Labor and Congress of Industrial Organizations AFL-CIO is acceptable in all references.
Headquarters is in Washington.

American Federation of Musicians Use this full name on first reference.
The shortened form *Musicians' union* is acceptable on second reference.
Headquarters is in New York.

American Federation of State, County and Municipal Employees Use this full name on first reference to prevent confusion with other unions that represent government workers. AFSCME is acceptable on second reference.
Headquarters is in Washington.

American Federation of Teachers Use this full name on first reference to prevent confusion with other unions that represent teachers. AFT is acceptable on second reference.
Headquarters is in Washington.

American Federation of Television and Radio Artists AFTRA is acceptable on second reference.
Headquarters is in New York.

American Hospital Association AHA is acceptable on second reference. Also: *the hospital association, the association.*
Headquarters is in Chicago.

American International Group Inc. AIG is acceptable on second reference. Headquarters is in New York.

Americanisms Words and phrases that have become part of the English language as spoken in the United States are listed with a star in Webster's New World College Dictionary.

Most Americanisms are acceptable in news stories, but let the context be the guide.

American Legion Capitalize also *the Legion* in second reference. Members are *Legionnaires*, just as members of the Lions Club are *Lions*.

Legion and *Legionnaires* are capitalized because they are not being used in their common noun sense. A *legion* (lowercase) is a large group of soldiers or, by derivation, a large number of items: *His friends are legion.* A *legionnaire* (lowercase) is a member of such a legion.

See **fraternal organizations and service clubs**.

American Medical Association *AMA* is acceptable on second reference. Also: *the medical association, the association.*

Headquarters is in Chicago.

American Newspaper Publishers Association See **Newspaper Association of America**.

American Petroleum Institute *API* is acceptable on second reference.

Headquarters is in Washington.

American Postal Workers Union This union represents clerks and similar employees who work inside post offices.

Use the full name on first reference to prevent confusion with the National Association of Letter Carriers. The shortened form *Postal Workers union* is acceptable on second reference.

Headquarters is in Washington.

American Press Institute *API* is acceptable on second reference.

Headquarters is in Reston, Va.

American Society for the Prevention of Cruelty to Animals This organization is limited to the five boroughs of New York City and neighboring Suffolk County in providing animal adoption services, although it has offices elsewhere that offer legal advice and other services to other animal welfare organizations. *ASPCA* is acceptable on second reference.

See **Society for the Prevention of Cruelty to Animals**.

American Society of Composers, Authors and Publishers *ASCAP* is acceptable on second reference.

Headquarters is in New York.

American Stock Exchange The exchange is part of NYSE Euronext. In second reference: *the American Exchange, the Amex* or *the exchange.*

American Telephone & Telegraph Co. See **AT&T Inc**.

AmeriCorps

Amex See **American Stock Exchange**.

amid Not *amidst.*

amidships

ammunition See **weapons**.

amnesty See **pardon, parole, probation**.

amok Not *amuck.*

among, between The maxim that *between* introduces two items and *among* introduces more than two covers most questions about how to use these words: *The funds were divided among Ford, Carter and McCarthy.*

However, *between* is the correct word when expressing the relationships of three or more items considered one pair at a time: *Negotiations on a debate format are under way between the network and the Ford, Carter and McCarthy committees.*

As with all prepositions, any pronouns that follow these words must be in the objective case: *among us, between him and her, between you and me.*

ampersand (&) Use the ampersand when it is part of a company's formal name or composition title: *House & Garden, Procter & Gamble, Wheeling & Lake Erie Railway.*

The ampersand should not otherwise be used in place of *and*, except for some accepted abbreviations: *B&B, R&B.*

amplitude modulation *AM* is acceptable in all references.

a.m., p.m. Lowercase, with periods. Avoid the redundant *10 a.m. this morning.*

Amsterdam The city in the Netherlands stands alone in datelines.

Amtrak This acronym, drawn from the words *American travel by track*, may be used in all references to the *National Railroad Passenger Corp.* Do not use *AMTRAK.*

The corporation was established by Congress in 1970 to take over intercity passenger operations from railroads that wanted to drop passenger service. Amtrak contracts with railroads for the use of their tracks and of certain other operating equipment and crews.

Amtrak is subsidized in part by federal funds appropriated yearly by Congress and administered through the Department of Transportation.

Amtrak headquarters is in Washington.

AMVETS Acceptable in all references for *American Veterans*, the organization formerly known as *American Veterans of World War II, Korea, and Vietnam.*

Headquarters is in Washington.

anchorman, anchorwoman
Not *anchor* or *co-anchor.*

anemia, anemic

Anglican Communion The name for the worldwide association of the 22 national Anglican churches.

Each national church is independent. A special position of honor is accorded to the archbishop of Canterbury, as the pre-eminent officer in the original Anglican body, the Church of England.

The test of membership in the Anglican Communion traditionally has been whether a church has been in communion with the See of Canterbury. No legislative or juridical ties exist, however.

BELIEFS: Anglicans believe in the Trinity, the humanity and divinity of Christ, the virginity of Mary, salvation through Christ, and everlasting heaven and hell.

A principal difference between Roman Catholics and Anglicans is still the dispute that led to the formation of the Church of England — refusal to acknowledge that the pope, as bishop of Rome, has ruling authority over other bishops. See **catholic, catholicism**.

ANGLICAN CHURCHES: Members of the Anglican Communion, in addition to the Church of England, include the Scottish Episcopal Church, the Anglican Church of Canada, and, in the United States, the Protestant Episcopal Church.

See **Episcopal Church**.

Anglo- Always capitalized. No hyphen when the word that follows is in lowercase:

Anglomania   Anglophobe
Anglophile

Use a hyphen when the word that follows is capitalized:

Anglo-American   Anglo-Indian
Anglo-Catholic   Anglo-Saxon

angry *At* someone or *with* someone.

animals Do not apply a personal pronoun to an animal unless its sex has been established or the animal has a name: *The dog was scared; it barked. Rover was scared; he barked. The cat, which was scared, ran to its basket. Susie the cat, who was scared, ran to her basket. The bull tosses his horns.*

Capitalize the name of a specific animal, and use Roman numerals to show sequence: *Bowser, Whirlaway II.*

For breed names, follow the spelling and capitalization in Webster's New World College Dictionary. For breeds not listed in the dictionary, capitalize words derived from proper nouns; use lowercase elsewhere: *basset hound, Boston terrier.*

anniversary Avoid *first anniversary*, the redundant *one-year anniversary* and terms such as *six-month anniversary* (or other time spans less than a year). Similarly, avoid *first annual.*

anno Domini See **A.D.**

annual An event cannot be described as *annual* until it has been held in at least two successive years.

Do not use the term *first annual.* Instead, note that sponsors plan to hold an event annually.

annual meeting Lowercase in all uses.

anonymous sources Whenever possible, we pursue information on the record. When a source insists on background or off-the-record ground rules, we must adhere to a strict set of guidelines.

Under AP's rules, material from anonymous sources may be used only if:

—The material is information and not opinion or speculation, and is vital to the news report.

—The information is not available except under the conditions of anonymity imposed by the source.

—The source is reliable, and in a position to have accurate information.

Reporters who intend to use material from anonymous sources must get approval from their news managers.

Explain in the story why the source requested anonymity. And, when it's relevant, describe the source's motive for disclosing the information.

The story also must provide attribution that establishes the source's credibility; simply quoting *a source* is not allowed. Be as descriptive as possible about the source of information. If space is limited, use *source* as a last resort. *Official* or similar word will often suffice, including in headlines.

See **source**.

another *Another* is not a synonym for *additional*; it refers to an element that somehow duplicates a previously stated quantity.

Right: *Ten people took the test; another 10 refused.*

Wrong: *Ten people took the test; another 20 refused.*

Right: *Ten people took the test; 20 others refused.*

Antarctic, Antarctica, Antarctic Ocean

ante- The rules in **prefixes** apply, but in general, no hyphen. Some examples:

antebellum   antedate

anthems See **composition titles**. Lowercase the term *national anthem*.

anti- Hyphenate all except the following words, which have specific meanings of their own:

antibiotic	antipasto
antibody	antiperspirant
anticlimax	antiphon
antidepressant	antiphony
antidote	antipollution
antifreeze	antipsychotic
antigen	antiseptic
antihistamine	antiserum
antiknock	antithesis
antimatter	antitoxin
antimony	antitrust
antiparticle*	antitussive

*And similar terms in physics such as *antiproton*.

This approach has been adopted in the interests of readability and easily remembered consistency.

It's *anti-lock* in Webster's New World College Dictionary. But note these Stylebook exceptions to Webster's spellings:

anti-abortion	anti-labor
anti-aircraft	anti-social
anti-bias	anti-war
anti-inflation	

See **Antichrist, anti-Christ**.

Antichrist, anti-Christ

Antichrist is the proper name for the individual the Bible says will challenge Christ.

The adjective *anti-Christ* would be applied to someone or something opposed to Christ.

anticipate, expect

Anticipate means to expect and prepare for something; *expect* does not include the notion of preparation:

They expect a record crowd. They have anticipated it by adding more seats to the auditorium.

Antiochian Orthodox Christian Archdiocese of North America

Formed in 1975 by the merger of the Antiochian Orthodox Christian Arch-diocese of New York and All North America and the Archdiocese of Toledo, Ohio, and Dependencies in North America. It is under the jurisdiction of the patriarch of Antioch.

See **Eastern Orthodox churches**.

antitrust Any law or policy designed to encourage competition by curtailing monopolistic power and unfair business practices.

anti-virus, anti-spyware

anybody, any body, anyone, any one

One word for an indefinite reference: *Anyone can do that.*

Two words when the emphasis is on singling out one element of a group: *Any one of them may speak up.*

AOL Acceptable in all references for *AOL Inc.* The Internet company was spun off from Time Warner Inc. in 2009. Headquarters is in New York. Do not use its former name, *America Online*.

AP Acceptable on second reference for *The Associated Press*.

Do not capitalize *the* when it precedes *AP*.

See **Associated Press**.

apostolic delegate, papal nuncio

An *apostolic delegate* is a Roman Catholic diplomat chosen by the pope to be his envoy to the church in a nation that does not have formal diplomatic relations with the Vatican.

A *papal nuncio* is the pope's envoy to a nation with which the Vatican has diplomatic relations.

apostrophe (') See entry in **Punctuation** section.

app Short for application. A program that runs inside another service. Many cellphones allow *applications* to be downloaded to expand their functions. *App* is acceptable on first reference. Explain the term in the body of the story.

Appalachia In the broadest sense, the word applies to the entire region along the Appalachian Mountains, which extend from Maine into northern Alabama.

In a sense that often suggests economic depression and poverty, the reference is to sections of eastern Tennessee, eastern Kentucky, southeastern Ohio and the western portion of West Virginia.

The Appalachian Regional Commission, established by federal law in 1965, has a mandate to foster development in 397 counties in 13 states — all of West Virginia and parts of Alabama, Georgia, Kentucky, Maryland, Mississippi, New York, North Carolina, Ohio, Pennsylvania, South Carolina, Tennessee and Virginia.

When the word *Appalachia* is used, specify the extent of the area in question.

Appalachian Mountains Or simply: *the Appalachians.*

appeals court See **U.S. Court of Appeals**.

Apple Inc. Headquarters is in Cupertino, Calif.

apposition A decision on whether to put commas around a word, phrase or clause used in apposition depends on whether it is essential to the meaning of the sentence (no commas) or not essential (use commas).

See **essential phrases, nonessential phrases** for examples.

appreciation Increase in value of property, as opposed to *depreciation.*

approve See **adopt, approve, enact, pass**.

April Fools' Day

Aqua-Lung A trademark for an underwater breathing apparatus. See **scuba**.

Arabic names In general, use an English spelling that approximates the way a name sounds in Arabic.

If an individual has a preferred spelling in English, use that. If usage has established a particular spelling, use that.

Problems in transliteration of Arabic names often are traceable to pronunciations that vary from region to region. The *g*, for example, is pronounced like the *g* of *go* mainly in Egypt, and the *j* of *joy* in the rest of the Arab world. Thus it is *Gamal* in Egypt and *Jamal* in nations on the peninsula. Follow local practice in deciding which letter to use.

Arabs commonly are known by two names (*Hassan Nasrallah*), or by three (*Mohammed Mahdi Akef*). Follow the individual's preference on first reference. On second reference, use only the final name in the sequence.

The articles *al-* or *el-* may be used or dropped depending on the person's preference or established usage. (*Ayman al-Zawahri, al-Zawahri,* or *Moammar Gadhafi, Gadhafi*). The article *al-* or *el-* should not be capitalized.

The Arabic word for son (*ibn* or

bin) is sometimes part of a name. On second reference, it is often dropped, using only the final name. In cases of personal preference or common usage, it should be retained. (*Osama bin Laden, bin Laden; Abdul-Aziz bin Baz, bin Baz*).

The word *abu* or *abou*, meaning *father of*, occasionally is used as a last name (*Abdel-Halim Abou Ghazala*). Capitalize and repeat it on second reference: *Abou Ghazala*.

The word *abdul*, meaning "servant of (God)," generally does not stand alone as a name, except sometimes in South Asia and Afghanistan. It is used in combination with a second name (an Arabic word for an attribute of God). This combination should be hyphenated, unless the individual prefers otherwise, and capitalized (*Adil Abdul-Mahdi, Abdul-Mahdi*). In Egypt and some other countries, *Abdul* is often written *Abdel*, reflecting local pronunciation.

For royalty, the titles *king, emir, sheik* and *imam* are used, but *prince* usually replaces *emir*. Some Arabs are known only by the title and a given name on first reference (*King Abdullah*). Others are known by a complete name (*Sheik Mohammed bin Rashid Al Maktoum*). Follow the common usage on first reference. On second reference, drop the title and use only the first name (*Abdullah, Mohammed*). The full names of many Gulf royals include the word *Al*, which in their case should be capitalized without a hyphen since it means *family of*.

The *al* should be capitalized in front of most Muslim and Arab institutions, universities, newspapers and major mosques, as in *Al-Azhar*, the university in Cairo; *Al-Aqsa*, the Jerusalem mosque, and the newspaper *Al-Ahram*.

Arabic numerals The numerical figures 0, 1, 2, 3, 4, 5, 6, 7, 8, 9.

In general, use Arabic forms unless denoting the sequence of wars or establishing a personal sequence for people or animals. See **Roman numerals**.

Separate entries list more details and examples. For a full list, see **numerals**.

arbitrage Buying currencies, commercial bills or securities in one market and selling them at the same time in another to make a profit on the price discrepancy.

arbitrate, mediate Both terms are used in reports about labor negotiations, but they should not be interchanged.

One who *arbitrates* hears evidence from all people concerned, then hands down a decision.

One who *mediates* listens to arguments of both parties and tries by the exercise of reason or persuasion to bring them to an agreement.

arch- No hyphen after this prefix unless it precedes a capitalized word:

archbishop	arch-Republican
archenemy	archrival

archaeology

archbishop See **Episcopal Church**; **Roman Catholic Church**; and **religious titles**.

archbishop of Canterbury In general, lowercase *archbishop* unless it is used before the name of the individual who holds the office.

Capitalize *Archbishop of Canterbury* standing alone only when it is used in a story that also refers to members of Britain's nobility. See **nobility** for the relevant guidelines.

archdiocese Capitalize as part of a proper name: *the Archdiocese* *of Chicago, the Chicago Archdiocese.* Lowercase when it stands alone.

See the entry for the particular denomination in question.

arctic Lowercase for adjective meaning frigid; capitalize for region around the North Pole. **Arctic Circle, arctic fox, Arctic Ocean**

are A unit of surface measure in the metric system, equal to 100 square meters.

An *are* is equal to approximately 1,076.4 square feet or 119.6 square yards.

See **hectare** and **metric system**.

area codes See **telephone numbers**.

Argentine The preferred term for the people and culture of Argentina.

Arizona Abbreviate *Ariz.* in datelines or stories. Postal code: *AZ*
See **state names**.

Arkansas Abbreviate *Ark.* in datelines or stories. Postal code: *AR*
See **state names**.

Armenian Church of America The term encompasses two independent dioceses that cooperate in some activities: the Eastern Diocese of the Armenian Church of America, for areas outside California, and the Western Diocese of the Armenian Church of America, which serves California.

See **Eastern Orthodox Churches**.

army Capitalize when referring to U.S. forces: *the U.S. Army, the Army, Army regulations.* Do not use the abbreviation *USA.*

Use lowercase for the forces of other nations: *the French army.*

This approach has been adopted for consistency, because many foreign nations do not use *army* as the proper name.

See **military academies** and **military titles**.

arrest To avoid any suggestion that someone is being judged before a trial, do not use a phrase such as *arrested for killing.* Instead, use *arrested on a charge of killing.* If a charge hasn't been filed, *arrested on suspicion of,* or a similar phrase, should be used.

For guidelines on related words, see **accused; allege;** and **indict**.

arrive It requires the preposition *at.* Do not omit, as airline dispatchers often do in: *He will arrive LaGuardia.*

artifact

artillery See **weapons**.

artworks Lowercase impressionism, modernism and other art styles and movements unless used in formal titles of shows or exhibits with quotation marks. Exception: *Bauhaus* is capitalized as the name of a school. *Gothic, Renaissance* and other historical periods are capitalized for art and architecture from those ages. Titles of paintings are enclosed in quotes: *"Mona Lisa."* Sculptures are capitalized without quotes: *The Thinker, Michelangelo's Pieta.*

See **composition titles**.

as See **like, as**.

ASCII An acronym for *American Standard Code for Information Interchange.* A numeric code used to represent the letters of the Roman alphabet, numbers and punctuation marks. Use of the acronym on first reference is acceptable if it is identified as a code.

ashcan, ashtray

Ashoura The Shiite Muslim holiday marking the death of Hussein, the grandson of Prophet Muhammad, at the Battle of Karbala in present-day Iraq in the 7th century.

Ash Wednesday The first day of Lent, 46 days before Easter. See **Easter** and **Lent**.

Asian-American A person of Asian birth or descent who lives in the U.S. When possible, refer to a person's country of origin. For example: *Filipino-American* or *Indian-American*. Follow the person's preference. See **nationalities and races** and **race**.

Asian, Asiatic Use *Asian* or *Asians* when referring to people.

Some Asians regard *Asiatic* as offensive when applied to people.

Asian flu

Asian subcontinent In popular usage the term applies to Bangladesh, Bhutan, India, Nepal, Pakistan, Sikkim and the island nation of Sri Lanka (formerly Ceylon) at the southeastern tip of India.

For definitions of the terms that apply to other parts of Asia, see **Far East**; **Middle East**; and **Southeast Asia**.

as if The preferred form, but *as though* is acceptable.

Asperger's syndrome After Hans Asperger, an Austrian pediatrician. An autism-like disorder.

assassination Use the term only if it involves the murder of a politically important or prominent individual by surprise attack.

assassination, date of A prominent person is shot one day and dies the next. Which day was he assassinated? The day he was attacked.

assassin, killer, murderer An *assassin* is one who kills a politically important or prominent person.

A *killer* is anyone who kills with a motive of any kind.

A *murderer* is one who is convicted of murder in a court of law.

Preferred use: *Joe Smith was convicted of second-degree murder.*

See **execute** and the **homicide, murder, manslaughter** entry.

assault, battery Popularly, *assault* almost always implies physical contact and sudden, intense violence.

Legally, however, *assault* means simply to threaten violence, as in pointing a pistol at an individual without firing it. *Assault and battery* is the legal term when the victim was touched by the assaulter or something the assaulter put in motion.

assembly Capitalize when part of the proper name for the lower house of a legislature: *the California Assembly*. Retain capitalization if the state name is dropped but the reference is specific:

SACRAMENTO, Calif. (AP) — The state Assembly ...

If a legislature is known as a general assembly: *the Missouri General Assembly, the General Assembly, the assembly*. *Legislature* also may be used as the proper name, however. See **legislature**.

Lowercase all plural uses: *the California and New York assemblies*.

assemblyman, assemblywoman Do not abbreviate. See **legislative titles**.

assets Everything a company or an individual owns or is owed.

Assets may be broken down as:

Current assets: cash, investments, money due to a corporation, unused raw materials and inventories of finished but unsold products.

Fixed assets: buildings, machinery and land.

Intangible assets: patents and goodwill.

See **goodwill**.

asset-backed security A financial security backed by loans, leases, credit-card debt, royalties, a company's accounts receivables, etc. *ABS* should not be used in copy.

asset, fixed Plant, land, equipment, long-term investments that cannot be readily liquefied without disturbing the operation of the business.

assistant Do not abbreviate. Capitalize only when part of a formal title before a name: *Assistant Secretary of State Richard Boucher*. Whenever practical, however, an appositional construction should be used: *Richard Boucher, assistant secretary of state*.

See **titles**.

associate Never abbreviate. Apply the same capitalization norms listed under **assistant**.

Associated Press, The The newsgathering cooperative dating from 1846.

Use *The Associated Press* on first reference (the capitalized article is part of the formal name).

On second reference, *AP* or *the AP* (no capital on *the*) may be used.

The address is 450 W. 33rd Street, New York, NY 10001. The telephone number is 212-621-1500.

Online: http://www.ap.org

See **AP**.

Association Do not abbreviate. Capitalize as part of a proper name: *American Medical Association*.

asterisk Do not use the symbol. It rarely translates and in many cases cannot be seen by AP computers or received by newspaper or other computers.

astronaut It is not a formal title. Do not capitalize when used before a name: *astronaut John Glenn*.

AT&T Inc. The full name of the business formerly known as American Telephone & Telegraph Co. AT&T was acquired in 2005 by its former subsidiary, SBC Communications Inc., which renamed itself AT&T. Headquarters is in Dallas.

atheist See **agnostic, atheist**.

athlete's foot, athlete's heart

Atlanta The city in Georgia stands alone in datelines.

Atlantic Ocean

Atlantic Standard Time, Atlantic Daylight Time Used in the Maritime Provinces of Canada and in Puerto Rico.

See **time zones**.

at large Usually two words for an individual representing more than a single district: *congressman at large, councilman at large*.

But it is *ambassador-at-large* for an ambassador assigned to no particular country.

ATM Acceptable in all references for *automated teller machine*.

Do not use the redundant *ATM machine*.

Atomic Age It began Dec. 2, 1942, at the University of Chicago with the creation of the first self-sustaining nuclear chain reaction.

attache It is not a formal title. Always lowercase.

attorney general, attorneys general Never abbreviate. Capitalize only when used as a title before a name: *Attorney General Eric Holder*.
See **titles**.

attorney, lawyer In common usage the words are interchangeable.

Technically, however, an *attorney* is someone (usually, but not necessarily, a lawyer) empowered to act for another. Such an individual occasionally is called an *attorney in fact*.

A *lawyer* is a person admitted to practice in a court system. Such an individual occasionally is called an *attorney at law*.

Do not abbreviate. Do not capitalize unless it is an officeholder's title: *defense attorney Perry Mason, attorney Perry Mason, District Attorney Hamilton Burger*.
See **lawyer**.

attribution AP news reports must attribute facts not gathered or confirmed on our own, whether the pickup is from a newspaper, website, broadcaster or blog, U.S. or international, AP member or subscriber. AP reports must also credit other organizations when they break a story and AP matches or further develops it.

augur A transitive verb. Do not follow it with the preposition for: *The tea leaves augur a time of success.*

author A noun used for both men and women. Do not use it as a verb.

automaker, automakers

automatic See **pistol** and **weapons**.

automobiles Capitalize brand names: *Buick, Ford, Mustang, Accord, Toyota, Taurus, Saturn*. Lowercase generic terms: *Corvette convertible, Caravan minivan*.

Auto Train Rail service that carries passengers and their cars. Owned and operated by Amtrak.

autoworker, autoworkers One word when used generically.
But *United Auto Workers* when referring to the union.

autumn See **seasons**.

avenue Abbreviate only with a numbered address. See **addresses**.

average, mean, median, norm *Average* refers to the result obtained by dividing a sum by the number of quantities added together: *The average of 7, 9, 17 is 33 divided by 3, or 11.*

Mean, in its sense used in arithmetic and statistics, is an *average* and is determined by adding the series of numbers and dividing the sum by the number of cases: *The mean temperature of five days with temperatures of 67, 62, 68, 69, 64 is 66.*

Median is the middle number of points in a series arranged in order of size: *The median grade in the group of 50, 55, 85, 88, 92 is 85. The average is 74.*

Norm implies a standard of average performance for a given group: *The child was below the norm for his age in reading comprehension.*

average of The phrase takes a plural verb in a construction such as: *An average of 100 new jobs are created daily.*

averse See **adverse, averse**.

Avianca Headquarters of this airline is in Bogota, Colombia.

aviator Use for both men and women.

awards and decorations Capitalize them: *Bronze Star*, *Medal of Honor*, etc.
See **Nobel Prize** and **Pulitzer Prizes**.

awe-struck

awhile (adv.)**, a while** *He plans to stay awhile (adv.). He plans to stay for a while (n.).*

AWOL Acceptable in all references for *absent without leave*.

ax Not *axe*.
The verb forms: *ax, axed, axing*.

Axis The alliance of Germany, Italy and Japan during World War II.

Baby Bells A collective description of the regional telephone companies formed out of the breakup of the Bell System of AT&T in 1984. Avoid except in quotes.

baby boomer Lowercase, no hyphen.

baby-sit, baby-sitting, baby-sat, baby sitter

baccalaureate

Bachelor of Arts, Bachelor of Science *A bachelor's degree* or *bachelor's* is acceptable in any reference.
See **academic degrees** for guidelines on when the abbreviations *B.A.* or *B.S.* are acceptable.

backfire In wildfires, this term is for a fire set along the inner edge of a fireline to consume the fuel in the fire's path or change its direction.

back up (v.) **backup** (n. and adj.)

backward Not backwards.

backyard One word in all uses.

bad, badly *Bad* should not be used as an adverb. It does not lose its status as an adjective, however, in a sentence such as *I feel bad*. Such a statement is the idiomatic equivalent of *I am in bad health*. An alternative, *I feel badly*, could be interpreted as meaning that your sense of touch was bad.
See **good, well**.

Baghdad The city in Iraq stands alone in datelines.

Bagram Air Field The preferred spelling for the U.S. base in Afghanistan.

Baha'i A monotheistic religion founded in the 1860s by Baha'u'llah, a Persian nobleman considered a prophet by the Baha'is. Baha'u'llah taught that all religions represent progressive stages in the revelation of God's will, leading to the unity of all people and faiths. The Baha'is have no clergy; they are governed by local, national and international elected councils. The international governing body, the Universal House of Justice, is based in Haifa, Israel. Its U.S. offices are in Evanston, Ill.

Bahamas In datelines, give the name of the city or town followed by *Bahamas*:
NASSAU, Bahamas (AP) —
In stories, use *Bahamas, the Bahamas* or *the Bahama Islands* as the construction of a sentence dictates.
Identify a specific island in the text if relevant.

bail *Bail* is money or property that will be forfeited to the court if an accused individual fails to appear for trial. It may be posted as follows:

—The accused may deposit with the court the full amount or its equivalent in collateral such as a deed to property.

—A friend or relative may make such a deposit with the court.

—The accused may pay a professional bail bondsman a percentage of the total figure. The bondsman, in turn, guarantees the court that it will receive from him the full amount in the event the individual fails to appear for trial.

It is correct in all cases to say that an accused *posted bail* or *posted a bail bond* (the money held by the court is a form of bond). When a distinction is desired, say that the individual *posted his own bail*, that *bail was posted by a friend or relative*, or that *bail was obtained through a bondsman*.

Bakelite A trademark for a type of plastic resin.

Bakery, Confectionery, Tobacco Workers and Grain Millers International Union The shortened form *Bakery Workers union* is acceptable in all references.

Headquarters is in Washington.

balance of payments, balance of trade The *balance of payments* is the difference between the amount of money that leaves a nation and the amount that enters it during a period of time.

The *balance of payments* is determined by computing the amount of money a nation and its citizens send abroad for all purposes — including goods and services purchased, travel, loans, foreign aid, etc. — and subtracting from it the amount that foreign nations send into the nation for similar purposes.

The *balance of trade* is the differ-ence between the monetary value of the goods a nation imports and the goods it exports.

An example illustrating the difference between the two:

The United States and its citizens might send $10 billion abroad — $5 billion for goods, $3 billion for loans and foreign aid, $1 billion for services and $1 billion for tourism and other purposes.

Other nations might send $9 billion into the United States — $6 billion for U.S. goods, $2 billion for services and $1 billion for tourism and other purposes.

The United States would have a *balance-of-payments* deficit of $1 billion but a *balance-of-trade* surplus of $1 billion.

balance sheet A listing of assets, liabilities and net worth showing the financial position of a company at the specific time. A bank balance sheet is generally referred to as a statement of condition.

ballclub, ballpark, ballplayer, ballroom

balloon mortgage A mortgage whose amortization schedule will not extinguish the debt by the end of the mortgage term, leaving a large payment (called balloon payment) of the remaining principal balance to be paid at that time.

ballpoint pen

baloney Foolish or exaggerated talk.

The sausage or luncheon meat is *bologna*.

Baltimore The city in Maryland stands alone in datelines.

Band-Aid A trademark for a type of adhesive bandage.

Bangkok The city in Thailand stands alone in datelines.

Bank of America Corp. Formed from the 1998 merger of BankAmerica and NationsBank and the 2004 merger with FleetBoston Financial. Acquired Merrill Lynch & Co. in 2009. Headquarters is in Charlotte, N.C. Note that the corporation's research department is styled *Banc of America Securities*.

bankruptcy Federal courts have exclusive jurisdiction over bankruptcy cases and each of the 94 federal judicial districts handles bankruptcy matters. The primary purposes of the federal bankruptcy laws are to give honest debtors a "fresh start" in life by relieving them of most debts, and to repay creditors in an orderly manner to the extent debtors have property available for payment. Bankruptcies can be voluntary or involuntary.

Chapter 7 of the Bankruptcy Code is available to both individual and business debtors. Its purpose is to achieve a fair distribution to creditors of the debtor's available non-exempt property. It provides a fresh financial start for individuals, although not all debt is wiped away; debts for certain taxes, fraudulently incurred credit card debt, family support obligations — including child support and alimony — and most student loans must still be repaid. The bankruptcy law that took effect in October 2005 limits Chapter 7 as an option for many Americans: Those deemed by a "means test" to have at least $100 a month left over after paying certain debts and expenses must file a five-year repayment plan under the more restrictive Chapter 13 instead. When a company files for Chapter 7, it usually leads to liquidation. But a company in Chapter 7 proceedings can continue to operate under the direction of a court trustee until the matter is settled, and if it can settle with creditors in the interim, it may not have to be liquidated.

Chapter 11 of the Bankruptcy Code is available for both business and consumer debtors. Its purpose is to rehabilitate a business as a going concern or reorganize an individual's finances through a court-approved reorganization plan. When referring to such a filing, say the company is seeking Chapter 11 protection. This action frees a company from the threat of creditors' lawsuits while it reorganizes its finances. The debtor's reorganization plan must be accepted by a majority of its creditors. Unless the court rules otherwise, the debtor remains in control of the business and its assets.

Chapter 12 of the Bankruptcy Code is designed to give special debt relief to a family farmer with regular income from farming.

Chapter 13 of the Bankruptcy Code is likely to be required for an increasing percentage of individuals seeking to wipe the slate clean. Those deemed by a "means test" to have at least $100 a month left over after paying certain debts and expenses will have to file a five-year repayment plan under Chapter 13 allowing unsecured creditors to recover part of all of what they are owed.

Chapter 15 was added to the Bankruptcy Code in 2005 and covers U.S. filings that are secondary to bankruptcy cases filed overseas. Courts can authorize trustees to act in a foreign country on behalf of a bankruptcy estate in a Chapter 15 proceeding. It represents the U.S. adoption of a model law on cross-border bankruptcy developed by the United Nations.

baptism See **sacraments**.

Baptist churches It is incorrect to apply the term church to any Baptist unit except the local church.

The largest of the more than 20 Baptist bodies in the United States is the Southern Baptist Convention; most of its members are in the South, although it has churches nationwide.

The largest Northern body is American Baptist Churches in the U.S.A.

Blacks predominate in three other large Baptist bodies, the National Baptist Convention of America, the National Baptist Convention U.S.A. Inc., and the Progressive National Baptist Convention Inc.

The roster of Baptist bodies in the United States also includes the Baptist General Conference, the Conservative Baptist Association of America, the General Association of Regular Baptist Churches, the General Association of General Baptists, and the North American Baptist General Conference.

The Baptist World Alliance, a voluntary association of Baptist bodies throughout the world, organizes the Baptist World Congress meetings. Headquarters is in Washington.

CLERGY: All members of the Baptist clergy may be referred to as *ministers*. *Pastor* applies if a minister leads a congregation.

On first reference, use *the Rev.* before the name of a man or woman. On second reference, use only the last name.

See **religious titles**.

See **religious movements** for definitions of some descriptive terms that often apply to Baptists but are not limited to them.

barbiturate

bar mitzvah The Jewish rite of passage and family celebration that marks a boy's 13th birthday. Judaism regards the age of 13 as the benchmark of religious maturity. *Bar mitzvah* translates as "one who is responsible for the Commandments."

Some congregations have instituted the *bas mitzvah* or *bat mitzvah*, a similar ceremony for girls.

baron, baroness See **nobility**.

barrel A standard barrel in U.S. measure contains 31.5 gallons.

A standard barrel in British and Canadian measure contains 36 imperial gallons.

In international dealings with crude oil, a standard barrel contains 42 U.S. gallons or 35 imperial gallons.

See the **oil** entry for guidelines on computing the volume and weight of petroleum products.

barrel, barreled, barreling

barrister See **lawyer**.

barroom

bartender Preferred in all references. Do not use *bar maid*.

BASIC A computer programming language. Acronym for *Beginners' All-Purpose Symbolic Instruction Code*. Use of acronym on first reference is acceptable if it is identified as a programming language.

basis point One one-hundredth of one percentage point. Changes in interest rates are measured in basis points. If the Federal Reserve's target rate was 2 percent and it was cut by 50 basis points, the new rate would be 1.5 percent.

battalion Capitalize when used with a figure to form a name: *the 3rd Battalion, the 10th Battalion*.

battlefield Also: *battlefront*,

battleground, battleship. But *battle station*.

bay Capitalize as an integral part of a proper name: *Hudson Bay, San Francisco Bay*.

Capitalize also *San Francisco Bay Area* or *the Bay Area* as the popular name for the nine-county region that has San Francisco as its focal point.

bazaar A fair. *Bizarre* means unusual.

B.C. Acceptable in all references to a calendar year in the period *before Christ*.

Because the full phrase would be *in the year 43 before Christ*, the abbreviation *B.C.* is placed after the figure for the year: *43 B.C.*

See **A.D.**

bear market A period of generally declining stock prices over a prolonged period, generally defined as a 20 percent or larger decline in broad stock indexes such as the Standard & Poor's 500.

bearer bond A bond for which the owner's name is not registered on the books of the issuing company. Interest and principal is thus payable to the bondholder.

bearer stock Stock certificates that are not registered in any name. They are negotiable without endorsement and transferable by delivery.

bed-and-breakfast *B&B* is acceptable on second reference.

bedbug

because, since Use *because* to denote a specific cause-effect relationship: *He went because he was told.*

Since is acceptable in a causal

sense when the first event in a sequence led logically to the second but was not its direct cause: *They went to the game, since they had been given the tickets.*

before Christ See **B.C.**

Beijing The city in China (formerly Peking) stands alone in datelines.

Beirut The city in Lebanon stands alone in datelines.

Bell Labs The research and development division of *Alcatel-Lucent*. It was previously called AT&T Bell Laboratories after the breakup of the Bell system in 1984 and was spun off from *AT&T* in 1996 as part of the formation of Lucent Technologies.

bellwether

Belo Corp. Owns television stations, including WFAA-TV in Dallas/Fort Worth, KHOU-TV in Houston, KING-TV in Seattle/Tacoma and KTVK-TV in Phoenix, along with websites and regional cable news channels. Spun off newspaper properties into A.H. Belo Corp. in February 2008. Headquarters is in Dallas.

A.H. Belo Corp. Owner of The Dallas Morning News, The Providence (R.I.) Journal, The Press-Enterprise in Riverside, Calif., and the Denton Record-Chronicle in Texas. Spun off in February 2008 from Belo Corp., which now has just the broadcast stations. Headquarters is in Dallas.

benefit, benefited, benefiting

Benelux Belgium, the Netherlands and Luxembourg.

If *Benelux* is used, explain that it is an inclusive word for these three nations.

Ben-Gurion International Airport Located at Lod, Israel, about 10 miles southeast of Tel Aviv.
See **airport**.

Berkshire Hathaway Inc. Headquarters is in Omaha, Neb.

Berlin The city in Germany stands alone in datelines.

Berlin Wall

Bermuda collar, Bermuda grass, Bermuda shorts

beside, besides *Beside* means at the side of.
Besides means in addition to.

besiege

best-seller Hyphenate in all uses.

betting odds Use figures and a hyphen: *The odds were 5-4, he won despite 3-2 odds against him.*

bettor A person who bets.

between See **among, between**.

bi- The rules in **prefixes** apply, but in general, no hyphen. Some examples:
bifocal	bimonthly
bilateral	bipartisan
bilingual	

biannual, biennial *Biannual* means twice a year and is a synonym for the word *semiannual*.
Biennial means every two years.

Bible Capitalize, without quotation marks, when referring to the Scriptures in the Old Testament or the New Testament. Capitalize also related terms such as the *Gospels, Gospel of St. Mark, the Scriptures, the Holy Scriptures*.

Lowercase *biblical* in all uses.
Lowercase *bible* as a nonreligious term: *My dictionary is my bible.*
Do not abbreviate individual books of the Bible.
Old Testament is a Christian designation; Hebrew Bible or Jewish Bible is the appropriate term for stories dealing with Judaism alone.
The standard names and order of Old Testament books as they appear in Protestant Bibles are: Genesis, Exodus, Leviticus, Numbers, Deuteronomy, Joshua, Judges, Ruth, 1 Samuel, 2 Samuel, 1 Kings, 2 Kings, 1 Chronicles, 2 Chronicles, Ezra, Nehemiah, Esther, Job, Psalms, Proverbs, Ecclesiastes, Song of Solomon, Isaiah, Jeremiah, Lamentations, Ezekiel, Daniel, Hosea, Joel, Amos, Obadiah, Jonah, Micah, Nahum, Habakkuk, Zephaniah, Haggai, Zechariah, Malachi.
Jewish Bibles contain the same 39 books, in different order. Roman Catholic Bibles follow a different order, usually use some different names, and include the seven Deuterocanonical books (called the Apocrypha by Protestants): Tobit, Judith, 1 Maccabees, 2 Maccabees, Wisdom, Sirach, Baruch.
The books of the New Testament, in order: Matthew, Mark, Luke, John, Acts, Romans, 1 Corinthians, 2 Corinthians, Galatians, Ephesians, Philippians, Colossians, 1 Thessalonians, 2 Thessalonians, 1 Timothy, 2 Timothy, Titus, Philemon, Hebrews, James, 1 Peter, 2 Peter, 1 John, 2 John, 3 John, Jude, Revelation.
Citation listing the number of chapter and verse(s) use this form: *Matthew 3:16, Luke 21:1-13, 1 Peter 2:1.*

Bible Belt Those sections of the United States, especially in the South and Middle West, where fundamentalist religious beliefs prevail. Use with care, because in certain contexts it can give offense. See **religious movements**.

bicycle

Big Board Acceptable on second reference for the *New York Stock Exchange*.

big brother One's older brother is a *big brother*. *Big Brother* (capitalized) means under the watchful eye of big government, from George Orwell's "1984."

Capitalize also in reference to members of Big Brothers Big Sisters of America Inc. The organization has headquarters in Philadelphia.

Big Three automakers A

phrase that in the past generally referred to *General Motors*, *Ford* and *Chrysler*. Given that these companies are no longer the top automakers globally, the phrase *Detroit Three* has begun to be used instead of *Big Three*.

bigwig

billion A thousand million. For forms, see **millions, billions**.

Bill of Rights The first 10 amendments to the Constitution.

bimonthly Means every other month. *Semimonthly* means twice a month.

bin Laden, Osama Use *bin Laden* on all references except at the start of a sentence. It is the family preference for the last name, which is an exception to the general rule on Arabic names. He founded al-Qaida and was killed by U.S. forces in Pakistan in May 2011.

bioterrorism

bird flu Preferred term for avian influenza, the virus that infects mostly poultry and other birds. The deadly form is caused by the H5N1 strain.

birthday Capitalize as part of the name for a holiday: *Washington's Birthday*. Lowercase in other uses.

bishop See **religious titles** and the entry for the denomination in question.

bit Acceptable in all references as an abbreviation for *binary digit*. Actual data take the form of electrical impulses. These can be thought of as either on or off or 1 and 0. The pulses are bits.

biweekly Means every other week. *Semiweekly* means twice a week.

bizarre Unusual. A fair is a *bazaar*.

black Acceptable for a person of the black race. *African-American* is acceptable for an American black person of African descent. (Use *Negro* only in names of organizations or in quotations.) Do not use colored as a synonym. See **African-American**, **colored**, **nationalities and races** and **race**.

BlackBerry, BlackBerrys A popular device that combines mobile email and a cellphone. Manufactured by *Research in Motion Ltd.*, whose name is commonly abbreviated *RIM* on second reference.

Black Muslims See **Muslim(s)**.

blackout, brownout A *blackout* is a total power failure over a large area or the concealing of lights that might be visible to enemy raiders.

The term *rolling blackout* is used by electric companies to describe a situation in which electric power to some sections temporarily is cut off on a rotating basis to assure that voltage will meet minimum standards in other sections.

A *brownout* is a small, temporary voltage reduction, usually from 2 percent to 8 percent, implemented to conserve electric power.

blast off (v.) **blastoff** (n. and adj.)

Blessed Sacrament, Blessed Virgin

blind See **disabled, handicapped, impaired**.

blizzard See **weather terms**.

bloc, block A *bloc* is a coalition of people, groups or nations with the same purpose or goal.

Block has more than a dozen definitions, but a political alliance is not one of them.

blog A website where short entries are usually (but not always) presented in reverse chronological order, with the newest entry first. Can be news, commentary, photos, video or any combination of the above and other items. An update to a blog is a *blog post* or *blog entry*. Blogs can also be distributed outside the website context via RSS feed.

blond, blonde Use *blond* as a noun for males and as an adjective for all applications: She has *blond* hair.

Use *blonde* as a noun for females.

blood alcohol content The concentration of alcohol in blood. It is usually measured as weight per volume. For example, 0.02 percent means 0.02 grams of alcohol per deciliter of an individual's blood. The legal limit for intoxication in most states is 0.08 percent. *The jury found he was driving with a blood alcohol level above Florida's 0.08 limit.*

bloodbath One word, an exception to Webster's New World College Dictionary.

bloodhound

Bloomberg LP A provider of financial news and information. Its Bloomberg News service, which started in 1990, provides news to newspapers worldwide and to financial professionals. Bloomberg LP also owns the magazine Bloomberg Businessweek and has television and radio divisions. The company is privately owned and has its headquarters in New York.

blue chip stock Stock in a company known for its long-established record of making money and paying dividends. The term *Internet blue chip* is sometimes used to describe some of the largest and longest-lasting online companies like *Yahoo* and *eBay*, but should be avoided except in quotations from analysts and the like.

Bluetooth A standard for short-range wireless transmissions, such as in headsets, that enable hands-free use of cellphones.

Blu-ray Disc A successor to the DVD, *Blu-ray Disc* is a standard used to deliver high-definition video and other digital content.

B'nai B'rith See **fraternal organizations and service clubs**.

board Capitalize only when an integral part of a proper name. See **capitalization**.

board of aldermen See **city council**.

board of directors, board of trustees Always lowercase. See **organizations and institutions**.

board of supervisors See **city council**.

boats, ships A *boat* is a watercraft of any size but generally is used to indicate a small craft. A *ship* is a large, seagoing vessel.

The word *boat* is used, however, in some words that apply to large craft: *ferryboat, PT boat*.

Use *it*, not the pronoun *she*, in references to boats and ships.

Use Arabic or Roman numerals in the names of boats and ships: *the Queen Elizabeth 2* or *QE2*; *Titan I, Titan II*.

The reference for military ships is Jane's Fighting Ships; for nonmilitary ships, Lloyd's Register of Shipping.

bobblehead

body mass index A measurement calculated from weight and height. *BMI* is acceptable on second reference. To calculate: multiply weight in pounds by 703, divide by height in inches, divide again by height in inches. An easy-to-use Web calculator: http://www.nhlbisupport.com/bmi/

Boeing Co. Formerly Boeing Aircraft Co.

Headquarters is in Chicago.

Bogota The city in Colombia carries the country name in datelines.

bona fide

bondholder

bond ratings Standard & Poor's, Moody's Investors Service and Fitch Ratings sell information — mainly to institutional investors — about what they view as the relative risk of various issues of debt. They also charge companies, municipalities and even foreign governments that wish to sell debt and have it rated. The ratings are a fundamental way for investors to form an opinion on whether they are likely to be repaid, and then decide whether the interest rate is high enough to compensate for the risk that they may get back none or only a portion of their investment (in the case of a bankruptcy or some other adverse event). The ratings also effectively set benchmarks for how much interest companies will have to pay to sell bonds, commercial paper, preferred stock and for bank loans they obtain. The higher the grade, the lower the interest rate a borrower must pay.

Standard & Poor's bond ratings, for example, include 10 categories that are referred to as investment-grade, from AAA to BBB-, given to borrowers with the strongest ability to repay. Another six categories, from BB+ to CCC-, are assigned to more speculative securities that are commonly referred to as *junk* or *high-yield debt*. The lowest category, D, is for securities that are in payment default.

A reduction in the rating of a company's debt to non-investment-grade can force some mutual funds and pension funds to sell those bonds because they are prohibited from holding junk debt.

book publishers Major U.S. publishers are:

Hachette Book Group USA, (formerly Time Warner Books), a division of French media company Lagardere SCA

HarperCollins Publishers, owned by News Corp.

Houghton Mifflin Harcourt

Hyperion Books, owned by The Walt Disney Co.

Macmillan (formerly Holtz-brinck), including Farrar, Straus & Giroux, St. Martin's Press, Henry Holt and Picador

Penguin Group (USA), including Penguin Press, G.P. Putnam's Sons and Viking, owned by Pearson PLC

Perseus Book Group

Random House Inc., including the Crown Publishing Group, the Knopf Doubleday Publishing Group and the Random House Publishing Group.

Scholastic Books, owned by Scholastic Corp.

Simon & Schuster Inc., owned by CBS Corp.

W.W. Norton and Co.

John Wiley & Sons Inc.

Books on Tape A trademark for a brand of audiobooks. Use a generic term such as *audiotape* or *audiocassette*.

book titles See **composition titles**.

book value The difference between a company's assets and liabilities.

The *book value per share* of common stock is the *book value* divided by the number of common shares outstanding.

Bosnia-Herzegovina The country has been divided into a Bosnian Serb republic and a Muslim-Croat federation since 1995. Both have wide autonomy but share a common presidency, parliament and government. In datelines: *SARAJEVO, Bosnia-Herzegovina*. The people are *Bosnians*.

Bosporus, the Not the Bosporus Strait.

Boston The city in Massachusetts stands alone in datelines.

Boston terrier

boulevard Abbreviated only with a numbered address. See **addresses**.

bowlegged

box office (n.) **box-office** (adj.)

boy Applicable until 18th birthday is reached. Use *man* or *young man* afterward.

boycott, embargo A *boycott* is an organized refusal to buy a particular product or service, or to deal with a particular merchant or group of merchants.

An *embargo* is a legal restriction against trade. It usually prohibits goods from entering or leaving a country.

boyfriend, girlfriend

Boy Scouts The full name of the national organization is *Boy Scouts of America*. Headquarters is in Irving, Texas.

Cub Scouting is for boys 8 through 10. Members are *Cub Scouts* or *Cubs*.

Boy Scouting is for boys 11 through 17. Members are *Boy Scouts* or *Scouts*.

Exploring is a separate program open to boys and girls from high school age through 20. Members are *Explorers*, not *Explorer Scouts*. Members of units that stress nautical programs are *Sea Explorers*.

Venturing, originally part of the *Exploring* division, is for young adults, 14 through 20.

See **Girl Scouts**.

BP PLC Formerly British Petroleum. *BP* is acceptable in all references.

Headquarters is in London.

bra Acceptable in all references for *brassiere*.

brackets See entry in **Punctuation** chapter.

Brahman, Brahmin *Brahman* applies to the priestly Hindu caste and a breed of cattle.

Brahmin applies to aristocracy in general: *Boston Brahmin*.

brand names When they are used, capitalize them.

Brand names normally should be used only if they are essential to a story.

Sometimes, however, the use of a brand name may not be essential but is acceptable because it lends an air of reality to a story: *He fished a Camel from his shirt pocket* may be preferable to the less specific *cigarette*.

When a company sponsors a sports or other event identified only by the company's name, use the name on first reference: Example: *Buick Open*.

However, when an event is clearly identifiable without the company's name, drop the name on first reference and include the sponsor name elsewhere in the story or at the bottom as an Editor's Note. Example: *FedEx Orange Bowl* would be identified in the story only as *Orange Bowl*.

Also use a separate paragraph to provide the name of a sponsor when the brand name is not part of the formal title.

See **trademark** entry.

brand-new (adj.)

break in (v.) **break-in** (n. and adj.)

break up (v.) **breakup** (n. and adj.)

breast-feed, breast-feeding, breast-fed

Breathalyzer Trademarked name for a device to test blood-alcohol level. Use a generic description if the brand is unknown.

bride, bridegroom, bridesmaid *Bride* is appropriate in wedding stories, but use *wife* or *spouse* in other circumstances.

brigadier See **military titles**.

Britain Acceptable in all references for *Great Britain*, which consists of England, Scotland and Wales.

See **United Kingdom**.

British Airways PLC Headquarters of this airline is in Harmondsworth, England.

British, Briton(s) The people of Great Britain: the English, the Scottish, the Welsh. *Brits* is slang.

British Broadcasting Corp. *BBC* is acceptable in all references.

British Columbia The Canadian province bounded on the west by the Pacific Ocean. Do not abbreviate.

See **datelines**.

British Commonwealth See **Commonwealth, the**.

British thermal unit The amount of heat required to increase the temperature of a pound of water 1 degree Fahrenheit. *Btu* (the same for singular and plural) is acceptable on second reference.

British ton See **ton**.

British Virgin Islands Use with a community name in datelines on stories from these islands. Do not abbreviate.

Specify an individual island in the text if relevant.

See **datelines**.

broadcast The past tense also is *broadcast*, not *broadcasted*.

broadcast networks Major U.S. networks are:

ABC, owned by The Walt Disney Co.

CBS, owned by CBS Corp.

NBC, part of NBCUniversal, which is controlled by Comcast Corp. Under a deal completed in January 2011, Comcast owns 51 percent while General Electric Co. owns the rest after selling a majority stake in the venture.

Fox, owned by News Corp.

PBS, a private, nonprofit organization owned and operated by public television stations

The CW, a joint venture between Time Warner Inc.'s Warner Bros. unit and CBS Corp.

Telemundo, part of NBCUniversal

Univision Communications Inc.

Broadway, off-Broadway, off-off-Broadway When applied to stage productions, these terms refer to distinctions made by union contracts, not to location of a theater.

Actors' Equity Association and unions representing craft workers have one set of pay scales for *Broadway* productions (generally those in New York City theaters of 300 or more seats) and a lower scale for smaller theaters, classified as *off-Broadway* houses.

The term *off-off-Broadway* refers to workshop productions that may use Equity members for a limited time at substandard pay. Other

unions maintain a hands-off policy, agreeing with the Equity attitude that actors should have an opportunity to develop their talents in offbeat roles without losing their Equity memberships.

Bronze Age The age characterized by the development of bronze tools and weapons, from 3500 to 1000 B.C. Regarded as coming between the Stone Age and the Iron Age.

Brotherhood of Locomotive Engineers and Trainmen *BLET* is acceptable on second reference.

Headquarters is in Cleveland.

Brothers Generally abbreviate as *Bros.* in formal company names: *Warner Bros.*, but follow the spelling preferred by the company.

For possessives: *Warner Bros.' profits*.

brownout See **blackout, brownout**.

brunette Use *brunette* as a noun for females. Use *brown-haired* for males.

Brussels The city in Belgium stands alone in datelines.

Btu The same in singular and plural. See **British thermal unit**.

Bubble Wrap A registered trademark. Unless the trademark name is important to the story, use *cushioning* or *packaging material*.

Budapest The capital of Hungary. In datelines, follow it with *Hungary*.

Buddha, Buddhism A major religion founded in India about 500 B.C. by Buddha. Buddha, which means enlightened one, was the name given to Siddhartha Gautama by his followers.

Most of Buddhism's followers are in India, Tibet, China, Japan, Korea and Southeast Asia.

Buddhists believe that correct thinking and self-denial will enable the soul to reach nirvana, a state of release into ultimate enlightenment and peace. Until nirvana is reached, believers cannot be freed from the cycle of death and rebirth.

There are four major groups within Buddhism.

—Hinayana or Theravada: Followers stress monastic discipline and attainment of nirvana by the individual through meditation. It is dominant among Buddhists in Cambodia, Laos, Myanmar, Thailand and Sri Lanka.

—Mahayana: Followers lay stress on idealism. The ideal life is that of virtue and wisdom. The sect is found mostly in Japan, Korea and eastern China.

—Mantrayana: Major centers for this group are in the Himalayas, Mongolia and Japan. It is similar to Mahayana but also has a structure of spiritual leaders and disciples, believes in various evil spirits and deities, uses magic, and has secret rituals.

—Zen: Followers seek enlightenment through introspection and intuition. The doctrines are again similar to Mahayana and like Mantrayana there is a loose structure of leaders and disciples. This group is found mostly in Japan.

Bufferin A trademark for buffered aspirin.

bug, tap A concealed listening device designed to pick up sounds in a room, an automobile, or such is a *bug*.

A *tap* is a device attached to a telephone circuit to pick up conversations on the line.

building Never abbreviate. Capitalize the proper names of buildings, including the word *building* if it is an integral part of the proper name: *the Empire State Building*.

build up (v.) **buildup** (n. and adj.)

bull's-eye

bullet See **weapons**.

bullfight, bullfighter, bullfighting

bullion Unminted precious metals of standards suitable for coining.

bullpen One word, for the place where baseball pitchers warm up, and for a pen that holds cattle.

bull market A period of generally rising stock prices over a prolonged period, generally defined as a 20 percent or larger increase in broad stock indexes such as the Standard & Poor's 500.

bureau Capitalize when part of the formal name for an organization or agency: *the Bureau of Labor Statistics*.

Lowercase when used alone or to designate a corporate subdivision: *the Washington bureau of The Associated Press*.

Bureau of Alcohol, Tobacco, Firearms and Explosives ATF is acceptable in subsequent references to this agency of the Department of Justice. (Note the *Explosives* part of the name.)

burglary, larceny, robbery, theft Legal definitions of *burglary* vary, but in general a *burglary* involves entering a building (not necessarily by breaking in) and remaining unlawfully with the intention of committing a crime.

Larceny is the legal term for the wrongful taking of property. Its non-legal equivalents are *stealing* or *theft.*

Robbery in the legal sense involves the use of violence or threat in committing larceny. In a wider sense it means to plunder or rifle, and may thus be used even if a person was not present: *His house was robbed while he was away.*

Theft describes a larceny that did not involve threat, violence or plundering.

USAGE NOTE: You *rob* a person, bank, house, etc., but you *steal* the money or the jewels.

Burlington Northern Santa Fe LLC The freight railroad, with headquarters in Fort Worth, Texas, is now owned by Berkshire Hathaway Inc.

burn To copy data, audio or video to optical media (such as a CD, a DVD or a Blu-ray Disc) with a laser.

burqa The all-covering dress worn by some Muslim women.

bus, buses Transportation vehicles. The verb forms: *bus, bused, busing.*
See **buss, busses**.

bushel A unit of dry measure equal to 4 pecks or 32 dry quarts. The metric equivalent is approximately 35.2 liters.

To convert to liters, multiply by 35.2 (5 bushels x 35.2 equals 176 liters).
See **liter**.

business editor Capitalize when used as a formal title before a name. See **titles**.

business names See **company names**.

buss, busses Kisses. The verb forms: *buss, bussed, bussing.*
See **bus, buses**.

by- The rules in **prefixes** apply, but in general, no hyphen. Some examples:

byline	byproduct
bypass	bystreet

By-election is an exception. See the next entry.

by-election A special election held between regularly scheduled elections. The term most often is associated with special elections to the British House of Commons.

bylaw

bylines Use only if the reporter was in the datelined community to gather the information reported.

Nicknames should not be used unless they specifically are requested by the writer.

byte A computer "word" made up of bits. The most common size *byte* contains eight bits, or binary digits. *Bytes* are a measure of information storage.

cabinet Capitalize references to a specific body of advisers heading executive departments for a president, king, governor, etc.: *The president-elect said he has not made his Cabinet selections.*

See **department** for a listing of all the U.S. Cabinet departments.

cable networks Major U.S. cable networks are:

A&E, owned by A&E Television Networks, a joint venture of Hearst Corp., The Walt Disney Co. and Comcast Corp.'s NBCUniversal

AMC (also We tv, IFC and Sundance Channel) owned by AMC Networks Inc.

Animal Planet, owned by Discovery Communications Inc.

Bravo, owned by Comcast Corp.'s NBCUniversal

Cartoon Network, owned by Time Warner Inc.

CNBC, owned by Comcast Corp.'s NBCUniversal

CNN, owned by Time Warner Inc.

Comedy Central, owned by Viacom Inc.

Discovery Channel, owned by Discovery Communications Inc.

Disney Channel and Disney XD, owned by The Walt Disney Co.

Epix, owned by Viacom Inc., Metro-Goldwyn-Mayer Inc. and Lions Gate Entertainment Corp.

E! Entertainment Television, owned by Comcast Corp.'s NBCUniversal

ESPN, 80 percent owned by The Walt Disney Co. and 20 percent owned by Hearst Corp.

Fox News Channel, owned by News Corp.

FX, owned by News Corp.

G4, owned by Comcast Corp.'s NBCUniversal

Golf Channel, owned by Comcast Corp.'s NBCUniversal

HBO, owned by Time Warner Inc.

History, owned by A&E Television Networks, a joint venture of Hearst Corp., The Walt Disney Co. and Comcast Corp.'s NBCUniversal

Lifetime, owned by A&E Television Networks, a joint venture of Hearst Corp., The Walt Disney Co. and Comcast Corp.'s NBCUniversal

MSNBC, owned by Comcast Corp.'s NBCUniversal

MTV, Nickelodeon, VH1, owned by Viacom Inc.

NFL Network, owned by the National Football League

OWN: The Oprah Winfrey Network, a joint venture of Discovery Communications Inc. and Oprah Winfrey

Oxygen, owned by Comcast Corp.'s NBCUniversal

PBS Kids Sprout, a joint venture of Comcast Corp.'s NBCUniversal, HIT Entertainment, PBS and Sesame Workshop

Syfy, owned by Comcast Corp.'s NBCUniversal

Showtime, owned by CBS Corp.

Starz, owned by Liberty Media Corp.

The Style Network, owned by Comcast Corp.'s NBCUniversal

TNT, TBS and Turner Classic Movies, owned by Time Warner Inc.

Travel Channel, 65 percent owned by Scripps Networks Interactive Inc. and 35 percent owned by Cox Communications Inc.

TV One, whose investors include Radio One Inc., Comcast Corp., DirecTV, Constellation Ventures, Syndicated Communications and Opportunity Capital Partner

USA Network, owned by Comcast Corp.'s NBCUniversal

Versus, owned by Comcast Corp.'s NBCUniversal

The Weather Channel, owned by Comcast Corp.'s NBCUniversal, Bain Capital LLC and The Blackstone Group

cactus, cactuses

cadet See **military academies**.

Cairo The city in Egypt stands alone in datelines.

caliber The form: *.38-caliber pistol*.
See **weapons**.

California Abbreviate *Calif.* in datelines or stories. Postal code: *CA*
See **state names**.

call letters Use all caps. Use hyphens to separate the type of station from the base call letters: *WBZ-AM, WBZ-FM, WBZ-TV*.

Citizens band operators, since 1983, are not required to be licensed by the Federal Communications Commission. Identification of such stations, either by the call sign previously assigned or made up by the operator, including the letter *K*, the operator's initials and the operator's ZIP code, is optional.

Amateur radio stations, which operate with greater power than citizens band stations and on different frequencies, typically mix letters and figures: *K2LRX*.

See **channel**; **citizens band**; **radio station**; and **television station**.

call up (v.) **call-up** (n. and adj.)

Cameroon See **geographic names**.

campaign manager Do not treat as a formal title. Always lowercase.
See **titles**.

Camp Fire Boys and Girls The full name of the national organization formerly known as Camp Fire Inc. Founded in 1910 as Camp Fire Girls, the name was changed to Camp Fire Inc., in 1979, and again in 1993 to reflect the inclusion of boys. Headquarters is in Kansas City, Mo.

Both girls and boys are included in all levels of the organization. Boys and girls in kindergarten through second grades are *Starflights*. Children in third through fifth grades are *Adventure* club members. Children in sixth through eighth grades are *Discovery* members. Youths in ninth through 12th grades are *Horizon* members.

Canada Montreal, Quebec City and Toronto stand alone in datelines. For all other datelines, use the city name and the name of the province or territory spelled out.

The 10 provinces of Canada are Alberta, British Columbia, Manitoba, New Brunswick, Newfoundland and Labrador (but usually known as just Newfoundland), Nova Scotia, Ontario, Prince Edward Island, Quebec and Saskatchewan.

The three territories are the Yukon, the Northwest Territories, and Nunavut (created April 1, 1999).

The provinces have substantial

autonomy from the federal government.

The territories are administered by the federal government, although residents of the territories do elect their own legislators and representatives to Parliament.

See **datelines**.

Canada goose

Canadian Broadcasting Corp.
CBC is acceptable in all references within contexts such as a television column. Otherwise, do not use *CBC* until second reference.

Canadian Press, The Canada's multimedia news agency. Its Francophone counterpart is La Presse Canadienne. Do not abbreviate *CP*.

canal Capitalize as an integral part of a proper name: *the Suez Canal*.

Canal Zone Do not abbreviate. No longer used except when referring to the Panama Canal area during the time it was controlled by the United States, exclusively or jointly with Panama, 1904-1999.

cancel, canceled, canceling, cancellation

cannon, canon A *cannon* is a weapon. See **weapons**.

A *canon* is a law or rule, particularly of a church, or a musical composition.

cannot

cant The distinctive stock words and phrases used by a particular sect or class.

See **dialect**.

cantor See **Jewish congregations**.

Canuck This reference to a

Canadian is sometimes considered derogatory. It should be avoided except when in quoted matter or in terms used in Canada, such as references to the hockey team, the *Vancouver Canucks*.

canvas, canvass *Canvas* is heavy cloth.

Canvass is a noun and a verb denoting a survey.

cape Capitalize as part of a proper name: *Cape Cod*, *Cape Hatteras*. Lowercase when standing alone.

Although local practice may call for capitalizing *the Cape* when the rest of the name is clearly understood, always use the full name on first reference.

Cape Canaveral, Fla. Formerly Cape Kennedy. See **John F. Kennedy Space Center**.

capital The city where a seat of government is located. Do not capitalize.

When used in a financial sense, *capital* describes money, equipment or property used in a business by a person or corporation.

See **Capitol**.

capital gain, capital loss The difference between what a *capital* asset cost and the price it brought when sold.

capitalization In general, avoid unnecessary capitals. Use a capital letter only if you can justify it by one of the principles listed here.

Many words and phrases, including special cases, are listed separately in this book. Entries that are capitalized without further comment should be capitalized in all uses.

If there is no relevant listing in this book for a particular word or phrase, consult Webster's New World College Dictionary. Use lowercase if the dictionary lists it as an acceptable form for the sense in which the word is being used.

As used in this book, *capitalize* means to use uppercase for the first letter of a word. If additional capital letters are needed, they are called for by an example or a phrase such as use *all caps.*

Some basic principles:

PROPER NOUNS: Capitalize nouns that constitute the unique identification for a specific person, place, or thing: *John, Mary, America, Boston, England.*

Some words, such as the examples just given, are always proper nouns. Some common nouns receive proper noun status when they are used as the name of a particular entity: *General Electric, Gulf Oil.*

PROPER NAMES: Capitalize common nouns such as *party, river, street* and *west* when they are an integral part of the full name for a person, place or thing: *Democratic Party, Mississippi River, Fleet Street, West Virginia.*

Lowercase these common nouns when they stand alone in subsequent references: *the party, the river, the street.*

Lowercase the common noun elements of names in plural uses: *the Democratic and Republican parties, Main and State streets, lakes Erie and Ontario.* Exception: plurals of formal titles with full names are capitalized: *Presidents Jimmy Carter and Gerald R. Ford.*

Among entries that provide additional guidelines are:

animals	**monuments**
brand names	**nationalities**
building	**and races**
committee	**nicknames**
Congress	**non-U.S.**
datelines	**governmental**
days of the week	**bodies**

directions and	**non-U.S.**
regions	**legislative**
family names	**bodies**
food	**organizations**
geographic names	**and institutions**
governmental bodies	**planets**
heavenly bodies	**plants**
historical periods	**police department**
and events	**religious references**
holidays and	**seasons**
holy days	**trademarks**
legislature	**unions**
months	

POPULAR NAMES: Some places and events lack officially designated proper names but have popular names that are the effective equivalent: *the Combat Zone* (a section of downtown Boston), *the Main Line* (a group of Philadelphia suburbs), *the South Side* (of Chicago), *the Badlands* (of South Dakota), *the Street* (the financial community in the Wall Street area of New York).

The principle applies also to shortened versions of the proper names of one-of-a-kind events: *the Series* (for the World Series), *the Derby* (for the Kentucky Derby). This practice should not, however, be interpreted as a license to ignore the general practice of lowercasing the common noun elements of a name when they stand alone.

DERIVATIVES: Capitalize words that are derived from a proper noun and still depend on it for their meaning: *American, Christian, Christianity, English, French, Marxism, Shakespearean.*

Lowercase words that are derived from a proper noun but no longer depend on it for their meaning: *french fries, herculean, malapropism, pasteurize, quixotic, venetian blind.*

SENTENCES: Capitalize the first word in a statement that stands as a sentence. See **sentences** and **parentheses**.

In poetry, capital letters are used

for the first words of some phrases that would not be capitalized in prose. See **poetry**.

COMPOSITIONS: Capitalize the principal words in the names of books, movies, plays, poems, operas, songs, radio and television programs, works of art, etc. See **composition titles**, **magazine names** and **newspaper names**.

TITLES: Capitalize formal titles when used immediately before a name. Lowercase formal titles when used alone or in constructions that set them off from a name by commas.

Use lowercase at all times for terms that are job descriptions rather than formal titles.

See **academic titles**, **courtesy titles**, **legislative titles**, **military titles**, **nobility**, **religious titles** and **titles**.

ABBREVIATIONS: Capital letters apply in some cases. See **abbreviations and acronyms**.

Capitol Capitalize *U.S. Capitol* and *the Capitol* when referring to the building in Washington: *The meeting was held on Capitol Hill in the west wing of the Capitol.*

Follow the same practice when referring to state capitols: *The Virginia Capitol is in Richmond. Thomas Jefferson designed the Capitol of Virginia.*

See **capital**.

captain See **military titles** for military and police usage.

Lowercase and spell out in such uses as *team captain Carl Yastrzemski.*

carat, caret, karat The weight of precious stones, especially diamonds, is expressed in *carats*. A carat is equal to 200 milligrams or about 3 grains.

A *caret* is a writer's and a proofreader's mark.

The proportion of pure gold used with an alloy is expressed in *karats*.

carbine See **weapons**.

cardholder, credit card holder

cardinal See **Roman Catholic Church**.

cardinal numbers See **numerals**.

CARE CARE USA has its headquarters in Atlanta. CARE International is based in Geneva. They refer to themselves simply as *CARE*.

carefree

caretaker

Caribbean See **Western Hemisphere**.

carmaker, carmakers

car pool (n.) **carpool** (v.)

carry-on

carry-over (n. and adj.)

cash on delivery The abbreviation *c.o.d.* is preferred in all references.

caster, castor *Caster* is a roller. *Castor* is the spelling for the oil and the bean from which it is derived.

catalog, cataloged, cataloger, cataloging, catalogist

Caterpillar A trademark for a brand of crawler tractor. The formal name of the company is *Caterpillar Inc.* Headquarters is in Peoria, Ill.

Use lowercase for the wormlike larva of various insects.

Cathay Pacific Airways Ltd. Headquarters of this airline is in Hong Kong.

catholic, catholicism Use *Roman Catholic Church, Roman Catholic* or *Roman Catholicism* in the first references to those who believe that the pope, as bishop of Rome, has the ultimate authority in administering an earthly organization founded by Jesus Christ.

Most subsequent references may be condensed to *Catholic Church, Catholic* or *Catholicism. Roman Catholic* should continue to be used, however, if the context requires a distinction between Roman Catholics and members of other denominations who often describe themselves as Catholic. They include some high church Episcopalians (who often call themselves *Anglo-Catholics*), members of Eastern Orthodox churches, and members of some national Catholic churches that have broken with Rome. Among churches in this last category are the Polish National Catholic Church and the Lithuanian National Catholic Church.

Lowercase *catholic* where used in its generic sense of general or universal, meanings derived from a similar word in Greek.

Those who use *Catholic* in a religious sense are indicating their belief that they are members of a universal church that Jesus Christ left on Earth.

cats See **animals**.

CAT scan See **CT scan**.

cattle See **animals**.

Caucasian

cave in (v.) **cave-in** (n. and adj.)

CB See **citizens band radio**.

CBS The formal name is CBS Corp., which was created in December 2005 when Viacom Inc. split into two companies. Headquarters is in New York. In addition to *CBS Television Network*, the company also owns *CBS Radio*, a group of local television stations, *Simon & Shuster* book publishing and the *Showtime* cable network.

CD See **compact disc**.

CD-ROM Acronym for *compact disc* acting as *read-only memory. CD-ROM disc* is redundant.

cease-fire, cease-fires (n. and adj.) The verb form is *cease fire*.

celebrant, celebrator Reserve *celebrant* for someone who conducts a religious rite: *He was the celebrant of the Mass.*

Use *celebrator* for someone having a good time: *The celebrators kept the party going until 3 a.m.*

cellophane Formerly a trademark, now a generic term.

cellphone

Celsius Use this term rather than *centigrade* for the temperature scale that is part of the metric system.

The Celsius scale is named for Anders Celsius, a Swedish astronomer who designed it. In it, zero represents the freezing point of water, and 100 degrees is the boiling point at sea level.

To convert to Fahrenheit, multiply a Celsius temperature by 9, divide by 5 and add 32 (25 x 9 equals 225, divided by 5 equals 45, plus 32 equals 77 degrees Fahrenheit).

When giving a Celsius temperature, use these forms: *40 degrees Celsius* or *40 C* (note the space and no period after the capital *C*) if degrees and Celsius are clear from the context.

See **Fahrenheit** and **metric system**.

cement *Cement* is the powder mixed with water and sand or gravel to make *concrete*. The proper term is *concrete* (not *cement*) *pavement*, *blocks*, *driveways*, etc.

censer, censor, censure A *censer* is a container in which incense is burned.

To *censor* is to prohibit or restrict the use of something.

To *censure* is to condemn.

census Capitalize only in specific references to the *U.S. Census Bureau*. Lowercase in other uses: *the census data was released Tuesday*.

Centers for Disease Control and Prevention Located in Atlanta, the Centers for Disease Control and Prevention is part of the U.S. Department of Health and Human Services and works to control and prevent infectious and chronic diseases and promote good health. The centers also work with state and local health officials to provide specialized services.

On first reference, use *Centers for Disease Control and Prevention*. Precede with *national*, *federal* or *U.S.* if needed for clarity. *CDC* is acceptable on second reference and takes a singular verb.

Online:
http://www.cdc.gov

centi- A prefix denoting one-hundredth of a unit. Move a decimal point two places to the left in converting to the basic unit: *155.6 centimeters equals 1.556 meters*.

centigrade See **Celsius**.

centimeter One-hundredth of a meter.

There are 10 millimeters in a centimeter.

To convert to inches, multiply by 0.4 (5 centimeters x 0.4 equals 2 inches).

See **meter**; **metric system**; and **inch**.

Central America See **Western Hemisphere**.

Central Asia The region includes Kyrgyzstan, Kazakhstan, Turkmenistan, Tajikistan, and Uzbekistan.

central bank A bank having responsibility for controlling a country's monetary policy.

Central Conference of American Rabbis See **Jewish Congregations**.

Central Intelligence Agency *CIA* is acceptable in all references.

The formal title for the individual who heads the agency is *director of central intelligence*. On first reference: *Director David Petraeus of the CIA, Director of Central Intelligence David Petraeus*, or *CIA Director David Petraeus*.

Central Standard Time (CST), Central Daylight Time (CDT) See **time zones**.

cents Spell out the word *cents* and lowercase, using numerals for amounts less than a dollar: *5 cents, 12 cents*. Use the *$* sign and decimal system for larger amounts: *$1.01, $2.50*.

century Lowercase, spelling out numbers less than 10: *the first century, the 20th century*.

For proper names, follow the organization's practice: *20th Century Fox, Twentieth Century Fund, Twentieth Century Limited*.

CEO Acceptable in all references for *chief executive officer*. Use *chief financial officer* and *chief operating officer* on first reference, and *CFO* and *COO* thereafter. Always spell out lesser-known "C-level" positions like *chief administrative officer* or *chief risk officer*.

cesarean section *C-section* is acceptable on second reference.

Ceylon It is now *Sri Lanka*, which should be used in datelines and other references to the nation.

The people may be referred to as *Ceylonese* (n. or adj.) or *Sri Lankans*. The language is *Sinhalese*.

cha-cha

chain saw

chairman, chairwoman
Capitalize as a formal title before a name: *company Chairman Henry Ford, committee Chairwoman Margaret Chase Smith*.

Do not capitalize as a casual, temporary position: *meeting chairman Robert Jones*.

Do not use *chairperson, chair* or *co-chair* unless it is an organization's formal title for an office.

See **titles**.

chamber of deputies See **foreign legislative bodies**.

chancellor The translation to English for the first minister in the governments of Germany and Austria. Capitalize when used before a name.

See **premier, prime minister** and **titles**.

changeable

changeover

Change to Win An affiliation of unions launched in 2005. Its members are the International Brotherhood of Teamsters, the Service Employees International Union, the United Farm Workers of America and the United Food and Commercial Workers International Union.

change up (v.) **change-up** (n. and adj.)

channel Capitalize when used with a figure; lowercase elsewhere: *She turned to Channel 3. No channel will broadcast the game.*

Also: *the English Channel*, but the channel on second reference.

chapters Capitalize *chapter* when used with a numeral in reference to a section of a book or legal code. Always use Arabic figures: *Chapter 1, Chapter 20*.

Lowercase when standing alone.

character, reputation *Character* refers to moral qualities.

Reputation refers to the way a person is regarded by others.

charge off A loan that no longer is expected to be repaid and is written off as a bad debt.

charismatic groups See **religious movements**.

Charleston, Charlestown, Charles Town *Charleston* is the name of the capital of West Virginia and a port city in South Carolina.

Charlestown is a section of Boston.

Charles Town is the name of a small city in West Virginia.

chauffeur

chauvinism, chauvinist The

words mean unreasoning devotion to one's race, sex, country, etc., with contempt for other races, sexes, countries, etc.

The terms come from Nicolas Chauvin, a soldier of Napoleon I, who was famous for his devotion to the lost cause.

check-in (n. and adj.) **check in** (v.)

checkout (n. and adj.) **check out** (v.)

check up (v.) **checkup** (n.)

Chemical Mace A trademark, usually shortened to *Mace*, for a brand of tear gas that is packaged in an aerosol canister and temporarily stuns its victims.

Chennai Indian city formerly known as Madras.

chess In stories, the names and pieces are spelled out, lowercase: *king, queen, bishop, pawn, knight, rook, kingside, queenside, white, black*.

Use the algebraic notation in providing tabular summaries.

In algebraic notation, the "ranks" are the horizontal rows of squares. The ranks take numbers, 1 to 8, beginning on white's side of the board.

The "files" are the vertical rows of squares. They take letters, a through h, beginning on white's left.

Thus, each square is identified by its file letter and rank number.

In the starting position, white's queen knight stands on *b1*, the queen on *d1*, the king on *e1*; black's queen knight stands on *b8*, the queen on *d8*, the king on *e8*, and so on.

Other features of the system follow:

—DESIGNATION OF PIECES: The major pieces are shown by a capital letter: *K* for king, *Q* for queen, *R* for rook, *B* for bishop and *N* for knight. No symbol is used for the pawn.

—MOVES BY PIECES: Shown by the letter of the piece (except for the pawn) and the destination square. For instance, *Bb5* means the bishop moves to square b5.

—MOVES BY PAWNS: Pawn moves are designated only by the name of the destination square. Thus, *e4* means the pawn on the e file moves to e4.

—CASTLING: It is written as *0-0* for the kingside and *0-0-0* for the queenside. *Kingside* is the side of the board (right half from white's point of view, left half from black's), on which each player's king starts. The other half is *queenside*.

—CAPTURES BY PIECES: A capture is recorded using an x after the letter for the capturing piece. For instance, if white's bishop captures the black pawn at the f6 square, it is written *Bxf6*.

—CAPTURES BY PAWNS: When a pawn captures a piece, the players name the file the pawn was on and the square where it made the capture. If white's pawn on a g file captured black's pawn on f6 square, the move would be *gxf6*. If black's pawn on an f file captured white's, it would be *fxg5*.

—CHECK: Use plus sign.

—AMBIGUITY: If more than one piece of the same type can move to a square, the rank number or file letter of the origination square is added. Thus, if a rook on d1 were to move to d4, but another rook also could move there, instead of *Rd4* the move would be given as *R1d4*. If there are black knights on c6 and e6, and the one on e6 moves to d4, the move is given as *Ned4*.

The form, taken from a 1993 championship match:

	Short (White)	Karpov (Black)
1.	e4	c5
2.	Nf3	d6
3.	d4	cxd4
4.	Nxd4	Nf6
5.	Nc3	a6
6.	Bc4	e6
7.	Bb3	Nbd7
8.	f4	Nc5
9.	f5	Be7
10.	Qf3	O-O
11.	Be3	e5
12.	Nde2	b5
13.	Bd5	Rb8
14.	b4	Ncd7
15.	O-O	Nxd5
16.	Nxd5	Bb7
17.	Nec3	Nf6
18.	Rad1	Bxd5
19.	Nxd5	Nxd5
20.	Rxd5	Rc8
21.	Qg4	f6
22.	Rf3	Rxc2
23.	Rh3	Rf7
24.	Qh5	h6
25.	Qg6	Kf8
26.	Bxh6	gxh6
27.	Rxh6	Qb6+
28.	Rc5	Bd8
29.	Rh8+	Ke7
30.	Rh7	Rxh7
31.	Qxh7+	Kf8

Draw agreed.

Chevron Corp. Created by the takeover by Chevron (formerly Standard Oil Co. of California) of Texaco in 2001. Headquarters is in San Ramon, Calif. (Name changed from ChevronTexaco in 2005.)

Chevy Not *Chevie* or *Chevvy*. This nickname for the *Chevrolet* should be used only in automobile features or in quoted matter.

Chicago The city in Illinois stands alone in datelines.

Chicago Board of Trade Commodity trading market where con-

tracts are traded for Treasury bonds, corn, soybeans, wheat, gold, silver, etc. Owned by CME Group. See **CME Group**.

Chicago Board Options Exchange Set up by the Chicago Board of Trade, it is the world's largest options exchange.

Chicano Sometimes used by Mexican-Americans in the Southwest. Not interchangeable with *Mexican-American*. Use only if a person's preference. See **Hispanic**, **Latino**, **nationalities and races**, and **race**.

chickenpox

chief Capitalize as a formal title before a name: *She spoke to police Chief Michael Codd. He spoke to Chief Michael Codd of the New York police.*
Lowercase when it is not a formal title: *union chief Walter Reuther.* See **titles**.

chief justice Capitalize only as a formal title before a name: *Chief Justice John Roberts.* The officeholder is the chief justice of the United States, not of the Supreme Court. See **judge**.

child care Two words, no hyphen, in all cases.

children In general, call children 15 or younger by their first name on second reference. Use the last name, however, if the seriousness of the story calls for it, as in a murder case, for example. For ages 16 and 17, use judgment, but generally go with the surname unless it's a light story. Use the surname for those 18 and older. See **privacy**.

Chile The nation.

chilly Moderately cold.

China When used alone, it refers to the nation that includes the mainland, Hong Kong and Macau. Use China in mainland datelines; Hong Kong and Macau stand alone in datelines.

Use *People's Republic of China*, *Communist China* and *mainland China* only in direct quotations or when needed to distinguish the mainland and its government from Taiwan. Use *Red China* only in direct quotes.

For datelines on stories from the island of Taiwan, use the name of a community and *Taiwan*. In the body of a story, use *Taiwan* for references to the government based on the island. Use the formal name of the government, the *Republic of China*, when required for legal precision.

China Eastern Airlines Corp. Ltd. Headquarters is in Shanghai.

China Southern Airlines Headquarters is in Guangzhou, China.

Chinese names A variety of systems are used for spelling Chinese names. For personal and place names from China, use the official Chinese spelling system known as *Pinyin*: *Senior leader Deng Xiaoping, Beijing,* or *Zhejiang province*.

In personal names, Chinese generally place surnames first and then given names, *Deng Xiaoping*. Second reference should be the family name, *Deng* in this case.

Some Chinese have Westernized their names, putting their given names or the initials for them first or sometimes using both an English name and a Chinese name: *P.Y. Chen, Jack Wang, Frank Hsieh Chang-ting*. In general, follow an individual's preferred spelling.

Normally Chinese women do not take their husbands' surnames. Use the courtesy titles *Mrs., Miss,* or *Ms.* only when specifically requested.

The Pinyin spelling system eliminates the hyphen or apostrophe previously used in many given names. Use the new spelling for *Mao Zedong* and *Zhou Enlai*, but keep the traditional American spelling for such historical figures as *Sun Yat-sen* and *Chiang Kai-shek*.

If the new Pinyin spelling of a proper noun is so radically different from the traditional American spelling that a reader might be confused, provide the Pinyin spelling followed by the traditional spelling in parentheses. For example, the city of *Fuzhou (Foochow)*. Or use a descriptive sentence: *Fuzhou, long known in the West as Foochow, is the capital of Fujian province, on China's eastern coast.*

Use the traditional American spellings for these place names: *China, Inner Mongolia, Shanghai, Tibet.*

Follow local spellings in stories dealing with Hong Kong and Taiwan.

chip In electronics, a sliver of semiconducting material (usually but not always silicon) on which an integrated circuit is fabricated. Chips perform a variety of functions, including processing information (microprocessors) and storing information (memory chips).

chipmaker (n.) **chipmaking** (adj.)

Christian Church (Disciples of Christ) The parentheses and the words they surround are part of the formal name.

The body owes its origins to an early-19th-century frontier movement to unify Christians.

The Disciples, led by Alexander Campbell in western Pennsylvania, and the Christians, led by Barton W. Stone in Kentucky, merged in 1832.

The local church is the basic organizational unit.

National policies are developed

by the General Assembly, made up of representatives chosen by local churches and regional organizations.

The church lists 831,000 members.

All members of the clergy may be referred to as *ministers*. *Pastor* applies if a minister leads a congregation.

On first reference, use *the Rev.* before the name of a man or woman. On second reference, use only the last name.

See **religious titles**.

Christian Science Church See Church of Christ, Scientist.

Christmas, Christmas Day

Dec. 25. The federal legal holiday is observed on Friday if Dec. 25 falls on a Saturday, on Monday if it falls on a Sunday.

Never abbreviate *Christmas* to *Xmas* or any other form.

church Capitalize as part of the formal name of a building, a congregation or a denomination; lowercase in other uses: *St. Mary's Church, the Roman Catholic Church, the Catholic and Episcopal churches, a Roman Catholic church, a church.*

Lowercase in phrases where the church is used in an institutional sense: *She believes in the separation of church and state. The pope said the church opposes abortion.*

See **religious titles** and the entry for the denomination in question.

Churches of Christ Thousands of independent U.S. congregations cooperate under this name. They sponsor numerous educational activities, primarily radio and television programs.

Each local church is autonomous and operates under a governing board of elders. The minister is an evangelist, addressed by members as *Brother*. The ministers do not use clergy titles. Do not precede their names by a title.

The churches do not regard themselves as a denomination. Rather, they stress a nondenominational effort to preach what they consider basic Bible teachings. The churches also teach that baptism is an essential part of the salvation process.

See **religious movements**.

churchgoer

Church of Christ, Scientist

This denomination was founded in 1879 by Mary Baker Eddy. Her teachings are contained in "Science and Health with Key to the Scriptures," which, along with the Bible, she ordained as the impersonal pastor of the church.

The Mother Church in Boston is the international headquarters. Its government provides for a board of directors, which transacts the business of the Mother Church.

A branch church, governed by its own democratically chosen board, is named First Church of Christ, Scientist, or Second Church, etc., according to the order of its establishment in a community.

The terms *Christian Science Church* or *Churches of Christ, Scientist*, are acceptable in all references to the denomination.

The word *Christian* is used because its teachings are based on the word and works of Jesus Christ. The word *Science* is used to reflect the concept that the laws of God are replicable and can be proved in healing sickness and sin.

The church is composed entirely of lay members and does not have clergy in the usual sense. Both men and women may serve as *readers*, *practitioners*, or *lecturers*.

The preferred form for these titles is to use a construction that sets them off from a name with commas. Capitalize them only when used as a formal title immediately before a name. Do not continue use of the title in subsequent references.

The terms *reverend* and *minister* are not applicable. Do not use *the Rev.* in any references.

See **religious titles**.

Church of England See Anglican Communion.

Church of Jesus Christ of Latter-day Saints, The

Note the capitalization and punctuation of *Latter-day*. *Mormon church*, *LDS church* or the *Latter-day Saints* can be used, but the official name is preferred in first reference in a story dealing primarily with church activities.

Members are referred to as *Latter-day Saints* or *Mormons*, the latter based on the church's sacred Book of Mormon.

The church is based on revelations that Joseph Smith said were brought to him in the 1820s by heavenly messengers.

The headquarters is in Salt Lake City, Utah, but millions of its members live outside the U.S .

Church hierarchy is composed of men known as general authorities. Among them, the policymaking body is the First Presidency, made up of a president and two or more counselors. It has final authority in all spiritual and worldly matters.

CLERGY: All worthy young men over the age of 12 are members of the priesthood. They can be ordained elders after age 18, usually after graduating from high school and before serving as missionaries. They may later become high priests, or bishops.

The only formal titles are *president* (for the head of the First Presidency), *bishop* (for members of the Presiding Bishopric and for local bishops) and *elder* (for other general authorities and church missionaries). Capitalize these formal titles

before a name on first reference; use only the last name on second reference.

The terms *minister* or *the Rev.* are not used.

See **religious titles**.

SPLINTER GROUPS: The term Mormon is not properly applied to the other Latter Day Saints churches that resulted from the split after Smith's death.

Among them is the Community of Christ, headquartered in Independence, Mo. From 1860 to 2001, it was called the Reorganized Church of Jesus Christ of Latter Day Saints (note the lack of a hyphen and the capitalized Day).

CIA CIA is acceptable in all references.

The formal title for the individual who heads the agency is *director of central intelligence*. On first reference: *Director David Petraeus of the CIA, Director of Central Intelligence David Petraeus*, or *CIA Director David Petraeus*.

cigarette

Cincinnati The city in Ohio stands alone in datelines.

CIO See AFL-CIO.

Cisco Systems Inc. Headquarters is in San Jose, Calif.

cities and towns Capitalize them in all uses. See **datelines** for guidelines on when they should be followed by a state or a country name.

Capitalize official titles, including separate political entities such as *East St. Louis, Ill.*, or *West Palm Beach, Fla.*

The preferred form for the section of a city is lowercase: *the west end, northern Los Angeles*. But capitalize widely recognized names for the sections of a city: *South Side* (Chicago), *Lower East Side* (New York).

See **city**.

Citigroup Inc. Formed from the combination of Travelers Group and Citicorp in 1998. *Citibank* is its banking unit. Headquarters is in New York.

citizen, resident, subject, national, native A *citizen* is a person who has acquired the full civil rights of a nation either by birth or naturalization. Cities and states in the United States do not confer citizenship. To avoid confusion, use *resident*, not *citizen*, in referring to inhabitants of states and cities.

Citizen is also acceptable for those in the United Kingdom, or other monarchies where the term *subject* is often used.

National is applied to a person residing away from the nation of which he or she is a citizen, or to a person under the protection of a specified nation.

Native is the term denoting that an individual was born in a given location.

citizens band Without an apostrophe after the *s,* based on widespread practice.

CB is acceptable on second reference.

The term describes a group of radio frequencies set aside by the Federal Communications Commission for local use at low power by individuals or businesses.

The Federal Communications Commission no longer requires a license to operate a CB station. Identification of such stations, either by the call sign previously assigned or made up by the operator, composed of the letter *K,* the operator's initials and the operator's ZIP code, is optional.

city Capitalize *city* if part of a proper name, an integral part of an official name, or a regularly used nickname: *Kansas City, New York City, Windy City, City of Light, Fun City.*

Lowercase elsewhere: *a Texas city; the city government; the city Board of Education;* and all *city of* phrases: *the city of Boston.*

Capitalize when part of a formal title before a name: *City Manager Francis McGrath.* Lowercase when not part of the formal title: *city Health Commissioner Frank Smith.*

See **city council** and **governmental bodies**.

city commission See the next entry.

city council Capitalize when part of a proper name: *the Boston City Council.*

Retain capitalization if the reference is to a specific council but the context does not require the city name:

BOSTON (AP) — The City Council ...

Lowercase in other uses: *the council, the Boston and New York city councils, a city council.*

Use the proper name if the body is not known as a city council: *the Miami City Commission, the City Commission, the commission; the Louisville Board of Aldermen, the Board of Aldermen, the board.*

Use *city council* in a generic sense for plural references: *the Boston, Louisville and Miami city councils.*

city editor Capitalize as a formal title before a name. See **titles**.

city hall Capitalize with the name of a city, or without the name of a city if the reference is specific: *Boston City Hall, City Hall.*

Lowercase plural uses: *the Boston*

and New York city halls.

Lowercase generic uses, including: *You can't fight city hall.*

citywide

civil cases, criminal cases

A *civil case* is one in which an individual, business or agency of government seeks damages or relief from another individual, business or agency of government. Civil actions generally involve a charge that a contract has been breached or that someone has been wronged or injured.

A *criminal case* is one that the state or the federal government brings against an individual charged with committing a crime.

Civil War

clean up (v.) cleanup (n. and adj.)

clear-cut (adj.)

clerical titles See religious titles.

Cleveland The city in Ohio stands alone in datelines.

clientele

cloak-and-dagger

Clorox A trademark for a brand of bleach.

closed shop A *closed shop* is an agreement between a union and an employer that requires workers to be members of a union before they may be employed.

A *union shop* requires workers to join a union within a specified period after they are employed.

An *agency shop* requires that the workers who do not want to join the union pay the union a fee instead of union dues.

A *guild shop*, a term often used when the union is The Newspaper Guild, is the same as a *union shop*.

See the **right-to-work** entry for an explanation of how some states prohibit contracts that require workers to join unions.

closely held corporation A corporation in which stock shares and voting control are concentrated in the hands of a small number of investors, but for which some shares are available and traded on the market.

close-up (n. and adj.)

cloture Not *closure*, for the parliamentary procedure for closing debate.

Whenever practical, use a phrase such as closing debate or ending debate instead of the technical term.

CME Group Inc. Parent of the Chicago Board of Trade and the Chicago Mercantile Exchange, which operates the Globex electronic trading platform and live trading floors. Its products include futures and options based on interest rates, equity indexes, foreign exchange, agricultural commodities, energy and alternative investment products, such as weather and real estate. Headquarters is in Chicago.

CNN Acceptable in all references for the *Cable News Network*. Owned by Time Warner Inc.

co- Retain the hyphen when forming nouns, adjectives and verbs that indicate occupation or status:

co-author	co-pilot
co-chairman	co-respondent
	(in a divorce suit)
co-defendant	co-signer
co-host	co-sponsor
co-owner	co-star
co-partner	co-worker

(Several are exceptions to Webster's New World College Dictionary in the interests of consistency.)

Use no hyphen in other combinations:

coed	cooperate
coeducation	cooperative
coequal	coordinate
coexist	coordination
coexistence	

Cooperate, coordinate and related words are exceptions to the rule that a hyphen is used if a prefix ends in a vowel and the word that follows begins with the same vowel.

Co. See **company, companies**.

coast Lowercase when referring to the physical shoreline: *Atlantic coast, Pacific coast, east coast*.

Capitalize when referring to regions of the United States lying along such shorelines: *the Atlantic Coast states, a Gulf Coast city, the West Coast, the East Coast*.

Do not capitalize when referring to smaller regions: *the Virginia coast*.

Capitalize *the Coast* when standing alone only if the reference is to the West Coast.

coastal waters See **weather terms**.

Coast Guard Capitalize when referring to this branch of the U.S. armed forces, a part of the Department of Homeland Security: *the U.S. Coast Guard, the Coast Guard, Coast Guard policy*. Do not use the abbreviation *USCG*, except in quotes.

Use lowercase for similar forces of other nations.

This approach has been adopted for consistency, because many foreign nations do not use *coast guard* as the proper name.

See **military academies**.

Coast Guardsman Capitalize as a proper noun when referring to

an individual in a U.S. Coast Guard unit: *He is a Coast Guardsman*.

Lowercase *guardsman* when it stands alone.

See **military titles**.

coastline

coattails

cocaine The slang term *coke* should appear only in quoted matter.

Crack is a refined cocaine in crystalline rock form.

c.o.d. Preferred in all references for *cash on delivery* or *collect on delivery*.

coed The preferred term as a noun is *female student*, but *coed* is acceptable as an adjective to describe coeducational institutions. No hyphen.

Cold War Capitalize when referring specifically to the post-World War II rivalry between the United States and the former Soviet Union. Use only in the historic sense.

collateral Stock or other property that a borrower is obliged to turn over to a lender if unable to repay a loan.

See **loan terminology**.

collateralized debt obligations Debt, including bonds or mortgages, that is pooled, sliced up and resold to investors.

collectibles

collective nouns Nouns that denote a unit take singular verbs and pronouns: *class, committee, crowd, family, group, herd, jury, orchestra, team*.

Some usage examples: *The committee is meeting to set its agenda. The jury reached its verdict. A herd of cattle was sold.*

Team names and musical group names that are plural take plural verbs. *The Yankees are in first place. The Jonas Brothers are popular.*

Team or group names with no plural forms also take plural verbs: *The Miami Heat are battling for third place.* Other examples: *Orlando Magic, Oklahoma City Thunder, Utah Jazz.*

Many singular names take singular verbs: *Coldplay is on tour. Boston is favored in the playoffs. The Cardinal is in the NCAA tournament.*

But some proper names that are plural in form take a singular verb: *Brooks Brothers is holding a sale.*

PLURAL IN FORM: Some words that are plural in form become collective nouns and take singular verbs when the group or quantity is regarded as a unit.

Right: *A thousand bushels is a good yield.* (A unit.)

Right: *A thousand bushels were created.* (Individual items.)

Right: *The data is sound.* (A unit.)

Right: *The data have been carefully collected.* (Individual items.)

collectors' item

college Capitalize when part of a proper name: *Dartmouth College.*

See **organizations and institutions**.

College of Cardinals See **Roman Catholic Church**.

collide, collision Two objects must be in motion before they can *collide*. A moving train cannot *collide* with a stopped train.

colloquialisms The word describes the informal use of a language. It is not local or regional in nature, as dialect is.

Webster's New World College Dictionary identifies many words as colloquial with the label *Informal*.

Many colloquial words and phrases characteristic of informal writing and conversation are acceptable in some contexts but out of place in others. Examples include *pal* and *nail*.

Other colloquial words normally should be avoided because they are pejorative. Webster's New World College Dictionary notes, for example, that *ain't* is informal, a "dialectal or nonstandard usage," although "widely used informally by educated speakers." Many still consider it illiterate and it should not be used in news stories unless needed to illustrate nonstandard speech in writing.

See **dialect**.

colon See entry in **Punctuation** chapter.

colonel See **military titles**.

colonial Capitalize *Colonial* as a proper adjective in all references to the *Colonies*. (See the next entry.)

colonies Capitalize only for the British dependencies that declared their independence in 1776, now known as the United States.

Colorado Abbreviate *Colo.* in datelines or stories. Postal code: *CO*

See **state names**.

colorblind

colored In some societies, including the United States, the word is considered derogatory and should not be used.

In some countries of Africa, it is used to denote individuals of mixed racial ancestry. Whenever the word is used, place it in quotation marks and provide an explanation of its meaning.

Columbus Day Oct. 12. The federal legal holiday is the second Monday in October.

coma A state of unconsciousness in which the eyes are closed and the patient can't be aroused as if simply asleep. There is no sign of a sleep-wake cycle, or of any awareness of self or environment. The patient cannot communicate or hear, and shows no emotion. Any movement is purely reflex. This is the first stage after a severe brain injury; the patient may recover partially or completely, die, or progress to a vegetative or minimally conscious state.
See **minimally conscious state** and **vegetative state**.

combat, combated, combating

combustible

Comcast Corp. Headquarters is in Philadelphia.

comedian Use for both men and women.

comma See entry in **Punctuation** chapter.

commander See **military titles**.

commander in chief Capitalize only if used as a formal title before a name.
See **titles**.

commercial paper Short-term loans, issued primarily by corporations, to finance their daily needs, such as making payroll. Historically, a lower cost alternative to bank loans.

commissioner Do not abbreviate. Capitalize when used as a formal title.
See **titles**.

commitment

committee Do not abbreviate. Capitalize when part of a formal name: *the House Appropriations Committee.*
Do not capitalize committee in shortened versions of long committee names: *the Special Senate Select Committee to Investigate Improper Labor-Management Practices,* for example, became *the rackets committee.*
See **subcommittee**.

commodities futures contract A contract to purchase or sell a specific amount of a given commodity at a specified future date.

commodity The products of mining or agriculture before they have undergone extensive processing.

common stock, preferred stock An ownership interest in a corporation.
If other classes of stock are outstanding, the holders of common stock are the last to receive dividends and the last to receive payments if a corporation is dissolved. The company may raise or lower common stock dividends as its earnings rise or fall.
When preferred stock is outstanding and company earnings are sufficient, a fixed dividend is paid. If a company is liquidated, holders of preferred stock receive payments up to a set amount before any money is distributed to holders of common stock.

commonwealth A group of people united by their common interests.
See **state**.

Commonwealth of Independent States Founded Dec. 8, 1991, the organization is made up of 11 of the former republics of the USSR, or Soviet Union. Russia is the largest and richest. Three other former republics — Latvia, Lithuania and Estonia — became independent nations earlier in 1991. (The Soviet Union was formally dissolved in December 1991. Its last leader, Mikhail Gorbachev, resigned on Dec. 25, 1991.)

The republics (with adjective form in parentheses):

Armenia (Armenian); Azerbaijan (Azerbaijani); Belarus (Belarusian); Kazakhstan (Kazakh); Kyrgyzstan (Kyrgyz); Moldova (Moldovan); Russia (Russian); Tajikistan (Tajik); Turkmenistan (Turkmen); Ukraine (no *the*) (Ukrainian); Uzbekistan (Uzbek). Georgia (Georgian) quit CIS in 2008.

DATELINES: MOSCOW stands alone. Follow all other datelines with the name of the state. *ALMATY, Kazakhstan.*

Commonwealth, the Formerly the British Commonwealth. The members of this frcc association of sovereign states recognize the British sovereign as head of the Commonwealth. Some also recognize the sovereign as head of their state; others do not.

The members are: Antigua and Barbuda, Australia, Bahamas, Bangladesh, Barbados, Belize, Botswana, Brunei, Cameroon, Canada, Cyprus, Dominica, Fiji, Gambia, Ghana, Grenada, Guyana, India, Jamaica, Kenya, Kiribati, Lesotho, Malawi, Malaysia, Maldives, Malta, Mauritius, Mozambique, Namibia, Nauru, New Zealand, Nigeria, Pakistan (suspended after the 1999 military coup; suspension lifted 2004), Papua New Guinea, St. Kitts and Nevis, St. Lucia, St. Vincent and the Grenadines, Samoa, Seychelles, Sierra Leone, Singapore, Solomon Islands, South Africa, Sri Lanka, Swaziland, Tanzania, Tonga, Trinidad and Tobago, Tuvalu, Uganda, United Kingdom, Vanuatu and Zambia. (Zimbabwe withdrew in 2003.)

Communications Workers of America The shortened form *Communications Workers union* is acceptable in all references.

Headquarters is in Washington.

communism, communist See **political parties and philosophies**.

commutation A legal term for a change of sentence or punishment to one that is less severe.

See **pardon, parole, probations**.

compact disc *CD* is acceptable in all references.

company, companies Use *Co.* or *Cos.* when a business uses either word at the end of its proper name: *Ford Motor Co., American Broadcasting Cos.*

If *company* or *companies* appears alone in second reference, spell the word out.

The forms for possessives: *Ford Motor Co.'s profits, American Broadcasting Cos.' profits.*

company (military) Capitalize only when part of a name: *Company B.* Do not abbreviate.

company names For a company's formal name, consult the national stock exchanges: the New York Stock Exchange, www.nyse.com, or Nasdaq, www.nasdaq.com. AP staffers may also reference an alphabetical list of all company names, with stock ticker abbreviations, at http://biz.ap.org. See below for 125 major U.S. companies and 70 major non-U.S. companies.

Do not use a comma before *Inc.* or *Ltd.*, even if it is included in the formal name.

You must include the full company name somewhere in the story. This ensures the story will be among the search results on major websites.

The formal name need not be used on first reference — for example, *Costco* is acceptable for *Costco Wholesale Corp.* — but it should be contained in the body of any story in which the subject matter could affect a company's business. For example, include the corporate name in a story on an earnings report, or in a story on a plane crash that could affect the airline's stock price. However, the corporate name might be irrelevant in a story about a political candidate's appearance at a local retail outlet.

When the full corporate name is NOT in the story, it should be included in a self-contained paragraph separated from the bottom of the story by a dash: *American Airlines is a unit of AMR Corp.*, or *Disney's full corporate name is The Walt Disney Co.* If more than one company is listed, each should be in a self-contained paragraph below the dash.

Generally, follow the spelling and capitalization preferred by the company: *eBay.* But capitalize the first letter if it begins a sentence.

Do not use all-capital-letter names unless the letters are individually pronounced: *BMW.* Others should be uppercase and lowercase. *Ikea*, not *IKEA*; *USA Today*, not *USA TODAY.*

Do not use symbols such as exclamation points, plus signs or asterisks that form contrived spellings that might distract or confuse a reader. Use *Yahoo*, not *Yahoo!*; *Toys R Us*, not *Toys "R" Us*; *E-Trade*, not *E*Trade.*

Use an ampersand only if it is part of the company's formal name, but not otherwise in place of *and.*

Use *the* lowercase unless it is part of the company's formal name.

Here are 125 major U.S. companies, listed alphabetically with ticker symbols and headquarters:

3M Co. (MMM) St. Paul, Minn.

Abbott Laboratories (ABT) Abbott Park, Ill.

Aetna Inc. (AET) Hartford, Conn.

Alcoa Inc. (AA) Pittsburgh

Allstate Corp. (ALL) Northbrook, Ill.

Altria Group Inc. (MO) Richmond, Va.

Amazon.com Inc. (AMZN) Seattle

American Express Co. (AXP) New York

American International Group Inc. (AIG) New York

Amgen Inc. (AMGN) Thousand Oaks, Calif.

AMR Corp. (AMR) Fort Worth, Texas

Anadarko Petroleum Corp. (APC) The Woodlands, Texas

Apple Inc. (AAPL) Cupertino, Calif.

AT&T Inc. (T) Dallas

Bank of America Corp. (BAC) Charlotte, N.C.

Berkshire Hathaway Inc. (BRK.A) Omaha, Neb.

Best Buy Co. Inc. (BBY) Richfield, Minn.

Biogen Idec Inc. (BIIB) Weston, Mass.

Boeing Co. (BA) Chicago

Bristol-Myers Squibb Co. (BMY) New York

Carnival Corp. (CCL) Miami

Caterpillar Inc. (CAT) Peoria, Ill.

CBS Corp. (CBS) New York

Chevron Corp. (CVX) San Ramon, Calif.

Cisco Systems Inc. (CSCO) San Jose, Calif.

Citigroup Inc. (C) New York

Coca-Cola Co. (KO) Atlanta

Colgate-Palmolive Co. (CL) New York

Comcast Corp. (CMCSA) Philadelphia

ConAgra Foods Inc. (CAG) Omaha, Neb.

ConocoPhillips (COP) Houston

Costco Wholesale Corp. (COST) Issaquah, Wash.

CVS Caremark Corp. (CVS) Woonsocket, R.I.

Deere & Co. (DE) Moline, Ill.

Dell Inc. (DELL) Round Rock, Texas

Delta Air Lines Inc. (DAL) Atlanta

DirecTV Group Inc. (DTV) El Segundo, Calif.

Dow Chemical Co. (DOW) Midland, Mich.

Duke Energy Corp. (DUK) Charlotte, N.C.

DuPont Co. (DD) Wilmington, Del.

eBay Inc. (EBAY) San Jose, Calif.

Eli Lilly & Co. (LLY) Indianapolis

EMC Corp. (EMC) Hopkinton, Mass.

Exelon Corp. (EXC) Chicago

Exxon Mobil Corp. (XOM) Irving, Texas

FedEx Corp. (FDX) Memphis, Tenn.

Ford Motor Co. (F) Dearborn, Mich.

General Dynamics Corp. (GD) Falls Church, Va.

General Electric Co. (GE) Fairfield, Conn.

General Mills Inc. (GIS) Minneapolis

General Motors Co. (GM) Detroit

Goldman Sachs Group Inc. (GS) New York

Google Inc. (GOOG) Mountain View, Calif.

Halliburton Co. (HAL) Houston

Hewlett-Packard Co. (HPQ) Palo Alto, Calif.

H.J. Heinz Co. (HNZ) Pittsburgh

Home Depot Inc. (HD) Atlanta

Honeywell International Inc. (HON) Morristown, N.J.

Intel Corp. (INTC) Santa Clara, Calif.

International Business Machines Corp. (IBM) Armonk, N.Y.

J. C. Penney & Co. (JCP) Plano, Texas

Johnson & Johnson (JNJ) New Brunswick, N.J.

Johnson Controls Inc. (JCI) Milwaukee

JPMorgan Chase & Co. (JPM) New York

Kellogg Co. (K) Battle Creek, Mich.

Kimberly-Clark Corp. (KMB) Irving, Texas

Kraft Foods Inc. (KFT) Northfield, Ill.

Kroger Co., The (KR) Cincinnati.

Lockheed Martin Corp. (LMT) Bethesda, Md.

Lowe's Cos. (LOW) Mooresville, N.C.

Macy's Inc. (M) Cincinnati.

Marathon Oil Corp. (MRO) Houston

MasterCard Inc. (MA) Purchase, N.Y.

McDonald's Corp. (MCD) Oak Brook, Ill.

McKesson Corp. (MCK) San Francisco

Medco Health Solutions, Inc. (MHS) Franklin Lakes, N.J.

Medtronic Inc. (MDT) Minneapolis

Merck & Co. (MRK) Whitehouse Station, N.J.

MetLife Inc. (MET) New York

Microsoft Corp. (MSFT) Redmond, Wash.

Monsanto Co. (MON) St. Louis

Morgan Stanley (MS) New York

Newmont Mining Corp. (NEM) Greenwood Village, Colo.

News Corp. (NWSA) New York

Nike Inc. (NKE) Beaverton, Ore.

Norfolk Southern Corp. (NSC) Norfolk, Va.

Northrop Grumman Corp. (NOC) Los Angeles

Occidental Petroleum Corp.

(OXY) Los Angeles

Oracle Corp. (ORCL) Redwood City, Calif.

PepsiCo Inc. (PEP) Purchase, N.Y.

Pfizer Inc. (PFE) New York

Philip Morris International (PM) Richmond, Va.

PNC Financial Services Group Inc. (PNC) Pittsburgh

Procter & Gamble Co. (PG) Cincinnati

Prudential Financial Inc. (PRU) Newark, N.J.

Qualcomm Inc. (QCOM) San Diego

Raytheon Co. (RTN) Waltham, Mass.

Schlumberger Ltd. (SLB) Houston

Sears Holdings Corp. (SHLD) Hoffman Estates, Ill.

Simon Property Group Inc. (SPG) Indianapolis

Southwest Airlines Co. (LUV) Dallas

Sprint Nextel Corp. (S) Reston, Va.

Starbucks Corp. (SBUX) Seattle

Target Corp. (TGT) Minneapolis

Texas Instruments Inc. (TXN) Dallas

Time Warner Inc. (TWX) New York

Travelers Cos. (TRV) St. Paul, Minn.

Tyson Foods Inc. (TSN) Springdale, Ark.

Union Pacific Corp. (UNP) Omaha, Neb.

United Continental Holdings Inc. (UAL) Chicago

UnitedHealth Group Inc. (UNH) Minnetonka, Minn.

United Parcel Service Inc. (UPS) Atlanta

United States Steel Corp. (X) Pittsburgh

United Technologies Corp. (UTX) Hartford, Conn.

US Bancorp (USB) Minneapolis

Verizon Communications Inc. (VZ) New York

Viacom Inc. (VIA) New York

Visa Inc. (V) Foster City, Calif.

Walgreen Co. (WAG) Deerfield, Ill.

Wal-Mart Stores Inc. (WMT) Bentonville, Ark.

Walt Disney Co., The (DIS) Burbank, Calif.

WellPoint Inc. (WLP) Indianapolis

Wells Fargo & Co. (WFC) San Francisco

Whirlpool Corp. (WHR) Benton Harbor, Mich.

Xerox Corp. (XRX) Norwalk, Conn.

Yahoo Inc. (YHOO) Sunnyvale, Calif.

Here are 70 major non-U.S. companies, listed alphabetically with headquarters:

Allianz SE, Munich

America Movil S.A.B. de C.V., Mexico City

Anheuser-Busch InBev, Leuven, Belgium

ArcelorMittal, Luxembourg

AstraZeneca PLC, London

Baidu Inc. Beijing

Banco Santander SA, Madrid

Bank of China, Beijing

Barrick Gold Corp., Toronto

Bayer AG, Leverkusen, Germany

BHP Billiton Ltd., Melbourne, Australia

BMW Group, Munich

BP PLC, London

Carrefour SA, Paris

China Construction Bank Corp., Beijing

China Mobile Ltd., Beijing

China Petroleum & Chemical Corp. or Sinopec, Beijing

CNOOC Ltd., Beijing

Credit Suisse Group, Zurich

Daimler AG, Stuttgart, Germany

Deutsche Bank, Frankfurt

Deutsche Telekom AG, Bonn,

Germany
 Diageo PLC, London
 Electricite de France, Paris
 ELF Aquitaine Group, Paris
 Eni SpA, Rome
 E.ON AG, Dusseldorf, Germany
 European Aeronautic Defence &
Space Co., Amsterdam
 France Telecom, Paris
 OAO Gazprom, Moscow
 GlaxoSmithKline PLC, London
 Honda Motor Co., Tokyo
 HSBC Holdings PLC, London
 Industrial and Commercial Bank
of China, Beijing
 L'Oreal SA, Paris
 LVMH Moet Hennessy Louis
Vuitton, Paris
 Mitsubishi UFJ Financial Group
Inc., Tokyo
 Nestle SA, Vevey, Switzerland
 Nintendo Co., Kyoto, Japan
 Nippon Telegraph & Telephone
Corp., Tokyo
 Nissan Motor Co., Tokyo
 Nokia Corp., Espoo, Finland
 Novartis AG, Basel, Switzerland
 Novo Nordisk A/S, Bagsværd,
Denmark
 PetroChina Ltd., Beijing
 Petroleo Brasileiro, Rio de Ja-
neiro
 Ranbaxy Laboratories Ltd., New
Delhi
 Reliance Industries Ltd., Mum-
bai, India
 Rio Tinto Group, London and
Melbourne, Australia
 Roche Holding AG, Basel, Swit-
zerland
 Royal Dutch Shell PLC, The
Hague, Netherlands
 SABMiller, London
 Samsung Electronics Co., Seoul,
South Korea
 Sanofi-Aventis, Paris
 SAP AG, Walldorf, Germany
 Siemens AG, Munich
 Societe Generale Group, Paris
 Sony Corp., Tokyo
 Tata Group, Mumbai, India

 Telefonica SA, Madrid
 Tesco PLC, London
 Teva Pharmaceutical Industries
Ltd., Petach Tikvah, Israel
 Total SA, Paris
 Toyota Motor Corp., Toyota City,
Japan
 UBS AG, Zurich
 Unilever NV, London and Rotter-
dam, Netherlands
 Vale SA, Rio de Janeiro
 Vivendi, Paris
 Vodafone Group PLC, Newbury,
UK
 Volkswagen AG, Wolfsburg, Ger-
many
 Xstrata plc, Zug, Switzerland

compared to, compared with
Use *compared to* when the intent is to assert, without the need for elaboration, that two or more items are similar: *She compared her work for women's rights to Susan B. Anthony's campaign for women's suffrage.*

Use *compared with* when juxtaposing two or more items to illustrate similarities and/or differences: *His time was 2:11:10, compared with 2:14 for his closest competitor.*

compatible

complacent, complaisant
Complacent means self-satisfied.
Complaisant means eager to please.

complementary, complimentary
The husband and wife have complementary careers.
They received complimentary tickets to the show.

complement, compliment
Complement is a noun and a verb denoting completeness or the process of supplementing something: *The ship has a complement of 200 sailors and 20 officers. The tie complements his suit.*

Compliment is a noun or a verb that denotes praise or the expression of courtesy: *The captain complimented the sailors. She was flattered by the compliments on her project.*

compose, comprise, constitute

Compose means to create or put together. It commonly is used in both the active and passive voices: *She composed a song. The United States is composed of 50 states. The zoo is composed of many animals.*

Comprise means to contain, to include all or embrace. It is best used only in the active voice, followed by a direct object: *The United States comprises 50 states. The jury comprises five men and seven women. The zoo comprises many animals.*

Constitute, in the sense of form or make up, may be the best word if neither *compose* nor *comprise* seems to fit: *Fifty states constitute the United States. Five men and seven women constitute the jury. A collection of animals can constitute a zoo.*

Use *include* when what follows is only part of the total: *The price includes breakfast. The zoo includes lions and tigers.*

composition titles

Apply the guidelines listed here to book titles, computer game titles, movie titles, opera titles, play titles, poem titles, album and song titles, radio and television program titles, and the titles of lectures, speeches and works of art.

The guidelines, followed by a block of examples:

—Capitalize the principal words, including prepositions and conjunctions of four or more letters.

—Capitalize an article — *the, a, an* — or words of fewer than four letters if it is the first or last word in a title.

—Put quotation marks around the names of all such works except the Bible and books that are primarily catalogs of reference material. In addition to catalogs, this category includes almanacs, directories, dictionaries, encyclopedias, gazetteers, handbooks and similar publications. Do not use quotation marks around such software titles as WordPerfect or Windows.

—Translate a foreign title into English unless a work is generally known by its foreign name. An exception to this is reviews of musical performances. In those instances, generally refer to the work in the language it was sung in, so as to differentiate for the reader. However, musical compositions in Slavic languages are always referred to in their English translations.

EXAMPLES: *"The Star-Spangled Banner," "The Rise and Fall of the Third Reich," "Gone With the Wind," "Of Mice and Men," "For Whom the Bell Tolls," "Time After Time,"* the NBC-TV *"Today"* program, the *"CBS Evening News," "The Mary Tyler Moore Show."* See television program names for further guidelines and examples.

Reference works: *Jane's All the World's Aircraft; Encyclopaedia Britannica; Webster's New World Dictionary of the American Language, Second Edition.*

Names of most websites and apps are capitalized without quotes: *Facebook, Foursquare.*

Exception: *"FarmVille"* and similar computer game apps are in quotes.

Foreign works: *Rousseau's "War,"* not *Rousseau's "La Guerre."* But: *Leonardo da Vinci's "Mona Lisa."* Mozart's *"The Marriage of Figaro"* if sung in English but *"Le Nozze di Figaro"* if sung in Italian. Mozart's *"The Magic Flute"* if sung in English but *"Die Zauberfloete"* if sung in German. *"Die Walkuere"* and *"Goetterdaemmerung"* from Wagner's

"*Der Ring des Nibelungen*" if sung in German but "*The Valkyrie*" and "*The Twilight of the Gods*" from "*The Ring of the Nibelung*" if sung in English. Janacek's "*From the House of the Dead*," not Janacek's "*Z Mrtveho Domu.*"

— For other classical music titles, use quotation marks around the composition's nicknames but not compositions identified by its sequence.

EXAMPLES: *Dvorak's "New World Symphony." Dvorak's Symphony No. 9.*

compound adjectives See **hyphen** entry in **Punctuation** chapter.

comptroller, controller *Comptroller* generally is the accurate word for government financial officers.

The U.S. comptroller of the currency is an appointed official in the Treasury Department who is responsible for the chartering, supervising and liquidation of banks organized under the federal government's National Bank Act.

Controller generally is the proper word for financial officers of businesses and for other positions such as *air traffic controller*.

Capitalize *comptroller* and *controller* when used as the formal titles for financial officers. Use lowercase for *aircraft controller* and similar occupational applications of the word.

See **titles**.

concentration camps For World War II camps in countries occupied by Nazi Germany, do not use phrases like *Polish death camps* that confuse the location and the perpetrators. Use instead, for example, *death camps in Nazi-occupied Poland.*

conclave A private or secret meeting. In the Roman Catholic Church it describes the private meeting of cardinals to elect a pope.

concrete See **cement**.

Confederate States of America The formal name of the states that seceded during the Civil War. The shortened form *the Confederacy* is acceptable in all references.

Conference Board, The The capitalized article is part of the formal name of the business organization.

confess, confessed In some contexts the words may be erroneous.

See **admit**.

confidant (n.) A male friend to whom one confides secrets. The female spelling is *confidante*.

confirmation See **sacraments**.

conglomerate A corporation that has diversified its operations, usually by acquiring enterprises in widely varied industries.

Congo In datelines:
KINSHASA, Congo (AP) —
BRAZZAVILLE, Republic of Congo (AP) —
Use *Congo* or *the Congo*, as the construction of a sentence dictates, in second references.

Congress Capitalize *U.S. Congress* and *Congress* when referring to the U.S. Senate and House of Representatives. Although *Congress* sometimes is used as a substitute for the House, it properly is reserved for reference to both the Senate and House.

Capitalize *Congress* also if referring to a foreign body that uses the term, or its equivalent in a foreign language, as part of its formal name: *the Argentine Congress, the Congress.*

See **non-U.S. legislative bodies**.

Lowercase when used as a synonym for *convention* or in second reference to an organization that uses the word as part of its formal name: *the Congress of Racial Equality, the congress.*

congressional Lowercase unless part of a proper name: *congressional salaries, the Congressional Quarterly, the Congressional Record.*

Congressional Directory Use this as the reference source for questions about the federal government that are not covered by this stylebook.

congressional districts Use figures and capitalize district when joined with a figure: *the 1st Congressional District, the 1st District.*

Lowercase *district* whenever it stands alone.

Congressional Record A daily publication of the proceedings of Congress including a complete stenographic report of all remarks and debates.

congressman, congresswoman Use only in reference to members of the U.S. House of Representatives.

See **legislative titles**.

Congress of Racial Equality *CORE* is acceptable on second reference.

Headquarters is in New York.

Connecticut Abbreviate *Conn.* in datelines or stories. Postal code: *CT*

See **state names**.

connote, denote *Connote* means to suggest or imply something beyond the explicit meaning: *To some people, the word "marriage" connotes too much restriction.*

Denote means to be explicit about the meaning: *The word "demolish" denotes destruction.*

ConocoPhillips Headquarters is in Houston.

consensus

conservative See **political parties and philosophies**.

Conservative Judaism See **Jewish congregations**.

constable Capitalize when used as a formal title before a name. See **titles**.

constitute See **compose, comprise, constitute**.

constitution Capitalize references to the U.S. Constitution, with or without the *U.S.* modifier: *The president said he supports the Constitution.*

When referring to constitutions of other nations or of states, capitalize only with the name of a nation or a state: *the French Constitution, the Massachusetts Constitution, the nation's constitution, the state constitution, the constitution.*

Lowercase in other uses: *the organization's constitution.*

Lowercase *constitutional* in all uses.

consulate A *consulate* is the residence of a consul in a foreign city. It handles the commercial affairs and personal needs of citizens of the appointing country.

Capitalize with the name of a nation; lowercase without it: *the French Consulate, the U.S. Consulate, the consulate.*

See **embassy** for the distinction between a consulate and an embassy.

consul, consul general, consuls general Capitalize when used as a formal title before a noun.
See **titles**.

consumer credit Loans extended to individuals or small businesses usually on an unsecured basis, and providing for monthly repayment. Also referred to as installment credit or personal loans.

Consumer Financial Protection Bureau Created by Congress under the 2010 financial overhaul to oversee mortgages, payday loans and other consumer borrowing. It aimed to close regulatory gaps exposed by the 2008 financial crisis. *CFPB* is acceptable on second reference.

consumer price index A measurement of changes in the retail prices of a constant marketbasket of goods and services. It is computed by comparing the cost of the marketbasket at a fixed time with its cost at subsequent or prior intervals.

It is issued monthly by the Bureau of Labor Statistics, an agency of the Labor Department. It should not be referred to as a *cost-of-living index*, because it does not include the impact of income taxes and Social Security taxes on the cost of living, nor does it reflect changes in buying patterns that result from inflation. It is, however, the basis for computing cost-of-living raises in many union contracts.

The preferred form for second reference is *the index*. Confine *CPI* to quoted material.

Consumer Product Safety Commission

contagious

contemptible

continent The seven continents, in order of their land size: Asia, Africa, North America, South America, Europe, Antarctica and Australia.

Capitalize *the Continent* and *Continental* only when used as synonyms for Europe or European. Lowercase in other uses such as: *the continent of Europe, the European continent, the African and Asian continents*.

Continental Airlines Use this spelling of *Airlines*, which Continental has adopted for its public identity. It now is a unit of United Continental Holdings Inc., based in Chicago.

Continental Divide The ridge along the Rocky Mountains that separates rivers flowing east from those that flow west.

continental shelf, continental slope Lowercase. The *shelf* is the part of a continent that is submerged in relatively shallow sea at gradually increasing depths, generally up to about 600 feet below sea level.

The *continental slope* begins at the point where the descent to the ocean bottom becomes very steep.

continual, continuous *Continual* means a steady repetition, over and over again: *The merger has been the source of continual litigation.*

Continuous means uninterrupted, steady, unbroken: *All she saw ahead of her was a continuous stretch of desert.*

Contra, Contras Uppercase when used to describe former Nicaraguan rebel groups.

contractions Contractions reflect informal speech and writing. Webster's New World College Dictionary includes many entries for contractions: *aren't* for *are not*, for example.

Avoid excessive use of contractions. Contractions listed in the dictionary are acceptable, however, in informal contexts where they reflect the way a phrase commonly appears in speech or writing.

See **colloquialisms** and **quotations in the news**.

contrasted to, contrasted with Use *contrasted to* when the intent is to assert, without the need for elaboration, that two items have opposite characteristics: *He contrasted the appearance of the house today to its ramshackle look last year.*

Use *contrasted with* when juxtaposing two or more items to illustrate similarities and/or differences: *He contrasted the Republican platform with the Democratic platform.*

control, controlled, controlling

controller See **comptroller, controller**.

controversial An overused word; avoid it.

convention Capitalize as part of the name for a specific national or state political convention: *the Democratic National Convention, the Republican State Convention.*

Lowercase in other uses: *the national convention, the state convention, the convention, the annual convention of the American Medical Association.*

convertible bond See **loan terminology**.

convict (v.) Follow with preposition *of*, not *for*: *He was convicted of murder.*

convince, persuade You may be *convinced that* something or *of*

something. You must be *persuaded* to *do* something.

Example: *John convinced Marsha of his good intentions. John persuaded Marsha to marry him.*

cookie, cookies A file many websites place on computers to save identifying information.

cooperate, cooperative But *co-op* as a short term of *cooperative*, to distinguish it from *coop*, a cage for animals.

Cooperative for Assistance and Relief Everywhere See **CARE**.

coordinate, coordination

cop Be careful in the use of this colloquial term for *police officer*. It may be used in lighter stories and in casual, informal descriptions, but often is a derogatory term out of place in serious police stories.

Copenhagen The city in Denmark carries the country name in datelines.

copter Acceptable shortening of *helicopter*. But use it only as a noun or adjective. It is not a verb.

copy editor Seldom a formal title. Also: *copy editing, copy edit*. See **titles**.

copyright (n., v. and adj.) *A copyright story.*

Use *copyrighted* only as the past tense of the verb: *He copyrighted the article.*

See **Copyright Infringement** in **Briefing on Media Law** section.

co-respondent In a divorce suit.

Corn Belt The region in the north-central Midwest where much corn and corn-fed livestock are raised. It extends from western Ohio to eastern Nebraska and northeastern Kansas.

Corp. See **corporation**.

corporal See **military titles**.

corporate names See **company names**.

corporation An entity that is treated as a person in the eyes of the law. It is able to own property, incur debts, sue and be sued.

Abbreviate *corporation* as *Corp.* when a company or government agency uses the word at the end of its name: *the Federal Deposit Insurance Corp.*

Spell out *corporation* when it occurs elsewhere in a name: *the Corporation for Public Broadcasting.*

Spell out and lowercase *corporation* whenever it stands alone.

The form for possessives: *Chevron Corp.'s profits.*

corps Capitalize when used with a word or a figure to form a proper name: *the Marine Corps, the Signal Corps, the 9th Corps.*

Capitalize when standing alone only if it is a shortened reference to *U.S. Marine Corps.*

The possessive form is *corps'* for both singular and plural: *one corps' location, two corps' assignments.*

corral, corralled, corralling

correctional facility, correctional institution See **prison, jail**.

Corsica Use instead of *France* in datelines on stories from communities on this island.

Cortes The Spanish parliament. See **foreign legislative bodies**.

cosmonaut A Russian or Soviet astronaut.

cost of living The amount of money needed to pay taxes and to buy the goods and services deemed necessary to make up a given standard of living, taking into account changes that may occur in tastes and buying patterns.

The term often is treated incorrectly as a synonym for the *U.S. Consumer Price Index*, which does not take taxes into account and measures only price changes, keeping the quantities constant over time.

Hyphenate when used as a compound modifier: *The cost of living went up, but he did not receive a cost-of-living raise.*

See **consumer price index** and **inflation**.

cost-plus

Cotton Belt The region in the South and Southwestern sections of the United States where much cotton is grown.

council, councilor, councilman, councilwoman A deliberative body and those who are members of it.

See **counsel** and **legislative titles**.

Council of Economic Advisers A group of advisers who help the U.S. president prepare his annual economic report to Congress and recommend economic measures to him throughout the year.

counsel, counseled, counseling, counselor, counselor at law To *counsel* is to advise. A *counselor* is one who advises.

A *counselor at law* (no hyphens for consistency with *attorney at law*) is a lawyer. See **lawyer**.

count, countess See **nobility**.

counter- The rules in **prefixes** apply, but in general, no hyphen.

Some examples:

counteract	counterproposal
countercharge	counterspy
counterfoil	

countryside

county Capitalize when an integral part of a proper name: *Dade County, Nassau County, Suffolk County.*

Capitalize the full names of county governmental units: *the Dade County Commission, the Orange County Department of Social Services, the Suffolk County Legislature.*

Retain capitalization for the name of a county body if the proper noun is not needed in the context; lowercase the word *county* if it is used to distinguish an agency from state or federal counterparts: *the Board of Supervisors, the county Board of Supervisors; the Department of Social Services, the county Department of Social Services.* Lowercase *the board, the department,* etc. whenever they stand alone.

Capitalize *county* if it is an integral part of a specific body's name even without the proper noun: *the County Commission, the County Legislature.* Lowercase *the commission, the legislature,* etc. when not preceded by the word *county.*

Capitalize as part of a formal title before a name: *County Manager John Smith.* Lowercase when it is not part of the formal title: *county Health Commissioner Frank Jones.*

Avoid *county of* phrases where possible, but when necessary, always lowercase: *the county of Westchester.*

Lowercase plural combinations: *Westchester and Rockland counties.*

Apply the same rules to similar terms such as *parish.*

See **governmental bodies**.

county court In some states, it is not a court but the administrative body of a county. In most cases, the *court* is presided over by a *county judge*, who is not a judge in the traditional sense but the chief administrative officer of the county.

The terms should be explained if they are not clear in the context.

Capitalize all references to a specific *county court*, and capitalize *county judge* when used as a formal title before a name. Do not use *judge* alone before a name except in direct quotations.

Examples:

SEVIERVILLE, Tenn. (AP) — A reluctant County Court approved a school budget today that calls for a 10 percent tax increase for property owners.

The county had been given an ultimatum by the state: Approve the budget or shut down the schools.

The chief administrative officer, County Judge Ray Reagan, said ...

coup d'etat The word *coup* usually is sufficient.

couple When used in the sense of two people, the word takes plural verbs and pronouns: *The couple were married Saturday and left Sunday on their honeymoon. They will return in two weeks.*

In the sense of a single unit, use a singular verb: *Each couple was asked to give $10.*

couple of The *of* is necessary. Never use *a couple tomatoes* or a similar phrase.

The phrase takes a plural verb in constructions such as: *A couple of tomatoes were stolen.*

coupon See **loan terminology** for its meaning in a financial sense.

course numbers Use Arabic numerals and capitalize the subject when used with a numeral: *History 6, Philosophy 209.* Otherwise, lowercase: *calculus, world history.*

court decisions Use figures and a hyphen: *The Supreme Court ruled 5-4, a 5-4 decision.* The word *to* is not needed, but use hyphens if it appears in quoted matter: *The court ruled 5-to-4, the 5-to-4 decision.*

court districts See **court names**.

courtesy titles Refer to both men and women by first and last name, without courtesy titles, on first reference: *Susan Smith* or *Robert Smith.* Refer to both men and women by last name, without courtesy titles, in subsequent references. Use the courtesy titles *Mr., Miss, Ms.* or *Mrs.* only in direct quotations or after first reference when a woman specifically requests it: for example, where a woman prefers to be known as *Mrs. Smith* or *Ms. Smith.*

When it is necessary to distinguish between two people who use the same last name, as in married couples or brothers and sisters, use the first and last name, without courtesy title.

In cases where a person's gender is not clear from the first name or from the story's context, indicate the gender by using *he* or *she* in subsequent reference.

courthouse Capitalize with the name of a jurisdiction: *the Cook County Courthouse, the U.S. Courthouse.* Lowercase in other uses: *the county courthouse, the courthouse, the federal courthouse.*

Court House (two words) is used in the proper names of some communities: *Appomattox Court House, Va.*

court-martial, court-martialed, courts-martial

court names Capitalize the full proper names of courts at all levels.

Retain capitalization if *U.S.* or a state name is dropped: *the U.S.*

Supreme Court, the Supreme Court, the state Superior Court, the Superior Court, Superior Court.

For courts identified by a numeral: *2nd District Court, 8th U.S. Circuit Court of Appeals.*

For additional details on federal courts, see **judicial branch** and separate listings under **U.S.** and the court name.

See **judge** for guidelines on titles before the names of judges.

Court of St. James's Note the *'s.* The formal name for the royal court of the British sovereign. Derived from St. James's Palace, the former scene of royal receptions.

courtroom

cover up (v.) **cover-up** (n. and adj.)

Cox Enterprises Inc. Privately held communications company with headquarters in Atlanta. It operates cable TV, newspapers, TV and radio. It also owns Valpak, the direct-marketing service.

CPR Acceptable in all references for *cardiopulmonary resuscitation.*

crack up (v.) **crackup** (n. and adj.)

crawfish Not *crayfish.* An exception to Webster's New World College Dictionary based on the dominant spelling in Louisiana, where it is a popular delicacy.

credit default swaps A form of insurance that promises payment to investors in mortgage securities and other bonds if the borrower defaults. The market is unregulated, prone to sloppy documentation and has no central clearinghouse.

Creutzfeldt-Jakob disease A

rare degenerative brain disorder. Another form, *variant Creutzfeldt-Jakob disease*, is related to mad cow disease. The word *"variant"* is needed to distinguish it from the classic *Creutzfeldt-Jakob disease*, which is not related to mad cow disease. See **mad cow disease**.

criminal cases See **civil cases, criminal cases**.

crisis, crises

crisscross

criterion, criteria

cross-examine (v.) **cross-examination** (n.)

crossfire

crossover (n. and adj.)

cross rate The rate of exchange between two currencies calculated by referring to the rates between each and a third currency.

cross section (n.) **cross-section** (v.)

crosstown

CRT Abbreviation for *cathode-ray tube*. Do not use. In stories referring to the TV component, *picture tube* is preferred.

CSX Corp. Freight railroad, with headquarters in Jacksonville, Fla.

CT scan *Computerized tomography*, a method of making multiple X-ray images of the body or parts of the body and using a computer to construct, from those images, cross-sectional views. (Formerly known as *CAT scan*.)

Cub Scouts See **Boy Scouts**.

cup Equal to 8 fluid ounces. The approximate metric equivalents are 240 milliliters or 0.24 of a liter.

To convert to liters, multiply by 0.24 (14 cups x 0.24 = 3.36 liters, or 3,360 milliliters).

See **liter**.

curate See **religious titles** and **Social Media Guidelines**.

cure-all

Curia See **Roman Catholic Church**.

currency conversions Currency conversions are necessary in stories that use foreign currency to make clear for readers how a number translates into dollars. But conversions should be used sparingly and preferably not in the lead unless it's a significant part of a story. A conversion is generally needed only the first time a currency is mentioned. The reader can make the necessary conversions after that.

Do not convert amounts that are not current because exchange rates change over time.

When conversions are needed, use the $ sign to report U.S. dollar amounts and the € sign for euros. To type a euro sign, press Alt + Shift + 4.

Examples:

LONDON (AP) - BT Group PLC, Britain's largest phone company, on Thursday reported quarterly earnings rose 18 percent but said it would slash 6,000 more jobs by March to keep costs down and maintain its profits.

Net profit for the three months to Sept. 30 was 400 million pounds ($595 million), compared with 339 million pounds a year earlier, when profits were hit by a 232 million-pound one-time restructuring charge. Restructuring charges this year were 72 percent lower at just 65 million pounds.

PARIS (AP) - Airbus parent com-

pany EADS said Friday it rebounded to a profit in the third quarter thanks to lower costs for restructuring and fewer delays to aircraft programs. But it warned that continued setbacks in production of its military transporter will make achieving its full-year target challenging.

European Aeronautic Defence & Space Co. NV made a net profit of €679 million ($850 million) in the July-September period, compared with a €776 million loss a year ago.

For all other currencies, following the amount, spell out the name of the currency followed in parentheses by the equivalent in U.S. dollars. *Japan approved a 1.8 trillion yen ($18 billion) extra budget to partially finance an economic stimulus package.*

When dealing with a dollar currency of a country other than the United States, use the following abbreviations before the amount on second and subsequent references:

AU$ Australian dollars
CA$ Canadian dollars
SG$ Singapore dollars
NZ$ New Zealand dollars
HK$ Hong Kong dollars
NT$ New Taiwan dollars
ZW$ Zimbabwe dollars

Treasurer Wayne Swan approved a 16 billion Australian dollar ($10.74 billion) deal. Swan said AU$8 billion would be reserved for capital expenditure.

currency depreciation, currency devaluation A nation's money *depreciates* when its value falls in relation to the currency of other nations or in relation to its own prior value.

A nation's money is *devalued* when its value is reduced in relation to the currency of other nations, either deliberately by the government or through market forces.

When a nation devalues its currency, the goods it imports tend to become more expensive. Its exports tend to become less expensive in other nations and thus more competitive.

See **devaluations**.

curtain raiser

Customs Capitalize in U.S. Immigration and Customs Enforcement and in U.S. Customs and Border Protection, both agencies of the Department of Homeland Security.

Lowercase elsewhere: *a customs official, a customs ruling, she went through customs.*

cut back (v.) **cutback** (n. and adj.)

cut off (v.) **cutoff** (n. and adj.)

cyber-, cyberspace *Cyberspace* is a term popularized by William Gibson in the novel "Neuromancer" to refer to the digital world of computer networks. It has spawned numerous words with *cyber-* prefixes, but try to avoid most of these coinages. When the combining form is used, follow the general rule for prefixes and do not use a hyphen before a word starting with a consonant: *cyberattack, cyberbullying, cybercafe, cybersecurity.*

cyclone See **weather terms**.

Cyclone A trademark for a brand of chain-link fence.

cynic, skeptic A *skeptic* is a doubter.

A *cynic* is a disbeliever.

czar Not *tsar*. It was a formal title only for the ruler of Russia and some other Slavic nations.

Lowercase in all other uses.

Dacron A trademark for a brand of polyester fiber.

dad Uppercase only when the noun substitutes for a name as a term of address: *Hi, Dad!*

Daimler AG German luxury automaker. Divested its *Chrysler* unit in August 2007. Brands are *Mercedes-Benz, smart* and *Maybach.* Based in Stuttgart, Germany.

dalai lama The traditional high priest of Lamaism, a form of Buddhism practiced in Tibet and Mongolia. *Dalai lama* is a title rather than a name, but it is all that is used when referring to the man. Capitalize *Dalai Lama* in references to the holder of the title, in keeping with the principles outlined in the **nobility** entry.

Dallas The city in Texas stands alone in datelines.

dam Capitalize when part of a proper name: *Hoover Dam.*

damage, damages *Damage* is destruction: *Authorities said damage from the storm would total more than $1 billion.*

Damages are awarded by a court as compensation for injury, loss, etc.: *The woman received $25,000 in damages.*

dame See **nobility**.

damn it Use instead of *dammit,* but like other profanity it should be avoided unless there is a compelling reason.

See **obscenities, profanities, vulgarities**.

dangling modifiers Avoid modifiers that do not refer clearly and logically to some word in the sentence.

Dangling: *Taking our seats, the game started.* (*Taking* does not refer to the subject, *game,* nor to any other word in the sentence.)

Correct: *Taking our seats, we watched the opening of the game.* (*Taking* refers to *we,* the subject of the sentence.)

Dardanelles, the Not *the Dardanelles Strait.*

Dark Ages The period beginning with the fall of Rome in 476 and ending about the 10th century. The term is derived from the idea that this period in Europe was characterized by intellectual stagnation, widespread ignorance and poverty.

dark horse

dash See entry in **Punctuation** chapter.

data A plural noun, it normally takes plural verbs and pronouns.

See the **collective nouns** entry, however, for an example of when *data* may take singular verbs and pronouns.

databank

database One word.

data center

data processing (n. and adj.)
Do not hyphenate the adjective.

date line Two words for the
imaginary line that separates one
day from another.
See the **international date line**
entry.

datelines Datelines on stories
should contain a city name, entirely
in capital letters, followed in most
cases by the name of the state,
county or territory where the city is
located.
DOMESTIC DATELINES: A list
of domestic cities that stand alone
in datelines follows. The norms that
influenced the selection were the
population of the city, the population of its metropolitan region, the
frequency of the city's appearance
in the news, the uniqueness of its
name, and experience that has
shown the name to be almost synonymous with the state or nation
where it is located.
No state with the following:

ATLANTA	MILWAUKEE
BALTIMORE	MINNEAPOLIS
BOSTON	NEW ORLEANS
CHICAGO	NEW YORK
CINCINNATI	OKLAHOMA CITY
CLEVELAND	PHILADELPHIA
DALLAS	PHOENIX
DENVER	PITTSBURGH
DETROIT	ST. LOUIS
HONOLULU	SALT LAKE CITY
HOUSTON	SAN ANTONIO
INDIANAPOLIS	SAN DIEGO
LAS VEGAS	SAN FRANCISCO
LOS ANGELES	SEATTLE
MIAMI	WASHINGTON

Stories from all other U.S. cit-
ies should have both the city and
state name in the dateline, including
KANSAS CITY, Mo., and *KANSAS
CITY, Kan.*
Spell out *Alaska, Hawaii, Idaho,
Iowa, Maine, Ohio, Texas* and *Utah.*
Abbreviate others as listed in this
book under the full name of each
state.
Use *Hawaii* on all cities outside
Honolulu. Specify the island in the
text if needed.
Follow the same practice for
communities on islands within the
boundaries of other states: *EDGAR-
TOWN, Mass.,* for example, not *ED-
GARTOWN, Martha's Vineyard.*
REGIONAL CIRCUITS: On state
wires, additional cities in a state or
region may stand alone if requested
by the newspapers served.
U.S. POSSESSIONS: Apply the
guidelines listed below in the IS-
LAND NATIONS AND TERRITO-
RIES section and the OVERSEAS
TERRITORIES section.
INTERNATIONAL DATELINES:
These international locations stand
alone in datelines:

AMSTERDAM	MEXICO CITY
BAGHDAD	MILAN
BANGKOK	MONACO
BEIJING	MONTREAL
BEIRUT	MOSCOW
BERLIN	MUNICH
BRUSSELS	NEW DELHI
CAIRO	PANAMA CITY
DJIBOUTI	PARIS
DUBLIN	PRAGUE
GENEVA	QUEBEC CITY
GIBRALTAR	RIO DE JANEIRO
GUATEMALA CITY	ROME
HAVANA	SAN MARINO
HELSINKI	SAO PAULO
HONG KONG	SHANGHAI
ISLAMABAD	SINGAPORE
ISTANBUL	STOCKHOLM
JERUSALEM	SYDNEY
JOHANNESBURG	TOKYO
KUWAIT CITY	TORONTO
LONDON	VATICAN CITY

LUXEMBOURG   VIENNA
MACAU   ZURICH
MADRID

In addition, use *UNITED NA-TIONS* alone, without a *N.Y.* designation, in stories from *U.N.* headquarters.

BALKANS: With the independence of Montenegro from Serbia-Montenegro formalized in 2006, use a Montenegro-only dateline, such as *PODGORICA, Montenegro*. Stories originating in Serbia carry a Serbia-only dateline: *BELGRADE, Serbia*. With the independence of Kosovo in 2008, use Kosovo in the dateline, such as *PRISTINA, Kosovo*.

CANADIAN DATELINES: Datelines on stories from Canadian cities other than Montreal, Quebec City and Toronto should contain the name of the city in capital letters followed by the name of the province. Do not abbreviate any province or territory name.

COMMONWEALTH OF INDEPENDENT STATES: For cities in the former Soviet Union, datelines include city and republic name: *AL-MATY, Kazakhstan*.

OTHER NATIONS: Stories from other international cities that do not stand alone in datelines should contain the name of the country or territory (see the next section) spelled out.

SPELLING AND CHOICE OF NAMES: In most cases, the name of the nation in a dateline is the conventionally accepted short form of its official name: *Argentina*, for example, rather than *Republic of Argentina*. (If in doubt, look for an entry in this book. If none is found, follow Webster's New World College Dictionary.)

Note these special cases:

–Instead of *United Kingdom*, use *England, Northern Ireland, Scotland* or *Wales*.

–For divided nations, use the commonly accepted names based on geographic distinctions: *North Korea, South Korea*.

–Use an article only with *El Salvador*. For all others, use just a country name – *Gambia, Netherlands, Philippines*, etc.

See *geographic names* for guidelines on spelling the names of international cities and nations not listed here or in separate entries.

ISLAND NATIONS AND TERRITORIES: When reporting from nations and territories that are made up primarily of islands but commonly are linked under one name, use the city name and the general name in the dateline. Identify an individual island, if needed, in the text:

Examples:
British Virgin Islands
Netherlands Antilles
Indonesia   Philippines

OVERSEAS TERRITORIES: Some overseas territories, colonies and other areas that are not independent nations commonly have accepted separate identities based on their geographic character or special status under treaties. In these cases, use the commonly accepted territory name after a city name in a dateline.

Examples:

Bermuda	Martinique
Corsica	Puerto Rico
Faeroe Islands	Sardinia
Greenland	Sicily
Guadeloupe	Sikkim
Guam	Tibet

WITHIN STORIES: In citing other cities within the body of a story:

—No further information is necessary if a city is in the same state as the datelined city. Make an exception only if confusion would result.

—Follow the city name with further identification in most cases where it is not in the same state or nation as the dateline city. The additional identification may be omitted, however, if no confusion would result. There is no need, for example, to refer to *Boston, Mass.*, in a story datelined *NEW YORK*.

—Provide a state or nation identification for the city if the story has no dateline. However, cities that stand alone in datelines may be used alone in undated stories if no confusion would result.

dateline selection A dateline should tell the reader that the AP obtained the basic information for the story in the datelined city.

Do not, for example, use a Washington dateline on a story written primarily from information that a newspaper reported under a Washington dateline. Use the home city of the newspaper instead.

This rule does not preclude the use of a story with a dateline different from the home city of a newspaper if it is from the general area served by the newspaper.

Use an international dateline only if the basic information in a story was obtained by a full- or part-time correspondent physically present in the datelined community.

If a radio broadcast monitored in another city was the source of information, use the dateline of the city where the monitoring took place and mention the fact in the story.

When a story has been assembled from sources in widely separated areas, use no dateline.

When a datelined story contains supplementary information obtained in another city, make that point clear in the context. Do not put parentheses around such material, however, unless the correspondent in the datelined community was cut off from incoming communications. Note the following examples:

—Material from another area was available in the datelined city:

LONDON (AP) — Prime Minister Harold Wilson submitted his resignation today.

In Washington, a State Department spokesman said the change in government leadership would have no effect on negotiations involving the Common Market.

—Material from another area was not available to the correspondent in the dateline city because communications from the outside world were cut off:

PHNOM PENH, Cambodia (AP) — Khmer Rouge troops pushed into Phnom Penh today, barely hours after the United States ran down the Stars and Stripes and abandoned Cambodia to the Communists.

(In Washington, the State Department said Americans evacuated in a mass airlift had arrived safely aboard aircraft carriers and at bases in Thailand.)

dates Always use Arabic figures, without *st, nd, rd* or *th*. See **months** for examples and **punctuation** guidelines.

daughter-in-law, daughters-in-law

Daughters of the American Revolution *DAR* is acceptable on second reference.

Headquarters is in Washington.

day care Two words, no hyphen, in all uses.

daylight saving time Not *savings*. No hyphen.

When linking the term with the name of a time zone, use only the word *daylight*: *Eastern Daylight Time, Pacific Daylight Time*, etc.

Lowercase *daylight saving time* in all uses and *daylight time* whenever it stands alone.

A federal law specifies that daylight time applies from 2 a.m. on the second Sunday of March until 2 a.m. on the first Sunday of November in areas that do not specifically exempt themselves.

See **time zones**.

daylong, dayslong

Day One Capitalize and spell out as a chronological device for summarizing multi-day events such as Day One, Day Two. Lowercase in casual or conversational references.

days of the week Capitalize them. Do not abbreviate, except when needed in a tabular format: *Sun, Mon, Tue, Wed, Thu, Fri, Sat* (three letters, without periods, to facilitate tabular composition).
See **time element**.

daytime

day to day, day-to-day Hyphenate when used as a compound modifier: *They have extended the contract on a day-to-day basis.*

D.C. See **District of Columbia**.

D-Day June 6, 1944, the day the Allies invaded Western Europe in World War II.

DDT Preferred in all references for the insecticide *dichlorodiphenyltrichloroethane*.

de See **foreign names**.

deacon See the entry for the individual's denomination.

dead center

dead end (n.) **dead-end** (adj.)

Dead Sea Scrolls

deaf See **disabled, handicapped, impaired**.

deaf-mute Avoid the term. The preferred form is to say that an individual cannot hear or speak. A *mute* person may be deaf or may be able to hear.

Do not use *deaf and dumb*.

dean Capitalize when used as a formal title before a name: *Dean John Jones, Deans John Jones and Susan Smith.*
Lowercase in other uses: *John Jones, dean of the college; the dean.*

dean's list Lowercase in all uses: *He is on the dean's list. She is a dean's list student.*

deathbed (n. and adj.)

death row

debt The money a company or individual owes a creditor.

debt service The outlay necessary to meet all interest and principal payments during a given period.

decades Use Arabic figures to indicate decades of history. Use an apostrophe to indicate numerals that are left out; show plural by adding the letter *s*: *the 1890s, the '90s, the Gay '90s, the 1920s, the mid-1930s.*
See **historical periods and events**.

deci- A prefix denoting one-tenth of a unit. Move the decimal point one place to the left in converting to the basic unit: 15.5 decigrams = 1.55 grams.

decimal units Use a period and numerals to indicate decimal amounts. Decimalization should not exceed two places in textual material unless there are special circumstances.
For amounts less than 1, use the numeral zero before the decimal point: 0.03. When the decimal is 1 or less, the type of measurement should be singular: 0.35 meter, 0.55 cubic foot, 0.75 kilometer.
See **fractions**.

Declaration of Independence
Lowercase *the declaration* whenever
it stands alone.

decorations See **awards and
decorations**.

deep-sea (adj.)

Deep South Capitalize both
words when referring to the region
that consists of Alabama, Georgia,
Louisiana, Mississippi and South
Carolina.

deep water (n.) **deep-water**
(adj.)

default The failure to meet a
financial obligation, the failure to
make payment either of principal
or interest when due or a breach or
nonperformance of the terms of a
note or mortgage.

defendant

defense Do not use it as a verb.

defense attorney Always lowercase, never abbreviate.
See **attorney** and **titles**.

defense spending *Military
spending* usually is the more precise
term.

definitely Overused as a vague
intensifier. Avoid it.

deflation A decrease in the general price level, which results from a
decrease in total spending relative to
the supply of available goods on the
market. Deflation's immediate effect
is to increase purchasing power.

degree-day See **weather terms**.

degrees See **academic degrees**.

deity Lowercase. See **gods** and
religious references.

dek- (before a vowel), **deka-**
(before a consonant) A prefix denoting 10 units of a measure. Move the
decimal point one place to the right
to convert to the basic unit: 15.6
dekameters = 156 meters.

Delaware Abbreviate *Del.* in
datelines or stories. Postal code: *DE*
Only Rhode Island is smaller in
area. See **state names**.

delegate The formal title for
members of the lower houses of
some legislatures. Do not abbreviate. Capitalize only before their
names. See **legislative titles**.
Always lowercase in other uses:
convention delegate Richard Henry Lee.

Delta Air Lines Inc. Headquarters is in Atlanta.

demagogue, demagoguery

**democrat, democratic, Demo-
cratic Party** See the **political parties and philosophies** entry.

**Democratic Governors Asso-
ciation** No apostrophe.

**Democratic National Com-
mittee** On the second reference: *the
national committee, the committee* or
the DNC.
Similarly: *Democratic State Committee, Democratic County Committee,
Democratic City Committee, the state
committee, the city committee, the committee.*

demolish, destroy Both mean
to do away with something completely. Something cannot be partially *demolished* or *destroyed*. It is
redundant to say *totally demolished*
or *totally destroyed.*

denote See **connote, denote**.

Denver The city in Colorado stands alone in datelines.

depart Follow it with a preposition: *He will depart from LaGuardia. She will depart at 11:30 a.m.*

department The following are the U.S. government departments: *Department of Agriculture* (*USDA* acceptable on second reference); *Department of Commerce*; *Department of Defense* (*DOD* or *Pentagon* acceptable on second reference); *Department of Education*; *Department of Energy* (*DOE* acceptable on second reference); *Department of Health and Human Services* (*HHS* acceptable on second reference); *Department of Homeland Security* (*DHS* acceptable on second reference); *Department of Housing and Urban Development* (*HUD* acceptable on second reference); *Department of the Interior*; *Department of Justice* (*DOJ* acceptable on second reference); *Department of Labor*; *Department of State*; *Department of Transportation* (*DOT* acceptable on second reference); *Department of the Treasury*, and *Department of Veterans Affairs* (*VA* acceptable on second reference).

It is preferable to list the subject first in stories, such as the *Agriculture Department* and *Commerce Department*. Exceptions are *Department of Health and Human Services*, *Department of Homeland Security*, *Department of Housing and Urban Development* and *Department of Veterans Affairs*.

Avoid acronyms when possible. A phrase such as *the department* is preferable on second reference because it is more readable and avoids alphabet soup.

Lowercase *department* in plural uses, but capitalize the proper name element: *the departments of Labor and Justice*.

A shorthand reference to the proper name element also is capitalized: *Kissinger said, "State and Justice must resolve their differences."* But: *Henry Kissinger, the secretary of state.*

Lowercase *the department* whenever it stands alone.

Do not abbreviate *department* in any usage.

TITLES: In stories with U.S. datelines, do not include U.S. before the titles of Secretary of State or other government officials, except where necessary for clarity. Examples: *Secretary of State Hillary Rodham Clinton, Attorney General Eric Holder.*

In stories with international datelines, include U.S. before the titles: *U.S. Secretary of State Hillary Rodham Clinton, U.S. Attorney General Eric Holder.* Exceptions: *President Barack Obama, Vice President Joe Biden.*

See **academic departments**.

dependent (n. and adj.)

depreciation The reduction in the value of capital goods due to wear and tear or obsolescence.

Estimated depreciation may be deducted from income each year as one of the costs of doing business.

depression Capitalize *Depression* and *the Great Depression* when referring to the worldwide economic hard times generally regarded as having begun with the stock market collapse of Oct. 28-29, 1929.

Lowercase in other uses: *the depression of the 1970s*.

depths See **dimensions**.

deputy Capitalize as a formal title before a name. See **titles**.

derivative A contract whose value depends on the financial performance of its underlying assets, such as mortgages, stock or traded commodities. Credit default swaps are one form of derivative.

derogatory terms Do not use derogatory terms except in direct quotes, and then only when their use is an integral, essential part of the story.

See **obscenities, profanities, vulgarities, word selection**.

-designate Hyphenate: *chairman-designate*. Capitalize only the first word if used as a formal title before a name.

See **titles**.

destroy See **demolish, destroy**.

detective Do not abbreviate. Capitalize before a name only if it is a formal rank: *police Detective Frank Serpico, private detective Richard Diamond*.

See **titles**.

detente

detention center See **prison, jail**.

Detroit The city in Michigan stands alone in datelines.

Deutsche Lufthansa AG The headquarters of this airline is Frankfurt, Germany.

devaluations Devaluations occur when the value of a country's currency goes down in its relation to another currency. This may happen by government decree, or through market forces. Devaluations are expressed in percentages, but the normal method of figuring a percentage change won't work. Use the following rules:

Say currency A is quoted in a set of units to currency B. When currency A is devalued, 1) take the new exchange rate and subtract the old exchange rate, 2) divide the answer by the new exchange rate and 3) multiply the answer by 100 to get the percentage devaluation.

Example:

9.5 (new rate) minus 6.3 (old rate) = 3.2

3.2 divided by 9.5 = 0.3368

0.3368 times 100 = 33.68421 (or 34 percent).

The ruble has been devalued against the dollar by 34 percent.

devil But capitalize *Satan*.

diabetes There are two main forms of this disease: Type 1, formerly called juvenile diabetes, and Type 2, the most common kind, formerly called adult-onset diabetes.

dialect The form of language peculiar to a region or a group, usually in matters of pronunciation or syntax. Dialect should be avoided, even in quoted matter, unless it is clearly pertinent to a story.

There are some words and phrases in everyone's vocabulary that are typical of a particular region or group. Quoting dialect, unless used carefully, implies substandard or illiterate usage.

When there is a compelling reason to use dialect, words or phrases are spelled phonetically, and apostrophes show missing letters and sounds: *"Din't ya yoosta live at Toidy-Toid Street and Sekun' Amya? Across from da moom pitchers?"*

See **colloquialisms** and **quotes in the news**.

dialogue (n.)

diarrhea

Dictaphone A trademark for a brand of dictation recorder.

dictionaries For spelling, style and usage questions not covered in this stylebook, consult Webster's New World College Dictionary, Fourth Edition, published by Wiley.

Use the first spelling listed in Webster's New World College Dictionary unless a specific exception is listed in this book.

If Webster's New World College Dictionary provides different spellings in separate entries (*tee shirt* and *T-shirt*, for example), use the spelling that is followed by a full definition (*T-shirt*).

If Webster's New World College Dictionary provides definitions under two different spellings for the same sense of a word, either use is acceptable. For example, *although* or *though*.

If there is no listing in either this book or Webster's New World College Dictionary, the backup dictionary is Webster's Third New International Dictionary, published by Merriam-Webster Inc.

Webster's New World College Dictionary is also the first reference for geographic names not covered in this stylebook. See **geographic names**.

die-hard (n. and adj.)

Diet The Japanese parliament. See **foreign legislative bodies**.

dietitian

different Takes the preposition *from*, not *than*.

differ from, differ with To *differ from* means to be unlike.

To *differ with* means to disagree.

dilemma It means more than a problem. It implies a choice between two unattractive alternatives.

dimensions Use figures and spell out *inches, feet, yards*, etc., to indicate depth, height, length and width. Hyphenate adjectival forms before nouns.

EXAMPLES: *He is 5 feet 6 inches tall, the 5-foot-6-inch man, the 5-foot man, the basketball team signed a 7 footer.*

The car is 17 feet long, 6 feet wide and 5 feet high. The rug is 9 feet by 12 feet, the 9-by-12 rug.

The storm left 5 inches of snow.

The building has 6,000 square feet of floor space.

Use an apostrophe to indicate feet and quote marks to indicate inches (5'6") only in very technical contexts.

Diners Club No apostrophe, in keeping with the practice the company has adopted for its public identity. Only its incorporation papers still read Diners' Club. Parent company Citigroup Inc. sold Diners Club to Discover Financial Services LLC in 2008.

diocese Capitalize as part of a proper name: *the Diocese of Rochester, the Rochester Diocese, the diocese.*

See **Episcopal Church** and **Roman Catholic Church**.

directions and regions In general, lowercase *north, south, northeast, northern,* etc., when they indicate compass direction; capitalize these words when they designate regions.

Some examples:

COMPASS DIRECTIONS: *He drove west. The cold front is moving east.*

REGIONS: *A storm system that developed in the Midwest is spreading eastward. It will bring showers to the East Coast by morning and to the entire Northeast by late in the day. Showers and thunderstorms were forecast in the Texas Panhandle. High temperatures will prevail throughout the Western states.*

The North was victorious. The

South will rise again. Settlers from the East went to the West in search of new lives. The customs of the East are different from those of the West. The Northeast depends on the Midwest for its food supply.

She has a Southern accent. He is a Northerner. Asian nations are opening doors to Western businessmen. The candidate developed a Southern strategy.

The storm developed in the South Pacific. European leaders met to talk about supplies of oil from Southeast Asia.

WITH NAMES OF NATIONS: Lowercase unless they are part of a proper name or are used to designate a politically divided nation: *northern France, eastern Canada, the western United States.*

But: *Northern Ireland, South Korea.*

WITH STATES AND CITIES: The preferred form is to lowercase directional or area descriptions when referring to a section of a state or city: *western Montana, southern Atlanta.*

But capitalize compass points:

—When part of a proper name: *North Dakota, West Virginia.*

—When used in denoting widely known sections: *Southern California, West Texas, the South Side of Chicago, the Lower East Side of New York.* If in doubt, use lowercase.

IN FORMING PROPER NAMES: When combining with another common noun to form the name for a region or location: *the North Woods, the South Pole, the Far East, the Middle East, the West Coast* (the entire region, not the coastline itself — see **coast**), *the Eastern Shore* (see separate entry), *the Western Hemisphere.*

dis- The rules in **prefixes** apply, but in general, no hyphen. Some examples:

dismember	disservice
dissemble	dissuade

disabled, handicapped, impaired In general, do not describe an individual as disabled or handicapped unless it is clearly pertinent to a story. If a description must be used, try to be specific. *An ad featuring actor Michael J. Fox swaying noticeably from the effects of Parkinson's disease drew nationwide attention.*

Avoid descriptions that connote pity, such as *afflicted with* or *suffers from multiple sclerosis.* Rather, *has multiple sclerosis.*

Some terms include:

cripple Often considered offensive when used to describe a person who is lame or disabled.

disabled A general term used for a physical or mental disability. Do not use *mentally retarded.*

handicap It should be avoided in describing a disability.

blind Describes a person with complete loss of sight. For others, use terms such as *visually impaired* or *person with low vision.*

deaf Describes a person with total hearing loss. For others, use *partial hearing loss* or *partially deaf.* Avoid using *deaf-mute.* Do not use *deaf and dumb.*

mute Describes a person who physically cannot speak. Others with speaking difficulties are *speech impaired.*

wheelchair user People use wheelchairs for independent mobility. Do not use *confined to a wheelchair,* or *wheelchair-bound.* If a wheelchair is needed, say why.

disc, disk Use the *disc* spelling for phonograph records and related terms (*disc jockey*), optical and laser-based devices (a *Blu-ray Disc*) and for *disc brake.* Use *disk* for computer-related references and medical references, such as a *slipped disk.*

disc jockey *DJ* is acceptable on second reference in a column or other special context. Use announcer in other contexts.

discount Interest withheld when a note, draft or bill is purchased.

discount rate The rate of interest charged by the Federal Reserve on loans it makes to member banks. This rate has an influence on the rates banks then charge their customers.

discreet, discrete *Discreet* means prudent, circumspect: *"I'm afraid I was not very discreet," she wrote.*

Discrete means detached, separate: *There are four discrete sounds from a quadraphonic system.*

diseases Do not capitalize *arthritis, emphysema, leukemia, pneumonia,* etc.

When a disease is known by the name of a person identified with it, capitalize only the individual's name: *Alzheimer's disease, Parkinson's disease,* etc.

Avoid such expressions as: *He is battling cancer. She is a stroke victim.* Use neutral, precise descriptions: *He has stomach cancer. She is a stroke patient.*

See **disabled, handicapped, impaired**.

disinterested, uninterested *Disinterested* means impartial, which is usually the better word to convey the thought.

Uninterested means that someone lacks interest.

dispel, dispelled, dispelling

disposable personal income The income that a person retains after deductions for income taxes, Social Security taxes, property taxes and for other payments such as fines and penalties to various levels of government.

Disposall A trademark for a type of mechanical garbage disposer.

dissociate Not *disassociate*.

distances Use figures for 10 and above, spell out one through nine: *He walked four miles.*

district Always spell it out. Use a figure and capitalize *district* when forming a proper name: *the 2nd District.*

district attorney Capitalize when used as a formal title before a name: *District Attorney Hamilton Burger.*

DA acceptable on second reference.

See **titles**.

district court See **court names** and **U.S. District Court**.

District of Columbia Abbreviate as *D.C.* in datelines or stories. Postal code: *DC*

See **state names**.

Do not use *D.C.* in conjunction with the federal district of Washington unless it could be confused with other Washingtons.

The district, rather than *D.C.*, should be used in subsequent references.

dive, dived or **dove, diving**

divided nations See **datelines** and entries under the names of these nations.

dividend In a financial sense, the word describes the payment per share that a corporation distributes to its stockholders as their return on the money they have invested in its stock.

See **profit terminology**.

division See **organizations and institutions**; **military units**; and **political divisions**.

divorcee The fact that a woman has been divorced should be mentioned only if a similar story about a man would mention his marital status.

When the woman's marital status is relevant, it seldom belongs in the lead. Avoid stories that begin: *A 35-year-old divorcee* ...The preferred form is to say in the body of the story that a woman is divorced.

Dixie cup A trademark for a paper drinking cup.

Djibouti Stands alone in datelines for the East African country and capital.

DNA Acceptable for all reference to deoxyribonucleic acid, which carries genetic information in the cell.

DNS Abbreviation for the *Domain Name System*, an international network of Internet domain servers, names and addresses. Spell out on first reference.

doctor Use *Dr.* in first reference as a formal title before the name of an individual who holds a doctor of dental surgery, doctor of medicine, doctor of optometry, doctor of osteopathic medicine, doctor of podiatric medicine, or doctor of veterinary medicine: *Dr. Jonas Salk.*

The form *Dr.*, or *Drs.*, in a plural construction, applies to all first-reference uses before a name, including direct quotations.

If appropriate in the context, *Dr.* also may be used on first reference before the names of individuals who hold other types of doctoral degrees. However, because the public

frequently identifies *Dr.* only with physicians, care should be taken to ensure that the individual's specialty is stated in first or second reference. The only exception would be a story in which the context left no doubt that the person was a dentist, psychologist, chemist, historian, etc.

In some instances it also is necessary to specify that an individual identified as *Dr.* is a physician. One frequent case is a story reporting on joint research by physicians, biologists, etc.

Do not use *Dr.* before the names of individuals who hold only honorary doctorates.

Do not continue the use of *Dr.* in subsequent references.

See **academic degrees**; **courtesy titles**; and **religious titles**.

Doctors Without Borders Use English translation in copy for the French group, Medecins Sans Frontieres.

dogs See **animals**.

dollars Always lowercase. Use figures and the $ sign in all except casual references or amounts without a figure: *The book cost $4. Dad, please give me a dollar. Dollars are flowing overseas.*

For specified amounts, the word takes a singular verb: *He said $500,000 is what they want.*

For amounts of more than $1 million, use up to two decimal places. Do not link the numerals and the word by a hyphen: *He is worth $4.35 million. He is worth exactly $4,351,242. He proposed a $300 billion budget.*

The form for amounts less than $1 million: *$4, $25, $500, $1,000, $650,000.*

See **cents**.

domain names The address used to locate a particular website or reach an email system. In email addresses, it is the portion to the right of the @ sign. It includes a suffix defining the type of entity, such as ".com" (for commerce, the most common suffix); ".net" initially for network service providers, but often used when ".com" is unavailable; ".org" (organizations); ".edu" (educational institutions); ".gov" (U.S. government) and ".mil" (U.S. military). There are also country-code suffixes (such as ".fr" for France, ".us" for the United States).

domino, dominoes

"don't ask, don't tell" The law
barring gays from serving in the U.S. military if they acknowledged their sexual orientation. The 1993 law was repealed by Congress in 2010, effective in 2011. Gays now may serve openly.

door to door, door-to-door
Hyphenate when used as a compound modifier: *He is a door-to-door salesman.*

But: *He went from door to door.*

DOS An acronym for *disk operating system*. Spell out.

do's and don'ts

dot-com An informal description of companies that do business mainly on the Internet.

double-click

double-faced

Dow Jones & Co. The company,
a subsidiary of News Corp., publishes The Wall Street Journal and Barron's National Business and Financial Weekly. It also operates the Dow Jones News Service.

For stock market watchers, it provides the Dow Jones industrial average, the Dow Jones transportation average, the Dow Jones utility average, and the Dow Jones composite average.

Headquarters is in New York.

Dow Jones industrial average
The market indicator comprises 30 leading U.S. stocks. Executives of Dow Jones Indexes choose the companies in the average. Always use the full name on first reference in stories. On subsequent references, use *the Dow*.

-down Follow Webster's New
World College Dictionary. Some examples, all nouns and/or adjectives:

breakdown	rundown
countdown	sit-down

All are two words when used as verbs.

down- The rules in **prefixes**
apply, but in general, no hyphen. Some examples:

downgrade	downtown

Down East Use only in reference to Maine.

download To get information
from another server or computer.

down payment

downside risk The probability
that the price of an investment will fall.

downstage

downstate Lowercase unless
part of a proper name: *downstate Illinois.* But: *the Downstate Medical Center.*

Down syndrome Not *Down's,*
for the genetic, chromosomal disorder first reported in 1866 by Dr. J. Langdon Down.

Down Under Australia, New Zealand and environs.

DPA *Deutsche Presse-Agentur GmbH* is an international news agency with headquarters in Hamburg, Germany, owned by a cooperative of German newspaper publishers and radio and television stations. It was founded in 1949. *DPA* is acceptable in all references.

Dr. See **doctor**.

drama See **composition titles**.

Dramamine A trademark for a brand of motion sickness remedy.

dreidel Toy spinning top for Jewish celebrations.

dressing room

drive See **addresses**.

drive-in (n.)

driver's license(s)

drive-thru (n. and adj.)

drop out (v.) **dropout** (n.)

drought

drowned, was drowned If a person suffocates in water or other fluid, the proper statement is that the individual *drowned*. To say that someone *was drowned* implies that another person caused the death by holding the victim's head under the water.

Drug Enforcement Administration *DEA* on second reference.

drugmaker

drugs Because the word *drugs* has come to be used as a synonym for narcotics in recent years, *medicine* is frequently the better word to specify that an individual is taking medication.

drugstore

drunk, drunken *Drunk* is the spelling of the adjective used after a form of the verb *to be*: *He was drunk*.
Drunken is the spelling of the adjective used before nouns: *a drunken driver, drunken driving*.
DUI, driving under the influence; *DWI, driving while intoxicated*; follow official state usage.

drunkenness

DSL Abbreviation acceptable in all references for *digital subscriber line*, for high-speed access to the Internet over a telephone network.

Dublin The city in Ireland stands alone in datelines.

duel A contest between two people. Three people cannot duel.

duffel

DUI/DWI Abbreviation for *driving under the influence* or *driving while intoxicated*. Acceptable on second reference or subsequent to a description of *drunken driving*. See **drunk, drunken**.

duke, duchess See **nobility**.

dumping The selling of a product in a foreign market at a price lower than the domestic price. It is usually done by a monopoly when it has such a large output that selling entirely in the domestic market would substantially reduce the price.

Dumpster Trademark for a large metal trash bin.

Use trash bin or trash container instead.

Dunklrk Use this spelling rather than *Dunkerque*, in keeping with widespread practice.

du Pont, E.I. Note the spelling of the name of the U.S. industrialist born in France. Use *du Pont* on second reference.

The company named after him is *E.I. du Pont de Nemours & Co.* of Wilmington, Del. Capitalize the shortened form *DuPont* (no space, capital P) in keeping with company practice. The shortened form is acceptable in all references.

See **foreign names**.

durable goods Long-lasting goods such as appliances that are bought by consumers.

dust storm See **weather terms**.

Dutch auction A bidding process where the price is lowered until the lowest price at which all securities will sell becomes the set price. Used on Treasury auctions and in risk arbitrage.

DVD Abbreviation for *digital video disc* (or *digital versatile disc*), similar to CD-ROMs, but able to hold more music, video or data.

The abbreviation is acceptable in all references.

DVR Acceptable on second reference for *digital video recorder*. TiVo is the trademark for one type of *DVR*. Do not use *TiVo* to describe the generic *DVRs* offered by many cable systems.

dwarf The preferred term for people with a medical or genetic condition resulting in short stature. Plural is *dwarfs*.

dyed-in-the-wool (adj.)

dyeing, dying *Dyeing* refers to changing colors.

Dying refers to death.

each Takes a singular verb.

each other, one another Two people look at *each other.*

More than two look at *one another.*

Either phrase may be used when the number is indefinite: *We help each other. We help one another.*

earl, countess See **nobility**.

earmark

earth Generally lowercase; capitalize when used as the proper name of the planet. *She is down-to-earth. How does the pattern apply to Mars, Jupiter, Earth, the sun and the moon? The astronauts returned to Earth. He hopes to move heaven and earth.*

See **planets**.

earthquakes Over a million earthquakes occur in the world each year. Most strike remote regions or are so small they cannot be felt.

The best source for information on major earthquakes is the National Earthquake Information Center operated by the U.S. Geological Survey in Golden, Colo.

Online sources:

http://earthquake.usgs.gov

http://earthquake.usgs.gov/regional/neic

http://earthquake.usgs.gov/earthquakes/pager

http://earthquake.usgs.gov/earthquakes/shakemap

Earthquake magnitudes are measures of earthquake size calculated from ground motion recorded on seismographs. The Richter scale, named for Dr. Charles F. Richter, is no longer widely used.

Magnitudes are usually reported simply as *magnitude 6.7*, for example. Hyphenate as a compound modifier: *magnitude-6.7 quake.*

In the first hours after a quake, earthquake size should be reported as a *preliminary magnitude of 6.7.* Early estimates are often revised, and it can be several days before seismologists calculate a final figure.

The most commonly used measure is the *moment magnitude*, related to the area of the fault on which an earthquake occurs, and the amount the ground slips.

The magnitude scale being used should be specified only when necessary. An example would be when two centers are reporting different magnitudes because they are using different scales. The various scales usually differ only slightly.

With each scale, every increase of one number, say from 5.5 to 6.5, means that the quake's magnitude is 10 times as great. Theoretically, there is no upper limit to the scales.

A quake of magnitude 2.5 to 3 is the smallest generally felt by people.

—Magnitude 4: The quake can cause moderate damage.

—Magnitude 5: The quake can cause considerable damage.

—Magnitude 6: The quake can

cause severe damage.

—Magnitude 7: A major earthquake, capable of widespread, heavy damage.

—Magnitude 8: An earthquake capable of tremendous damage.

Depth is a key factor in determining how damaging an earthquake will be. The closer to the surface an earthquake starts, the more ground shaking and potential damage it will cause, particularly in places without strict building codes. The strength of the earth shaking decreases the farther a quake gets from its source, so a deeper quake weakens as it gets closer to the surface.

Quakes are divided into three categories: shallow, intermediate and deep. Shallow quakes are at depths of less than 70 km (43 miles) and are the ones that have broader damage. Intermediate quakes are between 70 km and 300 km depth (43 miles to 186 miles) and deep are deeper than 300 km (186 miles).

To show the importance of depth in two similarly sized earthquakes: In 1994 in Northridge, Calif., a 6.7-magnitude quake struck at a depth of 12 miles (18 km), caused tens of billions of dollars' worth of damage and killed 60 people. In 2001, a 6.8-magnitude quake struck Seattle at a depth of 33 miles (51 km); the damage was only in the millions and only a few people were killed.

The magnitude and depth of an earthquake can change as scientists get more information from seismic stations and should be reported as *preliminary magnitude* and *preliminary depth*.

The deadliest quake on record occurred in Shaanxi province of China, Jan. 23, 1556. It killed 830,000 people, the largest number of fatalities on record from an earthquake.

A series of major quakes struck the region around New Madrid, Mo., in the winter of 1811-1812. The shock was felt over a wide area from St. Louis, Mo., to Memphis, Tenn. The area was sparsely populated at the time and there were no instruments to measure the power of the quake, but the land was raised as much as 30 feet in some areas, and subsidence elsewhere created Reelfoot Lake in western Tennessee.

NOTABLE QUAKES since 1900, according to the U.S. Geological Survey's list, based on magnitude or the amount of damage and arranged by number of fatalities:

—July 27, 1976, Tangshan, China, magnitude 7.5. Official casualty figure is 255,000 deaths. Estimated death toll as high as 655,000, 799,000 injured and extensive damage in the area. This is probably the greatest death toll from an earthquake in the last four centuries, and the second greatest in recorded history.

—Jan. 12, 2010, Haiti, 7.0. More than 300,000 people were killed, 300,000 injured, 1.3 million displaced, about 105,000 homes destroyed and 208,000 damaged in the Port-au-Prince area and much of southern Haiti, according to government estimates.

—Dec. 26, 2004, Sumatra, 9.1. This is the third-largest earthquake in the world since 1900 and the largest since the 1964 Prince William Sound, Alaska, earthquake. In total, 228,000 people were killed or were missing and presumed dead in 14 countries due to the quake and ensuing tsunami.

—Dec. 16, 1920, Haiyuan, Ningxia, China, 7.8. Total destruction in the Lijunbu-Haiyuan-Ganyanchi area. Estimated death toll of 200,000.

—Sept. 1, 1923, Kanto, Japan, 7.9.

Extreme destruction in the Tokyo-Yokohama area from the earthquake and subsequent firestorms, 143,000 dead.

—Oct. 5, 1948, Ashgabat, Turkmenistan, 7.3, 110,000 killed.

—May 12, 2008, Eastern Sichuan, China, 7.9, 87,600.

—Oct. 8, 2005, Pakistan, 7.6, 86,000.

—Dec. 28, 1908, Messina, Italy, 7.2, 72,000.

—May 31, 1970, Chimbote, Peru, 7.4, 70,000.

—June 20, 1990, Western Iran, 7.4, 40,000 to 50,000.

—May 22, 1927, Gulang, China, 7.6, 40,900.

—Dec. 26, 1939, Erzincan, Turkey, 7.8, 32,700.

—Jan. 13, 1915, Avezzano, Italy, 7.0, 32,610.

—Dec. 26, 2003, Southeastern Iran, 6.6, 31,000.

—May 30, 1935, Quetta, Pakistan, 7.6, 30,000.

—Jan. 25, 1939, Chillan, Chile, 7.8, 28,000.

—Dec. 7, 1988, Spitak, Armenia, 6.8, 25,000.

—Feb. 4, 1976, Guatemala, 7.5, 23,000.

—Jan. 26, 2001, Gujarat, India, 7.6, 20,000.

—March 11, 2011, Japan, 9.0, quake and tsunami killed more than 18,000, displaced 450,000 and caused radiation leaks from damaged reactors at a nuclear power plant.

OTHER NOTABLE QUAKES SINCE 1900:

–April 18, 1906, San Francisco, 7.8, death toll varies from 300 to 6,000.

–May 22, 1960, Valdivia, Chile, 9.5, most powerful earthquake recorded in the world killed 1,655 and injured 3,000.

–March 27, 1964, Prince William Sound, Alaska, 9.2, quake and tsunami killed 128.

–Dec. 23, 1972, Nicaragua, 6.2, 5,000 killed.

–Sept. 19, 1985, Mexico City, 8.0, at least 9,500 killed.

–Oct. 17, 1989, Loma Prieta, Calif., 6.9, 63 killed and 3,757 injured.

–Jan. 17, 1994, Northridge, Calif., 6.7, 60 dead and more than 7,000 injured.

–Jan. 17, 1995, Kobe, Japan, 6.9, 5,500 killed.

–Feb. 22, 2011, near Christchurch, New Zealand, 6.3, at least 166 killed.

OTHER TERMS: The word *temblor* (not *tremblor*) is a synonym for *earthquake*.

The word *epicenter* refers to the point on Earth's surface above the underground center, or focus, of an earthquake.

east, eastern See **directions and regions**.

Easter In the computation used by the Latin Rite of the Roman Catholic Church and by Protestant churches, it falls on the first Sunday after the first full moon that occurs on or after March 21. If the full moon falls on a Sunday, Easter is the next Sunday.

Easter may fall, therefore, between March 22 and April 25 inclusive.

Easter egg A hidden "surprise" in a program, a website, a DVD or a television show, such as an extra level of a computer game or a message.

Eastern Europe No longer a separate political unit, but can be used in specific references to the region. Use only in historic sense. (Also *Western Europe*.)

Eastern Hemisphere The half of the Earth made up primarily of Africa, Asia, Australia and Europe.

Eastern Orthodox churches

The term applies to a group of churches that have roots in the earliest days of Christianity and do not recognize papal authority over their activities.

Churches in this tradition were part of the undivided Christendom that existed until the Great Schism of 1054. At that time, many of the churches in the western half of the old Roman Empire accorded the bishop of Rome supremacy over other bishops. The result was a split between eastern and western churches.

The autonomous churches that constitute Eastern Orthodoxy are organized along mostly national lines. They recognize the patriarch of Constantinople (modern-day Istanbul) as their leader. He convenes councils, but his authority is otherwise that of a "first among equals."

Eastern orthodox churches include the Greek Orthodox Church and the Russian Orthodox Church.

In the United States, organizational lines are based on the national backgrounds of various ethnic groups. The largest is the Greek Orthodox Archdiocese of America. Next is the Orthodox Church in America, which includes people of Bulgarian, Romanian, Russian and Syrian descent.

The churches have their own disciplines on matters such as married clergy — a married man may be ordained, but a priest may not marry after ordination.

Some of these churches call the archbishop who leads them a *metropolitan*; others use the term *patriarch*. He normally heads the principal archdiocese within a nation. Working with him are other archbishops, bishops, priests and deacons.

Archbishops and bishops frequently follow a monastic tradition in which they are known only by a first name. When no last name is used, repeat the title before the sole name in subsequent references.

Some forms: *Metropolitan Theodosius, archbishop of Washington and metropolitan of America and Canada.* On second reference: *Metropolitan Theodosius. Archbishop* may be replaced by *the Most Rev.* on first reference. *Bishop* may be replaced by *the Rt. Rev.* on first reference.

Use *the Rev.* before the name of a priest on first reference.

See **religious titles**.

Eastern Rite churches The term applies to a group of Catholic churches that are organized along ethnic lines traceable to the churches established during the earliest days of Christianity.

These churches accept the authority of the pope, but they have considerable autonomy in ritual and questions of discipline such as married clergy — a married man may be ordained, but marriage is not permitted after ordination.

Among the churches of the Eastern Rite are the Antiochean-Maronite, Armenian Catholic, Byzantine-Byelorussian, Byzantine-Russian, Byzantine-Ruthenian, Byzantine-Ukrainian and Chaldean Catholic.

Eastern Seaboard Synonym for *East Coast.*

Eastern Shore A region on the east side of Chesapeake Bay, including parts of Maryland and Virginia.

Eastern Shore is not a synonym for *East Coast.*

Eastern Standard Time (EST), Eastern Daylight Time (EDT) See **time zones**.

easygoing

eBay Inc. The online auctioneer is based in San Jose, Calif. Lowercase "*e*" unless it's the start of a sentence.

e-book The electronic, nonpaper version of a book or publication, sold digitally and commonly consumed on an *e-book reader* or *e-reader*, such as Amazon's Kindle.

E. coli Acceptable in all references for *Escherichia coli O157:H7 bacteria*.

ecology The study of the relationship between organisms and their surroundings. It is not synonymous with *environment*.
Right: *The laboratory is studying the ecology of man and the desert.*
Wrong: *Even so simple an undertaking as maintaining a lawn affects ecology.* (Use *environment* instead.)

ecosystem

ecotourism

Ecstasy Capitalize (no quote marks) this and other synthetic drug names.

Ecuadorean The term for the people and culture of Ecuador.

editor Capitalize *editor* before a name only when it is an official corporate or organizational title. Do not capitalize as a job description.
See **titles**.

editor-in-chief Use hyphens and capitalize when used as a formal title before a name: *Editor-in-Chief Horace Greeley*. The hyphens, reflecting industry usage, are an exception to Webster's New World College Dictionary.

See **titles**.

eerie

EFE An international news agency with headquarters in Madrid, Spain. It was founded in 1939.

effect See **affect, effect**.

e.g. Meaning *for example*, it is always followed by a comma.

Eglin Air Force Base, Fla.

Eid al-Adha Meaning "Feast of Sacrifice," this most important Islamic holiday marks the willingness of the Prophet Ibrahim (Abraham to Christians and Jews) to sacrifice his son. During the holiday, which in most places lasts four days, Muslims slaughter sheep or cattle, distribute part of the meat to the poor and eat the rest. The holiday begins on the 10th day of the Islamic lunar month of Dhul-Hijja, during the annual hajj pilgrimage to Mecca.

Eid al-Fitr A three-day holiday marking the end of Ramadan, Islam's holy month of fasting.

either Use it to mean one or the other, not both.
Right: *She said to use either door.*
Wrong: *There were lions on either side of the door.*
Right: *There were lions on each side of the door. There were lions on both sides of the door.*

either...or, neither...nor The nouns that follow these words do not constitute a compound subject; they are alternate subjects and require a verb that agrees with the nearer subject:
Neither they nor he is going. Neither he nor they are going.

El Al Israel Airlines. An *El Al air-*

liner is acceptable in any reference.
Headquarters in Tel Aviv.

elder For its use in religious contexts, see the entry for an individual's denomination.

elderly Use this word carefully and sparingly. Do not refer to a person as *elderly* unless it is clearly relevant to the story.

It is appropriate in generic phrases that do not refer to specific individuals: *concern for the elderly, a home for the elderly*, etc.

If the intent is to show that an individual's faculties have deteriorated, cite a graphic example and give attribution for it. Use age when available and appropriate.

Apply the same principle to terms such as *senior citizen*.

-elect Always hyphenate and lowercase: *President-elect Barack Obama*.

Election Day, election night The first Tuesday after the first Monday in November.

election returns Use figures, with commas every three digits starting at the right and counting left. Use the word *to* (not a hyphen) in separating different totals listed together: *Jimmy Carter outpolled Gerald Ford 40,827,292 to 39,146,157 in 1976*.

Use the word *votes* if there is any possibility that the figures could be confused with a ratio: *Nixon outpolled McGovern 16 votes to 3 votes in Dixville Notch*.

Do not attempt to create adjectival forms such as *the 40,827,292-39,146,157 vote*.

See **vote tabulations**.

Electoral College But *electoral vote(s)*.

electrocardiogram *EKG* is acceptable on second reference.

eleventh Spell out only in the phrase *the eleventh hour*, meaning at the last moment; otherwise use the numeral.

ellipsis See entry in **Punctuation** chapter.

El Salvador The use of the article in the name of the nation helps to distinguish it from its capital, *San Salvador*.

Use *Salvadoran(s)* in references to citizens of the nation.

email Acceptable in all references for *electronic mail*. Many *email* or Internet addresses use symbols such as the *at* symbol (@), or the *tilde* (~) that cannot be transmitted correctly by some computers. When needed, spell them out and provide an explanatory editor's note. Use a hyphen with other *e-* terms: *e-book, e-business, e-commerce*.

embargo See **boycott, embargo**.

embargo times See **release times**.

embarrass, embarrassing, embarrassed, embarrassment

embassy An *embassy* is the official office of an ambassador in a foreign country and the office that handles the political relations of one nation with another.

A *consulate*, the office of a consul in a foreign city, handles the commercial affairs and personal needs of citizens of the appointing country.

Capitalize with the name of a nation; lowercase without it: *the French Embassy, the U.S. Embassy, the embassy*.

emcee, emceed, emceeing A

phrase such as: *He was the master of ceremonies* is preferred.

emergency room *ER* is acceptable on second reference.

emeritus This word often is added to formal titles to denote that individuals who have retired retain their rank or title.

When used, place *emeritus* after the formal title, in keeping with the general practice of academic institutions: *Professor Emeritus Samuel Eliot Morison, Dean Emeritus Courtney C. Brown, Publisher Emeritus Barnard L. Colby.*

Or: *Samuel Eliot Morison, professor emeritus of history; Courtney C. Brown, dean emeritus of the faculty of business; Barnard L. Colby, publisher emeritus.*

emigrate, immigrate One who leaves a country *emigrates* from it.

One who comes into a country *immigrates.*

The same principle holds for *emigrant* and *immigrant.*

Emirates Airlines Headquarters is in Dubai, United Arab Emirates.

Emmy, Emmys The annual awards by the Academy of Television Arts & Sciences (for prime-time programming; based in Los Angeles) and the National Academy of Television Arts and Sciences (for daytime, news and sports; based in New York).

emoticon A typographical cartoon or symbol generally used to indicate mood or appearance, as :-) and often looked at sideways. Also known as *smileys.*

employee

empty-handed

enact See **adopt, approve, enact, pass**.

encyclopedia But follow the spelling of formal names: *Encyclopaedia Britannica.*

enforce But *reinforce.*

engine, motor An *engine* develops its own power, usually through internal combustion or the pressure of air, steam or water passing over vanes attached to a wheel: *an airplane engine, an automobile engine, a jet engine, a missile engine, a steam engine, a turbine engine.*

A *motor* receives power from an outside source: *an electric motor, a hydraulic motor.*

England London stands alone in datelines. Use *England* after the names of other English communities in datelines.

See **datelines** and **United Kingdom**.

enroll, enrolled, enrolling

en route Always two words.

ensign See **military titles**.

ensure, insure, assure Use *ensure* to mean guarantee: *Steps were taken to ensure accuracy.*

Use *insure* for references to insurance: *The policy insures his life.*

Use *assure* to mean to make sure or give confidence: *She assured us the statement was accurate.*

entitled Use it to mean a right to do or have something. Do not use it to mean titled.

Right: *She was entitled to the promotion.*

Right: *The book was titled "Gone With the Wind."*

enumerations See examples in

dash and **periods** entries in **Punctuation** chapter.

envelop (v.) Other verb forms: *enveloping, enveloped*. But: *envelope* (n.)

environment See **ecology**.

Environmental Protection Agency *EPA* is acceptable on second reference.

envoy Not a formal title. Lowercase.
See **titles**.

epicenter The point on the Earth's surface above the underground center, or focus, of an earthquake.
See **earthquakes**.

epidemic, pandemic An *epidemic* is the rapid spreading of disease in a certain population or region; a *pandemic* is an *epidemic* that has spread worldwide.

epidemiology

Episcopal Church Acceptable in all references for the *Protestant Episcopal Church in the United States of America*, the U.S. national church that is a member of the Anglican Communion.

The church is governed nationally by two bodies — the permanent Executive Council and the General Convention, which meets every three years.

After the council, the principal organizational units are, in descending order of size, provinces, dioceses or missionary districts, local parishes and local missions.

The National Council is composed of bishops, priests, laymen and laywomen. One bishop is designated the leader and holds the for-

mal title of presiding bishop.

The General Convention has final authority in matters of policy and doctrine. All acts must pass both of its houses — the House of Bishops and the House of Deputies. The latter is composed of an equal number of clergy and lay delegates from each diocese.

A province is composed of several dioceses. Each has a provincial synod made up of a house of bishops and a house of deputies. The synod's primary duty is to coordinate the work of the church in its area.

Within a diocese, a bishop is the principal official. He is helped by the Diocesan Convention, which consists of all the clergy in the diocese and lay representatives from each parish.

The parish or local church is governed by a vestry, composed of the pastor and lay members elected by the congregation.

The clergy consists of bishops, priests, deacons and brothers. A priest who heads a parish is described as a *rector* rather than a pastor.

For first reference to bishops, use *Bishop* before the individual's name: *Bishop John M. Allin*. An acceptable alternative in referring to U.S. bishops is *the Rt. Rev.* The designation *the Most Rev.* is used before the names of the archbishops of Canterbury and York.

For first references, use *the Rev.* before the name of a priest, *Deacon* before the name of a deacon.
See **Anglican Communion** and **religious titles**.

Episcopal, Episcopalian *Episcopal* is the adjective form; use *Episcopalian* only as a noun referring to a member of the Episcopal Church: *She is an Episcopalian*. But: *She is an Episcopal priest*.

Capitalize *Episcopal* when referring to the Episcopal Church. Use lowercase when the reference is simply to a body governed by bishops.

epoch See **historical periods and events**.

equal An adjective without comparative forms.

When people speak of a *more equal* distribution of wealth, what is meant is *more equitable*.

Equal Employment Opportunity Commission *EEOC* is acceptable on second reference.

equal, equaled, equaling

equally as Do not use the words together; one is sufficient.

Omit the *equally* shown here in parentheses: *She was (equally) as wise as Marilyn.*

Omit the *as* shown here in parentheses: *She and Marilyn were equally (as) wise.*

equal time *Equal time* applies to the Federal Communications Commission regulation that requires a radio or television station to provide a candidate for political office with air time equal to any time that an opponent receives beyond the coverage of news events.

equator Always lowercase.

equitable See **equal**.

equity When used in a financial sense, *equity* means the value of property beyond the amount that is owed on it.

A *stockholder's equity* in a corporation is the value of the shares he holds.

A *homeowner's equity* is the difference between the value of the house and the amount of the unpaid mortgage.

ERA Acceptable in all references to baseball's *earned run average*.

eras See **historical periods and events**.

e-reader Or *e-book reader*. Devices such as Amazon's Kindle, Barnes & Noble's Nook and Sony's Reader used to display electronic books and other digital publications. Other devices, including laptops and Apple's iPad, have e-reader software that can perform similar functions.

escalator Formerly a trademark, now a generic term.

escalator clause A clause in a contract providing for increases or decreases in wages, prices, etc., based on fluctuations in the cost of living, production, expenses, etc.

Eskimo, Eskimos Some, especially in northern Canada, use the term *Inuit* for these native peoples of northern North America. Follow the preference of those involved in the story.

ESOP Acronym for *employee stock ownership plan*. Spell out on first reference.

essential clauses, nonessential clauses These terms are used in this book instead of *restrictive clause* and *nonrestrictive clause* to convey the distinction between the two in a more easily remembered manner.

Both types of clauses provide additional information about a word or phrase in the sentence.

The difference between them is that the *essential clause* cannot be eliminated without changing the meaning of the sentence — it so *restricts* the meaning of the word or phrase that its absence would lead to a substantially different interpretation of what the author meant.

The *nonessential clause,* however, can be eliminated without altering the basic meaning of the sentence — it does not *restrict* the meaning so significantly that its absence would radically alter the author's thought.

PUNCTUATION: An essential clause must not be set off from the rest of a sentence by commas. A nonessential clause must be set off by commas.

The presence or absence of commas provides the reader with critical information about the writer's intended meaning. Note the following examples:

—*Reporters who do not read the Stylebook should not criticize their editors.* (The writer is saying that only one class of reporters, those who do not read the Stylebook, should not criticize their editors. If the *who ... Stylebook* phrase were deleted, the meaning of the sentence would be changed substantially.)

—*Reporters, who do not read the Stylebook, should not criticize their editors.* (The writer is saying that all reporters should not criticize their editors. If the *who ... Stylebook* phrase were deleted, this meaning would not be changed.)

USE OF WHO, WHOM, THAT, WHICH. See separate entries on **that (conjunction); that, which (pronouns); who, whom**.

That is the preferred pronoun to introduce essential clauses that refer to an inanimate object or an animal without a name. *Which* is the only acceptable pronoun to introduce a nonessential clause that refers to an inanimate object or an animal without a name.

The pronoun *which* occasionally may be substituted for *that* in the introduction of an essential clause that refers to an inanimate object or an animal without a name. In general, this use of *which* should appear only when *that* is used as a conjunction to introduce another clause in the same sentence: *He said Monday that the part of the army which suffered severe casualties needs reinforcement.*

See **that (conjunction)** for guidelines on the use of *that* as a conjunction.

essential phrases, nonessential phrases These terms are used in this book instead of *restrictive phrase* and *nonrestrictive phrase* to convey the distinction between the two in a more easily remembered manner.

The underlying concept is the one that also applies to clauses:

An *essential phrase* is a word or group of words critical to the reader's understanding of what the author had in mind.

A *nonessential phrase* provides more information about something. Although the information may be helpful to the reader's comprehension, the reader would not be misled if the information were not there.

PUNCTUATION: Do not set an essential phrase off from the rest of a sentence by commas:

We saw the award-winning movie "One Flew Over the Cuckoo's Nest." (No comma, because many movies have won awards, and without the name of the movie the reader would not know which movie was meant.)

They ate dinner with their daughter Julie. (Because they have more than one daughter, the inclusion of Julie's name is critical if the reader is to know which daughter is meant.)

Set off nonessential phrases by commas:

We saw the 1975 winner in the Academy Award competition for best picture, "One Flew Over the Cuckoo's Nest." (Only one movie won the award. The name is informative, but even without the name no other movie could be meant.)

They ate dinner with their daughter Julie and her husband, David. (Julie has only one husband. If the phrase read *and her husband David*, it would suggest that she had more than one husband.)

The company chairman, Henry Ford II, spoke. (In the context, only one person could be meant.)

Indian corn, or maize, was harvested. (*Maize* provides the reader with the name of the corn, but its absence would not change the meaning of the sentence.)

DESCRIPTIVE WORDS: Do not confuse punctuation rules for nonessential clauses with the correct punctuation when a nonessential word is used as a descriptive adjective. The distinguishing clue often is the lack of an article or pronoun:

Right: *Julie and husband Jeff went shopping. Julie and her husband, Jeff, went shopping.*

Right: *Company Chairman Henry Ford II made the announcement. The company chairman, Henry Ford II, made the announcement.*

ETF Abbreviation for *exchange-traded fund*. A security that tracks a benchmark much as a mutual fund does, but trades throughout market days like a stock on the exchange. Spell out on first reference.

ethanol Fuel additive distilled from mashed and fermented grain. Gasoline blends are written as a percentage of *ethanol*, e.g., *E85 for 85 percent ethanol and 15 percent gasoline.*

euro The common currency of 17 of the 27 members of the European Union, known as the *eurozone*: Austria, Belgium, Cyprus, Estonia, Finland, France, Germany, Greece, Ireland, Italy, Luxembourg, Malta, Netherlands, Portugal, Slovakia, Slovenia and Spain. Some smaller countries and territories also use the *euro*, either through agreement with the EU or as a de-facto currency.

Plural is *euros*.

eurodollar A U.S. dollar on deposit in a European bank, including foreign branches of U.S. banks.

European Community See **European Union**.

European Union *EU* (no periods). The 27-nation European Union, based in Brussels, was created by the Treaty on European Union, which was signed in February 1992 and took effect Nov. 1, 1993. Its executive body is the 27-member European Commission, which runs the EU's day-to-day affairs, drafts European laws and, after their adoption by governments, ensures their enforcement across the bloc. It also represents the EU in international trade negotiations and conducts antitrust investigations. The EU created the positions of president and foreign minister in 2010 in an effort to give the bloc greater prominence in world affairs. It also gave the European Parliament more powers in making EU laws. The EU is an outgrowth of the 1958 European Economic Community, which itself was formed out of the 1952 European Coal and Steel Community. The six founding members are: France, Germany, Italy, Netherlands, Belgium and Luxembourg. Other members are: Austria, Britain, Bulgaria, Cyprus, Czech Republic, Denmark, Estonia, Finland, Greece, Hungary, Ireland, Latvia, Lithuania, Malta, Poland, Portugal, Romania, Slovakia, Slovenia, Spain and Sweden.

eurozone See **euro**.

evangelical See **religious movements**.

Evangelical Friends Alliance See **Quakers**.

evangelism See **religious movements**.

evangelist Capitalize only in reference to the men credited with writing the Gospels: *The four Evangelists were Matthew, Mark, Luke and John.*

In lowercase, it means a preacher who makes a profession of seeking conversions.

eve Capitalize when used after the name of a holiday: *New Year's Eve, Christmas Eve.* But: *the eve of Christmas.*

every day (adv.) **everyday** (adj.)

every one, everyone Two words when it means each individual item: *Every one of the clues was worthless.*

One word when used as a pronoun meaning all persons: *Everyone wants his life to be happy.* (Note that *everyone* takes singular verbs and pronouns.)

ex- Use no hyphen for words that use *ex-* in the sense of *out of*:
excommunicate   expropriate

Hyphenate when using *ex-* in the sense of *former*:
ex-convict   ex-president

Do not capitalize *ex-* when attached to a formal title before a name: *ex-President Richard Nixon.* The prefix modifies the entire term: *ex-New York Gov. Mario Cuomo*; not *New York ex-Gov.*

Usually *former* is better.

exaggerate

except See **accept, except**.

exclamation point See entry in **Punctuation** chapter.

execute To *execute* a person is to kill him in compliance with a military order or judicial decision.

See **assassin, killer, murderer** and **homicide, murder, manslaughter**.

executive branch Always lowercase.

executive director Capitalize before a name only if it is a formal corporate or organizational title.

See **titles**.

Executive Mansion Capitalize only in references to the White House.

executor Use for both men and women.

Not a formal title. Always lowercase.

See **titles**.

exorcise, exorcism

expel, expelled, expelling

Explorers See **Boy Scouts**.

Export-Import Bank of the United States *Export-Import Bank* is acceptable in all references; *Ex-Im Bank* is acceptable on second reference.

Headquarters is in Washington.

extol, extolled, extolling

extra- Do not use a hyphen when *extra* means *outside of* unless the prefix is followed by a word beginning with *a* or a capitalized word:
extralegal   extraterrestrial
extramarital   extraterritorial
But:
extra-alimentary   extra-Britannic
Follow *extra-* with a hyphen when it is part of a compound modifier describing a condition beyond

the usual size, extent or degree:

extra-base hit	extra-large book
extra-dry drink	extra-mild taste

extraordinary loss, extraordinary income See **profit terminology**.

extrasensory perception *ESP* is acceptable on second reference.

extreme unction See **sacraments**.

Exxon Mobil Corp. Energy corporation formed from the 1999 acquisition by Exxon of Mobil, both formerly part of Standard Oil. *Exxon Mobil* is acceptable on second reference.

Headquarters is in Irving, Texas, with exploration, production and chemical operations based in Houston.

eye, eyed, eyeing

eyestrain

eye to eye, eye-to-eye Hyphenate when used as a compound modifier: *an eye-to-eye confrontation*.

eyewitness

Facebook See **social networking**.

face to face When a story says two people meet for discussions, talks or debate, it is unnecessary to say they met *face to face*.

fact-finding (adj.)

factor A financial organization whose primary business is purchasing the accounts receivable of other firms, at a discount, and taking the risk and responsibilities of making collection.

Faeroe Islands Use in datelines after a community name in stories from this group of Danish islands in the northern Atlantic Ocean between Iceland and the Shetland Islands.

Fahrenheit The temperature scale commonly used in the United States.

The scale is named for Gabriel Daniel Fahrenheit, a German physicist who designed it. In it, the freezing point of water is 32 degrees and the boiling point is 212 degrees.

To convert to Celsius, subtract 32 from Fahrenheit figure, multiply by 5 and divide by 9 (77 - 32 = 45, times 5 = 225, divided by 9 = 25 degrees Celsius.)

In cases that require mention of the scale, use these forms: *86 degrees Fahrenheit* or *86 F* (note the space and no period after the *F*) if degrees and Fahrenheit are clear from the context.

See **Celsius** and **Kelvin**.

For guidelines on when Celsius temperatures should be used, see **metric system** entry.

TEMPERATURE CONVERSIONS

Following is a temperature conversion table. Celsius temperatures have been rounded to the nearest whole number.

F	C	F	C	F	C
-26	-32	19	-7	64	18
-24	-31	21	-6	66	19
-22	-30	23	-5	68	20
-20	-29	25	-4	70	21
-18	-28	27	-3	72	22
-17	-27	28	-2	73	23
-15	-26	30	-1	75	24
-13	-25	32	0	77	25
-11	-24	34	1	79	26
-9	-23	36	2	81	27
-8	-22	37	3	82	28
-6	-21	39	4	84	29
-4	-20	41	5	86	30
-2	-19	43	6	88	31
0	-18	45	7	90	32
1	-17	46	8	91	33
3	-16	48	9	93	34
5	-15	50	10	95	35
7	-14	52	11	97	36
9	-13	54	12	99	37
10	-12	55	13	100	38
12	-11	57	14	102	39
14	-10	59	15	104	40
16	-9	61	16	106	41
18	-8	63	17	108	42

fall See **seasons**.

fallout (n.)

false titles Often derived from occupational titles or other labels. Always lowercase. See **titles**.

family names Capitalize words denoting family relationships only when they precede the name of a person or when they stand unmodified as a substitute for a person's name: *I wrote to Grandfather Smith. I wrote Mother a letter. I wrote my mother a letter.*

Fannie Mae A government-controlled company that helps provide money for the U.S. housing market by buying residential mortgages and packaging pools of those loans for sale to investors. The company, whose name is short for *Federal National Mortgage Association*, was seized by the government in September 2008 and is overseen by the Federal Housing Finance Agency.

FAQ Abbreviation for *frequently asked questions*.

Far East The easternmost portions of the continent of Asia: China, Japan, North and South Korea, Taiwan, Hong Kong and the eastern portions of Russia.
Confine *Far East* to this restricted sense. Use the *Far East and Southeast Asia* when referring to a wider portion of eastern Asia.
See **Asian subcontinent** and **Southeast Asia**.

far-flung (adj.)

farmworker

far-off (adj.)

far-ranging (adj.)

farsighted When used in a medical sense, it means that a person can see objects at a distance but has difficulty seeing materials at close range.

farther, further Farther refers to physical distance: *He walked farther into the woods.*
Further refers to an extension of time or degree: *She will look further into the mystery.*

Far West For the U.S. region, generally west of the Rocky Mountains.

FASB Abbreviation for *Financial Accounting Standards Board*. Spell out on first reference.

fascism, fascist See **political parties and philosophies**.

Fatah A secular Palestinian party and former guerrilla movement founded by Yasser Arafat. Do not use with the prefix *al-*.

father Use *the Rev.* in first reference before the names of Episcopal, Orthodox and Roman Catholic priests. Use *Father* before a name only in direct quotations.
See **religious titles**.

Father's Day The third Sunday in June.

father-in-law, fathers-in-law

Father Time

fax Preferable for *facsimile* or *facsimile machine* in all uses.

faze, phase *Faze* means to embarrass or disturb: *The snub did not faze her.*
Phase denotes an aspect or stage: *They will phase in a new system.*

FBI Acceptable in all references for *Federal Bureau of Investigation*.

102

feather bedding, featherbedding *Feather bedding* is a mattress stuffed with feathers.

Featherbedding is the practice of requiring an employer to hire more workers than needed to handle a job.

features They are not exempt from normal style rules. See **special contexts** for guidelines on some limited exceptions.

federal Use a capital letter for the architectural style and for corporate or governmental bodies that use the word as part of their formal names: *the Federal Trade Commission.* (See separate entries for governmental agencies.)

Lowercase when used as an adjective to distinguish something from state, county, city, town or private entities: *federal assistance, federal court, the federal government, a federal judge.*

Also: *federal District Court* (but *U.S. District Court* is preferred) and *federal Judge Ann Aldrich* (but *U.S. District Judge Ann Aldrich* is preferred).

Federal Aviation Administration *FAA* is acceptable on second reference.

Federal Bureau of Investigation *FBI* is acceptable in all references. To avoid alphabet soup, however, use *the bureau* in some references.

Federal Communications Commission *FCC* is acceptable on second reference.

federal court Always lowercase.
The preferred form for first reference is to use the proper name of the court. See entries under **U.S.** and the court name.

Do not create nonexistent entities such as *Manhattan Federal Court.*

Instead, use *a federal court in Manhattan.*

See **judicial branch**.

Federal Crop Insurance Corp. Do not abbreviate.

Federal Deposit Insurance Corp. The Federal Deposit Insurance Corp. is the government agency that insures deposits in banks and thrifts. *FDIC* is acceptable on second reference.

Federal Emergency Management Agency *FEMA* is acceptable on second reference.

Federal Energy Regulatory Commission This agency replaced the Federal Power Commission in 1977. It regulates interstate natural gas and electricity transactions.

FERC is acceptable on second reference, but *the agency* or *the commission* is preferred.

Federal Farm Credit Board Do not abbreviate.

Federal Farm Credit System The federally chartered cooperative banking system that provides most of the nation's agricultural loans. The system is cooperatively owned by its farm borrowers and is made up of the regional banks that issue operating and mortgage loans through local land bank associations and production credit associations.

federal funds, federal funds rate Money in excess of what the Federal Reserve says a bank must have on hand to back up deposits. The excess can be lent overnight to banks that need more cash on hand to meet their reserve requirements. The interest rate of these loans is the *federal funds rate.* Its target rate is set by the Federal Reserve's policymaking panel, the Federal Open

Market Committee. See **Federal Reserve System**.

Federal Highway Administration Reserve the *FHA* abbreviation for the *Federal Housing Administration*.

Federal Home Loan Bank Board Do not abbreviate.

Federal Home Loan Mortgage Corp. See **Freddie Mac**.

Federal Housing Administration *FHA* is acceptable on second reference.

federal legal holidays See **holidays and holy days**.

Federal Mediation and Conciliation Service Do not abbreviate. Use *the service* on second reference.

Federal National Mortgage Association See **Fannie Mae**.

Federal Register This publication, issued every workday, is the legal medium for recording and communicating the rules and regulations established by the executive branch of the federal government.

Individuals or corporations cannot be held legally responsible for compliance with a regulation unless it has been published in the Register.

In addition, executive agencies are required to publish in advance some types of proposed regulations.

Federal Reserve The central bank of the United States. It comprises the Federal Open Market Committee, which sets interest rates; the Federal Reserve Board, the regulatory body made up of Fed governors in Washington; and the Federal Reserve System, which includes the Fed in Washington and 12 regional Fed banks. Use *Federal Reserve* on first reference, *the Fed* on second reference.

Federal Trade Commission *FTC* is acceptable on second reference.

FedEx Use this official brand name for the *Federal Express* delivery service company. The formal name of the parent company is *FedEx Corp*. Headquarters is in Memphis, Tenn.

felony, misdemeanor A *felony* is a serious crime. A *misdemeanor* is a minor offense against the law.

A fuller definition of what constitutes a felony or misdemeanor depends on the governmental jurisdiction involved.

At the federal level, a *misdemeanor* is a crime that carries a potential penalty of no more than a year in jail. A *felony* is a crime that carries a potential penalty of more than a year in prison. Often, however, a statute gives a judge options such as imposing a fine or probation in addition to or instead of a jail or prison sentence.

A *felon* is a person who has been convicted of a *felony*, regardless of whether the individual actually spends time in confinement or is given probation or a fine instead.

Convicted felon is redundant.

See **prison, jail**.

female Use *female* as an adjective, not *woman*. *She is the first female governor of North Carolina.*

Ferris wheel

ferryboat

fertility rate As calculated by the federal government, it is the number of live births per 1,000 females age 15 through 44 years.

fewer, less In general, use *fewer* for individual items, *less* for bulk or quantity.

Wrong: *The trend is toward more machines and less people.* (People in this sense refers to individuals.)

Wrong: *She was fewer than 60 years old.* (Years in this sense refers to a period of time, not individual years.)

Right: *Fewer than 10 applicants called.* (Individuals.)

Right: *I had less than $50 in my pocket.* (An amount.) But: *I had fewer than 50 $1 bills in my pocket.* (Individual items.)

Fez The preferred spelling for the city in Morocco.

fiance (man) **fiancee** (woman)

Fiberglas Note the single *s*. A trademark for fiberglass or glass fiber.

field house

figuratively, literally *Figuratively* means in an analogous sense, but not in the exact sense. *He bled them white.*

Literally means in an exact sense; do not use it figuratively.

Wrong: *He literally bled them white.* (Unless the blood was drained from their bodies.)

figure The symbol for a number: *the figure 5.*
See **numerals**.

filibuster To *filibuster* is to make long speeches to obstruct the passage of legislation.

A legislator who used such methods also is a *filibuster*, not a *filibusterer*.

Filipinos The people of the Philippines.

film noir

filmgoer

filmmaker

film ratings See **movie ratings**.

financial editor Capitalize only as a formal title before a name.
See **titles**.

financial institutions Here are 15 major U.S. financial institutions, with their ticker symbols and headquarters:

Allstate Corp. (ALL) Northbrook, Ill.

American Express Co. (AXP) New York

Bank of America Corp. (BAC) Charlotte, N.C.

Bank of New York Mellon Corp. (BK) New York

Charles Schwab Corp. (SCHW) San Francisco

Citigroup Inc. (C) New York

Goldman Sachs Group Inc. (GS) New York

JPMorgan Chase & Co. (JPM) New York

MetLife Inc. (MET) New York

Morgan Stanley (MS) New York

PNC Financial Services Group Inc. (PNC) Pittsburgh

Prudential Financial Inc. (PRU) Newark, N.J.

Travelers Cos. (TRV) New York

U.S. Bancorp (USB) Minneapolis

Wells Fargo & Co. (WFC) San Francisco

Finland A Nordic state, not part of Scandinavia.

firearms See **weapons**.

fire department See the **governmental bodies** entry for the basic rules on capitalization.

See **titles** and **military titles** for guidelines on titles.

firefight

firefighter, fireman The preferred term to describe a person who fights fire is *firefighter*.

One meaning of *fireman* is a person who tends fires in a furnace. *Fireman* is also an acceptable synonym for *firefighter*.

firewall A device or software designed to stop malicious or unauthorized Internet traffic from reaching a computer or local data network. Some firewalls also inspect outgoing traffic.

firm A business partnership is correctly referred to as a *firm*: *He joined a law firm*.

Do not use *firm* in references to an incorporated business entity. Use *the company* or *the corporation* instead.

first class, first-class Hyphenate as a modifier before a noun. *The restaurant was first class. It was a first-class restaurant.*

first degree, first-degree Hyphenate when used as a compound modifier: *It was murder in the first degree. He was convicted of first-degree murder.*

first family Always lowercase.

firsthand (adj. and adv.)

first lady Not a formal title. Do not capitalize, even when used before the name of a chief of state's wife.

See **titles**.

first quarter, first-quarter Hyphenate when used as a compound modifier: *He scored in the first quarter. The team took the lead on his first-quarter goal.*

fiscal, monetary *Fiscal* applies to budgetary matters.

Monetary applies to money supply.

fiscal year The 12-month period that a corporation or governmental body uses for bookkeeping purposes.

The federal government's fiscal year starts three months ahead of the calendar year — fiscal 2007, for example, ran from Oct. 1, 2006, to Sept. 30, 2007.

fitful It means restless, not a condition of being fit.

fjord

flack, flak *Flack* is slang for press agent. Avoid using in copy.

Flak is a type of anti-aircraft fire, hence figuratively a barrage of criticism.

flagpole, flagship

flail, flay To *flail* is to swing the arms widely.

To *flay* is, literally, to strip off the skin by whipping. Figuratively, *to flay* means to tongue-lash a person.

flair, flare *Flair* is conspicuous talent or style.

Flare is a verb meaning to blaze with sudden, bright light or to burst out in anger. It is also a noun meaning a flame.

flak See **flack, flak.**

flare up (v.) **flare-up** (n.) See **flair, flare.**

flash flood See **weather terms.**

flat-panel TV, flat-screen TV A flat-panel television set contains no cathode-ray tube or optical path, which means it can be thinner than a tube-based TV set. The two most popular technologies are plasma displays and liquid-crystal displays, or LCDs. Flat-screen TVs have a flat front glass surface, as opposed to the convex surfaces of older CRT sets. The term can apply to CRT sets and rear-projection sets that are not flat panels.

flaunt, flout *To flaunt* is to make an ostentatious or defiant display: *She flaunted her intelligence.*

To flout is to show contempt for: *He flouts the law.*

fleet Use figures and capitalize *fleet* when forming a proper name: *the 6th Fleet.*

Lowercase *fleet* whenever it stands alone.

flier, flyer *Flier* is the preferred term for an aviator or a handbill. *Flyer* is the proper name of some trains and buses: *The Western Flyer.*

flip-flop

float Money that has been committed but not yet credited to an account, like a check that has been written but has not yet cleared.

flood plain

floods, flood stage See **weather terms**.

floodwaters

floor leader Treat it as a job description, lowercased, rather than a formal title: *Republican floor leader John Smith.*

Do not use when a formal title such as *majority leader, minority leader* or *whip* would be the accurate description.

See **legislative titles** and **titles**.

Florida Abbreviate *Fla.* in date-lines or stories. Postal code: *FL*

See **state names**.

Florida Keys A chain of small islands extending southwest from the southern tip of mainland Florida.

Cities, or the islands themselves, are followed by *Fla.* in datelines: *KEY WEST, Fla. (AP) —*

flounder, founder A *flounder* is a fish; to *flounder* is to move clumsily or jerkily, to flop about: *The fish floundered on land.*

To founder is to bog down, become disabled or sink: *The ship floundered in the heavy seas for hours, then foundered.*

flout See **flaunt, flout**.

flowers See **plants**.

fluid ounce Equal to 1.8 cubic inches, 2 tablespoons or 6 teaspoons. The metric equivalent is approximately 30 milliliters.

To convert to milliliters, multiply by 30 (3 ounces x 30 equals 90 milliliters).

See **liter**.

flu-like

fluorescent

flush To become red in the face. See **livid**.

flyer See **flier, flyer**.

FM Acceptable in all references for the *frequency modulation* system of radio transmission.

f.o.b. Acceptable on first reference for *free on board*, meaning a seller agrees to put a commodity on a truck or ship, etc., at no charge, but transportation costs must be paid by the buyer.

-fold No hyphen: *twofold, fourfold* and *hundredfold.*

folk singer, folk song

following The word usually is a noun, verb or adjective: *He has a large following. He is following his conscience. The following statement was made.*

Although Webster's New World College Dictionary records its use as a preposition, the preferred word is *after: He spoke after dinner.* Not: *He spoke following dinner.*

follow-up (n. and adj.) Use two words (no hyphen) in verb form.

food Most food names are lowercase: *apples, cheese, peanut butter.*

Capitalize brand names and trademarks: *Roquefort cheese, Tabasco sauce.*

Most proper nouns or adjectives are capitalized when they occur in a food name: *Boston brown bread, Russian dressing, Swiss cheese, Waldorf salad.*

Lowercase is used, however, when the food does not depend on the proper noun or adjective for its meaning: *french fries.*

If a question arises, check the separate section on **Food Guidelines.** If there is no entry, follow Webster's New World College Dictionary. Use lowercase if the dictionary lists it as an acceptable form for the sense in which the word is used.

The same principles apply to foreign names for foods: *mousse de saumon* (salmon mousse), *pomme de terre* (literally, "apple of the earth" — for potato), *salade Russe* (Russian salad).

Food and Agriculture Organization Not *Agricultural. FAO* is acceptable on second reference to this U.N. agency.

Food and Drug Administration *FDA* is acceptable on second reference.

foodborne (adj.)

foot The basic unit of length in the measuring system that has been used in the United States. Its origin was a calculation that this was the length of the average human foot.

The metric equivalent is exactly 30.48 centimeters, which may be rounded to 30 centimeters for most comparisons.

For most conversions to centimeters, it is adequate to multiply 30 (5 feet x 30 equals 150 centimeters). For more exact figures, multiply by 30.48 (5 feet x 30.48 equals 152.4 centimeters).

To convert to meters, multiply by .3 (5 feet x .3 equals 1.5 meters).

See **centimeter; meter;** and **dimensions**.

foot-and-mouth disease Not *hoof-and-mouth disease.*

forbear, forebear *To forbear* is to avoid or shun.

A *forebear* is an ancestor.

forbid, forbade, forbidding

force majeure A condition permitting a company to depart from the strict terms of a contract because of an event or effect that can't be reasonably controlled.

forcible rape A redundancy that usually should be avoided. It may be used, however, in stories dealing with both rape and statutory rape, which does not necessarily involve the use of force.

Ford Motor Co. Use *Ford* on second reference.

Headquarters is in Dearborn, Mich.

fore- The rules in **prefixes** apply, but in general, no hyphen. Some examples:

forebrain	foregoing
forefather	foretooth

There are three nautical exceptions, based on long-standing practice:

fore-topgallant	fore-topsail
fore-topmast	

forecast Use *forecast* also for the past tense, not *forecasted*.
See **weather terms**.

foreclosure The process by which a lender seizes property from a mortgage holder who has failed to make payments and is in default.

forego, forgo To *forego* means to go before, as in *foregone conclusion*.

To *forgo* means to abstain from, as in: *He decided to forgo his senior year of eligibility*.

foreign governmental bodies
See **non-U.S. governmental bodies**.

foreign legislative bodies See **non-U.S. legislative bodies**.

foreign money Generally, amounts of foreign money mentioned in news stories should be converted to dollars. If it is necessary to mention the foreign amount, provide the dollar equivalent in parentheses.

The basic monetary units of nations are listed in Webster's New World College Dictionary under "Monetary Units." Use, as appropriate, the official exchange rates, which change from day to day on the world's markets.

foreign names For foreign place names, use the primary spelling in Webster's New World College Dictionary. If it has no entry, follow the National Geographic Atlas of the World.

For personal names, follow the individual's preference for an English spelling if it can be determined. Otherwise:

—Use the nearest phonetic equivalent in English if one exists: *Alexander Solzhenitsyn*, for example, rather than *Aleksandr*, the spelling that would result from a transliteration of the Russian letters into the English alphabet.

If a name has no close phonetic equivalent in English, express it with an English spelling that approximates the sound in the original language: *Anwar Sadat*.

In general, lowercase particles such as *de, der, la, le,* and *van, von* when part of a given name: *Charles de Gaulle, Baron Manfred von Richthofen*. But follow individual preferences, as in *bin Laden*, or Dutch names such as *Van Gogh* or *Van der Graaf*. Capitalize the particles when the last names start a sentence: *De Gaulle spoke to von Richthofen*.

For additional guidelines, see **Arabic names; Chinese names; Portuguese names; Russian names; Spanish names**.

foreign words Some foreign words and abbreviations have been accepted universally into the English language: *bon voyage*; *versus, vs.*; *et cetera, etc.* They may be used without explanation if they are clear in the context.

Many foreign words and their abbreviations are not understood universally, although they may be used in special applications such as medical or legal terminology. If such a word or phrase is needed in a story, place it in quotation marks and provide an explanation: *"ad astra per aspera," a Latin phrase meaning "to the stars through difficulty."*

foreman, forewoman Seldom a formal title. Never use foreperson.

formal titles See **titles**.

former Always lowercase. But retain capitalization for a formal title used immediately before a name: *former President Bill Clinton.*

Formica A trademark for a brand of laminated plastic.

formula, formulas Use figures in writing formulas, as illustrated in the entries on metric units.

forsake, forsook, forsaken

fort Do not abbreviate, for cities or for military installations.
In datelines for cities:
FORT LAUDERDALE, Fla. (AP)
—
In datelines for military installations:
FORT BRAGG, N.C. (AP) —

fortuneteller, fortunetelling

forty, forty-niner *'49er* is acceptable.

forward Not *forwards.*

foul, fowl *Foul* means offensive, out of line.
A *fowl* is a bird, especially the larger domestic birds used as food: chickens, ducks, turkeys.

founder See **flounder, founder**.

Founding Fathers Capitalize when referring to the creators of the U.S. Constitution.

Four-H Club *4-H Club* is preferred. Members are *4-H'ers.*

Foursquare A location-based social network. Users check in at certain places or businesses, collect rewards for visits and track friends who use the service.

four-star general

Fourth Estate Capitalize when used as a collective name for journalism and journalists.
The description is attributed to Edmund Burke, who is reported to have called the reporters' gallery in Parliament a "Fourth Estate."
The three estates of early English society were the Lords Spiritual (the clergy), the Lords Temporal (the nobility) and the Commons (the bourgeoisie).

Fourth of July, July Fourth Also *Independence Day.* The federal legal holiday is observed on Friday if July 4 falls on a Saturday, on Monday if it falls on a Sunday.

4x4 *Four-wheel drive* is preferred, unless *4x4* is part of the car model's proper name.

401(k) (no space)

fracking See **hydraulic fracturing**.

fractions Spell out amounts less than 1 in stories, using hyphens between the words: *two-thirds, four-fifths, seven-sixteenths,* etc.
Use figures for precise amounts larger than 1, converting to decimals whenever practical.
When using fractional characters, remember that most newspaper type fonts can set only 1/8, 1/4, 3/8, 1/2, 5/8, 3/4 and 7/8 as one unit; for mixed numbers, use 1 1/2, 2 5/8, etc. with a full space between the whole number and the fraction. Other fractions require a hyphen and individual figures, with a space between the whole number and the fraction: 1 3-16, 2 1-3, 5 9-10.
In tabular material, use figures exclusively, converting to decimals if the amounts involve extensive

use of fractions that cannot be expressed as a single character.
See **percent**.

fragment, fragmentary *Fragment* describes a piece or pieces broken from the whole: *She sang a fragment of the song.*

Fragmentary describes disconnected and incomplete parts: *Early returns were fragmentary.*

frame up (v.) **frame-up** (n.)

Frankfurt The city in Germany carries the name of the country in datelines.

fraternal organizations and service clubs Capitalize the proper names: *American Legion, Lions Club, Independent Order of Odd Fellows, Rotary Club.*

Capitalize also words describing membership: *He is a Legionnaire, a Lion, an Odd Fellow, an Optimist and a Rotarian.* See **American Legion** for the rationale on *Legionnaire.*

Capitalize the formal titles of officeholders when used before a name.
See **titles**.

Freddie Mac A government-controlled company that helps provide money for the U.S. housing market by buying residential mortgages and packaging pools of those loans for sale to investors. The company, whose name is short for *Federal Home Loan Mortgage Corp.*, was seized by the government in September 2008 and is overseen by the Federal Housing Finance Agency.

free-for-all (n. and adj.)

freelance (v. and adj.) **freelancer** (n.)

freely floating Describes an exchange rate that is allowed to

fluctuate in response to supply and demand in the foreign markets.

free on board See **f.o.b.**

freewheeling

freeze-dry, freeze-dried, freeze-drying

freezing drizzle, freezing rain See **weather terms**.

French Canadian, French Canadians Without a hyphen. An exception to the normal practice in describing a dual ethnic heritage.

French Foreign Legion Retain capitalization if shortened to the Foreign Legion.

Lowercase *the legion* and *legionnaires*. Unlike the situation with the American Legion, the French Foreign Legion is a group of active soldiers.

frequency modulation *FM* is acceptable in all references.

frequent flier

Friends General Conference, Friends United Meeting See **Quakers**.

Frigidaire A trademark for a brand of refrigerator.

Frisbee A trademark for a plastic disc thrown as a toy. Use *Frisbee disc* for the trademarked version and *flying disc* for other generic versions.

Frontier Airlines Holdings Inc. Headquarters is in Denver.

front line (n.) **front-line** (adj.)

frontman

front page (n.) **front-page** (adj.)

front-runner

frost See **weather terms**.

fruits See **food**.

FTP The abbreviation stands for *File Transfer Protocol*, a common procedure for transferring files on the *Internet*. The abbreviation is acceptable in second reference.

fulfill, fulfilled, fulfilling

full- Hyphenate when used to form compound modifiers:

full-dress	full-page
full-fledged	full-scale
full-length	

See the listings that follow and Webster's New World College Dictionary for the spelling of other combinations.

full-body scanner

full faith and credit bond See **loan terminology**.

full house Three of a kind and a pair in poker.

full time, full-time Hyphenate when used as a compound modifier: *He works full time. She has a full-time job.*

fulsome It means disgustingly excessive. Do not use it to mean lavish or profuse.

fundamentalist See **religious movements**.

fundraising, fundraiser One word in all cases.

funnel cloud See **weather terms**.

furlough

further See **farther, further**.

fuselage

fusillade

futures *Futures* contracts are agreements to deliver a quantity of goods, generally commodities, at a specified price at a certain time in the future. *Options*, which also are widely traded on the nation's commodities exchanges, give buyers the right but not the obligation to buy or sell something at a certain price within a specified period.

The purpose of the futures exchanges is to transfer the risk of price fluctuations from people who don't want the risk, such as farmers or metals processors, to speculators who are willing to take a gamble on making big profits.

Major U.S. commodities markets are the Chicago Board Options Exchange, Chicago Board of Trade, Chicago Mercantile Exchange, New York Mercantile Exchange, the New York Cotton Exchange, and the Coffee, Sugar and Cocoa Exchange.

F-word See **obscenities, profanities, vulgarities**.

GAAP The acronym stands for *generally accepted accounting principles*. Spell out on first reference.

gage, gauge A *gage* is a security or a pledge.

A *gauge* is a measuring device. *Gauge* is also a term used to designate the size of shotguns. See **weapons**.

gaiety

gale See **weather terms**.

gallon Equal to 128 fluid ounces. The metric equivalent is approximately 3.8 liters. There are 42 gallons in a barrel of oil.

To convert to liters, multiply by 3.8 (3 gallons x 3.8 = 11.4 liters).

See **imperial gallon**; **liter**; and **metric system**.

Gallup poll Prepared by the Gallup Organization, Princeton, N.J.

gambling Preferred term for playing games of chance. Avoid use of the term *gaming* except in quotations or proper names.

game plan

gaming See **gambling**.

gamut, gantlet, gauntlet A *gamut* is a scale of notes or any complete range or extent.

A *gantlet* is a flogging ordeal, literally or figuratively.

A *gauntlet* is a glove. *To throw down the gauntlet* means to issue a challenge. To *take up the gauntlet* means to accept a challenge.

Gannett Co. The largest owner of U.S. newspapers, including *USA Today*, the top-selling newspaper in the United States. Also owns television stations. Headquarters is in McLean, Va.

garnish, garnishee *Garnish* means to adorn or decorate.

As a verb, *garnishee* (*garnisheed*, *garnisheeing*) means to attach a debtor's property or wages to satisfy a debt. As a noun, it identifies the individual whose property was attached.

gauge See **gage, gauge**.

gay Used to describe men and women attracted to the same sex, though *lesbian* is the more common term for women. Preferred over *homosexual* except in clinical contexts or references to sexual activity.

Include sexual orientation only when it is pertinent to a story, and avoid references to "sexual preference" or to a gay or alternative "lifestyle."

Gazprom Russia's state-controlled gas monopoly. Corporate name is *OAO Gazprom*. Headquarters is in Moscow.

GED A trademark abbreviation for General Educational Development tests, a battery of five exams designed by the American Council on Education to measure high school equivalency. *GED* should be used as an adjective, not as a noun. Those passing the tests earn a *GED diploma* or *certificate*, not a *GED*.

G-8 Use a hyphen in the abbreviated form for the *Group of Eight*, made up of representatives of the major industrial nations, Britain, Canada, France, Germany, Italy, Japan, Russia and the United States. (The *G-7* or *Group of Seven* — all the aforementioned except Russia — deals with economic issues.) A general description rather than the full name is preferred on first reference: *Leading industrial nations.* See **G-20**.

general assembly See **legislature** for its treatment as the name of a state's legislative body.

Capitalize when it is the formal name for the ruling or consultative body of an organization: *the General Assembly of the World Council of Churches.*

General Assembly (U.N.) *General Assembly* may be used on the first reference in a story under a United Nations dateline.

Use *U.N. General Assembly* in other first references, *the General Assembly* or *the assembly* in subsequent references.

general court Part of the official proper name for the legislatures in Massachusetts and New Hampshire. Capitalize specific references with or without the state name: *the Massachusetts General Court, the General Court.*

In keeping with the accepted practice, however, *Legislature* may be used instead and treated as a proper name. See **legislature**.

Lowercase *legislature* in a generic use such as: *The General Court is the legislature in Massachusetts.*

General Dynamics Corp. Headquarters is in Falls Church, Va.

General Electric Co. *GE* is acceptable on second reference.

Headquarters is in Fairfield, Conn.

general, general of the air force, general of the army See **military titles**.

general manager Capitalize only as a formal title before a name: corporate *General Manager Jim Smith.* Lowercase as a job description for sports teams: *Giants general manager Jerry Reese.*

See **titles**.

General Motors Co. *GM* is acceptable on second reference.

Headquarters is in Detroit.

general obligation bond See **loan terminology**.

General Services Administration *GSA* is acceptable on second reference.

Geneva The city in Switzerland stands alone in datelines.

Geneva Conventions Note the final *s.*

gentile Generally, any person not Jewish; often, specifically a Christian. But to Mormons it is anyone not a Mormon.

gentleman Do not use as a synonym for *man.* See **lady**.

genus, species In scientific or biological names, capitalize the first, or generic, Latin name for the class of plant or animal and lowercase the species that follows: *Homo sapiens, Tyrannosaurus rex.*

In second references, use the abbreviated form: *P. borealis, T. rex.*

geographic names The basic guidelines:

DOMESTIC: Do not use the postal abbreviations for state names. For acceptable abbreviations, see entries in this book under each state's name. See **state names** for rules on when the abbreviations may be used.

Abbreviate *Saint* as *St.* (But abbreviate *Sault Sainte Marie* as *Sault Ste. Marie.*)

FOREIGN: The first source for the spelling of all foreign place names is Webster's New World College Dictionary as follows:

—Use the first-listed spelling if an entry gives more than one.

—If the dictionary provides different spellings in separate entries, use the spelling that is followed by a full description of the location.

If the dictionary does not have an entry, use the first-listed spelling in the National Geographic Atlas of the World.

Online: http://www.nationalgeographic.com

NEW NAMES: Follow the styles adopted by the United Nations and the U.S. Board on Geographic Names on new cities, new independent nations and nations that change their names.

DATELINES: See the **datelines** entry.

CAPITALIZATION: Capitalize common nouns when they form an integral part of a proper name, but lowercase them when they stand alone: *Pennsylvania Avenue, the avenue; the Philippine Islands, the islands; the Mississippi River, the river.*

Lowercase common nouns that are not a part of a specific name: *the Pacific islands, the Swiss mountains, Zhejiang province.*

For additional guidelines, see **addresses**; **capitalization**; **directions and regions**; and **island**.

Georgia Abbreviate *Ga.* in datelines or stories. Postal code: *GA*
See **state names**.

German measles Also known as *rubella*.

Germany *East Germany* and *West Germany* were reunited as of Oct. 3, 1990. *Berlin* stands alone in datelines.

getaway (n.)

get-together (n.)

ghetto, ghettos Do not use indiscriminately as a synonym for the sections of cities inhabited by minorities or the poor. *Ghetto* has a connotation that government decree has forced people to live in a certain area.

In most cases, *section, district, slum area* or *quarter* is the more accurate word.

gibe, jibe *To gibe* means to taunt or sneer: *They gibed him about his mistakes.*

Jibe means to shift direction or, colloquially, to agree: *They jibed their ship across the wind. Their stories didn't jibe.*

Gibraltar, Strait of Not *Straits*. The entrance to the Mediterranean from the Atlantic Ocean. The British colony on the peninsula that juts into the strait stands alone in datelines as *GIBRALTAR*.

GIF Acronym for *Graphics Interchange Format*, a compression format for images. *GIF* is acceptable in copy but should be explained in the story. Use lowercase in a file name.

giga- A prefix denoting 1 billion units of a measure. Move a decimal point nine places to the right, adding zeros if necessary, to convert to the basic unit: 5.5 gigatons = 5,500,000,000 tons.

gigabyte A unit of storage capacity in a computer system, loosely equal to 1 billion bytes. Abbreviate *GB*.

GI, GIs Believed to have originated as an abbreviation for *government issue* supplies, it describes military personnel in general, but normally is used for the Army. (No periods is an exception to the general rule for two-letter abbreviations.)
Soldier is preferred unless the story contains the term in quoted matter or involves a subject such as the *GI Bill of Rights*.

Ginnie Mae Commonly used for *Government National Mortgage Association*.

girl Applicable until 18th birthday is reached. Use *woman* or *young woman* afterward.

girlfriend, boyfriend

Girl Scouts The full name of the national organization is *Girl Scouts of the United States of America*. Headquarters is in New York. Note that *Girl Scout Cookies* is a trademark name.
Girls 6 through 8 are *Brownie Girl Scouts* or *Brownies*. Girls 9 through 11 are *Junior Girl Scouts* or *Juniors*. Girls 12 through 14 are *Cadette Girl Scouts* or *Cadettes*. Girls 15 through 17 are *Senior Girl Scouts* or *Seniors*.
See **Boy Scouts**.

glamour One of the few *our* endings still used in American writing. But the adjective is *glamorous*.

GlaxoSmithKline PLC Headquarters is in London.

Global Positioning System See **GPS**.

global warming, climate change The terms can be used interchangeably.

globe-trotter, globe-trotting But the proper name of the basketball team is the *Harlem Globetrotters*.

GMT For *Greenwich Mean Time*. See **time zones**.

gobbledygook

go-between (n.)

godchild, goddaughter Also: *godfather, godliness, godmother, godsend* and *godson*. Always lowercase.

gods and goddesses Capitalize *God* in references to the deity of all monotheistic religions. Capitalize all noun references to the deity: *God the Father, Holy Ghost, Holy Spirit*, etc. Lowercase personal pronouns: *he, him, thee, thou*.
Lowercase *gods* and *goddesses* in references to the deities of polytheistic religions.
Lowercase *god, gods* and *goddesses* in references to false gods: *He made money his god*.
See **religious references**.

Godspeed

go-go

Goldman Sachs Group Inc. Headquarters is in New York.

goodbye

Good Conduct Medal

Good Friday The Friday before Easter.

good Samaritan But uppercase when used in a title: *Good Samaritan Hospital.*

good, well *Good* is an adjective that means something is as it should be or is better than average.

When used as an adjective, *well* means suitable, proper, healthy. When used as an adverb, *well* means in a satisfactory manner or skillfully.

Good should not be used as an adverb. It does not lose its status as an adjective in a sentence such as *I feel good.* Such a statement is the idiomatic equivalent of *I am in good health.* An alternative, *I feel well,* could be interpreted as meaning that your sense of touch was good.

See **bad, badly** and **well**.

good will, goodwill One word when used as the financial term referring to the amount by which the purchase price exceeds the fair value of an acquired company's net assets. Accounting rules require companies to evaluate *goodwill* yearly and take write-downs, known as impairment charges, to reflect any diminished value.

Google A trademark for a Web search engine. *Google, Googling* and *Googled* are used informally as a verb for searching for information on the Internet. Headquarters of *Google Inc.* is in Mountain View, Calif.

GOP Grand Old Party. *GOP* is acceptable on second reference for *Republican Party.*

Gospel(s), gospel Capitalize when referring to any or all of the first four books of the New Testament: *the Gospel of St. John, the Gos-*

pels.

Lowercase in other references: *She is a famous gospel singer.*

government Always lowercase, never abbreviate: *the federal government, the state government, the U.S. government.*

Government Accountability Office The *Government Accountability Office* is a nonpartisan congressional agency that audits federal programs. (Formerly the General Accounting Office.)

GAO is acceptable on second reference.

governmental bodies Follow these guidelines:

FULL NAME: Capitalize the full proper names of governmental agencies, departments and offices: *The U.S. Department of State, the Georgia Department of Human Resources, the Boston City Council, the Chicago Fire Department.*

WITHOUT JURISDICTION: Retain capitalization in referring to a specific body if the dateline or context makes the name of the nation, state, county, city, etc. unnecessary: *The Department of State* (in a story from Washington), *the Department of Human Resources* or *the state Department of Human Resources* (in a story from Georgia), *the City Council* (in a story from Boston), *the Fire Department* or *the city Fire Department* (in a story from Chicago).

Lowercase further condensations of the name: *the department, the council,* etc.

For additional guidance see **assembly; city council; committee; congress; legislature; House of Representatives; Senate; Supreme Court of the United States;** and **supreme courts of the states**.

FLIP-FLOPPED NAMES: Retain capital names for the name of a governmental body if its formal name is flopped to delete the word *of*: *the State Department, the Human Resources Department.*

GENERIC EQUIVALENTS: If a generic term has become the equivalent of a proper name in popular use, treat it as a proper name: *Walpole State Prison,* for example, even though the proper name is the *Massachusetts Correctional Institute-Walpole.*

For additional examples, see **legislature**; **police department**; and **prison, jail**.

PLURALS, NONSPECIFIC REFERENCES: All words that are capitalized when part of a proper name should be lowercased when they are used in the plural or do not refer to a specific, existing body. Some examples:

All states except Nebraska have a state senate. The town does not have a fire department. The bill requires city councils to provide matching funds. The president will address the lower houses of the New York and New Jersey legislatures.

NON-U.S. BODIES: The same principles apply. See **non-U.S. governmental bodies** and **non-U.S. legislative bodies**.

government, junta, regime A *government* is an established system of political administration: *the U.S. government.*

A *junta* is a group or council that often rules after a coup: *A military junta controls the nation.* A *junta* becomes a government after it establishes a system of political administration.

The word *regime* is a synonym for *political system: a democratic regime, an authoritarian regime.* It also may mean the period in which a person or system was in power, often with a negative connotation: *Gadhafi's regime,* the *Nazi regime.*

An *administration* consists of officials who make up the executive branch of a government: *the Reagan administration.*

governor Capitalize and abbreviate as *Gov.* or *Govs.* when used as a formal title before one or more names.

See the next entry and **titles**.

governor general, governors general The formal title for the British sovereign's representatives in Canada and elsewhere.

Do not abbreviate in any use.

GPA Acceptable in all references for *grade-point average.*

GPS Acceptable in all references to *Global Positioning System.* If a descriptive word is used following, use it in lowercase: *The GPS satellite.*

grade, grader Hyphenate in combining forms: *a fourth-grade pupil, a 12th-grade student, first-grader, 10th-grader.*

graduate (v.) *Graduate* is correctly used in the active voice: *She graduated from the university.*

It is correct, but unnecessary, to use the passive voice: *He was graduated from the university.*

Do not, however, drop *from: John Adams graduated from Harvard.* Not: *John Adams graduated Harvard.*

grain The smallest unit in the system of weights that has been used in the United States. It originally was defined as the weight of 1 grain of wheat.

It takes 437.5 grains to make an ounce. There are 7,000 grains to a pound.

See **ounce (weight)** and **pound**.

gram The basic unit of mass in the metric system. It is equal to approximately one-twenty-eighth of an ounce. To convert to ounces, multiply by .035 (86 grams x .035 equals 3 ounces).

See **metric system**.

grammar

granddad, granddaughter
Also: *grandfather, grandmother,*
grandson.

grand jury Always lowercase:
a Los Angeles County grand jury, the
grand jury.
This style has been adopted
because, unlike the case with city
council and similar governmental
units, a jurisdiction frequently has
more than one grand jury session.

Grand Old Party *GOP* is acceptable as a synonym for *Republican*
Party on second reference.

grant-in-aid, grants-in-aid

gray Not grey. But:
greyhound.

great- Hyphenate *great-grandfa-*
ther, great-great-grandmother, etc.
Use *great grandfather* only if the
intended meaning is that the grandfather was a great man.

Great Atlantic & Pacific Tea
Co. Inc. *A&P* is acceptable in all ref-
erences.
Headquarters is in Montvale, N.J.

Great Britain It consists of Eng-
land, Scotland and Wales, but not
Northern Ireland.
Britain is acceptable in all refer-
ences.
See **United Kingdom**.

Great Depression See **Depres-**
sion.

greater Capitalize when used
to define a community and its surrounding region: *Greater Boston*.

Great Lakes The five, from the
largest to the smallest: Lake Superi-
or, Lake Huron, Lake Michigan, Lake
Erie, Lake Ontario.

Great Plains Capitalize *Great*
Plains or *the Plains* when referring
to the U.S. prairie lands that extend
from North Dakota to Texas and
from the Rocky Mountains east
toward the Mississippi River valley.
Use *northern Plains, southwestern*
Plains, etc., when referring to a portion of the region.

Great Recession The recession that began in December 2007
and became the longest and deepest
since the Great Depression of the
1930s. It occurred after losses on
subprime mortgages battered the
U.S. housing market. The National
Bureau of Economic Research said it
officially ended in June 2009, having
lasted 18 months.

Greek Orthodox Archdiocese
of America See **Eastern Orthodox**
churches.

Greek Orthodox Church See
Eastern Orthodox churches.

Green Berets See **special forces**.

Greenwich Mean Time (GMT)
See **time zones** and **meridians**.

gringo A derogatory term for a
foreigner, especially an American, in
parts of Latin America. Use only in
direct quotes when essential to the
story. See **nationalities and races**.

grisly, grizzly *Grisly* is horrify-
ing, repugnant.
Grizzly means grayish or is a
short form for *grizzly bear*.

gross domestic product The
sum of all goods and services produced within a nation's borders. In
the U.S., it is calculated quarterly by

the Commerce Department.
Lowercase in all uses, but *GDP* is acceptable in later references.

Groundhog Day Feb. 2.

groundskeeper

groundswell

ground zero

group Takes singular verbs and pronouns: *The group is reviewing its position.*

grown-up (n. and adj.)

G-string

G-20 Use a hyphen in the abbreviated form for the *Group of 20*, made up of representatives of industrial and emerging-market nations. A general description rather than the full name is preferred on first reference: *Leading rich and developing nations.* Members are the European Union and the following 19 countries: Argentina, Australia, Brazil, Britain, Canada, China, France, Germany, India, Indonesia, Italy, Japan, Mexico, Russia, Saudi Arabia, South Africa, South Korea, Turkey and the United States.

Guadalupe (Mexico)

Guadeloupe (West Indies)

Guam Use in datelines after the name of a community. See **datelines**.

Guangzhou City in China formerly known as Canton.

guarantee Preferred to *guaranty*, except in proper names.

guard Usually a job description, not a formal title. See **titles**.

guardsman See **National Guard**

and **Coast Guardsman**.

Guatemala City Stands alone in datelines.

gubernatorial

guerrilla Unorthodox soldiers and their tactics.

guest Do not use as a verb except in quoted matter. (An exception to a use recorded by Webster's New World College Dictionary.)

Guinness World Records The book is published by Guinness World Records Ltd.

Gulf, Gulf Coast Capitalize when referring to the region of the United States lying along the Gulf of Mexico. Also: *Mexico's Gulf Coast* or *Gulf Coast of Mexico.*
See **coast**.

Gulf Stream But the racetrack is *Gulfstream Park.*

gunbattle, gunboat, gunfight, gunfire, gunpoint, gunpowder

gung-ho A colloquialism to be used sparingly.

guns See **weapons**.

guru

Gypsy, Gypsies Capitalize references to the nomadic ethnic group also known as *Roma*. Either is acceptable. In Europe, where most Gypsies live, they are widely referred to as *Roma*. The word should be explained: *Gypsies, also known as Roma.* Lowercase otherwise: *gypsy cab, gypsy-cab driver, gypsy moth.* See **Roma**.

gypsy moth

habeas corpus A writ ordering a person in custody to be brought before a court. It places the burden of proof on those detaining the person to justify the detention.

When *habeas corpus* is used in a story, define it.

hacker The term has evolved to mean one who uses computer skills to unlawfully penetrate proprietary computer systems.

Hades But lowercase *hell.*

Hague, The In datelines:
THE HAGUE, *Netherlands* (AP)

In text: *The Hague.*

hajj The pilgrimage to Mecca required of every Muslim who can afford it. The person making the *hajj* is a *hajji.*

half It is not necessary to use the preposition *of*: *half the time* is correct, but *half of the time* is not wrong.

half- Follow Webster's New World College Dictionary. Hyphenate if not listed there.

Some frequently used words without a hyphen:
halfback   halftone
halfhearted   halftrack

Also: *halftime*, in keeping with widespread practice in sports copy.

Some frequently used combinations that are two words without a hyphen:
half brother   half size
half dollar   half sole (n.)
half note   half tide

Some frequently used combinations that include a hyphen:
half-baked   half-life
half-blood   half-moon
half-cocked   half-sole (v.)
half-hour   half-truth

half day (n.) **half-day** (adj.)

half-mast, half-staff On ships and at naval stations ashore, flags are flown at *half-mast.*

Elsewhere ashore, flags are flown at *half-staff.*

hallelujah

Halley's comet After Edmund Halley, an English astronomer who predicted the comet's appearance once every 75 years. It was last seen in 1985-86.

Halliburton Co. Headquarters is in Houston.

Halloween

halo, halos

Hamas A Palestinian Islamic political party, which has an armed wing of the same name. The word is an acronym for the Arabic words for *Islamic Resistance Movement.*

Hamburg The city in Germany

carries the country name in date-lines.

handheld (n.) **hand-held** (adj.)

handicapped See **disabled, handicapped, impaired.**

handmade

hand-picked

hands off, hands-off Hyphenate when used as a compound modifier: *He kept his hands off the matter. He follows a hands-off policy.*

hand to hand, hand-to-hand, hand to mouth, hand-to-mouth Hyphenate when used as compound modifiers: *The cup was passed from hand to hand. They live a hand-to-mouth existence.*

hand-washing

hangar, hanger A *hangar* is a building.
A *hanger* is used for clothes.

hang, hanged, hung One *hangs* a picture, a criminal or oneself.
For past tense or the passive, use *hanged* when referring to executions or suicides, *hung* for other actions.

hangover

hang-up (n.) **hang up** (v.)

Hanukkah The Jewish Festival of Lights, an eight-day commemoration of rededication of the Temple by the Maccabees after their victory over the Syrians.
Usually occurs in December but sometimes falls in late November.

harass, harassment

harelip Avoid. *Cleft lip* is preferred.

Haram al-Sharif Arabic for *Noble Sanctuary*, the Muslim name for the walled, elevated area in Jerusalem's Old City that was the site of the ancient Jewish temples. Better known as the *Temple Mount*, the area now houses the centuries-old Dome of the Rock shrine and Al-Aqsa mosque. Muslims believe Prophet Muhammad made his night journey to heaven from the site.

hard line (n.) **hard-line** (adj.) **hard-liner** (n.)

Harper's Magazine Not to be confused with Harper's Bazaar.

Harris Poll Prepared by Harris Interactive of New York.

Hartford Financial Services Group Inc. Headquarters is in Hartford, Conn.

Havana The city in Cuba stands alone in datelines.

Hawaii Do not abbreviate the state name in datelines or stories. Postal code: *HI*
Hawaiians are members of an ethnic group indigenous to the Hawaiian Islands and are also called *Native Hawaiians.* Use *Hawaii resident* for anyone living in the state.
The state comprises 132 islands about 2,400 miles southwest of San Francisco. Collectively, they are the *Hawaiian Islands.*
The largest island in land area is Hawaii. Honolulu and Pearl Harbor are on Oahu, where more than 80 percent of the state's residents live.
Honolulu stands alone in datelines. Use *Hawaii* after all other cities in datelines, specifying the island in the text, if needed.
See **datelines** and **state names.**

Hawaiian Airlines Headquarters is in Honolulu.

Hawaii Standard Time The time zone used in Hawaii. There is no daylight saving time in Hawaii.

headlines Only the first word and proper nouns are capitalized.

Follow story style in spelling, but use numerals for all numbers and single quotes for quotation marks. Exception: use *US*, *UK* and *UN* (no periods) in all headlines.

For U.S. states in headlines, no periods for those abbreviated with two capital letters: NY, NJ, NH, NM, NC, SC, ND, SD and RI. Also DC. Other states retain periods: Ga., Ky., Mont., Conn.

Online: For online subscribers so desiring, AP systems convert headlines to a version with all words capitalized.

headlong

head-on (adj., adv.)

headquarters May take a singular or a plural verb.

headscarf, headscarves

health care

hearing examiner See **administrative law judge**.

hearsay

heart attack, heart failure, cardiac arrest A *heart attack* (myocardial infarction) occurs when one or more arteries supplying blood to the heart become blocked. *Heart failure* is a chronic condition that occurs when a weakened heart can no longer effectively pump blood. *Cardiac arrest,* or *sudden cardiac arrest*, occurs when the heart suddenly stops beating. It can be due to a *heart attack*, a heart rhythm problem, or as a result of trauma.

heaven

heavenly bodies Capitalize the proper names of planets, stars, constellations, etc.: *Mars, Arcturus, the Big Dipper, Aries.* See **earth**.

For comets, capitalize only the proper noun element of the name: *Halley's comet.*

Lowercase sun and moon, but capitalize them if their Greek or Latin names are used: *Helios, Luna.*

Capitalize nouns and adjectives derived from the proper names of planets: *Martian, Venusian,* but lowercase adjectives derived from other heavenly bodies: *solar, lunar.*

hect- (before a vowel), **hecto-** (before a consonant) A prefix denoting 100 units of a measure. Move a decimal point two places to the right, adding zeros if necessary, to convert to the basic unit: 5.5 hectometers = 550 meters.

hectare A unit of surface measure in the metric system equal to 100 ares or 10,000 square meters.

A hectare is equal to 2.47 acres, 107,639.1 square feet or 11,959.9 square yards.

To convert to acres, multiply by 2.47 (5 hectares x 2.47 = 12.35 acres). See **are** and **metric system**.

hedge fund Unregulated funds that pool money from wealthy investors and trade in everything from commodities to real estate to complex derivative investments. The private investment funds use sophisticated techniques to try to achieve higher returns than the stock market.

hedging A method of selling for future delivery whereby a dealer protects himself from falling prices between the time he buys a product and the time he resells or processes it. A miller, for example, who buys wheat to convert to flour will sell a similar quantity of wheat he doesn't own at near the price at which he bought his own. He will agree to deliver it at the same time his flour is ready for market. If at that time the price of wheat and therefore flour has fallen, he will lose on the flour but can buy the wheat at a low price and deliver it at a profit. If prices have risen, he will make an extra profit on his flour which he will have to sacrifice to buy the wheat for delivery. But either way he has protected his profit.

he, him, his, thee, thou Personal pronouns referring to the deity are lowercase.
See **deity**.

heights See **dimensions**.

heliport

hell But capitalize *Hades*.

Hells Angels

Helsinki The city in Finland stands alone in datelines.

helter-skelter

hemisphere Capitalize *Northern Hemisphere, Western Hemisphere*, etc.
Lowercase *hemisphere* in other uses: *the Eastern and Western hemispheres, the hemisphere*.

hemorrhage

hemorrhoid

her Do not use this pronoun in reference to nations or ships, except in quoted matter.
Use *it* instead.

here The word is frequently redundant, particularly in the lead of a datelined story. Use only if there is some specific need to stress that the

event being reported took place in the community.
If the location must be stressed in the body of the story, repeat the name of the datelined community, both for the reader's convenience and to avoid problems if the story is topped with a different dateline.

Her Majesty Capitalize when it appears in quotations or is appropriate before a name as the long form of a formal title.
For other purposes, use the woman's name or *the queen*.
See **nobility**.

heroin The narcotic, originally a trademark.

heroes

hertz This term, the same in singular or plural, has been adopted as the international unit of frequency equal to one cycle per second.
In contexts where it would not be understood by most readers, it should be followed by a parenthetical explanation: *15,400 hertz (cycles per second)*.
Do not abbreviate.

Hewlett-Packard Co. *HP* (no hyphen) is acceptable on second reference. Headquarters is in Palo Alto, Calif.

Hezbollah The Lebanese Shiite Muslim political party, which has an armed wing of the same name. The word means *party of God* in Arabic.

hideaway

hideout

high blood pressure Preferred term. Avoid using *hypertension*.

high definition (n.) **high-definition** (adj.) The term refers to moving-image hardware and content that produces at least 720 lines of vertical resolution. *HD* is acceptable on second reference. *HDTV* is acceptable on second reference for a high-definition television set. A U.S. DVD or analog TV broadcast has 480 lines of vertical resolution — neither is HD.

high-five (n.) **high-fived** (v.)

high-rise (n. and adj.)

high-tech

highway designations Use these forms, as appropriate in the context, for highways identified by number: *U.S. Highway 1, U.S. Route 1, U.S. 1, state Route 34, Route 34, Interstate Highway 495, Interstate 495.* On second reference only for *Interstate*: *I-495.*

When a letter is appended to a number, capitalize it but do not use a hyphen: *Route 1A.*

See **addresses**.

highway patrol Capitalize if used in the formal name of a police agency: *the Kansas Highway Patrol, the Highway Patrol.* Lowercase *highway patrolman* in all uses.

See **state police**.

hijab The headscarf worn by Muslim women.

hike Acceptable as a verb for increasing or raising prices sharply.

hillbilly Usually a derogatory term for an Appalachian backwoods or mountain person. Avoid unless in direct quotes or special context. *Mountaineer* is a suggested alternative.

Hindu, Hinduism The dominant religion of India and the world's third-largest religion, after Christianity and Islam.

The basic teaching is that the soul never dies, but is reborn each time the body dies. The soul may be reborn in either human or animal form. The rule of karma states that no matter how small the action or thought of an individual, it will affect how the soul will be reborn in the next generation. The cycle of death and rebirth continues until a soul reaches spiritual perfection. At that point the soul is united in total enlightenment and peace with the supreme being and the cycle is ended.

There are a number of gods and goddesses, all of whom are different focuses of the one supreme being. The primary gods are Brahma, Vishnu, called the preserver, and Siva, the destroyer. Vishnu has had important human incarnations as Krishna and Rama. The primary goddess is Devi, who is also known as Durga, Kali, Sarasvati, Lakshimi and other names. She represents in her forms either motherhood and good fortune or destruction. There are thousands of other deities and saints that also may receive prayers and offerings.

Hindus also believe that animals have souls and many are worshipped as gods. There are thousands of sects, and organization runs from virtually none to very strict depending on the group. There is no formal clergy.

hip-hop

Hiroshima On Aug. 6, 1945, this Japanese city and military base were the targets of the first atomic bomb dropped as a weapon. The explosion had the force of 20,000 tons (20 kilotons) of TNT. It destroyed more than four square miles and killed or injured 140,000 people, according to an official count taken between August and December 1945. Hiroshima city officials say the toll may be

220,000 if including those who died after December 1945 of non-acute injuries or radiation.

his, her Do not presume maleness in constructing a sentence, but use the pronoun *his* when an indefinite antecedent may be male or female: *A reporter tries to protect his sources.* (Not *his or her* sources, but note the use of the word *reporter* rather than *newsman*.)

Frequently, however, the best choice is a slight revision of the sentence: *Reporters try to protect their sources.*

His Majesty Capitalize when it appears in quotations or is appropriate before a name as the long form of a formal title.

For other purposes, use the man's name or *king*.

See **nobility**.

Hispanic A person from — or whose ancestors were from — a Spanish-speaking land or culture. *Latino* and *Latina* are sometimes preferred. Follow the person's preference. Use a more specific identification when possible, such as *Cuban, Puerto Rican* or *Mexican-American*. See **Latino, nationalities and races,** and **race**.

Hispaniola The island shared by the Dominican Republic and Haiti. See **Western Hemisphere**.

historical periods and events Capitalize the names of widely recognized epochs in anthropology, archaeology, geology and history: *the Bronze Age, the Dark Ages, the Middle Ages, the Pliocene Epoch.*

Capitalize also widely recognized popular names for the periods and events: *the Atomic Age, the Boston Tea Party, the Civil War, the Exodus* (of the Israelites from Egypt), *the Great Depression, Prohibition.*

Lowercase *century*: *the 18th century*.

Capitalize only the proper nouns or adjectives in general descriptions of a period: *ancient Greece, classical Rome, the Victorian era, the fall of Rome.*

For additional guidance, see separate entries in this book for other epochs, events and historical periods. If this book has no entry, follow the capitalization in Webster's New World College Dictionary, using lowercase if the dictionary lists it as an acceptable form for the sense in which the word is used.

historic, historical A *historic* event is an important occurrence, one that stands out in history.

Any occurrence in the past is a *historical* event.

history Avoid the redundant *past history*.

hit and run (v.) **hit-and-run** (n. and adj.)

hitchhike, hitchhiker

Hitler, Adolf Not *Adolph*.

HIV See **AIDS**.

H.J. Heinz Co. Headquarters is in Pittsburgh.

hocus-pocus

hodgepodge

Hodgkin lymphoma After Dr. Thomas Hodgkin, the English physician who first described the disease of the lymph nodes. Formerly called *Hodgkin's disease*.

Non-Hodgkin lymphoma, spelled without a possessive, is the more common type and spreads rapidly, especially among older people and those with HIV infections.

ho-hum

holding company A company whose principal assets are the securities it owns in companies that actually provide goods or services.

The usual reason for forming a holding company is to enable one corporation and its directors to control several companies by holding a majority of their stock.

hold up (v.) **holdup** (n. and adj.)

holidays and holy days Capitalize them: *New Year's Eve, New Year's Day, Groundhog Day, Easter, Hanukkah*, etc.

The legal holidays in federal law are New Year's, Martin Luther King Jr. Day, Washington's Birthday, Memorial Day, Independence Day, Labor Day, Columbus Day, Veterans Day, Thanksgiving and Christmas. See individual entries for the official dates and when they are observed if they fall on a weekend.

The designation of a day as a federal legal holiday means that federal employees receive the day off or are paid overtime if they must work. Other requirements that may apply to holidays generally are left to the states. Many follow the federal lead in designating a holiday, but they are not required to do so.

Holy Communion See **sacraments**.

Holy Father The preferred form is to use *the pope* or *the pontiff*, or to give the individual's name.

Use *Holy Father* in direct quotations or special contexts where a particular literary effect is desired.

Holy Land Capitalize the biblical region.

holy orders See **sacraments**.

Holy See The headquarters of the Roman Catholic Church in Vatican City.

Holy Spirit Now preferred over *Holy Ghost* in most usage.

Holy Week The week before Easter.

homebuilder

homebuyer, homeowner

Home Depot Inc. Headquarters is in Atlanta.

home equity line of credit HELOC A line of credit secured by a home. Borrowers can draw on it for a fixed period set by the lender, usually five to 10 years.

homefront

homemade

home page Two words. The "front" page of a particular website.

home-school (v.) **home-schooler** (n.) **home-schooled** (adj.) **home schooling** (n.)

hometown Use a comma to set off an individual's hometown when it is placed in apposition to a name, whether *of* is used or not: *Tim Johnson, of Vermillion, S.D.; Mary Richards, Minneapolis.*

homicide, murder, manslaughter *Homicide* is a legal term for slaying or killing.

Murder is malicious, premeditated homicide. Some states define certain homicides as murder if the killing occurs in the course of armed robbery, rape, etc.

Manslaughter is homicide without malice or premeditation.

A *homicide* should not be described as murder unless a person has been convicted of that charge.

Unless authorities say premeditation was obvious, do not say that a victim *was murdered* until someone has been convicted in court. Instead, say that a victim *was killed* or *slain*.

Examples:

An officer pulled over 29-year-old John White, who was arrested and charged with murder, according to Andrew Johnson, the county sheriff's spokesman.

The 66-year-old amateur photographer has pleaded not guilty to four counts of first-degree murder for the slaying of four women.

The killings occurred between 1977 and 1979. Prosecutors say Adams raped, tortured and robbed some of them before killing them.

Cook County Sheriff James Jones says a shooting that left one woman dead and a man injured appears to be a murder-suicide.

See **execute** and **assassin, killer, murderer**.

Hong Kong Stands alone in datelines.

Honolulu The city in Hawaii stands alone in datelines. It is on the island of Oahu.
See **Hawaii**.

honorary degrees All references to honorary degrees should specify that the degree was honorary.

Do not use *Dr.* before the name of an individual whose only doctorate is honorary.

honorary titles See **nobility**.

hoof-and-mouth disease Use *foot-and-mouth disease*.

hooky

hopefully The traditional meaning is in a hopeful manner. Also acceptable is the modern usage: *it's hoped, we hope*.

Correct: *"You're leaving soon?" she asked hopefully.*

Correct: *Hopefully, we'll be home before dark.*

horsepower

horse races Capitalize their formal names: *Kentucky Derby, Preakness, Belmont Stakes*, etc.

horses' names Capitalize. See **animals**.

hotel Capitalize as part of the proper name for a specific hotel: *the Waldorf-Astoria Hotel*.

Lowercase when standing alone or used in an indefinite reference to one hotel in a chain: *The city has a Sheraton hotel*.

hotline A telephone line for use in an emergency or a crisis, especially between government leaders.

hot spot Two words, for descriptions of the area where computers can connect wirelessly, or for global trouble spots, or areas of intense heat in general.

hourlong, hourslong

household, housing unit In the sense used by the Census Bureau, a *household* is made up of all occupants of a *housing unit*. A *household* may contain more than one family or may be used by one person.

A *housing unit*, as defined by the bureau, is a group of rooms or single room occupied by people who do not live and eat with any other person in the structure. It must have either direct access from the outside or through a common hall, or have a kitchen or cooking equipment for the exclusive use of the occupants.

House of Commons, House of Lords
The two houses of the British Parliament.

On second reference: *Commons* or *the Commons, Lords* or *the Lords*.

House of Representatives
Capitalize when referring to a specific governmental body: *the U.S. House of Representatives, the Massachusetts House of Representatives*.

Capitalize shortened references that delete the words *of Representatives*: *the U.S. House, the Massachusetts House*.

Retain capitalization if *U.S.* or the name of a state is dropped but the reference is to a specific body.

BOSTON (AP) — The House has adjourned for the year.

Lowercase plural uses: *the Massachusetts and Rhode Island houses*.

Apply the same principle to similar legislative bodies such as *the Virginia House of Delegates*.

See **organizations and institutions** for guidelines on how to handle the term when it is used by a nongovernmental body.

Houston
The city in Texas stands alone in datelines.

howitzer
See **weapons**.

HTML
For *HyperText Markup Language*. (Lowercase in Web addresses.) In stories, describe as *the Web programming language known as HTML*.

HTTP
For *Hypertext Transfer Protocol*. (Lowercase in Web addresses.) In stories, describe as *the start of all Web addresses*.

Huffington Post
The Huffington Post news website is affiliated with AOL. It's *HuffPost* in shortened form.

human, human being
Human is preferred, but either is acceptable.

Humane Society of the United States
An animal protection agency headquartered in Washington. It operates 10 regional offices across the country, but has no formal affiliation with the many local organizations that use the name *Humane Society*.

Humvee
A trademark for a four-wheeled military vehicle, built by AM General and used by U.S. and allied forces. *Hummer* is the sport utility vehicle.

hurricane
Capitalize hurricane when it is part of the name that weather forecasters assign to a storm: *Hurricane Hazel*.

But use *it* and *its* — not *she, her* or *hers* or *he, him* or *his* — in pronoun references.

And do not use the presence of a woman's name as an excuse to attribute sexist images of women's behavior to a storm. Avoid, for example, such sentences as: *The fickle Hazel teased the Louisiana coast.*

See **weather terms**.

hush-hush

hybrid
A vehicle that can be powered by more than one energy source, for example, a car with a gasoline engine and an electric motor. See **engine, motor**.

hydraulic fracturing
A technique used by the energy industry to extract oil and gas from rock by injecting high-pressure mixtures of water, sand or gravel and chemicals. The short form is *fracking*, a term considered pejorative by the industry.

hydro- The rules in **prefixes** apply, but in general, no hyphen. Some examples:

hydroelectric   hydrophobia

hyper- The rules in **prefixes** apply, but in general, no hyphen. Some examples:

hyperactive   hypercritical

hyperlink A link from one part of a Web page to another page, as a restaurant home page with a link to its menu.

hypertension Preferred term is *high blood pressure.*

hypertext A system of linking electronic documents.

hyphen See entry in **Punctuation** chapter.

I

Iberia Airlines Headquarters of this airline is in Madrid.

IBM Acceptable as first reference for *International Business Machines Corp.*
Headquarters is in Armonk, N.Y.

ICBM, ICBMs Acceptable on first reference for *intercontinental ballistic missile(s)*, but the term should be defined in the body of a story.
Avoid the redundant *ICBM missiles*.

ice age Lowercase, because it denotes not a single period but any of a series of cold periods marked by glaciation alternating with periods of relative warmth.
Capitalize the proper nouns in the names of individual ice ages, such as the *Wisconsin ice age*.
The most recent series of ice ages happened during the *Pleistocene* epoch, which began about 1.6 million years ago. During that time, glaciers sometimes covered much of North America and northwestern Europe.
The present epoch, the *Holocene* or *Recent*, began about 10,000 years ago, when the continental glaciers had retreated to Antarctica and Greenland.

ice storm See **weather terms**.

Idaho Do not abbreviate in datelines or stories. Postal code: *ID* See **state names**.

i.e. Abbreviation for the Latin *id est* or *that is* and is always followed by a comma.

IED Abbreviation for *improvised explosive device*. *IED* is acceptable on second reference. *Roadside bomb* is preferable.

iftar The breaking of the daily fast during the holy Islamic month of Ramadan.

illegal Use *illegal* only to mean a violation of the law. Be especially careful in labor-management disputes, where one side often calls an action by the other side illegal. Usually it is a charge that a contract or rule, not a law, has been violated.

illegal immigrant Used to describe someone who has entered a country illegally or who resides in a country in violation of civil or criminal law. Acceptable variations include *living in the country without legal permission*. Use of these terms, as with any terms implying illegalities, must be based on reliable information about a person's true status. Unless quoting someone, AP does not use the terms *illegal alien, an illegal, illegals* or the term *undocumented*.

illegitimate Do not refer to the child of unmarried parents as illegitimate. If it is pertinent to the story at all, use an expression such as *whose mother was not married, whose parents were not married* or *was born to an unmarried teenager.*

Illinois Abbreviate *Ill.* in datelines or stories. Postal code: *IL* See **state names.**

illusion See **allusion, illusion.**

IM Abbreviation for *instant message*; sometimes used as a verb: *IMing, IMed.* Acceptable on second reference for *instant messaging.*

imam Lowercase when describing the leader of a prayer in a Muslim mosque. Capitalize before a name when used as the formal title for a Muslim leader or ruler. See **religious titles.**

Imax Corp. Headquarters is in Mississauga, Ontario.

immigrate See **emigrate, immigrate.**

impassable, impassible, impassive *Impassable* means that passage is impossible: *The bridge was impassable.*
Impassible and *impassive* describe lack of sensitivity to pain or suffering. Webster's New World College Dictionary notes, however, that *impassible* suggests an inability to be affected, while *impassive* implies only that no reaction was noticeable: *She was impassive throughout the ordeal.*

impeachment The constitutional process accusing an elected official of a crime in an attempt to remove the official from office. Do not use as a synonym for *conviction* or *removal from office.*

impel, impelled, impelling

imperial gallon The standard British gallon, equal to 277.42 cubic inches or about 1.2 U.S. gallons.
The metric equivalent is approximately 4.5 liters.
See **liter.**

imperial quart One-fourth of an imperial gallon.

implausible

imply, infer Writers or speakers *imply* in the words they use.
A listener or reader *infers* something from the words.

impostor

impromptu It means without preparation or advance thought.

improvised explosive device IED is acceptable on second reference. *Roadside bomb* is preferable.

in, into *In* indicates location: *He was in the room.*
Into indicates motion: *She walked into the room.*

-in Precede with a hyphen:
break-in   walk-in
cave-in   write-in

in- No hyphen when it means *not*:
inaccurate   insufferable
Other uses without a hyphen:
inbound   infighting
indoor   inpatient (n., adj.)
infield
A few combinations take a hyphen, however:
in-depth   in-house
in-group   in-law
Follow Webster's New World College Dictionary when in doubt.

"in" When employed to indicate that something is in vogue, use quotation marks only if followed by a noun: *It was the "in" thing to do. Raccoon coats are in again.*

inasmuch as

Inauguration Day Capitalize only when referring to the total collection of events that include inauguration of a U.S. president; lowercase in other uses: *Inauguration Day is Jan. 20. The inauguration day for the change has not been set.*

inbox

Inc. See **incorporated**.

inch Equal to one-twelfth of a foot.
The metric equivalent is exactly 2.54 centimeters.
To convert to centimeters, multiply by 2.54 (6 inches x 2.54 equals 15.24 centimeters).
See **centimeter**; **foot**; and **dimensions**.

inches per second A rating used for the speed of tape recorders.
The abbreviation *ips* (no periods) is acceptable on first reference in specialized contexts such as a records column; otherwise do not use *ips* until second reference.

include Use *include* to introduce a series when the items that follow are only part of the total: *The price includes breakfast. The zoo includes lions and tigers.*
Use *comprise* when the full list of individual elements is given: *The zoo comprises 100 types of animals, including lions and tigers.*
See **compose, comprise, constitute**.

income See **profit terminology**.

incorporated Abbreviate and capitalize as *Inc.* when used as a part of a corporate name. Do not set off with commas: *Time Warner Inc. announced* ...
See **company names**.

incorporator Do not capitalize

when used before a name.
See **titles**.

incredible, incredulous *Incredible* means unbelievable.
Incredulous means skeptical.

incur, incurred, incurring

Independence Day *July Fourth* or *Fourth of July* also are acceptable.
The federal legal holiday is observed on Friday if July 4 falls on a Saturday, on Monday if it falls on a Sunday.

index, indexes

Index of Leading Economic Indicators A composite of 10 economic measurements developed to help forecast shifts in the direction of the U.S. economy.
It is compiled by the Conference Board, a private business-sponsored research group, which took it over from the Commerce Department in 1995.

Indiana Abbreviate *Ind.* in datelines or stories. Postal code: *IN*
See **state names**.

Indianapolis The city in Indiana stands alone in datelines.

Indian Ocean See **oceans**.

Indians *American Indian* or *Native American* is acceptable for those in the U.S. Follow the person's preference. Where possible, be precise and use the name of the tribe: He is a *Navajo* commissioner. In stories about American Indians, such words as *wampum, warpath, powwow, teepee, brave, squaw*, etc., can be disparaging and offensive. In Alaska, the indigenous groups include *Aleuts, Eskimos* and *Indians*. See **Native American, nationalities and races**, and **race**.

indict Use *indict* only in connection with the legal process of bringing charges against an individual or corporation.

To avoid any suggestion that someone is being judged before a trial, do not use phrases such as *indicted for killing* or *indicted for bribery*. Instead, use *indicted on a charge of killing* or *indicted on a bribery charge*.

For guidelines on related words, see **accused**; **allege**; and **arrest**.

indigenous A term used to refer to original inhabitants of a place. *Aboriginal leaders welcomed a new era of indigenous relations in Australia. Bolivia's indigenous peoples represent some 62 percent of the population.* See **nationalities and races**, and **race**.

indiscreet, indiscrete *Indiscreet* means lacking prudence. Its noun form is *indiscretion*.

Indiscrete means not separated into distinct parts. Its noun form is *indiscreteness*.

indiscriminate, indiscriminately

individual retirement account *IRA* is acceptable on second reference.

indispensable

indo- Usually hyphenated and capitalized:

Indo-Aryan Indo-Hittite
Indo-German Indo-Iranian
But: *Indochina*.

Indochina Formerly French Indochina, now divided into Cambodia, Laos and Vietnam.

Indochinese Peninsula Located here are the nations of Cambodia, Laos, Myanmar, Thailand and Vietnam.

Indonesia Use after the name of a community in datelines on stories from this nation.

Specify an individual island, if needed, in the text.

indoor (adj.) **indoors** (adv.)

infant Applicable to children through 12 months old.

infantile paralysis The preferred term is *polio*.

inflation A sustained increase in prices. The result is a decrease in the purchasing power of money.

There are two basic types of inflation:

—*Cost-push inflation* occurs when rising costs are the chief reason for the increased prices.

—*Demand-pull inflation* occurs when the amount of money available exceeds the amount of goods and services available for sale.

infra- The rules in **prefixes** apply, but in general, no hyphen. Some examples:

infrared infrastructure

infrastructure An economy's capital in the form of roads, railways, water supplies, educational facilities, health services, etc., without which investment in factories can't be fully productive.

initial public offering *IPO* acceptable on second reference.

initials Use periods and no space when an individual uses initials instead of a first name: *H.L. Mencken*.

Do not give a name with a single initial (*J. Jones*) unless it is the individual's preference or a first name cannot be learned.

See **middle initials**.

injuries They are *suffered*, not *sustained* or *received*.

in-law

Inner Light See **Quakers**.

innocent, not guilty In court cases, plea situations and trials, *not guilty* is preferable to *innocent*, because it is more precise legally. (However, special care must be taken to prevent omission of the word *not*.) When possible, say a defendant was *acquitted* of criminal charges.

innocuous

innuendo

inoculate

input Do not use as a verb in describing the introduction of data into a computer.

inquire, inquiry Not *enquire*, *enquiry*.

insignia Same form for singular and plural.

insofar as

in spite of *Despite* means the same thing and is shorter.

Institute for Supply Management Produces monthly reports on manufacturing and service sectors. *ISM* acceptable on second reference.

Intel Corp. Headquarters is in Santa Clara, Calif.

inter- The rules in **prefixes** apply, but in general, no hyphen. Some examples:
inter-American   interstate
interracial

intercontinental ballistic missile See **ICBM, ICBMs**.

Internal Revenue Service *IRS* is acceptable on second reference.
Capitalize also *Internal Revenue*, but lowercase *the revenue service*.

International Association of Machinists and Aerospace Workers The shortened form *Machinists* union is acceptable in all references.
Headquarters is in Washington.

International Bank for Reconstruction and Development *World Bank* is acceptable in all references.
Headquarters is in Washington.

International Brotherhood of Electrical Workers Use the full name on first reference to avoid confusion with the United Electrical, Radio and Machine Workers of America.
IBEW is acceptable on second reference.
Headquarters is in Washington.

International Brotherhood of Teamsters, Chauffeurs, Warehousemen and Helpers of America *Teamsters* union is acceptable in all references. See **Teamsters union**.

International Court of Justice The principal judicial organ of the United Nations, established at The Hague in 1945.
The court is not open to individuals. It has jurisdiction over all matters specifically provided for either in the U.N. charter or in treaties and conventions in force. It also has jurisdiction over cases referred to it by U.N. members and by nonmembers such as Switzerland that subscribe to the court statute.
The court serves as the successor

to the Permanent Court of International Justice of the League of Nations, which also was known as the World Court.

On second reference use *international court* or *world court* in lowercase. Do not abbreviate.

International Criminal Police Organization *Interpol* is acceptable in all references.

Headquarters is in Lyon, France.

international date line The imaginary line drawn north and south through the Pacific Ocean, largely along the 180th meridian.

By international agreement, when it is 12:01 a.m. Sunday just west of the line, it is 12:01 a.m. Saturday just east of it.

See **time zones**.

International Energy Agency

Paris-based energy adviser for developed nations. *IEA* acceptable on second reference.

International Labor Organization *ILO* is acceptable on second reference.

Headquarters is in Geneva.

International Longshore and Warehouse Union *ILWU* is acceptable on second reference.

Headquarters is in San Francisco.

International Longshoremen's Association *ILA* is acceptable on second reference.

Headquarters is in New York.

International Monetary Fund

IMF is acceptable on second reference. Headquarters is in Washington.

A supply of money supported by subscriptions of member nations, for the purpose of stabilizing international exchange and promoting orderly and balanced trade. Member nations may obtain foreign currency needed, making it possible to correct temporary maladjustments in their balance of payments without currency depreciation.

International Space Station

International Telecommunications Satellite Organization

ITSO is acceptable on first reference, but the body of the story should identify it as the shortened form of the full name.

(The original name was International Telecommunications Satellite Consortium.)

Headquarters is in Washington.

Internet A decentralized, worldwide network of computers that can communicate with each other. In later references, *the Net* is acceptable.

The World Wide Web, like email, is a subset of the Internet. They are not synonymous and should not be used interchangeably in stories.

USE IN STORIES: Be acutely aware of the potential dangers of using information from Internet and email sources. Email headers are easily forged, and websites may be set up by fraudulent groups. Be sure of the authenticity and correctness before using the information.

All such information, from computer disk data to email to material posted on the Internet, falls into the "tangible form" category that is subject to copyright protection as well as libel guidelines.

INTERNET ADDRESSES: The current Internet address system based on domain names — such as "ap.org" — was developed in the 1980s. See **domain names**.

Website addresses are also known as Uniform Resource Locators, or URLs. Follow the spelling and capitalization of the website owner. In stories, try to use the name of the website rather than the Web address, the way you'd refer to *the Empire State Building* in the physical world and not *350 Fifth Avenue.* So it's *Facebook,* not *Facebook.com.* Use ".com" only if it's part of the legal name, as in *Amazon.com Inc.*

If an Internet address falls at the end of a sentence, use a period. If an address breaks between lines, split it directly after a slash or a dot that is part of the address, without an inserted hyphen. Use the *http://* protocol at the start of the Web address, as well as other starts, such as *ftp://*.

When a story prominently mentions a specific website or Web service, include within the text the full Internet address with *http://* and set it off with commas. Add additional addresses to the end of a story when they provide additional information, even when they aren't specifically referred to in a story.

An example:

PASADENA, Calif. (AP) — NASA abandoned any real hope Tuesday for the missing-in-action Mars Polar Lander and promised to investigate every aspect of the failed mission and delay future expeditions to the Red Planet if necessary.

The last, best chance to make radio contact with the spacecraft yielded only silence early Tuesday. A somber Richard Cook, the spacecraft's operations manager at NASA's Jet Propulsion Laboratory, said the flight team had "played its last ace." ...

Online:
http://marslander.jpl.nasa.gov
http://mars.ucla.edu

Avoid URLs that are particularly lengthy and complicated, unless essential to guide the reader to a particular document. Consider a URL abbreviation service such as bit.ly.

Some symbols in Internet addresses, such as the "at" sign, the equal sign, the underscore and the tilde, result in garbles in some newspaper computers. This is the case when referring to specific videos on YouTube or specific documents at other sites. Spell them out instead and provide an explanatory note, or use a URL abbreviation service.

See separate listings for some commonly used Internet, computer and telecommunications terms.

OPERATIONS: No single individual, organization or government runs the Internet, and anyone may connect to the network by following the TCP/IP protocols.

However, the U.S. government has tremendous influence over the Internet by controlling the Domain Name System. The government has delegated the policy-making authority to the Internet Corporation for Assigned Names and Numbers, but it retains veto power over the Marina del Rey, California, nonprofit group. See **Web**.

Internet Explorer Microsoft Corp.'s Web browser

Interpol Acceptable in all references for *International Criminal Police Organization.*

intifada An Arabic term for the Palestinian uprising against Israel.

intra- Within, inside. The rules in **prefixes** apply, but in general, no hyphen. Some examples:
intracity   intraparty

intranet A private network inside a company or organization, only for internal use.

IOU, IOUs

Iowa Do not abbreviate in datelines or stories. Postal code: *IA*
See **state names**.

IP address *Internet Protocol address*, a numeric address given to a computer connected to the Internet. Spell out on first reference. Most users type in domain names as stand-ins for IP addresses, and domain name servers help with the translation in the background. Traditional IP addresses take the form of four numbers from 0 to 255 connected by dots, as in xx.xx.xx.xx. See **domain names**.

iPad A touch-screen computer that is much like an iPod but is larger and can be connected to cellular data networks. Use *IPad* when the word starts a sentence or headline.

iPhone Apple Inc.'s smartphone. Use *IPhone* when the word starts a sentence or headline.

iPod A digital media player sold by Apple Inc. Use *IPod* when the word starts a sentence or headline.

ips See **inches per second**.

IQ Acceptable in all references for intelligence quotient.

Iran The nation formerly called Persia. It is not an Arab country.

The official name of the country is the *Islamic Republic of Iran*.

Uppercase *Islamic Revolution* when referring to the 1979 event.

The people are *Iranians*, not *Persians* or *Irani*.

The official language is *Persian*, also known as *Farsi*.

Iraq The Arab nation coinciding roughly with ancient Mesopotamia.

Its people are *Iraqis*. The dialect of Arabic is *Iraqi*.

Ireland Acceptable in most references to the independent nation known formally as the Irish Republic.

Use *Irish Republic* when a distinction must be made between this nation and *Northern Ireland*, a part of the United Kingdom.

Irish Republican Army An outlawed paramilitary group committed to overthrowing Northern Ireland and its links with Britain. Its formal name is Provisional IRA. It was founded in 1969 with the aim of abolishing Northern Ireland as a predominantly British Protestant state. Its members claim direct lineage to the old IRA, which wrested the predominantly Catholic rest of Ireland from British control following a 1919-21 rebellion.

IRA is acceptable, but *Irish Republican Army* should be spelled out somewhere in the story.

Sinn Fein (pronounced "shin fane") is a legal political party that is linked with the *IRA*, but not technically a wing of it.

irregardless A double negative. *Regardless* is correct.

Islam Followers are called Muslims. Their holy book is the Quran, which according to Islamic belief was revealed by Allah (God) to the Prophet Muhammad in the seventh century in Mecca and Medina. The place of worship is a mosque. The weekly holy day, the equivalent of the Christian sabbath, is Friday.

It is the religion of more than 1 billion people in the world, making it the world's second-largest faith, after Christianity. Although Arabic is the language of the Quran and Muslim prayers, not all Arabs are Muslims and not all Muslims are Arabs. Most of the world's Muslims live in a wide belt that stretches halfway around the world: across West Africa and North Africa, through the Arab countries of the Middle East and on to Turkey, Iran, Afghanistan, Pakistan and other Asian countries, parts of the former Soviet Union and western China, to Indonesia and the southern Philippines.

There are two major divisions in Islam:

—*Sunni* The biggest single sect in Islam, comprising about 85 percent of all Muslims. Nations with Sunni majorities include Egypt, Saudi Arabia and most other Arab nations, as well as non-Arab Turkey and Afghanistan. Most Palestinian Muslims and most West African Muslims are Sunnis.

The Saudis sometimes are referred to as Wahhabi Muslims. This is a subgroup within the Sunni branch of Islam.

—*Shiite* The second-largest sect. Iran is the only nation with an overwhelming Shiite majority. Iraq, Lebanon and Bahrain have large Shiite communities, in proportion to their overall populations.

(The schism between Sunni and Shiite stems from the early days of Islam and arguments over Muhammad's successors as caliph, the spiritual and temporal leader of Muslims during that period. The Shiites wanted the caliphate to descend through Ali, Muhammad's son-in-law. Ali eventually became the fourth caliph, but he was murdered; Ali's son al-Hussein was massacred with his fighters at Karbala, in what is now Iraq. Shiites considered the later caliphs to be usurpers. The Sunnis no longer have a caliph.)

Titles for the clergy vary from sect to sect and from country to country, but these are the most common:

Grand Mufti — The highest authority in Quranic law and interpretation, a title used mostly by Sunnis.

Sheik — Used by most clergymen in the same manner that the Rev. is used as a Christian clerical title, especially common among Sunnis. (Not all sheiks are clergymen. *Sheik*

can also be a secular title of respect or nobility.)

Ayatollah — Used by Shiites, especially in Iran, to denote senior clergymen, such as *Ayatollah Ruhollah Khomeini.*

Hojatoleslam — A rank below ayatollah.

Mullah — Lower-level clergy.

Imam — Used by some sects as a title for the prayer leader at a mosque. Among the Shiites, it usually has a more exalted connotation.

The adjective is *Islamic. Islamist* is an advocate of Political Islam, the philosophy that the Quran should rule all aspects of life — religious, political and personal. *Islamic fundamentalist* should not be used as a synonym for *Islamic militant* or *radical.*

Islamabad The city in Pakistan stands alone in datelines.

Islamic holy days See **Ashoura**, **Eid al-Adha**, **Eid al-Fitr** and **Ramadan**. Because the Muslim faith operates on the lunar calendar, these holidays fall on different days each year on the Western calendar.

Islamist Supporter of government in accord with the laws of Islam. Those who view the Quran as a political model encompass a wide range of Muslims, from mainstream politicians to militants known as *jihadi.*

island Capitalize *island* or *islands* as part of a proper name: *Prince Edward Island, the Hawaiian Islands.*

Lowercase *island* and *islands* when they stand alone or when the reference is to the islands in a given area: *the Pacific islands.*

Lowercase all *island of* constructions: *the island of Nantucket.*

U.S. DATELINES: For communities on islands within the boundaries of the United States, use the community name and the state name:

EDGARTOWN, Mass. (AP) —

Honolulu stands alone, however.

DATELINES ABROAD: If an island has an identity of its own (*Bermuda, Prince Edward Island, Puerto Rico, Sardinia, Taiwan,* etc.) use the community name and the island name:

HAMILTON, Bermuda (AP) —

Havana, Hong Kong, Macau and *Singapore* stand alone, however.

If the island is part of a chain, use the community name and the name of the chain:

MANILA, Philippines (AP) —

Identify the name of the island in the text if relevant: *Manila is on the island of Luzon.*

For additional guidelines, see **datelines**.

Istanbul The city in Turkey stands alone in datelines.

it Use this pronoun, rather than *she*, in references to nations and ships.

IT Abbreviation for *information technology; IT* is acceptable on second reference.

italics AP does not italicize words in news stories. Italics are used in Stylebook entries to highlight examples of correct and incorrect usage.

it's, its *It's* is a contraction for *it is* or *it has: It's up to you. It's been a long time.*

Its is the possessive form of the neuter pronoun: *The company lost its assets.*

IUD Acceptable on second reference for *intrauterine device.*

IV Acceptable in all references for *intravenous.*

Ivy League Brown University, Columbia University, Cornell University, Dartmouth College, Harvard University, Princeton University, the University of Pennsylvania and Yale University.

Jacuzzi Trademark for a brand of whirlpool products. Generic terms are whirlpool bath or whirlpool spa.

jail Not interchangeable with *prison*. See **prison, jail**.

Jane's All the World's Aircraft, Jane's Fighting Ships The reference sources for questions about aircraft and military ships not covered in this book.

The reference for nonmilitary ships is Lloyd's Register of Shipping.

Japan Airlines Corp. *JAL* is acceptable on second reference.

Headquarters is in Tokyo.

Japan Current A warm current flowing from the Philippine Sea east of Taiwan and northeast past Japan.

jargon The special vocabulary and idioms of a particular class or occupational group.

In general, avoid jargon. When it is appropriate in a special context, include an explanation of any words likely to be unfamiliar to most readers.

See **dialect**.

Java A trademark of Sun Microsystems Inc. for a computer programming language that can be run across the Internet and a number of computer systems.

JavaScript A scripting language, developed by Netscape, designed to run inside Web pages.

Jaws of Life Trademark name for the tool used to pry open parts of a vehicle to free those trapped inside.

Jaycees Members of the U.S. Junior Chamber of Commerce, affiliated with the worldwide body, Junior Chamber International.

See **fraternal organizations and service clubs** and **Junior Chamber of Commerce**.

J.C. Penney Co. Headquarters is in Plano, Texas.

jeep, Jeep Lowercase the military vehicle. Capitalize if referring to the civilian vehicle, a brand of Chrysler Group LLC.

Jehovah's Witnesses The denomination was founded in Pittsburgh in 1872 by Charles Taze Russell, a former Congregationalist layman.

Witnesses do most of their work through three legal corporations: the Watch Tower Bible and Tract Society of Pennsylvania, the Watchtower Bible and Tract Society of New York Inc., and, in England, the International Bible Students Association. A governing body consisting largely of the principal officers of the corporations oversees the denomination.

Jehovah's Witnesses believe that they adhere to the oldest religion on Earth, the worship of Almighty God revealed in the Bible as Jehovah.

They regard civil authority as necessary and obey it "as long as its laws do not contradict God's law." Witnesses refuse to bear arms, salute the flag or participate in secular government.

They refuse blood transfusions as being against the Bible, citing the section of Leviticus that reads: "Whatsoever man ... eats any manner of blood, I will cut him off from among his people."

There are no formal titles, but there are three levels of ministry: *publishers* (baptized members who do evangelistic work), *regular pioneers*, who devote greater time to activities, and *special pioneers* (full-time workers).

Jemaah Islamiyah Southeast Asian Islamic radical group. The words are Arabic for *Islamic congregation*, or *Islamic group*.

Jerusalem The city in Israel stands alone in datelines.

Jesus The central figure of Christianity, he also may be called *Jesus Christ* or *Christ*.

Personal pronouns referring to him are lowercase.

JetBlue Airways Corp. Headquarters of this airline is in Forest Hills, N.Y.

jet, jetliner, jet plane See **aircraft terms**.

Jet Ski A registered trademark of Kawasaki for a type of personal watercraft.

Jew Use for men and women.

Jewish congregations A Jewish congregation is autonomous. No synods, assemblies or hierarchies control the activities of an individual synagogue.

In the United States, there are three major expressions of Judaism:

1. Orthodox Judaism. Most of its congregations are represented nationally by the Union of Orthodox Jewish Congregations of America. Most of its rabbis are members of the Rabbinical Council of America.

2. Reform Judaism. Its national representatives are the Union for Reform Judaism and the Central Conference of American Rabbis.

3. Conservative Judaism. Its national representatives are the United Synagogue of Conservative Judaism and the Rabbinical Assembly.

Conservative and Reform are the largest branches of Judaism, well exceeding the Orthodox and the very small Reconstructionist branches.

Jews generally believe that a divine kingdom will be established on Earth, opening a messianic era that will be marked by peace and bliss. They also believe that they have a mandate from God to work toward this kingdom.

The only formal titles in use are *rabbi*, for the spiritual leader of a congregation, and *cantor*, for the individual who leads the congregation in song. Capitalize these titles before an individual's full name on first reference. On second reference, use only the last name.

See **religious titles** and **Zionism**.

Jewish holy days See separate listings for **Hanukkah, Passover, Purim, Rosh Hashana, Shavuot, Sukkot** and **Yom Kippur**.

The High Holy Days are Rosh Hashana and Yom Kippur. All Jewish holy days and the Jewish Sabbath start at sunset before the day marked on most calendars.

jibe See **gibe, jibe**.

Jiddah, Saudi Arabia

jihad Arabic noun used to refer to the Islamic concept of the struggle to do good. In particular situations, that can include *holy war*, the meaning extremist Muslims commonly use.

job descriptions Always lowercase. See **titles**.

Johannesburg The city in South Africa stands alone in datelines.

John F. Kennedy Space Center Located in Cape Canaveral, Fla., it is the National Aeronautics and Space Administration's principal launch site for manned spacecraft.
Kennedy Space Center is acceptable in all references.
For datelines on launch stories: *CAPE CANAVERAL, Fla. (AP) —*
See **Lyndon B. Johnson Space Center**.

Johns Hopkins University No apostrophes.

Johnson & Johnson Headquarters is in New Brunswick, N.J.

Joint Chiefs of Staff Also: *the Joint Chiefs*. But lowercase *the chiefs* or *the chiefs of staff*.

JPEG, JPG Acronyms for *Joint Photographic Experts Group*, one of two common types of image compression mechanisms used on the World Wide Web (along with *GIF*). Acronyms acceptable in all references.

JPMorgan Chase & Co. Formed from the 2000 merger of J.P. Morgan & Co. with Chase Manhattan Corp. and the 2004 merger with Bank One Corp. Acquired Bear Stea-

rns Cos. and Washington Mutual Inc. in 2008. Headquarters is in New York.

Jr. See **junior, senior**.

judge Capitalize before a name when it is the formal title for an individual who presides in a court of law. Do not continue to use the title in second reference.
Do not use *court* as part of the title unless confusion would result without it:
—No *court* in the title: *U.S. District Judge John Bates, District Judge John Bates, federal Judge John Bates, Judge John Bates, U.S. Circuit Judge Priscilla Owen, appellate Judge Priscilla Owen.*
—*Court* needed in the title: *Juvenile Court Judge John Jones, Criminal Court Judge John Jones, Superior Court Judge Robert Harrison, state Supreme Court Judge William Cushing.*
When the formal title *chief judge* is relevant, put the court name after the judge's name: *Chief Judge Royce Lamberth of the U.S. District Court in Washington, D.C.; Chief Judge Karen J. Williams of the 4th U.S. Circuit Court of Appeals.*
Do not pile up long court names before the name of a judge. Make it *Judge John Smith of Allegheny County Common Pleas Court*. Not: *Allegheny County Common Pleas Court Judge John Smith.*
Lowercase *judge* as an occupational designation in phrases such as *contest judge Simon Cowell.*
See **administrative law judge**; **court names**; **judicial branch**; **justice**; and **magistrate**.

judge advocate The plural: *judge advocates*. Also: *judge advocate general, judge advocates general.*
Capitalize as a formal title before a name.
See **titles**.

judgment

judicial branch Always lower-case.

The federal court system that exists today as the outgrowth of Article 3 of the Constitution is composed of the Supreme Court of the United States, the U.S. Court of Appeals, U.S. District Courts, and the U.S. Customs Court. There are also four district judges for U.S. territories.

U.S. bankruptcy and magistrate judges are fixed-term judges serving in U.S. District Courts. Magistrate judges are generalist judges who preside in cases referred from U.S. district judges. Bankruptcy judges are specialized judges whose authority is restricted to bankruptcy issues.

The U.S. Tax Court and the U.S. Court of Military Appeals for the Armed Forces are not part of the judicial branch as such.

For more detail on all federal courts, see separate entries under the names listed here.

Judicial Conference of the United States This policymaking body for the courts of the judicial branch meets twice a year. Its 27 members are the chief justice of the United States, the chief judges of the 12 regional circuit courts of appeals, the chief judge of the Federal Circuit Court of Appeals, a district judge from each of the regional circuits, and the chief judge of the Court of International Trade.

Day-to-day functions are handled by the Administrative Office of U.S. Courts.

jukebox

jumbo jet Any very large jet plane, including the Airbus A380, Boeing 747, the DC-10, the L-1011 and the C-5A.

jumbo loan A home loan that exceeds $417,000 in much of the country, except in high-cost areas such as California and the Northeast, where the limit can go as high as $729,750 for 2009. Consumers who need to take out home loans above that amount typically pay higher interest rates because government-controlled mortgage finance companies Fannie Mae and Freddie Mac can't buy loans above those limits.

Junior Chamber of Commerce A volunteer organization of young men and women involved in civic service and leadership training.

Members are called *Jaycees*.

U.S. headquarters is in Tulsa, Okla.; international headquarters in Coral Gables, Fla.

See **Jaycees**.

junior, senior Abbreviate as *Jr.* and *Sr.* only with full names of persons or animals. Do not precede by a comma: *Martin Luther King Jr.*

The notation *II* or *2nd* may be used if it is the individual's preference. Note, however, that *II* and *2nd* are not necessarily the equivalent of *junior* — they often are used by a grandson or nephew.

If necessary to distinguish between father and son in second reference, use the *elder Smith* or the *younger Smith*.

See **names**.

junk bonds Also known as non-investment-grade bonds, these corporate debt securities provide high yields to investors to compensate for their higher-than-normal credit risk. They are typically issued by companies with a lot of debt to repay loans, fund takeovers or buy out stockholders.

junta See **government, junta, regime**.

jury The word takes singular verbs and pronouns: *The jury has been sequestered until it reaches a verdict.*

Include racial breakdown only if relevant.

Do not capitalize: *a U.S. District Court jury, a federal jury, a Massachusetts Superior Court jury, a Los Angeles County grand jury.*

See **grand jury**.

justice Capitalize before a name when it is the formal title. It is the formal title for members of the U.S. Supreme Court and for jurists on some state courts. In such cases, do not use *judge* in first or subsequent references.

See **judge**; **Supreme Court of the United States**; and **titles**.

justice of the peace Capitalize as a formal title before a name. Do not abbreviate.

See **titles**.

juvenile delinquent Juveniles may be declared delinquents in many states for anti-social behavior or for breaking the law. In some states, laws prohibit publishing or broadcasting the names of juvenile delinquents.

Follow the local law unless there is a compelling reason to the contrary. Consult with regional editors if you believe such an exception is warranted.

See **privacy**.

K Use *K* in references to modem transmission speeds, in keeping with standard usage: *a 56K modem* (no space after numeral).

The abbreviation should not be used to mean 1,000 or $1,000.

Kabul The city in Afghanistan carries the name of the country in datelines.

kaffiyeh The men's headdress in Arab countries.

Kansas Abbreviate *Kan.* in datelines or stories. Postal code: *KS*
See **state names**.

Kansas City Use *KANSAS CITY, Kan.,* or *KANSAS CITY, Mo.,* in datelines to avoid confusion between the two.

Kansas City Southern Freight railroad, with headquarters in Kansas City, Mo. It is the parent of Kansas City Southern Railway Co. and Kansas City Southern de Mexico SA and it holds a 50 percent stake in Panama Canal Railway Co.

karat See **carat, caret, karat**.

Katmandu Preferred spelling for the capital of Nepal.

Kelvin scale A scale of temperature based on, but different from, the Celsius scale. It is used primarily in science to record very high and very low temperatures. The Kelvin scale starts at zero and indicates the total absence of heat (absolute zero).

Zero on the Kelvin scale is equal to minus 273.16 degrees Celsius and minus 459.67 degrees Fahrenheit.

The freezing point of water is 273.16 kelvins. The boiling point of water is 373.16 kelvins. (Note temperatures on the Kelvin scale are called *kelvins*, not *degrees*. The symbol, a capital K, stands alone with no degree symbol.)

To convert from Celsius to Kelvin, add 273.16 to the Celsius temperature.

See **Celsius** and **Fahrenheit**.

Kennedy Space Center See **John F. Kennedy Space Center**.

Kentucky Abbreviate *Ky.* in datelines or stories. Postal code: *KY*

Legally a commonwealth, not a state.

See **state names**.

kerosene Formerly a trademark, now a generic term.

keynote address Also: *keynote speech*.

KGB Acceptable on first reference, but the story should contain a phrase identifying it as the former Russian secret police and intelligence agency.

The initials stand for the Russian

words meaning *Committee for State Security*.

kibbutz An Israeli collective settlement.

The plural is *kibbutzim*.

kidnap, kidnapped, kidnapping, kidnapper

killer See **assassin, killer, murderer**.

kilo- A prefix denoting 1,000 units of a measure. Move a decimal point three places to the right, adding zeros if necessary, to convert to the basic unit: 10.5 kilograms equals 10,500 grams.

kilobyte A unit of measurement for digital data storage. In the metric system, a *kilobyte* is 1,000 bytes; in computer binary terms, it is 1,024 bytes. Thus, 64KB means 64 times 1,024 bytes, or 65,536 bytes (not 64,000). Abbreviate *KB*. (Similarly, *MB* for megabytes, *GB* for gigabytes.) Note no space when used with numerals: *a 400KB file*.

Use *Kb* in abbreviations for kilobits and *Kbps* for kilobits per second.

kilocycles The new term is *kilohertz*.

kilogram The metric term for 1,000 grams.

A kilogram is equal to approximately 2.2 pounds or 35 ounces.

To convert to pounds, multiply by 2.2 (9 kilograms x 2.2 equals 19.8 pounds).

See **gram**; **metric system**; and **pound**.

kilohertz Equals 1,000 hertz (1,000 cycles per second), replacing *kilocycles* as the correct term in applications such as broadcast frequencies. Spell out on first reference. Abbreviate *kHz*.

kilometer The metric term for 1,000 meters. Abbreviate *km*.

A kilometer is equal to approximately 3,281 feet, or five-eighths (0.62) of a mile.

To convert to miles, multiply by 0.62 (5 kilometers x 0.62 equals 3.1 miles).

See **meter**; **metric system**; and **miles**.

kilometers per hour The abbreviation *kph* is acceptable in all references.

kiloton, kilotonnage A unit used to measure the power of nuclear explosions. One kiloton has the explosive force of 1,000 tons of TNT.

The atomic bomb dropped Aug. 6, 1945, on Hiroshima, Japan, in the first use of the bomb as a weapon had an explosive force of 20 kilotons.

A *megaton* has the force of a million tons of TNT. A *gigaton* has the force of a billion tons of TNT.

kilowatt-hour The amount of electrical energy consumed when 1,000 watts are used for one hour.

The abbreviation *kwh* is acceptable on second reference.

kindergarten

king Capitalize only when used before the name of royalty: *King George VI*. Continue in subsequent references that use the king's given name: *King George*, not *George*.

Lowercase *king* when it stands alone.

Capitalize in plural uses before names: *Kings George and Edward*.

Lowercase in phrases such as *strikeout king Nolan Ryan*.

See **nobility** and **titles**.

Kitty Litter A brand of absorbent material used in cat litter boxes. Use a generic term such as *cat box filler*.

Kleenex A trademark for a brand of facial tissue.

Kmart No hyphen, no space, lowercase *m*.
See **Sears Holdings Corp**.

Knesset The Israeli parliament. See **foreign legislative bodies**.

knight See **nobility**.

Knights of Columbus *K. of C.* or *the Knights* may be used on second reference.
See **fraternal organizations and service clubs**.

K-9

knot A knot is 1 nautical mile (6,076.10 feet) per hour. It is redundant to say *knots per hour*.
To convert knots into approximate statute miles per hour, multiply knots by 1.15.
Always use figures: *Winds were at 7 to 9 knots; a 10-knot wind*.
See **nautical mile**.

know-how

Kodak A trademark for photographic products made by Eastman Kodak Co. in Rochester, N.Y.

Kolkata Indian city formerly known as Calcutta.

Koran Use *Quran* in all references except when preferred by an organization or in a specific title or name. See **Quran**.

Korea The Korean Peninsula remains in a technical state of war, divided by the *Demilitarized Zone* into *North Korea*, officially the *Democratic*

People's Republic of Korea, and *South Korea*, officially the *Republic of Korea*. On follow-ups, the *North* and the *South* are acceptable. The abbreviations *NKorea* and *SKorea* are used only in headlines. *DMZ* is acceptable on second reference.

Korean Airlines Co. Ltd. Headquarters of this airline is in Seoul, Korea.

Korean names The style and spelling of names in North Korea and South Korea follow each government's standard policy for transliterations unless the subject has a personal preference.
North Korean names are written as three separate words, each starting with a capital letter: *Kim Jong Il*. Use *Kim* on second reference.
South Korean names are written as two names, with the given name hyphenated and a lowercase letter after the hyphen: *Lee Myung-bak*. Use *Lee* on second reference.
For South Korean place names, use the revised Romanized spellings introduced by the South Korean government in 2000: *Incheon* (formerly Inchon), *Busan* (formerly Pusan).
In both Koreas, the family name comes first.

Korean War But lowercase *Korean conflict*.

kosher Always lowercase.

Kosovo The capital is Pristina.

kowtow

K2 world's second-tallest mountain. No hyphen.

kudos It means credit or praise for an achievement.
The word is singular and takes singular verbs.

Ku Klux Klan A secretive society organized in the South after the Civil War to assert white supremacy, often using violence. The organization splintered, and not all successor groups use the full name. But each may be referred to as *Ku Klux Klan*, and *KKK* may be used on second reference.

Kuomintang The Chinese Nationalist political party. Do not follow with the word *party*. *Tang* means party.

Kuril Islands Use in datelines after a community name in stories from these islands. Name an individual island, if needed, in the text.

Explain in the text that a small portion of the archipelago is claimed by Japan but most are part of Russia.

Kuwait City This capital city of Kuwait stands alone in datelines.

Kwanzaa A seven-day celebration, based on African festivals, from Dec. 26 through Jan. 1. The name comes from the Swahili for "first fruits."

Kyodo News The nonprofit international news agency is based in Tokyo. It was founded in 1945. *Kyodo* is acceptable on second reference.

la See **foreign names** entry.

Labor Day The first Monday in September.

Laborers' International Union of North America The shortened form *Laborers' union* is acceptable in all references.

Headquarters is in Washington.

Labrador The mainland portion of the Canadian province of Newfoundland and Labrador.

Use *Newfoundland* in datelines after the name of a community. Specify in the text that it is in Labrador.

Ladies' Home Journal

lady Do not use as a synonym for *woman*. *Lady* may be used when it is a courtesy title or when a specific reference to fine manners is appropriate without patronizing overtones.

See **nobility**.

lake Capitalize as part of a proper name: *Lake Erie, Canandaigua Lake, the Finger Lakes.*

Lowercase in plural uses: *lakes Erie and Ontario; Canandaigua and Seneca lakes.*

lame duck (n.) **lame-duck** (adj.)

LAN Acronym for *local area net-*

work, which links computers within a geographically limited area. Acronym acceptable on first reference but spell out in copy.

Land Rover No hyphen. A trademark for a brand of all-terrain vehicle. Parent company Ford Motor Co. sold Land Rover and its Jaguar vehicle group to India's Tata Motors Ltd. in 2008.

languages Capitalize the proper names of languages and dialects: *Aramaic, Cajun, English, Gullah, Persian, Serbo-Croatian, Yiddish.*

laptop

larceny See **burglary, larceny, robbery, theft**.

last Avoid the use of *last* as a synonym for *latest* if it might imply finality. *The last time it rained, I forgot my umbrella*, is acceptable. But: *The last announcement was made at noon* may leave the reader wondering whether the announcement was the final announcement, or whether others are to follow.

The word *last* is not necessary to convey the notion of most recent when the name of a month or day is used:

Preferred: *It happened Wednesday. It happened in April.* Correct, but redundant: *It happened last Wednesday.*

But: *It happened last week. It happened last month.*

Lastex A trademark for a type of elastic yarn.

Last Supper

Las Vegas The city in Nevada stands alone in datelines. Do not confuse with Las Vegas, N.M.

late Do not use it to describe someone's actions while alive.
Wrong: *Only the late senator opposed this bill.* (The senator was not dead at that time.)

latex A resin-based substance used in making elastic materials and paints.

Latin America See Western Hemisphere.

Latino Often the preferred term for a person from — or whose ancestors were from — a Spanish-speaking land or culture or from Latin America. *Latina* is the feminine form. Follow the person's preference. Use a more specific identification when possible, such as *Cuban, Puerto Rican, Brazilian* or *Mexican-American*. See **Hispanic, nationalities and races**, and **race**.

Latin Rite See Roman Catholic Church.

latitude and longitude *Latitude*, the distance north or south of the equator, is designated by parallels. *Longitude*, the distance east or west of Greenwich, England, is designated by meridians.
Use these forms to express degrees of latitude and longitude: *New York City lies at 40 degrees 45 minutes north latitude and 74 degrees 0 minutes west longitude; New York City lies south of the 41st parallel north and along the 74th meridian west.*

Latter Day Saints, Latter-day Saints See **Church of Jesus Christ of Latter-day Saints**.

laws Capitalize legislative acts but not bills: *the Taft-Hartley Act, the Kennedy bill.*

lawsuit *Civil lawsuit* is redundant.

lawyer A generic term for all members of the bar.
An *attorney* is someone legally appointed or empowered to act for another, usually, but not always, a lawyer. An *attorney at law* is a lawyer.
A *barrister* is an English lawyer who is specially trained and appears exclusively as a trial lawyer in higher courts. He is retained by a solicitor, not directly by the client. There is no equivalent term in the United States.
Counselor, when used in a legal sense, means a person who conducts a case in court, usually, but not always, a lawyer. A *counselor at law* is a lawyer. *Counsel* frequently is used collectively for a group of counselors.
A *solicitor* in England is a lawyer who performs legal services for the public. A solicitor appears in lower courts but does not have the right to appear in higher courts, which are reserved to barristers.
A *solicitor* in the United States is a lawyer employed by a governmental body. *Solicitor* is generally a job description, but in some agencies it is a formal title.
Solicitor general is the formal title for a chief law officer (where there is no attorney general) or for the chief assistant to the law officer (when there is an attorney general). Capitalize when used before a name.
Do not use *lawyer* as a formal title.
See **attorney, lawyer** and **titles**.

lay, lie The action word is *lay*. It takes a direct object. *Laid* is the form for its past tense and its past participle. Its present participle is *laying*.

Lie indicates a state of reclining along a horizontal plane. It does not take a direct object. Its past tense is *lay*. Its past participle is *lain*. Its present participle is *lying*.

When *lie* means to make an untrue statement, the verb forms are *lie, lied, lying*.

Some examples:
PRESENT OR FUTURE TENSES:
Right: *I will lay the book on the table. The prosecutor tried to lay the blame on him.*

Wrong: *He lays on the beach all day. I will lay down.*

Right: *He lies on the beach all day. I will lie down.*

IN THE PAST TENSE:
Right: *I laid the book on the table. The prosecutor has laid the blame on him.*

Right: *He lay on the beach all day. He has lain on the beach all day. I lay down. I have lain down.*

WITH THE PRESENT PARTICIPLE:
Right: *I am laying the book on the table. The prosecutor is laying the blame on him.*

Right: *He is lying on the beach. I am lying down.*

layoff (n.), **lay off** (v.)

Leaning Tower of Pisa

leatherneck Lowercase this nickname for a member of the U.S. Marine Corps. It is derived from the leather lining that was formerly part of the collar on the Marine uniform.

lectern, podium, pulpit, rostrum A speaker stands *behind a lectern, on a podium* or *rostrum,* or *in the pulpit.*

lecturer A formal title in the Christian Science Church. An occupational description in other uses.

lectures Capitalize and use quotation marks for their formal titles, as described in **composition titles**.

left hand (n.) **left-handed** (adj.) **left-hander** (n.)

leftist, ultra-leftist In general, avoid these terms in favor of a more precise description of an individual's political philosophy.

Ultra-leftist suggests an individual who subscribes to a communist view or one holding that liberal or socialist change cannot come within the present form of government.

See **radical** and **rightist, ultra-rightist**.

left wing (n.) **left-wing** (adj.) **left-winger** (n.) Generally try to avoid in describing political leanings.

legal holiday See **holidays and holy days**.

legion, legionnaire See **American Legion** and **French Foreign legion**.

Legionnaires' disease The disease takes its name from an outbreak at the Pennsylvania American Legion convention held at the Bellevue-Stratford Hotel in Philadelphia in July 1976. The bacterium believed to be responsible is found in soil and grows in water, such as air-conditioning ducts, storage tanks and rivers.

legislative titles FIRST-REFERENCE FORM: Use *Rep., Reps., Sen.* and *Sens.* as formal titles before one or more names. Spell out and lowercase *representative* and *senator* in other uses.

Spell out other legislative titles in all uses. Capitalize formal titles such as *assemblyman, assemblywoman, city councilor, delegate,* etc., when they are used before a name. Lowercase in other uses.

Add *U.S.* or state before a title only if necessary to avoid confusion: *U.S. Rep. Don Young of Alaska now has a Republican primary opponent, state Rep. Gabrielle LeDoux of Kodiak.*

In stories with international datelines, include *U.S.* before legislative titles.

FIRST-REFERENCE PRACTICE: The use of a title such as *Rep.* or *Sen.* in first reference is normal in most stories. It is not mandatory, however, provided an individual's title is given later in the story.

Deletion of the title on first reference is frequently appropriate, for example, when an individual has become well known: *Barack Obama declared Americans were ready to "cast aside cynicism" as he looked for a convincing win in the Democratic contest. The Illinois senator was leading in the polls.*

SECOND REFERENCE: Do not use legislative titles before a name on second reference unless they are part of a direct quotation.

CONGRESSMAN, CONGRESSWOMAN: *Rep.* and *U.S. Rep.* are the preferred first-reference forms when a formal title is used before the name of a U.S. House member. The words *congressman* or *congresswoman,* in lowercase, may be used in subsequent references that do not use an individual's name, just as *senator* is used in references to members of the Senate.

Congressman and *congresswoman* should appear as capitalized formal titles before a name only in direct quotation.

ORGANIZATIONAL TITLES: Capitalize titles for formal, organizational offices within a legislative body when they are used before a name: *House Speaker John Boehner, Senate Majority Leader Harry Reid, House Minority Leader Nancy Pelosi, Senate Republican Whip Jon Kyl, Senate Judiciary Committee Chairman Patrick Leahy, President Pro Tem Daniel Inouye.*

See **party affiliation** and **titles**.

legislature Capitalize when preceded by the name of a state: *the Kansas Legislature.*

Retain capitalization when the state name is dropped but the reference is specifically to that state's legislature:

TOPEKA, Kan. (AP) — Both houses of the Legislature adjourned today.

Capitalize *legislature* in subsequent specific references and in such constructions as: *the 100th Legislature, the state Legislature.*

Although the word *legislature* is not part of the formal, proper name for the lawmaking bodies in many states, it commonly is used that way and should be treated as such in any story that does not use the formal name.

If a given context or local practice calls for the use of a formal name such as *Missouri General Assembly,* retain the capital letters if the name of the state can be dropped, but lowercase the word *assembly* if it stands alone. Lowercase *legislature* if a story uses it in a subsequent reference to a body identified as a general assembly.

Lowercase *legislature* when used generically: *No legislature has approved the amendment.*

Use *legislature* in lowercase for all plural references: *The Arkansas and Colorado legislatures are considering the amendment.*

In 49 states the separate bodies are a senate and a *house* or *assembly.* The *Nebraska Legislature* is a unicameral body.

See **assembly**; **general assembly**; **governmental bodies**; **House of Representatives**; and **Senate**.

Lent The period from Ash Wednesday through Holy Saturday, the day before Easter. The 40-day Lenten period for penance, suggested by Christ's 40 days in the desert, does not include the six Sundays between Ash Wednesday and Easter.

See **Easter** for the method of computing when Easter occurs.

lesbian See **gay**.

-less No hyphen before this suffix:

childless	waterless
tailless	

less See **fewer, less**.

let up (v.) **letup** (n. and adj.)

leverage The use of borrowed assets by a business to enhance the return of the owner's equity. The expectation is that the interest rate charged will be lower than the earnings made on the money.

leveraged buyout A corporate acquisition in which the bulk of the purchase price is paid with borrowed money. The debt then is repaid with the acquired company's cash flow, with money raised by the sale of its assets or by the later sale of the entire company.

Levi's A trademark for a brand of jeans.

liabilities When used in a financial sense, the word means all the claims against a corporation.

They include accounts payable, wages and salaries due but not paid, dividends declared payable, taxes payable, and fixed or long-term ob-

ligations such as bonds, debentures and bank loans.

See **assets**.

liaison

liberal, liberalism See **political parties and philosophies**.

Libor The rate that international banks charge for short-term loans to each other. Libor, an acronym for the London Interbank Offered Rate, is calculated every business day.

lie See **lay, lie**.

lie in state Only people who are entitled to a state funeral may formally lie in state. In the United States, this occurs in the rotunda in the Capitol.

Those entitled to a state funeral are a president, a former president, a president-elect or any other person designated by the president.

Members of Congress may lie in state, and a number have done so. The decision is either house's to make, although the formal process normally begins with a request from the president.

Those entitled to an official funeral, but not to lie in state, are the vice president, the chief justice, Cabinet members and other government officials when designated by the president.

lieutenant See **military titles**.

lieutenant governor Capitalize and abbreviate as *Lt. Gov.* or *Lt. Govs.* when used as a formal title before one or more names both inside and outside quotations. Lowercase and spell out in all other uses.

See **titles**.

life-size

life span

lifestyle

lifetime

lift off (v.) **liftoff** (n. and adj.)

light, lighted, lighting *Lit* is acceptable as the past tense form.

lightning The electrical discharge.

light-year The distance that light travels in one year at the rate of 186,282 miles per second. It works out to about 5.88 trillion miles (5,878,612,800,000 miles).

likable

-like Do not precede this suffix by a hyphen unless the letter l would be tripled or the main element is a proper noun:

bill-like	Norwalk-like
businesslike	shell-like

An exception is *flu-like*.

like- Follow with a hyphen when used as a prefix meaning similar to:

like-minded	like-natured

No hyphen in words that have meanings of their own:

likelihood	likewise
likeness	

like, as Use *like* as a preposition to compare nouns and pronouns. It requires an object: *Jim blocks like a pro.*

The conjunction *as* is the correct word to introduce clauses: *Jim blocks the linebacker as he should.*

limousine

linage, lineage *Linage* is the number of lines.

Lineage is ancestry or descent.

Lincoln's Birthday Capitalize *birthday* in references to the holiday.

Lincoln was born Feb. 12. His birthday is not a federal legal holiday.

line numbers Use figures and lowercase the word line in naming individual lines of a text: *line 1, line 9.* But: *the first line, the 10th line.*

linoleum Formerly a trademark, now a generic term.

lion's share The term comes from an Aesop fable in which the lion took all the spoils of a joint hunt.

Use it to mean the whole of something, or the best and biggest portion.

Do not use it to mean majority.

liquefied natural gas Natural gas that has been cooled to minus 260 degrees Fahrenheit, making it liquid. The process reduces the volume of the gas, making it easier to transport. *LNG* is acceptable on second reference.

liquefy

liquidation When used in a financial sense, the word means the process of converting stock or other assets into cash.

When a company is liquidated, the cash obtained is first used to pay debts and obligations to holders of bonds and preferred stock. Whatever cash remains is distributed on a per-share basis to the holders of common stock.

liquidity The ease with which assets can be converted to cash without loss in value. The faster it can be sold, the more liquid it is.

Listserv A trademark for a software program for setting up and maintaining discussion groups through email.

liter The basic unit of volume in the metric system. It is defined as the volume occupied by 1 kilogram of distilled water at 4 degrees Celsius. It works out to a total of 1,000 cubic centimeters (1 cubic decimeter).

It takes 1,000 milliliters to make a liter.

A liter is equal to approximately 34 fluid ounces or 1.06 liquid quarts. A liter equals 0.91 of a dry quart. The metric system makes no distinction between dry volume and liquid volume.

To convert to liquid quarts, multiply by 1.06 (4 liters x 1.06 equals 4.24 liquid quarts).

To convert to dry quarts, multiply by 0.91 (4 liters x 0.91 equals 3.64 dry quarts).

To convert to liquid gallons, multiply by 0.26 (8 liters x 0.26 equals 2.08 gallons).

See **gallon; kilogram; metric system; quart (dry);** and **quart (liquid).**

literally See **figuratively, literally.**

literature See **composition titles.**

Little League, Little League Baseball The official name of the worldwide youth baseball and softball organization and its affiliated local leagues.

livable

livid It is not a synonym for *fiery, bright, crimson, red* or *flaming.* If a person turns *livid* with rage, his face becomes ashen or pale. It can mean *blue, bluish gray, gray, dull white, dull purple* or *grayish black.*

Lloyds Bank International Ltd. A prominent bank with headquarters in London.

Lloyd's of London A self-regulating market of insurance. Founded in Britain in 1680, it relies on individual investors worldwide, known as Names, along with several hundred companies, to provide the money for underwriting insurance.

Lloyd's Register of Shipping The reference source for questions about nonmilitary ships not covered in this book.

It is published by Lloyd's Register — Fairplay Ltd. in Surrey, U.K.

loan terminology Note the meanings of these terms in describing loans by governments and corporations:

bond A certificate issued by a corporation or government stating the amount of a loan, the interest to be paid, the time for repayment and the collateral pledged if payment cannot be made. Repayment generally is not due for a long period, usually seven years or more.

collateral Stock or other property that a borrower is obligated to turn over to a lender if unable to repay a loan.

convertible bond A bond carrying the stipulation that it may be exchanged for a specific amount of stock in the company that issued it.

coupon A slip of paper attached to a bond that the bondholder clips at specified times and returns to the issuer for payment of the interest due.

debenture A certificate stating the amount of a loan, the interest to be paid and the time for repayment, but not providing collateral. It is backed only by the corporation's reputation and promise to pay.

default A person, corporation or government is in default if it fails to meet the terms for repayment.

full faith and credit bond An alternate term for general obligation bond, often used to contrast such a bond with a moral obligation bond.

general obligation bond A bond that has had the formal approval of either the voters or their legislature. The government's promise to repay the principal and pay the interest is constitutionally guaranteed on the strength of its ability to tax the population.

maturity The date on which a bond, debenture or note must be repaid.

moral obligation bond A government bond that has not had the formal approval of either the voters or their legislature. It is backed only by the government's "moral obligation" to repay the principal and interest on time.

municipal bond A general obligation bond issued by a state, country, city, town, village, possession or territory, or a bond issued by an agency or authority set up by one of these governmental units. In general, interest paid on municipal bonds is exempt from federal income taxes. It also usually is exempt from state and local taxes if held by someone living within the state of issue.

note A certificate issued by a corporation or government stating the amount of a loan, the interest to be paid and the collateral pledged in the event payment cannot be made. The date for repayment is generally more than a year after issue but not more than seven or eight years later. The shorter interval for repayment is the principal difference between a note and a bond.

revenue bond A bond backed only by the revenue of the airport, turnpike or other facility that was built with the money it raised.

Treasury borrowing A *Treasury bill* is a certificate representing a loan to the federal government that matures in three, six or 12 months. A *Treasury note* may mature in one

to 10 years or more. A *Treasury bond* matures in more than 10 years. Because Treasurys carry the full backing of the government, they are viewed as the safest investment.

loan (n.) **lend** (v.) The preferred usage.

loath (adj.) **loathe** (v.) Note the difference. She is *loath* to leave. He *loathes* bureaucracy.

local Avoid the irrelevant use of the word.

Irrelevant: *The injured were taken to a local hospital.*

Better: *The injured were taken to a hospital.*

local of a union Always use a figure and capitalize *local* when giving the name of a union subdivision: *Local 123 of the United Auto Workers.*

Lowercase *local* standing alone in plural uses: *The local will vote Tuesday. He spoke to locals 2, 4 and 10.*

See **union names**.

Lockheed Martin Corp. Headquarters is in Bethesda, Md.

lodges See **fraternal organizations and service clubs**.

login, logon, logoff (n.) But use as two words in verb form: *I log in to my computer.*

London The city in England stands alone in datelines.

long distance, long-distance Always a hyphen in reference to telephone calls: *We keep in touch by long-distance. He called long-distance. She took the long-distance call.*

In other uses, hyphenate only when used as a compound modifier: *She traveled a long distance. She made a long-distance trip.*

longitude See **latitude and longitude**.

longshoreman Capitalize *longshoreman* only if the intended meaning is that the individual is a member of the International Longshore and Warehouse Union or the International Longshoremen's Association.

long term, long-term Hyphenate when used as a compound modifier: *We will win in the long term. He has a long-term assignment.*

long time, longtime *They have known each other a long time. They are longtime partners.*

long ton Also known as a *British ton.* Equal to 2,240 pounds. See **ton**.

Lord's Supper See **sacraments**.

Los Angeles The city in California stands alone in datelines. *LA* is acceptable on second reference.

Louisiana Abbreviate *La.* in datelines or stories. Postal code: *LA* See **state names**.

Low Countries Belgium, Luxembourg and Netherlands.

lowercase One word (n., v., adj.) when referring to the absence of capital letters. Originally from printers' practice.

LSD Acceptable in all references for *lysergic acid diethylamide.*

Lt. Gov. See **lieutenant governor**.

Lucite A trademark for an acrylic plastic.

Lufthansa German Airlines See **Deutsche Lufthansa AG**.

Lutheran churches The basic unit of government in Lutheran practice is the congregation. It normally is administered by a council, headed either by the senior pastor or a lay person elected from the membership of the council. The council customarily consists of a congregation's clergy and elected lay people.

The three major Lutheran bodies in the United States merged on Jan. 1, 1988, into a new organization, the Evangelical Lutheran Church in America , which is now the largest Lutheran group in the U.S.

The Lutheran Church in America had been the largest and most geographically spread of the three and was formed in 1962 from a merger of four bodies with Danish, Finnish, German and Swedish backgrounds. It merged with the American Lutheran Church, a mostly Midwestern group formed in 1960 through a merger of four bodies with Danish, German and Norwegian backgrounds, and the relatively small west-central Association of Evangelical Lutheran Churches.

The Lutheran Church-Missouri Synod, founded in 1847, is a separate and distinct body.

Lutheran teachings go back to Martin Luther, a 16th-century Roman Catholic priest whose objections to elements of Roman Catholic practice began the movement known as the Protestant Reformation.

Members of the clergy are known as *ministers.* Pastor applies if a minister leads a congregation.

On first reference, use *the Rev.* before the name of a man or woman. On second reference, use only the last name.

See **religious titles**.

Luxembourg Stands alone in datelines.

-ly Do not use a hyphen between adverbs ending in *-ly* and adjectives they modify: *an easily remembered rule, a badly damaged island, a fully informed woman.*

See the compound modifiers section of the **hyphen** entry.

Lycra Unless referring to the trademark fiber or fabric, use a generic term such as *spandex* or *elastic* or *stretch fabric.*

Lyndon B. Johnson Space Center Formerly the Manned Spacecraft Center. Located in Houston, it is the National Aeronautics and Space Administration's principal control and training center for manned spaceflight.

Johnson Space Center is acceptable in all references.

In datelines:

HOUSTON (AP) —

See **John F. Kennedy Space Center**.

Macau Stands alone in datelines. Spelling is an exception to Webster's New World College Dictionary.

Mace A trademark, shortened from *Chemical Mace*, for a brand of tear gas that is packaged in an aerosol canister and temporarily stuns its victims.

machine gun (n.) **machine-gun** (v. and adj.) **machine-gunner**, **machine-gun fire**
See **weapons**.

Mach number Named for Ernst Mach, an Austrian physicist, the figure represents the ratio of the speed of an object to the speed of sound in the surrounding medium, such as air, through which the object is moving.
A rule of thumb for speed of sound is approximately 750 mph at sea level and approximately 660 mph at 30,000 feet above sea level.
A body traveling at *Mach 1* would be traveling at the speed of sound. *Mach 2* would equal twice the speed of sound.

mad cow disease Acceptable for bovine spongiform encephalopathy, a progressive neurological disease that afflicts cattle. The disorder caused in humans by eating meat from diseased cattle is called *variant Creutzfeldt-Jakob disease*. See **Creutzfeldt-Jakob disease**.

Madrid The city in Spain stands alone in datelines.

Mafia Secret criminal organization operating mainly in the U.S. and Italy and engaged in illegal activities such as gambling, drug-dealing and prostitution. Lowercase as a synonym for organized crime.

magazine names Capitalize the initial letters of the name but do not place it in quotes. Lowercase *magazine* unless it is part of the publication's formal title: *Harper's Magazine, Newsweek magazine, Time magazine.*
Check the masthead if in doubt.

magistrate Capitalize when used as a formal title before a name. Use *magistrate judge* when referring to the fixed-term judge who presides in U.S. District Court and handles cases referred by U.S. district judges. See **titles**.

mailman *Letter carrier* is preferable because many women hold this job.

Maine Do not abbreviate *Maine* in datelines or stories. Postal code: *ME*
See **state names**.

mainland China See **China**.

major See **military titles**.

majority leader Capitalize when used as a formal title before a name: *Majority Leader John Boehner.* Lowercase elsewhere.
See **legislative titles** and **titles**.

majority, plurality *Majority* means more than half of an amount.

Plurality means more than the next highest number.

COMPUTING MAJORITY: To describe how large a majority is, take the figure that is more than half and subtract everything else from it: If 100,000 votes were cast in an election and one candidate received 60,000 while opponents received 40,000, the winner would have a *majority* of 20,000 votes.

COMPUTING PLURALITY: To describe how large a plurality is, take the highest number and subtract from it the next highest number: If, in the election example above, the second-place finisher had 25,000 votes, the winner's *plurality* would be 35,000 votes.

Suppose, however, that no candidate in this example had a majority. If the first-place finisher had 40,000 votes and the second-place finisher had 30,000, for example, the leader's *plurality* would be 10,000 votes.

USAGE: When *majority* and *plurality* are used alone, they take singular verbs and pronouns: *The majority has made its decision.*

If a plural word follows an *of* construction, the decision on whether to use a singular or plural verb depends on the sense of the sentence: *A majority of two votes is not adequate to control the committee. The majority of the houses on the block were destroyed.*

-maker Follow Webster's New World College Dictionary. For words not in this book, if the word combination is not listed, use two words for the verb form and hyphenate any noun or adjective forms: *chip-maker*. Exceptions: *drugmaker, policymaker, coffee maker.*

make up (v.) **makeup** (n., adj.)

Malaysia Airlines Headquarters of this airline is in Subang, Malaysia.

Maldives Use this official name with a community name in a dateline: *MALE, Maldives.* Refer to the country in the body of the story as *the Maldives: The president won a referendum on the Maldives' future form of government.*

Mallorca Use instead of Spain in datelines on stories from communities on this island.

manageable

manager Capitalize when used as a formal title before a name: *City Manager Dick O'Connell.*

Do not capitalize in job descriptions, including sports teams: *Mets manager Terry Collins.*

See **titles**.

managing editor Capitalize when used as a formal title before a name.

See **titles**.

Manitoba A province of central Canada. Do not abbreviate.

See **datelines**.

man, mankind Either may be used when both men and women are involved and no other term is convenient. In these cases, do not use duplicate phrases such as *a man or a woman* or *mankind and womankind.*

Frequently the best choice is a substitute such as *humanity, a person* or *an individual.*

See **women**.

manslaughter See **homicide, murder, manslaughter**.

mantel, mantle A *mantel* is a shelf. A *mantle* is a cloak.

Maoism (Maoist) The communist philosophy and policies of Mao Zedong. See **political parties and philosophies**.

Marcellus Shale Capitalize major geologic formations.

Mardi Gras Literally *fat Tuesday*, the term describes a day of merrymaking on the Tuesday before Ash Wednesday.

In New Orleans and many Roman Catholic countries, the Tuesday celebration is preceded by a week or more of parades and parties.

margin The practice of purchasing securities in part with borrowed money, using the purchased securities as collateral in anticipation of an advance in the market price. If the advance occurs, the purchaser may be able to repay the loan and make a profit. If the price declines, the stock may have to be sold to settle the loan. The margin is the difference between the amount of the loan and the value of the securities used as collateral.

marijuana

Marines Capitalize when referring to U.S. forces: *the U.S. Marines, the Marines, the Marine Corps, Marine regulations*. Do not use the abbreviation *USMC*.

Capitalize *Marine* when referring to an individual in a Marine Corps unit: *He is a Marine*.

Do not describe *Marines* as soldiers, which is generally associated with the Army. Use *troops* if a generic term is needed.

Maritime Provinces The Canadian provinces of Nova Scotia, New Brunswick and Prince Edward Island.

marketbasket, marketplace

mark to market An accounting requirement that securities must be valued at their current price, rather than the purchase price or the price they might fetch later. Also called "fair value."

marquess, marchioness, marquis, marquise See **nobility**.

Marseille Preferred spelling for the French city.

Marshall Islands Named for John Marshall, a British explorer.

In datelines, give the name of a city and *Marshall Islands*. List the name of an individual island in the text.

marshal, marshaled, marshaling, Marshall *Marshal* is the spelling for both the verb and the noun: *Marilyn will marshal her forces. Erwin Rommel was a field marshal*.

Marshall is used in proper names: *George C. Marshall, John Marshall, the Marshall Islands*.

Martin Luther King Jr. Day Federal holiday honoring Martin Luther King Jr., who was born Jan. 15, 1929, is on the third Monday in January. It was first celebrated in 1986.

Marxism (Marxist) The system of thought developed by Karl Marx and Friedrich Engels. See **political parties and philosophies**.

Maryland Abbreviate *Md.* in datelines or stories. Postal code: *MD* See **state names**.

Mason-Dixon Line The boundary line between Pennsylvania and Maryland, generally regarded as separating the North from the South. (Named for 18th-century surveyors Charles Mason and Jeremiah Dixon, the line later was extended to West Virginia.)

Mass It is *celebrated*, not *said*. Always capitalize when referring to the ceremony, but lowercase any preceding adjectives: *high Mass, low Mass, requiem Mass.*

In Eastern Orthodox churches the correct term is *Divine Liturgy*.
See **Roman Catholic Church**.

Massachusetts Abbreviate *Mass.* in datelines or stories. Legally a commonwealth, not a state. Postal code: *MA*
See **state names**.

Master of Arts, Master of Science, Master of Business Administration Abbreviated *M.A., M.S.* but *MBA*. A *master's degree* or a *master's* is acceptable in any reference.
See **academic degrees**.

matrimony See **sacraments**.

maturity In a financial sense, the date on which a bond, debenture or note must be repaid. See **loan terminology**.

May Day, mayday *May Day* is May 1, often observed as a festive or political holiday.
Mayday is the international distress signal, from the French *m'aider*, meaning "help me."

mayors' conference See **U.S. Conference of Mayors**.

McClatchy Co. U.S. newspaper publisher with headquarters in Sacramento, Calif. Owns dailies including *The Miami Herald, The Charlotte (N.C.) Observer* and *The Sacramento Bee*.

McDonald's Corp. Headquarters is in Oak Brook, Ill.

M.D. A word such as *physician* or *surgeon* is preferred. The periods in the abbreviation are an exception to Webster's New World College Dictionary.
See **doctor** and **academic titles**.

meager

mean See **average, mean, median, norm**.

mecca Lowercase in the metaphorical sense; capitalize the city in Saudi Arabia.

Medal of Freedom It is now the *Presidential Medal of Freedom*. See entry under that name.

Medal of Honor The nation's highest military honor, awarded by Congress for risk of life in combat beyond the call of duty. Use *Medal of Honor recipient* or a synonym, but not *winner*.
There is no *Congressional Medal of Honor*.

medevac Acceptable abbreviation for *medical evacuation*, especially in referring to aircraft used to transport wounded military personnel.

Medfly Mediterranean fruit fly. The capital *M* is an exception to Webster's New World College Dictionary.

media In the sense of mass communication, such as magazines, newspapers, the news services, radio, television and online, the word is plural: *The news media are resisting attempts to limit their freedom.*

median See **average, mean, median, norm**.

MediaNews Group Inc. Privately held U.S. newspaper publisher with headquarters in Denver. Owns dailies including *The Denver Post, San Jose Mercury News* and *The Detroit News.*

mediate See **arbitrate, mediate.**

Medicaid A federal-state program that helps pay for health care for the needy, aged, blind and disabled, and for low-income families with children.

A state determines eligibility and which health services are covered. The federal government reimburses a percentage of the state's expenditures.

Medicare The federal health care insurance program for people aged 65 and over, and for the disabled. Eligibility is based mainly on eligibility for Social Security.

Medicare helps pay charges for hospitalization, for stays in skilled nursing facilities, for physician's charges and for some associated health costs. There are limitations on the length of stay and type of care.

In Canada, *Medicare* refers to the nation's national health insurance program.

medicine See **drugs, medicine.**

medieval

mega- A prefix denoting 1 million units of a measure. Move the decimal point six places to the right, adding zeros if necessary, to convert to the basic unit: 5.5 megatons = 5,500,000 tons.

megabyte A unit of storage capacity in computer systems, loosely 1 million bytes. Abbreviate *MB.*

megahertz A measure of radio frequency or the speed of a computer processor, equal to a million

hertz, or cycles per second. Spell out on first reference. Abbreviate *MHz.*

melee

Melkite Church See **Eastern Rite churches.**

memento, mementos

memo, memos

memorandum, memorandums

Memorial Day Formerly May 30. The federal legal holiday is the last Monday in May.

menorah Candelabrum with nine branches used for Hanukkah.

menswear Not *men's wear.*

mentally disabled The preferred term, not *mentally retarded.* See **disabled, handicapped, impaired.**

Mercedes-Benz Note hyphen in this division of Daimler AG.

merchant marine Lowercase in referring to the ships of a nation used in commerce. Capitalize only in references to the organization the Merchant Marine or the U.S. Merchant Marine Academy. Members are *merchant mariners* or *merchant crewmen,* but not marines.

Merck & Co. Headquarters is in Whitehouse Station, N.J.

merger Few business combinations are truly a merger of equals, so be precise and sparing in the use of the word *merger.* It is not a synonym for acquisition or takeover, which should be the preferred descriptive in most stories. Use the following rules for deciding whether it's a merger or acquisition, and as a guide in concluding who is the acquirer and the company being taken over:

—Is one of the companies' stock being used as the currency? If the answer is yes, that's usually a good sign that company is the acquirer and it is not a merger.

—What is the message from the exchange ratio in stock transactions? Typically when shareholders of Company A are offered new shares in a combined company at a 1-for-1 ratio, and Company B shares are exchanged at something less or more (i.e., each Company B will be exchanged for 0.47 percent of a share of the new company), it's an indication that Company A's stock is being used as the basis for the transaction. But it also could be a sign that the companies' boards have agreed to a merger that uses a formula to compensate for the differing market value (total number of shares multiplied by the closing stock price the day before the announcement) of the two companies to come up with an exchange ratio for stock in the new company.

—What is the message from the stock movements after the announcement? Shares of companies being acquired typically rise and shares of the acquirer often fall after the announcement. Not always, of course, but that's usually the case because most bidders pay a premium, or an above-market price, for the shares of the company being acquired, and investors often are worried about the amount of debt the acquirer is taking on to complete the transaction.

—Whose cash is being used to fund the cash portion of a transaction? If the announcement says Company A's cash will be used or that its existing lines of credit will be tapped to pay for Company B's shares, that's a strong indication that Company A is the acquirer.

—Which company's executives are filling most of the top management roles? The key distinction usually is who gets the CEO slot. But if one of the two CEOs is named to head the company for a limited period (say two years or less) before his fellow CEO takes over, that's a good sign of a political compromise to paper over the fact that the second CEO's company is going to be in charge long term.

—Which company will end up with the majority of the seats on the new board of directors? This is often a key tie breaker. When Company A and Company B insist it's a merger of equals and other checklist items are inconclusive, if one ends up with 60 percent of the board seats and the other gets 40 percent, that's a good indication of which is going to be in charge. Also, make sure you get not only the short-term makeup of the board of the combined company, but also whether there were any deals cut for some members to retire in short order.

—Where will the company be headquartered? Since CEOs typically do the negotiating and they typically aren't anxious to move, this can be an informative tell.

meridians Use numerals and lowercase to identify the imaginary locater lines that ring the globe from north to south through the poles. They are measured in units of 0 to 180 degrees east and west of the *prime meridian*, which runs through Greenwich, England.

Examples: *33rd meridian* (if location east or west of Greenwich is obvious), *1st meridian west, 100th meridian*.

See **latitude and longitude**.

merry-go-round

Mesa Air Group Inc. Headquarters of this airline is in Phoenix.

messiah Capitalize in religious uses, such as references to the promised deliverer of the Jews or to Jesus in Christianity. Lowercase when referring to the liberator of a people or country.

metadata Data about data. Examples of metadata include descriptors indicating when information was created, by whom and in what format. Do not use in a story without an explanation of what information is being revealed in a given set of metadata: *Investigators determined that Johnson wrote the document by analyzing its metadata, which indicated that it had been saved on his computer.*

meter The basic unit of length in the metric system.

It is equal to approximately 39.37 inches, which may be rounded off to 39.5 inches in most comparisons.

It takes 100 centimeters to make a meter.

It takes 1,000 meters to make a kilometer.

To convert to inches, multiply by 39.37 (5 meters x 39.37 = 196.85 inches).

To convert to yards, multiply by 1.1 (5 meters x 1.1 = 5.5 yards).

See **inch**; **metric system**; and **yards**.

Methodist churches The term *Methodist* originated as a nickname applied to a group of 18th-century Oxford University students known for their methodical application to Scripture study and prayer.

The principal Methodist body in the United States is the United Methodist Church, which also has some member conferences outside the United States. It was formed in 1968 by the merger of the Methodist Church and the Evangelical United Brethren Church and has a world-wide membership.

The government of the United Methodist Church follows a stratified pattern from the General Conference through several intermediate conferences down to the local congregation.

The General Conference, which meets every four years, has final authority in all matters.

A Methodist bishop presides over a "church area," which may embrace one or more annual conferences. Bishops have extensive administrative powers, including the authority to place, transfer and remove local church pastors, usually in consultation with district superintendents.

Districts in each conference are responsible for promotion of mission work, support of colleges, hospitals and publications, and examination of candidates for the ministry.

Members of a congregation form a charge conference. It elects officers to a board that assists the pastor.

Methodism in the United States also includes three major black denominations: the African Methodist Episcopal Church, the African Methodist Episcopal Zion Church and the Christian Methodist Episcopal Church.

Methodists believe in the Trinity and the humanity and divinity of Christ. There are two sacraments, baptism and the Lord's Supper.

Ordained individuals are known as *bishops* and *ministers*. *Pastor* applies if a minister leads a congregation.

For first references to bishops use the word: *Bishop W. Kenneth Goodson* of Richmond, Va.

For first reference to ministers, use *the Rev.* before the name of a man or woman. On second reference, use only the last name.

See **religious titles**.

metric system For U.S. members, use metric terms only in situations where they are universally accepted forms of measurement (*16 mm film*) or where the metric distance is an important number in itself: *He vowed to walk 100 kilometers (62 miles) in a week.*

Normally, the equivalent should be in parentheses after the metric figure. A general statement, however, such as *A kilometer equals about five-eighths of a mile*, would be acceptable to avoid repeated use of parenthetical equivalents in a story that uses *kilometers* many times.

To avoid the need for long strings of figures, prefixes are added to the metric units to denote fractional elements or large multiples. The prefixes are: *pico-* (one-trillionth), *nano-* (one-billionth), *micro-* (one-millionth), *milli-* (one-thousandth), *centi-* (one-hundredth), *deci-* (one-tenth), *deka-* (10 units), *hecto-* (100 units), *kilo-* (1,000 units), *mega-* (1 million units), *giga-* (1 billion units), *tera-* (1 trillion units). Entries for each prefix show how to convert a unit preceded by the prefix to the basic unit.

In addition, separate entries for

METRIC CONVERSION CHART

INTO METRIC			OUT OF METRIC		
multiply	*by this number*	*to get*	*multiply*	*by this number*	*to get*
LENGTH					
inches	2.54	centimeters	millimeters	0.04	inches
foot	30	centimeters	centimeters	0.39	inches
yards	0.91	meters	meters	3.28	feet
miles	1.61	kilometers	kilometers	0.62	miles
AREA					
sq. inches	6.45	sq. centimeters	sq. centimeters	0.16	sq. inches
sq. feet	0.09	sq. meters	sq. meters	0.2	sq. yards
sq. yards	0.84	sq. meters	sq. kilometers	0.39	sq. miles
sq. miles	2.59	sq. kilometers	hectares	2.47	acres
acres	0.39	hectares			
MASS (weight)					
ounces	28	grams	grams	0.035	ounces
pounds	0.45	kilograms	kilograms	2.2	pounds
short ton	0.91	metric ton	metric ton	1.1	short tons
VOLUME					
teaspoons	5	milliliters	milliliters	0.03	fluid ounces
tablespoons	15	milliliters	liters	2.1	pints
fluid ounces	30	milliliters	liters	1.06	quarts
cups	0.24	liters	liters	0.26	gallons
pints	0.47	liters	cubic meters	35	cubic feet
quarts	0.95	liters	cubic meters	1.3	cubic yards
gallons	3.79	liters			
cubic feet	0.03	cubic meters			
cubic yards	0.76	cubic meters			
TEMPERATURE					
Fahrenheit to Celsius	Subtract 32, then divide by 1.8		Celsius to Fahrenheit	Multiply by 1.8, then add 32	

gram, **meter**, **liter**, **Celsius** and other frequently used metric units define them and give examples of how to convert them to equivalents in the terminology that has been used in the United States.

Similarly, entries for **pound**, **inch**, **quart**, **Fahrenheit**, etc., contain examples of how to convert these terms to metric forms.

Online: http://www.megaconverter.com/mega2/

ABBREVIATIONS: The abbreviation *mm* for millimeter is acceptable in references to film widths (*8 mm film*) and weapons (*a 105 mm cannon*). (Note space between numeral and abbreviation.)

The principal abbreviations, for reference in the event they are used by a source, are: *g* (gram), *kg* (kilogram), *t* (metric ton), *m* (meter), *cm* (centimeter), *km* (kilometer), *mm* (millimeter), *L* (liter, capital *L* to avoid confusion with the figure *1*) and *mL* (milliliter).

metric ton Equal to approximately 2,204.62 pounds. See **ton**.

Metro-Goldwyn-Mayer Inc.
MGM is acceptable in all references.

Headquarters is in Santa Monica, Calif.

Mexico There are 31 states and Mexico City, the capital and an independent federal district run by a city government. The states are Aguascalientes, Baja California, Baja California Sur, Campeche, Coahuila, Colima, Chiapas, Chihuahua, Durango, Guanajuato, Guerrero, Hidalgo, Jalisco, Mexico, Michoacan, Morelos, Nayarit, Nuevo Leon, Oaxaca, Puebla, Queretaro, Quintana Roo, San Luis Potosi, Sinaloa, Sonora, Tabasco, Tamaulipas, Tlaxcala, Veracruz, Yucatan and Zacatecas.

Mexican states elect their own governor and legislators. Congress is made up of two houses: the lower House of Deputies, with 500 members, and the Senate, with 128 members.

In datelines, use only the city and country.

Mexico City The city in Mexico stands alone in datelines.

Miami The city in Florida stands alone in datelines.

mic (n.) Informal form of *microphone*.

Michigan Abbreviate *Mich.* in datelines or stories. Postal code: *MI* See **state names**.

micro- A prefix denoting one-millionth of a unit.

Move the decimal point six places to the left in converting to the basic unit: 2,999,888.5 microseconds = 2.9998885 seconds.

Microsoft Corp. Headquarters is in Redmond, Wash.

mid- No hyphen unless a capitalized word follows: *midair, mid-America, mid-Atlantic, midsemester* and *midterm*.

But use a hyphen when *mid-* precedes a figure: *mid-30s.*

Middle Ages A.D. 476 to approximately A.D. 1450.

Middle Atlantic States As defined by the U.S. Census Bureau, they are New Jersey, New York and Pennsylvania.

Less formal references often consider Delaware part of the group. See **Northeast region**.

middle class (n.) **middle-class** (adj.)

Middle East The term applies to southwest Asia west of Pakistan and Afghanistan (Iran, Iraq, Israel, Kuwait, Jordan, Lebanon, Oman, Bahrain, Qatar, Saudi Arabia, Syria, the eastern part of Turkey known also as Asia Minor, United Arab Emirates and Yemen), and northeastern Africa (Egypt and Sudan).

Popular usage once distinguished between the *Near East* (the westerly nations in the listing) and the *Middle East* (the easterly nations), but the two terms now overlap, with current practice favoring *Middle East* for both areas.

Use *Middle East* unless *Near East* is used by a source in a story.

Mideast is also acceptable, but *Middle East* is preferred.

middle initials Use according to a person's preference.

Include middle initials in stories where they help identify a specific individual. Examples include casualty lists and stories naming the accused in a crime. A middle initial may be dropped if a person does not use one or is publicly known without it: *Mickey Mantle* (not *Mickey C.*), *the Rev. Billy Graham* (not *Billy F.*).

See **names**.

middleman

middle names Use them only with people who are publicly known that way (*James Earl Jones*), or to prevent confusion with people of the same name.

See **middle initials; names**.

Middle West Definitions vary, but the term generally applies to the 12 states that the U.S. Census Bureau includes in the *Midwest* region. See **Midwest region**.

The shortened form *Midwest* is acceptable in all references.

The forms for adjectives are *Middle Western, Midwestern*.

See **directions and regions**.

midget Considered offensive when used to describe a person of short stature. *Dwarf* is the preferred term for people with that medical or genetic condition. See **dwarf**.

midnight Do not put a 12 in front of it. It is part of the day that is ending, not the one that is beginning.

midshipman See **military academies**.

Midwest region As defined by the U.S. Census Bureau, the region (previously designated the North Central region) is broken into two divisions.

The East North Central states are Indiana, Illinois, Michigan, Ohio and Wisconsin.

The West North Central states are Iowa, Kansas, Minnesota, Missouri, Nebraska, North Dakota and South Dakota.

See **Northeast region; South**; and **West** for the bureau's other regional breakdowns.

MiG The *i* in this designation for a type of Russian fighter jet is lowercase because it is the Russian word for *and*. The initials are from the last names of the designers, Arten Mikoyan and Mikhail Gurevich.

The forms: *MiG-19, MiG-21s*.

See **aircraft names**.

Milan The city in Italy stands alone in datelines.

mile Also called a statute mile, it equals 5,280 feet.

The metric equivalent is approximately 1.6 kilometers.

To convert to kilometers, multiply by 1.6 (5 miles x 1.6 equals 8 kilometers).

See **foot**; **kilometer**; **knot**; and **nautical mile**.

Use figures for amounts under 10 in dimensions, formulas and speeds: *The farm measures 5 miles by 4 miles. The car slowed to 7 mph. The new model gets 4 miles more per gallon.*

Spell out below 10 in distances: *He drove four miles.*

miles per gallon The abbreviation *mpg* is acceptable in all references.

miles per hour The abbreviation *mph* is acceptable in all references.

military academies Capitalize *U.S. Air Force Academy, U.S. Coast Guard Academy, U.S. Merchant Marine Academy, U.S. Military Academy, U.S. Naval Academy.* Retain capitalization if the *U.S.* is dropped: *the Air Force Academy,* etc.

Lowercase *academy* whenever it stands alone.

Cadet is the proper title on first reference for men and women enrolled at the Army, Air Force, Coast Guard and Merchant Marine academies. *Midshipman* is the proper title for men and women enrolled at the Naval Academy.

Use the appropriate title on first reference. On second reference, use only the last name.

military titles Capitalize a military rank when used as a formal title before an individual's name.

See the lists that follow to determine whether the title should be spelled out or abbreviated in regular text.

On first reference, use the appropriate title before the full name of a member of the military.

In subsequent references, do not continue using the title before a name. Use only the last name.

Spell out and lowercase a title when it is substituted for a name:

Gen. John Allen is the top U.S. commander in Afghanistan. The general endorsed the idea.

In some cases, it may be necessary to explain the significance of a title: *Army Sgt. Maj. John Jones described the attack. Jones, who holds the Army's highest rank for enlistees, said it was unprovoked.*

In addition to the ranks listed on the next page, each service has ratings such as *machinist, radarman, torpedoman,* etc., that are job descriptions. Do not use any of these designations as a title on first reference. If one is used before a name in a subsequent reference, do not capitalize or abbreviate it.

Moreover, each service branch has its own systems of abbreviating officer and enlisted ranks -- e.g., COL for colonel in the Army, CMDR for Navy commander -- that vary widely from AP style. However, the Department of Defense uses AP's military titles in news releases because the abbreviations are easily understood.

ABBREVIATIONS: The abbreviations, with the highest ranks listed first:

MILITARY TITLES

Rank	Usage before a name

ARMY

Commissioned Officers

general	Gen.
lieutenant general	Lt. Gen.
major general	Maj. Gen.
brigadier general	Brig. Gen.
colonel	Col.
lieutenant colonel	Lt. Col.
major	Maj.
captain	Capt.
first lieutenant	1st Lt.
second lieutenant	2nd Lt.

Warrant Officers

chief warrant officer five (CW5)	Chief Warrant Officer 5
chief warrant officer four (CW4)	Chief Warrant Officer 4
chief warrant officer three (CW3)	Chief Warrant Officer 3

chief warrant officer two (CW2)	Chief Warrant Officer 2
warrant officer (WO1)	Warrant Officer

Enlisted Personnel

sergeant major of the Army	Sgt. Maj. of the Army
command sergeant major	Command Sgt. Maj.
sergeant major	Sgt. Maj.
first sergeant	1st Sgt.
master sergeant	Master Sgt.
sergeant first class	Sgt. 1st Class
staff sergeant	Staff Sgt.
sergeant	Sgt.
corporal	Cpl.
specialist	Spc.
private first class	Pfc.
private	Pvt.

NAVY, COAST GUARD

Commissioned Officers

admiral	Adm.
vice admiral	Vice Adm.
rear admiral upper half	Rear Adm.
rear admiral lower half	Rear Adm.
captain	Capt.
commander	Cmdr.
lieutenant commander	Lt. Cmdr.
lieutenant	Lt.
lieutenant junior grade	Lt. j.g.
ensign	Ensign

Warrant Officers

chief warrant officer	Chief Warrant Officer

Enlisted Personnel

master chief petty officer of the Navy	Master Chief Petty Officer of the Navy
master chief petty officer	Master Chief Petty Officer
senior chief petty officer	Senior Chief Petty Officer
chief petty officer	Chief Petty Officer
petty officer first class	Petty Officer 1st Class
petty officer second class	Petty Officer 2nd Class
petty officer third class	Petty Officer 3rd Class
seaman	Seaman
seaman apprentice	Seaman Apprentice
seaman recruit	Seaman Recruit

MARINE CORPS

Ranks and abbreviations for commissioned officers are the same as those in the Army. Warrant officer ratings follow the same system used in the Navy. There are no specialist ratings.

Others

sergeant major of the Marine Corps	Sgt. Maj. of the Marine Corps
sergeant major	Sgt. Maj.
master gunnery sergeant	Master Gunnery Sgt.
first sergeant	1st Sgt.
master sergeant	Master Sgt.
gunnery sergeant	Gunnery Sgt.
staff sergeant	Staff Sgt.
sergeant	Sgt.
corporal	Cpl.
lance corporal	Lance Cpl.
private first class	Pfc.
private	Pvt.

AIR FORCE

Ranks and abbreviations for commissioned officers are the same as those in the Army.

Enlisted Designations

chief master sergeant of the Air Force	Chief Master Sgt. of the Air Force
chief master sergeant	Chief Master Sgt.
senior master sergeant	Senior Master Sgt.
master sergeant	Master Sgt.
technical sergeant	Tech. Sgt.
staff sergeant	Staff Sgt.
senior airman	Senior Airman
airman first class	Airman 1st Class
airman	Airman
airman basic	Airman

PLURALS: Add *s* to the principal element in the title: *Majs. John Jones and Robert Smith; Maj. Gens. John Jones and Robert Smith; Spcs. John Jones and Robert Smith.*

RETIRED OFFICERS: A military rank may be used in first reference before the name of an officer who has retired if it is relevant to a story. Do not, however, use the military abbreviation *Ret.*

Instead, use *retired* just as *former* would be used before the title of a civilian: *They invited retired Army Gen. John Smith.*

FIREFIGHTERS, POLICE OFFICERS: Use the abbreviations listed here when a military-style title is used before the name of a firefighter or police officer outside a direct quotation. Add *police* or *fire* before the title if needed for clarity: *police Sgt. William Smith, fire Capt. David Jones.*

Spell out titles such as *detective* that are not used in the armed forces.

military units Use Arabic figures and capitalize the key words when linked with the figures: *1st Infantry Division* (or *the 1st Division*), *5th Battalion, 395th Field Artillery, 7th Fleet.*

But: *the division, the battalion, the artillery, the fleet.*

millennium

milli- A prefix denoting one-thousandth of a unit. Move the decimal three places to the left in converting to the basic unit: 1,567.5 millimeters equals 1.5675 meters.

milligram One-thousandth of a gram.

Equal to approximately one-twenty-eight-thousandth of an ounce.

To convert to ounces, multiply by 0.000035 (140 milligrams x 0.000035 equals 0.0049 ounce).

See **metric system**.

milliliter One-thousandth of a liter.

Equal to approximately one-fifth of a teaspoon.

Thirty milliliters equals 1 fluid ounce.

To convert to teaspoons, multiply by 0.2 (5 milliliters x 0.2 equals 1 teaspoon).

See **liter** and **metric system**.

millimeter One-thousandth of a meter.

It takes 10 millimeters to make a centimeter.

To convert to inches, multiply by 0.04 (5 millimeters x 0.04 is 0.2 of an inch).

May be abbreviated as *mm* when used with a numeral in first or subsequent references to film or weapons: *35 mm film, 105 mm artillery piece.* (Note space after numeral.)

See **meter**; **metric system**; and **inch**.

millions, billions Use figures with *million* or *billion* in all except casual uses: *I'd like to make a billion dollars.* But: *The nation has 1 million citizens. I need $7 billion.*

Do not go beyond two decimal places. *7.51 million people, $256 billion, 7,542,500 people, $2,565,750,000.* Decimals are preferred where practical: *1.5 million.* Not: *1 1/2 million.*

Do not mix *millions* and *billions* in the same figure: *2.6 billion.* Not: *2 billion 600 million.*

Do not drop the word *million* or *billion* in the first figure of a range: *He is worth from $2 million to $4 million.* Not: *$2 to $4 million,* unless you really mean $2.

Note that a hyphen is not used to join the figures and the word *million* or *billion,* even in this type of phrase: *The president submitted a $300 billion budget.*

Milwaukee The city in Wisconsin stands alone in datelines.

mindset

mini- The rules in **prefixes** apply, but in general, no hyphen. Some examples:

miniseries   miniskirt
minivan

minimally conscious state In this condition, the eyes are open, but the patient shows only minimal and intermittent signs of awareness of self and environment and responds only inconsistently when asked to gesture, move or speak. At times, the patient may be able to reach for objects, indicate yes or no and follow objects with the eyes, but a given patient may not be able to do all these things.
See **coma** and **vegetative state**.

minister It is not a formal title in most religions, with exceptions such as the Nation of Islam, and is not capitalized. Where it is a formal title, it should be capitalized before the name: *Minister John Jones*.
See **religious titles** and the entry for an individual's denomination.

ministry See **foreign governmental bodies**.

Minneapolis The city in Minnesota stands alone in datelines.

Minnesota Abbreviate *Minn.* in datelines or stories. Postal code: *MN* See **state names**.

minority leader Treat the same as *majority leader*. See that entry and **legislative titles**.

minuscule Not miniscule.

minus sign Use a hyphen, not a dash, but use the word *minus* if there is any danger of confusion.
Use a word, not a minus sign, to indicate temperatures below zero: *minus 10* or *5 below zero*.

MIRV, MIRVs Acceptable on first reference for *multiple independently targetable re-entry vehicle(s)*.

Explain in the text that a *MIRV* is an intercontinental ballistic missile with several warheads, each of which can be directed to a different target.

misdemeanor See **felony, misdemeanor**.

mishap A minor misfortune. People are not killed in *mishaps*.

Miss See **courtesy titles**.

missile names Use Arabic figures and capitalize the proper name but not the word *missile*: *Pershing 2 missile*.
See **ABM**; **ICBM**; **MIRV**; and **SAM**.

Mississippi Abbreviate *Miss.* in datelines or stories. Postal code: *MS* See **state names**.

Missouri Abbreviate *Mo.* in datelines or stories. Postal code: *MO* See **state names**.

mixed martial arts Generic term for bouts featuring boxing, wrestling, taekwondo, judo and other disciplines. Do not use *ultimate fighting* as a synonym. It is a registered trademark for events sanctioned by Ultimate Fighting Championship. See **Ultimate Fighting**.

mix up (v.) **mix-up** (n. and adj.)

Mobil Corp. See **Exxon Mobil**.

mock-up (n.)

model numbers See **serial numbers**.

modem Acceptable in all references for the acronym formed from *modulator* and *demodulator*.

mom Uppercase only when the noun substitutes for a name as a term of address: *Hi, Mom!*

Monaco After the Vatican, the world's smallest state.

The *Monaco* section stands alone in datelines. The other two sections, *La Condamine* and *Monte Carlo*, are followed by *Monaco*:

MONTE CARLO, Monaco (AP) —

Monday morning quarterback One who second-guesses.

monetary See the **fiscal, monetary** entry.

monetary units See **cents**; **dollars**; and **pounds**.

moneymaker

monsignor See **Roman Catholic Church**.

Montana Abbreviate *Mont.* in datelines or stories. Postal code: *MT* See **state names**.

Montessori method After Maria Montessori, a system of training young children. It emphasizes training of the senses and guidance to encourage self-education.

monthlong, monthslong

months Capitalize the names of months in all uses. When a month is used with a specific date, abbreviate only *Jan., Feb., Aug., Sept., Oct., Nov.* and *Dec.* Spell out when using alone, or with a year alone.

When a phrase lists only a month and a year, do not separate the year with commas. When a phrase refers to a month, day and year, set off the year with commas.

EXAMPLES: *January 1972 was a cold month. Jan. 2 was the coldest day of the month. His birthday is May*

8. Feb. 14, 1987, was the target date. She testified that it was Friday, Dec. 3, when the accident occurred.

In tabular material, use these three-letter forms without a period: *Jan, Feb, Mar, Apr, May, Jun, Jul, Aug, Sep, Oct, Nov, Dec.*

See **dates** and **years**.

Montreal The city in Canada stands alone in datelines.

monuments Capitalize the popular names of monuments and similar public attractions: *Lincoln Memorial, Statue of Liberty, Washington Monument, Leaning Tower of Pisa,* etc.

moon Lowercase. See **heavenly bodies**.

mo-ped Hyphen is an exception to Webster's New World College Dictionary.

mop up (v.) **mop-up** (n. and adj.)

moral obligation bond See **loan terminology**.

more than See **over**.

Morgan Stanley Headquarters is in New York.

Mormon church Acceptable in references to *The Church of Jesus Christ of Latter-day Saints*, but the official name is preferred in first reference in a story dealing primarily with church activities.

See **Church of Jesus Christ of Latter-day Saints, The**.

mortgage A loan secured by property. The contract between the borrower and the lender gives the lender the right to take possession and resell the property it if the borrower defaults. See **adjustable-rate mortgage** and **balloon mortgage**.

mortgage-backed security A bond backed by home or commercial mortgage payments. These provide income from payments of the underlying mortgages.

Moscow The city in Russia stands alone in datelines.

mosquito, mosquitoes

Mother's Day The second Sunday in May.

mother-in-law, mothers-in-law

Mother Nature

motor See the **engine, motor** entry.

mount Spell out in all uses, including the names of communities and of mountains: *Mount Clemens, Mich.*; *Mount Everest.*

mountains Capitalize as part of a proper name: *Appalachian Mountains, Ozark Mountains, Rocky Mountains.*
Or simply: *the Appalachians, the Ozarks, the Rockies.*

Mountain Standard Time (MST), Mountain Daylight Time (MDT) See **time zones**.

Mountain States As defined by the U.S. Census Bureau, the eight are Arizona, Colorado, Idaho, Montana, Nevada, New Mexico, Utah and Wyoming.

mouse, mice Use *mice* as the plural form of hand-held computer-input devices.

moviegoer

movie ratings The ratings used by the Motion Picture Association of America are:
G — General audiences. All ages admitted.
PG — Parental guidance suggested. Some material may not be suitable for children.
PG-13 — Special *parental guidance* strongly suggested for children under 13. Some material may be inappropriate for young children.
R — Restricted. Under 17 requires accompanying parent or adult guardian.
NC-17 — No one under 17 admitted.
When the ratings are used in news stories or reviews, use these forms as appropriate: *the movie has an R rating, an R-rated movie, the movie is R-rated.*

movie studios Major U.S. studios are:
Columbia TriStar, owned by Sony Corp.
Dimension, owned by The Weinstein Co.
Disney, owned by The Walt Disney Co.
DreamWorks SKG Inc., owned by Steven Spielberg, Stacey Snider and Reliance Big Entertainment
DreamWorks Animation SKG Inc.
Focus Features, unit of Universal Pictures, part of Comcast's NBCUniversal
Twentieth Century Fox, owned by News Corp.
Fox Searchlight, owned by News Corp.
IFC Films, owned by AMC Networks Inc.
Lionsgate, owned by Lions Gate Entertainment Corp. (the brand Lionsgate is one word, the corporate name is two)
MGM Studios and United Artists, owned by Metro-Goldwyn-Mayer Inc., which is owned by a group of

former creditors including Highland Capital, Anchorage Advisors and Carl Icahn.

Miramax, owned by Filmyard Holdings LLC, whose investors include Ron Tutor, Colony Capital LLC, Tom Barrack and Qatar Holding LLC.

Newmarket Films, independent

New Line Cinema, a brand of Time Warner Inc.'s Warner Bros.

Paramount Pictures and Paramount Vantage, owned by Viacom Inc.

Pixar Animation Studios, owned by The Walt Disney Co.

Relativity Media LLC

Rogue Pictures, a unit of Relativity Media LLC

Screen Gems, owned by Sony Corp.

Sony Pictures Classics, owned by Sony Corp.

Summit Entertainment LLC, independent

THINKFilm, independent

Touchstone, owned by The Walt Disney Co.

Universal Pictures, owned by Comcast's NBCUniversal

Warner Bros., owned by Time Warner Inc.

The Weinstein Co.

movie titles See **composition titles**.

MPEG-2 An international standard for digital video compression and decompression. *MPEG* is an acronym for *Moving Picture Experts Group*.

mpg Acceptable in all references for *miles per gallon*.

mph Acceptable in all references for *miles per hour* or *miles an hour*.

MP3 A popular audio compression format on the Internet.

MRI Magnetic resonance imaging, a noninvasive diagnostic procedure used to render images of the inside of an object. It is primarily used in medical imaging to demonstrate pathological or other physiological alterations of living tissues. *MRI* is acceptable on first reference and in all uses.

Mr., Mrs. See **courtesy titles**.

MRSA Abbreviation for *methicillin-resistant Staphylococcus aureus*. *MRSA* is acceptable on first reference but include full name in story.

Ms. This is the spelling and punctuation for all uses of the courtesy title, including direct quotations.

There is no plural. If several women who prefer *Ms.* must be listed in a series, repeat *Ms.* before each name.

See **courtesy titles** for guidelines on when to use *Ms.*

Muhammad The chief prophet and central figure of the Islamic religion, *Prophet Muhammad*. Use other spellings only if preferred by a specific person for his own name or in a title or the name of an organization.

mujahedeen Lowercase when using the Arabic for *holy warriors*; uppercase if it is part of the name of a group. The Iranian opposition group is *Mujahedeen-e-Khalq*. The singular for *holy warrior* is *mujahed*.

mullah An Islamic leader or teacher, often a general title of respect for a learned man.

multi- The rules in prefixes apply, but in general, no hyphen. Some examples:

multicolored   multimillion

multilateral   multimillionaire

Mumbai India's largest city, formerly known as Bombay.

Munich The city in Germany stands alone in datelines.

municipal bond See **loan terminology**.

murder See **homicide, murder, manslaughter**.

murderer See **assassin, killer, murderer**.

Murphy's law The law is: *If something can go wrong, it will.*

music Capitalize, but do not use quotation marks, on descriptive titles for orchestral works: *Bach's Suite No. 1 for Orchestra*; *Beethoven's Serenade for Flute, Violin and Viola.* If the instrumentation is not part of the title but is added for explanatory purposes, the names of the instruments are lowercased: *Mozart's Sinfonia Concertante in E flat major* (the common title) *for violin and viola.* If in doubt, lowercase the names of the instruments.

Use quotation marks for nonmusical terms in a title: *Beethoven's "Eroica" Symphony.* If the work has a special full title, all of it is quoted: *"Symphonie Fantastique," "Rhapsody in Blue."*

In subsequent references, lowercase *symphony, concerto*, etc.

See **composition titles**.

music companies Major U.S. music companies:

A&M/Octone Records, a joint venture between Octone Records and Universal Music Group, a subsidiary of Vivendi SA

Angel Records, owned by EMI Group Ltd.

Astralwerks, owned by EMI Group Ltd.

Atlantic Records Group, which includes Atlantic Records, Atlantic Nashville, Elektra and Roadrunner Records, owned by Warner Music Group Corp.

Bad Boy Records, owned by Bad Boy Worldwide Entertainment Group, a private company founded by Sean "Diddy" Combs and half-owned by Warner Music Group Corp.

Blue Note, owned by EMI Group Ltd.

BNA Records, owned by Sony Music Entertainment Inc., a Sony Corp. subsidiary

Capitol, Capitol Latin and Capitol Nashville, owned by EMI Group Ltd.

Columbia Records and Columbia Nashville, owned by Sony Music Entertainment Inc., a Sony Corp. subsidiary

Decca Music Group, which includes Decca Records and Decca Broadway. A unit of Universal Music Group, a subsidiary of Vivendi SA, a French media and telecommunications company

EMI, EMI Classics, EMI CMG, and EMI Televisa Music, owned by EMI Group Ltd.

Epic Records, owned by Sony Music Entertainment Inc., a Sony Corp. subsidiary

Interscope Geffen A&M, which includes Interscope Records, Geffen Records and A&M Records. Owned by Universal Music Group, a subsidiary of Vivendi SA

Island Def Jam Music Group, which includes Island Records, Def Jam Records and Mercury Records. A unit of Universal Music Group, a subsidiary of Vivendi SA

LaFace Records, owned by Sony Music Entertainment Inc., a Sony Corp. subsidiary

Legacy Records, owned by Sony Music Entertainment Inc., a Sony Corp. subsidiary

Lost Highway Records, owned by Universal Music Group, a subsidiary of Vivendi SA

Machete Music, owned by Universal Music Group, a subsidiary of Vivendi SA

Manhattan Records, owned by EMI Group Ltd.

Maverick Records, owned by Warner Music Group Corp.

Mercury Records, owned by Universal Music Group, a subsidiary of Vivendi SA

Motown Records, including Universal Motown and Classic Motown, owned by Universal Music Group, a subsidiary of Vivendi SA

Mute Records, owned by EMI Group Ltd.

Nonesuch Records, owned by Warner Music Group Corp.

Parlophone, owned by EMI Group Ltd.

Provident Label Group, owned by Sony Music Entertainment Inc., a Sony Corp. subsidiary

RCA Records and RCA Records Label Nashville, owned by Sony Music Entertainment Inc., a Sony Corp. subsidiary

Reprise Records, owned by Warner Music Group Corp.

Rhino Entertainment, which includes Rhino Records, owned by Warner Music Group Corp.

Roc Nation, a joint venture between rapper Jay-Z and Live Nation Entertainment Inc.

Show Dog/Universal Music, owned by Universal Music Group, a subsidiary of Vivendi SA

Sire Records, owned by Warner Music Group Corp.

Sony Masterworks, owned by Sony Music Entertainment Inc., a Sony Corp. subsidiary

Sony Music Latin, owned by Sony Music Entertainment Inc., a Sony Corp. subsidiary

UMG Nashville, which includes MCA Nashville Records, Mercury

Nashville Records and Lost Highway Records, owned by Universal Music Group, a subsidiary of Vivendi SA

Uni Records, owned by Universal Music Group, a subsidiary of Vivendi SA

Universal Motown Records Group, which includes Universal Motown Records and Universal Republic Records. Owned by Universal Music Group, a subsidiary of Vivendi SA

Universal Music Classical, owned by Universal Music Group, a subsidiary of Vivendi SA

Universal Music Enterprises, which includes UMe Records and Verve Records. Owned by Universal Music Group, a subsidiary of Vivendi SA

Universal Music Latin Entertainment, owned by Universal Music Group, a subsidiary of Vivendi SA

Universal Republic Records, owned by Universal Music Group, a subsidiary of Vivendi SA

Verity Gospel Music Group, owned by Sony Music Entertainment Inc., a Sony Corp. subsidiary

Virgin, owned by EMI Group Ltd.

Warner Bros. Records, owned by Warner Music Group Corp.

Warner Nashville, owned by Warner Music Group Corp.

musket See **weapons**.

Muslims The preferred term to describe adherents of Islam.

A *Black Muslim* is a member of a predominantly black Islamic sect in the United States. However, the term is considered derogatory by members of the sect, who call themselves *Muslims*.

Muzak A trademark for a type of recorded background music.

Myanmar Use this name for the country and the language. Use

Myanmar people or *Myanmar* for the inhabitants. (Formerly Burma.)

myriad (adj.) Note word is not followed by *of*: *The myriad books in the library.*

N

n. See **nouns**.

naive

names In general, use only last names on second reference, unless an individual requests otherwise. See **Arabic names**, **Chinese names**, **Korean names**, **Russian names** and **Spanish names**.

When it is necessary to distinguish between two people who use the same last name, as in married couples or brothers and sisters, use the first and last name. See **courtesy titles**.

In stories involving juveniles, generally refer to them on second reference by surname if they are 16 or older and by first name if they are 15 or younger. Exceptions would be if they are involved in serious crimes or are athletes or entertainers.

nano- A prefix denoting one-billionth of a unit. Move the decimal point nine places to the left in converting to the basic unit: 2,999,888,777.5 nanoseconds equals 2.9998887775 seconds.

naphtha

narrow-minded

Nasdaq The nation's largest all-electronic stock market. Formerly an acronym, it is now a proper name. Parent company is Nasdaq Stock Market Inc.

national See **citizen, resident, subject, national, native**.

National Aeronautics and Space Administration *NASA* is acceptable in all references.

national anthem Lowercase. But: *"The Star-Spangled Banner."*

National Association for the Advancement of Colored People *NAACP* is acceptable on first reference to avoid a cumbersome lead, but provide the full name in the body of the story.

Headquarters is in Baltimore.

National Association of Letter Carriers The shortened form *Letter Carriers union* is acceptable in all references.

Headquarters is in Washington.

National Baptist Convention of America See **Baptist churches**.

National Baptist Convention U.S.A. Inc. See **Baptist churches**.

National Broadcasting Co. See **NBC**.

national chairman Capitalize when used before the name of the individual who heads a political party: *Democratic National Chairman Tim Kaine.*

National Council of the

Churches of Christ in the U.S.A.

This interdenominational, cooperative body includes most major Protestant and Eastern Orthodox denominations in the United States.

The shortened form *National Council of Churches* is acceptable in all references.

Headquarters is in New York. See **World Council of Churches**.

National Education Association *NEA* is acceptable on

second reference.

Headquarters is in Washington.

National FFA Organization

Formerly the Future Farmers of America. *FFA* is acceptable on second reference.

Headquarters is in Alexandria, Va.

National Governors Association Represents the

governors of the 50 states and five territories.

Its office is in Washington.

National Guard Capitalize

when referring to U.S. or state-level forces, or foreign forces when that is the formal name: *the National Guard, the Guard, the Iowa National Guard, Iowa's National Guard, National Guard troops, the Iraqi National Guard*. On second reference, *the guard*.

When referring to an individual in a National Guard unit, use National Guardsman: *He is a National Guardsman.*

Lowercase *guardsman* when it stands alone.

See **military titles**.

National Hurricane Center

See **weather terms**.

National Institutes of Health

This agency within the Department of Health and Human Services is the principal biomedical research arm of the federal government.

Its institutes are: National Cancer Institute; National Eye Institute; National Heart, Lung and Blood Institute; National Human Genome Research Institute; National Institute on Aging; National Institute on Alcohol Abuse and Alcoholism; National Institute of Allergy and Infectious Diseases; National Institute of Arthritis and Musculoskeletal and Skin Diseases; National Institute of Biomedical Imaging and Bioengineering; National Institute of Child Health and Human Development; National Institute on Drug Abuse; National Institute on Deafness and Other Communication Disorders; National Institute of Diabetes and Digestive and Kidney Diseases; National Institute of Dental and Craniofacial Research; National Institute of Environmental Health Sciences; National Institute of General Medical Sciences; National Institute of Mental Health; National Institute of Neurological Disorders and Stroke; and National Institute of Nursing Research; and National Library of Medicine.

Its centers are: Center for Information Technology; Center for Scientific Review; John E. Fogarty International Center; National Center for Complementary and Alternative Medicine; National Center on Minority Health and Health Disparities; National Center for Research Resources; and NIH Clinical Center.

All the agencies are in Bethesda, Md., except the National Institute of Environmental Health Sciences, which is in Research Triangle Park, N.C.

nationalist Lowercase when referring to a partisan of a country. Capitalize only when referring to alignment with a political party for

which this is the proper name.
See **political parties and philosophies**.

Nationalist China See **China**.

nationalities and races Capitalize the proper names of nationalities, peoples, races, tribes, etc.: *Arab, Arabic, African, American, Caucasian, Cherokee, Chinese* (both singular and plural), *Eskimo* (plural *Eskimos*), *French Canadian, Japanese* (singular and plural), *Jew, Jewish, Nordic, Sioux, Swede*, etc.

See **race** for guidelines on when racial identification is pertinent in a story.

Use derogatory terms only in direct quotes when essential to the story and flag the contents in an editor's note.

National Labor Relations Board *NLRB* is acceptable on second reference.

National League of Cities Its
members are the governments of cities with 30,000 or more residents, and some state and municipal leagues.

It is separate from the U.S. Conference of Mayors, whose membership is limited to mayors of cities with 30,000 or more residents. The organizations often engage in joint projects, however.

The office is in Washington.

National Newspaper Association A newspaper association representing community newspapers, their owners, publishers and editors. *NNA* is acceptable on second reference.

Headquarters is at the Missouri School of Journalism, Columbia, Mo.

National Organization for Women Not *of*. *NOW* is acceptable on second reference.

Headquarters is in Washington.

National Park Service A bureau of the Interior Department, it manages the 391 units of the National Park System, which includes 58 national parks as well as monuments, battlefields, historic sites and seashores, and the White House. It was created in 1916, although the first national park, Yellowstone, was established much earlier in 1872. The National Park Service also helps administer dozens of affiliated sites, the National Register of Historic Places, National Heritage Areas, National Wild and Scenic Rivers, National Historic Landmarks, and National Trails. On second reference, *Park Service*.

National Rifle Association
NRA is acceptable on second reference.

Headquarters is in Washington.

National Weather Service *The weather service* (lowercase) may be used in any reference.
See **weather terms**.

Nation of Islam The nationalist religious movement traces its origins in 1930 to W.D. Fard, also known as Wali Fard, who called for racial separation. Elijah Muhammad took over the leadership in 1934, holding the post until his death in 1975. A son, Warith (Wallace) Dean Muhammad, succeeded to the leadership and pointed the movement toward integration and traditional Islam. Louis Farrakhan led a militant faction into a separatist movement in 1976.

The Nation of Islam does not release membership figures.

Use the title *minister* on first reference to clergymen: *Minister Louis Farrakhan*.

nationwide

native See **citizen, resident, subject, national, native**.

Native American Acceptable for those in the U.S. Follow the person's preference. Where possible, be precise and use the name of the tribe: He is a *Navajo* commissioner. In stories about American Indians, such words or terms as *wampum*, *warpath*, *powwow*, *teepee*, *brave*, *squaw*, etc., can be disparaging and offensive. See **Indians**, **nationalities and races**, and **race**.

Nativity scene Only the first word is capitalized.

NATO Acceptable in all references for the *North Atlantic Treaty Organization*.

Naugahyde A trademark for a brand of simulated leather.

nautical mile It equals 1 minute of arc of a great circle of the Earth or 6,076.11549 feet, or 1,852 meters. To convert to approximate statute miles (5,280 feet), multiply the number of nautical miles by 1.15.
See **knot**.

naval, navel Use *naval* in copy pertaining to a navy.
A *navel* is a bellybutton.
A *navel orange* is a seedless orange, so named because it has a small depression, like a navel.

naval station Capitalize only as part of a proper name: *Norfolk Naval Station*.

navy Capitalize when referring to U.S. forces: *the U.S. Navy, the Navy, Navy policy*. Do not use the abbreviation *USN*.
Lowercase when referring to the naval forces of other nations: *the British navy*.
This approach has been adopted for consistency, because many foreign nations do not use *navy* as the proper name.
See **military academies** and **military titles**.

Nazi, Nazism Derived from the German for the National Socialist German Workers' Party, the fascist political party founded in 1919 and abolished in 1945. Under Adolf Hitler, it seized control of Germany in 1933.
See **political parties and philosophies**.

NBC Acceptable in all references to the *National Broadcasting Co.* NBC is part of NBCUniversal, which is controlled by Comcast Corp. Under a deal completed in January 2011, Comcast owns 51 percent while General Electric Co. owns the rest after selling a majority stake in the venture.

NCR Corp. Formerly National Cash Register Co.
Headquarters is in Dayton, Ohio.

nearsighted When used in a medical sense, it means an individual can see well at close range but has difficulty seeing objects at a distance.

Nebraska Abbreviate *Neb.* in datelines or stories. Postal code: *NE*
See **state names**.

negligee

neither...nor See **either...or, neither...nor**.

Nestle Headquarters is in Vevey, Switzerland.

Netherlands In datelines, give

the name of the community followed by *Netherlands*:

MAASTRICHT, *Netherlands* (AP)
—

In stories: *the Netherlands* or *Netherlands* as the construction of a sentence dictates.

Netherlands Antilles In datelines, give the name of the community followed by *Netherlands Antilles*. Do not abbreviate.

Identify an individual island, if needed, in the text.

net income, net profit See **profit terminology**.

Nevada Abbreviate *Nev.* in datelines or stories. Postal code: *NV*
See **state names**.

never-ending

New Brunswick One of the three Maritime Provinces of Canada. Do not abbreviate.
See **datelines**.

New Delhi The city in India stands alone in datelines.

New England Connecticut, Maine, Massachusetts, New Hampshire, Rhode Island and Vermont.

Newfoundland This Canadian province, officially renamed Newfoundland and Labrador in 2001, comprises the island of Newfoundland and the mainland section of Labrador. Do not abbreviate.

In datelines, use Newfoundland after the names of all cities and towns. Specify in the text whether the community is on the island or in Labrador.
See **datelines**.

New Hampshire Abbreviate *N.H.* in datelines or stories. Postal code: *NH*

See **state names**.

New Jersey Abbreviate *N.J.* in datelines or stories. Postal code: *NJ*
See **state names**.

New Mexico Abbreviate *N.M.* in datelines or stories. Postal code: *NM*
See **state names**.

New Orleans The city in Louisiana stands alone in datelines.

News Corp. Global media conglomerate controlled by Rupert Murdoch and based in New York. Units include *Twentieth Century Fox*; the *Fox* broadcast network; a group of television stations; a cable networks group that includes *Fox News Channel*, *FX* and several sports channels; satellite TV broadcasters including *Sky Italia* and a significant stake in *BSkyB*; newspapers in the United Kingdom and Australia and the *New York Post* and *Dow Jones & Co.*, publisher of *The Wall Street Journal*, in the United States; magazines and the book publisher *HarperCollins*.

Newspaper Association of America Formerly the American Newspaper Publishers Association. *NAA* is acceptable in second reference. Also *the newspaper association*, *the association*.

Headquarters is in Vienna, Va.

Newspaper Guild-Communications Workers of America, The Formerly the American Newspaper Guild, it is a union for newspaper and news service employees, generally those in the news and business departments.

On second reference: *the Guild*. Headquarters is in Washington.

The News Media Guild, formerly the Wire Service Guild, is the local representing employees of The Associated Press.

newspaper names Capitalize *the* in a newspaper's name if that is the way the publication prefers to be known. Do not place name in quotes.

Lowercase *the* before newspaper names if a story mentions several papers, some of which use *the* as part of the name and some of which do not.

Where location is needed but is not part of the official name, use parentheses: *The Huntsville (Ala.) Times.*

Consult the International Newspaper Data Book published by Editor & Publisher to determine whether a two-name combination is hyphenated.

newspapers The 20 largest U.S. newspapers by circulation, with owners, according to the Audit Bureau of Circulations:

The Wall Street Journal, Dow Jones & Co., part of News Corp.

USA Today, Gannett Co.

The New York Times, The New York Times Co.

Daily News, New York, real estate billionaire Mortimer B. Zuckerman

Los Angeles Times, Tribune Co.

San Jose (Calif.) Mercury News, MediaNews Group Inc.

New York Post, News Corp.

The Washington Post, The Washington Post Co.

Chicago Tribune, Tribune Co.

The Dallas Morning News, A.H. Belo Corp.

Newsday, Long Island, N.Y., Cablevision Systems Corp.

Chicago Sun-Times, Sun-Times Media LLC.

Houston Chronicle, Hearst Corp.

The Denver Post, MediaNews Group Inc.

The Philadelphia Inquirer, Philadelphia Media Network Inc.

Star Tribune, Minneapolis, Star Tribune Media Co. LLC

The Arizona Republic, Gannett Co.

The Orange County (Calif.) Register, Freedom Communications Inc.

The Plain Dealer, Cleveland, Advance Publications Inc.

The Seattle Times, Blethen Corp.

newsstand

New Testament See **Bible**.

New World The Western Hemisphere.

New Year's, New Year's Day, New Year's Eve But: *What will the new year bring?*

The federal legal holiday is observed on Friday if Jan. 1 falls on a Saturday, on Monday if it falls on a Sunday.

New York Abbreviate *N.Y.* in datelines or stories. Postal code: *NY*

Use *New York state* when a distinction must be made between state and city. See **state names**.

New York City Use *NEW YORK* in datelines, not the name of an individual community or borough such as *Flushing* or *Queens.*

Identify the borough in the body of the story if pertinent.

New York Stock Exchange *NYSE* is acceptable on second reference as an adjective for the stock exchange or the exchange for other references. Its parent company is NYSE Euronext Inc., which was formed in 2007 by the takeover by NYSE Group Inc. of Euronext NV, a Paris-based exchange operator with operations in several European countries. Its shares are publicly traded. Headquarters is in New York.

The New York Times Co.
Owner of The New York Times, The Boston Globe, the International Herald Tribune and other daily newspapers. Also owns About.com website. Headquarters is in New York.

NGO *Nongovernmental organization.* Usually refers to a nonprofit, humanitarian organization. Use *NGO* sparingly and only on second reference.

nicknames A nickname should be used in place of a person's given name in news stories only when it is the way the individual prefers to be known: *Jimmy Carter.*

When a nickname is inserted into the identification of an individual, use quotation marks: *Sen. Henry M. "Scoop" Jackson.* Also: *Jackson is known as "Scoop."*

In sports stories and sports columns, commonly used nicknames may be substituted for a first name without the use of quotation marks: *Babe Ruth, Dizzy Dean, Boomer Esiason, Tubby Smith, Tiger Woods, Magic Johnson,* etc. But in sports stories where the given name is used, and in all news stories: *Paul "Bear" Bryant.*

Capitalize without quotation marks such terms as *Sunshine State, the Old Dominion, Motown, the Magic City, Old Hickory, Old Glory, Galloping Ghost.*

See **names**.

nightclub

nighttime

9/11 Acceptable in all references to describe the attacks in the United States on Sept. 11, 2001.

911 Acceptable for the U.S. emergency call number.

niqab The veil worn by the most conservative Muslim women, in which, at most, only the eyes show.

nitpicking

nitty-gritty

No. Use as the abbreviation for *number* in conjunction with a figure to indicate position or rank: *No. 1 man, No. 3 choice.*

Do not use in street addresses, with this exception: *No. 10 Downing St.,* the residence of Britain's prime minister.

Do not use in the names of schools: *Public School 19.*

Nobel Prize, Nobel Prizes
The five established under terms of the will of Alfred Nobel are: Nobel Peace Prize, Nobel Prize in chemistry, Nobel Prize in literature, Nobel Prize in physics, Nobel Prize in physiology or medicine. (Note the capitalization styles.)

The Nobel Memorial Prize in Economic Sciences (officially it is the cumbersome Bank of Sweden Prize in Economic Sciences in Memory of Alfred Nobel) is not a Nobel Prize in the same sense. The Central Bank of Sweden established it in 1968 as a memorial to Alfred Nobel. References to this prize should include the word *Memorial* to help make this distinction. Explain the status of the prize in the story when appropriate.

Nobel Prize award ceremonies are held on Dec. 10, the anniversary of Alfred Nobel's death in 1896. The award ceremony for peace is in Oslo and the other ceremonies are in Stockholm.

Capitalize *prize* in references that do not mention the category: *He is a Nobel Prize winner. She is a Nobel Prize-winning scientist.*

Lowercase *prize* when not linked with the word *Nobel: The peace prize was awarded Monday.*

nobility References to members of the nobility in nations that have a system of rank present special problems because nobles frequently are known by their titles rather than their given or family names. Their titles, in effect, become their names.

The guidelines here relate to Britain's nobility. Adapt them as appropriate to members of nobility in other nations.

Orders of rank among British nobility begin with the royal family. The term *royalty* is reserved for the families of living and deceased sovereigns.

Next, in descending order, are dukes, marquesses (also called marquises), earls, viscounts and barons. There are also life peers who are appointed to serve in the House of Lords and hold their titles only for their own lifetimes. On first reference to a life peer, use the person's ordinary name, e.g., *Margaret Thatcher* or *Jeffrey Archer*. Elsewhere, if relevant, explain that the person has been appointed to the House of Lords.

Occasionally the sovereign raises an individual to the nobility and makes the title inheritable by the person's heirs, but the practice is increasingly rare.

Sovereigns also confer honorary titles, which do not make an individual a member of the nobility. The principal designations, in descending order, are baronet and knight.

In general, the guidelines in **courtesy titles** and **titles** apply. However, honorary titles and titles of nobility are capitalized when they serve as an alternate name.

Some guidelines and examples:

ROYALTY: Capitalize *king, queen, prince* and *princess* when they are used directly before one or more names; lowercase when they stand alone:

Queen Elizabeth II, Queen Eliza-

beth II of the United Kingdom of Great Britain and Northern Ireland, the queen. Kings George and Edward. Queen Mother Elizabeth, the queen mother.

Also capitalize a longer form of the sovereign's title when its use is appropriate in a story or it is being quoted: *Her Majesty Queen Elizabeth.*

Use *Prince* or *Princess* before the names of a sovereign's children: *Princess Anne, the princess*; *Prince Charles.*

In references to the queen's husband first reference should be Prince Philip (not Duke of Edinburgh, commonly used in Britain).

The male heir to the throne normally is designated *Prince of Wales*, and the title becomes, in common usage, an alternate name. Capitalize when used: *The queen invested her eldest son as Prince of Wales. Prince Charles is now the Prince of Wales. The prince is married. His wife, Camilla, is called the Duchess of Cornwall.*

Prince Charles' eldest son is Prince William. Prince William's wife, the former Kate Middleton, is the Duchess of Cambridge.

DUKE: The full title — *Duke of Wellington*, for example — is an alternate name, capitalized in all uses. Lowercase duke when it stands alone.

The designation *Arthur, Duke of Wellington*, is appropriate in some cases, but never *Duke Arthur* or *Lord Arthur.*

The wife of a duke is a *duchess*: *the Duchess of Wellington, the duchess*, but never *Duchess Diana* or *Lady Diana.*

A duke normally also has a lesser title. It is commonly used for his eldest son if he has one. Use the courtesy titles *Lord* or *Lady* before the first names of a duke's children.

Some examples:

Lady Jane Wellesley, only daughter of the eighth Duke of Wellington, has been linked romantically with Prince Charles, heir to the British throne. The eldest of Lady Jane's four brothers is Arthur Charles, the Marquess Douro. The Wellingtons, whose family name is Wellesley, are not of royal blood. However, they rank among the nation's most famous aristocrats thanks to the first duke, the victor at Waterloo.

MARQUESS, MARQUIS, EARL, VISCOUNT, BARON: The full titles serve as alternate names and should be capitalized. Frequently, however, the holder of such a title is identified as a lord: *The Marquess of Bath*, for example, more commonly is known as *Lord Bath*.

Use *Lady* before the name of a woman married to a man who holds one of these titles. The wife of a marquess is a marchioness, the wife of a marquis is a marquise, the wife of an earl is a countess (earl is the British equivalent of count), the wife of a viscount is a viscountess, the wife of a baron is a baroness.

Use *Lord* or *Lady* before the first names of the children of a marquess.

Use *Lady* before the first name of an earl's daughter. *The Honorable* often appears before the names of sons of earls, viscounts and barons who do not have titles. Their names should stand alone in news stories, however.

The Honorable also appears frequently before the names of unmarried daughters of viscounts and barons. In news stories, however, use a full name on first reference.

Some examples:

Queen Elizabeth gave her sister's husband, Antony Armstrong-Jones, the title Earl of Snowdon. Their son, David, is the Viscount Linley. They also have a daughter, Lady Sarah Armstrong-Jones. Lord Snowdon, a photographer, was known as Antony Armstrong-Jones before he received his title.

BARONET, KNIGHT: *Sir John*

Smith on first reference and *Smith* on second.

Do not use both an honorary title and a title of military rank or authority, such as *prime minister*, before a name.

Use *Lady* before the name of the wife of a baronet or knight.

For a woman who has received an honor in her own right, use *Dame* before her name: *Dame Margot Fonteyn* on first reference, *Fonteyn* on second.

nobody

noisome, noisy *Noisome* means offensive, noxious.

Noisy means clamorous.

Nokia Corp. Headquarters is in Espoo, Finland.

nolo contendere The literal meaning is, "I do not wish to contend." Terms such as *no contest* or *no-contest plea* are acceptable in all references.

When a defendant in a criminal case enters this plea, it means that he is not admitting guilt but is stating that he will offer no defense. The person is then subject to being judged guilty and punished as if he had pleaded guilty or had been convicted. The principal difference is that the defendant retains the option of denying the same charge in another legal proceeding.

no man's land

non- The rules of **prefixes** apply, but in general no hyphen when forming a compound that does not have special meaning and can be understood if *not* is used before the base word. Use a hyphen, however, before proper nouns or in awkward combinations, such as *non-nuclear*.

nonaligned nations A political

rather than economic or geographic term used primarily during the Cold War. Although nonaligned nations do not belong to Western or Eastern military alliances or blocs, they profess not to be neutral, like Switzerland, but activist alternatives.

Do not confuse *nonaligned* with *Third World*, although some Third World nations may belong to the nonaligned group.

See **Third World**.

noncombat, noncombatant

none It usually means no single one. When used in this sense, it always takes singular verbs and pronouns: *None of the seats was in its right place.*

Use a plural verb only if the sense is no two or no amount: *None of the consultants agree on the same approach. None of the taxes have been paid.*

nonprofit

nonrestrictive clauses See **essential clauses, nonessential clauses**.

non-U.S. governmental bodies Capitalize the names of the specific governmental agencies and departments, either with the name of the nation or without it if clear in the context: *French Foreign Ministry, the Foreign Ministry.*

Lowercase *the ministry* or a similar term when standing alone.

non-U.S. legislative bodies In general, capitalize the proper name of a specific legislative body abroad: *the Knesset, the Diet.*

The most frequent names in use are *Congress, National Assembly* and *Parliament.*

GENERIC USES: Lowercase *parliament* or a similar term only when used generically to describe a body for which the formal name is being

given: *the Diet, Japan's parliament.*

PLURALS: Lowercase *parliament* and similar terms in plural constructions: *the parliaments of England and France, the English and French parliaments.*

INDIVIDUAL HOUSES: The principle applies also to individual houses of the nation's legislature, just as *Senate* and *House* are capitalized in the United States:

ROME (AP) — New leaders have taken control in the Chamber of Deputies.

Lowercase *assembly* when used as a shortened reference to national assembly.

In many countries, *national assembly* is the name of a unicameral legislative body. In some, such as France, it is the name for the lower house of a legislative body known by some other name such as *parliament.*

noon Do not put a 12 in front of it.

See **midnight** and **times**.

no one

Norfolk Southern Corp.
Freight railroad, with headquarters in Norfolk, Va.

norm See **average, mean, median, norm**.

North America See **Western Hemisphere**.

North Atlantic Treaty Organization *NATO* is acceptable in all references.

North Carolina Abbreviate *N.C.* in datelines or stories. Postal code: NC
See **state names**.

North Dakota Abbreviate *N.D.* in datelines or stories. Postal code: ND

See **state names**.

Northeast region As defined by the U.S. Census Bureau, the nine-state region is broken into two divisions — the *New England* states and the *Middle Atlantic* states.

Connecticut, Maine, Massachusetts, New Hampshire, Rhode Island and Vermont are the *New England* states.

New Jersey, New York and Pennsylvania are classified as the *Middle Atlantic* states.

See **Midwest region; South**; and **West** for the bureau's other regional breakdowns.

Northern Ireland Use *Northern Ireland* after the names of all communities in datelines.

See **datelines** and **United Kingdom**.

north, northern, northeast, northwest See **directions and regions**.

Northrop Grumman Corp. Headquarters is in Los Angeles.

North Slope The portion of Alaska north of Brooks Range, a string of mountains extending across the northern part of the state.

North Warning System A system of long-range radar stations along the 70th parallel in North America. Previous system, known as the Distant Early Warning (DEW) line, was deactivated in 1985.

Northwest Territories A territorial section of Canada. Do not abbreviate. Use in datelines after the names of all cities and towns in the territory.

See **Canada**.

note For use in a financial sense,

see **loan terminology**.

nouns The abbreviation *n.* is used in this book to identify the spelling of the noun forms of words frequently misspelled.

Novartis AG Headquarters is in Basel, Switzerland.

Nova Scotia One of the three Maritime Provinces of Canada. Do not abbreviate.

See **datelines**.

Novocain A trademark for a drug used as a local anesthetic.

nowadays

NPR Acceptable in all references to National Public Radio. Producer and distributor of noncommercial news, talk and entertainment programming. Headquarters is in Washington, D.C.

Nuclear Non-Proliferation Treaty Global agreement intended to limit the spread of nuclear weapons. It provides civilian nuclear trade in exchange for a pledge from nations not to pursue nuclear weapons.

Nuclear Regulatory Commission This commission has taken over the regulatory functions previously performed by the Atomic Energy Commission.

NRC is acceptable on second reference, but *the agency* or *the commission* is preferred.

nuclear terminology In reporting on nuclear energy, include the definitions of appropriate terms, especially those related to radiation.

core The part of a nuclear reactor that contains its fissionable fuel. In a reactor core, atoms of fuel, such as uranium, are split. This releases energy in the form of heat which, in turn, is used to boil water for steam. The steam powers a turbine, and the turbine drives a generator to produce electricity.

fission The splitting of the nucleus of an atom, releasing energy.

meltdown The worst possible nuclear accident in which the reactor core overheats to such a degree that the fuel melts. If the fuel penetrates its protective housing, radioactive materials will be released into the environment.

rad The standard unit of measurement for absorbed radiation. A *millirad* is a thousandth of a rad. There is considerable debate among scientists whether there is any safe level of absorption.

radiation Invisible particles or waves given off by radioactive material, such as uranium. Radiation can damage or kill body cells, resulting in latent cancers, genetic damage or death.

rem The standard unit of measurement of absorbed radiation in living tissue, adjusted for different kinds of radiation so that 1 rem of any radiation will produce the same biological effect. A millirem is a thousandth of a rem.

A diagnostic chest X-ray involves less than 10 millirems of radiation. Each American, on average, receives 360 millirems of radiation a year from natural "background" sources, such as cosmic rays, and man-made sources, such as diagnostic X-rays. There is considerable debate among scientists over the safety of repeated low doses of radiation.

roentgen The standard measure of X-ray exposure.

uranium A metallic, radioactive element used as fuel in nuclear reactors.

numerals A numeral is a figure, letter, word or group of words expressing a number.

Roman numerals use the letters *I, V, X, L, C, D* and *M*. Use Roman numerals for wars and to show personal sequence for animals and people: *World War II, Native Dancer II, King George VI, Pope John XXIII*. See **Roman numerals**.

Arabic numerals use the figures *1, 2, 3, 4, 5, 6, 7, 8, 9* and *0*. Use Arabic forms unless Roman numerals are specifically required. See **Arabic numerals**.

The figures *1, 2, 10, 101*, etc. and the corresponding words — *one, two, ten, one hundred one*, etc. — are called *cardinal numbers*. The term *ordinal number* applies to *1st, 2nd, 10th, 101st, first, second, tenth, one hundred first*, etc.

Follow these guidelines in using numerals:

SENTENCE START: Spell out a numeral at the beginning of a sentence. If necessary, recast the sentence. There is one exception — a numeral that identifies a calendar year.

Wrong: *993 freshmen entered the college last year.*

Right: *Last year 993 freshmen entered the college.*

Right: *1976 was a very good year.*

CASUAL USES: Spell out casual expressions:

A thousand times no! Thanks a million. He walked a quarter of a mile.

PROPER NAMES: Use words or numerals according to an organization's practice: *3M, Twentieth Century Fund, Big Ten*.

FRACTIONS: See the **fractions** entry.

DECIMALS: See the **decimal units** entry.

FIGURES OR WORDS?

For ordinals:

—Spell out *first* through *ninth* when they indicate sequence in time or location: *first base, the First Amendment, he was first in line.* Starting with *10th* use figures.

—Use *1st, 2nd, 3rd, 4th*, etc. when the sequence has been assigned in forming names. The principal examples are geographic, military and political designations such as *1st Ward, 7th Fleet* and *1st Sgt.* See examples in the separate entries listed below.

For cardinal numbers, consult the following separate entries:

act numbers	**latitude and longitude**
addresses	**mile**
ages	**millions, billions**
aircraft names	**monetary units**
amendments to the Constitution	**No.**
betting odds	**page numbers**
century	**parallels**
channel	**percent**
chapters	**political divisions**
congressional districts	**proportions**
course numbers	**ratios**
court decisions	**recipes**
court names	**room numbers**
dates	**route numbers**
decades	**scene numbers**
decimal units	**serial numbers**
dimensions	**sizes**
distances	**spacecraft designations**
district	
earthquakes	**speeds**
election returns	**telephone**
fleet	**temperatures**
formula	**times**
fractions	**weights**
highway designations	**years**

SOME PUNCTUATION AND USAGE EXAMPLES:

—*Act 1, Scene 2*
—*a 5-year-old girl*
—*3 ounces*
—*4-foot-long*
—*4-foot fence*
—*3-week-old war,* but *three-week war*
—*"The president's speech lasted 18 1/2 minutes,"* she said.
—*DC-10* but *747B*
—*a 5-4 court decision*
—*2nd District Court*

—*the 1980s, the '80s*
—*the House voted 230-205.* (Fewer than 1,000 votes.)
—*Jimmy Carter outpolled Gerald Ford 40,827,292 to 39,146,157.* (More than 1,000 votes.)
—*Carter outpolled Ford 10 votes to 2 votes in Little Junction.* (To avoid confusion with ratio.)
—*5 cents, $1.05, $650,000, $2.45 million*
—*No. 3 choice,* but *Public School 3*
—*0.6 percent, 1 percent, 6.5 percent*
—*a pay increase of 12-15 percent.* Or: *a pay increase of between 12 and 15 percent*
Also: *from $12 million to $14 million*
—*a ratio of 2-to-1, a 2-1 ratio*
—*1 in 4 voters*
—*a 4-3 score*
—*350-262-4600*
—*minus 10, zero, 60 degrees*

OTHER USES: For uses not covered by these listings: Spell out whole numbers below 10, use figures for 10 and above. Typical examples: *They had three sons and two daughters. They had a fleet of 10 station wagons and two buses. She ran four miles, and he walked 11.*

IN A SERIES: Apply the appropriate guidelines: *They had 10 dogs, six cats and 97 hamsters. They had four four-room houses, 10 three-room houses and 12 10-room houses.*

nuns See **sister**.

Nuremberg Use this spelling for the city in Germany, instead of Nuernberg, in keeping with widespread practice.

N-word See **obscenities, profanities, vulgarities**.

nylon Not a trademark.

oasis, oases

OB-GYN Acceptable in all references for obstetrics and gynecology, a medical specialty.

obscenities, profanities, vulgarities Do not use them in stories unless they are part of direct quotations and there is a compelling reason for them.

Try to find a way to give the reader a sense of what was said without using the specific word or phrase. If a profanity, obscenity or vulgarity must be used, flag the story at the top:
Eds: Story includes vulgarity (or graphic content, etc.)
Confine the offending language, in quotation marks, to a separate paragraph that can be deleted easily by editors who do not want to use it.

In reporting profanity that normally would use the words *damn* or *god*, lowercase *god* and use the following forms: *damn, damn it, goddamn it.* (Do not change *damn it* to *darn it.*)

If a full quote that contains an obscenity, profanity or vulgarity cannot be dropped but there is no compelling reason for the offensive language, replace the letters of the offensive word with hyphens, using only an initial letter. In some stories or scripts, it may be better to replace the offensive word with a generic descriptive in parentheses, e.g., *(vulgarity)* or *(obscenity)*.

When the subject matter of a story may be considered offensive, but the story does not contain quoted profanity, obscenities or vulgarities, flag the story at the top:
Eds: Story may be offensive to some readers.
For guidelines on racial or ethnic slurs, see **nationalities and races**.

Occupational Safety and Health Administration *OSHA* is acceptable on second reference.

occupational titles They are always lowercase. See **titles**.

occur, occurred, occurring Also: *occurrence.*

ocean The five, from the largest to the smallest: Pacific Ocean, Atlantic Ocean, Indian Ocean, Antarctic Ocean, Arctic Ocean.

Lowercase *ocean* standing alone or in plural uses: *the ocean, the Atlantic and Pacific oceans.*

oceangoing

odd- Follow with a hyphen:
odd-looking   odd-numbered
See **betting odds**.

oddsmaker

off-Broadway, off-off-Broadway See **Broadway, off-Broadway, off-off-Broadway**.

offering The issue or sale of a company stock or bond. A company usually will sell financial securities to the public to raise capital.

office Capitalize *office* when it is part of an agency's formal name: *Office of Management and Budget.*
Lowercase all other uses, including phrases such as: *the office of the attorney general, the U.S. attorney's office.*
See **Oval Office**.

officeholder

Office of Thrift Supervision U.S. Treasury Department bureau that regulates the nation's savings and loan industry. *OTS* is acceptable on second reference.

offline No hyphen is an exception to Webster's New World College Dictionary.

off of The *of* is unnecessary: *He fell off the bed.* Not: *He fell off of the bed.*

off-, -off Follow Webster's New World College Dictionary. Hyphenate if not listed there.
Some commonly used combinations with a hyphen:

off-color	off-white
off-peak	send-off

Some combinations without a hyphen:

cutoff	offside
liftoff	offstage
offhand	playoff
offset	standoff
offshore	takeoff

off-site Hyphenated. Also: *on-site.*

offstage

Ohio Do not abbreviate in datelines or stories. Postal code: *OH*
See **state names**.

oil In shipping, oil and oil products normally are measured by the ton. For news stories, convert these tonnage figures to gallons.
There are 42 gallons to each barrel of oil. The number of barrels per ton varies, depending on the type of oil product.

OIL EQUIVALENCY TABLE

Type of Product	Barrels Per Short Ton (2,000 lbs.)	Barrels Per Metric Ton (2,204.6 lbs.)	Barrels Per Long Ton (2,240 lbs.)
crude oil, foreign	6.349	6.998	7.111
crude oil, domestic	6.770	7.463	7.582
gasoline and naphtha	7.721	8.511	8.648
kerosene	7.053	7.775	7.900
distillate fuel oil	6.580	7.253	7.369
residual fuel oil	6.041	6.660	6.766
lubricating oil	6.349	6.998	7.111
lubricating grease	6.665	7.346	7.464
wax	7.134	7.864	7.990
asphalt	5.540	6.106	6.205
coke	4.990	5.500	5.589
road oil	5.900	6.503	6.608
jelly and petrolatum	6.665	7.346	7.464
liquefied pet. gas	10.526	11.603	11.789
Gilsonite	5.515	6.080	6.177

To convert tonnage to gallons:
—Determine the type of oil.
—Consult the table below to find out how many barrels per ton for that type of oil.

Multiply the number of tons by the number of barrels per ton. The result is the number of barrels in the shipment.
—Multiply the number of barrels by 42. The result is the number of gallons.

EXAMPLE: A tanker spills 20,000 metric tons of foreign crude petroleum. The table shows 6.998 barrels of foreign crude petroleum per metric ton. Multiply 6.998 x 20,000 equals 139,960 barrels. Multiply 139,960 x 42 is 5,878,320 gallons.

TABLE: The table on the previous page is based on figures supplied by the American Petroleum Institute.

oil companies Here are 10 major global oil companies, with their headquarters:
Exxon Mobil Corp., Irving, Texas
PetroChina Co. Ltd., Beijing
Royal Dutch Shell PLC, The Hague, Netherlands
Chevron Corp., San Ramon, Calif.
Petroleo Brasileiro SA, Rio de Janeiro
Gazprom OAO, Moscow
BP PLC, London
Total SA, Courbevoie, France
China Petroleum & Chemical Corp., Beijing
Eni S.p.A., Rome

OK, OK'd, OK'ing, OKs Do not use *okay*.

Oklahoma Abbreviate *Okla.* in datelines or stories. Postal code: *OK* See **state names**.

Oklahoma City The city in

Oklahoma stands alone in datelines.

Old City of Jerusalem The walled part of the city.

Old South The South before the Civil War.

Old Testament See **Bible**.

old-time, old-timer, old times

Old West The American West as it was being settled in the 19th century.

Old World The Eastern Hemisphere: Asia, Europe, Africa. The term also may be an allusion to European culture and customs.

Olympic Airways Headquarters is in Athens, Greece.

Olympics Capitalize all references to the international athletic contests: *the Olympics, the Winter Olympics, the Olympic Games, an Olympic-size pool,* but lowercase *the games* when used alone.
An Olympic-size pool is 50 meters long by 25 meters wide.

on Do not use *on* before a date or day of the week when its absence would not lead to confusion, except at the beginning of a sentence: *The meeting will be held Monday. He will be inaugurated Jan. 20. On Sept. 3, the committee will meet to discuss the issue.*
Use *on* to avoid an awkward juxtaposition of a date and a proper name: *John met Mary on Monday. He told Reagan on Thursday that the bill was doomed.*
Use *on* also to avoid any suggestion that a date is the object of a transitive verb: *The House killed on Tuesday a bid to raise taxes. The Senate postponed on Wednesday its consideration of a bill to reduce import duties.*

one- Hyphenate when used in writing fractions:

one-half   one-third

Use phrases such as *a half* or *a third* if precision is not intended.

See **fractions**.

one another See **each other, one another**.

one person, one vote The adjective form: *one-person, one-vote. He supports the principle of one person, one vote. The one-man, one-vote rule.*

Supreme Court rulings all use the phrase *one person, one vote*, not *one man, one vote.*

one-sided

onetime, one-time, one time
He is the onetime (former) heavyweight champion. She is the one-time (once) winner in 2003. He did it one time.

online One word in all cases for the computer connection term.

online trading Buying or selling financial securities and/or currencies through a brokerage's Internet-based proprietary trading platforms.

onstage

Ontario This Canadian province is the nation's first in total population and second to Quebec in area. Do not abbreviate.

See **datelines**.

OPEC Acceptable in all references for the Organization of the Petroleum Exporting Countries.

Founded in 1960, OPEC has 12 members: Algeria, Angola, Ecuador, Iran, Iraq, Kuwait, Libya, Nigeria, Qatar, Saudi Arabia, United Arab Emirates and Venezuela.

Headquarters is in Vienna, Austria.

operas See **composition titles**.

opinion polls See **polls and surveys**.

opossum The only North American marsupial. No apostrophe is needed to indicate missing letters in a phrase such as *playing possum.*

option In the financial world, it is a contract that gives an investor the right, but not the obligation, to buy (call) or sell (put) a security or other financial asset at an agreed-upon price (strike price) during a certain period of time or on a specific date (exercise date).

Oracle Corp. Headquarters is in Redwood City, Calif.

oral, verbal, written Use *oral* to refer to spoken words: *He gave an oral promise.*

Use *written* to refer to words committed to paper: *We had a written agreement.*

Use *verbal* to compare words with some other form of communication: *His tears revealed the sentiments that his poor verbal skills could not express.*

ordinal numbers See **numerals**.

Oregon Abbreviate *Ore.* in datelines or stories. Postal code: *OR*
See **state names**.

Organization of American States *OAS* is acceptable on second reference. Headquarters is in Washington.

organizations and institutions Capitalize the full names of organizations and institutions: *the American Medical Association; First Presbyterian Church; General Motors Corp.; Harvard University, Harvard*

University Medical School; the Procrastinators Club; the Society of Professional Journalists.

Retain capitalization if *Co., Corp.* or a similar word is deleted from the full proper name: *General Motors.* See company, companies; corporation; and incorporated.

SUBSIDIARIES: Capitalize the names of major subdivisions: *the Pontiac Motor Division of General Motors.*

INTERNAL ELEMENTS: Use lowercase for internal elements of an organization when they have names that are widely used generic terms: *the board of directors of General Motors, the board of trustees of Columbia University, the history department of Harvard University, the sports department of the Daily Citizen-Leader.*

Capitalize internal elements of an organization when they have names that are not widely used generic terms: *the General Assembly of the World Council of Churches, the House of Delegates of the American Medical Association, the House of Bishops and House of Deputies of the Episcopal Church.*

FLIP-FLOPPED NAMES: Retain capital letters when commonly accepted practice flops a name to delete the word of: *Harvard School of Dental Medicine, Harvard Dental School.*

Do not, however, flop formal names that are known to the public with the word of: *Massachusetts Institute of Technology,* for example, not *Massachusetts Technology Institute.*

ABBREVIATIONS AND ACRONYMS: Some organizations and institutions are widely recognized by their abbreviations: *Alcoa, GOP, NAACP, NATO.* For guidelines on when such abbreviations may be used, see the individual listings and the entries under abbreviations and acronyms and second reference.

Orient, Oriental Do not use when referring to East Asian nations and their peoples. *Asian* is the acceptable term for an inhabitant of those regions. See **nationalities and races** and **race**.

original equipment manufacturer A company that builds components or systems that are used in production of another company's systems or products. *OEM* is acceptable on second reference.

Orlon A trademark for a form of acrylic fiber similar to nylon.

orthodox Capitalize when referring to membership in or the activities of an Eastern Orthodox church. See **Eastern Orthodox Churches**.

Capitalize also in phrases such as *Orthodox Judaism* or *Orthodox Jew.* See **Jewish congregations**.

Do not describe a member of an Eastern Orthodox church as a *Protestant.* Use a phrase such as *Orthodox Christian* instead.

Lowercase *orthodox* in nonreligious uses: *an orthodox procedure.*

Orthodox Church in America See **Eastern Orthodox churches**.

Oscar, Oscars See **Academy Awards**.

Oslo The city in Norway carries the country name in datelines.

Ottawa The capital of Canada carries Ontario, the province name, in datelines.

Ouija A trademark for a board used in seances.

ounce (dry) Units of dry volume are not customarily carried to this level.

See **pint (dry)**.

ounce (liquid) See **fluid ounce**.

ounce (weight) It is defined as 437.5 grains.

The metric equivalent is approximately 28 grams.

To convert to grams, multiply by 28 (5 ounces x 28 = 140 grams).

See **grain** and **gram**.

-out Follow Webster's New World College Dictionary. Hyphenate nouns and adjectives not listed there.

Some frequently used words (all nouns):

cop-out	hide-out
fade-out	pullout
fallout	walkout
flameout	washout

Two words for verbs:

fade out	walk out
hide out	wash out
pull out	

out- Follow Webster's New World College Dictionary. Hyphenate if not listed there.

Some frequently used words:

outargue	outpost
outbox	output
outdated	outscore
outfield	outstrip
outfox	outtalk
outpatient (n., adj.)	

outbreak For disease references, reserve for larger numbers of an illness, not a few cases.

Outer Banks The sandy islands along the North Carolina coast.

out of bounds But as a modifier: *out-of-bounds. The ball went out of bounds. He took an out-of-bounds pass.*

out of court, out-of-court *They settled out of court. He accepted an out-of-court settlement.*

outperform

outsourcing A business practice used by companies to reduce costs by transferring work previously performed in-house to outside suppliers.

outstanding shares Stock held by shareholders of a company.

Oval Office The White House office of the president.

-over Follow Webster's New World College Dictionary. Hyphenate if not listed there.

Some frequently used words (all are nouns, some also are used as adjectives):

carry-over	stopover
holdover	walkover
takeover	

Use two words when any of these occurs as a verb.

See **suffixes**.

over It generally refers to spatial relationships: *The plane flew over the city.*

More than is preferred with numerals: *Their salaries went up more than $20 a week.*

over- Follow Webster's New World College Dictionary. A hyphen seldom is used. Some frequently used words:

overbuy	overrate
overexert	override

See the **overall** entry.

overall A single word in adjectival and adverbial use: *Overall, the Democrats succeeded. Overall policy.*

The word for the garment is *overalls.*

over-the-counter stock A stock that isn't listed and traded on an organized exchange. OTC stocks are traditionally those of smaller companies that don't meet the listing requirements of the New York

Stock Exchange or Nasdaq Stock
Market. *OTC* is acceptable on second reference. See **Pink Sheets**.

owner Not a formal title. Always
lowercase: *Dallas Cowboys owner
Jerry Jones.*

Oyez Not *oyes.* The cry of court
and public officials to command
silence.

Ozark Mountains Or simply:
the Ozarks.

PAC Acronym for *political action committee*. Raises money and makes contributions to campaigns of political candidates or parties. At the federal level, contribution amounts are limited by law and may not come from corporations or labor unions. Enforcement overseen by the Federal Election Commission. *PAC* acceptable on first reference; spell out in body of story. A *super PAC* is a *political action committee* that may raise and spend unlimited amounts of money, including from corporations and unions, to campaign independently for candidates for federal office. Its activities must be reported to the FEC, but are not otherwise regulated if not coordinated with the candidate or campaign.

pacemaker Formerly a trademark, now a generic term for a device that electronically helps a person's heart maintain a steady beat.

Pacific Ocean See **ocean**.

Pacific Standard Time (PST), Pacific Daylight Time (PDT) See **time zones**.

page numbers Use figures and capitalize *page* when used with a figure. When a letter is appended to the figure, capitalize it but do not use a hyphen: *Page 1, Page 10, Page 20A*.
One exception: *It's a Page One story*.

paintings See **composition titles**.

palate, palette, pallet *Palate* is the roof of the mouth.
A *palette* is an artist's paint board.
A *pallet* is a bed.

Palestine Liberation Organization Not *Palestinian*. *PLO* is acceptable in all references.

pan- Prefix meaning "all" takes no hyphen when combined with a common noun:
panchromatic   pantheism
Most combinations with *pan-* are proper nouns, however, and both *pan-* and the proper name it is combined with are capitalized:
Pan-African   Pan-Asiatic
Pan-American

Panama City The city in Panama stands alone in datelines.

pantsuit

pantyhose

papal nuncio Do not confuse with an *apostolic delegate*. See **apostolic delegate, papal nuncio**.

paparazzi (plural), **paparazzo** (singular) A photographer, often a freelancer, who takes candid shots often in an intrusive manner of celebrities.

Pap test (or **smear**) After George Papanicolaou, the U.S. anatomist who developed this test for cervical cancer.

parallel, paralleled, paralleling

parallels Use figures and lowercase to identify the imaginary locater lines that ring the globe from east to west. They are measured in units of 0 to 90 degrees north or south of the equator.

Examples: *4th parallel north, 89th parallel south*, or, if location north or south of the equator is obvious: *19th parallel.*

See **latitude and longitude**.

pardon, parole, probation The terms often are confused, but each has a specific meaning. Do not use them interchangeably.

A *pardon* forgives and releases a person from further punishment. It is granted by a chief of state or a governor. By itself, it does not expunge a record of conviction, if one exists, and it does not by itself restore civil rights.

A *general pardon*, usually for political offenses, is called *amnesty*.

Parole is the release of a prisoner before the sentence has expired, on condition of good behavior. It is granted by a parole board, part of the executive branch of government, and can be revoked only by the board.

Probation is the suspension of sentence for a person convicted, but not yet imprisoned, on condition of good behavior. It is imposed and revoked only by a judge.

parentheses See entry in **Punctuation** chapter.

Parent Teacher Association
PTA is acceptable in all references.

pari-mutuel

Paris The city in France stands alone in datelines.

parish Capitalize as part of the formal name for a church congregation or a governmental jurisdiction: *St. John's Parish, Jefferson Parish.*

Lowercase standing alone or in plural combinations: *the parish, St. John's and St. Mary's parishes, Jefferson and Plaquemines parishes.*

See **county** for additional guidelines on governmental jurisdictions.

parishioner Note spelling for this member of a parish, an administrative district of various churches, particularly Roman Catholic and Anglican churches. Do not use for Judaism or non-hierarchal Protestant denominations.

Parkinson's disease After James Parkinson, the English physician who described this degenerative disease of later life.

Parkinson's law After C. Northcote Parkinson, the British economist who came to the satirical conclusion that work expands to fill the time allotted to it.

parliament See **foreign legislative bodies**.

parliamentary Lowercase unless part of a proper name.

parole See **pardon, parole, probation**.

partial quotes See **quotation marks** in the **Punctuation** chapter.

particles See **foreign names** entry.

part time, part-time Hyphenate when used as a compound modifier: *She works part time. She has a part-time job.*

party See **political parties and philosophies**.

party affiliation Let relevance be the guide in determining whether to include a political figure's party affiliation in a story.

Party affiliation is pointless in some stories, such as an account of a governor accepting a button from a poster child.

It will occur naturally in many political stories.

For stories between these extremes, include party affiliation if readers need it for understanding or are likely to be curious about what it is.

GENERAL FORMS: When party designation is given, use any of these approaches as logical in constructing a story:

—*Republican Sen. Jim DeMint of South Carolina said ...*

—*Sen. Jim DeMint, R-S.C., said ...*

—*Sen. Jim DeMint also spoke. The South Carolina Republican said ...*

—*Rep. Frank Lucas of Oklahoma, the senior Republican on the House Agriculture Committee, said he supports the amendment.*

In stories about party meetings, such as a report on the Republican National Convention, no specific reference to party affiliation is necessary unless an individual is not a member of the party in question.

SHORT-FORM PUNCTUATION: Set short forms such as *R-S.C.* off from a name by commas, as illustrated above.

Use *R-* for Republicans, *D-* for Democrats, and *I-* for independents: *Sen. Joseph Lieberman, I-Conn., spoke with Sen. Bernie Sanders, I-Vt.*

FORM FOR U.S. HOUSE MEMBERS: The normal practice for U.S. House members is to identify them by party and state. In contexts where state affiliation is clear and home city is relevant, such as a state election roundup, identify representatives by party and city: *U.S. Reps. Ander Crenshaw, R-Jacksonville, and Kendrick Meek, D-Miami.* If this option is used, be consistent throughout the story.

FORM FOR STATE LEGISLATORS: Short-form listings showing party and home city are appropriate in state stories. For national stories, the normal practice is to say that the individual is a *Republican* or *Democrat.* Use a short-form listing only if the legislator's home city is relevant.

See **legislative titles**.

pass See **adopt, approve, enact, pass**.

passenger mile One passenger carried one mile, or its equivalent, such as two passengers carried one-half mile.

passer-by, passers-by

Passover The weeklong Jewish commemoration of the deliverance of the ancient Hebrews from slavery in Egypt. Occurs in March or April.

Capitalize *Seder* in references to the *Passover* feast commemorating the exodus.

pasteurize

pastor See **religious titles** and the entry for the individual's denomination.

pat-down (n. and adj.)

patriarch Lowercase when describing someone of great age and dignity.

Capitalize as a formal title before a name in some religious uses. See **Eastern Orthodox churches**; **religious titles**; and **Roman Catholic Church**.

patrolman, patrolwoman Capitalize before a name only if the word is a formal title. In some cities, the formal title is *police officer*.

See **titles**.

patrol, patrolled, patrolling

payload

PDA Abbreviation for *personal digital assistant*. Acceptable in all references.

PDF Abbreviation for *Portable Document Format*. A file format that allows a document to be shared among several types of computers without losing its formatting. Abbreviation is acceptable in all references.

peacekeeping

peacemaker, peacemaking

peace offering

peacetime

peacock It applies only to the male. The female is a *peahen*. Both are *peafowl*.

peasant Avoid the term, which is often derogatory, in referring to farm laborers (except in quotes or an organization name).

peck A unit of dry measure equal to 8 dry quarts or one-fourth of a bushel.

The metric equivalent is approximately 8.8 liters.

To convert to liters, multiply by 8.8 (5 pecks x 8.8 = 44 liters).

See **liter**.

pedal, peddle When riding a bicycle or similar vehicle, you *pedal* it.

When selling something, you may *peddle* it.

peddler

penance See **sacraments**.

peninsula Capitalize as part of a proper name: *the Florida Peninsula, the Upper Peninsula of Michigan, the Korean Peninsula, the Indochina Peninsula.*

penitentiary See **prison, jail**.

Pennsylvania Abbreviate *Pa.* in datelines or stories. Postal code: *PA*

Legally a commonwealth, not a state. See **state names**.

Pennsylvania Dutch The individuals are of German descent. The word *Dutch* is a corruption of *Deutsch*, the German word for "German."

Pentecost The seventh Sunday after Easter.

Pentecostalism See **religious movements**.

people's Use this possessive form when the word occurs in the formal name of a nation: *the People's Republic of China.*

Use this form also in such phrases as *the people's desire for freedom.*

people, persons Use *person* when speaking of an individual: *One person waited for the bus.*

The word *people* is preferred to *persons* in all plural uses. For example: *Thousands of people attended the fair. What will people say? There were 17 people in the room.*

Persons should be used only when it is in a direct quote or part of a title as in *Bureau of Missing Persons.*

People also is a collective noun that takes a plural verb when used to refer to a single race or nation: *The American people are united.* In this sense, the plural is *peoples*: *The peoples of Africa speak many languages.*

PepsiCo Inc. Note the in-capped *C*. Formerly the Pepsi-Cola Co. Headquarters is in Purchase, N.Y.

percent One word. It takes a singular verb when standing alone or when a singular word follows an *of* construction: *The teacher said 60 percent was a failing grade. He said 50 percent of the membership was there.*

It takes a plural verb when a plural word follows an *of* construction: *He said 50 percent of the members were there.*

Use figures for percent and percentages: *1 percent, 2.5 percent* (use decimals, not fractions), *10 percent, 4 percentage points.*

For a range, *12 to 15 percent*, or *between 12 and 15 percent.*

For amounts less than 1 percent, precede the decimal with a zero: *The cost of living rose 0.6 percent.*

periods See entry in the **Punctuation** chapter.

perk A shortened form of *perquisite*, often used by legislators to describe fringe benefits. In the state of New York, legislators also use the word *lulu* to describe the benefits they receive in lieu of pay.

permissible

per-share earnings Also earnings per share.

Persian Gulf Use this long-established name for the body of water off the southern coast of Iran.

Some Arab nations call it the *Arabian Gulf*. Use *Arabian Gulf* only in direct quotations and explain in the text that the body of water is more commonly known as the *Persian Gulf*.

personifications Capitalize them: *Grim Reaper, Father Time, Mother Nature, Old Man Winter, Sol,* etc.

-persons Do not use coined words such as *chairperson* or *spokesperson* in regular text.

Instead, use *chairman* or *spokesman* if referring to a man or the office in general. Use *chairwoman* or *spokeswoman* if referring to a woman. Or, if applicable, use a neutral word such as *leader* or *representative*.

Use *chairperson* or similar coinage only in direct quotations or when it is the formal description for an office.

persons See **people, persons**.

persuade See **convince, persuade**.

Peter Principle It is: Employees are promoted until they reach their level of incompetence.

From the book by Laurence J. Peter.

Petroleo Brasileiro Headquarters is in Rio de Janeiro.

petty officer See **military titles**.

Pfizer Inc. Headquarters is in New York.

phase See **faze, phase**.

Ph.D., Ph.D.s The preferred form is to say a person *holds a doctorate* and name the individual's area of specialty.

See **academic degrees** and **doctor**.

phenomenon, phenomena

Philadelphia The city in Pennsylvania stands alone in datelines.

Philippines In datelines, give the name of a city or town followed by *Philippines*:

MANILA, *Philippines* (AP) —

Specify the name of an individual island, if needed, in the text.

In stories: *the Philippines* or *the Philippine Islands* as the construction of a sentence dictates.

The people are *Filipinos.* The language is *Filipino,* an offshoot of Tagalog.

phishing A form of Internet fraud that aims to steal personal information such as credit cards, Social Security numbers, user IDs and passwords.

Phoenix The city in Arizona stands alone in datelines.

Photoshop Trademark for a brand of photo-editing software.

physician assistant No apostrophe in this medical profession title.

piano, pianos

pica A unit of measure in printing, equal to a fraction less than one-sixth of an inch.

A pica contains 12 points.

picket, pickets, picketed, picket line *Picket* is both the verb and the noun. Do not use *picketer.*

pickup (n. and adj.)

picnic, picnicked, picnicking, picnicker

pico- A prefix denoting one-trillionth of a unit. Move the decimal point 12 places to the left in converting to the basic unit: 2,999,888,777,666.5 picoseconds equals 2.9998887776665 seconds.

pigeon

pigeonhole (n. and v.)

Pikes Peak No apostrophe. After Zebulon Montgomery Pike, a U.S. general and explorer. The 14,115-foot peak is in the Rockies of central Colorado.

pile up (v.) **pileup** (n., adj.)

pill Do not capitalize in references to oral contraceptives. Use *birth control pill* on first reference if necessary for clarity.

pilot Not a formal title. Do not capitalize before a name.
See **titles**.

pingpong A synonym for *table tennis.*

The trademark name is *Ping-Pong.*

Pink Sheets A daily publication compiled by the National Quotation Bureau with bid and ask prices of over-the-counter stocks. See **over-the-counter stocks**.

pint (dry) Equal to 33.6 cubic inches, or one-half of a dry quart.

The metric equivalent is approximately 0.55 of a liter.

To convert to liters, multiply by 0.55 (5 dry pints x 0.55 is 2.75 liters). See **liter** and **quart (dry)**.

pint (liquid) Equal to 16 fluid ounces, or two cups.

The approximate metric equivalents are 470 milliliters or 0.47 of a liter.

To convert to liters, multiply by 0.47 (4 pints x 0.47 is 1.88 liters). See **liter**.

Pinyin The official Chinese spelling system.
See **Chinese names**.

pipeline

Pittsburgh The city in Pennsylvania stands alone in datelines.

The spelling is *Pittsburg* (no *h*) for communities in California, Illinois, Kansas, New Hampshire, Oklahoma and Texas.

plains See **Great Plains**.

planets Capitalize the proper names of planets: *Jupiter, Mars, Mercury, Neptune, Saturn, Uranus, Venus.* (*Pluto* was redefined as a dwarf planet by the International Astronomical Union in 2006.)

Capitalize *Earth* when used as the proper name of our planet: *The astronauts returned to Earth.*

Capitalize nouns and adjectives derived from the proper names of planets and other heavenly bodies: *Martian, Venusian.* But lowercase adjectives derived from other heavenly bodies: *solar, lunar.*

See **earth** and **heavenly bodies**.

planning Avoid the redundant *future planning.*

plants In general, lowercase the names of plants, but capitalize proper nouns or adjectives that occur in a name.

Some examples: *tree, fir, white fir, Douglas fir; Scotch pine; clover, white clover, white Dutch clover.*

If a botanical name is used, capitalize the first word; lowercase others: *pine tree (Pinus), red cedar (Juniperus virginiana), blue azalea (Callicarpa americana), Kentucky coffee tree (Gymnocladus dioica).*

play titles See **composition titles**.

plead, pleaded, pleading Do not use the colloquial past tense form, *pled.*

Pledge of Allegiance

Plexiglas Note the single *s*. A trademark for plastic glass.

plow

plurality See **majority, plurality**.

plurals Follow these guidelines in forming and using plural words:

MOST WORDS: Add *s*: *boys, girls, ships, villages.*

WORDS ENDING IN CH, S, SH, SS, X and Z: Add *es*: *churches, lenses, parishes, glasses, boxes, buzzes.* (*Monarchs* is an exception.)

WORDS ENDING IN IS: Change *is* to *es*: *oases, parentheses, theses.*

WORDS ENDING IN Y: If *y* is preceded by a consonant or *qu*, change *y* to *i* and add *es*: *armies, cities, navies, soliloquies.* (See PROPER NAMES below for an exception.)

Otherwise add *s*: *donkeys, monkeys.*

WORDS ENDING IN O: If *o* is preceded by a consonant, most plurals require *es*: *buffaloes, dominoes, echoes, heroes, potatoes.* But there are exceptions: *pianos.* See individual entries in this book for many of these exceptions.

WORDS ENDINGS IN F: In general, change *f* to *v* and add *es*: *leaves, selves.* (*Roof, roofs* is an exception.)

LATIN ENDINGS: Latin-root words ending in *us* change *us* to *i*: *alumnus, alumni.* (Words that have taken on English endings by common usage are exceptions: *prospectuses, syllabuses.*)

Most ending in *a* change to *ae*: *alumna, alumnae (formula, formulas* is an exception).

Most ending in *um* add *s*: *memorandums, referendums, stadiums.* Among those that still use the Latin ending: *addenda, curricula, media.*

Use the plural that Webster's New World College Dictionary lists as most common for a particular sense of word.

FORM CHANGE: *man, men; child, children; foot, feet; mouse, mice;* etc.

Caution: When *s* is used with any of these words it indicates possession and must be preceded by an apostrophe: *men's, children's,* etc.

WORDS THE SAME IN SINGULAR AND PLURAL: *corps, chassis, deer, moose, sheep,* etc.

The sense in a particular sentence is conveyed by the use of a singular or plural verb.

WORDS PLURAL IN FORM, SINGULAR IN MEANING: Some take singular verbs: *measles, mumps, news.*

Others take plural verbs: *grits, scissors.*

COMPOUND WORDS: Those written solid add *s* at the end: *cupfuls, handfuls, tablespoonfuls.*

For those that involve separate words or words linked by a hyphen, make the most significant word plural:

—Significant word first: *adjutants general, aides-de-camp, attorneys general, courts-martial, daughters-in-law, passers-by, postmasters general, presidents-elect, secretaries-general, sergeants major.*

—Significant word in the middle: *assistant attorneys general, deputy chiefs of staff.*

—Significant word last: *assistant attorneys, assistant corporation counsels, deputy sheriffs, lieutenant colonels, major generals.*

WORDS AS WORDS: Do not use *'s: His speech had too many "ifs," "ands" and "buts."* (Exception to Webster's New World College Dictionary.)

PROPER NAMES: Most ending in *es* or *s* or *z* add *es: Charleses, Joneses, Gonzalezes.*

Most ending in *y* add *s* even if preceded by a consonant: *the Duffys, the Kennedys, the two Kansas Citys.* Exceptions include *Alleghenies* and *Rockies.*

For others, add *s: the Carters, the McCoys, the Mondales.*

FIGURES: Add *s: The custom began in the 1920s. The airline has two 727s. Temperatures will be in the low 20s. There were five size 7s.*

(No apostrophes, an exception to Webster's New World College Dictionary guideline under "apostrophe.")

SINGLE LETTERS: Use *'s: Mind your p's and q's. He learned the three R's and brought home a report card with four A's and two B's. The Oakland A's won the pennant.*

MULTIPLE LETTERS: Add *s: She knows her ABCs. I gave him five IOUs. Four VIPs were there.*

PROBLEMS, DOUBTS: Separate entries in this book give plurals for troublesome words and guidance on whether certain words should be used with singular or plural verbs and pronouns. See also **collective nouns** and **possessives**.

For questions not covered by this book, use the plural that Webster's New World College Dictionary lists as most common for a particular sense of a word.

Note also the guidelines that the dictionary provides under its "plural" entry.

p.m., a.m. Lowercase, with periods. Avoid the redundant *10 p.m. tonight.*

pocket veto Occurs only when Congress has adjourned. If Congress is in session, a bill that remains on the president's desk for 10 days becomes law without his signature. If Congress adjourns, however, a bill that fails to get his signature within 10 days is vetoed.

Many states have similar procedures, but the precise requirements vary.

podcast A downloadable audio program.

podium See **lectern, podium, pulpit, rostrum**.

poetry See **composition titles** for guidelines on the names of poems.

Capitalize the first word in a line of poetry unless the author deliberately has used lowercase for a special effect. Do not, however, capitalize the first word on indented lines that must be created simply because the writer's line is too long for the available printing width.

poinsettia Note the *ia*.

point Do not abbreviate. Capitalize as part of a proper name: *Point Pleasant*.

point-blank

point (printing) As a unit of measure in printing, a *point* equals a fraction less than a seventy-second of an inch. A pica contains 12 *points*. See **pica**.

poison pill In the financial world, a strategy used by corporations to discourage a hostile takeover by another company or investor group.

Polaroid A trademark for Polaroid Land instant-picture cameras and for transparent material containing embedded crystals capable of polarizing light.

police department In communities where this is the formal name, capitalize *police department* with or without the name of the community: *the Los Angeles Police Department, the Police Department*.

If a police agency has some other formal name such as *Division of Police*, use that name if it is the way the department is known to the public. If the story uses *police department* as a generic term for such an agency, put *police department* in lowercase.

If a police agency with an unusual formal name is known to the public as a *police department*, treat *police department* as the name, capitalizing it with or without the name of the community. Use the formal name only if there is a special reason in the story.

If the proper name cannot be determined for some reason, such as the need to write about a police agency from a distance, treat *police department* as the proper name, capitalizing it with or without the name of the community.

Lowercase *police department* in plural uses: *the Los Angeles and San Francisco police departments*.

Lowercase *the department* whenever it stands alone.

police titles See **military titles** and **titles**.

policymaker, policymaking

polio The preferred term for *poliomyelitis* and *infantile paralysis*.

Politburo Acceptable in all references for the *Political Bureau of the Communist Party*.

political divisions Use Arabic figures and capitalize the accompanying word when used with the figures: *1st Ward, 10th Ward, 3rd Precinct, 22nd Precinct, the ward, the precinct*.

political parties and philosophies Capitalize both the name of the party and the word *party* if it is customarily used as part of the organization's proper name: *the Democratic Party, the Republican Party*.

Capitalize *Communist, Conserva-*

tive, *Democrat, Liberal, Republican, Socialist*, etc., when they refer to a specific party or its members. Lowercase these words when they refer to political philosophy (see examples below).

Lowercase the name of a philosophy in noun and adjective forms unless it is the derivative of a proper name: *communism, communist; fascism, fascist*. But: *Marxism, Marxist; Nazism, Nazi*.

EXAMPLES: *John Adams was a Federalist, but a man who subscribed to his philosophy today would be described as a federalist. The liberal Republican senator and his Conservative Party colleague said they believe that democracy and communism are incompatible. The Communist said he is basically a socialist who has reservations about Marxism.*

See **convention** and **party affiliation**.

politicking

politics Usually it takes a plural verb: *My politics are my own business.*

As a study or science, it takes a singular verb: *Politics is a demanding profession.*

polls and surveys Stories based on public opinion polls must include basic information for an intelligent evaluation of the results. Carefully word such stories to avoid exaggerating the meaning of poll results.

Every story based on a poll should include answers to these questions:

1. Who did the poll and who paid for it? Start with the polling firm, media outlet or other organization that conducted the poll. Be wary of polls paid for by candidates or interest groups; their release of poll results may be done selectively and is often a campaign tactic or publicity ploy. Any reporting of such polls

must highlight the poll's sponsor, so readers can be aware of potential bias from such sponsorship.

2. How many people were interviewed? How were they selected? Only a poll based on a scientific, random sample of a population — in which every member of the population has a known probability of inclusion — can be considered a valid and reliable measure of that population's opinions. Among surveys that do not meet this criterion:

• Samples drawn from panels of people who volunteer for online polls. These cannot be considered representative of larger populations because panel members are self-selected — often including "professional respondents" who sign up for numerous surveys to earn money or win prizes — and exclude people without Internet access. (Online panels recruited randomly from the entire population, with Internet access provided to those who don't already have it, are valid.)

• Balloting via websites, cell-phone text messaging or calls to 900 numbers. These too are self-selected samples, and results are subject to manipulation via blog and email campaigns and other methods. If such unscientific pseudo-polls are reported for entertainment value, they must never be portrayed as accurately reflecting public opinion and their failings must be highlighted.

3. Who was interviewed? A valid poll reflects only the opinions of the population that was sampled. A poll conducted only in urban areas of a country cannot be considered nationally representative; people in rural areas often have different opinions from those in cities. Many political polls are based on interviews with registered voters, since registration is usually required for voting. Polls may be based on "likely

voters" closer to an election; if so, ask the pollster how that group was identified and what percentage of the voting population it totaled. Are there far more "likely voters" in the poll than turnout in comparable past elections would suggest?

4. How was the poll conducted — by telephone or some other way? Avoid polls in which computers conduct telephone interviews using a recorded voice. Among the problems of these surveys are that they do not randomly select respondents within a household, and they cannot exclude children from adult samples

5. When was the poll taken? Opinion can change quickly, especially in response to events.

6. What are the sampling error margins for the poll and for subgroups mentioned in the story? The polling organization should provide sampling error margins, which are expressed as "plus or minus X percentage points," not "percent." The margin varies inversely with sample size: the fewer people interviewed, the larger the sampling error. If the opinions of a subgroup — women, for example — are important to the story, the sampling error for that subgroup should be noted. (Some pollsters release survey results to the first decimal place, which implies a greater degree of precision than is possible from a sampling. Round poll results to whole numbers. However, the sampling error margin — a statistical calculation — may be reported to the first decimal place.)

Also consider the wording and order of the questions asked in the poll. Small differences in question wording can cause big differences in results, and the results for one question may be affected by preceding questions. The exact question wording need not be in every poll story unless it is crucial or controversial.

When writing and editing poll stories, here are areas for close attention:

—Do not exaggerate poll results. In particular, with pre-election polls, these are the rules for deciding when to write that the poll finds one candidate is leading another:

• If the difference between the candidates is more than twice the sampling error margin, then the poll says one candidate is leading.

• If the difference is less than the sampling error margin, the poll says that the race is close, that the candidates are "about even." (Do not use the term "statistical dead heat," which is inaccurate if there is any difference between the candidates; if the poll finds the candidates are tied, say they're tied.)

• If the difference is at least equal to the sampling error but no more than twice the sampling error, then one candidate can be said to be "apparently leading" or "slightly ahead" in the race.

—Comparisons with other polls are often newsworthy. Earlier poll results can show changes in public opinion. Be careful comparing polls from different polling organizations. Different poll techniques can cause differing results.

—Sampling error is not the only source of error in a poll, but it is one that can be quantified. Question wording and order, interviewer skill and refusal to participate by respondents randomly selected for a sample are among potential sources of error in surveys.

—No matter how good the poll, no matter how wide the margin, the poll does not say one candidate will win an election. Polls can be wrong and the voters can change their minds before they cast their ballots.

pontiff Not a formal title. Always lowercase.

Ponzi scheme A fraudulent investing technique that promises high rates of return with little risk to investors. In the scheme, money provided by new investors is used to pay seeming high returns to early-stage investors to suggest the enterprise is prosperous. The scheme collapses when required redemptions exceed new investments. Named for Charles Ponzi, who set up such an illegal pyramid scheme in the 1920s as a way for investors to make money through international currency transactions. The largest fraud in U.S. history was perpetrated by Bernard Madoff, a New York financier who was sentenced to 150 years in prison after admitting to bilking investors of an estimated $20 billion.

pooh-pooh

pope Capitalize when used as a formal title before a name; lowercase in all other uses: *Pope Paul spoke to the crowd. At the close of his address, the pope gave his blessing.*
See **Roman Catholic Church** and **titles**.

popular names See **capitalization**.

pore, pour The verb *pore* means to gaze intently or steadily: *She pored over her books.*
The verb *pour* means to flow in a continuous stream: *It poured rain. He poured the coffee.*

port, starboard Nautical for left and right (when facing the bow, or forward). Port is left. Starboard is right. Change to *left* or *right* unless in direct quotes.

Portuguese names The family names of both the father and mother usually are considered part of a person's full name. In everyday use, customs sometimes vary with individuals and countries.

The normal sequence is given name, mother's family name, father's family name: *Maria Santos Ferreira.*

On second reference, use only the father's family name (*Ferreira*), unless the individual prefers or is widely known by a multiple last name (*Ferreira Castro*).

Some Portuguese use an *e* (for *and*) between the two names: *Joao Canto e Castro.* This would not be split on second reference, but would be *Canto e Castro.*

When a surname is preceded by *da, do, dos,* or *das,* include it in the second reference. *Jorge da Costa,* for example, would be *da Costa* on second reference.

A married woman adds her husband's surname to the end of hers. If *Maria Santos Ferreira* married *Joao Costa da Silva,* her full name would be *Maria Ferreira da Silva.*

Occasionally, a woman may choose not to take her husband's surname for personal reasons or because the mother's family has an aristocratic or famous surname. Use both surnames if the individual's choice is not known.

possessives Follow these guidelines:
PLURAL NOUNS NOT ENDING IN S: Add *'s*: *the alumni's contributions, women's rights.*
PLURAL NOUNS ENDING IN S: Add only an apostrophe: *the churches' needs, the girls' toys, the horses' food, the ships' wake, states' rights, the VIPs' entrance.*
NOUNS PLURAL IN FORM, SINGULAR IN MEANING: Add only an apostrophe: *mathematics' rules, measles' effects.* (But see INANIMATE OBJECTS below.)
Apply the same principle when a plural word occurs in the formal

name of a singular entity: *General Motors' profits, the United States' wealth.*

NOUNS THE SAME IN SINGULAR AND PLURAL: Treat them the same as plurals, even if the meaning is singular: *one corps' location, the two deer's tracks, the lone moose's antlers.*

SINGULAR NOUNS NOT ENDING IN S: Add *'s: the church's needs, the girl's toys, the horse's food, the ship's route, the VIP's seat.*

Some style guides say that singular nouns ending in *s* sounds such as *ce, x,* and *z* may take either the apostrophe alone or *'s.* See SPECIAL EXPRESSIONS, but otherwise, for consistency and ease in remembering a rule, always use *'s* if the word does not end in the letter *s: Butz's policies, the fox's den, the justice's verdict, Marx's theories, the prince's life, Xerox's profits.*

SINGULAR COMMON NOUNS ENDING IN S: Add *'s* unless the next word begins with *s: the hostess's invitation, the hostess' seat; the witness's answer, the witness' story.*

SINGULAR PROPER NAMES ENDING IN S: Use only an apostrophe: *Achilles' heel, Agnes' book, Ceres' rites, Descartes' theories, Dickens' novels, Euripides' dramas, Hercules' labors, Jesus' life, Jules' seat, Kansas' schools, Moses' law, Socrates' life, Tennessee Williams' plays, Xerxes' armies.*

SPECIAL EXPRESSIONS: The following exceptions to the general rule for words not ending in *s* apply to words that end in an *s* sound and are followed by a word that begins with *s: for appearance' sake, for conscience' sake, for goodness' sake.* Use *'s* otherwise: *the appearance's cost, my conscience's voice.*

PRONOUNS: Personal interrogative and relative pronouns have separate forms for the possessive. None involve an apostrophe: *mine, ours, your, yours, his, hers, its, theirs, whose.*

Caution: If you are using an apostrophe with a pronoun, always double-check to be sure that the meaning calls for a contraction: *you're, it's, there's, who's.*

Follow the rules listed above in forming the possessives of other pronouns: *another's idea, others' plans, someone's guess.*

COMPOUND WORDS: Applying the rules above, add an apostrophe or *'s* to the word closest to the object possessed: *the major general's decision, the major generals' decisions, the attorney general's request, the attorneys general's request.* See the **plurals** entry for guidelines on forming the plurals of these words.

Also: *anyone else's attitude, John Adams Jr.'s father, Benjamin Franklin of Pennsylvania's motion.* Whenever practical, however, recast the phrase to avoid ambiguity: *the motion by Benjamin Franklin of Pennsylvania.*

JOINT POSSESSION, INDIVIDUAL POSSESSION: Use a possessive form after only the last word if ownership is joint: *Fred and Sylvia's apartment, Fred and Sylvia's stocks.*

Use a possessive form after both words if the objects are individually owned: *Fred's and Sylvia's books.*

DESCRIPTIVE PHRASES: Do not add an apostrophe to a word ending in *s* when it is used primarily in a descriptive sense: *citizens band radio, a Cincinnati Reds infielder, a teachers college, a Teamsters request, a writers guide.*

Memory Aid: The apostrophe usually is not used if *for* or *by* rather than *of* would be appropriate in the longer form: *a radio band for citizens, a college for teachers, a guide for writers, a request by the Teamsters.*

An *'s* is required, however, when a term involves a plural word that does not end in *s: a children's hospital, a people's republic, the Young Men's Christian Association.*

DESCRIPTIVE NAMES: Some

governmental, corporate and institutional organizations with a descriptive word in their names use an apostrophe; some do not. Follow the user's practice: *Actors' Equity, Diners Club, the Ladies' Home Journal, the National Governors Association.* See separate entries for these and similar names frequently in the news.

QUASI POSSESSIVES: Follow the rules above in composing the possessive form of words that occur in such phrases as *a day's pay, two weeks' vacation, three days' work, your money's worth.*

Frequently, however, a hyphenated form is clearer: *a two-week vacation, a three-day job.*

DOUBLE POSSESSIVE: Two conditions must apply for a double possessive — a phrase such as *a friend of John's* — to occur: 1. The word after *of* must refer to an animate object, and 2. The word before *of* must involve only a portion of the animate object's possessions.

Otherwise, do not use the possessive form of the word after *of*: *The friends of John Adams mourned his death.* (All the friends were involved.) *He is a friend of the college.* (Not *college's,* because college is inanimate.)

Memory Aid: This construction occurs most often, and quite naturally, with the possessive forms of personal pronouns: *He is a friend of mine.*

INANIMATE OBJECTS: There is no blanket rule against creating a possessive form for an inanimate object, particularly if the object is treated in a personified sense. See some of the earlier examples, and note these: *death's call, the wind's murmur.*

In general, however, avoid excessive personalization of inanimate objects, and give preference to an *of* construction when it fits the make-up of the sentence. For example, the earlier references to *mathematics' rules* and *measles' effects* would better be phrased: *the rules of mathematics, the effects of measles.*

post- Follow Webster's New World College Dictionary. Hyphenate if not listed there.

Some words without a hyphen:

postdate	postnuptial
postdoctoral	postoperative
postelection	postscript
postgame	postwar
postgraduate	

Some words that use a hyphen:

post-bellum	post-mortem
post-convention	

Post-it A trademark for small pieces of paper with an adhesive strip on the back that can be attached to documents.

post office It may be used but it is no longer capitalized because the agency is now the *U.S. Postal Service.*

Use lowercase in referring to an individual office: *I went to the post office.*

post-traumatic stress disorder

pothole

pound (monetary) The English pound sign is not used. Convert the figures to dollars in most cases. Use a figure and spell out *pounds* if the actual figure is relevant.

pound (weight) Equal to 16 ounces. The metric equivalent is approximately 454 grams, or 0.45 kilograms.

To convert to kilograms, multiply the number of pounds by 0.45 (20 pounds x 0.45 equals 9 kilograms).

See **gram** and **kilogram**.

pour See **pore, pour**.

poverty level An income level

judged inadequate to provide a family or individual with the essentials of life. The figure for the United States is adjusted regularly to reflect changes in the Consumer Price Index.

practitioner See **Church of Christ, Scientist**.

Prague The city in the Czech Republic stands alone in datelines.

pre- The rules in **prefixes** apply. The following examples of exceptions to first-listed spellings in Webster's New World College Dictionary are based on the general rule that a hyphen is used if a prefix ends in a vowel and the word that follows begins with the same vowel:

pre-election	pre-establish
pre-eminent	pre-exist
pre-empt	

Otherwise, follow Webster's New World College Dictionary, hyphenating if not listed there. Some examples:

prearrange	prehistoric
precondition	preignition
precook	prejudge
predate	premarital
predecease	prenatal
predispose	prenuptial
preflight	pretax
pregame	pretest
preheat	prewar

Some hyphenated coinage, not listed in the dictionary:

pre-convention	pre-noon

preacher A job description, not a formal religious title. Do not capitalize.

See **titles** and **religious titles**.

precincts See **political divisions**.

preferred stock An ownership in a company that has no voting rights but pays a fixed dividend and has a higher claim on the company's assets and earnings than common stock.

prefixes See separate listings for commonly used prefixes.

Generally do not hyphenate when using a prefix with a word starting with a consonant.

Three rules are constant, although they yield some exceptions to first-listed spellings in Webster's New World College Dictionary:

—Except for *cooperate* and *coordinate*, use a hyphen if the prefix ends in a vowel and the word that follows begins with the same vowel.

—Use a hyphen if the word that follows is capitalized.

—Use a hyphen to join doubled prefixes: *sub-subparagraph*.

premiere A first performance.

premier, prime minister These two titles often are used interchangeably in translating to English the title of an individual who is the first minister in a national government that has a council of ministers.

Prime minister is the correct title throughout the Commonwealth, formerly the British Commonwealth. See **Commonwealth** for a list of members.

Prime minister is the best or traditional translation from most other languages. For consistency, use it throughout the rest of the world with these exceptions:

—Use *chancellor* in Austria and Germany.

—Follow the practice of a nation if there is a specific preference that varies from this general practice. For example, use *premier* in China.

Premier is also the correct title for the individuals who lead the provincial governments in Canada and Australia.

See **titles**.

Presbyterian churches Presbyterian denominations typically have four levels of authority - individual congregations, presbyteries, synods and a general assembly.

Congregations are led by a pastor, who provides guidance in spiritual matters, and by a session, composed of ruling elders chosen by the congregation to represent the members in matters of government and discipline.

A presbytery is composed of all the ministers and an equal number of ruling elders, including at least one from each congregation, in a given district. Although the next two levels are technically higher, the presbytery has the authority to rule on many types of material and spiritual questions.

Presbyteries unite to form a synod, whose members are elected by the presbyteries. A synod generally meets once a year to decide matters such as the creation of new presbyteries and to pass judgment on appeals and complaints that do not affect the doctrine or constitution of the church.

A general assembly, composed of delegations of pastors and ruling elders from each presbytery, meets yearly to decide issues of doctrine and discipline within a Presbyterian body. It also may create new synods, divide old ones and correspond with general assemblies of other Presbyterian bodies.

The northern and southern branches of Presbyterianism merged in 1983 to become the Presbyterian Church (U.S.A.). Formerly, Presbyterianism in the United States was concentrated in two bodies. The principal body in the North was the United Presbyterian Church in the United States of America. The Presbyterian Church in the United States was the principal Southern body.

There are also several distinctly conservative Presbyterian denominations, the largest of them the Presbyterian Church in America. Be careful to specify the denomination being written about.

Presbyterians believe in the Trinity and the humanity and divinity of Christ. Baptism, which may be administered to children, and the Lord's Supper are the only sacraments.

All Presbyterian clergymen may be described as *ministers*. Pastor applies if a minister leads a congregation.

On first reference, use *the Rev.* before the name of a man or woman. On second reference, use only the last name.

See **religious titles**.

presently Use it to mean *in a little while* or *shortly*, but not to mean *now*.

presidency Always lowercase.

president Capitalize *president* only as a formal title before one or more names: *President Barack Obama, Presidents Gerald R. Ford and Jimmy Carter.*

Lowercase in all other uses: *The president said today. He is running for president. Lincoln was president during the Civil War.*

See **titles**.

FULL NAMES: Use the first and family name on first reference to a current or former U.S. president or the president-elect: *former President Jimmy Carter, President Barack Obama, President-elect Barack Obama.* On subsequent references, use only the last name.

For presidents of other nations and of organizations and institutions, capitalize president as a formal title before a full name: *President Nicolas Sarkozy of France, President John Smith of Acme Corp.*

On second reference, use only the last name.

presidential Lowercase unless part of a proper name.

Presidential Medal of Free-dom This is the nation's highest civilian honor. It is given by the president, on the recommendation of the Distinguished Civilian Service Board, for "exceptionally meritorious contribution to the security of the United States or other significant public or private endeavors."

Until 1963 it was known as the Medal of Freedom.

Presidents Day Not adopted by the federal government as the official name of the Washington's Birthday holiday. However, some federal agencies, states and local governments use the term.

presiding officer Always lowercase.

press conference *News conference* is preferred.

press secretary Seldom a formal title. For consistency, always use lowercase, even when used before an individual's name.

(The formal title for the person who serves a U.S. president in this capacity is *assistant to the president for press relations*.)

See **titles**.

pretax

pretense, pretext A *pretext* is something that is put forward to conceal a truth: *He was discharged for tardiness, but the reason given was only a pretext for general incompetence.*

A *pretense* is a false show, a more overt act intended to conceal personal feelings: *My profuse compliments were all pretense.*

preventive

price-earnings ratio The price of a share of stock divided by earnings per share for a 12-month period.

Ratios in AP stock tables reflect earnings for the most recent 12 months.

For example, a stock selling for $60 per share and earning $6 per share would be selling at a price-earnings ratio of 10-to-1. *P/E* is acceptable on second reference.

See **profit terminology**.

PricewaterhouseCoopers

priest A vocational description, not a formal title. Do not capitalize.

See **religious titles** and the entries for the **Roman Catholic Church** and **Episcopal Church**.

prima-facie (adj.)

primary Do not capitalize: *the New Hampshire primary, the Democratic primary, the primary.*

primary day Use lowercase for any of the days set aside for balloting in a primary.

prime meridian See **meridians**.

prime minister See **premier, prime minister**.

prime rate A benchmark rate used by banks to set interest charges on a variety of corporate and consumer loans, including some adjustable home mortgages, revolving credit cards and business loans extended to their most creditworthy customers. Banks almost always raise or lower their rates by a similar amount on the same day Federal Reserve policymakers change their target for overnight loans between banks, known as the *federal funds rate.*

prime time (n.) **prime-time** (adj.)

Prince Edward Island One of the three Maritime Provinces of

Canada. Do not abbreviate.

See **datelines**.

prince, princess Capitalize when used as a royal title before a name; lowercase when used alone: *Prince Charles, the prince.*

See **nobility**.

principal, principle *Principal* is a noun and adjective meaning someone or something first in rank, authority, importance or degree: *She is the school principal. He was the principal player in the trade. Money is the principal problem.*

Principle is a noun that means a fundamental truth, law, doctrine or motivating force: *They fought for the principle of self-determination.*

prior to *Before* is less stilted for most uses. *Prior to* is appropriate, however, when a notion of requirement is involved: *The fee must be paid prior to the examination.*

prisoner(s) of war *POW(s)* is acceptable on second reference.

Hyphenate when used as a compound modifier: *a prisoner-of-war trial.*

prison, jail Do not use the two words interchangeably.

DEFINITIONS: *Prison* is a generic term that may be applied to the maximum security institutions often known as *penitentiaries* and to the medium security facilities often called *correctional institutions* or *reformatories.* All such facilities usually confine people serving sentences for felonies.

A *jail* is normally used to confine people serving sentences for misdemeanors, people awaiting trial or sentencing on either felony or misdemeanor charges, and people confined for civil matters such as failure to pay alimony and other types of contempt of court.

See **felony, misdemeanor**.

The guidelines for capitalization:

PRISONS: Many states have given elaborate formal names to their prisons. They should be capitalized when used, but commonly accepted substitutes should also be capitalized as if they were proper names. For example, use either *Massachusetts Correctional Institution-Walpole* or *Walpole State Prison* for the maximum security institution in Massachusetts.

Do not, however, construct a substitute when the formal name is commonly accepted: It is the *Colorado State Penitentiary*, for example, not *Colorado State Prison*.

On second reference, any of the following may be used, all in lowercase: *the state prison, the prison, the state penitentiary, the penitentiary*.

Use lowercase for all plural constructions: *the Colorado and Kansas state penitentiaries*.

JAILS: Capitalize *jail* when linked with the name of the jurisdiction: *Los Angeles County Jail*. Lowercase *county jail, city jail* and *jail* when they stand alone.

FEDERAL INSTITUTIONS: Maximum security institutions are known as *penitentiaries*: *the U.S. Penitentiary at Lewisburg* or *Lewisburg Penitentiary* on first reference; *the federal penitentiary* or *the penitentiary* on second reference.

Medium security institutions include the word *federal* as part of their formal names: *the Federal Correctional Institution at Danbury, Connecticut*. On second reference: *the correctional institution, the federal prison, the prison*.

Most federal facilities used to house people awaiting trial or serving sentences of a year or less have the proper name *Federal Detention Center*. The term *Metropolitan Correctional Center* is being adopted for some new installations. On second reference: *the detention center, the correctional center.*

privacy Do not identify juveniles (under 18) who are accused of crimes, even if other news media do so or police release names. Also, do not transmit images that would reveal their identity.

Do not identify, in text or through images, juveniles (under 18) who are witnesses to crimes.

Do not identify, in text or through images, persons who say they have been sexually assaulted, and use discretion in naming victims of other extremely severe abuse.

Exceptions may be made in extraordinary cases only with the approval of the Standards Center or the manager on duty at the Nerve Center. Issues that may weigh in a decision include the severity of the alleged crime; whether police have formally released the juvenile's name; and whether the juvenile has been formally charged as an adult. Other considerations might include public safety, such as when the youth is the subject of a manhunt; or widespread publication of the juvenile suspect's name, making the identity de facto public knowledge.

In some situations, state or national laws may determine whether the person's name can be published.

Sometimes a person may be identified by AP in an abduction or manhunt situation, and it develops later that – because of a sexual assault or other reason – the name should not be used. In such cases, with approval by the Standards Center or the manager on duty at the Nerve Center, it may be appropriate to withdraw the identification from future coverage. AP may also consider identifying the victim of a sexual assault if the individual comes forward publicly and agrees to be identified.

Consult with the Standards Center or Nerve Center on all questions about these policies.

private See **military titles**.

privatization The process of transferring a government-owned enterprise to private ownership.

privilege, privileged

pro- Use a hyphen when coining words that denote support for something. Some examples:

pro-labor   pro-business
pro-peace   pro-war

No hyphen when *pro* is used in other senses: *produce, profile, pronoun, proactive,* etc.

probation See **pardon, parole, probation**.

problem-solving

Procter & Gamble Co. *P&G* is acceptable on second reference. Headquarters is in Cincinnati.

producer price index An index of changes in wholesale prices, produced by the Bureau of Labor Statistics, U.S. Department of Labor, and used as a gauge of inflation. Spell the index name lowercase.

profanity See **obscenities, profanities, vulgarities**.

professor Never abbreviate. Lowercase before a name, but capitalize Professor Emeritus as a conferred title before a name: *Professor Emeritus Susan Johnson.* Do not continue in second reference unless part of a quotation.

See **academic titles, emeritus** and **titles**.

profit-sharing (n. and adj.) The hyphen for the noun is an exception to Webster's New World College Dictionary.

profit-sharing plan A plan that gives employees a share in the profits of the company. Each employee receives a percentage of those profits based on the company's earnings.

profit-taking (n. and adj.) Avoid this term. It means selling a security after a recent rapid rise in price. It is inaccurate if the seller bought the security at a higher price, watched it fall, then sold it after a recent rise but for less than he bought it. In that case, he would be cutting his losses, not taking his profit.

profit terminology Note the meanings of the following terms in reporting a company's financial status. Always be careful to specify whether the figures given apply to quarterly or annual results.

The terms, listed in the order in which they might occur in analyzing a company's financial condition:

dividend The amount paid per share per year to holders of common stock. Payments generally are made in quarterly installments.

The dividend usually is a portion of the earnings per share. However, if a company shows no profit during a given period, it may be able to use earnings retained from profitable periods to pay its dividend on schedule.

earnings per share (or **loss per share**, for companies posting a net loss) The figure obtained by dividing the number of outstanding shares of common stock into the amount left after dividends have been paid on any preferred stock.

extraordinary loss, extraordinary income An expense or source of income that does not occur on a regular basis, such as a loss due to a major fire or the revenue from the sale of a subsidiary. Extraordinary items should be identified in any report on the company's financial status to avoid creating the false impression that its overall profit trend has suddenly plunged or soared.

gross profit The difference between the sales price of an item or service and the expenses directly attributed to it, such as the cost of raw materials, labor and overhead linked to the production effort.

income before taxes Gross profits minus companywide expenses not directly attributed to specific products or services. These expenses typically include interest costs, advertising and sales costs, and general administrative overhead.

net income, profit, earnings The amount left after taxes and preferred dividends have been paid.

Some of what remains may be paid in dividends to holders of common stock. The rest may be invested to obtain interest revenue or spent to acquire new buildings or equipment to increase the company's ability to make further profits.

To avoid confusion, do not use the word *income* alone — always specify whether the figure is *income before taxes* or *net income*.

The terms *profit* and *earnings* commonly are interpreted as meaning the amount left after taxes. The terms *net profit* and *net earnings* are acceptable synonyms.

return on investment A percentage figure obtained by dividing the company's assets into its net income.

revenue The amount of money a company took in, including interest earned and receipts from sales, services provided, rents and royalties.

The figure also may include excise taxes and sales taxes collected for the government. If it does, the fact should be noted in any report on revenue. The singular form is preferable in most uses.

sales The money a company received for the goods and services it sold.

In some cases the figure includes receipts from rents and royalties. In others, particularly when rentals and royalties make up a large portion of a company's income, figures for these activities are listed separately.

pro forma In the financial world, it describes a method of calculating a company's sales and earnings as if changes in circumstances existed throughout an entire period covered by a financial report. Pro forma figures are often given for companies that have been involved in a merger or acquisition, gone public or emerged from bankruptcy reorganization. Unlike earnings based on generally accepted accounting principles, pro forma earnings do not comply with any standardized rules or regulations.

Prohibition Capitalize when referring to the period that began when the 18th Amendment to the Constitution prohibited the manufacture, sale or transportation of alcoholic liquors.

The amendment was declared ratified Jan. 29, 1919, and took effect Jan. 16, 1920. It was repealed by the 21st Amendment, which took effect Dec. 5, 1933, the day it was declared ratified.

pronouncers When necessary to use a pronouncer, put it in parentheses immediately following the word or name. The syllable to be stressed should be in caps with an apostrophe: *acetaminophen (a-see-tuh-MIHN'-oh-fen)*.

Here are the basic sounds represented by AP phonetic symbols:

Vowels	Consonants
a — apple, bat	g — got, beg
ah — father, hot	j — gem, job
ahr — part, car	k — cap, keep
aw — law, long	ch — chair
ay — ace, fate	s — see
eh — bed	sh — shut
ehr — merry	y — yes
ee — see, tea	z — zoom
ih — pin, middle	zh — mirage
oh — go, oval	kh — guttural "k"
oo — food, two	
or — for, torn	
ow — cow	
oy — boy	
u — foot, put	
uh — puff	
ur — burden, curl	
y, eye — ice, time	

propeller

proper nouns See **capitalization**.

prophecy (n.) **prophesy** (v.)

proportions Always use figures: *2 parts powder to 6 parts water.*

proposition Do not abbreviate. Capitalize when used with a figure in describing a ballot question: *He is uncommitted on Proposition 15.*

prosecutor Capitalize before a name when it is the formal title. In most cases, however, the formal title is a term such as *attorney general, state's attorney* or *U.S. attorney.* If so, use the formal title on first reference.

Lowercase *prosecutor* if used before a name on a subsequent reference, generally to help the reader distinguish between prosecutor and defense attorney without having to look back to the start of the story.

See **titles**.

prostate gland

protective tariff A duty high enough to assure domestic producers against any effective competition from foreign producers.

Protestant Episcopal Church See **Episcopal Church**.

Protestant, Protestantism

Capitalize these words when they refer either to denominations formed as a result of the break from the Roman Catholic Church in the 16th century or to the members of these denominations.

Church groups covered by the term include Anglican, Baptist, Congregational, Methodist, Lutheran, Presbyterian and Quaker denominations. See separate entries for each.

Protestant is not generally applied to Christian Scientists, Jehovah's Witnesses or Mormons.

Do not use *Protestant* to describe a member of an Eastern Orthodox church. Use a phrase such as *Orthodox Christian* instead.

See **religious movements**.

protester

prove, proved, proving
Use *proven* only as an adjective: *a proven remedy*.

provinces
Names of provinces are set off from community names by commas, just as the names of U.S. states are set off from city names: *They went to Halifax, Nova Scotia, on their vacation.*

Do not capitalize province: *They visited the province of Nova Scotia. The earthquake struck Shensi province.*

See **datelines**.

proviso, provisos

provost marshal
The plural: *provost marshals.*

proxy
An authorization for someone else to vote on behalf of a shareholder at a company's annual shareholder meeting. *Proxy fight* is a strategy used by an acquiring company or investor group in its attempt to gain control of a target company; the acquirer tries to convince other shareholders that the management of the target company should be replaced or a specific corporate action be taken. *Proxy statement* is a document that disclosed important information about issues to be discussed at an annual meeting. It includes the qualifications of management and board directors, serves as a ballot for elections to the board of directors and provides detailed information about executive compensation.

PTA
Acceptable in all references for *Parent Teacher Association*.

PT boat
Acceptable in all references for *patrol torpedo boat*, a small, fast attack vessel used by the U.S. Navy in World War II.

Public Broadcasting Service
An association of public television stations organized to buy and distribute programs selected by a vote of the members.

PBS is acceptable on first reference only within contexts such as a television column. Otherwise, do not use *PBS* until second reference.

public schools
Use figures and capitalize *public school* when used with a figure: *Public School 3, Public School 10.*

If a school has a commemorative name: *Benjamin Franklin School.*

publisher
Capitalize when used as a formal title before an individual's name: *Publisher Isaiah Thomas of the Massachusetts Spy.*

See **titles**.

Puerto Rico
Do not abbreviate. See **datelines**.

Pulitzer Prizes
These yearly awards for outstanding work in journalism and the arts were endowed by the late Joseph Pulitzer, publisher of the old New York World, and first

given in 1917. They are awarded by the trustees of Columbia University on recommendation of an advisory board.

Capitalize *Pulitzer Prize*, but lowercase the categories: *Pulitzer Prize for public service, Pulitzer Prize for fiction*, etc.

Also: *She is a Pulitzer Prize winner. He is a Pulitzer Prize-winning author.*

pull back (v.) **pullback** (n.)

pull out (v.) **pullout** (n.)

pull up (v.) **pullup** (n.)

pulpit See **lectern, podium, pulpit, rostrum**.

punctuation The punctuation entries in this book refer to guidelines rather than rules. Guidelines should not be treated casually, however.

See **Punctuation** chapter for separate entries under: **apostrophe**; **brackets**; **colon**; **comma**; **dash**; **ellipsis**; **exclamation point**; **hyphen**; **parentheses**; **periods**; **question mark**; **quotation marks**; and **semicolon**.

Purim The Jewish Feast of Lots, commemorating Esther's deliverance of the Jews in Persia from a massacre plotted by Haman. Occurs in February or March.

push-button (n., adj.)

push up (v.) **pushup** (n., adj.)

put out (v.) **putout** (n.)

pygmy Capitalize only when referring specifically to any of several races of unusually small African or Asian peoples.

Q-and-A format Use *Q-and-A* within the body of a story. See **question mark** in **Punctuation** chapter.

Qantas Airways Ltd. Headquarters of this airline is in Mascot, Australia.

QE2 Acceptable on second reference for the ocean liner Queen Elizabeth 2.

(But use a Roman numeral for the monarch: *Queen Elizabeth II.*)

Q-tips A trademark for a brand of cotton swabs.

Quakers This informal name may be used in all references to members of the *Religious Society of Friends*, but always include the full name in a story dealing primarily with Quaker activities.

The denomination originated with George Fox, an Englishman who objected to Anglican emphasis on ceremony. In the 1640s, he said he heard a voice that opened the way for him to develop a personal relationship with Christ, described as the Inner Light, a term based on the Gospel description of Christ as the "true light."

Brought to court for opposing the established church, Fox tangled with a judge who derided him as a "quaker" in reference to his agitation over religious matters.

The basic unit of Quaker organization is the weekly meeting, which corresponds to the congregation in other churches.

Various yearly meetings form larger associations that assemble at intervals of a year or more. The largest is the Friends United Meeting. Its 15 yearly meeting members represent about half the Friends in the world.

Others include the Evangelical Friends Alliance and the Friends General Conference. Members of the conference include some yearly meetings that also are affiliated with the Friends United Meeting.

Fox taught that the Inner Light emancipates a person from adherence to any creed, ecclesiastical authority or ritual forms.

There is no recognized ranking of clergy over lay people. However, there are meeting officers, called *elders* or *ministers*. Many Quaker ministers, particularly in the Midwest and West, use *the Rev.* before their names and describe themselves as *pastors*.

Capitalize *elder*, *minister* or *pastor* when used as a formal title before a name. Use *the Rev.* before a name on first reference if it is a minister's practice. On second reference, use only the last name.

See **religious titles**.

quakes See **earthquakes**.

quart (dry) Equal in volume to 67.2 cubic inches. The metric equivalent is approximately 1.1 liters.

To convert to liters, multiply by 1.1 (5 dry quarts x 1.1 is 5.5 liters). See **liter**.

quart (liquid) Equal in volume to 57.75 cubic inches. Also equal to 32 fluid ounces.

The approximate metric equivalents are 950 milliliters or 0.95 of a liter.

To convert to liters, multiply by 0.95 (4 quarts x 0.95 is 3.8 liters). See **liter**.

quasar Acceptable in all references for a *quasi-stellar astronomical object*, often a radio source.

Quebec Use *Quebec City* without the name of the province in datelines.

Do not abbreviate any reference to the province of *Quebec*, Canada's largest in area and second largest in population.

The people are *Quebecois*. See **datelines**.

queen Capitalize only when used before the name of royalty: *Queen Elizabeth II*. Continue in second references that use the queen's given name: *Queen Elizabeth*.

Lowercase *queen* when it stands alone.

Capitalize in plural uses: *Queens Elizabeth and Victoria*. See **nobility** and **titles**.

queen mother A widowed queen who is mother of the reigning monarch. See **nobility**.

question mark See entry in **Punctuation** chapter.

questionnaire

quick-witted

quiet period Avoid using this term. In the investing world, it is commonly thought to be the period following a company's initial public offering or just before earnings are reported in which it is subject to possible sanctions by the U.S. Securities and Exchange Commission for making public disclosures. But since SEC rules only prohibit disclosures that go beyond what the company has stated in SEC filings, the term *quiet period* is a misnomer.

quotation marks See entry in **Punctuation** chapter.

quotations in the news Never alter quotations even to correct minor grammatical errors or word usage. Casual minor tongue slips may be removed by using ellipses but even that should be done with extreme caution. If there is a question about a quote, either don't use it or ask the speaker to clarify.

If a person is unavailable for comment, detail attempts to reach that person. (*Smith was out of the country on business; Jones did not return phone messages left at the office.*)

Do not use substandard spellings such as *gonna* or *wanna* in attempts to convey regional dialects or informal pronunciations, except to help a desired touch or to convey an emphasis by the speaker.

Follow basic writing style and use abbreviations where appropriate, as in *No. 1, St., Gov., Sen.* and *$3*.

FULL vs. PARTIAL QUOTES: In general, avoid fragmentary quotes. If a speaker's words are clear and concise, favor the full quote. If cumbersome language can be paraphrased fairly, use an indirect construction, reserving quotation marks for sensitive or controversial passages that must be identified specifically as coming from the speaker.

CONTEXT: Remember that you can misquote someone by giving a startling remark without its modifying passage or qualifiers. The manner of delivery sometimes is part of the context. Reporting a smile or a deprecatory gesture may be as important as conveying the words themselves.

OFFENSIVE LANGUAGE: See the **obscenities, profanities, vulgarities** entry.

PUNCTUATION: See the **quotation marks** entry in the **Punctuation** chapter.

Quran The preferred spelling for the Muslim holy book. Use the spelling *Koran* only if preferred by a specific organization or in a specific title or name.

rabbi See **Jewish congregations**.

Rabbinical Assembly See **Jewish congregations**.

Rabbinical Council of America See **Jewish congregations**.

race Identification by race is pertinent:

—In biographical and announcement stories that involve significant, groundbreaking or historic events, such as being elected U.S. president, named to the U.S. Supreme Court or other notable occurrences. *Barack Obama is the first black U.S. president. Sonia Sotomayor is the first Hispanic justice of the U.S. Supreme Court. Jeremy Lin is the first American-born NBA player of Chinese or Taiwanese descent.*

—For suspects sought by the police or missing person cases using police or other credible, detailed descriptions. Such descriptions apply for all races. The racial reference should be removed when the individual is apprehended or found.

—When reporting a demonstration or disturbance involving race or such issues as civil rights or slavery.

In other situations with racial overtones, use news judgment.

Do not use racially derogatory terms unless they are part of a quotation that is essential to the story.

See **obscenities, profanities, vulgarities** and **nationalities and races**.

racket Not *racquet*, for the light bat used in tennis and badminton.

rack, wrack The noun *rack* applies to various types of framework; the verb *rack* means to arrange on a rack, to torture, trouble or torment: *He was placed on the rack. She racked her brain.*

The noun *wrack* means ruin or destruction, and generally is confined to the phrase *wrack and ruin* and *wracked with doubt* (or *pain*).

The verb *wrack* has substantially the same meaning as the verb *rack*, the latter being preferred.

radar A lowercase acronym for *radio detection and ranging*. Radar acceptable in all references.

radical In general, avoid this description in favor of a more precise definition of an individual's political views.

When used, it suggests that an individual believes change must be made by tearing up the roots or foundation of the present order.

Although *radical* often is applied to individuals who hold strong socialist or communist views, it also is applied at times to individuals who believe an existing form of government must be replaced by a more authoritarian or militaristic one.

See **leftist, ultra-leftist** and **rightist, ultra-rightist**.

radio Capitalize and use before a name to indicate an official or state-funded broadcast voice: *Radio Free Europe, Radio France International.*

Lowercase and place after the name when indicating only that the information was obtained from broadcasts in a city. *Mexico City radio*, for example, is the form used in referring to reports that are broadcast on various stations in the Mexican capital.

radio station Use lowercase: *radio station WHEC*.
See **call letters**.

railroads Railroads can be characterized as either freight carriers or passenger railroads. Freight carriers with U.S. operations:
Canadian National Railway Co., parent of the Illinois Central and Wisconsin Central Ltd.
Burlington Northern Santa Fe, a unit of Berkshire Hathaway Inc.
Canadian Pacific Railway Ltd., parent of Dakota, Minnesota & Eastern Railroad Corp.
CSX Corp.
Kansas City Southern
Norfolk Southern Corp.
Union Pacific Corp

U.S. passenger and commuter railroads include:
Amtrak
Bay Area Rapid Transit (BART) (San Francisco)
Los Angeles County Light Rail
Massachusetts Bay Commuter Railroad Co.
Metropolitan Atlanta Rapid Transit Authority (MARTA)
Metropolitan Transportation Authority (including Long Island Railroad and Metro North)
New Jersey Transit Corp.
Northeast Illinois Regional Commuter Railroad Corp. (Metra)
Southeast Pennsylvania Transportation Authority (SEPTA)
Washington Metropolitan Area Transit Authority (Metro)

rainstorm See **weather terms**.

raised, reared Only humans may be *reared*.
All living things, including humans, may be *raised*.

RAM Acronym for *random access memory*, the "working memory" of a computer into which programs can be introduced and then executed. *RAM* is acceptable in all uses.

Ramadan The Muslim holy month, marked by daily fasting from dawn to sunset, ending with the Islamic holiday of Eid al-Fitr. Avoid using *holiday* on second reference.

ranges The form: *$12 million to $14 million*. Not: *$12 to $14 million*. Also: *A pay increase of 12-15 percent*. Or: *A pay increase of between 12 and 15 percent*.

rank and file (n.) **rank-and-file** (adj.)

rarely It means seldom. *Rarely ever* is redundant, but *rarely if ever* often is the appropriate phrase.

ratings agency A company that measures the creditworthiness of companies, municipalities and countries. A ratings agency gauges an entity's ability to repay its debt and assigns a rating based on that assessment. The better the rating, the lower the cost for an entity to borrow money. The three main international ratings agencies are Standard & Poor's, a unit of McGraw-Hill Companies Inc.; Moody's Investors Service, a unit of Moody's Corp.; and Fitch Ratings, a unit of Fimalac SA of Paris.

ratios Use figures and hyphens: *the ratio was 2-to-1, a ratio of 2-to-1, a 2-1 ratio*. As illustrated, the word *to* should be omitted when the numbers precede the word *ratio*.
Always use the word *ratio* or a

phrase such as *a 2-1 majority* to avoid confusion with actual figures.

ravage, ravish *To ravage* is to wreak great destruction or devastation: *Union troops ravaged Atlanta.*

To ravish is to abduct, rape or carry away with emotion: *Soldiers ravished the women.*

Although both words connote an element of violence, they are not interchangeable. Buildings and towns cannot be *ravished*.

rayon Not a trademark.

re- The rules in **prefixes** apply. The following examples of exceptions to first-listed spellings in Webster's New World College Dictionary are based on the general rule that a hyphen is used if a prefix ends in a vowel and the word that follows begins with the same vowel:

re-elect	re-enlist
re-election	re-enter
re-emerge	re-entry
re-employ	re-equip
re-enact	re-establish
re-engage	re-examine

For many other words, the sense is the governing factor:

recover (regain)	re-cover (cover again)
reform (improve)	re-form (form again)
resign (quit)	re-sign (sign again)

Otherwise, follow Webster's New World College Dictionary. Use a hyphen for words not listed there unless the hyphen would distort the sense.

reader See **Church of Christ, Scientist**.

Realtor The term *real estate agent* is preferred. Use *Realtor* only if there is a reason to indicate that the individual is a member of the National Association of Realtors.

reared See **raised, reared**.

rebut, refute *Rebut* means to

argue to the contrary: *He rebutted his opponent's statement.*

Refute connotes success in argument and almost always implies an editorial judgment. Instead, use *deny, dispute, rebut* or *respond to.*

receivership A legal action in which a court appoints a *receiver* to manage a business while the court tries to resolve problems that could ruin the business, such as insolvency. *Receivership* is often used in federal bankruptcy court proceedings. But it also can be used for nonfinancial troubles such as an ownership dispute.

In bankruptcy proceedings, the court appoints a trustee called a *receiver* who attempts to settle the financial difficulties of the company while under protection from creditors.

recession A falling-off of economic activity that may be a temporary phenomenon or could continue into a depression.

recession-proof

recipes Always use figures. See **fractions**.

Do not use abbreviations. Spell out *teaspoon, tablespoon,* etc.

See the **food** entry for guidelines on when to capitalize the names of foods.

recision The preferred spelling is *rescission*.

reconnaissance

Reconstruction The process of reorganizing the Southern states after the Civil War.

record Avoid the redundant *new record*.

rector See **religious titles**.

recur, recurred, recurring Not *reoccur*.

Red Capitalize when used as a political, geographic or military term: *the Red army*.

red-haired, redhead, redheaded All are acceptable for a person with red hair.
Redhead also is used colloquially to describe a type of North American diving duck.

red-handed (adj. and adv.)

red-hot

redneck From the characteristic sunburned neck acquired in the fields by farm laborers. It refers to poor, white rural residents of the South and often is a derogatory term.

re-elect, re-election

refer See **allude, refer**.

referable

reference works Capitalize their proper names.
Do not use quotation marks around the names of books that are primarily catalogs of reference material. In addition to catalogs, this category includes almanacs, directories, dictionaries, encyclopedias, gazetteers, handbooks, school yearbooks and similar publications.
EXAMPLES: *Congressional Directory, Webster's New World College Dictionary, the AP Stylebook*. But: *"The Careful Writer"* and *"The Elements of Style."*
See the bibliography for the principal reference works used in preparing this book.

referendum, referendums

reformatory See **prison, jail**.

Reform Judaism See **Jewish congregations**.

refugee A person who is forced to leave his home or country to escape war, persecution or natural disaster.

refute See **rebut, refute**.

regime See **government, junta, regime**.

regions See **directions and regions**.

reign, rein The leather strap for controlling a horse is a *rein*, hence figuratively: *seize the reins, give free rein to, put a checkrein on*.
Reign is the period a ruler is on the throne: *The king began his reign*.

release times Follow these guidelines; consult online Stylebook for story formats:
TIME SET BY SOURCE FOR PUBLICATION OR BROADCAST OF A STORY: If a source provides material on condition that it not be published or broadcast until a specific time (sometimes known as a release embargo), the story should move on a Hold for Release (HFR) basis.
TIME SET BY SOURCE FOR WIRE MOVEMENT: If a source provides material on condition that it not be transmitted in any form to members or subscribers until a specific time (sometimes known as a wire embargo or wire movement embargo), the material should be held until that time. Consult New York if any problems arise.
AP ADVANCES: AP stories sent in advance for use on a specific date are considered released for publication and broadcast at 6:30 p.m. Eastern time the night before that date.

religious affiliations Capitalize the names and the related terms applied to members of the orders: *He is a member of the Society of Jesus. He is a Jesuit.*

religious movements The terms that follow have been grouped under a single entry because they are interrelated and frequently cross denominational lines.

evangelical Historically, *evangelical* was used as an adjective describing Protestant dedication to conveying the message of Christ. Today it also is used as a noun, referring to a category of doctrinally conservative Protestants. They emphasize the need for a definite, adult commitment or conversion to faith in Christ and the duty of all believers to persuade others to accept Christ.

Evangelicals make up some conservative denominations and are numerous in broader denominations. Evangelicals stress both doctrinal absolutes and vigorous efforts to win others to belief.

The National Association of Evangelicals is an interdenominational, cooperative body of relatively small, conservative Protestant denominations.

evangelism The word refers to activity directed outside the church fold to influence others to commit themselves to faith in Christ, to his work of serving others and to infuse his principles into society's conduct.

Styles of evangelism vary from direct preaching appeals at large public meetings to practical deeds of carrying the name of Christ, indirectly conveying the same call to allegiance to him.

The word *evangelism* is derived from the Greek *evangelion*, which means the gospel or good news of Christ's saving action in behalf of humanity.

fundamentalist The word gained usage in an early-20th century fundamentalist-modernist controversy within Protestantism. In recent years, however, *fundamentalist* has to a large extent taken on pejorative connotations except when applied to groups that stress strict, literal interpretations of Scripture and separation from other Christians.

In general, do not use *fundamentalist* unless a group applies the word to itself.

liberal In general, avoid this word as a descriptive classification in religion. It has objectionable implications to many believers.

Acceptable alternate descriptions include *activist, more flexible* and *broadview.*

Moderate is appropriate when used by the contending parties, as is the case in the conflict between the moderate or more flexible wing of a denomination and conservatives, who argue for literal interpretations of biblical passages others consider symbolic.

Do not use the term *Bible-believing* to distinguish one faction from another, because all Christians believe the Bible. The differences are over interpretations.

neo-Pentecostal, charismatic These terms apply to a movement that has developed within mainline Protestant and Roman Catholic denominations since the mid-20th century. It is distinguished by its emotional expressiveness, spontaneity in worship, speaking or praying in "unknown tongues" and healing. Participants often characterize themselves as "spirit-filled" Christians.

Unlike the earlier Pentecostal movement, which led to separate denominations, this movement has swelled within major churches.

Pentecostalism A movement that arose in the early 20th century and separated from historic Protestant denominations. It is distinguished by the belief in tangible manifestations of the Holy Spirit, often in demonstrative, emotional ways such as speaking in "unknown tongues" and healing.

Pentecostal denominations include the Assemblies of God, the Pentecostal Holiness Church, the United Pentecostal Church Inc. and the International Church of the Foursquare Gospel founded by Aimee Semple McPherson.

religious references The basic guidelines:

DEITIES: Capitalize the proper names of monotheistic deities: *God, Allah, the Father, the Son, Jesus Christ, the Son of God, the Redeemer, the Holy Spirit,* etc.

Lowercase pronouns referring to the deity: *he, him, his, thee, thou, who, whose, thy,* etc.

Lowercase *gods* in referring to the deities of polytheistic religions.

Capitalize the proper names of pagan and mythological gods and goddesses: *Neptune, Thor, Venus,* etc.

Lowercase such words as *god-awful, goddamn, godlike, godliness, godsend.*

LIFE OF CHRIST: Capitalize the names of major events in the life of Jesus Christ in references that do not use his name: *The doctrines of the Last Supper, the Crucifixion, the Resurrection and the Ascension are central to Christian belief.*

But use lowercase when the words are used with his name: *The ascension of Jesus into heaven took place 40 days after his resurrection from the dead.*

Apply the principle also to events in the life of his mother: *He cited the doctrines of the Immaculate Conception and the Assumption.* But: *She referred to the assumption of Mary into heaven.*

RITES: Capitalize proper names for rites that commemorate the Last Supper or signify a belief in Christ's presence: *the Lord's Supper, Holy Communion, Holy Eucharist.*

Lowercase the names of other sacraments. See **sacraments**.

Capitalize *Benediction* and the *Mass.* But: *a high Mass, a low Mass, a requiem Mass.*

HOLY DAYS: Capitalize the names of holy days. See **holidays and holy days** and separate entries for major Christian, Jewish and Muslim feasts.

OTHER WORDS: Lowercase *heaven, hell, devil, angel, cherub, an apostle, a priest,* etc.

Capitalize *Hades* and *Satan.*

For additional details, see **Bible**, entries for frequently used religious terms, the entries for major denominations, **religious movements** and **religious titles**.

Religious Society of Friends
See **Quakers**.

religious titles The first reference to a clergyman or clergywoman normally should include a capitalized title before the individual's name.

In many cases, *the Rev.* is the designation that applies before a name on first reference. Use *the Rev. Dr.* only if the individual has an earned doctoral degree (doctor of divinity degrees frequently are honorary) and reference to the degree is relevant.

On second reference to members of the clergy, use only a last name: *the Rev. Billy Graham* on first reference, *Graham* on second. If known only by a religious name, repeat the title: *Pope Benedict XVI* on first reference, *Benedict, the pope* or *the pontiff* on second; *Metropolitan Herman* on first reference, *Metropolitan Herman* or *the metropolitan* on second.

Detailed guidance on specific titles and descriptive words such as *priest* and *minister* is provided in the entries for major denominations. In general, however:

CARDINALS, ARCHBISHOPS,

BISHOPS: The preferred form for first reference is to use *Cardinal, Archbishop* or *Bishop* before the individual's name: *Cardinal Daniel DiNardo, archbishop of Galveston-Houston.* On second reference: *DiNardo* or *the cardinal.*

Substitute *the Most Rev.* if applicable and appropriate in the context: *He spoke to the Most Rev. Jose Gomez, archbishop of San Antonio.* On second reference: *Gomez* or *the archbishop.*

Entries for individual denominations tell when *the Most Rev., the Very Rev.,* etc., are applicable.

MINISTERS AND PRIESTS: Use *the Rev.* before a name on first reference.

Substitute *Monsignor* before the name of a Roman Catholic priest who has received this honor.

Do not routinely use *curate, father, pastor* and similar words before an individual's name. If they appear before a name in a quotation, capitalize them.

RABBIS: Use *Rabbi* before a name on first reference. On second reference, use only the last name.

NUNS: Always use *Sister,* or *Mother* if applicable, before a name: *Sister Agnes Rita* in all references if the nun uses only a religious name; *Sister Mary Ann Walsh* on first reference if she uses a surname. *Walsh* on subsequent references.

OFFICEHOLDERS: The preferred first-reference form for those who hold church office but are not ordained clergy in the usual sense is to use a construction that sets the title apart from the name by commas. Capitalize the formal title of an office, however, if it is used directly before an individual's name.

reluctant, reticent *Reluctant* means unwilling to act: *He is reluctant to enter the primary.*

Reticent means unwilling to speak: *The candidate's husband is reticent.*

Reorganized Church of Jesus Christ of Latter Day Saints Not

properly described as a *Mormon church.* See the explanation under **Church of Jesus Christ of Latter-day Saints**.

representative, Rep. See **legislative titles** and **party affiliation**.

republic Capitalize *republic* when used as part of a nation's full, formal name: *the Republic of Argentina.*

See **datelines**.

Republic Airways Holdings Inc. Headquarters of this airline is in Indianapolis.

Republican Governors Association No apostrophe.

Republican National Committee On second reference: *the national committee, the committee* and *the RNC.*

Similarly: *Republican State Committee, Republican County Committee, Republican City Committee, the state committee, the county committee, the city committee, the committee.*

Republican, Republican Party

GOP may be used on second reference.

See **political parties and philosophies**.

reputation See **character, reputation**.

rescission

Reserve Capitalize when referring to U.S. armed forces, as in *Army Reserve.* Lowercase in reference to members of these backup forces: *reserves,* or *reservists.*

Reserve Officers' Training Corps The *s'* is military practice. *ROTC* is acceptable in all references.

When the service is specified, use *Army ROTC, Navy ROTC* or *Air Force ROTC,* not *AROTC, NROTC* or *AFROTC.*

resident See **citizen, resident, subject, national, native**.

resistible

restaurateur

restrictive clauses See **essential clauses, nonessential clauses**.

restrictive phrases See **essential phrases, nonessential phrases**.

Retail Clerks International Union See **United Food and Commercial Workers International Union**.

retail sales The sales of retail stores, including merchandise sold and receipts for repairs and similar services.

A business is considered a *retail store* if it is engaged primarily in selling merchandise for personal, household or farm consumption.

Reuters See **Thomson Reuters Corp**.

Rev. When this description is used before an individual's name, precede it with the word *"the"* because, unlike the case with *Mr.* and *Mrs.*, the abbreviation *Rev.* does not stand for a noun.

If an individual also has a secular title such as *Rep.*, use whichever is appropriate to the context.

See **religious titles**.

revenue See **profit terminology**.

revenue bond See **loan terminology**.

reverse auction An auction where the winning bidder is the one willing to take the lowest price. In a reverse auction for subprime mortgage loans, for instance, a bank offering to sell a bundle of bad loans for 50 cents on the dollar would beat a bank offering to sell its loans for 60 cents on the dollar.

revolution Capitalize when part of a name for a specific historical event: *the American Revolution, the Bolshevik Revolution, the French Revolution.*

The Revolution, capitalized, also may be used as a shorthand reference to the *American Revolution.* Also: *the Revolutionary War.*

Lowercase in other uses: *a revolution, the revolution, the American and French revolutions.*

revolutions per minute The abbreviation *rpm* is acceptable on first reference in specialized contexts such as an auto column. Otherwise do not use it until second reference.

revolving credit Describes an account on which the payment is any amount less than the total balance, and the remaining balance carried forward is subject to finance charges.

Rh factor Also: *Rh negative, Rh positive.*

Rhode Island Abbreviate *R.I.* in datelines or stories. Postal code: *RI*

Smallest of the 50 states in total land area: 1,049 square miles. See **state names**.

Rhodes scholar Lowercase *scholar* and *scholarship.*

rhythm and blues *R&B* is acceptable on second reference.

RIA Novosti A Russian government news agency, based in Moscow. Successor to the Soviet Information Bureau (1941-1960) and the Novosti Press Agency (1961-1990).

Richter scale No longer widely used. See **earthquakes**.

RICO An acronym for *Racketeer Influenced and Corrupt Organizations Act*. Acceptable on second reference, but *anti-racketeering* or *anti-corruption law* is preferred.

rifle See **weapons**.

rifle, riffle To *rifle* is to plunder or steal.
To *riffle* is to leaf rapidly through a book or pile of papers.

right hand (n.) **right-handed** (adj.) **right-hander** (n.)

rightist, ultra-rightist In general, avoid these terms in favor of more precise descriptions of an individual's political philosophy.
Ultra-rightist suggests an individual who subscribes to rigid interpretations of a conservative doctrine or to forms of fascism that stress authoritarian, often militaristic, views.
See **radical** and **leftist, ultra-leftist**.

right of way, rights of way

right-to-work (adj.) A *right-to-work* law prohibits a company and a union from signing a contract that would require the affected workers to be union members.
See **closed shop** for definitions of various agreements that require union membership.

right wing (n.), **right-wing** (adj.) **right-winger** (n.) Generally try to avoid in describing political leanings.

Ringling Bros. and Barnum & Bailey Note the *and, &*.
The circus is owned by Feld Entertainment Inc., headquartered in Vienna, Va.

Rio de Janeiro The city in Brazil stands alone in datelines.

Rio Grande Not *Rio Grande River*. *Rio* means river in Spanish.

rip off (v.) **rip-off** (n. and adj.)

river Capitalize as part of a proper name: *the Mississippi River*.
Lowercase in other uses: *the river, the Mississippi and Missouri rivers*.

road Do not abbreviate. See **addresses**.

robbery See **burglary, larceny, robbery, theft**.

Roche Holding AG Headquarters is in Basel, Switzerland.

rock 'n' roll But *Rock and Roll Hall of Fame*.

Rocky Mountains Or simply: *the Rockies*.

roll call (n.) **roll-call** (adj.)

Rollerblade A trademark for a brand of in-line skates.

rollover The selling of new securities to pay off old ones coming due or the refinancing of an existing loan.

Rolls-Royce Note the hyphen in this trademark for a make of automobile.

Rolodex A trademark for a brand of rotary card file.

ROM Acronym for *read-only memory*, computer memory whose contents cannot be modified. *ROM* acceptable in all references.

Roma Capitalize references to the nomadic ethnic group also known as *Gypsies*. Either is acceptable. In the United States, they are widely referred to as *Gypsies*. The word should be explained: *Roma, also known as Gypsies*. See **Gypsy, Gypsies**.

Roman Catholic Church The church teaches that its bishops have been established as the successors of the apostles through generations of ceremonies in which authority was passed down by a laying-on of hands.

Responsibility for teaching the faithful and administering the church rests with the bishops. However, the church holds that the pope has final authority over their actions because he is the bishop of Rome, the office that it teaches was held by the Apostle Peter at his death.

The Curia serves as a form of governmental cabinet. Its members, appointed by the pope, handle both administrative and judicial functions.

The pope also chooses members of the College of Cardinals, who serve as his principal counselors. When a new pope must be chosen, they meet in a conclave to select a new pope by majority vote. In practice, cardinals are bishops, but there is no requirement that a cardinal be a bishop.

In the United States, the church's principal organizational units are archdioceses and dioceses. They are headed, respectively, by archbishops and bishops, who have final responsibility for many activities within their jurisdictions and report directly to Rome.

The church counts more than 1 billion members worldwide. In the United States it has more than 65 million members, making it the largest single body of Christians in the nation.

Roman Catholics believe in the Trinity — that there is one God who exists as three divine persons, the Father, the Son and the Holy Spirit. They believe that the Son became man as Jesus Christ.

In addition to the Holy Eucharist, there are six other sacraments — baptism, confirmation, penance (often called the sacrament of reconciliation), matrimony, holy orders, and the sacrament of the sick (formerly extreme unction).

The clergy below pope are, in descending order, cardinal, archbishop, bishop, monsignor, priest and deacon. In religious orders, some men who are not priests have the title *brother*.

Capitalize *pope* when used as a title before a name: *Pope Benedict XVI, Pope Paul*. Lowercase in all other uses. See **titles**.

The first-reference forms for other titles follow. Use only last names on second reference.

Cardinals: *Cardinal Daniel DiNardo*. The usage *Daniel Cardinal DiNardo*, a practice traceable to the nobility's custom of identifications such as *William, Duke of Norfolk*, is still used in formal documents but otherwise is considered archaic.

Archbishops: *Archbishop Daniel DiNardo*, or *the Most Rev. Daniel DiNardo, archbishop of Galveston-Houston*.

Bishops: *Bishop William Lori*, or *the Most Rev. William Lori, bishop of Bridgeport, Conn.*

Monsignors: *Monsignor Martin Krebs*. Do not use the abbreviation *Msgr*. Do not use *the Rt. Rev.* or *the Very Rev.* — this distinction between types of monsignors no longer is made.

Priests: *the Rev. James Martin*.

See **religious titles**.

Romania

Romanian Orthodox Church
The Romanian Orthodox Church in America is an autonomous archdiocese of the Romanian Orthodox Church. The Romanian Orthodox Episcopate of America is an autonomous archdiocese within the Orthodox Church in America.
See **Eastern Orthodox churches**.

Roman numerals They use letters (*I, X,* etc.) to express numbers.

Use Roman numerals for wars and to establish personal sequence for people and animals: *World War I, Native Dancer II, King George V.* Also for certain legislative acts (*Title IX*) and pro football Super Bowls.

Use Arabic numerals in all other cases. See **Arabic numerals** and **numerals**.

In Roman numerals, the capital letter *I* equals 1, *V* equals 5, *X* equals 10, *L* equals 50, *C* equals 100, *D* equals 500 and *M* equals 1,000.

Other numbers are formed from these by adding or subtracting as follows:

—The value of a letter following another of the same or greater value is added: *III* equals 3.

—The value of a letter preceding one of greater value is subtracted: *IV* equals 4.

Rome The city in Italy stands alone in datelines.

room numbers Use figures and capitalize *room* when used with a figure: *Room 2, Room 211.*

rooms Capitalize the names of specially designated rooms: *Blue Room, Lincoln Room, Oval Office, Persian Room.*

rosary It is *recited* or *said*, never *read*. Always lowercase.

Rosh Hashana The Jewish new year. Occurs in September or October.

rostrum See **lectern, podium, pulpit, rostrum**.

ROTC See **Reserve Officers' Training Corps**.

round up (v.) **roundup** (n.)

route numbers Do not abbreviate *route.* Use figures and capitalize route when used with a figure: *U.S. Route 70, state Route 1A.*
See **highway designations**.

Royal Dutch Shell PLC A 2005 unification of Royal Dutch Petroleum and Shell Transport & Trading Co., with headquarters in The Hague, Netherlands. The company specializes in petroleum and related products. Holdings include Shell Oil Co., a U.S. corporation, with headquarters in Houston.

royal titles See **nobility**.

RSS An abbreviation for *Really Simple Syndication.* A protocol for subscribing to and distributing feeds that notify people of new entries on news sites, blogs, podcasts or other online information sources. *RSS* is acceptable in all references. Also *RSS feed.*

RSVP The abbreviation for the French *repondez s'il vous plait,* it means *please reply.*

rubber stamp (n.) **rubber-stamp** (v. and adj.)

rubella Also known as *German measles.*

runner-up, runners-up

running mate

rush hour (n.) **rush-hour** (adj.)

Russia See **Commonwealth of Independent States**.

Russian names When a first name in Russian has a close phonetic equivalent in English, use the equivalent in translating the name: *Alexander Solzhenitsyn* rather than *Aleksandr*, the spelling that would result from a transliteration of the Russian letter into the English alphabet.

When a first name has no close phonetic equivalent in English, express it with an English spelling that approximates the sound in Russian: *Dmitry, Nikita, Sergei*, for example.

For last names, use the English spelling that most closely approximates the pronunciation in Russian. Exception: the *"ev"* ending of names like Gorbachev may be pronounced "yov."

If an individual has a preference for an English spelling that is different from the one that would result by applying these guidelines, follow the individual's preference.

Women's last names have feminine endings. But use them only if the woman is not married or if she is known under that name (*the ballerina Maya Plissetskaya*). Otherwise, use the masculine form: *Raisa Gorbachev*, not *Gorbacheva*.

Russian names never end in *off*, except for common mistransliterations such as *Rachmaninoff*. Instead, the transliterations should end in *ov*: *Romanov*. Also, Russian names end in *"sky,"* rather than *"ski"* typical of Polish surnames.

Russian Orthodox Church See **Eastern Orthodox churches**.

Russian Revolution Also: *the Bolshevik Revolution*.

Rust Belt Areas of the Midwest and Northeast where factories are old and closed.

Ryanair Holdings PLC Headquarters of this airline is in Dublin, Ireland.

Sabbath Capitalize in religious references.

saboteur

Sacagawea

sacraments Capitalize the proper names used for a sacramental rite that commemorates the life of Jesus Christ or signifies a belief in his presence: *the Lord's Supper, Holy Communion, Holy Eucharist.*

Lowercase the names of other sacraments: *baptism, confirmation, penance* (now often called the *sacrament of reconciliation*), *matrimony, holy orders,* and *the sacrament of anointing the sick* (formerly *extreme unction*).

See entries for the major religious denominations and **religious references**.

sacrilegious

Saddam Use *Saddam* in second reference to Iraq's Saddam Hussein.

Safeway Inc. Formerly Safeway Stores. Headquarters is in Pleasanton, Calif.

saint Abbreviate as *St.* in the names of saints, cities and other places: *St. Jude; St. Paul, Minn.; St. John's, Newfoundland; St. Lawrence Seaway.*

But see the entries for **Saint John** and **Sault Ste. Marie.**

Saint John The spelling for the city in New Brunswick.

To distinguish it from *St. John's, Newfoundland.*

salable

SALT See **Strategic Arms Reduction Treaty (START)**

Salt Lake City The city in Utah stands alone in datelines.

salvo, salvos

SAM, SAMs Acceptable on second reference for *surface-to-air missile(s).*

Samsung Electronics Headquarters is in Seoul, South Korea.

Sanaa The capital of Yemen. The double-a retains the Arabic pronunciation of San'a, AP's former spelling.

San Antonio The city in Texas stands alone in datelines.

sandbag (n. and v.) The verbs: *sandbagged, sandbagging.* And: *sandbagger.*

San Diego The city in California stands alone in datelines.

sandstorm See **weather terms**.

San Francisco The city in California stands alone in datelines.

sanitarium, sanitariums

San Marino Use alone in datelines on stories from the Republic of San Marino.

Santa Claus

Sao Paulo The city in Brazil stands alone in datelines.

Sardinia Use instead of Italy in datelines on stories from communities on this island.

SARS Acceptable in all references for *severe acute respiratory syndrome*, but it should be spelled out somewhere in the story.

Saskatchewan A province of Canada north of Montana and North Dakota. Do not abbreviate.
See **datelines**.

SAT Use only the initials in referring to the previously designated Scholastic Aptitude Test or the Scholastic Assessment Test. Example: *The students scored above average on the SAT.*

Satan But lowercase *devil* and *satanic*.

satellite communications The
following are some generally used technical terms dealing with satellite communications.
uplink The transmission from the ground to the satellite.
downlink The transmission from the satellite to the ground.
footprint The area on the ground in which a transmission from a particular satellite can be received.
earth station Sending or receiving equipment on the ground for a satellite.
transponder The equipment on

a satellite that receives from the ground and sends to the ground. A satellite usually has a number of *transponders*.
geosynchronous A satellite orbit in which the satellite appears to always be in the same place in reference to the Earth. Most communications satellites are in geosynchronous orbits. Also *geostationary*.

satellites See **spacecraft designations**.

Saturday night special See **weapons**.

Saudi Arabia Use *Saudi* as the adjective in referring to the people or culture of Saudi Arabia. It's *Saudi diplomacy*, not Saudi Arabian diplomacy. For the Saudi monarchy, follow the style on British and other monarchies. *Foreign Minister Prince Saud Al-Faisal* would be *Prince Saud* on first reference and *Saud* on second reference.

Saudi Arabian Oil Co. *Saudi Aramco* is acceptable on second reference. Formerly the Arabian American Oil Co.

Sault Ste. Marie, Mich., Sault Ste. Marie, Ontario The abbreviation is *Ste.* instead of *St.* because the full name is *Sault Sainte Marie*.

savings and loan associations
Once limited to accepting deposits and making home mortgage loans, they are not banks. Since enactment of the Financial Institutions Reform Recovery and Enforcement Act in 1989, they have been regulated by the Office of Thrift Supervision. Use *the association* on second reference.

savior Use this spelling for all senses, rather than the alternate form, *saviour*.

scene numbers Capitalize scene when used with a figure: *Scene 2; Act 2, Scene 4.*

But: *the second scene, the third scene.*

scheme Do not use as a synonym for *a plan* or *a project.*

school Capitalize when part of a proper name: *Public School 3, Madison Elementary School, Doherty Junior High School, Crocker High School.*

scissors Takes plural verbs and pronouns: *The scissors are on the table. Leave them there.*

scotch barley, scotch broth, scotch salmon, scotch sour

Scotch tape A trademark for a brand of transparent tape.

Scotland Use *Scotland* after the names of Scottish communities in datelines.

See **datelines** and **United Kingdom**.

Scot, Scots, Scottish A native of Scotland is a *Scot.* The people are the *Scots,* not the *Scotch.*

Somebody or something is *Scottish.*

screen saver

E.W. Scripps Co. Owner of the Commercial Appeal in Memphis, Tenn., the Knoxville (Tenn.) News Sentinel, the Ventura County (Calif.) Star, other newspapers and broadcast properties. Its United Media unit distributes Peanuts, Dilbert and other comics. Spun off Scripps Networks Interactive Inc. on July 1, 2008. Sponsors annual spelling bee.

Headquarters is in Cincinnati.

Scripps Networks Interac-

tive Inc. Owner of HGTV, Food Network, DIY Network and other national television networks. Spun off from E.W. Scripps Co. on July 1, 2008. Headquarters is in Cincinnati.

Scripture, Scriptures Capitalize when referring to the religious writings in the Bible.

See **Bible**.

scuba Lowercased acronym for *self-contained underwater breathing apparatus.*

Scud missile

sculptor Use for both men and women.

scurrilous

Sea Islands A chain of islands off the coasts of South Carolina, Georgia and Florida.

Islands within the boundaries of South Carolina include Parris Island, Port Royal Island, and St. Helena Island.

Those within Georgia include Cumberland Island (largest in the chain), St. Simons Island and St. Catherines Island (no apostrophes), and Sea Island.

Amelia Island is within the boundaries of Florida.

Several communities have names taken from the island name — Port Royal is a town on Port Royal Island, Sea Island is a resort on Sea Island, and St. Simons Island is a village on St. Simons Island.

In datelines:
PORT ROYAL, S.C. (AP) —
ST. SIMONS ISLAND, Ga. (AP) —

SEAL(s) A special operations force of the Navy. The acronym is for *sea, air, land.*

See **special forces**.

seaman See **military titles**.

Sears Holdings Corp. The company formed when Kmart Holding Corp. bought Sears, Roebuck & Co. in 2005. Headquarters is in Hoffman Estates, Ill.

seasons Lowercase *spring, summer, fall, winter* and derivatives such as *springtime* unless part of a formal name: *Dartmouth Winter Carnival, Winter Olympics, Summer Olympics*.

Seattle The city in the state of Washington stands alone in datelines.

second guess (n.) The verb form: *second-guess*. Also: *second-guesser*.

second hand (n.) **secondhand** (adj. and adv.)

second-rate (adj.)

second reference When used in this book, the term applies to all subsequent references to an organization or individual within a story.

Acceptable abbreviations and acronyms for organizations frequently in the news are listed under the organization's full name. A few prominent acronyms acceptable on first reference also are listed alphabetically according to the letters of the acronym.

The listing of an acceptable term for second reference does not mean that it always must be used after the first reference. Often a generic word such as *the agency, the commission* or *the company* is more appropriate and less jarring to the reader. At other times, the full name may need to be repeated for clarity.

For additional guidelines that apply to organizations, see **abbreviations and acronyms** and **capitalization**.

For additional guidelines that apply to individuals, see **courtesy titles** and **titles**.

secretary Capitalize before a name only if it is an official corporate or organizational title. Do not abbreviate.
See **titles**.

secretary-general With a hyphen. Capitalize as a formal title before a name: *Secretary-General Ban Ki-moon*.
See **titles**.

secretary of state Capitalize as a formal title before a name.
See **titles**.

secretary-treasurer With a hyphen. Capitalize as a formal title before a name.
See **titles**.

Secret Service A federal agency administered by the Department of Homeland Security.

The *Secret Service Uniformed Division*, which protects the president's residence and offices and the embassies in Washington, formerly was known as the Executive Protective Service.

section Capitalize when used with a figure to identify part of a law or bill: *Section 14B of the Taft-Hartley Act*.

Securities and Exchange Commission *SEC* is acceptable on second reference.

The related legislation is the *Securities Exchange Act* (no *and*).

securitization Bundling together individual assets, such as mortgages, and selling stakes to investors.

Security Council (U.N.) *Se-*

curity Council may be used on first reference in stories under a United Nations dateline. Use *U.N. Security Council* in other first references.

Retain capitalization of *Security Council* in all references.

Lowercase *council* whenever it stands alone.

Seeing Eye dog A trademark for a guide dog trained by Seeing Eye Inc. of Morristown, N.J. *Guide dog* is preferred in all references.

seesaw

self- Always hyphenate:
self-assured   self-government
self-defense

sell out (v.) **sellout** (n.)

semi- The rules in **prefixes** apply, but in general, no hyphen. Some examples:
semifinal   semiofficial
semi-invalid   semitropical

semiannual Twice a year, a synonym for *biannual*.

Do not confuse it with *biennial*, which means every two years.

semicolon See entry in **Punctuation** chapter.

semitrailer Or *tractor-trailer*, but not *semi-tractor trailer*.

Senate Capitalize all specific references to governmental legislative bodies, regardless of whether the name of the state or nation is used: *the U.S. Senate, the Senate, the Virginia Senate, the state Senate, the Senate.*

Lowercase plural uses: *the Virginia and North Carolina senates.*

See **governmental bodies**.

The same principles apply to non-U.S. bodies. See **non-U.S. legislative bodies**.

Lowercase references to non-governmental bodies: *the student senate at Yale.*

senatorial Always lowercase.

senator, Sen. See **legislative titles** and **party affiliation**.

send off (v.) **send-off** (n.)

senior See **junior, senior**.

senior citizen Use the term sparingly. See **elderly**.

sentences Capitalize the first word of every sentence, including quoted statements and direct questions:
Patrick Henry said, "I know not what course others may take, but as for me, give me liberty or give me death."

Capitalize the first word of a quoted statement if it constitutes a sentence, even if it was part of a larger sentence in the original: *Patrick Henry said, "Give me liberty or give me death."*

In direct questions, even without quotation marks: *The story answers the question, Where does true happiness really lie?*

Use a single space between sentences.

See **ellipsis** in **Punctuation** chapter and **poetry**.

Sept. 11 The term for describing the attacks in the United States on Sept. 11, 2001. Use 2001 if needed for clarity. Also acceptable is 9/11. See **9/11**.

Sept. 11 memorial Acceptable in all references to the *National September 11 Memorial & Museum* at *ground zero*. Add location for other memorials with similar names.

sergeant See **military titles**.

sergeant-at-arms

serial numbers Use figures and capital letters in solid form (no hyphens or spaces unless the source indicates they are an integral part of the code): *A1234567*.

server A computer program that responds to requests from remote computers on a network. A Web server, for instance, hosts websites and delivers pages to users upon demand. A file server, in another example, stores and delivers documents to users on a network. A server typically runs on a specialized computer, though most of today's PCs are capable of running such software.

serviceable

service clubs See **fraternal organizations and service clubs**.

serviceman, servicewoman But *service member*.

sesquicentennial A 150-year period.

set up (v.) **setup** (n. and adj.)

Seven Seas Arabian Sea, Atlantic Ocean, Bay of Bengal, Mediterranean Sea, Persian Gulf, Red Sea, South China Sea.

Seventh-day Adventist Church The denomination is traceable to the preaching of William Miller of New Hampton, New York, a Baptist layman who said his study of the Book of Daniel showed that the end of the world would come in the mid-1840s.

When the prediction did not come true, the Millerites split into smaller groups. One, influenced by visions described by Ellen Harmon, later the wife of James White, is the precursor of the Seventh-day Adventist practice today.

The church has four constituent levels: 1. Local churches. 2. Local conferences of churches for a state or part of a state. 3. Union conferences of a number of local conferences. 4. The General Conference.

The General Conference in Session and the General Conference Executive Committee are the highest administrative authorities.

The headquarters is in Silver Spring, Md.

The description *adventist* is based on the belief that a second coming of Christ is near. *Seventh-day* derives from the contention that the Bible requires observing the seventh day of the week as the Sabbath.

Baptism, by immersion, is reserved for those old enough to understand its meaning. Baptism and the Lord's Supper are the only sacraments.

The head of the General Conference holds the formal title of *president*. The formal titles for ministers are *pastor* or *elder*. Capitalize them when used immediately before a name on first reference. On second reference, use only the last name.

The designation *the Rev.* is not used.

See **religious titles**.

Seven Wonders of the World The Egyptian pyramids, the hanging gardens of Babylon, the Mausoleum at Halicarnassus, the temple of Artemis at Ephesus, the Colossus of Rhodes, the statue of Zeus by Phidias at Olympia and the Pharos or lighthouse at Alexandria.

sewage Use this term, not *sewerage*, for both the waste matter and the drainage system.

sexism See **man, mankind** and **women**.

sexually transmitted diseases *STDs* is acceptable on second reference.

shah Capitalize when used as a title before a name: *Shah Mohammad Reza Pahlavi of Iran.*
The Shah of Iran commonly is known only by this title, which is, in effect, an alternate name. Capitalize *Shah of Iran* in references to the holder of the title; lowercase subsequent references as *the shah.*
The practice is based on the guidelines in the **nobility** entry.

shake up (v.) **shake-up** (n. and adj.)

shall, will Use *shall* to express determination: *We shall overcome. You and he shall stay.*
Either *shall* or *will* may be used in first-person constructions that do not emphasize determination: *We shall hold a meeting. We will hold a meeting.*
For second- and third-person constructions, use *will* unless determination is stressed: *You will like it. She will not be pleased.*
See **should, would** and **subjunctive mood**.

Shanghai The city in China stands alone in datelines.

shape up (v.) **shape-up** (n. and adj.)

Shariah Islamic law.

Shavuot The Jewish Feast of Weeks, commemorating the receiving of the Ten Commandments. Occurs in May or June.

she Do not use this pronoun in references to ships or nations.
Use *it* instead.

Sheet Metal Workers International Association The shortened form *Sheet Metal Workers union* is acceptable in all references.
Headquarters is in Washington.

Sheetrock A trademark for a brand of gypsum wallboard.

sheik A title for a religious or tribal leader. Also used as a term of respect. Use this spelling unless the individual named personally prefers *sheikh. Sheikh* also is used in certain Arab names, such as the Egyptian city of *Sharm el-Sheikh.*

shell See **weapons**.

sheriff Capitalize when used as a formal title before a name. See **titles**.

ships See **boats, ships**.

Shiite The spelling for this branch of Islam. Plural is *Shiites.* The alternate spelling *Shia* is acceptable in quotes. See **Islam**.

shirt sleeve, shirt sleeves (n.) **shirt-sleeve** (adj.)

shoeshine, shoestring

shopworn

short An investment term used to describe the position held by individuals who sell stock that they do not yet own by borrowing from their broker in order to deliver to the purchaser.
A person selling short is betting that the price of the stock will fall.

shortchange

short covering The purchase of a security to repay shares of a security borrowed from a broker.

short-lived (adj.) *A short-lived plan. The plan was short-lived.*

short sale A sale of securities that are not owned by the sellers at the time of sale but which they intend to purchase or borrow in time to make delivery. Short selling is a bet that a stock's price will fall.

short ton Equal to 2,000 pounds. See **ton**.

shot See **weapons**.

shotgun See **weapons**.

should, would Use *should* to express an obligation: *We should help the needy.*
Use *would* to express a customary action: *In the summer we would spend hours by the seashore.*
Use *would* also in constructing a conditional past tense, but be careful:
Wrong: *If Soderholm would not have had an injured foot, Thompson would not have been in the lineup.*
Right: *If Soderholm had not had an injured foot, Thompson would not have been in the lineup.*
See **subjunctive mood**.

shoutout (n.) **shout out** (v.)

showcase, showroom

show off (v.) **showoff** (n.)

shrubs See **plants**.

shut down (v.) **shutdown** (n.)

shut-in

shut off (v.) **shut-off** (n.)

shut out (v.) **shutout** (n.)

(sic) Do not use *(sic)* unless it is in the matter being quoted. To show that an error, peculiar usage or spelling is in the original, use a note to editors at the top of the story, below the summary line but ahead of a byline.

— — —

Eds. note: [**Eds: The spelling cabob is in the original document.**]
or
Eds. note: [**Eds: The spelling Jorga is correct.**]

Sicily Use instead of Italy in datelines on stories from communities on this island.

side by side, side-by-side *They walked side by side. The stories received side-by-side display.*

Siemens AG Headquarters is in Munich.

Sierra Nevada, the Not *Sierra Nevada mountains* or *Sierra Nevada mountain range.* (*Sierra* means mountain range.)

sightseeing, sightseer

sign-up (n. and adj.) **sign up** (v.)

Silicon Valley The high-tech region encompassing the northern Santa Clara Valley and adjacent areas of Northern California.

Sinai Not the *Sinai.* But: *the Sinai Desert, the Sinai Peninsula.*

Singapore Stands alone in datelines.

Singapore Airlines Headquarters of this airline is in Singapore.

single-handed, single-handedly

sir See **nobility**.

sister Capitalize in all references before the names of nuns.

If no surname is given, the name is the same in all references: *Sister Agnes Rita.*

If a surname is used in first reference, drop the given name and sister on second reference: *Sister Mary Ann Walsh* on first reference, *Walsh* in subsequent references.

Use *Mother* the same way when referring to a woman who heads a group of nuns.

See **religious titles**.

sister-in-law, sisters-in-law

sit down (v.) **sit-down** (n. and adj.)

sit in (v.) **sit-in** (n. and adj.)

sit up (v.) **situp** (n.)

sizable

sizes Use figures: *a size 8 dress, size 40 long, 10 1/2B shoes, a 34 1/2 sleeve.*

skeptic See **cynic, skeptic**.

Skid Road, Skid Row The term originated as *Skid Road* in the Seattle area, where dirt roads were used to skid logs to the mill. Over the years, *Skid Road* became a synonym for the area where loggers gathered, usually down among the rooming houses and saloons.

In time, the term spread to other cities as a description for sections, such as the Bowery in New York, that were havens for derelicts. In the process, *row* replaced *road* in many references.

Use *Skid Road* for this section in Seattle; either *Skid Road* or *Skid Row* for other areas.

skillful

ski, skis, skier, skied, skiing Also: *ski jump, ski jumping.*

SkyWest Inc. Headquarters of this airline is in St. George, Utah.

slang In general, avoid slang, the highly informal language that is outside of conventional or standard usage.

See **colloquialisms** and **dialect**.

slash Acceptable in descriptive phrases such as 24/7 or 9/11, but otherwise confine its use to special situations, as with fractions or denoting the ends of a line in quoted poetry.

slaying See **homicide, murder, manslaughter**.

sledgehammer

sleet See **weather terms**.

sleight of hand

slideshow

slowdown (n.) **slow down** (v.)

slumlord

slush fund

small-arms fire

small-business man ✓

smartphone An advanced mobile device, such as an iPhone, that can be used to check email, browse the Web and download applications.

smash up (v.) **smashup** (n. and adj.)

Smithsonian Institution Not *Smithsonian Institute.*

smoke bomb, smoke screen

smokejumper One word, lowercase, for the firefighter who gets to fires by aircraft and parachute.

Smokey Or *Smokey Bear*. Not *Smokey the Bear*.
But: *A smoky room.*

smolder Not *smoulder*.

SMS An abbreviation for *Short Message Service*. *Text messaging* is preferred.

sneaked Preferred as past tense of *sneak*. Do not use the colloquial *snuck*.

snowdrift, snowfall, snowflake, snowman, snowplow, snowshoe, snowstorm, snowsuit

so called (adv.) **so-called** (adj.) Use sparingly. Do not follow with quotation marks. Example: *He is accused of trading so-called blood diamonds to finance the war.*

socialist, socialism See **political parties and philosophies**.

social media Online tools that people use to connect with one another, including social networks. See section on **Social Media Guidelines**.

social networking A practice by which people meet, interact and share information online through the use of such sites as *Facebook* or *Twitter*.

Social Security Capitalize all references to the U.S. system.
The number groups are hyphenated: *123-45-6789*
Lowercase generic uses such as: *Is there a social security program in Sweden?*

social titles See **courtesy titles**.

Society for the Prevention of Cruelty to Animals *SPCA* is acceptable on second reference.
The *American Society for the Prevention of Cruelty to Animals* is limited to the five boroughs of New York City.
The autonomous chapters in other cities ordinarily precede the organization by the name of the city: On first reference, *the San Francisco Society for the Prevention of Cruelty to Animals*; on second, *the San Francisco SPCA* or *SPCA* as appropriate in the context.

Society of Friends See **Quakers**.

Society of Professional Journalists (no longer the Society of Professional Journalists, Sigma Delta Chi). On second reference: *SPJ*.

soft-spoken

software titles Capitalize but do not use quotation marks around such titles as WordPerfect or Windows, but use quotation marks for computer games: *"Where in the World Is Carmen Sandiego?"*

solicitor See **lawyer**.

soliloquy, soliloquies

solvency The ability to pay expenses and debt on time and continue operating. An insolvent company typically has to seek bankruptcy protection from creditors.

Somali A person from Somalia, or an adjective for something linked to Somalia. Do not use *Somalian*.

song titles See **composition titles**.

son-in-law, sons-in-law

SOS The distress signal.
S.O.S (no final period) is a trademark for a brand of soap pad.

sound barrier The speed of sound is no longer a true barrier because aircraft have exceeded it. See **Mach number**.

soundstage

source Avoid the term if possible. Be as specific as possible about the source of information. If space is limited, use *source* as a last resort. *Official* or a similar word will often suffice, including in headlines. See **anonymous sources**.

source code The basic blueprint of a computer program.

South As defined by the U.S. Census Bureau, the 16-state region is broken into three divisions.

The four *East South Central* states are Alabama, Kentucky, Mississippi and Tennessee.

The eight *South Atlantic* states are Delaware, Florida, Georgia, Maryland, North Carolina, South Carolina, Virginia and West Virginia.

The four *West South Central* states are Arkansas, Louisiana, Oklahoma and Texas.

There is no official U.S. Census Bureau definition of Southeast.

See **Midwest region**; **Northeast region**; and **West** for the bureau's other regional breakdowns.

South America See **Western Hemisphere**.

South Carolina Abbreviate *S.C.* in datelines or stories. Postal code: *SC*

See **state names**.

South Dakota Abbreviate *S.D.* in datelines or stories. Postal code: *SD*

See **state names**.

Southeast Asia The nations of the Indochinese Peninsula and the islands southeast of it: Cambodia, Indonesia, Laos, Malaysia, Myanmar, Papua New Guinea, the Philippines, Singapore, Thailand and Vietnam.

See **Asian subcontinent** and **Far East**.

south, southern, southeast, southwest See **directions and regions**.

Southwest Airlines Inc. Headquarters of this airline is in Dallas.

Soviet Union See **Commonwealth of Independent States**.

Space Age It began with the launching of Sputnik 1 on Oct. 4, 1957.

space agency See **National Aeronautics and Space Administration**.

space centers See **John F. Kennedy Space Center** and **Lyndon B. Johnson Space Center**.

spacecraft designations Use Arabic figures and capitalize the name: *Gemini 7, Apollo 11, Pioneer 10.*

spaceship

space shuttle Lowercase *space shuttle*, but capitalize a proper name.

The space shuttle is a reusable winged aircraft capable of carrying people and cargo into Earth orbit. It is designed to take off vertically with the aid of booster rockets. After an orbital mission, re-entry begins with the firing of engines that send the craft back into Earth's atmosphere. The final leg of the return trip is a powerless glide to a landing strip.

spacewalk

spam, Spam Use *spam* in all references to unsolicited commercial or bulk email, often advertisements. Use *Spam*, a trademark, to refer to a canned meat product.

Spanish-American War

Spanish names The family names of both the father and mother usually are considered part of a person's full name. In everyday use, customs sometimes vary with individuals and countries.

The normal sequence is given name, father's family name, mother's family name: *Gabriel Garcia Marquez*.

On second reference, use only the father's family name (*Garcia*), unless the individual prefers or is widely known by a multiple last name (*Garcia Marquez*).

Some individuals use a *y* (for *and*) between the two surnames to ensure that both names are used together (including second references): *Gabriel Garcia y Marquez*.

A married woman sometimes uses her father's name, followed by the particle *de* (for *of*) and her husband's name. A woman named *Irma Perez* who married a man named *Anibal Gutierrez* would be known as *Irma Perez de Gutierrez*.

speaker Capitalize as a formal title before a name. Generally, it is a formal title only for the speaker of a legislative body: *Speaker John Boehner*.
See **titles**.

special contexts When this term is used in this book, it means that the material described may be used in a regular column devoted to a specialized subject or when a particular literary effect is suitable.

Special literary effects generally are suitable only in feature copy, but even there they should be used with care. Most feature material should follow the same style norms that apply to regular news copy.

special forces Do not use interchangeably with *special operations forces*. Capitalize when referring specifically to the *U.S. Army Special Forces*, also known as Green Berets. Others, such as Navy SEALs or Army Rangers, should be called *special operations forces*.

species Same in singular and plural. Use singular or plural verbs and pronouns depending on the sense: *The species has been unable to maintain itself. Both species are extinct.*
See **genus, species**.

speeches Capitalize and use quotation marks for their formal titles, as described in **composition titles**.

speechmaker, speechmaking

speed of sound See **Mach number**.

speeds Use figures. *The car slowed to 7 mph, winds of 5 to 10 mph, winds of 7 to 9 knots, 10-knot wind.*
Avoid extensively hyphenated constructions such as *5-mile-per-hour winds*.

speed up (v.) **speedup** (n. and adj.)

spelling The basic rule when in doubt is to consult this book followed by, if necessary, a dictionary under conditions described in the **dictionaries** entry.

Memory Aid: Noah Webster developed the following rule of thumb for the frequently vexing question of whether to double a final consonant in forming the present participle and past tense of a verb:

—If the stress in pronunciation is on the first syllable, do not double the consonant: *combat, combating, combated; cancel, canceling, canceled.*

—If the stress in pronunciation is on the second syllable, double the consonant unless confusion would result: *incur, incurred, incurring.* An exception, to avoid confusion with *buss,* is *bus, bused, busing.*

Avoid spelling simplifications such as *lite.* Exception: *thru* allowed in some compounds: *drive-thru, writethru.*

British spellings, when they differ from American, are acceptable only in particular cases such as formal or composition titles: *Jane's Defence Weekly, Labour Party.*

spill, spilled, spilling Not *spilt* in the past tense.

spinoff (n.) A distribution that occurs when the company forms a separate company out of a division, a subsidiary or other holdings. The shares of the new company are distributed proportionately to the parent company holders.

Spirit Airlines Headquarters is in Miramar, Fla.

split infinitive See **verbs**.

spokesman, spokeswoman But not *spokesperson.* Use a *representative* if you do not know the sex of the individual.

sports writer This is an exception to Webster's New World College Dictionary.

sport utility vehicle No plural *s* in *sport*; no hyphen.

SUV is acceptable on first reference.

spot market A market for buying or selling commodities or foreign exchange for immediate delivery and for cash payment.

spot price The price of a commodity available for immediate sale and delivery. The term is also used to refer to foreign exchange transactions.

spouse Use when some of the people involved may be either gender. For example: *physicians and their spouses,* not *physicians and their wives.*

spring See **seasons**.

springtime

sputnik Usually lowercase, but capitalize when followed by a figure as part of a proper name: *Sputnik 1.*

It is Russian for *satellite.*

squall See **weather terms**.

square Do not abbreviate. Capitalize when part of a proper name: *Washington Square.*

Sri Lanka Formerly Ceylon. Use *Sri Lanka* in datelines and other references to the nation.

The people may be called either *Sri Lankans* or *Ceylonese.*

Before the nation was called Ceylon, it was Serendip, whence comes the word *serendipity.*

SRO Acceptable on second reference for *standing room only.*

SST Acceptable in all references for a *supersonic transport.*

stadium, stadiums Capitalize only when part of a proper name: *Dodger Stadium.*

Stalin, Josef Not *Joseph.*

stall Use care when using *stall* in this sense. When an automobile *stalls*, the engine stops. This may not be true when an airplane *stalls*; it pitches forward or sideways because of a lack of air speed.

stamp, stomp Both are acceptable, but *stamp* is preferred.

stanch, staunch *Stanch* is a verb: *He stanched the flow of blood.*
Staunch is an adjective: *She is a staunch supporter of equality.*

stand-alone (adj.)

Standard & Poor's 500 index The market indicator most professional investors use to determine how stocks are performing. It encompasses 500 top companies in leading U.S. industries. Many mutual funds use it as the benchmark they measure their own performance against. Always use the full name on first reference. On subsequent references, use *S&P 500.*

standard-bearer

standard time Capitalize *Eastern Standard Time, Pacific Standard Time*, etc., but lowercase *standard time* when standing alone.
See **time zones**.

stand in (v.) **stand-in** (n. and adj.)

stand off (v.) **standoff** (n. and adj.)

stand out (v.) **standout** (n. and adj.)

starboard Nautical for *right*, when facing the bow, or forward. See **port, starboard**.

"The Star-Spangled Banner"

But lowercase *the national anthem.*

startup One word (n. and adj.) to describe a new business venture. An exception to Webster's New World College Dictionary preference.

state Lowercase in all *state of* constructions: *the state of Maine, the states of Maine and Vermont.*
Four states — Kentucky, Massachusetts, Pennsylvania and Virginia — are legally commonwealths rather than states. The distinction is necessary only in formal uses: *The commonwealth of Kentucky filed a suit.* For simple geographic reference: *Tobacco is grown in the state of Kentucky.*
Do not capitalize *state* when used simply as an adjective to specify a level of jurisdiction: *state Rep. William Smith, the state Transportation Department, state funds.*
Apply the same principle to phrases such as *the city of Chicago, the town of Auburn*, etc.
See also **state names**.

statehouse Capitalize all references to a specific statehouse, with or without the name of the state: *The Vermont Statehouse is in Montpelier. The governor will visit the Statehouse today.*
Lowercase plural uses: *the Massachusetts and Rhode Island statehouses.*

state names Follow these guidelines:
STANDING ALONE: Spell out the names of the 50 U.S. states when they stand alone in textual material. Any state name may be condensed, however, to fit typographical requirements for tabular material.
EIGHT NOT ABBREVIATED: The names of eight states are never abbreviated in datelines or text: *Alaska, Hawaii, Idaho, Iowa, Maine, Ohio, Texas* and *Utah.*

Memory Aid: Spell out the names of the two states that are not part of the contiguous United States and of the continental states that are five letters or fewer.

ABBREVIATIONS REQUIRED: Use the state abbreviations listed at the end of this section:

—In conjunction with the name of a city, town, village or military base in most datelines. See **datelines** for examples and exceptions for large cities.

—In conjunction with the name of a city, county, town, village or military base in text. See examples in Punctuation section below. See **datelines** for guidelines on when a city name may stand alone in the body of a story.

—In short-form listings of party affiliation: *D-Ala.*, *R-Mont.* See **party affiliation** entry for details.

Following are the state abbreviations, which also appear in the entries for each state (postal code abbreviations in parentheses):

Ala. (AL)	Md. (MD)	N.D. (ND)
Ariz. (AZ)	Mass. (MA)	Okla. (OK)
Ark. (AR)	Mich. (MI)	Ore. (OR)
Calif. (CA)	Minn. (MN)	Pa. (PA)
Colo. (CO)	Miss. (MS)	R.I. (RI)
Conn. (CT)	Mo. (MO)	S.C. (SC)
Del. (DE)	Mont. (MT)	S.D. (SD)
Fla. (FL)	Neb. (NE)	Tenn. (TN)
Ga. (GA)	Nev. (NV)	Vt. (VT)
Ill. (IL)	N.H. (NH)	Va. (VA)
Ind. (IN)	N.J. (NJ)	Wash. (WA)
Kan. (KS)	N.M. (NM)	W.Va. (WV)
Ky. (KY)	N.Y. (NY)	Wis. (WI)
La. (LA)	N.C. (NC)	Wyo. (WY)

These are the postal code abbreviations for the eight states that are not abbreviated in datelines or text: AK (Alaska), HI (Hawaii), ID (Idaho), IA (Iowa), ME (Maine), OH (Ohio), TX (Texas), UT (Utah). Also: District of Columbia (DC).

Use the two-letter Postal Service abbreviations only with full addresses, including ZIP code.

PUNCTUATION: Place one comma between the city and the state name, and another comma after the state name, unless ending a sentence or indicating a dateline: *He was traveling from Nashville, Tenn., to Austin, Texas, en route to his home in Albuquerque, N.M. She said Cook County, Ill., was Mayor Daley's stronghold.*

STATES IN HEADLINES: No periods for those abbreviated with two capital letters: NY, NJ, NH, NM, NC, SC, ND, SD and RI. Other states retain periods: Ga., Ky., Mont., Conn.

MISCELLANEOUS: Use *New York state* when necessary to distinguish the state from New York City.

Use *state of Washington* or *Washington state* when necessary to distinguish the state from the District of Columbia. (*Washington State* is the name of a university in the state of Washington.)

State of the Union Capitalize all references to the president's annual address.

Lowercase other uses: *"The state of the union is confused,"* the editor said.

state police Capitalize with a state name if part of the formal description for a police agency: *the New York State Police, the Virginia State Police.*

In most cases, state police standing alone is a shorthand reference for *state policemen* rather than a reference to the agency. For consistency and to avoid hairline distinctions about whether the reference is to the agency or the officers, lowercase the words *state police* whenever they are not preceded by a state name.

See **highway patrol**.

states' rights

statewide

stationary, stationery To stand still is to be *stationary*. Writing paper is *stationery*.

station wagon

status update A short string of words used on social networks to alert followers to a user's recent activities or point them to something of interest.

statute mile It equals 5,280 feet, or approximately 1.6 kilometers.

To convert to approximate nautical miles, multiply the number of statute miles by .869.

See **kilometer**; **knot**; **mile**; and **nautical mile**.

staunch See **stanch, staunch**.

stealth When used in connection with military aircraft, ships and vehicles it means the equipment is masked from various types of electronic detection. Stealth equipment can range from radar wave absorbing paint to electronic jamming devices. Like the *cruise* missile, always lowercase, no quotation marks.

stem cell

stepbrother, stepfather Also: *stepsister, stepmother*.

steppingstone

stifling

St. John's The city in the Canadian province of Newfoundland and Labrador.

Not to be confused with *Saint John, New Brunswick*.

St. Louis The city in Missouri stands alone in datelines.

stockbroker

Stockholm The city in Sweden stands alone in datelines.

stock index futures Futures contracts valued on the basis of indexes that track the prices of a specific group of stocks. The most widely traded is the future based on the Standard & Poor's 500 stock index. Speculators also trade options on index futures.

stock market prices With the stock markets' conversion to decimalization, prices are quoted in dollars and cents, not fractions. Use active verbs: *Shares rose 15 cents to $48.05 in afternoon trading.*

stopgap

storm See **weather terms**.

stormwater

storyline

storyteller

straight-laced, strait-laced Use *straight-laced* for someone strict or severe in behavior or moral views.

Reserve *strait-laced* for the notion of confinement, as in a corset.

strait Capitalize as part of a proper name: *Bering Strait, Strait of Gibraltar*.

But: *the Bosporus* and *the Dardanelles*. Neither is followed by *Strait*.

straitjacket

Strategic Arms Reduction Treaty *START* is acceptable on first reference to the treaty as long as it is made immediately clear which is being referred to.

Use the *strategic arms treaty* or the *treaties* in some references to avoid alphabet soup.

There are three START treaties:
—START I, signed in 1991.
—START II, signed in 1992. Ratified by U.S. Senate, but never took effect because Senate did not adopt the 1997 protocol and several amendments to Anti-Ballistic Missile treaty demanded by Russian Duma. Shelved by Russia in 2002 after U.S withdrew from ABM treaty.
—New START, signed in 2010.

Do not confuse with the *Strategic Arms Limitation Treaty* of 1979, known as *SALT*.

Strategic Defense Initiative

This is the official name of the research and development work on defense against a nuclear attack. *SDI* is the abbreviation and is acceptable on second reference. "Star Wars" has become synonymous with both and was derived from the movie series. If used, it must always be within quotation marks.

streaming A method of processing and delivering media in real time over the Internet. Videos on YouTube are an example of streaming content, as are many on-demand services like Netflix and Hulu.

street Abbreviate only with a numbered address. See **addresses**.

strikebreaker

strong-arm (v. and adj.)

strong-willed

stylebook One word when referring to the *AP Stylebook* and to *stylebooks* generically.

Styrofoam A trademark for a brand of plastic foam. Use the term *plastic foam* unless referring specifically to the trademarked product. (Note: Cups and other serving items are not made of *Styrofoam* brand

plastic foam.)

sub- The rules in **prefixes** apply, but in general, no hyphen. Some examples:

subbasement	submachine gun
subcommittee	suborbital
subculture	subtotal
subdivision	subzero

subcommittee Lowercase when used with the name of a legislative body's full committee: *a Ways and Means subcommittee*.

Capitalize when a subcommittee has a proper name of its own: *the Senate Permanent Subcommittee on Investigations*.

subject See **citizen, resident, subject, national, native**.

subjunctive mood Use the subjunctive mood of a verb for contrary-to-fact conditions, and expressions of doubts, wishes or regrets:

If I were a rich man, I wouldn't have to work hard.

I doubt that more money would be the answer.

I wish it were possible to take back my words.

Sentences that express a contingency or hypothesis may use either the subjunctive or the indicative mood depending on the context. In general, use the subjunctive if there is little likelihood that a contingency might come true:

If I were to marry a millionaire, I wouldn't have to worry about money.

If the bill passes as expected, it will provide an immediate tax cut.

See **should, would**.

submachine gun See **weapons**.

subpoena, subpoenaed, subpoenaing

subprime A class of borrowers characterized by tarnished credit histories. These borrowers usually entail greater risk for lenders so they are charged a higher interest rate for a loan.

successor

Sudan Use *Sudan* for the East African country whose capital is *Khartoum. South Sudan* is the country in the southern region that declared independence July 9, 2011. Its capital is *Juba.*

suffixes See separate listing for commonly used suffixes.

Follow Webster's New World College Dictionary for words not in this book.

If a word combination is not listed in Webster's New World College Dictionary, use two words for the verb form; hyphenate any noun or adjective forms.

suit, suite You may have a *suit* of clothes, a *suit* of cards, or be faced with a *lawsuit.*

There are *suites* of music, rooms and furniture.

Sukkot The Jewish Feast of Tabernacles, celebrating the fall harvest and commemorating the desert wandering of the Jews during the Exodus. Occurs in September or October.

summer See **seasons**.

summertime

sun Lowercase. See **heavenly bodies**.

sunbathe The verb forms: *sunbathed, sunbathing.* Also: *sunbather.*

Sun Belt Generally those states in the South and West, ranging from Florida and Georgia through the Gulf states into California.

super Avoid the slang tendency to use it in place of *excellent, wonderful,* etc.

super- The rules in **prefixes** apply, but in general, no hyphen. Some frequently used words:

superagency	superhighway
supercarrier	superpower
supercharge	supertanker

As with all prefixes, however, use a hyphen if the word that follows is capitalized: *super-Republican.*

Super Bowl

superconducting super collider

superintendent Do not abbreviate. Capitalize when used as a formal title before a name.
See **titles**.

superior court See **court names**.

supersede

supersonic See **Mach number**.

supersonic transport *SST* is acceptable in all references.

supra- The rules in **prefixes** apply, but in general, no hyphen. Some examples:

supragovernmental   supranational

Supreme Court of the United States Capitalize *U.S. Supreme Court* and also *the Supreme Court* when the context makes the *U.S.* designation unnecessary.

The chief justice is properly the *chief justice of the United States,* not *of the Supreme Court: Chief Justice John Roberts.*

The proper title for the eight other members of the court is *as-*

sociate justice. When used as a formal title before a name, it should be shortened to justice unless there are special circumstances: *Justice Ruth Bader Ginsburg, Associate Justice Ruth Bader Ginsburg.*

See **judge**.

supreme courts of the states

Capitalize with the state name (*the New Jersey Supreme Court*) and without the state name when the context makes it unnecessary: *the state Supreme Court, the Supreme Court.*

If a court with this name is not a state's highest tribunal, the fact should be noted. In New York, for example, the Supreme Court is a trial court. Appeals are directed to the Appellate Division of the Supreme Court. The state's highest court is the Court of Appeals.

surface-to-air missile(s)

SAM(s) may be used on second reference. Avoid the redundant *SAM missiles.*

SWAT Acronym for *Special Weapons and Tactics.*

swastika

sweatpants, sweatshirt,
sweatsuit These are exceptions to Webster's New World College Dictionary.

Swiss Switzerland's national airline is formally Swiss International Air Lines. Headquarters is in Zurich.

Sydney The city in Australia stands alone in datelines.

syllabus, syllabuses

synagogue Capitalize only when part of a formal name.

Synagogue Council of America See **Jewish congregations**.

sync Short for synchronization; not *synch*. Also, *syncing.*

synod A council of churches or church officials. See the entry for the denomination in question.

tablecloth

tablespoon, tablespoonfuls
Equal to three teaspoons or one-half a fluid ounce.
The metric equivalent is approximately 15 milliliters.
See **liter** and **recipes**.

table tennis See **pingpong**.

tablet A touch-screen device, such as an iPad or Kindle Fire, that can be connected to the Internet via Wi-Fi or cellular data networks.

tabular matter Exceptions may be made to the normal rules for abbreviations, as necessary to make material fit. But make any abbreviations as clear as possible.

tailspin

tail wind

Taiwan Use *Taiwan*, not *Formosa*, in references to the government in Taiwan and to the island itself.
See **China**.

take-home pay

take off (v.) **takeoff** (n. and adj.)

take out (v.) **takeout** (n. and adj.)

take over (v.) **takeover** (n. and adj.)

take up (v.) **takeup** (n. and adj.)

Taliban Extremist Islamic movement that ruled Afghanistan until driven out by U.S.-led coalition after the Sept. 11, 2001, attacks. The *Taliban* continue to operate as an insurgent force with adherents in Afghanistan and Pakistan. The name derives from the Arabic word for religious students. The word *Taliban* normally takes a plural verb.

Talmud The collection of writings that constitute the Jewish civil and religious law.

tanks Use Arabic figures, separated from letters by a hyphen: *M-60*. Plural: *M-60s*.

tape recording (n.), **tape-record** (v.)

taps Lowercase (without quotation marks) the bugle call for "lights out," also sounded at military funerals.

Target Corp. Headquarters is in Minneapolis.

Taser Trademark for stun gun. (Acronym for Thomas A. Swift's Electric Rifle.) Use the generic form if the brand is uncertain. Don't use verbs like *tasered*. Exception: When verb forms appear in direct quotations, use lowercase.

Tass Acceptable on first reference for the Russian government's news agency that is officially *ITAR-Tass*. *ITAR* is an acronym for *Information Telegraph Agency of Russia*.

tattletale

tax-free (adj.)

tea party Populist movement in the United States that opposes the Washington political establishment and espouses conservative and libertarian philosophy, including reduced government spending, lower taxes and reduction of the national debt and the federal budget deficit. Adherents are *tea partyers*. Formally named groups in the movement are capitalized: *Tea Party Express*.

teachers college No apostrophe.

team Use singular verb and pronoun "it" when referring to the team as a collective unit. However, the team name takes a plural verb: *The Orlando Magic are close to setting a franchise record.*
See **collective nouns**.

teammate

teamster Capitalize *teamster* only if the intended meaning is that the individual is a member of the International Brotherhood of Teamsters, Chauffeurs, Warehousemen and Helpers of America.

Teamsters union Acceptable in all references to the *International Brotherhood of Teamsters*.
See the entry under that name.

tear gas Two words. See also **Chemical Mace**.

teaspoon Equal to one-sixth of a fluid ounce, or one-third of a tablespoon.
The metric equivalent is approximately 5 milliliters.
See **liter**.

teaspoonful, teaspoonfuls Not *teaspoonsful*. See **recipes**.

Technicolor A trademark for a process of making color motion pictures.

teen, teenager (n.) **teenage** (adj.) Do not use *teen-aged*.

Teflon A trademark for a type of nonstick coating.

telecast (n.) **televise** (v.)

telephone numbers Use figures. The form: *212-621-1500*. For international numbers use 011 (from the United States), the country code, the city code and the telephone number: *011-44-20-7535-1515*. Use hyphens, not periods.
The form for toll-free numbers: *800-111-1000*.
If extension numbers are needed, use a comma to separate the main number from the extension: *212-621-1500, ext. 2*.

teleprompter It has become a generic term, no longer a trademark, for a type of television cuing device.

television program titles Follow the guidelines in **composition titles**.
Put quotation marks around *show* only if it is part of the formal name. The word *show* may be dropped when it would be cumbersome, such as in a set of listings.
(Italics are used here only to illustrate examples; do not use italics on the wires.)
In text or listing, treat programs

named after the star in any of the following ways: *"The Mary Tyler Moore Show," "Mary Tyler Moore"* or *the Mary Tyler Moore show.* But be consistent in a story or set of listings.

Use quotation marks also for the title of an episode: *"Chuckles Bites the Dust," an episode of "The Mary Tyler Moore Show."* Also: *"NBC Nightly News," the "Today" show, "The Tonight Show."*

television station The call letters alone are frequently adequate, but when this phrase is needed, use lowercase: *television station WTEV.*

telltale

temblor See **earthquakes**.

temperatures Use figures for all except *zero.* Use a word, not a minus sign, to indicate temperatures below zero.
Right: *The day's low was minus 10.*
Right: *The day's low was 10 below zero.*
Wrong: *The day's low was -10.*
Right: *The temperature rose to zero by noon.*
Right: *The day's high was expected to be 9 or 10.*
Also: *5-degree temperatures, temperatures fell 5 degrees, temperatures in the 30s* (no apostrophe).
Temperatures get *higher* or *lower*, but they don't get *warmer* or *cooler.*
Wrong: *Temperatures are expected to warm up in the area Friday.*
Right: *Temperatures are expected to rise in the area Friday.*
See **Fahrenheit**; **Celsius**; and **weather terms**.

Temple Mount The walled, elevated area in Jerusalem's Old City that was the site of the ancient Jewish temples. It now houses the centuries-old Dome of the Rock shrine and Al-Aqsa mosque and is known

to Muslims as the *Haram al-Sharif,* or *Noble Sanctuary.* Muslims believe Prophet Muhammad made his night journey to heaven from the site.

Ten Commandments Do not abbreviate or use figures.

tenderhearted

tenfold

Ten Most Wanted Fugitives The FBI's official list.

Tennessee Abbreviate *Tenn.* in datelines or stories. Postal code: *TN* See **state names**.

Tennessee Valley Authority *TVA* is acceptable on second reference.
Headquarters is in Knoxville, Tenn.

tera- A prefix denoting 1 trillion units of a measure. Move the decimal point 12 places to the right, adding zeros if necessary, to convert to the basic unit: 5.5 teratons = 5,500,000,000,000 tons.

terrace Do not abbreviate. See **addresses**.

Texas Do not abbreviate in datelines or stories. Postal code: *TX*
Second in total land area. See **state names**.

Texas Hold 'em The poker game.

texts, transcripts Follow normal style guidelines for capitalization, spelling and abbreviations in handling a text or transcript. Do not use a dateline.
Use quotation marks only for words or phrases that were quoted in the text or by the person who spoke.

Identify a change in speakers by starting a paragraph with the new speaker's name and a colon. Use normal second-reference forms if the speaker has been identified earlier; provide a full name and identification if the individual is being mentioned for the first time.

Use *Q:* for *question* and *A:* for *answer* at the start of paragraphs when these notations are adequate to identify a change in speakers.

See **ellipsis** in the **Punctuation** chapter for guidelines on condensing texts and transcripts.

text, texting, texted Acceptable in all usages as a verb for *to send a text message.*

Thai A native or the language of Thailand.

Siam and *Siamese* are historical only.

Use *siamese* for the cat.

Thai Airways International PLC Headquarters of this airline is in Bangkok, Thailand.

Thanksgiving, Thanksgiving Day The fourth Thursday in November.

that (conjunction) Use the conjunction *that* to introduce a dependent clause if the sentence sounds or looks awkward without it. There are no hard-and-fast rules, but in general:

—*That* usually may be omitted when a dependent clause immediately follows a form of the verb *to say*: *The president said he had signed the bill.*

—*That* should be used when a time element intervenes between the verb and the dependent clause: *The president said Monday that he had signed the bill.*

—*That* usually is necessary after

some verbs. They include: *advocate, assert, contend, declare, estimate, make clear, point out, propose* and *state.*

—*That* is required before subordinate clauses beginning with conjunctions such as *after, although, because, before, in addition to, until* and *while*: *Haldeman said that after he learned of Nixon's intention to resign, he sought pardons for all connected with Watergate.*

When in doubt, include *that.* Omission can hurt. Inclusion never does.

that, which (pronouns) Use *that* and *which* in referring to inanimate objects and to animals without a name. Use *that* for essential clauses, important to the meaning of a sentence, and without commas: *I remember the day that we met.* Use *which* for nonessential clauses, where the pronoun is less necessary, and use commas: *The team, which finished last a year ago, is in first place.*

(Tip: If you can drop the clause and not lose the meaning of the sentence, use *which*; otherwise, use *that.* A *which* clause is surrounded by commas; no commas are used with *that* clauses.)

See the **essential clauses, nonessential clauses** entry for guidelines on using *that* and *which* to introduce phrases and clauses.

theater Use this spelling unless the proper name is *Theatre*: *Shubert Theatre.*

theatergoer

theft See **burglary, larceny, robbery, theft**.

their, there, they're *Their* is a possessive pronoun: *They went to their house.*

There is an adverb indicating direction: *We went there for dinner.*

There also is used with the force of a pronoun for impersonal constructions in which the real subject follows the verb: *There is no food on the table.*

They're is a contraction for *they are.*

theretofore Use *until then.*

thermos Formerly a trademark, now a generic term for any vacuum bottle, although one manufacturer still uses the word as a brand name.

Lowercase *thermos* when it is used to mean any vacuum bottle; use *Thermos* when referring to the specific brand.

Third World The economically developing nations of Africa, Asia and Latin America.

Do not confuse with nonaligned, which is a political term. See **nonaligned nations**.

Thomson Reuters Corp. A news and data provider based in New York. It operates two main segments: the Professional division, which supplies information for law firms, accountants, health care providers and other professionals; and the Markets division, which serves investors and financial institutions. The company was formed out of Thomson Corp.'s 2008 acquisition of Reuters Group PLC, which includes the news agency named for Baron Paul Julius von Reuter, the founder. Use *Reuters* when referring to the news agency.

3-D

3M Trademark and official name of the company formerly known as Minnesota Mining & Manufacturing. Its products are known under the names *3M* and *Scotch*. Headquarters is in Maplewood, Minn.

three R's They are: *reading, 'riting and 'rithmetic.*

throwaway (n. and adj.)

thumbs-up, thumbs-down

thunderstorm See **weather terms**.

Tiananmen Square Large public square in central Beijing. Site of pro-democracy demonstrations in 1989 that ended in bloodshed.

tidbit

tie in (v.) **tie-in** (n. and adj.)

tie, tied, tying

tie up (v.) **tie-up** (n. and adj.)

tilde Do not use the symbol in standard AP wire transmissions. If necessary for Internet addresses, write out the word and put it in parentheses.

till Or *until.* But not *'til.*

time element Use the days of the week, not *today* or *tonight* in print copy.

Use Monday, Tuesday, etc., for days of the week within seven days before or after the current date.

Use the month and a figure where appropriate. See months for forms and punctuation.

Avoid such redundancies as *last Tuesday* or *next Tuesday.* The past, present or future tense used for the verb usually provides adequate indication of which Tuesday is meant: *He said he finished the job Tuesday. She will return Tuesday.*

Avoid awkward placements of the time element, particularly those that suggest the day of the week is the object of a transitive verb: *The police jailed Tuesday.* Potential remedies include the use of the word *on* (see the **on** entry), rephrasing the sentence, or placing the time element in a different sentence.

time of day The exact time of day that an event has happened or will happen is not necessary in most stories. Follow these guidelines to determine when it should be included and in what form:

SPECIFY THE TIME:

—Whenever it gives the reader a better picture of the scene: Did the earthquake occur when people were likely to be home asleep or at work? A clock reading for the time in the datelined community is acceptable although *pre-dawn hours* or *rush hour* often is more illustrative.

—Whenever the time is critical to the story: When will the rocket be launched? When will a major political address be broadcast? What is the deadline for meeting a demand?

DECIDING ON CLOCK TIME: When giving a clock reading, use the time in the datelined community.

If the story has no dateline, use the clock time in force where the event happened or will take place.

The only exception is a nationwide story or tabular listing that involves television or radio programs. Always use Eastern time, followed by *EDT* or *EST*, and specify whether the program will be broadcast simultaneously nationwide or whether times will vary because of separate transmissions for different time zones. If practical, specify those times in a separate paragraph.

ZONE ABBREVIATIONS: Use *EST*, *CDT*, *PST*, etc., after a clock time only if:

—The story involves travel or other activities, such as the closing hour for polling places or the time of a televised speech, likely to affect people or developments in more

than one time zone.

—The item involves television or radio programs. (See above.)

—The item has no dateline.

—The item is an advisory to editors.

CONVERT TO EASTERN TIME? Do not convert clock times from other time zones in the continental United States to Eastern time. If there is high interest in the precise time, add *CDT*, *PST*, etc., to the local reading to help readers determine their equivalent local time.

If the time is critical in a story from outside the continental United States, provide a conversion to Eastern time using this form:

The kidnappers set a 9 a.m. (3 a.m. EDT) deadline.

See **time zones** for additional guidance on forms.

timeout One word is an exception to Webster's New World College Dictionary.

times Use figures except for *noon* and *midnight.* Use a colon to separate hours from minutes: *11 a.m., 1 p.m., 3:30 p.m., 9-11 a.m., 9 a.m. to 5 p.m.*

Avoid such redundancies as *10 a.m. this morning, 10 p.m. tonight* or *10 p.m. Monday night.* Use *10 a.m.* or *10 p.m. Monday,* etc., as required by the norms in time element.

The construction *4 o'clock* is acceptable, but time listings with *a.m.* or *p.m.* are preferred.

See **midnight, noon** and **time zones**.

time sequences Spell out: *50 hours, 23 minutes, 14 seconds.* When using the abbreviated form, as in sports statistics or similar agate use, or subsequent references, the form is: *2:30:21.65* (hours, minutes, seconds, tenths, hundredths).

Time Warner Inc. Time Warner is one of the world's largest media conglomerates. It owns the *Warner Bros.* movie and TV studio; the *Time Inc.* magazine publishing group, which includes *Time, Sports Illustrated, People* and *Fortune*; and a group of cable networks including *HBO, CNN* and *TBS.* It spun off *Time Warner Cable Inc.* in 2009. The company was briefly known as AOL Time Warner Inc. after agreeing to be acquired by America Online Inc. in 2000, but changed its name back to just *Time Warner Inc.* in 2003. AOL was spun off in 2009. Headquarters is in New York.

time zones Capitalize the full name of the time in force within a particular zone: *Eastern Standard Time, Eastern Daylight Time, Central Standard Time,* etc.

Lowercase all but the region in short forms: *the Eastern time zone, Eastern time, Mountain time,* etc.

See **time of day** for guidelines on when to use clock time in a story.

Spell out *time zone* in references not accompanied by a clock reading: *Chicago is in the Central time zone.*

The abbreviations *EST, CDT,* etc., are acceptable on first reference for zones used within the continental United States, Canada and Mexico only if the abbreviation is linked with a clock reading: *noon EST, 9 a.m. PST.* (Do not set off the abbreviations with commas.)

Spell out all references to time zones not used within the contiguous United States: *When it is noon EDT, it is 1 p.m. Atlantic Standard Time and 8 a.m. Alaska Standard Time.*

One exception to the spelled-out form: *Greenwich Mean Time* may be abbreviated as *GMT* on second reference if used with a clock reading.

tip off (v.) **tipoff** (n. and adj.)

tiptop

titleholder

titles In general, confine capitalization to formal titles used directly before an individual's name.

The basic guidelines:

LOWERCASE: Lowercase and spell out titles when they are not used with an individual's name: *The president issued a statement. The pope gave his blessing.*

Lowercase and spell out titles in constructions that set them off from a name by commas: *The vice president, Nelson Rockefeller, declined to run again. Pope Benedict XVI, the current pope, does not plan to retire.*

COURTESY TITLES: See **courtesy titles** for guidelines on when to use *Miss, Mr., Mrs., Ms.* or no titles.

The forms *Mr., Mrs., Miss* and *Ms.* apply both in regular text and in quotations.

FORMAL TITLES: Capitalize formal titles when they are used immediately before one or more names: *Pope Benedict XVI, President Barack Obama, Vice Presidents John Jones and William Smith.*

A formal title generally is one that denotes a scope of authority, professional activity or academic activity: *Sen. Dianne Feinstein, Dr. Benjamin Spock, retired Gen. Colin Powell.*

Other titles serve primarily as occupational descriptions: *astronaut John Glenn, movie star John Wayne, peanut farmer Jimmy Carter.*

A final determination on whether a title is formal or occupational depends on the practice of the governmental or private organization that confers it. If there is doubt about the status of a title and the practice of the organization cannot be determined, use a construction that sets the name or the title off with commas.

ABBREVIATED TITLES: The

United States time zones

Hawaii does not observe daylight saving time.

Difference with GMT -10

Hawaii

-11 -10 -9 -8 -7

Alaska

-9 -8

Arizona does not observe daylight saving time. Pacific time is used from March until November. Otherwise, the state is on Mountain time.

PACIFIC -8

MOUNTAIN -7

CENTRAL -6

EASTERN -5

MEXICO

CANADA

Wash.

Ore.

Calif.

Nev.

Idaho

Utah

Ariz.

Mont.

Wyo.

N.M.

Colo.

Texas

Okla.

Kan.

Neb.

S.D.

N.D.

Minn.

Iowa

Mo.

Ark.

La.

Miss.

Ala.

Tenn.

Ill.

Wis.

Ind.

Mich.

Ky.

Ohio

W.Va.

Va.

Ga.

S.C.

N.C.

Fla.

Pa.

N.Y.

Vt. N.H.

Maine

Mass.

R.I.

Conn.

N.J.

Del.

Md.

-4

following formal titles are capitalized and abbreviated as shown when used before a name both inside and outside quotations: *Dr., Gov., Lt. Gov., Rep., Sen.* and certain military ranks listed in **military titles**.

All other formal titles are spelled out in all uses.

GOVERNMENT OFFICIALS: In stories with U.S. datelines, do not include *U.S.* before the titles of Secretary of State or other government officials, except where necessary for clarity. Examples: *Secretary of State Hillary Rodham Clinton, Attorney General Eric Holder.*

In stories with international datelines, include *U.S.* before the titles: *U.S. Secretary of State Hillary Rodham Clinton, U.S. Attorney General Eric Holder.* Exceptions: *President Barack Obama, Vice President Joe Biden.*

ROYAL TITLES: Capitalize *king, queen,* etc., when used directly before a name. See individual entries and **nobility**.

TITLES OF NOBILITY: Capitalize a full title when it serves as the alternate name for an individual. See **nobility**.

PAST AND FUTURE TITLES: A formal title that an individual formerly held, is about to hold or holds temporarily is capitalized if used before the person's name. But do not capitalize the qualifying word: *former President George W. Bush, deposed King Constantine, Attorney General-designate Griffin B. Bell, acting Mayor Peter Barry.*

LONG TITLES: Separate a long title from a name by a construction that requires a comma: *Charles Robinson, the undersecretary for economic affairs, spoke.* Or: *The undersecretary for economic affairs, Charles Robinson, spoke.*

UNIQUE TITLES: If a title applies only to one person in an organization, insert the word *the* in a construction that uses commas: *John Jones, the deputy vice president, spoke.*

ADDITIONAL GUIDANCE: Many commonly used titles and occupational descriptions are listed separately in this book, together with guidelines on whether and/or when they are capitalized. In these entries, the phrases *before a name* or *immediately before a name* are used to specify that capitalization applies only when a title is not set off from a name by commas.

See **academic titles**; **composition titles**; **legislative titles**; **military titles**; and **religious titles**.

tobacco, tobaccos

Tobago See **Trinidad and Tobago**.

today, tonight Use only in direct quotations and in phrases that do not refer to a specific day: *Customs today are different from those of a century ago.*

Use the day of the week in copy, not *today* or *tonight*.

Tokyo The city in Japan stands alone in datelines.

tomorrow Use only in direct quotations and in phrases that do not refer to a specific day: *The world of tomorrow will need additional energy resources.*

Use the day of the week in other cases.

ton There are three types:
A *short ton* is equal to 2,000 pounds.

A *long ton*, also known as a *British ton*, is equal to 2,240 pounds.

A *metric ton* is equal to 1,000 kilograms, or approximately 2,204.62 pounds.

CONVERSION EQUATIONS:
Short to long: Multiply by 0.89 (5 short tons x 0.89 = 4.45 long tons).

Short to metric: Multiply by 0.9

(5 short tons x 0.9 = 4.5 metric tons).

Long to short: Multiply by 1.12 (5 long tons x 1.12 = 5.6 short tons).

Long to metric: Multiply by 1.02 (5 long tons x 1.02 = 5.1 metric tons).

Metric to short: Multiply by 1.1 (5 metric tons x 1.1 = 5.5 short tons).

Metric to long: Multiply by 0.98 (5 metric tons x 0.98 = 4.9 long tons).

See **metric system**.

See **kiloton** for units used to measure the power of nuclear explosions.

See **oil** for formulas to convert the tonnage of oil shipments to gallons.

tonight See **today, tonight** entry.

tornado(es) See **weather terms**.

Toronto The city in Canada stands alone in datelines.

Tory, Tories An exception to the normal practice when forming the plural of a proper name ending in *y*.

The words are acceptable on second reference to the Conservative Party in Britain and its members.

Total SA Headquarters of French oil company is in Paris.

total, totaled, totaling The phrase *a total of* often is redundant.

It may be used, however, to avoid a figure at the start of a sentence: *A total of 650 people were killed in holiday traffic accidents.*

touch screen (n.) **touch-screen** (adj.)

toward Not *towards*.

town Apply the capitalization principles in **city**.

town council Apply the capitalization principles in **city council**.

Toyota Motor Corp. Headquarters is in Toyota City, Japan.

Toys R Us

trade in (v.) **trade-in** (n. and adj.)

trademark A trademark is a brand, symbol, word, etc., used by a manufacturer or dealer and protected by law to prevent a competitor from using it: *AstroTurf*, for a type of artificial grass, for example.

In general, use a generic equivalent unless the trademark name is essential to the story.

When a trademark is used, capitalize it.

Many trademarks are listed separately in this book, together with generic equivalents.

The International Trademark Association, located in New York, is a helpful source of information about trademarks. See **brand names**.

trade off (v.) **trade-off** (n. and adj.)

trade show

traffic, trafficked, trafficking

trampoline Formerly a trademark, now a generic term.

trans- The rules in **prefixes** apply, but in general, no hyphen. Some examples:

transcontinental	transsexual
transmigrate	transship
transoceanic	trans-Siberian

Also: *trans-Atlantic* and *trans-Pacific*. These are exceptions to Webster's New World College Dictionary in keeping with the general rule that a hyphen is needed when a prefix precedes a capitalized word.

transcripts See **texts, transcripts**.

transfer, transferred, transferring

transgender Use the pronoun preferred by the individuals who have acquired the physical characteristics of the opposite sex or present themselves in a way that does not correspond with their sex at birth.

If that preference is not expressed, use the pronoun consistent with the way the individuals live publicly. See **transsexual**.

Transportation Communications International Union
Formerly the Brotherhood of Railway, Airline and Steamship Clerks, Freight Handlers, Express and Station Employees. *TCU* is acceptable on second reference.

Headquarters is in Rockville, Md.

transsexual A person who changes gender by undergoing surgical procedures. See **transgender**.

travelogue Not *travelog*.

travel, traveled, traveling, traveler

treasurer Capitalize when used as a formal title immediately before a name. See **titles**.

Caution: The secretary of the U.S. Department of the Treasury is not the same person as the U.S. treasurer.

Treasurys Securities sold by the federal government to investors to fund its operations, cover the interest on U.S. government debt and pay off maturing securities. Because they carry the full backing of the government, Treasurys are viewed as the safest investment.

Treasury bills, Treasury bonds, Treasury notes See **loan terminology**.

trees See **plants**.

tribe, tribal Refers to a social group of linked families or communities sharing a common ancestry or culture and who may be part of a larger ethnic group, such as the *Cherokee tribe* of American Indians and the *Ngunnawal tribe* of Aborigines. *Ethnic group* is preferred when referring to ethnicity or ethnic violence. See **nationalities and races**.

Tribune Co. U.S. newspaper publishing and broadcasting company with headquarters in Chicago. Large-market titles include *Los Angeles Times*, *Chicago Tribune*, *The (Baltimore) Sun* and *The Hartford (Conn.) Courant*. Company filed for bankruptcy protection in December 2008 because of dwindling advertising revenue and a debt load of $13 billion, much of it from a transaction led by real estate mogul Sam Zell to take the company private.

trigger-happy

Trinidad and Tobago In datelines on stories from this island nation, use a community name followed by either *Trinidad* or *Tobago* — but not both — depending on where the community is located.

Trojan horse, Trojan War

troop, troops, troupe A *troop*, in its singular form, is a group of people, often military, or animals. *Troops*, in the plural, means several such groups. But when the plural appears with a large number, it is understood to mean individuals: *There were an estimated 150,000 troops in Iraq.* (But not: *Three troops were injured.*)

Use *troupe* only for ensembles of actors, dancers, singers, etc.

tropical depression See **weather terms**.

Truman, Harry S. With a period after the initial. Truman once said there was no need for the period because the S did not stand for a name. Asked in the early 1960s about his preference, he replied, "It makes no difference to me."

AP style has called for the period since that time.

trustee A person to whom another's property or the management of another's property is entrusted.

Do not capitalize if used before a name.

trusty A prison inmate granted special privileges as a trustworthy person.

Do not capitalize if used before a name.

try out (v.) **tryout** (n.)

tsar Use *czar.*

T-shirt

tsunami See **weather terms**.

tuberculosis *TB* is acceptable on second reference.

tune up (v.) **tuneup** (n. and adj.)

turboprop See **aircraft terms**.

turnpike Capitalize as part of a proper name: *the Pennsylvania Turnpike.* Lowercase *turnpike* when it stands alone.

See **highway designations**.

TV Acceptable as an abbreviated form of *television*, as a noun or adjective.

Twelve Apostles The disciples of Jesus. An exception to the normal practice of using figures for 10 and above.

20th Century Fox, Twentieth Century Limited Follow an organization's practice. See **company names**.

20-something

24/7

twin towers The two tallest buildings in the World Trade Center complex destroyed in the 9/11 attack. Also lowercase *north tower* and *south tower.*

Twitter A message-distribution system that allows users to post continual updates of up to 140 characters detailing their activities for followers or providing links to other content. The verb is *to tweet, tweeted.* A Twitter message is known as a *tweet.*

two-by-four Spell out the noun, which refers to any length of building lumber 2 inches thick by 4 inches wide.

typhoons Capitalize typhoon when it is part of the name that weather forecasters assign to a storm: *Typhoon Tilda.*

But use *it* and *its* — not *she, her* or *hers* — in pronoun references.

And do not use the presence of a woman's name as an excuse to attribute sexist images of women's behavior to a typhoon.

See **weather terms**.

U-boat A German submarine. Anything referring to a submarine should be *submarine* unless directly referring to a German vessel of World War I or II vintage.

UFO, UFOs Acceptable in all references for *unidentified flying object(s)*.

Ukrainian Catholic Church See **Eastern Rite churches**.

ukulele

Ulster Historically, one of the four Irish provinces, covering nine counties. Six of the counties became Northern Ireland, three became part of the Republic of Ireland. Avoid use as a synonym for *Northern Ireland*. See **United Kingdom**.

Ultimate Fighting A registered trademark. Use the generic term *mixed martial arts* for bouts featuring boxing, wrestling, taekwondo, judo and other disciplines. *Ultimate Fighting Championship* is acceptable for events sanctioned by that group.

ultra- The rules in **prefixes** apply, but in general, no hyphen. Some examples:

ultramodern	ultrasonic
ultranationalism	ultraviolet

umlaut This diacritical mark (two dots placed over the vowel to change its sound) should not be used in standard AP transmissions. Instead, use two regular letters when needed.

U.N. Use periods in *U.N.*, for consistency with U.S. within texts. In headlines, it's *UN* (no periods). See **United Nations**.

un- The rules in **prefixes** apply, but in general, no hyphen. Some examples:

un-American	unnecessary
unarmed	unshaven

Uncle Sam

Uncle Tom A term of contempt applied to a black person, taken from the main character in Harriet Beecher Stowe's novel "Uncle Tom's Cabin." It describes the practice of kowtowing to whites to curry favor.

Do not apply it to an individual. It carries potentially libelous connotations of having sold one's convictions for money, prestige or political influence.

under- The rules in **prefixes** apply, but in general, no hyphen. Some examples:

underdog	undersheriff
underground	undersold

underscore Do not use the symbol in Internet addresses; write out the word and put it in parentheses.

undersecretary One word. See **titles**.

underwater In the housing industry, the term for homeowners who owe more on their mortgages than their homes are worth.

under way Two words in virtually all uses: *The project is under way. The naval maneuvers are under way.*

One word only when used as an adjective before a noun in a nautical sense: *an underway flotilla.*

unemployment rate In the United States, this estimate of the number of unemployed residents seeking work is compiled monthly by the Bureau of Labor Statistics, an agency of the Labor Department.

Each month the bureau selects a nationwide cross section of the population and conducts interviews to determine the size of the U.S. workforce. The workforce is defined as the number of people with jobs and the number looking for jobs.

The unemployment rate is expressed as a percentage figure. The essential calculation involves dividing the total workforce into the number of people looking for jobs, followed by adjustments to reflect variable factors such as seasonal trends.

UNESCO Acceptable in all reference for the *United Nations Educational, Scientific and Cultural Organization.*

UNICEF Acceptable in all references for the *United Nations Children's Fund.* The words *International* and *Emergency*, originally part of the name, have been dropped.

unidentified flying object(s) *UFO* and *UFOs* are acceptable in all references.

Uniform Code of Military Justice The laws covering members of the U.S. armed forces.

uninterested See **disinterested, uninterested**.

union Capitalize when used as a proper name of the Northern states during the Civil War: *The Union defeated the Confederacy.*

union names The formal names of unions may be condensed to conventionally accepted short forms that capitalize characteristic words from the full name followed by union in lowercase.

Follow union practice in the use of the word worker in shortened forms: United Auto Workers, United Mine Workers.

When worker is used generically, make autoworkers and steelworkers one word in keeping with widespread practice; use two words for other job descriptions: bakery workers, mine workers.

See the local of a union entry and the individual entries for these unions frequently in the news:
Amalgamated Transit Union
American Federation of Government Employees
American Federation of Labor and Congress of Industrial Organizations
American Federation of Musicians
American Federation of State, County and Municipal Employees
American Federation of Teachers
American Federation of Television and Radio Artists
American Postal Workers Union
Communications Workers of America
International Association of Machinists and Aerospace Workers
International Brotherhood of Electrical Workers
International Brotherhood of Teamsters
International Longshore and Warehouse Union

International Longshoremen's Association

International Union of Bricklayers and Allied Craftworkers

International Union of Painters and Allied Trades

Laborers' International Union of North America

National Association of Letter Carriers

Newspaper Guild, The

Sheet Metal Workers International Association

UNITE HERE, (no hyphen), a merger of the Union of Needletrades, Industrial and Textile Employees with the Hotel Employees and Restaurant Employees.

United Auto Workers

United Brotherhood of Carpenters

United Electrical, Radio and Machine Workers of America

United Farm Workers

United Food and Commercial Workers International Union

United Mine Workers of America

United Steelworkers

Union Pacific Corp. Freight railroad, with headquarters in Omaha, Neb.

union shop See **closed shop.**

unique It means one of a kind. Do not describe something as *rather unique, most unique* or *very unique.*

United Arab Emirates Do not abbreviate, even in datelines.

Use *U.A.E.* (with periods) if quoted matter requires the abbreviation.

United Auto Workers The shortened form of the United Automobile, Aerospace and Agricultural Implement Workers of America is acceptable in all references. Headquarters is in Detroit.

United Brotherhood of Carpenters The shortened form *Carpenters union* is acceptable in all references.

Headquarters is in Washington.

United Church of Christ The Evangelical and Reformed Church merged with the Congregational Christian Churches in 1957 to form the United Church of Christ.

The word *church* is correctly applied only to an individual local church. Each such church is responsible for the doctrine, ministry and ritual of its congregation.

A small body of churches that did not enter the United Church of Christ is known as the National Association of Congregational Churches.

Jesus is regarded as man's savior, but no subscription to a set creed is required for membership.

Members of the clergy are known as *ministers. Pastor* applies if a minister leads a congregation.

On first reference, use *the Rev.* before the name of a man or woman. On second reference, use only the last name.

See **religious titles.**

United Continental Holdings Inc. This is the result of the merger of the airline companies Continental and UAL in 2010. Headquarters is in Chicago.

United Electrical, Radio and Machine Workers of America The shortened form *Electrical Workers union* is acceptable in all references.

Headquarters is in New York.

United Farm Workers Headquarters is in Keene, Calif.

United Food and Commercial Workers International Union

Formed by the merger of the Retail Clerks International Union and the Amalgamated Meat Cutters and Butcher Workmen of North America.

The shortened form *Food and Commercial Workers union* is acceptable in all references.

Headquarters is in Washington.

United Kingdom It consists of Great Britain and Northern Ireland.

Great Britain (or Britain) consists of England, Scotland and Wales.

Ireland is independent of the United Kingdom.

The abbreviation *U.K.* is acceptable as a noun or adjective. Use *UK* (no periods) in headlines.

See **datelines** and **Ireland**.

United Methodist Church See **Methodist churches**.

United Mine Workers of America The shortened forms *United Mine Workers* and *United Mine Workers union* are acceptable in all references.

UMW and *Mine Workers* are acceptable on second reference.

Use *mine workers* or *miners*, lowercase, in generic references to workers in the industry.

Headquarters is in Washington.

United Nations Abbrev: *U.N.* (no space). Use periods in *U.N.*, for consistency with U.S. within texts. In headlines, it's *UN* (no periods).

In datelines: *UNITED NATIONS (AP) —*

Use *U.N. General Assembly, U.N. Secretariat* and *U.N. Security Council* in first references not under a United Nations dateline.

General Assembly, the Secretariat and *Security Council* are acceptable in all references under a United Nations dateline and on second refer-

ence under other datelines.

Lowercase *the assembly* and *the council* when they stand alone.

See **UNESCO** and **UNICEF**.

United Presbyterian Church in the United States of America It no longer exists. See **Presbyterian churches** entry.

United Press International A privately owned news agency formed in 1958 as a merger of United Press and International News Service.

Use the full name on first reference. *UPI* is acceptable on second reference.

Headquarters is in Washington.

United Service Organizations *USO* is acceptable in all references.

United States Use periods in the abbreviation, *U.S.* within texts. In headlines, it's *US* (no periods).

United States Conference of Catholic Bishops Formerly the National Conference of Catholic Bishops, it is the national organization of Roman Catholic bishops.

United Steelworkers The shortened form of the United Steel, Paper and Forestry, Rubber, Manufacturing, Energy, Allied Industrial and Service Workers International Union is acceptable in all references. Headquarters is in Pittsburgh, Pa.

United Synagogue of Conservative Judaism Not *synagogues*. See **Jewish congregations**.

unprecedented It means having no precedent, unheard of. Often misused.

-up Follow Webster's New World College Dictionary. Hyphenate if not listed there.

Some frequently used words (all are nouns, some also are used as adjectives):

breakup	makeup
call-up	mix-up
change-up	mock-up
checkup	pileup
cleanup	pushup
close-up	roundup
cover-up	runners-up
crackup	setup
follow-up	shake-up
frame-up	shape-up
grown-up	smashup
hang-up	speedup
holdup	tie-up
letup	walk-up
lineup	windup

Use two words when any of these occurs as a verb.

See **suffixes**.

up- The rules in **prefixes** apply, but in general, no hyphen. Some examples:

upend	upstate
upgrade	uptown

UPI Acceptable on second references for *United Press International.*

uppercase One word (n., v., adj.) when referring to the use of capital letters, in keeping with printers' practice.

UPS Inc. Acceptable in all references to *United Parcel Service Inc.* Headquarters is in Atlanta.

upside down (adv.) **upside-down** (adj.) *The car turned upside down. The book is upside-down.*

upstage

upstate Always lowercase: *upstate New York.*

upward Not *upwards.*

URL *Uniform Resource Locator,* an Internet address. An example:
http://politics.ap.org/states/mi.html

http: is the protocol, or method of transfer.
// indicates a computer name follows.
politics is the server.
ap.org is the domain.
/states is the folder.
/mi.html indicates a file (*.html* is the file type).
When the *URL* does not fit entirely on one line, break it into two or more lines without adding a hyphen or other punctuation mark.
The URL should always be the last line on a story; other underdash material, such as a list of contributors to the story, goes above the URL.

U.S. The abbreviation is acceptable as a noun or adjective for *United States.* In headlines, it's *US* (no periods).

USA No periods in the abbreviated form for United States of America.

U.S. Agency for International Development *USAID* is acceptable on second reference.

U.S. Air Force See **air force**; **military academies**; and **military titles**.

US Airways Inc. Formerly USAir. Acquired by America West Holdings Corp. in 2005. The combined company retains the *US Airways* name. Headquarters is in Tempe, Ariz.

U.S. Army See **army**; **military academies**; and **military titles**.

U.S. Coast Guard See **coast guard**; **military academies**; and **military titles**.

U.S. Conference of Mayors The members are the mayors of cities with 30,000 or more residents.

See **National League of Cities**.

Use *the conference* or *the mayors' conference* on second reference.

There is no organization with the name *National Mayors' Conference*.

U.S. Court of Appeals The court is divided into 13 circuits as follows:

District of Columbia Circuit.

Federal Circuit.

1st Circuit: Maine, Massachusetts, New Hampshire, Rhode Island, Puerto Rico. Based in Boston.

2nd Circuit: Connecticut, New York, Vermont. Based in New York.

3rd Circuit: Delaware, New Jersey, Pennsylvania, Virgin Islands. Based in Philadelphia.

4th Circuit: Maryland, North Carolina, South Carolina, Virginia, West Virginia. Based in Richmond, Va.

5th Circuit: Louisiana, Mississippi, Texas. Based in New Orleans.

6th Circuit: Kentucky, Michigan, Ohio, Tennessee. Based in Cincinnati.

7th Circuit: Illinois, Indiana, Wisconsin. Based in Chicago.

8th Circuit: Arkansas, Iowa, Minnesota, Missouri, Nebraska, North Dakota, South Dakota. Based in St. Louis.

9th Circuit: Alaska, Arizona, California, Hawaii, Idaho, Montana, Nevada, Oregon, Washington, Guam. Based in San Francisco.

10th Circuit: Colorado, Kansas, New Mexico, Oklahoma, Utah, Wyoming. Based in Denver.

11th Circuit: Alabama, Florida and Georgia. Based in Atlanta.

The courts do not always sit in the cities where they are based. Sessions may be held in other major cities within each region.

REFERENCE FORMS: A phrase such as a *federal appeals court* is acceptable on first reference.

On first reference to the full name, use *U.S. Court of Appeals* or a full name: *8th U.S. Circuit Court of Appeals* or *the U.S. Court of Appeals for the 8th Circuit*.

U.S. Circuit Court of Appeals without a circuit number is a misnomer and should not be used.

In shortened and subsequent references: *the Court of Appeals, the 2nd Circuit, the appeals court, the appellate court(s), the circuit court(s), the court*.

Do not create nonexistent entities such as *the San Francisco Court of Appeals*. Make it *the U.S. Court of Appeals in San Francisco*.

JURISTS: The formal title for the jurists on the court is *judge*: *U.S. Circuit Judge Homer Thornberry* is preferred to *U.S. Appeals Judge Homer Thornberry*, but either is acceptable.

See **judge**.

U.S. Court of Appeals for the Armed Forces This court, not part of the judicial branch as such, is a civilian body established by Congress to hear appeals from actions of the Defense Department. It is based in Washington. (Formerly the U.S. Court of Military Appeals.)

U.S. Court of Appeals for the Federal Circuit Commonly known as the CAFC, it replaced U.S. Court of Claims and U.S. Court of Customs and Patent Appeals. It handles suits against the federal government and appeals involving customs, patents and copyright. It is based in Washington.

U.S. Customs and Border Protection An agency of the Department of Homeland Security, it includes the Border Patrol.

U.S. Court of Military Appeals See **U.S. Court of Appeals for the Armed Forces**.

U.S. Customs Court This court,

based in New York City, handles disputes over customs duties that arise at any U.S. port of entry.

U.S. District Courts There are 94. In shortened and subsequent references: *the District Court, the District Courts, the court.*

Judge is the formal title for District Court jurists: *U.S. District Judge Frank Johnson.* See **judge**.

usher Use for both men and women.

U.S. Immigration and Customs Enforcement *ICE* is the acronym for this investigative arm of the Department of Homeland Security. It incorporates the functions of the former Immigration and Naturalization Service, the former Customs service and the Federal Protective Service.

U.S. Marshals Service No apostrophe.

U.S. Military Academy See **military academies**.

U.S. Navy See **navy**; **military academies**; and **military titles**.

U.S. Postal Service Use *U.S. Postal Service* or *the Postal Service* on first reference. Retain capitalization of *Postal Service* in subsequent references to the agency.

Lowercase *the service* when it stands alone. Lowercase *post office* in generic references to the agency and to an individual office: *I went to the post office.*

USS For *United States Ship, Steamer* or *Steamship*, preceding the name of a vessel: *the USS Iowa.*

In datelines:
ABOARD USS IOWA (AP) —

U.S. Supreme Court See **Supreme Court of the United States**.

U.S. Tax Court This court handles appeals in tax cases.

Utah Do not abbreviate in datelines or stories. Postal code: *UT* See **state names**.

U-turn (n. and adj.)

v. See **verbs**.

vacuum

Valium A trademark for a brand of tranquilizer and muscle relaxant. It also may be called *diazepam*.

valley Capitalize as part of a full name: *the Mississippi Valley*.
Lowercase in plural uses: *the Missouri and Mississippi valleys*.

van, von See **foreign names**.

Vaseline A trademark for a brand of petroleum jelly.

Vatican City Stands alone in datelines.

v-chip

VCR Acceptable in all references to *videocassette recorder*.

VDT Abbreviation for *video display terminal*. Spell out.

V-E Day May 8, 1945, the day the surrender of Germany was announced, officially ending the European phase of World War II.

vegetables See **food**.

vegetative state A condition in which the eyes are open and can move, and the patient has periods of sleep and periods of wakefulness, but remains unconscious, unaware of self or others. The patient can't think, reason, respond, do anything on purpose, chew or swallow. Reaction to a sound or a sight is reflex. A vegetative state is labeled "persistent" if it lasts more than a month. It's generally considered permanent if it lasts longer than three months and was caused by lack of oxygen to the brain, or longer than 12 months when caused by traumatic injury.
See **coma** and **minimally conscious state**.

V-8 The engine.

Velcro Trademark for a nylon material that can be pressed together or pulled apart for easy fastening and unfastening. Use a generic term such as fabric fastener.

vendor

verbal See **oral, verbal, written**.

verbs The abbreviation *v.* is used in this book to identify the spelling of the verb forms of words frequently misspelled.
SPLIT FORMS: In general, avoid awkward constructions that split infinitive forms of a verb (*to leave, to help*, etc.) or compound forms (*had left, are found out*, etc.)
Awkward: *She was ordered to immediately leave on an assignment.*
Preferred: *She was ordered to leave immediately on an assignment.*

Awkward: *There stood the wagon that we had early last autumn left by the barn.*

Preferred: *There stood the wagon that we had left by the barn early last autumn.*

Occasionally, however, a split is not awkward and is necessary to convey the meaning:

He wanted to really help his mother.
Those who lie are often found out.
How has your health been?
The budget was tentatively approved.

Verizon Communications Inc.
Headquarters is in New York.

Vermont Abbreviate *Vt.* in datelines or stories. Postal code: *VT*
See **state names**.

vernacular The native language of a country or place. A vernacular term that has achieved widespread recognition may be used without explanation if appropriate in the context.

Terms not widely known should be explained when used. In general, they are appropriate only when illustrating vernacular speech.
See **colloquialisms** and **dialect**.

verses See **poetry** for guidelines on how to handle verses of poetry typographically.

versus Spell it out in ordinary speech and writing: *The proposal to revamp Medicare versus proposals to reform Medicare and Medicaid at the same time ...* In short expressions, however, the abbreviation *vs.* is permitted: *The issue of guns vs. butter has long been with us.*

For court cases, use *v: Marbury v. Madison.*

Very Rev. See **Episcopal Church**; **religious titles**; and **Roman Catholic Church**.

Veterans Affairs Formerly Veterans Administration, it became Cabinet level in March 1989 with the full title Department of Veterans Affairs. *VA* (no periods) is still used on second reference.

Veterans Day Formerly Armistice Day, Nov. 11, the anniversary of the armistice that ended World War I in 1918.

The federal legal holiday, observed on the fourth Monday in October during the mid-1970s, reverted to Nov. 11 in 1978.

Veterans of Foreign Wars
VFW is acceptable on second reference.

Headquarters is in Kansas City, Mo.

veto, vetoes (n.) The verb forms: *vetoed, vetoing.*

vice Use two words: *vice admiral, vice chairman, vice chancellor, vice consul, vice president, vice principal, vice regent, vice secretary.*

Several are exceptions to Webster's New World College Dictionary. The two-word rule has been adopted for consistency in handling the similar terms.

vice president Capitalize or lowercase following the same rules that apply to *president.* See **president** and **titles**.

Do not drop the first name on first reference.

vice versa

videocassette recorder *VCR* is acceptable in all references.

videodisc

video game Two words in all uses.

video recording Precise term for digital audio and visual recording. Digital has largely replaced videotaping.

videotape (n. and v.)

Vienna The city in Austria stands alone in datelines.

Vietnam

Vietnam War

vie, vied, vying

village Apply the capitalization principles in **city**.

VIP, VIPs Acceptable in all references for *very important person(s)*.

Virgin America Headquarters of this airline is in Burlingame, Calif.

Virgin Atlantic Airways Ltd. Headquarters is in Crawley, England.

Virginia Abbreviate *Va.* in datelines or stories. Postal code: *VA*
Legally a commonwealth, not a state. See **state names**.

Virgin Islands Use with a community name in datelines on stories from the U.S. Virgin Islands. Do not abbreviate.
Identify an individual island in the text if relevant.
See **datelines** and **British Virgin Islands**.

virus, worm A computer *virus* is any malicious, invasive program designed to infect and disrupt computers. A *worm* is a type of virus that spreads on networks such as the Internet, copying itself from one computer to another without human intervention.

viscount, viscountess See **nobility**.

V-J Day The day of victory for the Allied forces over Japan in World War II.
It is calculated both as Aug. 15, 1945, the day the fighting with Japan ended, and as Sept. 2, 1945, the day Japan officially surrendered.

V-neck (n. and adj.)

voice mail Two words.

Voice of America *VOA* is acceptable on second reference.

Volkswagen AG Headquarters is in Wolfsburg, Germany.

Volkswagen of America Inc. The name of the U.S. subsidiary of the German company *Volkswagen AG*.
U.S. headquarters is in Auburn Hills, Mich.

volley, volleys

Voodoo Capitalize when referring specifically to the religion, practiced primarily in Haiti and parts of Africa. Lowercase in other uses, especially when ascribing magical solutions to problems, as in *voodoo economics*.

vote-getter

vote tabulations Always use figures for the totals.
Spell out below 10 in other phrases related to voting: *by a five-vote majority, with three abstentions, four votes short of the necessary two-thirds majority.*
For results that involve fewer than 1,000 votes on each side, use these forms: *The House voted 230-205, a 230-205 vote.*

To make totals that involve more than 1,000 votes on a side easier to read, separate the figures with the word *to* to avoid hyphenated adjectival constructions. See **election returns** for examples.

vulgarities See **obscenities, profanities, vulgarities**.

Wahhabi Follower of a strict Muslim sect that adheres closely to the Quran; it's most powerful in Saudi Arabia.

waiter (male) **waitress** (female)

waitlist (n.) **wait-list** (v.)

wake-up call

Wales Use *Wales* after the names of Welsh communities in datelines.
See **datelines** and **United Kingdom**.

walk up (v.) **walk-up** (n. and adj.)

Wall Street When the reference is to the entire complex of financial institutions in the area rather than the actual street itself, *the Street* is an acceptable short form.
See **capitalization**.

Wal-Mart Stores Inc. Headquarters is in Bentonville, Ark.

Walt Disney Co., The Headquarters is in Burbank, Calif.

war Capitalize as part of the name of a specific conflict: *the Afghanistan War, the Iraq War, the Civil War, the Cold War, the Korean War, the Vietnam War, the War of 1812, World War I, World War II, the Gulf War.*

warden Capitalize as a formal title before a name. See **titles**.

wards Use figures. See **political divisions**.

warhead

war horse, warhorse Two words for a horse used in battle.
One word for a veteran of many battles: *He is a political warhorse.*

warlike

warlord

warrant officer See **military titles**.

wartime

washed-up (adj.)

Washington Abbreviate *Wash.* in datelines or stories. Postal code: *WA*
Never abbreviate when referring to the U.S. capital.
Use state of Washington or Washington state and Washington, D.C., or District of Columbia when the context requires distinction between the state and the federal district.
See **state** and **state names**.

The Washington Post Co. Owner of The Washington Post, Slate website and other media properties. Generates more than half of revenue from non-media properties, namely the Kaplan academic testing service and Cable One cable operator. Headquarters is in Washington, D.C.

Washington's Birthday Capitalize *birthday* in references to the holiday.

The date he was born is computed as Feb. 22. The federal legal holiday is the third Monday in February.

Some states and some organizations refer to it as *Presidents Day,* but the formal name has not changed.

wastebasket

waterspout See **weather terms**.

watt A unit of power, mostly associated with electricity. Electrical energy is measured in watt-hours (or kilowatt-hours or megawatt-hours). Do not use "megawatts per hour." Abbreviate *W, kW, MW.*

weapons *Gun* is an acceptable term for any firearm. Note the following definitions and forms in dealing with weapons and ammunition:

anti-aircraft A cannon or other weapon designed for defense against air attack. The form: *a 105 mm anti-aircraft gun.*

artillery A carriage-mounted cannon.

assault rifle A rifle that is capable of being fired in fully automatic and semi-automatic modes, at the user's option. Designed for, and used by, military forces. Also used by some law enforcement agencies. The form: *an M16 assault rifle, an AK-47 assault rifle.*

assault weapon A semi-automatic firearm similar in appearance to a fully automatic firearm or military weapon. Not synonymous with assault rifle, which can be used in

fully automatic mode. Wherever possible, be specific about the type of weapon: *semi-automatic rifle, semi-automatic shotgun* or *semi-automatic pistol.*

automatic A firearm that reloads automatically after each shot. Note there are differences between fully automatic and semi-automatic firearms. Be specific in usage. The form: *a .22-caliber automatic.*

buckshot See **shot**.

bullet The projectile fired by a rifle, pistol or machine gun. Together with metal casing, primer and propellant, it forms a *cartridge.*

caliber A measurement of the diameter of the inside of a gun barrel except for most shotguns. Measurement is in either millimeters or decimal fractions of an inch. The word *caliber* is not used when giving the metric measurement. The forms: *a 9 mm pistol, a .22-caliber rifle.*

cannon A weapon, usually supported on some type of carriage, that fires explosive projectiles. The form: *a 105 mm cannon.*

carbine A short, lightweight rifle, usually having a barrel length of less than 20 inches. The form: *an M3 carbine.*

cartridge See **bullet**.

clip A device to store multiple rounds of ammunition together as a unit, ready for insertion into the gun. Clips are generally used to load obsolete military rifles. *Clip* is not the correct term for detachable magazines commonly used in modern military rifles, submachine guns and semiautomatic pistols. See **magazine**.

Colt Named for Samuel Colt, it designates a make of weapon or ammunition developed for Colt handguns. The forms: *a Colt .45-caliber revolver, .45 Colt ammunition.*

fully automatic A firearm that fires continuously as long as the trigger is depressed. Examples include *machine guns* and *submachine guns*.

gauge The measure of the size of a shotgun. Gauge is expressed in terms of the number per pound of round lead balls with a diameter equal to the size of the barrel. The bigger the number, the smaller the shotgun.

The forms: *a 12-gauge shotgun, a .410-gauge shotgun.* The .410 actually is a caliber, but commonly is called a gauge.

handgun

howitzer A cannon shorter than a gun of the same caliber employed to fire projectiles at relatively high angles at a target, such as opposing forces behind a ridge. The form: *a 105 mm howitzer.*

M1, M16 These and similar combinations of a letter and figure(s) designate rifles used by the military. The forms: *an M1 rifle, an M16 rifle.*

machine gun A fully automatic gun that fires as long as the trigger is depressed. The form: *a .50-caliber Browning machine gun.*

magazine The ammunition storage and feeding device within or attached to a firearm. It may be fixed to the firearm or detachable.

Magnum A trademark for a type of high-powered cartridge with a larger case and a larger powder charge than other cartridges of approximately the same caliber. The form: *a .357 Magnum, a .44 Magnum.*

mortar Device used to launch a mortar shell; it is the shell, not the mortar, that is fired.

musket A heavy, large-caliber shoulder firearm fired by means of a matchlock, a wheel lock, a flintlock or a percussion lock. Its ammunition is a musket ball.

pistol A handgun that can be a single shot or a semi-automatic. Its size is measured in calibers. The form: *a .45-caliber pistol.*

revolver A handgun. Its cartridges are held in chambers in a cylinder that revolves. The form: *a .45-caliber revolver.*

rifle A firearm designed or made to be fired from the shoulder and having a rifled bore. It uses bullets or cartridges for ammunition. Its size is measured in calibers. The form: *a .22-caliber rifle.*

Saturday night special A compact, relatively inexpensive handgun.

semi-automatic A firearm that fires only once for each pull of the trigger. It reloads after each shot. The form: *a semi-automatic rifle, a semi-automatic weapon, a semi-automatic pistol.*

shell The word applies to military or naval ammunition and to shotgun ammunition.

shot Small lead or steel pellets fired by shotguns. A shotgun shell usually contains 1 to 2 ounces of shot. Do not use *shot* interchangeably with *buckshot*, which refers only to the largest shot sizes.

shotgun A firearm typically used to fire small spherical pellets called shot. *Shotguns* usually have a smooth bore barrel, but some contain a rifled barrel, which is used to fire a single projectile. Size is measured according to gauge, except for the .410, which is measured according to caliber. The form: *a 12-gauge shotgun.*

submachine gun A lightweight fully automatic gun firing handgun ammunition.

weather-beaten

weather bureau See **National Weather Service**.
Online:
www.noaa.gov

weatherman The preferred term is *weather forecaster*.

weather terms The following are based on definitions used by the National Weather Service. All temperatures are Fahrenheit.

blizzard Wind speeds of 35 mph or more and considerable falling and/or blowing of snow with visibility near zero. *Severe blizzard*, winds of 45 mph, temperature at or below 10 F and visibility reduced by snow to near zero.

coastal waters The waters within about 20 miles of the coast, including bays, harbors and sounds.

cyclone A storm with strong winds rotating about a moving center of low atmospheric pressure.

The word sometimes is used in the United States to mean *tornado* and in the Indian Ocean area to mean *hurricane*.

degree-day A unit of measurement describing how much the temperature differs from a standard average for one day. It is usually used to gauge the amount of heating or cooling needed for a building. If the standard average temperature for a day is 65 degrees, then a temperature of 10 below zero for 24 hours yields 75 degree-days.

dew point The temperature to which air must be cooled for dew to form. The higher the *dew point*, the more moisture in the air.

dust devil A small, rapidly rotating wind that is made visible by the dust, dirt or debris it picks up. Also called a *whirlwind*, it develops best on clear, dry, hot afternoons.

dust storm Visibility of one-half mile or less due to dust, wind speeds of 30 mph or more.

flash flood A sudden, violent flood. It typically occurs after a heavy rain or the melting of a heavy snow.

flash flood warning Warns that flash flooding is imminent or in progress. Those in the affected area should take necessary precautions immediately.

flash flood watch Alerts the public that flash flooding is possible.

Those in the affected area are urged to be ready to take additional precautions if a flash flood warning is issued or if flooding is observed.

flood Stories about floods usually tell how high the water is and where it is expected to crest. Such a story should also, for comparison, list flood stage and how high the water is above, or below, flood stage.

Wrong: *The river is expected to crest at 39 feet.*

Right: *The river is expected to crest at 39 feet, 12 feet above flood stage.*

freeze Describes conditions when the temperature at or near the surface is expected to be below 32 degrees during the growing season. Adjectives such as *severe* or *hard* are used if a cold spell exceeding two days is expected.

A freeze may or may not be accompanied by the formation of frost. However, use of the term *freeze* usually is restricted for occasions when wind or other conditions prevent frost.

freezing drizzle, freezing rain A drizzle or rain that falls as a liquid but freezes into glaze upon contact with the cold ground or surface structures.

frost Describes the formation of very small ice crystals, which might develop under conditions similar to dew except for the minimum temperatures involved. Phrases such as *frost in low places* or *scattered light frost* are used when appropriate.

funnel cloud A violent, rotating column of air that does not touch the ground, usually a pendant from a cumulonimbus cloud.

gale Sustained winds within the range of 39 to 54 mph (34 to 47 knots).

hail Precipitation in the form of irregular pellets or balls of ice. Showery precipitation in the form of irregular pellets or balls of ice more than 5 mm in diameter, falling from a cumulonimbus cloud.

heavy snow It generally means:

a. A fall accumulating to 4 inches or more in depth in 12 hours, or

b. A fall accumulating to 6 inches or more in depth in 24 hours.

high wind Normally indicates that sustained winds of 39 mph or greater are expected to persist for one hour or longer.

hurricane categories Hurricanes are ranked 1 to 5 according to what is known as the Saffir-Simpson scale of strength:

Category 1 — Hurricane has central barometric pressure of 28.94 inches or more and winds of 74 to 95 mph, is accompanied by a 4 to 5 foot storm surge and causes minimal damage.

Category 2 — Pressure 28.50 to 28.93 inches, winds from 96 to 110 mph, storm surge 6 to 8 feet, damage moderate.

Category 3 — Pressure 27.91 to 28.49 inches, winds from 111 to 130 mph, storm surge 9 to 12 feet, damage extensive.

Category 4 — Pressure 27.17 to 27.90 inches, winds from 131 to 155 mph, storm surge 13 to 18 feet, damage extreme.

Category 5 — Pressure less than 27.17 inches, winds greater than 155 mph, storm surge higher than 18 feet, damage catastrophic.

Only three *Category 5* storms have hit the United States since record-keeping began: the 1935 Labor Day hurricane that hit the Florida Keys and killed 600 people; Hurricane Camille, which devastated the Mississippi coast in 1969, killing 256 and leaving $1.4 billion damage, and Hurricane Andrew, which hit South Florida in 1992, killing 43 and causing $30.5 billion in damage.

hurricane eye The relatively calm area in the center of the storm. In this area winds are light and the sky often is covered only partly by clouds.

hurricane or typhoon A warm-core tropical cyclone in which the minimum sustained surface wind is 74 mph or more.

Hurricanes are spawned east of the international date line. Typhoons develop west of the line. They are known as cyclones in the Indian Ocean and Australia.

When a hurricane or typhoon loses strength (wind speed), usually after landfall, it is reduced to *tropical storm* status.

hurricane season The portion of the year that has a relatively high incidence of hurricanes. In the Atlantic, Caribbean and Gulf of Mexico, this is from June through November. In the eastern Pacific, it is May 15 through Nov. 30. In the central Pacific, it is June 1 through Nov. 30.

hurricane tide Same as **storm tide**.

hurricane warning Warns that one or both of these dangerous effects of a hurricane are expected in specified areas in 36 hours or less:

a. Sustained winds of 74 mph (64 knots) or higher, and/or

b. Dangerously high water or a combination of dangerously high water and exceptionally high waves, even though winds expected may be less than hurricane force.

hurricane watch An announcement for specific areas that a hurricane or incipient hurricane conditions may pose a threat to coastal and inland communities. A watch is issued 48 hours ahead of storm force winds.

ice storm warning Reserved for occasions when significant, and possibly damaging, accumulations of ice are expected.

ice storm, freezing drizzle, freezing rain Describes the freezing of drizzle or rain on objects as it strikes them. *Freezing drizzle* and *freezing rain* are synonyms for *ice storm*.

microburst Occurs when a mass of cooled air rushes downward out of a thunderstorm, hits the ground and rushes outward in all directions. A plane flying through a *microburst* at low altitude, as on final approach or takeoff, would at first experience a strong headwind and increased lift, followed by a strong tail wind and sharply decreased lift.

National Hurricane Center The National Weather Service's National Hurricane Center in Miami has overall responsibility for tracking and providing information about tropical depressions, tropical storms and hurricanes in the Atlantic Ocean, Gulf of Mexico, Caribbean Sea and eastern Pacific Ocean.

The service's Central Pacific Hurricane Center in Honolulu is responsible for hurricane information in the Pacific Ocean area north of the equator from 140 degrees west longitude to 180 degrees.

Online:
www.nhc.noaa.gov

nearshore waters The waters extended to five miles from shore.

nor'easter The term used by the National Weather Service for storms that either exit or move north along the East Coast, producing winds blowing from the northeast.

offshore waters The waters extending to about 250 miles from shore.

sandstorm Visibility of one-half mile or less due to sand blown by winds of 30 mph or more.

Santa Ana wind In Southern California, a weather condition in which strong, hot, dust-bearing winds descend to the Pacific Coast from inland desert regions.

severe blizzard Wind speeds of 45 mph or more, great density of falling and/or blowing snow with visibility frequently near zero and a temperature of 10 degrees or lower.

severe thunderstorm Describes either of the following:

a. Winds — Thunderstorm-related surface winds sustained or gusts

50 knots or greater.

b. Hail — Surface hail three-quarters of an inch in diameter or larger. The word *hail* in a watch implies hail at the surface and aloft unless qualifying phrases such as *hail aloft* are used.

sleet (one form of ice pellet) Describes generally solid grains of ice formed by the freezing of raindrops or the refreezing of largely melted snowflakes. Sleet, like small hail, usually bounces when hitting a hard surface.

sleet (heavy) Heavy sleet is a fairly rare event in which the ground is covered to a depth of significance to motorists and others.

snow avalanche bulletin Snow avalanche bulletins are issued by the U.S. Forest Service for avalanche-prone areas in the western United States.

squall A sudden increase of wind speed by at least 16 knots and rising to 25 knots or more and lasting for at least one minute.

storm tide Directional wave(s) caused by a severe atmospheric disturbance.

tidal wave Often used incorrectly as a synonym for *tsunami*. A large wave created by rising tide in a funnel-shaped inlet is called a *tidal bore*. Unusually large waves at sea are sometimes called *rogue waves*.

tornado A violent rotating column of air forming a pendant, usually from a cumulonimbus cloud, and touching the ground. It is often, but not always, visible as a funnel cloud, and usually is accompanied by a loud roaring noise. On a local scale, it is the most destructive of all atmospheric phenomena. Tornadoes can appear from any direction, but in the U.S. most move from southwest to northeast.

Tornado strength is measured by an enhanced F-scale rating from EF0 to EF5, which considers 28 different types of damage to structures and trees. It updates the original scale, which estimated wind strength. An EF2 or higher is considered a significant tornado.

Plural is *tornadoes*.

tornado warning A *tornado warning* is issued by a local National Weather Service office to warn the public of an existing tornado or one suspected to be in existence.

tornado watch A *tornado watch* alerts the public to the possibility of a tornado in the next several hours.

traveler's advisory Alerts the public that difficult traveling or hazardous road conditions are expected to be widespread.

tropical depression A tropical cyclone in which the maximum sustained surface wind is 38 mph (33 knots) or less.

tropical storm A warm core tropical cyclone in which the maximum sustained surface winds range from 39 to 73 mph (34 to 63 knots) inclusive.

tsunami (s.), **tsunamis** (pl.) A great sea wave or seismic sea wave caused by an underwater disturbance such as an earthquake, landslide or volcano. It can cause massive death and destruction as was

Heat index table

RELATIVE HUMIDITY

TEMP. F	40%	45%	50%	55%	60%	65%	70%	75%	80%	85%	90%	95%	100%
110	136												
108	130	137											
106	124	130	137										
104	119	124	131	137			APPARENT TEMPERATURE						
102	114	119	124	130	137								
100	109	114	118	124	129	136							
98	105	109	113	117	123	128	134						
96	101	104	108	112	116	121	126	132					
94	97	100	102	106	110	114	119	124	129	135			
92	94	96	99	101	105	108	112	116	121	126	131		
90	91	93	95	97	100	103	106	109	113	117	122	127	132
88	88	89	91	93	95	98	100	103	106	110	113	117	121
86	85	87	88	89	91	93	95	97	100	102	105	108	112
84	83	84	85	86	88	89	90	92	94	96	98	100	103
82	81	82	83	84	84	85	86	88	89	90	91	93	95
80	80	80	81	81	82	82	83	84	84	85	86	86	87

Wind chill factor table

AIR TEMPERATURE

WIND MPH	40	35	30	25	20	15	10	5	0	-5	-10	-15	-20	-25	-30	-35	-40	-45
						APPARENT TEMPERATURE												
5	36	31	25	19	13	7	1	-5	-11	-16	-22	-28	-34	-40	-46	-52	-57	-63
10	34	27	21	15	9	3	-4	-10	-16	-22	-28	-35	-41	-47	-53	-59	-66	-72
15	32	25	19	13	6	0	-7	-13	-19	-26	-32	-39	-45	-51	-58	-64	-71	-77
20	30	24	17	11	4	-2	-9	-15	-22	-29	-35	-42	-48	-55	-61	-68	-74	-81
25	29	23	16	9	3	-4	-11	-17	-24	-31	-37	-44	-51	-58	-64	-71	-78	-84
30	28	22	15	8	1	-5	-12	-19	-26	-33	-39	-46	-53	-60	-67	-73	-80	-87
35	28	21	14	7	0	-7	-14	-21	-27	-34	-41	-48	-55	-62	-69	-76	-82	-89
40	27	20	13	6	-1	-8	-15	-22	-29	-36	-43	-50	-57	-64	-71	-78	-84	-91
45	26	19	12	5	-2	-9	-16	-23	-30	-37	-44	-51	-58	-65	-72	-79	-86	-93
50	26	19	12	4	-3	-10	-17	-24	-31	-38	-45	-52	-60	-67	-74	-81	-88	-95
55	25	18	11	4	-3	-11	-18	-25	-32	-39	-46	-54	-61	-68	-75	-82	-89	-97
60	25	17	10	3	-4	-11	-19	-26	-33	-40	-48	-55	-62	-69	-76	-84	-91	-98

FROSTBITE TIME   30 min.   10 min.   5 min.

seen in the Indian Ocean *tsunami* in December 2004. *Tidal wave* was long used as a synonym for *tsunami*, but it is incorrect in that use.

typhoon See **hurricane or typhoon** in this listing.

waterspout A tornado over water.

wind chill index Also known as the *wind chill factor*. No hyphen.

The *wind chill* is a calculation that describes the combined effect of the wind and cold temperatures on exposed skin. The *wind chill index* would be minus 4, for example, if the temperature was 15 degrees and the wind was blowing at 25 mph — in other words, a temperature of 4 below zero with no wind.

The higher the wind at a given temperature, the lower the wind chill reading, although wind speeds above 40 mph have little additional cooling effect.

wind shear *Wind shear* is a sudden shift in wind direction and speed. It can prevent development of some storms and is sometimes visible when the wind shears off the top of a cloud to form an anvil.

winter storm warning Notifies the public that severe winter weather conditions are almost certain to occur.

winter storm watch Alerts the public to the possibility of severe winter weather conditions.

weather vane

Web Short form of *World Wide Web*, it is a service, or set of standards, that enables the publishing of multimedia documents on the Internet. The Web is not the same as the Internet, but is a subset; other applications, such as email, exist on the Internet.

It is generally credited as the concept of researcher Tim Berners-Lee, who developed the first practi-

cal system in 1989.

Also, *website, webcam, webcast* and *webmaster*. But as a short form and in terms with separate words, *the Web, Web page* and *Web feed*.

Caution:

Do not mistake the Internet for an encyclopedia, and the search engine for a table of contents. The Internet is a sprawling information repository. Anything you find should be assessed with the same care that you use for everything else. In particular, check these points:

• Who is sponsoring the page? Is the author identifiable and, if so, is that person pretending to be someone else? You should avoid anonymous pages just as you avoid anonymous sources.

• Is there contact information in case you want to follow up? One way to check who owns a page is the Whois query at http://www.network-solutions.com/whois/index.jsp. Keep in mind, however, that data are self-reported and could be incorrect.

• Is the domain type (".edu" or ".gov", for example) appropriate for the information provided? Websites set up by professional groups are generally more reliable than personal home pages.

• The source for the information on the page should be clearly stated, whether original or borrowed. Is it a primary or secondary source? Can it be checked somewhere else?

• Based on what you know, how accurate does the information seem? If there's something on the site that you know is incorrect, it's likely there are errors elsewhere.

• Are there any obvious signs of bias? One possible clue: the type of sites that this site links to.

• Is the page current? If it hasn't been updated lately, the information may be outdated. See **Internet**.

website A location on the World Wide Web that maintains one or more pages at a specific address. Also, *webcam*, *webcast* and *webmaster*. But as a short form and in terms with separate words, *the Web*, *Web page* and *Web feed*. See **Web**.

Webster's New World College Dictionary See **dictionaries**.

Webster's Third New International Dictionary See **dictionaries**.

weekend

weeklong, weekslong One word as an adjective.

weights Use figures: *The baby weighed 9 pounds, 7 ounces. She had a 9-pound, 7-ounce boy.*

weird, weirdo

well Hyphenate as part of a compound modifier: *She is a well-dressed woman.*
See **hyphen** in the **Punctuation** chapter for guidelines on compound modifiers.

well-being

well-informed

Wells Fargo & Co. Acquired Wachovia Corp. in 2009. Headquarters is in San Francisco.

well-to-do

well-wishers

West As defined by the U.S. Census Bureau, the 13-state region is broken into two divisions.
The eight *Mountain division* states are Arizona, Colorado, Idaho, Montana, Nevada, New Mexico, Utah and Wyoming.

The five *Pacific division* states are Alaska, California, Hawaii, Oregon and Washington.
See **Midwest region**; **Northeast region**; and **South** for the bureau's other three regional breakdowns.

Western Capitalize for the film or book genre, but lowercase the style of music better known as *country*.

Western Hemisphere The continents of North and South America, and the islands near them.
It frequently is subdivided as follows:
Caribbean The islands from the tip of Florida to the continent of South America, plus French Guiana, Guyana and Suriname on the northeastern coast of South America.
Major island elements are Cuba, Hispaniola (the island shared by the Dominican Republic and Haiti), Jamaica, Puerto Rico, and the West Indies islands.
Central America The narrow strip of land between Mexico and Colombia. Located there are Belize, Costa Rica, El Salvador, Guatemala, Honduras, Nicaragua and Panama.
Latin America The area of the Americas south of the United States where Romance languages (those derived from Latin) are dominant. It applies to most of the region south of the United States except areas with a British heritage: the Bahamas, Barbados, Belize, Grenada, Guyana, Jamaica, Trinidad and Tobago, and various islands in the West Indies. Suriname, the former Dutch Guiana, is an additional exception.
North America Canada, Mexico, the United States and the Danish territory of Greenland. When the term is used in more than its continental sense, it also may include the islands of the Caribbean.
South America Argentina, Bolivia,

Brazil, Chile, Colombia, Ecuador, Paraguay, Peru, Uruguay, Venezuela, and in a purely continental sense, French Guiana, Guyana and Suriname. Politically and psychologically, however, the latter three regard themselves as part of the Caribbean.

West Indies An island chain extending in an eastward arc between the southeastern United States and the northern shore of South America, separating the Caribbean Sea from the Atlantic Ocean and including the Bahamas, the Greater Antilles, and the Lesser Antilles.

Major island elements are the nations of Barbados, Grenada, and Trinidad and Tobago, plus smaller islands dependent in various degrees on:

—Britain: British Virgin Islands, Anguilla, and the West Indies Associated States, including Antigua, Dominica, St. Lucia, St. Vincent and St. Christopher-Nevis.

—France: Guadeloupe (composed of islands known as Basse-Terre and Grande-Terre, plus five other islands) and Martinique.

—Netherlands: Netherlands Antilles, composed of Aruba, Bonaire, Curacao, Saba, St. Eustatius and the southern portion of St. Martin Island (the northern half is held by France and is part of Guadeloupe).

—United States: U.S. Virgin Islands, principally St. Croix, St. John and St. Thomas.

West Indies See **Western Hemisphere**.

West Point Acceptable on second reference to the *U.S. Military Academy*.

See **military academies**.
In datelines:
WEST POINT, N.Y. (AP) —

West Virginia Abbreviate *W.Va.* (no space between *W.* and *Va.*) in

datelines or stories. Postal code: *WV*
See **state names**.

west, western See **directions and regions**.

Weyerhaeuser Co. Headquarters is in Federal Way, Wash.

wheat It is measured in bushels domestically, in metric tons for international trade.

There are 36.7 bushels of wheat in a metric ton.

wheelchair See **disabled, handicapped, impaired**.

whereabouts Takes a singular verb:
His whereabouts is a mystery.

wherever

which See **essential clauses, nonessential clauses**; **that, which**; and **who, whom**.

whip Capitalize when used as a formal title before a name. See **legislative titles** and **titles**.

whistle-blower

white-collar (adj.)

White House Do not personify it with phrases such as *the White House said*. Instead, use a phrase such as *a White House official said*.

white paper Two words, lowercase, when used to refer to a special report.

whitewash (n., v. and adj.)

wholehearted

wholesale price index A measurement of the changes in the average prices that businesses pay for a selected group of industrial commodities, farm products, processed foods and feed for animals.

Do not capitalize when referring to the U.S. producer price index, issued monthly by the Bureau of Labor Statistics, an agency of the Labor Department.

who's, whose *Who's* is a contraction for *who is*, not a possessive: *Who's there?*

Whose is the possessive: *I do not know whose coat it is.*

who, whom *Who* is the pronoun used for references to human beings and to animals with a name. It is grammatically the subject (never the object) of a sentence, clause or phrase: *The woman who rented the room left the window open. Who is there?*

Whom is used when someone is the object of a verb or preposition: *The woman to whom the room was rented left the window open. Whom do you wish to see?*

See **essential clauses, nonessential clauses** for guidelines on how to punctuate clauses introduced by *who, whom, that* and *which.*

whom See **who, whom.**

-wide No hyphen. Some examples:

citywide	nationwide
continentwide	statewide
countrywide	worldwide
industrywide	

wide- Usually hyphenated. Some examples:

wide-angle	wide-eyed
wide-awake	wide-open
wide-brimmed	

Exception: *widespread.*

widow, widower In obituaries: A man is *survived by his wife*, or *leaves his wife*. A woman is *survived by her husband*, or *leaves her husband*.

Guard against the redundant *widow (widower) of the late.*

widths See **dimensions**.

Wi-Fi For the wireless networking standards.

wiki Software that allows a group of users to add, delete, edit and share information on an intranet or Internet website.

WikiLeaks

Wikipedia An online encyclopedia whose entries are created and edited by its users, regardless of a person's expertise. May contain useful links, but should not be used as a primary source for stories.

wildlife

Wilkes-Barre, Pa.

will See **shall, will** and **subjunctive mood**.

Windbreaker A trademark for a brand of wind-resistant sports jacket.

wind chill index See **weather terms**.

window dressing (n.) **window-dress** (v.)

wind-swept

wind up (v.) **windup** (n. and adj.)

wingspan

winter See **seasons**.

wintertime

wiretap, wiretapper (n.) The verb forms: *wiretap, wiretapped, wiretapping.*

Wisconsin Abbreviate *Wis.* in datelines or stories. Postal code: WI See **state names**.

-wise No hyphen when it means *in the direction of* or *with regard to*. Some examples:

clockwise   otherwise
lengthwise   slantwise

Avoid contrived combinations such as *moneywise, religionwise*.

The word *penny-wise* is spelled with a hyphen because it is a compound adjective in which *wise* means *smart*, not an application of the suffix *-wise*. The same for *street-wise* in *the street-wise youth* (an exception to Webster's New World College Dictionary).

WMD Acceptable on second reference for weapons of mass destruction.

women Women should receive the same treatment as men in all areas of coverage. Physical descriptions, sexist references, demeaning stereotypes and condescending phrases should not be used.

To cite some examples, this means that:

—Copy should not assume maleness when both sexes are involved, as in *Jackson told newsmen* or in *the taxpayer ... he* when it easily can be said *Jackson told reporters* or *taxpayers ... they*.

—Copy should not express surprise that an attractive woman can be professionally accomplished, as in: *Mary Smith doesn't look the part, but she's an authority on ...*

—Copy should not gratuitously mention family relationships when there is no relevance to the subject, as in: *Golda Meir, a doughty grandmother, told the Egyptians today ...*

—Use the same standards for men and women in deciding whether to include specific mention of personal appearance or marital and family situation.

In other words, treatment of the sexes should be evenhanded and free of assumptions and stereotypes. This does not mean that valid and acceptable words such as *mankind* or *humanity* cannot be used. They are proper.

See **courtesy titles**; **divorcee**; **man, mankind**; and **-persons**.

word-of-mouth (n. and adj.)

word processing (adj.)

workbook, workday, workforce, workhorse, workout, workplace, workstation, workweek

workers' compensation

working class (n.) **working-class** (adj.)

World Bank Acceptable in all references for *International Bank for Reconstruction and Development*.

World Council of Churches
This is the main international, interdenominational cooperative body of Anglican, Eastern Orthodox, Protestant and old or national Catholic churches.

The Roman Catholic church is not a member but cooperates with the council in various programs.

Headquarters is in Geneva.

World Health Organization
WHO is acceptable on second reference.

Headquarters is in Geneva.

World Series Or *the Series* on second reference. A rare exception to the general principles under **capitalization**.

World War I, World War II

worldwide

worn-out

worship, worshipped, wor-shipper

worthwhile

would See **should, would**.

wrack See **rack, wrack**.

wracked The preferred spelling when used to say a person is *wracked with doubt* or *wracked with pain*.

write-down (n. and adj.) **write down** (v.) An accounting step a company makes when an asset or class of assets it holds falls in value. The decline in value is reflected in a reduction on the asset side of a company's balance sheet.

write in (v.) **write-in** (n. and adj.)

wrongdoing

Wyoming Abbreviate *Wyo.* in datelines or stories. Postal code: *WY* See **state names**.

XYZ

Xerox A trademark for a brand of photocopy machine. Never a verb. Use a generic term, such as photocopy.

Headquarters of *Xerox Corp.* is in Norwalk, Conn.

Xinhua News Agency The official news agency of the Chinese government is based in Beijing. It was founded in 1931 as the Red China News Agency and adopted its current name in 1937. *Xinhua* is acceptable on second reference.

XML For *Extensible Markup Language,* used to sort, search and format information.

X-ray (n., v. and adj.) Use for both the photographic process and the radiation particles themselves.

Yahoo A trademark for an online computer service. Headquarters of Yahoo Inc. is in Sunnyvale, Calif. Do not use the exclamation point in the formal corporate name.

yam Botanically, yams and sweet potatoes are not related, although several varieties of moist-fleshed sweet potatoes are popularly called *yams* in some parts of the United States.

yard Equal to 3 feet.

The metric equivalent is approximately 0.91 meter.

To convert to meters, multiply by 0.91 (5 yards x 0.91 = 4.55 meters). See **foot; meter;** and **distances**.

year-end (n. and adj.)

yearlong, yearslong

year-round (adj. and adv.)

years Use figures, without commas: *1975.* When a phrase refers to a month, day and year, set off the year with a comma: *Feb. 14, 1987, is the target date.* Use an *s* without an apostrophe to indicate spans of decades or centuries: *the 1890s, the 1800s.*

Years are the lone exception to the general rule in numerals that a figure is not used to start a sentence: *1976 was a very good year.*

See **A.D.; B.C.; century; historical periods and events;** and **months**.

yellow journalism The use of cheaply sensational methods to attract or influence readers. The term comes from the "Yellow Kid," a comic strip in the New York World in 1895.

Yellow Pages Capitalize in describing the business telephone directory.

yesterday Use only in direct quotations and in phrases that do not refer to a specific day: *Yesterday we were young.*

Use the day of the week in other cases.

yesteryear

Yom Kippur The Jewish Day of Atonement. Occurs in September or October.

Young Men's Christian Association The term *the Y* is acceptable in all references to the main organization, which has its headquarters in Chicago. Use *YMCA* when referring to a specific location: *the YMCA of Greater Louisville.*

Young Women's Christian Association *YWCA* is acceptable in all references.

Headquarters is in New York.

youth Applicable to boys and girls from age 13 until 18th birthday. Use *man* or *woman* for individuals 18 and older.

YouTube A video-serving network owned by Google Inc. that allows users to upload their own videos for access by anyone with a network connection.

yo-yo Formerly a trademark, now a generic term.

Yukon A territorial section of Canada. Do not abbreviate. Use in datelines after the names of communities in the territory.

See **Canada**.

yule, yuletide

Yum Brands Inc. Owner of the Pizza Hut, KFC and Taco Bell restaurant chains. Do not use the formal exclamation point in the corporate name. Headquarters of Yum Brands is in Louisville, Ky.

zero, zeros

zigzag

Zionism The effort of Jews to regain and retain their biblical homeland. It is based on the promise of God in the book of Genesis that Israel would forever belong to Abraham and his descendants as a nation.

The term is named for Mount Zion, the site of the ancient temple in Jerusalem. The Bible also frequently uses *Zion* in a general sense to denote the place where God is especially present with his people.

ZIP code Use all-caps *ZIP* for *Zoning Improvement Plan*, but always lowercase the word *code*.

Run the five digits together without a comma, and do not put a comma between the state name and the ZIP code: *New York, NY 10020.*

zip line

Zurich The city in Switzerland stands alone in datelines.

A GUIDE TO PUNCTUATION

There is no alternative to correct punctuation. Incorrect punctuation can change the meaning of a sentence, the results of which could be far-reaching.

Even if the meaning is not changed, bad punctuation, however inconsequential, can cause the reader to lose track of what is being said and give up reading a sentence.

The basic guideline is to use common sense.

—Punctuation is to make clear the thought being expressed.

—If punctuation does not help make clear what is being said, it should not be there.

"The Elements of Style" by William Strunk Jr. and E.B. White is a bible of writers. It states:

"Clarity, clarity, clarity. When you become hopelessly mired in a sentence, it is best to start fresh; do not try to fight your way through against terrible odds of syntax. Usually what is wrong is that the construction has become too involved at some point; the sentence needs to be broken apart and replaced by two or more shorter sentences."

This applies to punctuation. If a sentence becomes cluttered with commas, semicolons and dashes, start over.

These two paragraphs are full of commas and clauses; all of it equals too much for the reader to grasp:

The Commonwealth Games Federation, in an apparent effort to persuade other nations to ignore the spiraling boycott, ruled Sunday that Budd, a runner who has had a storied past on and off the track, and Cowley, a swimmer who competes for the University of Texas, were ineligible under the Commonwealth Constitution to compete for England in the 10-day event to be held in Edinburgh, Scotland, beginning July 24.

The decision on Budd, who has been the object of a number of demonstrations in the past, and Cowley followed an earlier announcement Sunday by Tanzania that it was joining Nigeria, Kenya, Ghana and Uganda in boycotting the games because of Britain's refusal to support economic sanctions against South Africa's government.

PUNCTUATION MARKS AND HOW TO USE THEM

apostrophe (') Follow these guidelines:

POSSESSIVES: See the **possessives** entry in main section.

PLURAL NOUNS NOT ENDING IN S: Add *'s: the alumni's contributions, women's rights.*

PLURAL NOUNS ENDING IN S: Add only an apostrophe: *the churches' needs, the girls' toys, the horses' food, the ships' wake, states' rights, the VIPs' entrance.*

NOUNS PLURAL IN FORM, SINGULAR IN MEANING: Add only an apostrophe: *mathematics' rules, measles' effects.* (But see INANIMATE OBJECTS below.)

Apply the same principle when a plural word occurs in the formal name of a singular entity: *General Motors' profits, the United States' wealth.*

NOUNS THE SAME IN SINGULAR AND PLURAL: Treat them the same as plurals, even if the meaning is singular: *one corps' location, the two deer's tracks, the lone moose's antlers.*

SINGULAR NOUNS NOT ENDING IN S: Add *'s: the church's needs, the girl's toys, the horse's food, the ship's route, the VIP's seat.*

Some style guides say that singular nouns ending in *s* sounds such as *ce, x,* and *z* may take either the apostrophe alone or *'s.* See SPECIAL EXPRESSIONS, but otherwise, for consistency and ease in remembering a rule, always use *'s* if the word does not end in the letter *s: Butz's policies, the fox's den, the justice's verdict, Marx's theories, the prince's life, Xerox's profits.*

SINGULAR COMMON NOUNS ENDING IN S: Add *'s* unless the next word begins with *s: the hostess's invitation, the hostess' seat; the wit-*ness's answer, the witness' story.

SINGULAR PROPER NAMES ENDING IN S: Use only an apostrophe: *Achilles' heel, Agnes' book, Ceres' rites, Descartes' theories, Dickens' novels, Euripides' dramas, Hercules' labors, Jesus' life, Jules' seat, Kansas' schools, Moses' law, Socrates' life, Tennessee Williams' plays, Xerxes' armies.* (An exception is *St. James's Palace.*)

SPECIAL EXPRESSIONS: The following exceptions to the general rule for words not ending in *s* apply to words that end in an *s* sound and are followed by a word that begins with *s: for appearance' sake, for conscience' sake, for goodness' sake.* Use *'s* otherwise: *the appearance's cost, my conscience's voice.*

PRONOUNS: Personal interrogative and relative pronouns have separate forms for the possessive. None involves an apostrophe: *mine, ours, your, yours, his, hers, its, theirs, whose.*

Caution: If you are using an apostrophe with a pronoun, always double-check to be sure that the meaning calls for a contraction: *you're, it's, there's, who's.*

Follow the rules listed above in forming the possessives of other pronouns: *another's idea, others' plans, someone's guess.*

COMPOUND WORDS: Applying the rules above, add an apostrophe or *'s* to the word closest to the object possessed: *the major general's decision, the major generals' decisions, the attorney general's request, the attorneys general's request.* See the **plurals** entry for guidelines on forming the plurals of these words.

Also: *anyone else's attitude, John Adams Jr.'s father, Benjamin Franklin of Pennsylvania's motion.* Whenever practical, however, recast the phrase to avoid ambiguity: *the motion by Benjamin Franklin of Pennsylvania.*

JOINT POSSESSION, INDIVIDUAL POSSESSION: Use a possessive form after only the last word if ownership is joint: *Fred and Sylvia's apartment, Fred and Sylvia's stocks.*

Use a possessive form after both words if the objects are individually owned: *Fred's and Sylvia's books.*

DESCRIPTIVE PHRASES: Do not add an apostrophe to a word ending in *s* when it is used primarily in a descriptive sense: *citizens band radio, a Cincinnati Reds infielder, a teachers college, a Teamsters request, a writers guide.*

Memory Aid: The apostrophe usually is not used if *for* or *by* rather than *of* would be appropriate in the longer form: *a radio band for citizens, a college for teachers, a guide for writers, a request by the Teamsters.*

An *'s* is required however, when a term involves a plural word that does not end in *s*: *a children's hospital, a people's republic, the Young Men's Christian Association.*

DESCRIPTIVE NAMES: Some governmental, corporate and institutional organizations with a descriptive word in their names use an apostrophe; some do not. Follow the user's practice: *Actors' Equity, Diners Club, the Ladies' Home Journal, the National Governors Association.* See separate entries for these and similar names frequently in the news.

QUASI POSSESSIVES: Follow the rules above in composing the possessive form of words that occur in such phrases as *a day's pay, two weeks' vacation, three days' work, your money's worth.*

Frequently, however, a hyphenated form is clearer: *a two-week vacation, a three-day job.*

DOUBLE POSSESSIVE: Two conditions must apply for a double possessive — a phrase such as *a friend of John's* — to occur: 1. The word after *of* must refer to an animate object, and 2. The word before *of* must involve only a portion of the animate object's possessions.

Otherwise, do not use the possessive form of the word after *of*: *The friends of John Adams mourned his death.* (All the friends were involved.) *He is a friend of the college.* (Not *college's,* because *college* is inanimate).

Memory Aid: This construction occurs most often, and quite naturally, with the possessive forms of personal pronouns: *He is a friend of mine.*

INANIMATE OBJECTS: There is no blanket rule against creating a possessive form for an inanimate object, particularly if the object is treated in a personified sense. See some of the earlier examples, and note these: *death's call, the wind's murmur.*

In general, however, avoid excessive personalization of inanimate objects, and give preference to an *of* construction when it fits the makeup of the sentence. For example, the earlier references to *mathematics' rules* and *measles' effects* would better be phrased: *the rules of mathematics, the effects of measles.*

OMITTED LETTERS: *I've, it's, don't, rock 'n' roll, 'tis the season to be jolly. He is a ne'er-do-well.* See **contractions** in main section.

OMITTED FIGURES: *The class of '62. The Spirit of '76. The '20s.*

PLURALS OF A SINGLE LETTER: *Mind your p's and q's. He learned the three R's and brought home a report card with four A's and two B's. The Oakland A's won the pennant.*

DO NOT USE: For plurals of numerals or multiple-letter combinations. See **plurals**.

brackets [] They cannot be transmitted over news wires. Use parentheses or recast the material.

See **parentheses**.

colon (:) The most frequent use of a colon is at the end of a sentence to introduce lists, tabulations, texts, etc.

Capitalize the first word after a colon only if it is a proper noun or the start of a complete sentence: *He promised this: The company will make good all the losses.* But: *There were three considerations: expense, time and feasibility.*

EMPHASIS: The colon often can be effective in giving emphasis: *He had only one hobby: eating.*

LISTINGS: Use the colon in such listings as time elapsed (*1:31:07.2*), time of day (*8:31 p.m.*), biblical and legal citations (*2 Kings 2:14; Missouri Code 3:245-260*).

DIALOGUE: Use a colon for dialogue. In coverage of a trial, for example:

Bailey: What were you doing the night of the 19th?

Mason: I refuse to answer that.

Q AND A: The colon is used for question-and-answer interviews:

Q: Did you strike him?

A: Indeed I did.

INTRODUCING QUOTATIONS: Use a comma to introduce a direct quotation of one sentence that remains within a paragraph. Use a colon to introduce long quotations within a paragraph and to end all paragraphs that introduce a paragraph of quoted material.

PLACEMENT WITH QUOTATION MARKS: Colons go outside quotation marks unless they are part of the quotation itself.

MISCELLANEOUS: Do not combine a dash and a colon.

comma (,) The following guidelines treat some of the most frequent questions about the use of commas. Additional guidelines on specialized uses are provided in separate entries such as **dates** and **scores**.

For detailed guidance, consult the punctuation section in the back of Webster's New World College Dictionary.

IN A SERIES: Use commas to separate elements in a series, but do not put a comma before the conjunction in a simple series: *The flag is red, white and blue. He would nominate Tom, Dick or Harry.*

Put a comma before the concluding conjunction in a series, however, if an integral element of the series requires a conjunction: *I had orange juice, toast, and ham and eggs for breakfast.*

Use a comma also before the concluding conjunction in a complex series of phrases: *The main points to consider are whether the athletes are skillful enough to compete, whether they have the stamina to endure the training, and whether they have the proper mental attitude.*

See **dash** and **semicolon** for cases when elements of a series contain internal commas.

WITH EQUAL ADJECTIVES: Use commas to separate a series of adjectives equal in rank. If the commas could be replaced by the word *and* without changing the sense, the adjectives are equal: *a thoughtful, precise manner; a dark, dangerous street.*

Use no comma when the last adjective before a noun outranks its predecessors because it is an integral element of a noun phrase, which is the equivalent of a single noun: *a cheap fur coat* (the noun phrase is *fur coat*); *the old oaken bucket; a new, blue spring bonnet.*

WITH NONESSENTIAL CLAUSES: A nonessential clause must be set off by commas. An essential clause must not be set off from the rest of a sentence by commas.

See **essential clauses, nonessential clauses** in the main section.

WITH NONESSENTIAL PHRAS-

ES: A nonessential phrase must be set off by commas. An essential phrase must not be set off from the rest of a sentence by commas.

See **essential phrases, nonessential phrases** in the main section.

WITH INTRODUCTORY CLAUSES AND PHRASES: A comma is used to separate an introductory clause or phrase from the main clause: *When he had tired of the mad pace of New York, he moved to Dubuque.*

The comma may be omitted after short introductory phrases if no ambiguity would result: *During the night he heard many noises.*

But use the comma if its omission would slow comprehension: *On the street below, the curious gathered.*

WITH CONJUNCTIONS: When a conjunction such as *and, but* or *for* links two clauses that could stand alone as separate sentences, use a comma before the conjunction in most cases: *She was glad she had looked, for a man was approaching the house.*

As a rule of thumb, use a comma if the subject of each clause is expressly stated: *We are visiting Washington, and we also plan a side trip to Williamsburg. We visited Washington, and our senator greeted us personally.* But no comma when the subject of the two clauses is the same and is not repeated in the second: *We are visiting Washington and plan to see the White House.*

The comma may be dropped if two clauses with expressly stated subjects are short. In general, however, favor use of a comma unless a particular literary effect is desired or if it would distort the sense of a sentence.

INTRODUCING DIRECT QUOTES: Use a comma to introduce a complete one-sentence quotation within a paragraph: *Wallace said, "She spent six months in Argen-*

tina and came back speaking English with a Spanish accent." But use a colon to introduce quotations of more than one sentence. See **colon**.

Do not use a comma at the start of an indirect or partial quotation: *He said the victory put him "firmly on the road to a first-ballot nomination."*

BEFORE ATTRIBUTION: Use a comma instead of a period at the end of a quote that is followed by attribution: *"Rub my shoulders," Miss Cawley suggested.*

Do not use a comma, however, if the quoted statement ends with a question mark or exclamation point: *"Why should I?" he asked.*

WITH HOMETOWNS AND AGES: Use a comma to set off an individual's hometown when it is placed in apposition to a name (whether *of* is used or not): *Mary Richards, Minneapolis, and Maude Findlay, Tuckahoe, N.Y., were there.*

If an individual's age is used, set it off by commas: *Maude Findlay, 48, Tuckahoe, N.Y., was present.*

WITH PARTY AFFILIATION, ACADEMIC DEGREES, RELIGIOUS AFFILIATIONS: See separate entries under each of these terms.

NAMES OF STATES AND NATIONS USED WITH CITY NAMES: *His journey will take him from Dublin, Ireland, to Fargo, N.D., and back. The Selma, Ala., group saw the governor.*

Use parentheses, however, if a state name is inserted within a proper name: *The Huntsville (Ala.) Times.*

WITH YES AND NO: *Yes, I will be there.*

IN DIRECT ADDRESS: *Mother, I will be home late. No, sir, I did not take it.*

SEPARATING SIMILAR WORDS: Use a comma to separate duplicated words that otherwise would be confusing: *What the problem is, is not clear.*

IN LARGE FIGURES: Use a comma for most figures greater than

999. The major exceptions are street addresses (1234 *Main St.*), broadcast frequencies (1460 *kilohertz*), room numbers, serial numbers, telephone numbers, and years (1876). See separate entries under these headings.

PLACEMENT WITH QUOTES: Commas always go inside quotation marks.

WITH FULL DATES: When a phrase refers to a month, day and year, set off the year with a comma: *Feb. 14, 1987, is the target date.*

See **semicolon**.

compound adjectives See the **hyphen** entry.

dash (–) Follow these guidelines:

ABRUPT CHANGE: Use dashes to denote an abrupt change in thought in a sentence or an emphatic pause: *We will fly to Paris in June — if I get a raise. Smith offered a plan — it was unprecedented — to raise revenues.*

SERIES WITHIN A PHRASE: When a phrase that otherwise would be set off by commas contains a series of words that must be separated by commas, use dashes to set off the full phrase: *He listed the qualities — intelligence, humor, conservatism, independence — that he liked in an executive.*

ATTRIBUTION: Use a dash before an author's or composer's name at the end of a quotation: *"Who steals my purse steals trash." — Shakespeare.*

IN DATELINES:

NEW YORK (AP) — The city is broke.

IN LISTS: AP uses dashes instead of bullets to introduce individual sections of a list. Capitalize the first word following the dash. Use periods, not semicolons, at the end of each section, whether it is a full sentence or a phrase. Example:

Jones gave the following reasons:

—*He never ordered the package.*
—*If he did, it didn't come.*
—*If it did, he sent it back.*
WITH SPACES: Put a space on both sides of a dash in all uses except the start of a paragraph and sports agate summaries.

ellipsis (...) In general, treat an ellipsis as a three-letter word, constructed with three periods and two spaces, as shown here.

Use an ellipsis to indicate the deletion of one or more words in condensing quotes, texts and documents. Be especially careful to avoid deletions that would distort the meaning.

An ellipsis also may be used to indicate a thought that the speaker or writer does not complete. Substitute a dash for this purpose, however, if the context uses ellipses to indicate that words actually spoken or written have been deleted.

Brief examples of how to use ellipses are provided after guidelines are given. More extensive examples, drawn from the speech in which President Richard Nixon announced his resignation, are in the sections below marked CONDENSATION EXAMPLE and QUOTATIONS.

SPACING REQUIREMENTS: In some computer editing systems the thin space must be used between the periods of the ellipsis to prevent them from being placed on two different lines when they are sent through a computer that handles hyphenation and justification.

Leave one regular space — never a thin — on both sides of an ellipsis: *I ... tried to do what was best.*

PUNCTUATION GUIDELINES: If the words that precede an ellipsis constitute a grammatically complete sentence, either in the original or in the condensation, place a period at the end of the last word before the ellipsis. Follow it with a regular space and an ellipsis: *I no longer have a strong enough political base.* ...

When the grammatical sense calls for a question mark, exclamation point, comma or colon, the sequence is word, punctuation mark, regular space, ellipsis: *Will you come?* ...

When material is deleted at the end of one paragraph and at the beginning of the one that follows, place an ellipsis in both locations.

CONDENSATION EXAMPLE: Here is an example of how the spacing and punctuation guidelines would be applied in condensing President Richard Nixon's resignation announcement:

Good evening. ...

In all the decisions I have made in my public life, I have always tried to do what was best for the nation. ...

... However, it has become evident to me that I no longer have a strong enough political base in ... Congress.

... As long as there was ... a base, I felt strongly that it was necessary to see the constitutional process through to its conclusion, that to do otherwise would be ... a dangerously destabilizing precedent for the future.

QUOTATIONS: In writing a story, do not use ellipses at the beginning and end of direct quotes:

"It has become evident to me that I no longer have a strong enough political base," Nixon said.

Not *"... it has become evident to me that I no longer have a strong enough political base ... ,"* Nixon said.

SPECIAL EFFECTS: Ellipses also may be used to separate individual items within a paragraph of show business gossip or similar material. Use periods after items that are complete sentences.

exclamation point (!) Follow these guidelines:

EMPHATIC EXPRESSIONS: Use the mark to express a high degree of surprise, incredulity or other strong emotion.

AVOID OVERUSE: Use a comma after mild interjections. End mildly exclamatory sentences with a period.

PLACEMENT WITH QUOTES: Place the mark inside quotation marks when it is part of the quoted material: *"How wonderful!" he exclaimed. "Never!" she shouted.*

Place the mark outside quotation marks when it is not part of the quoted material: *I hated reading Spenser's "Faerie Queene"!*

MISCELLANEOUS: Do not use a comma or a period after the exclamation mark:

Wrong: *"Halt!", the corporal cried.*
Right: *"Halt!" the corporal cried.*

hyphen (-) Hyphens are joiners. Use them to avoid ambiguity or to form a single idea from two or more words.

Use of the hyphen is far from standardized. It is optional in most cases, a matter of taste, judgment and style sense. But the fewer hyphens the better; use them only when not using them causes confusion. (*Small-business owner*, but *health care center*.) See individual entries in this book. If not listed here, use the first listed entry in Webster's New World College Dictionary. (amended example from small-businessman, in line with entry below.)

Some guidelines:

AVOID AMBIGUITY: Use a hyphen whenever ambiguity would result if it were omitted: *The president will speak to small-business men.* (*Businessmen* normally is one word. But *the president will speak to small businessmen* is unclear.)

Others: *He recovered his health. He re-covered the leaky roof.*

COMPOUND MODIFIERS: When a compound modifier — two or more words that express a single concept — precedes a noun, use hyphens to link all the words in the compound except the adverb *very* and all adverbs that end in *-ly*: *a first-quarter touchdown, a bluish-green dress, a full-time job, a well-known man, a better-qualified woman, a know-it-all attitude, a very good time, an easily remembered rule.*

Many combinations that are hyphenated before a noun are not hyphenated when they occur after a noun: *The team scored in the first quarter. The dress, a bluish green, was attractive on her. She works full time. His attitude suggested that he knew it all.*

But when a modifier that would be hyphenated before a noun occurs instead after a form of the verb *to be*, the hyphen usually must be retained to avoid confusion: *The man is well-known. The woman is quick-witted. The children are soft-spoken. The play is second-rate.*

The principle of using a hyphen to avoid confusion explains why no hyphen is required with *very* and *-ly* words. Readers can expect them to modify the word that follows. But if a combination such as *little-known man* were not hyphenated, the reader could logically be expecting *little* to be followed by a noun, as in *little man.* Instead, the reader encountering *little known* would have to back up mentally and make the compound connection on his own.

TWO-THOUGHT COMPOUNDS: *serio-comic, socio-economic.*

COMPOUND PROPER NOUNS AND ADJECTIVES: Use a hyphen to designate dual heritage: *Italian-American, Mexican-American.*

No hyphen, however, for *French Canadian* or *Latin American.*

PREFIXES AND SUFFIXES: See the **prefixes** and **suffixes** entries, and separate entries for the most frequently used prefixes and suffixes.

AVOID DUPLICATED VOWELS, TRIPLED CONSONANTS:

Examples: *anti-intellectual, pre-empt, shell-like.*

WITH NUMERALS: Use a hyphen to separate figures in **odds**, **ratios**, **scores**, some **fractions** and some **vote tabulations**. See examples in entries under these headings.

When large numbers must be spelled out, use a hyphen to connect a word ending in *-y* to another word: *twenty-one, fifty-five*, etc.

SUSPENSIVE HYPHENATION: The form: *He received a 10- to 20-year sentence in prison.*

parentheses ( ) In general, use parentheses around logos, as shown in **datelines**, but otherwise be sparing with them.

Parentheses are jarring to the reader. Because they do not appear on some news service printers, there is also the danger that material inside them may be misinterpreted.

The temptation to use parentheses is a clue that a sentence is becoming contorted. Try to write it another way. If a sentence must contain incidental material, then commas or two dashes are frequently more effective. Use these alternatives whenever possible.

There are occasions, however, when parentheses are the only effective means of inserting necessary background or reference information. When they are necessary, follow these guidelines:

WITHIN QUOTATIONS: If parenthetical information inserted in a direct quotation is at all sensitive, place an editor's note under a dash at the bottom of a story alerting copy desks to what was inserted.

PUNCTUATION: Place a period outside a closing parenthesis if the material inside is not a sentence (*such as this fragment*).

(*An independent parenthetical sentence such as this one takes a period before the closing parenthesis.*)

When a phrase placed in parentheses (*this one is an example*) might normally qualify as a complete sentence but is dependent on the surrounding material, do not capitalize the first word or end with a period.

MATERIAL FROM OTHER AREAS: If a story contains information from outside the datelined city, put the material in parentheses only if the correspondent in the datelined community was cut off from incoming communications. See **dateline selection**.

INSERTIONS IN A PROPER NAME: Use parentheses if a state name or similar information is inserted within a proper name: *The Huntsville (Ala.) Times*. But use commas if no proper name is involved: *The Selma, Ala., group saw the governor.*

NEVER USED: Do not use parentheses to denote a political figure's party affiliation and jurisdiction. Instead, set them off with commas, as shown under **party affiliation**.

Do not use (*cq*) or similar notation to indicate that an unusual spelling or term is correct. Include the confirmation in an editor's note at the top of a story.

periods (.) Follow these guidelines:

END OF DECLARATIVE SENTENCE: *The stylebook is finished.*

END OF A MILDLY IMPERATIVE SENTENCE: *Shut the door.*

Use an exclamation point if greater emphasis is desired: *Be careful!*

END OF SOME RHETORICAL QUESTIONS: A period is preferable if a statement is more a suggestion than a question: *Why don't we go.*

END OF AN INDIRECT QUESTION: *He asked what the score was.*

MANY ABBREVIATIONS: For guidelines, see **abbreviations and acronyms**. For the form of frequently used abbreviations, see the entry under the full name, abbreviation,

acronym or term.

INITIALS: *John F. Kennedy, T.S. Eliot* (No space between *T.* and *S.*, to prevent them from being placed on two lines in typesetting.)

Abbreviations using only the initials of a name do not take periods: *JFK, LBJ.*

ELLIPSIS: See **ellipsis**.

ENUMERATIONS: After numbers or letters in enumerating elements of a summary: 1. *Wash the car.* 2. *Clean the basement.* Or: A. *Punctuate properly.* B. *Write simply.*

PLACEMENT WITH QUOTATION MARKS: Periods always go inside quotation marks. See **quotation marks**.

SPACING: Use a single space after a period at the end of a sentence.

question mark (?) Follow these guidelines:

END OF A DIRECT QUESTION: *Who started the riot?*
Did he ask who started the riot? (The sentence as a whole is a direct question despite the indirect question at the end.)
You started the riot? (A question in the form of a declarative statement.)

INTERPOLATED QUESTION: *You told me — Did I hear you correctly? — that you started the riot.*

MULTIPLE QUESTIONS: Use a single question mark at the end of the full sentence:
Did you hear him say, "What right have you to ask about the riot?"
Did he plan the riot, employ assistants, and give the signal to begin?

Or, to cause full stops and throw emphasis on each element, break into separate sentences: *Did he plan the riot? Employ assistants? Give the signal to begin?*

CAUTION: Do not use question marks to indicate the end of indirect questions:
He asked who started the riot. To

ask why the riot started is unnecessary. I want to know what the cause of the riot was. How foolish it is to ask what caused the riot.

QUESTION-AND-ANSWER FORMAT: Do not use quotation marks. Paragraph each speaker's words:

Q: Where did you keep it?
A: In a little tin box.

PLACEMENT WITH QUOTATION MARKS: Inside or outside, depending on the meaning:

Who wrote "Gone With the Wind"?
He asked, "How long will it take?"

MISCELLANEOUS: The question mark supersedes the comma that normally is used when supplying attribution for a quotation: *"Who is there?" she asked.*

quotation marks (" ") The basic guidelines for open-quote marks (") and close-quote marks ("):

FOR DIRECT QUOTATIONS: To surround the exact words of a speaker or writer when reported in a story:

"I have no intention of staying," he replied.

"I do not object," he said, "to the tenor of the report."

Franklin said, "A penny saved is a penny earned."

A speculator said the practice is "too conservative for inflationary times."

RUNNING QUOTATIONS: If a full paragraph of quoted material is followed by a paragraph that continues the quotation, do not put close-quote marks at the end of the first paragraph. Do, however, put open-quote marks at the start of the second paragraph. Continue in this fashion for any succeeding paragraphs, using close-quote marks only at the end of the quoted material.

If a paragraph does not start with quotation marks but ends with a quotation that is continued in the next paragraph, do not use close-quote marks at the end of the introductory paragraph if the quoted material constitutes a full sentence. Use close-quote marks, however, if the quoted material does not constitute a full sentence. For example:

He said, "I am shocked and horrified by the incident.

"I am so horrified, in fact, that I will ask for the death penalty."

But: *He said he was "shocked and horrified by the incident."*

"I am so horrified, in fact, that I will ask for the death penalty," he said.

DIALOGUE OR CONVERSATION: Each person's words, no matter how brief, are placed in a separate paragraph, with quotation marks at the beginning and the end of each person's speech:

"Will you go?"
"Yes."
"When?"
"Thursday."

NOT IN Q-and-A: Quotation marks are not required in formats that identify questions and answers by Q: and A:. See **question mark** for example.

NOT IN TEXTS: Quotation marks are not required in full texts, condensed texts or textual excerpts. See **ellipsis**.

COMPOSITION TITLES: See **composition titles** for guidelines on the use of quotation marks in book titles, movie titles, etc.

NICKNAMES: See **nicknames**.

IRONY: Put quotation marks around a word or words used in an ironical sense: *The "debate" turned into a free-for-all.*

UNFAMILIAR TERMS: A word or words being introduced to readers may be placed in quotation marks on first reference:

Broadcast frequencies are measured in "kilohertz."

Do not put subsequent references to *kilohertz* in quotation marks. See **foreign words**.

AVOID UNNECESSARY FRAGMENTS: Do not use quotation marks to report a few ordinary words that a speaker or writer has used:

Wrong: *The senator said he would "go home to Michigan" if he lost the election.*

Right: *The senator said he would go home to Michigan if he lost the election.*

PARTIAL QUOTES: When a partial quote is used, do not put quotation marks around words that the speaker could not have used.

Suppose the individual said, *"I am horrified at your slovenly manners."*

Wrong: *She said she "was horrified at their slovenly manners."*

Right: *She said she was horrified at their "slovenly manners."*

Better when practical: Use the full quote.

QUOTES WITHIN QUOTES: Alternate between double quotation marks ("or") and single marks ('or'):

She said, "I quote from his letter, 'I agree with Kipling that "the female of the species is more deadly than the male," but the phenomenon is not an unchangeable law of nature,' a remark he did not explain."

Use three marks together if two quoted elements end at the same time: *She said, "He told me, 'I love you.'"*

(NOTE: Local style should ensure some differentiation between the single and double quotation marks, either with a "thin" space or by different typography, if not computer-programmed.)

PLACEMENT WITH OTHER PUNCTUATION: Follow these long-established printers' rules:

—The period and the comma always go within the quotation marks.

—The dash, the semicolon, the question mark and the exclamation point go within the quotation marks when they apply to the quoted matter only. They go outside when they apply to the whole sentence.

See **comma**.

semicolon (;) In general, use the semicolon to indicate a greater separation of thought and information than a comma can convey but less than the separation that a period implies.

The basic guidelines:

TO CLARIFY A SERIES: Use semicolons to separate elements of a series when the items in the series are long or when individual segments contain material that also must be set off by commas:

He is survived by a son, John Smith, of Chicago; three daughters, Jane Smith, of Wichita, Kan., Mary Smith, of Denver, and Susan, of Boston; and a sister, Martha, of Omaha, Neb.

Note that the semicolon is used before the final *and* in such a series.

Another application of this principle may be seen in the cross-references at the end of entries in this book. Because some entries themselves have a comma, a semicolon is used to separate references to multiple entries, as in: *See the* **felony, misdemeanor** *entry*; **pardon, parole, probation**; *and* **prison, jail**.

See **dash** for a different type of connection that uses dashes to avoid multiple commas.

TO LINK INDEPENDENT CLAUSES: Use semicolon when a coordinating conjunction such as *and, but* or *for* is not present: *The package was due last week; it arrived today.*

If a coordinating conjunction is present, use a semicolon before it only if extensive punctuation also is required in one or more of the individual clauses: *They pulled their boats from the water, sandbagged the retain-*

ing walls, and boarded up the windows; but even with these precautions, the island was hard-hit by the hurricane.

Unless a particular literary effect is desired, however, the better approach in these circumstances is to break the independent clauses into separate sentences.

PLACEMENT WITH QUOTES: Place semicolons outside quotation marks.

THE ASSOCIATED PRESS STATEMENT OF NEWS VALUES AND PRINCIPLES

For more than a century and a half, men and women of The Associated Press have had the privilege of bringing truth to the world. They have gone to great lengths, overcome great obstacles — and, too often, made great and horrific sacrifices — to ensure that the news was reported quickly, accurately and honestly. Our efforts have been rewarded with trust: More people in more places get their news from the AP than from any other source.

In the 21st century, that news is transmitted in more ways than ever before — in print, on the air and on the Web, with words, images, graphics, sounds and video. But always and in all media, we insist on the highest standards of integrity and ethical behavior when we gather and deliver the news.

That means we abhor inaccuracies, carelessness, bias or distortions.

It means we will not knowingly introduce false information into material intended for publication or broadcast; nor will we alter photo or image content. Quotations must be accurate, and precise.

It means we always strive to identify all the sources of our information, shielding them with anonymity only when they insist upon it and when they provide vital information — not opinion or speculation; when there is no other way to obtain that information; and when we know the source is knowledgeable and reliable.

It means we don't plagiarize.

It means we avoid behavior or activities that create a conflict of interest and compromise our ability to report the news fairly and accurately, uninfluenced by any person or action.

It means we don't misidentify or misrepresent ourselves to get a story. When we seek an interview, we identify ourselves as AP journalists.

It means we don't pay newsmakers for interviews, to take their photographs or to film or record them. It means we must be fair. Whenever we portray someone in a negative light, we must make a real effort to obtain a response from that person. When mistakes are made, they must be corrected — fully, quickly and ungrudgingly.

And ultimately, it means it is the responsibility of every one of us to ensure that these standards are upheld. Any time a question is raised about any aspect of our work, it should be taken seriously.

"I have no thought of saying The Associated Press is perfect. The frailties of human nature attach to it," wrote Melville Stone, the great general manager of the AP. But he went on to say that "the thing it is striving for is a truthful, unbiased report of the world's happenings ... ethical in the highest degree."

He wrote those words in 1914. They are true today.

* * *

The policies set forth in these pages are central to the AP's mission; any failure to abide by them is subject to review, and could result in disciplinary action, ranging from admonishment to dismissal, depending on the gravity of the infraction.

STANDARDS AND PRACTICES

ANONYMOUS SOURCES

Transparency is critical to our credibility with the public and our subscribers. Whenever possible, we pursue information on the record. When a newsmaker insists on background or off-the-record ground rules, we must adhere to a strict set of guidelines, enforced by AP news managers.

Under AP's rules, material from anonymous sources may be used only if:

1. The material is information and not opinion or speculation, and is vital to the news report.

2. The information is not available except under the conditions of anonymity imposed by the source.

3. The source is reliable, and in a position to have accurate information.

Reporters who intend to use material from anonymous sources must get approval from their news manager before sending the story to the desk. The manager is responsible for vetting the material and making sure it meets AP guidelines. The manager must know the identity of the source, and is obligated, like the reporter, to keep the source's identity confidential. Only after they are assured that the source material has been vetted should editors allow it to be transmitted.

Reporters should proceed with interviews on the assumption they are on the record. If the source wants to set conditions, these should be negotiated at the start of the interview. At the end of the interview, the reporter should try once again to move some or all of the information back on the record.

Before agreeing to use anonymous source material, the reporter should ask how the source knows the information is accurate, ensuring that the source has direct knowledge. Reporters may not agree to a source's request that AP not pursue additional comment or information.

The AP routinely seeks and requires more than one source. Stories should be held while attempts are made to reach additional sources for confirmation or elaboration. In rare cases, one source will be sufficient — when material comes from an authoritative figure who provides information so detailed that there is no question of its accuracy.

We must explain in the story why the source requested anonymity. And, when it's relevant, we must describe the source's motive for disclosing the information. If the story hinges on documents, as opposed to interviews, the reporter must describe how the documents were obtained, at least to the extent possible.

The story also must provide attribution that establishes the source's credibility; simply quoting "a source" is not allowed. We should be as descriptive as possible: "according to top White House aides" or "a senior official in the British Foreign Office." The description of a source must never be altered without consulting the reporter.

We must not say that a person declined comment when he or she is already quoted anonymously. And we should not attribute information to anonymous sources when it is obvious or well known. We should just state the information as fact.

Stories that use anonymous sources must carry a reporter's byline. If a reporter other than the bylined staffer contributes anonymous material to a story, that reporter should be given credit as a contributor to the story.

And all complaints and questions about the authenticity or veracity of anonymous material — from inside or outside the AP — must be promptly brought to the news manager's attention.

Not everyone understands "off the record" or "on background" to mean the same things. Before any interview in which any degree of anonymity is expected, there should be a discussion in which the ground rules are set explicitly.

These are the AP's definitions:

On the record. The information can be used with no caveats, quoting the source by name.

Off the record. The information cannot be used for publication.

Background. The information can be published but only under conditions negotiated with the source. Generally, the sources do not want their names published but will agree to a description of their position. AP reporters should object vigorously when a source wants to brief a group of reporters on background and try to persuade the source to put the briefing on the record. These background briefings have become routine in many venues, especially with government officials.

Deep background. The information can be used but without attribution. The source does not want to be identified in any way, even on condition of anonymity.

In general, information obtained under any of these circumstances can be pursued with other sources to be placed on the record.

ANONYMOUS SOURCES IN MATERIAL FROM OTHER NEWS SOURCES

Reports from other news organizations based on anonymous sources require the most careful scrutiny when we consider them for our report.

AP's basic rules for anonymous-source material apply to pickups as they do in our own reporting: The material must be factual and obtainable no other way. The story must be truly significant and newsworthy. Use of sourced material must be authorized by a manager. The story must be balanced, and comment must be sought.

Further, before picking up such a story we must make a bona fide effort to get it on the record, or, at a minimum, confirm it through our own sources. We shouldn't hesitate to hold the story if we have any doubts. If the source material is ultimately used, it must be attributed to the originating member and note their description of their sources.

AUDIO

AP's audio actualities must always tell the truth. We do not alter or manipulate the content of a newsmaker actuality in any way. Voice reports by AP correspondents may be edited to remove pauses or stumbles.

With the permission of a manager, overly long pauses by news subjects may be shortened.

The AP does permit the use of the subtle, standard audio processing methods of normalization of levels, general volume adjustments, equalization to make the sound clearer, noise reduction to reduce extraneous sounds such as telephone line noise, and fading in and out of the start and end of sound bites — provided the use of these methods does not conceal, obscure, remove or otherwise alter the content, or any portion of the content, of the audio. When an employee has questions about the use of such methods or the AP's requirements and limitations on audio editing, he or she should contact the desk supervisor prior to the transmission of any audio.

BYLINES

Bylines may be used only if the journalist was in the datelined location to gather the information reported. If a reporter in the field provides information to a staffer who writes the story, the reporter in the field gets the byline, unless the editor in charge determines that the byline should more properly go to the writer.

We give bylines to photographers, broadcast reporters and TV crew members who provide information without which there would be no story.

If multiple staffers report the story, the byline is the editor's judgment call. In general, the byline should go to the staffer who reported the key facts. Or, one staffer can take the byline for one cycle, and another for the following cycle.

A double byline or editor's note also can be used when more than one staffer makes a substantial contribution to the reporting or writing of a story. Credit lines recognize reporting contributions that are notable but don't call for a double byline.

If either of the staffers with a double byline was not in the datelined location, we should say who was where in a note at the story's end.

For roundups, the byline goes to the writer, with credit in an editor's note to the reporters who contributed substantial information.

Regarding credits for staffers who do voice or on-camera work: We do not use pseudonyms or "air names." Any exceptions — for instance, if a staffer has been known professionally by an air name for some time — must be approved by a manager.

CORRECTIONS/CORRECTIVES

Staffers must notify supervisory editors as soon as possible of errors or potential errors, whether in their work or that of a colleague. Every effort should be made to contact the staffer and his or her supervisor before a correction is moved.

When we're wrong, we must say so as soon as possible. When we make a correction in the current cycle, we point out the error and its fix in the editor's note. A correction must always be labeled a correction in the editor's note. We do not use euphemisms such as "recasts," "fixes," "clarifies" or "changes" when correcting a factual error.

A corrective corrects a mistake from a previous cycle. The AP asks papers or broadcasters that used the erroneous information to use the corrective, too.

For corrections on live, online stories, we overwrite the previous version. We send separate corrective stories online as warranted.

For graphics, we clearly label a correction with a FIX logo or bug, and clearly identify the material that has been corrected.

For photos, we move a caption correction and retransmit the photo with a corrected caption, clearly labeled as a retransmission to correct an error.

For video, corrections in scripts and/or shotlists are sent to clients as an advisory and are labeled as such.

For live broadcasts, we correct errors in the same newscast if at all possible. If not, we make sure the corrected information is used in the next appropriate live segment. Audio correspondent reports that contain factual errors are eliminated and, when possible, replaced with corrected reports.

DATELINES

A dateline tells the reader where we obtained the basic information for a story. In contrast, a byline tells the reader that a reporter was at the site of the dateline.

When a datelined story contains supplementary information obtained in another location — say, when an official in Washington comments on a disaster elsewhere — we should note it in the story.

The dateline for video or audio must be the location where the events depicted actually occurred. For voice work, the dateline must be the location from which the reporter is speaking; if that is not possible, the reporter should not use a dateline. If a reporter covers a story in one location but does a live report from a filing point in another location, the dateline is the filing point.

FABRICATIONS

Nothing in our news report — words, photos, graphics, sound or video — may be fabricated. We don't use pseudonyms, composite characters or fictional names, ages, places or dates. We don't stage or re-enact events for the camera or microphone, and we don't use sound effects or substitute video or audio from one event to another. We do not "cheat" sound by adding audio to embellish or fabricate an event. A senior editor must be consulted prior to the introduction of any neutral sound (ambient sound that does not affect the editorial meaning but corrects a technical fault).

We do not ask people to pose for photos unless we are making a portrait and then we clearly state that in the caption. We explain in the caption the circumstances under which photographs are made. If someone is asked to pose for photographs by third parties and that is reflected in AP-produced images, we say so in the caption. Such wording would be: ``XXX poses for photos."

GRAPHICS

We use only authoritative sources. We do not project, surmise or estimate in a graphic. We create work only from what we know.

We post or move a locator map only when we can confirm the location ourselves.

We create charts at visually proper perspectives to give an accurate representation of data. The information must be clear and concise. We do not skew or alter data to fit a visual need.

We credit our sources on every graphic, including graphics for which AP journalists have created the data set or database.

IMAGES

AP pictures must always tell the truth. We do not alter or digitally manipulate the content of a photograph in any way.

The content of a photograph must not be altered in Photoshop or by any other means. No element should be digitally added to or subtracted from any photograph. The faces or identities of individuals must not be obscured by Photoshop or any other editing tool. Only retouching or the use of the cloning tool to eliminate dust on camera sensors and scratches on scanned negatives or scanned prints are acceptable.

Minor adjustments in Photoshop are acceptable. These include cropping, dodging and burning, conversion into grayscale, and normal toning and color adjustments that should be limited to those minimally necessary for clear and accurate reproduction (analogous to the burning and dodging previously used in darkroom processing of images) and that restore the authentic nature of the photograph. Changes in density, contrast, color and saturation levels that substantially alter the original scene are not acceptable. Backgrounds should not be digitally blurred or eliminated by burning down or by aggressive toning. The removal of "red eye" from photographs is not permissible.

When an employee has questions about the use of such methods or the AP's requirements and limitations on photo editing, he or she should contact a senior photo editor prior to the transmission of any image.

On those occasions when we transmit images that have been provided and altered by a source — the faces obscured, for example — the caption must clearly explain it. Transmitting such images must be approved by a senior photo editor.

Except as described herein, we do not stage, pose or re-enact events. When we shoot video, environmental portraits, or photograph subjects in a studio care should be taken to avoid, misleading viewers to believe that the moment was spontaneously captured in the course of gathering the news. In the cases of portraits, fashion or home design illustrations, any intervention should be revealed in the caption and special instructions box so it can't be mistaken as an attempt to deceive.

For video, the AP permits the use of subtle, standard methods of improving technical quality, such as adjusting video and audio levels, color correcting due to white balance, eliminating buzzing, hums, clicks, pops, or overly long pauses or other technical faults, and equalization of audio to make the sound clearer — provided the use of these methods does not conceal, obscure, remove or otherwise alter the content, or any portion of the content, of the image. The AP also allows digitally obscuring faces to protect a subject's identity under certain circumstances. Such video must not be distributed without approval of the Editor of the Day or senior manager. In addition, video for online use and for domestic broadcast stations can be fonted with titles and logos.

Graphics, including those for television, often involve combining various photographic elements, which necessarily means altering portions of each photograph. The background of a photograph, for example, may be removed to leave the headshot of the newsmaker. This may then be combined with a logo representing the person's company or industry, and the two elements may be layered over a neutral background.

Such compositions must not misrepresent the facts and must not result in an image that looks like a photograph — it must clearly be a graphic.

Similarly, when we alter photos to use as graphics online, we retain the integrity of the image, limiting the changes to cropping, masking and adding elements like logos. Videos for use online can be altered to add graphical information such as titles and logos, to tone the image and to improve audio quality. It is permissible to display photos online using techniques such as 360-degree panoramas or dissolves as long as they do not alter the original images.

OBSCENITIES, PROFANITIES, VULGARITIES

We do not use obscenities, racial epithets or other offensive slurs in stories unless they are part of direct quotations and there is a compelling reason for them.

If a story cannot be told without reference to them, we must first try to find a way to give the reader a sense of what was said without using the specific word or phrase. If a profanity, obscenity or vulgarity is used, the story must be flagged at the top, advising editors to note the contents.

A photo containing something that could be deemed offensive must carry an editor's note flagging it.

When a piece of video or audio contains something that might be deemed offensive, we flag it in the written description (rundown, billboard and/or script) so clients know what they are getting. Recognizing that standards differ around the world, we tailor our advisories and selection of video and audio according to customer needs.

We take great care not to refer readers to Web sites that are obscene, racist or otherwise offensive, and we must not directly link our stories to such sites.

In our online service, we link the least offensive image necessary to tell the story. For photo galleries and interactive presentations we alert readers to the nature of the material in the link and on the opening page of the gallery or interactive. If an obscene image is necessary to tell the story, we blur the portion of the image considered offensive after approval of the department manager, and flag the video.

PRIVACY

We do not generally identify those who say they have been sexually assaulted or pre-teenage children who are accused of crimes or who are witnesses to them, except in unusual circumstances. Nor do we transmit photos or video that identify such persons. An exception would occur when an adult victim publicly identifies him/herself.

Senior editors/managers must be consulted about exceptions.

PROVIDING ATTRIBUTION

We should give the full name of a source and as much information as needed to identify the source and explain why he or she is credible. Where appropriate, include a source's age; title; name of company, organization or government department; and hometown.

If we quote someone from a written document — a report, email or news release — we should say so. Information taken from the Internet must be vetted according to our standards of accuracy and attributed to the original source. File, library or archive photos, audio or videos must be identified as such.

For lengthy stories, attribution can be contained in an extended editor's note, usually at the end, detailing interviews, research and methodology. The goal is to provide a reader with enough information to have full confidence in the story's veracity.

QUOTATIONS

The same care that is used to ensure that quotes are accurate should also be used to ensure that quotes are not taken out of context.

We do not alter quotations, even to correct grammatical errors or word usage. If a quotation is flawed because of grammar or lack of clarity, the writer must be able to paraphrase in a way that is completely true to the original quote. If a quote's meaning is too murky to be paraphrased accurately, it should not be used.

Ellipses should be used rarely.

When relevant, stories should provide information about the setting in which a quotation was obtained — for example, a press conference, phone interview or hallway conversation with the reporter. The source's affect and body language — perhaps a smile or deprecatory gesture — is sometimes as important as the quotation itself.

Use of regional dialects with nonstandard spellings should generally be limited to a writer's effort to convey a special tone or sense of place. In this case, as in any interview with a person not speaking his or her native language, it is especially important that their ideas be accurately conveyed. Always, we must be careful not to mock the people we quote.

Quotes from one language to another must be translated faithfully. If appropriate, we should note the language spoken.

The video or audio editing of quotations or soundbites must not alter the speaker's meaning. Internal editing of audio soundbites of newsmakers is not permitted. Shortened soundbites by cutaway or other video transition are permitted as long as the speaker's meaning is not altered or misconstrued. Sound edits on videotape are permitted under certain circumstances, such as a technical failure. They must be done only after approval by a senior editorial manager.

RESPONSES

We must make significant efforts to reach anyone who may be portrayed in a negative way in our stories, and we must give them a reasonable amount of time to get back to us before we move the story. What is "reasonable" may depend on the urgency and competitiveness of the story. If we don't reach the parties involved, we must explain in the story what efforts were made to do so.

USE OF OTHERS' MATERIAL

An AP staffer who reports and writes a story must use original content, language and phrasing. We do not plagiarize, meaning that we do not take the work of others and pass it off as our own.

But in some respects, AP staffers must deal with gray areas.

It is common for an AP staffer to include in his or her work passages from a previous AP story by another writer — generally background, or boilerplate. This is acceptable if the passages are short. Regardless, the reporter writing the story is responsible for the factual and contextual accuracy of the material.

Also, the AP often has the right to use material from its members and subscribers; we sometimes take the work of newspapers, broadcasters and other outlets, rewrite it and transmit it without credit.

There are rules, however. When the material is exclusive, controversial or sensitive, we always credit it. And we do not transmit the stories in their original form; we rewrite them, so that the approach, content, structure and length meet our requirements and reflect the broader audience we serve.

Similar rules apply when we use material from news releases. Under no circumstances can releases reach the wire in their original form; we can use information and quotes from releases, but we must check the material, augment it with information from other sources, and then write our own stories.

We apply the same judgment in picking up material from members or from news releases that we use when considering information we receive from other sources. We must satisfy ourselves, by our own reporting, that the material is credible. If it does not meet AP standards, we don't use it.

For video, if another broadcaster's material is required and distributed, the name of that broadcaster shall be advised on the accompanying shotlist.

Pickups of audio and of television graphics are credited in billboards/captions when the member requests it.

CONFLICTS OF INTEREST

The AP respects and encourages the rights of its employees to participate actively in civic, charitable, religious, public, social or residential organizations.

However, AP employees must avoid behavior or activities — political, social or financial — that create a conflict of interest or compromise our ability to report the news fairly and accurately, uninfluenced by any person or action. Nothing in this policy is intended to abridge any rights provided by the National Labor Relations Act.

Here is a sampler of AP practices on questions involving possible conflict of interest. It is not all-inclusive; if you are unsure whether an activity may constitute a conflict or the appearance of a conflict, consult your manager at the onset.

EXPRESSIONS OF OPINION

Anyone who works for the AP must be mindful that opinions they express may damage the AP's reputation as an unbiased source of news. They must refrain from declaring their views on contentious public issues in any public forum, whether in Web logs, chat rooms, letters to the editor, petitions, bumper stickers or lapel buttons, and must not take part in demonstrations in support of causes or movements.

FAVORS

Employees should not ask news sources or others they meet in a professional capacity to extend jobs or other benefits to anyone. They also should not offer jobs, internships or any benefits of being an AP employee to news sources.

FINANCIAL INTERESTS

Associated Press employees who regularly write or edit business or financial news must always avoid any conflict of interest or the appearance of any conflict of interest in connection with the performance of these duties. For these reasons, these employees must abide by the following rules and guidelines when making personal investment and financial decisions.

These employees must not own stock, equities or have any personal financial investment or involvement with any company, enterprise or industry that they regularly cover for the AP. A technology writer, for example, must not own any technology equities; a retail industry writer must not own the stock of any department store or corporate enterprise that includes department stores. Staff members who are temporarily assigned to such coverage or editorial duties must immediately notify a manager of possible conflicts to determine whether the assignment is appropriate. If necessary, employees might be asked either to divest or to suspend any activity involving their holdings.

Editors and writers who regularly cover the financial markets may not own stock in any company. They may invest in equity index-related products and publicly available diversified mutual funds or commodity pools.

Financial news employees must also avoid investment activities that are speculative or driven by day-trading or short-term profit goals because such activities may create the impression that the employee is seeking to drive market factors or is acting upon information that is not available to the public.

Instead, the personal financial activities and investments of these employees must be based upon the longer term and retirement savings. For these reasons, an employee covered by this policy should not buy and sell the same financial product within 60 days, unless he/she gains the permission of the department manager and is able to demonstrate financial need that is unrelated to information discussed or gained in the course of his/her employment. This trading limitation does not apply to equity-index funds, broadly diversified and publicly available mutual funds and commodity pools.

All employees must comply with federal and local laws concerning securities and financial transactions, including statutes, regulations and guidelines prohibiting actions based upon "inside information." All employees are reminded that they may not act upon, or inform any other person of, information gained in the course of AP employment, unless and until that information becomes known to the general public.

Employees should avoid any conflict of interest or the appearance of a conflict of interest in the investments and business interests of their spouses or other members of their household with whom they share finances. They are expected to make every effort to assure that no spouse or other member of their household has investment or business interests that could pose such a conflict.

Employees should be aware that the investment activities and/or financial interests of their spouses or other individuals with whom they share financial interests may make it inappropriate for them to accept certain assignments. Employees must consult with their managers before accepting any such assignment.

Employees who are asked to divest holdings will be given one year from the date of the request to do so, in order to give them the opportunity to avoid market fluctuations.

When this document requires the sale of stock holdings, an employee can satisfy this requirement by putting the shares into a blind trust (or into an equivalent financial arrangement) that meets the same goal: preventing an individual from knowing, at any given time, the specific holdings in the account and blocking an individual from controlling the timing of transactions in such holdings. If AP assigns a staff member to a new job where mandatory divestiture would impose a financial hardship even after the one-year grace period, AP will reimburse the staff member up to a maximum of $500 for the reasonable costs of setting up a blind trust.)

FREELANCE WORK
Individuals who seek to engage in non-AP work are subject to the following restrictions:

• Freelance work must not represent a conflict of interest for either the employee or the AP.

• Such activities may not interfere with the employees' job responsibilities, including availability for newsgathering.

• Such activities may not exploit the name of The Associated Press or the employee's position with the AP without permission of the AP.

• Inevitably, some employees will use material they accumulated in their AP work — notes, stories (either written or broadcast), images, videotape, graphics — for other-than-AP uses. The resulting product must be presented to the AP for its approval prior to submission to any outside publisher, purchaser or broadcaster. And under no circumstances should the AP incur expenses for research material that is not used for AP purposes.

FREE TICKETS

We do not accept free tickets to sports, entertainment or other events for anything other than coverage purposes. If we obtain tickets for a member or subscriber as a courtesy, they must be paid for, and the member should reimburse the AP.

GIFTS

Associated Press offices and staffers are often sent or offered gifts or other items — some of them substantial, some of them modest, some of them perishable — by sources, public relations agencies, corporations and others. Sometimes these are designed to encourage or influence AP news coverage or business, sometimes they are just "perks" for journalists covering a particular event. Whatever the intent, we cannot accept such items; an exception is made for trinkets like caps or mugs that have nominal value, approximately $25 or less. Otherwise, gifts should be politely refused and returned, or if that is impracticable, they should be given to charity.

Books, CDs, DVDs, and other items received for review may be kept for staffers' professional reference or donated to charities, but may not be sold for personal gain. In cases where restrictions forbid transfer to third parties, these items, usually CDs and DVDs should be recycled. Items of more than nominal value that are provided for testing, such as computer gear, must be returned.

AP and its employees may accept discounts from companies only if those discounts are standard and offered to other customers.

We do not accept unsolicited contest awards from any organization that has a partisan or financial interest in our coverage; nor do we enter such contests.

The aim in all dealings should be to underscore the AP's reputation for objectivity.

OFFICIAL SCORERS

Employees may not serve as official scorers at sports events.

OUTSIDE APPEARANCES

Employees frequently appear on radio and TV news programs as panelists asking questions of newsmakers; such appearances are encouraged.

However, there is potential for conflict if staffers are asked to give their opinions on issues or personalities of the day. Advance discussion and clearance from a staffer's supervisor are required.

Employees must inform a news manager before accepting honoraria and/ or reimbursement of expenses for giving speeches or participating in seminars at colleges and universities or at other educational events if such appearance makes use of AP's name or the employee represents himself or herself as an AP employee. No fees should be accepted from governmental bodies; trade, lobbying or special interest groups; businesses, or labor groups; or any group that would pose a conflict of interest. All appearances must receive prior approval from a staffer's supervisor.

POLITICAL ACTIVITIES

Editorial employees are expected to be scrupulous in avoiding any political activity, whether they cover politics regularly or not. They may not run for political office or accept political appointment; nor may they perform public relations work for politicians or their groups. Under no circumstances should they donate money to political organizations or political campaigns. They should use great discretion in joining or making contributions to other organizations that may take political stands.

Non-editorial employees must refrain from political activity unless they obtain approval from a manager.

When in doubt, staffers are encouraged to discuss any such concerns with their supervisors.

And a supervisor must be informed when a spouse — or other members of an employee's household — has any ongoing involvement in political causes, either professionally or personally.

TRIPS

If a trip is organized, and we think the trip is newsworthy, we go and pay our way. If we have a chance to interview a newsmaker on a charter or private jet, we reimburse the news source for the reasonable rate of the costs incurred — for example, standard airfare. There may be exceptional circumstances, such as a military trip, where it is difficult to make other travel arrangements or calculate the costs. Consult a manager for exceptions.

* * *

BRIEFING ON MEDIA LAW

INTRODUCTION

The legal standards that govern the work of reporters and editors have undergone significant change since the civil rights movement and the Vietnam War, as the courts have given new force and meaning to the First Amendment's protection of speech and press.

In *New York Times v. Sullivan* (1964), the Supreme Court held for the very first time that the First Amendment limits the ability of states to impose damages based upon the content of a statement, even when it may be false. Sixteen years later, in *Richmond Newspapers v. Virginia* (1980), the court reached the equally unprecedented conclusion that the First Amendment establishes an affirmative right for the press and public to compel access to information concerning the exercise of government power. The fallout from these two watershed cases has reshaped a great deal of the law that governs the publication of the news and the way it is gathered.

This chapter addresses some of the key legal issues facing journalists. With respect to newsgathering *activity*, it explores three topics of direct significance:

Access to government information, including the rules governing reporter's access to the courts and to government information generally;

Confidential sources, including the law relating to promises of confidentiality and the reporter's privilege; and

Newsgathering conduct, including common law and statutory rules that may create liability for actions taken while a reporter is seeking out the news.

With respect to news *content*, this chapter addresses the legal principles in three branches of the law that govern liability for the publication of information:

Defamation, including the elements of a claim arising from the publication of a *false* statement, and the common law and constitutional defenses to liability;

Privacy, including claims for the disclosure of private facts, misappropriation and "false light," which can arise when the facts reported are *true*; and

Copyright infringement, including the elements of a copyright claim and the "fair use" defense.

While the law can vary in significant ways from one state to another, particularly in its details, the broad principles affecting newsgathering and reporting are largely consistent, due in part to the federal constitutional principles protecting speech and the press that overlay state law. Reporters and editors naturally will become familiar over time with the particulars of media law in the places where they work, and this chapter is intended only as a general primer on some basic principles that are likely to apply across a range of situations. It should not be construed as legal advice and should not substitute for obtaining legal guidance when you are in doubt.

LEGAL PRINCIPLES OF NEWSGATHERING

Several legal rules have special importance to the way the news is gathered. This chapter takes up three of them: the affirmative rights that can be invoked to compel access to government *proceedings* and the release of government documents; the legal protections that often allow reporters to obtain information through a promise of confidentiality; and, the "laws of general applicability," such as intrusion, trespass, and misrepresentation, that reporters must usually follow, even when they inhibit the ability to seek out the news.

Access to government information

Public access to information about the actions of government is essential to the functioning of a democracy. In 1822, James Madison made just this point:

"A Popular Government, without popular information, or the means of acquiring it, is but a Prologue to a Farce or a Tragedy; or perhaps both. Knowledge will forever govern ignorance: And a people who mean to be their own Governors, must arm themselves with the power which knowledge gives."

The press and public have affirmative rights, both constitutional and statutory, to compel access to the type of government information that is essential to the functioning of our democracy. The right of access extends to official proceedings, including court trials, hearings, and the meetings of some legislative bodies and administrative agencies. Access rights also extend to the inspection of *documents* held by the government, with only specific exceptions. Given the independence of the three branches of government, the scope of access to judicial proceedings and court records is largely governed by constitutional and common law principles articulated by judges, while access to information in the executive and legislative branches are largely governed by statutes and administrative regulations.

These access rights are not absolute; they can be abridged in a number of situations. Nonetheless, clear legal standards define the scope of these rights and the procedures available to reporters to enforce them.

• Recognition of a First Amendment right of access

The articulation by the Supreme Court in 1980 of a constitutional *right* to certain information about the exercise of government power, and the delineation of the proper scope and application of that right over the ensuing years, would provide a fascinating case study of the meaning of a "living constitution." In *Richmond Newspapers* v. Virginia, the Supreme Court ruled for the first time that the First Amendment encompasses an affirmative, enforceable right of public access to criminal trials. As the court later explained the rationale for this new constitutional right, "a major purpose" of the First Amendment's protection of free speech, a free press and the right to petition the government is the public's need to know what the government is up to, if democracy is to function. Just as other provisions of the Bill of Rights have been read to imply the right to travel, a right to privacy, and the right to be presumed innocent, the court concluded that the First Amendment implies a right of the public to certain information concerning the direct exercise of government power.

In a series of subsequent rulings following *Richmond Newspapers*, the Supreme Court reaffirmed the existence of this constitutional right of access and defined its scope. In 1982, the court said that the right to attend a criminal trial applies even during the testimony of a minor victim of a sex crime. In *Globe Newspaper Co. v. Superior Court* (1982), the court struck down as unconstitutional a Massachusetts statute mandating closed proceedings during all such testimony, saying that the First Amendment right of access requires a judge to determine on a case-by-case basis whether the privacy concerns of a particular victim outweigh the public's right to attend and observe the proceedings. In 1984, the Supreme Court held that the right of access extends to the proceedings to select a jury in a criminal case, *Press-Enterprise Co. v. Superior Ct.*, and two years later said the right extends to preliminary hearings in a criminal prosecution. *Press-Enterprise Co. v Superior Ct.* The First Amendment protects the public's right to attend such judicial proceedings unless specific findings are made, on the record, demonstrating that a closed proceeding is essential in order to "preserve higher values," and any limitation imposed on public access must be narrowly tailored to serve that interest. In 2010, in *Presley v. Georgia*, the court held a trial judge must ensure that these standards are satisfied before a courtroom is closed to the public, even if no one objects to the closure.

While the Supreme Court has not substantively revisited the right of access in detail since 1986, lower federal and state courts have widely considered and applied the right to a large variety of judicial and administrative proceedings over the intervening years. Courts have recognized a constitutional right to attend a given type of proceeding if public access will generally play a positive role in the performance of the proceeding (encouraging diligent attention by officials, ensuring that proper procedures are followed, preventing perjury or other misconduct, facilitating public understanding of decisions made), and if it is the type of proceeding that historically has been open to the public. And the right has been held to extend to administrative proceedings conducted like trials, such as deportation hearings and agency adjudications.

The constitutional right is generally recognized to apply to all aspects of a criminal prosecution, except to matters involving a grand jury. Grand jury investigations historically have been completely secret, and this secrecy itself advances the important public policy of protecting innocent people in those cases where an investigation does not result in any criminal charge being filed. The right of access has been held to extend to civil trials and proceedings, although in some states there are important exceptions. Family Court proceedings, for example, raise significant privacy concerns, as do juvenile delinquency matters, and these are often closed to the public.

• Limits on constitutional access

As noted, the constitutional right to attend proceedings is not absolute. That a First Amendment right protects public access to the proceeding does not mean that a proceeding can never be closed to the press and public. The Supreme Court has identified four factors that must each be satisfied before the right of access may be restricted:

1. Those who want to close a proceeding must prove that holding a public proceeding would directly threaten some compelling interest, such as a defendant's right to a fair trial or the right of privacy, that outweighs the public interest in openness.

2. There must be no alternative short of closing the proceeding that could protect the threatened interest.

3. Any limitation on access must be as narrow as possible.

4. The limitation imposed must be effective in protecting the threatened interest or else closure may not be ordered.

Applying these factors, courts have required journalists and the public to be excluded from proceedings in a number of situations, such as during the testimony of a sexual assault victim whose identity has not previously been disclosed to the public, or during testimony by an undercover police officer whose effectiveness or safety would be jeopardized by public identification.

Sidebar conferences between the attorneys and the judge generally involve discussions intended to be kept confidential from the jury, but these discussions should usually be available to the press. A transcript is generally kept of such sidebar discussions and should be available for inspection as part of the record of the proceeding. To withhold the transcript of such a sidebar conference held during an open proceeding, the same four-part test would need to be met.

One recurring but unsettled issue concerns reporters' access to information identifying jurors, and their right to speak to jurors after a verdict. The Supreme Court has said specifically that the First Amendment right of access extends to jury selection proceedings, where names and other identifying information are normally disclosed. Some lower courts have concluded that this principle also requires disclosures of written juror questionnaires when they are used. Nonetheless, in some high profile cases such as the prosecutions of Martha Stewart, Michael Jackson, Illinois Gov. Rod Blagojevich, and baseball slugger Barry Bonds, courts have sought to keep the identities of jurors private during the trial or to minimize press contact with jurors following a verdict. Sometimes a judge will conduct jury selection by reference only to juror numbers, to prevent public disclosure of juror names or addresses before a trial is over. The U.S. Court of Appeals in Philadelphia has concluded in *United States v. Wecht,* (2008), that the public access right requires juror names to be disclosed before the start of a trial, but this position is not universally embraced. In other cases, courts have barred reporters from speaking with jurors long after a verdict is returned. Limitations on disclosure of juror identities before a verdict is returned are sometimes permitted, but restrictions after a verdict is returned can rarely be squared with the First Amendment right of access.

Reporters confronted with such court orders should seek legal advice on the validity of the restriction imposed.

• What to say if a hearing is about to be closed without prior notice

Because a constitutional right is at stake when a judicial proceeding is closed, the press has a right to be heard before a proceeding is closed to the public. The following statement should be read in court when confronted with an attempt to close a hearing without advance notice. It allows a reporter, when permitted to address the court, to state the basic concerns and to seek time for counsel to appear to make the legal argument. Any parts of the statement that are not applicable to a specific case can be changed or omitted:

May it please the Court, I am (name) of The Associated Press (or other news organization). I respectfully request the opportunity to register on the record an objection to closing this proceeding to the public. The Associated Press (or other organization) requests a hearing at which its counsel may present to the Court legal authority and arguments showing why any closure in this case would be improper.

The press and the public have a constitutional right to attend judicial proceedings, and may not be excluded unless the Court makes findings, on the record, that: (1) *closure is required to preserve a compelling constitutional interest,* (2) *no adequate alternatives to closure exist, and* (3) *the closure ordered is narrowly tailored to protect the threatened interest effectively.*

The Associated Press (or other news organization) submits that these findings cannot be made here, especially given the public interest in this proceeding. The public has a right to be informed of what transpires in this case, the positions being argued by the parties, and the factual basis for rulings made by the Court. The Court should avoid any impression that justice is being carried on in secret. The Associated Press (or other news organization) objects to any closure order and respectfully requests a hearing at which it can present full legal arguments and authority in support of this position. Thank you.

If the court will not allow a reporter to be heard, a brief written statement — handwritten is fine — should be delivered to the courtroom clerk, making these same points.

• A word about gag orders

The tension between the right of a free press and the right of a fair trial is nothing new. Finding an impartial jury for the treason trial of Aaron Burr in 1807 was difficult, the Supreme Court has noted, because few people in Virginia "had not formed some opinions concerning Mr. Burr or his case, from newspaper accounts." Nonetheless, an apparently increasing number of cases involving celebrity defendants or notorious crimes generating intense publicity have led to an increased number of orders preventing lawyers, parties to a case, and sometimes even witnesses, from discussing the case outside of the courtroom.

The Supreme Court has said that speech by attorneys, as officers of the court, may be regulated to protect the integrity of the judicial system. Orders more broadly barring the speech of other trial participants, including the parties and witnesses, are permitted only when absolutely necessary to ensure an accused's right to a fair trial. Such orders have been entered in cases involving extraordinary press coverage that threatens the ability to select an impartial jury, when other measures are not likely to mitigate the effects of unrestrained pretrial publicity.

A typical gag order does not prevent a reporter from asking questions, but it does bar trial participants and court officers from answering them. Because a gag order restricts access to news, a reporter has legal standing to challenge an order, and may be successful if a gag order was entered without adequate factual findings to justify the need for the specific restraint on speech imposed by the court, or if the order is overbroad in the categories of individuals restrained or the range of topics they are prohibited from discussing.

• Media protocols in high-profile cases

"Decorum orders" regulate the conduct of reporters covering high profile trials. Sometimes requested by the parties and sometimes imposed unilaterally by the court, these orders may restrict the use of cameras and recording devices at specific locations in and around the courthouse, direct that witnesses or jurors not be photographed as they come and go from court, restrict the use of cellphones, or impose other restrictions to protect the decorum of a trial and operations at the courthouse. In the aborted Kobe Bryant prosecution, for example, a Colorado state judge imposed a decorum order specifying such details as where cameras could be positioned outside the courthouse, limiting the times when reporters could enter or leave the courtroom, and specifying where reporters could sit, where they could park their cars and how they could enter the courthouse.

Restrictions on the actions of journalists that directly affect their ability to gather news must be narrowly tailored to protect a compelling governmental interest. Decorum orders that become necessary in high-profile cases to ensure safety, protect physical access to the courts by the public, or prevent interference with the integrity of the proceedings in the courtroom, are likely to be allowed as long as their terms are reasonable, content-neutral and limited to clearly defined restrictions on conduct within the courthouse and its immediate environs. A decorum order likely goes too far, however, if it also controls the content of a news report rather than just the conduct of a reporter. For example, for privacy reasons a court might restrict the taking of photographs of jurors as they enter or leave the courthouse, but could not properly bar the press from ever publishing the image of a juror, even if it were obtained through other sources. One restriction is limited to conduct at the courthouse; the other is aimed at the content of a news report.

• The right to attend other proceedings

In some instances, the constitutional right of access has been held to extend to proceedings beyond court hearings. For example, in 2004, the U.S. Court of Appeals in Cincinnati held that the public had a constitutional right to attend deportation proceedings conducted by the Immigration and Naturalization Service. (*Detroit Free Press v. Ashcroft*, 2002.) In 2001 the U.S. Court of Appeals in New York held that the right of access applied in transit agency tribunals to assess fines. (*New York Civ. Lib. Union v. N.Y.C. Transit Authority*, (2011)). The First Amendment right of access similarly has been found to extend to military courts-martial, proceedings of judicial review boards and hearings of the Federal Mine Safety and Health Administration.

Most states and the federal government also have statutes known as "open meetings laws" or "government in the sunshine" acts that protect the right of the public and the press to attend meetings of public authorities. These laws essentially provide that every meeting where a public board or public authority convenes to conduct business must be open to the public, with only limited exception. The federal law, for example, allows a meeting to be closed only if one of 10 identified categories of information are to be discussed, such as personnel and salary decisions. Even when a portion of a meeting is closed, a transcript or minutes must be prepared, and must be disclosed to the extent that release would not reveal the exempt information.

These access laws apply to executive agencies, but not to the legislative bodies, in most cases. Most state constitutions separately require open legislative sessions, although each house is usually free to make its own rules about access to committee meetings.

• The right of access applies to court documents

The right of access generally includes the right to inspect transcripts of open proceedings, evidence introduced at a trial and most motion papers, orders and other records of open court proceedings. Some courts have concluded that this right to inspect judicial records is implicit in the First Amendment right of access, holding that the right covers any documents relating to a proceeding that is itself subject to the First Amendment right of access.

Other courts analyzed the right of access to documents filed with the court as a common law right that may be more easily restricted, sometimes with unfortunate results. For example, in the famous case of *McConnell v. Federal Election Commission* (2003), a challenge to the constitutionality of the McCain-Feingold campaign finance reform act was decided by the courts entirely on the basis of written submissions, without any public evidentiary hearing. A massive record of some 100,000 pages was presented to the court, apparently detailing the types of campaign abuses that justified the restrictions on election speech imposed by Congress. Despite the public interest in knowing the factual basis for the competing arguments being made, the District of Columbia court concluded that the public had only a common law right to inspect the documents presented to the court, and that this right extended only to information "relied upon" by the court in reaching its decision. The court therefore rejected an application by several news organizations to inspect the evidence filed with the court, saying the public was only entitled to inspect specific pages of the record actually cited in the court's opinions. Other courts have rejected this limitation and have found a constitutional right of access to records submitted to courts in support of requests for judicial action, regardless of whether the court ultimately relies on the record, an approach embraced by the U.S. court of Appeals in New York (*Lugosh v. Pyramid Corp.*).

Whether the right to inspect court records is a constitutional right or a common law right is not fully settled in some areas of the country. Whatever the scope of the right to inspect court records, however, it does not generally extend to pretrial discovery documents and other litigation records that are not filed with the courts. While compelled public access to discovery has been afforded on rare occasions, involving highly newsworthy disputes, reporters generally have no right to require parties to a lawsuit to allow inspection of litigation material that is never filed with the court.

• Access to other government records

The federal Freedom of Information Act (FOIA), originally passed by Congress in 1966, creates a presumptive right of access to all documents held in the executive branch, other than documents in the possession of the president and his immediate staff. It does not cover Congress or the courts. All Cabinet agencies, independent agencies, regulatory commissions and government-owned corporations are covered.

Records made available for inspection under the act include virtually anything recorded in a physical medium that can be reproduced. This includes all documents, papers, reports, and letters in the government's possession, as well as films, photographs, sound recordings, databases, computer disks and tapes. A 1996 law expanded FOIA to require federal agencies, whenever possible, to share data in a specific format, such as on computer diskette or CD-ROM. The 1996 amendments also broadened citizen access to government by placing more information directly online.

The act contains nine exemptions that permit — but do not require — agencies to withhold information. Those exemptions are: (1) national security; (2) internal agency personnel rules; (3) information specifically exempt from disclosure by another law; (4) trade secrets; (5) internal agency memorandums and policy deliberations; (6) personal privacy; (7); law enforcement investigations; (8) federally regulated bank information; and (9) oil and gas well data.

Different agencies apply these exemptions in different ways even when issues ostensibly have already been settled in court. If you want something, ask for it. Let the government decide whether it has any grounds or willingness to deny your request. The statutory exemptions allow information to be withheld, but do not require it. Even an exempt document can be released at the government's discretion.

Because of the various exemptions, documents are often produced with large sections blacked out as "exempt." And, because of a lack of manpower assigned to implement the act, there are often long delays in getting documents at all. Under the law, information is supposed to be produced within 20 days, but there is no effective enforcement mechanism when an agency misses this deadline, short of going to court.

• Making a request under FOIA

There is no set format for making a FOIA request for documents. Although most agencies have adopted regulations describing specific steps to follow, any reasonably precise identification of the information sought, submitted to the proper person, will trigger an obligation for an agency to respond. Here are a few elementary steps to consider in making a FOIA request that may help avoid problems:

—Call the public information office of the agency you believe has the records before filing your request, to make sure you have the right agency and the right address for filing it. Ask if the information you are seeking could be released without a written FOIA request.

—Be as specific as possible about what you want. Give dates, titles, and authors for documents if you know them. In your letter, provide your telephone number, email address, and offer to supply any other information that might help narrow the search.

—Even if you are using the letterhead stationery of a news organization, state specifically that you are a reporter for that organization and plan to use the material in news stories. The act does not require you to state your purpose, but disclosures in the public interest are eligible for fee waivers, exemption waivers and in some cases expedited handling.

—Request a waiver of search and copying fees. To avoid delays if the waiver is denied, also state a limit you are prepared to pay, such as $100, without the agency's need to obtain your prior, specific consent.

—If you want field office files checked as well as those at headquarters, be sure to request that specifically. Some agencies, such as the FBI, will not check beyond the office where the request is submitted, unless asked. It is often good practice to send a separate request directly to the FOI officer at the field office of an agency in any event, if you think relevant documents exist there.

—Ask the agency to cite specific exemptions for each item it withholds in the event that any part of the request is denied.

—Request that redacted copies of documents be provided if only a specific portion of a document is subject to an exemption.

—If your initial request is denied, file an administrative appeal. Some agencies take a very different view on appeal. The denial letter will specify to whom the appeal must be sent and the deadline for making an appeal. If you do not first pursue an administrative appeal, you cannot go to court to compel release of the information.

—An appeal can be made through a simple letter that explains why the public will benefit from disclosure and asks for a review of the grounds on which the request was denied. Several exemptions require a balancing effort between private and public interests, and reviewers on an administrative appeal may be more likely to exercise their right to waive an exemption if a good case for disclosure is made.

You may want to consult FOIA experts or manuals before proceeding with a request. An FOI Service Center is maintained by the Reporters Committee for Freedom of the Press. The committee publishes a pamphlet with sample FOIA letters and appeal forms as well as analyses of the act. (Available on the Web at: http://www.rcfp.org/foiact/index.html.) The committee maintains a toll-free hot line (800-336-4243), 24 hours a day, seven days a week, with attorneys available to provide FOIA advice to journalists.

On the Web, the U.S. Department of Justice publishes a "Freedom of Information Act Guide," which gives the current government understanding of what is covered and not covered by each exemption, http://www.usdoj.gov/oip/foia_guide07.htm. Also on the Web, the U.S. Department of Justice publishes the "FOIA Reference Materials," which contains up-to-date copies of relevant statutes and recent cases, http://www.usdoj.gov/oip/04_7.html.

It is advisable to check on specific state freedom of information laws. Each individual state also has its own freedom of information laws that apply to state and local government agencies.

Issues concerning sources

For better or worse, some sources who possess important information of great public significance will speak to a journalist only if they are promised confidentiality. This has been true from the earliest history of an independent press in America. John Peter Zenger, whose New York trial in 1735 is best remembered for establishing the principle that truth must be a defense to a claim for libel, was also the first American newspaperman to establish the tradition that journalists will protect their sources to the point of imprisonment, refusing to divulge to British authorities the anonymous sources of material they claimed to be libelous.

The use of confidential sources remains an important means for reporters to uncover the news. Such sources make available to the public more than the sanitized "spin" of government and corporate press releases. Yale professor Alexander Bickel noted:

"Indispensable information comes in confidence from officeholders fearful of superiors, from businessmen fearful of competitors, from informers operating at the edge of the law who are in danger of reprisal from criminal associates, from people afraid of the law and government - sometimes rightly afraid, but as often from an excess of caution - and from men in all fields anxious not to incur censure for unorthodox or unpopular views." ("The Morality of Consent," 1975.)

In one study of some 10,000 news reports conducted in 2005, 13 percent of the front-page newspaper articles reviewed were based, at least in part, on anonymous sources.

Promising confidentiality to a source always raises a number of issues, legal and journalistic. If a reporter refuses to identify a source, there is always the potential that a publisher may be hauled into court or a reporter thrown into jail. If a publisher is sued for libel, having a story based on sources that were promised confidentiality creates an entirely separate set of concerns: it is hard to prove the "truth" of a statement if the source of the information cannot be revealed. In one recent case, a Massachusetts court entered a default judgment against the Boston Globe for refusing to reveal its confidential source for a story that became the subject of a libel claim. A jury subsequently awarded the plaintiff $2.1 million — a hefty price to pay to uphold a promise to a source.

• A promise to a source creates an enforceable agreement

A reporter who reveals the name or identity of someone who was promised confidentiality can be held liable for breach of the agreement.

The Supreme Court decided just this issue in *Cohen v. Cowles* (1991), a case involving "dirt" on one political candidate that was provided to a newspaper reporter on the eve of the election by a political consultant for the candidate's opponent. The reporter promised the consultant confidentiality. His editors, however, considered the identification of the source necessary for the public to weigh the significance of the new disclosures, and overruled the reporter. As a result, the no-longer confidential source lost his job, and sued. A jury verdict of $200,000 in favor of the spurned source was upheld by the Supreme Court, which found the First Amendment no defense to a claim for the damages caused by breaking a promise freely made.

The same result was reached by a New York court in a case involving a promise to mask someone's identity in a photograph. A journalist promised a man receiving treatment in an AIDS clinic that he would not be "identifiable" if he allowed his photograph to be taken. The journalist used a rear-angle setup and retouching techniques to obscure his identity, but the man's friends still recognized him when the photograph was published. The New York court held that the burden of carrying out the promise to disguise rested with the journalist who made the promise, and upheld the jury's award of damages to the patient.

Reporters can unwittingly create problems for themselves in making agreements with sources to protect confidentiality, or in failing to clarify with the source the meaning of an agreement. A few common-sense steps can minimize the risk that problems with sources will develop:

-Before making any promise, consider whether it is worth doing: How important is the information that the source is going to provide? Can the information be obtained or confirmed from any "on-the-record" source?

-If a promise of some protection is to be made, express it in terms of the steps that will be taken to protect the source rather than the result to be achieved. For example, promise a source to not use the name, or agree on how the source will be identified in the story (a "high-ranking military officer," or a "knowledgeable Defense Department official"), rather than promising "no one will know you gave me this information." If a photograph or videotape is involved, the key is still to promise a specific action ("I will photograph you only from behind") rather than promising a result ("no one will recognize you").

-Make sure the source has the same understanding of the scope of the promise made, as you do. Avoid using ambiguous terms as a shorthand for an agreement, such as "this will be off the record," or this is "confidential." Instead, be specific about the terms of the agreement and how far the promise extends. Must confidentiality be maintained if litigation results? If a court order requires disclosure? Or, will the source allow disclosure in certain situations?

-Follow through with any agreement, making sure to inform editors and others who need to know to carry out the promise. The broader the promise, the more the effort needed to make sure that it is upheld.

The bottom line is this: promises of confidentiality or anonymity should be made cautiously, and only after a determination that the risk of such promises is outweighed by the need for the information. When a promise is made, make sure it is as precise as possible, and then make sure it is carried out.

• Reporter's privilege

Given the importance of confidential sources, reporters have long asserted a right to protect the identity of those to whom confidentiality was promised. All states except Wyoming currently provide some level of protection for reporters who are called to testify about their sources. Thirty-three states and the District of Columbia have enacted "shield laws" that provide legal protection against the disclosure of sources; 18 additional states have recognized some form of a "reporter's privilege" through judicial decisions. About half of the state shield laws provide reporters with an absolute privilege not to disclose confidential sources, while the remainder establish a high standard that must be met before a reporter's promise of confidentiality can be pierced.

The existence and scope of the reporter's privilege is more confused in federal courts. There is no federal shield law, and the Supreme Court has addressed the "reporter's privilege" only once - in a ruling that is far from clear.

In *Branzburg v. Hayes* (1972), the Supreme Court considered claims of privilege asserted by three journalists who had been subpoenaed to reveal confidential information and sources before grand juries investigating possible criminal activity. The reporters had written stories describing the synthesizing of hashish, conversations with admitted drug users, and eyewitness accounts of events at Black Panther headquarters at a time of civil unrest in the surrounding neighborhood. In each instance, the journalist claimed a privilege under the First Amendment not to answer questions concerning confidential information and sources.

A closely divided Supreme Court held in a 5-4 ruling that it did not violate the First Amendment to require these journalists to testify in the grand jury investigations, conducted in good faith, concerning the identities of persons allegedly engaged in criminal conduct. The court, however, did not reject altogether the notion of a First Amendment privilege. To the contrary, the majority opinion expressed the view that its narrow focus should not apply to "the vast bulk of confidential relationships between reporters and their sources," and emphasized that even grand juries "must operate within the limits of the First Amendment as well as the Fifth."

Justice Lewis Powell cast the decisive fifth vote and wrote separately to underscore further the "limited nature" of the court's holding. He explained that reporters would still have access to the courts, and could move to quash a subpoena if confidential source information were being sought "without a legitimate need of law enforcement."

Court decisions over the ensuing decades have embraced a qualified reporter's privilege that accommodates the interests of the press and those who seek to obtain information through judicial process. The United States Courts of Appeals in 10 of the 12 federal circuits have specifically applied the First Amendment reporter's privilege in civil lawsuits.

Courts, however, have read *Branzburg* more restrictively in the criminal context, sometimes declining to recognize a privilege at all, or allowing only a very limited balancing of interests. Recently, three different federal appellate courts affirmed contempt citations requiring reporters to be jailed for refusing to reveal confidential sources sought in criminal investigations. In 2001, freelance writer Vanessa Leggett served nearly six months in a Texas prison for declining to reveal sources of information related to a notorious murder, almost four times longer than any prison term previously imposed on any reporter by any federal court. In 2004, James Taricani, a reporter for WJAR-TV in Rhode Island, completed a four-month sentence of home confinement for declining to reveal who leaked a videotape capturing alleged corruption by public officials in Providence. And, in 2005 The New York Times reporter Judith Miller was jailed in Virginia for several months for refusing to disclose her confidential source for a story she never wrote about CIA operative Valerie Plame.

These aggressive court actions in criminal investigations have encouraged private litigants and federal courts adjudicating their civil cases also to demand confidential information from reporters. In one civil suit, five reporters (including two Pulitzer Prize winners) were held in contempt and subjected to fines of $500 per day each for declining to reveal their confidential sources of information about Dr. Wen Ho Lee, who claimed information about him was provided to reporters by government agents in violation of the Privacy Act.

While the state of the reporter's privilege in the federal courts is somewhat unsettled, reporters have one additional protection in federal criminal investigations in the form of Department of Justice guidelines that severely limit the circumstances under which U.S. attorneys may attempt to subpoena reporters. Adopted by Attorney General Elliot Richardson in the wake of the Watergate scandal, these guidelines remain in effect and are published in the Code of Federal Regulations at 28 C.F.R. 50.10. In general, the guidelines adopt the following policies with respect to the issuance of subpoenas directed to journalists:

-All reasonable attempts must be made to obtain the information sought from other sources before a subpoena to a reporter is even considered,

-Negotiations for the information should be pursued with the reporter before a subpoena is sought.

-No subpoena may be issued to a reporter without the personal approval of the attorney general.

-The attorney general's approval may not be sought unless the information held by the reporter is essential to the investigation and not available from other sources.

-Except in exigent circumstances, subpoenas should be used only to verify published information and to confirm the accuracy of the circumstances surrounding published information.

These regulations provide the same types of protection contained in some state shield laws, and the Department of Justice has demonstrated in the past a serious desire to enforce these regulations strictly. Any time a subpoena is received by a reporter from a U.S. attorney, the first question to ask the attorney is: Did you comply with the media guidelines at 28 C.F.R. 50.10 before issuing this subpoena? Not infrequently, just asking the question results in the subpoena being withdrawn.

• Policies and practices for handling subpoenas
AP declines to provide any of its news stories and photos to non-subscribers

without a valid subpoena. Although AP does not invite subpoenas, it advises litigants and government officials that it will accept service of a validly issued subpoena narrowly requiring production of news stories and photos as they were transmitted, and will otherwise enforce its rights to resist disclosure to the full extent of the law.

Procedures for responding to a narrow subpoena for published material should be consistently applied, without taking sides, in order to preserve neutrality and objectivity, both in fact and in appearance. In appropriate cases, AP may provide a letter or affidavit authenticating a published story or photo, confirming that a fair and true copy has been provided of an item transmitted by AP on a particular date and time. Whenever possible, AP seeks reimbursement of its copying costs and other costs of compliance.

Subpoenas that go beyond published reports should be resisted routinely by AP reporters in order to avoid becoming perceived as an investigative arm of the government or private litigants. AP does not produce reporters' notes or photos or negatives which have not been moved, nor does it produce drafts or any editorial material, including internal memorandums concerning the newsgathering process. AP never reveals the identity of sources to whom it has promised confidentiality.

AP does not invite sanctions by ignoring subpoenas. It will affirmatively oppose subpoenas that seek privileged work-product and unpublished information of every kind.

A couple of practical pointers that can avoid subpoena problems:

-Always avoid giving out information about stories to lawyers over the phone. Providing information may only whet a lawyer's appetite to serve a subpoena, and it can create an argument that grounds for objecting to a subpoena have somehow been waived. It is always better to refer any questions from lawyers to AP's lawyers in New York.

-Subpoenas from criminal defense attorneys seeking published, local news copy to demonstrate the extent of pretrial publicity can often be deflected by reminding the litigants that AP has no means of determining whether or which AP members used AP copy. The reliable sources for information about what was disseminated to the public are articles stored in news databases and video clips available from television stations and electronic "clipping" services.

• Liability for newsgathering conduct

A reporter for Mother Jones won a national award in 1984 for posing as a job applicant at a chemical factory and covertly taking photographs documenting illegal pesticides being manufactured for the export market. That conduct today would more likely win a lawsuit.

In holding that a reporter's promise of confidentiality is legally binding, the Supreme Court in *Cohen v. Cowles* (1991) announced that "generally applicable" laws having only "incidental effects" on the ability of the press to gather the news do not offend the First Amendment. Ever since, a flow of lawsuits have been filed against reporters asserting claims for such "generally applicable" torts as intrusion, trespass, and fraud. From the muzzling effect of the tobacco industry's threat of "tortuous interference" liability against CBS for an expose based on a confidential source who was party to a standard confidentiality agreement as an employee of a tobacco company, through *Food Lion's* claim of trespass, fraud and breach of duty leveled against ABC and a spate of other hidden camera lawsuits, reporters since *Cohen v. Cowles*, have faced an increased number of claims alleging misconduct in the gathering of the news.

This section highlights briefly some of the legal theories that can create problems for the unwary reporter.

• Intrusion upon seclusion

A claim for intrusion exists in most states if someone intentionally commits a "highly offensive" intrusion upon another's solitude or seclusion, invading either a physical space or the private affairs of the plaintiff, such as reviewing private financial statements or personal email without permission. Intrusion claims against the press most commonly arise in three contexts: (1) surreptitious surveillance; (2) trespass of private property, and (3) instances where consent to enter a private setting for one purpose has been exceeded (as where a reporter gains access to information under false pretenses).

Intrusion is a branch of the law of privacy. Where the potentially offending conduct occurs is therefore important. For example, a person generally has no legitimate basis to complain if a picture is taken in a public place, but if the picture is taken in or around the person's home, a claim for intrusion may exist if the person had a "reasonable expectation" of privacy where the photograph was taken.

In one noted lawsuit a few years back, the family of an officer of a large health care corporation successfully obtained an injunction against the elaborate efforts of a news organization that was seeking information about the family. The organization's camera crew followed the children to school, and sat in a boat outside the family's Florida home with a camera equipped with a high-powered telescopic lens. In issuing an injunction, the court concluded that "a persistent course of hounding, harassment and unreasonable surveillance, even if conducted in a public or semi-public place," could support a claim for intrusion upon seclusion.

A claim for intrusion generally requires (1) an intentional intrusion, (2) that impinges upon the solitude or seclusion of another, or his private affairs, and (3) that would be highly offensive to a reasonable person. The term "highly offensive" is ill-defined, but can include harassing behavior, surreptitious surveillance, or the use of high-power lenses and listening devices to invade typically private places.

The tort of intrusion is based on wrongful conduct rather than on the publication of any information, so a claim may exist even when the news story being pursued is never published. For this reason, in many states it is no defense to an intrusion claim to assert the newsworthiness of the information that was being sought. The issue is whether a reasonable person would view the conduct as highly offensive under all the circumstances.

Some examples where courts have upheld claims for intrusion illustrate the nature of the tort:

—Two journalists in California, without discussing who they were, gained access to the home of a disabled veteran who purported to provide healing aids in the form of clay, minerals and herbs. While there, they surreptitiously photographed and tape-recorded the veteran, for use in a magazine report. The court allowed a claim for intrusion even though the reporters were invited into the home by the veteran. While a person takes the risk that someone allowed into their home is not what he seems, and even though a visitor is free to repeat anything he sees or hears, the court held that the homeowner's risk does not extend to the risk that secret photographs and recordings will be transmitted to the world at large.

—The unauthorized recording of an unplanned interview conducted when the plaintiff answered his own front door has similarly been held to constitute an actionable "intrusion," while secretly recording an interview of a person who stepped from their home onto a public sidewalk was held not to be an intrusion.

—Televising an image of a person's home is not an intrusion if the broadcast shows no more than what can be seen from the street, and secretly recording a conversation in a place of business was held not to be an intrusion if the reporter was invited into the office and the state wiretap law permitted the secret recording.

• Trespass

A person commits a trespass by entering property that is in the possession of another, without authorization or consent. To avoid a claim, permission must be obtained by an owner, a tenant or someone acting on their behalf. Like intrusion, a trespass claim arises from conduct in gathering news, not from the content of any report that may subsequently be published.

Permission to be on private property can be implied by custom or by the nature of the premises. For example, someone has implied permission to enter a store or restaurant during business hours, even though it may be located on private property. There is similarly an implied right to approach someone's house on a driveway or sidewalk to see if they are home. Permission, whether express or implied, can also be revoked. If a posted sign says "Do Not Enter," or if the owner came to the door and said to leave, remaining on the property would be a trespass.

Trespass is also a strict liability tort. Entering on someone's property without permission, even by accident or mistake, will constitute a trespass. On the other hand, trespass protects only against a physical invasion of property; it does not limit the collection or use of information gathered while on the property. The law of trespass does not restrict a reporter on a public sidewalk from using what can be seen or heard on the adjacent private property.

The impact of trespass on newsgathering is also tempered by the nature of the damages that may be recovered through a claim for trespass. The trespass tort is intended to protect property, not privacy or reputation. A trespasser therefore can be held responsible only for physical harm done while on the land and other injury that is a "natural consequence" of the trespass. Courts generally will not recognize injury to reputation or emotional distress caused by the later publication of a photograph obtained during a trespass to be a "natural consequence" of the trespass itself.

A vivid example of a trespass claim involved a television camera crew that was preparing a report on credit card fraud. The United States Secret Service obtained a warrant to search an apartment for evidence of credit card fraud, and a news magazine camera crew followed the Secret Service into the apartment. Part of the search was taped, including a sequence of a mother and child cowering on the couch asking not be photographed. In refusing to dismiss a lawsuit asserting claims for trespass and a constitutional tort (for improperly accompanying federal agents in executing a search warrant), an outraged court said the reporters "had no greater right than that of a common thief to be in the apartment." Like intrusion, the trespass was complete once the invasion of private property occurred. The trespass claim could be asserted even though the news report being pursued was never broadcast.

In situations rife with the potential for trespass, common sense can once again minimize the risk of litigation:

—Whenever possible, ask the property owner or those who appear to be in charge for permission to enter, or seek their approval to remain. In situations where police or fire officials have taken control of a crime or disaster scene, they may stand in for the owner and grant or deny access. Their presence does not defeat the owner's rights, however, and the owner can still require a reporter to leave private property.

—Always identify yourself — verbally, by displaying a press credential, and through insignias on clothing and cameras — so that those present know you are a reporter and will not assume you are part of any police or emergency response team. If not asked to leave, the very fact that your status as a reporter was disclosed may be sufficient to establish an implied consent to remain.

—If asked to leave, retire to the sidewalk, street, or other position on public property.

—Consent obtained through fraud or misrepresentation will not be considered valid consent and will not defeat a claim for trespass.

—Consent obtained from minors or others who are not legally capable of giving consent (mentally incapacitated people, for example) will not defeat a claim for trespass.

• Electronic eavesdropping

Both state and federal law regulate the electronic recording of conversations, including telephone conversations.

Under the federal law, a conversation may not be recorded without the consent of at least one of the participants. That means reporters are not prohibited by federal law from recording any conversation that they participate in, whether or not they disclose that the conversation is being recorded. But, leaving a hidden tape recorder in a room to record a conversation between others, secretly listening in on an extension phone and recording the conversation, or recording a telephone call picked up on a scanner or listening device, is a violation of federal law if done without permission of one of the parties.

The law in most states is similar to the federal law, allowing a conversation to be recorded so long as one party to the conversation consents. The laws in a minority of states are more strict, and prohibit recording any conversation unless permission is given by all the parties to the conversation. States where the consent of all parties is required in order to record a conversation are: California, Connecticut, Florida, Illinois, Maryland, Massachusetts, Michigan, Montana, Nevada, New Hampshire, Pennsylvania, and Washington. This requirement extends only to conversations where there is some expectation of privacy, and does not prohibit tape-recording at speeches, press conferences and similar public events.

• Misrepresentation and similar forms of wrongdoing

Laws of general applicability govern the actions of reporters, yet conduct that might sometimes be deemed "deceit," "misrepresentation" or "fraud" can be useful in ferreting out the news. Reporters are often less than candid in dealing with those from whom they want information. Recognizing this reality, some courts have held that claims such as fraud and misrepresentation cannot be pursued against journalists unless the wrong is "particularly egregious," or part of a broader pattern of wrongdoing. For example, courts have rejected claims for fraud based on a false message left on a telephone answering machine to induce the disclosure of information, and for fraudulently promising that no "ambush" techniques would be used if an interview were granted.

Other courts have been less willing to weigh the public interest in a news report against the allegedly wrongful conduct. In one instance, a judge allowed claims for fraud and breach of contract to proceed against Business Week after a reporter gained access to records of a credit reporting agency by misrepresenting that a subscription to the credit service was being sought in order to conduct background checks on potential Business Week employees. In reality, information was sought for an exposé on the credit-reporting industry, and the reporter promptly obtained the credit history of then-Vice President Dan Quayle without his consent. The court held that such "wanton misconduct" can result in liability, and allowed a recovery of the costs incurred by the credit agency as a result of the misrepresentation.

Remember, the basic rule is that reporters must obey rules and regulations when they are gathering the news. While there are some exceptions, the First Amendment will not generally provide a defense to a reporter who violates the law while gathering the news.

• *Special Considerations When Dealing with National Security Issues*

The Espionage Act (of 1917) makes it a federal crime to publish classified information that either (a) reveals the communications intelligence activities of the United States or any foreign country, or (b) discloses classified information obtained from a foreign government or military force through the "processes of communications intelligence." The Espionage Act also broadly makes it a crime for any unauthorized person either to communicate to another, or to retain possession of "information relating to national defense" if there is "reason to believe" the information could harm the U.S. or help a foreign nation or military force.

In the decades since the statute was enacted, there has never been a prosecution of a news organization for violating the Espionage Act, but there has been sabre-rattling from time to time. In December 2010, for example, Sen. Joseph Lieberman publicly called upon the Justice Department to investigate whether The New York Times had violated the Espionage Act by publishing confidential U.S. diplomatic cables it had obtained from WikiLeaks. The application of the Espionage Act to a news organization would raise significant First Amendment issues and might well run afoul of the doctrine barring application of criminal sanctions against the press for publishing truthful information on matters of public concern. It would also raise a number of significant issues, including the propriety of the classification of the information at issue; the vagueness and breadth of the statute when applied the press; and the lack of the meaning of "harm" to our national security and the burden proving it.

Given the uncertainty surrounding the Espionage Act, special care should be taken before accepting or communicating information known to be classified, and legal guidance sought where appropriate. Because the act is not literally limited to "classified" information, special care should be taken with any non-public information concerning official intelligence activities or communications with foreign governments.

In order to avoid exposure for possible conspiracy and "aiding and abetting" liability or both, it is also important to maintain a traditional source-news organization relationship with those individuals who may provide you with national security information.

LEGAL PRINCIPLES OF PUBLICATION

When a news report is published, the nature of its content poses three principal legal risks to a journalist: that the report contains incorrect information that harms someone's reputation, contains correct information that invades someone's privacy, or contains material that is subject to someone else's copyright. This section provides an overview of the law of libel, privacy and copyright infringement, by examining what a plaintiff is required to prove against news organizations to succeed on such claims and the defenses that are available.

Defamation

In 1967, shortly after *New York Times v. Sullivan* was handed down, Associate Justice John Harlan remarked that "the law of libel has changed substantially since the early days of the Republic." Unfortunately, the news stories that still generate the most claims of injury to reputation – the basis of libel – are still the run-of-the-mill.

Perhaps 95 of 100 libel suits result from the routine publication of charges of crime, immorality, incompetence or inefficiency. A Harvard Nieman report makes the point: "The gee-whiz, slam-bang stories usually aren't the ones that generate libel, but the innocent-appearing, potentially treacherous minor yarns from police courts and traffic cases, from routine meetings and from business reports."

Most lawsuits based on relatively minor stories result from factual error or inexact language – for example, getting the plea wrong or inaccurately making it appear that all defendants in a case face identical charges. Libel even lurks in such innocent-appearing stories as birth notices and wedding announcements. Turner Catledge, former managing editor of The New York Times, noted in his autobiography, "My Life and the Times," that people sometimes would "call in the engagement of two people who hate each other, as a practical joke." The fact that some New York newspapers have had to defend suits for such announcements illustrates the care and concern required in every editorial department.

In publishing, no matter what level of constitutional protection, there is just no substitute for accuracy.

• *What is libel?*

Libel is one side of the coin called "defamation," slander being the flip side. At its most basic, defamation means injury to reputation. Libel is generally distinguished from slander, in that a libel is written, or otherwise printed, whereas a slander is spoken. While defamation published in a newspaper universally is regarded as libel, it is perhaps not so self-evident that, in many states, defamation broadcast by television or radio also is considered libel, rather than slander: Because broadcast defamation is often recorded on tape and carried to a wide audience, it is viewed as more dangerous to reputation than a fleeting, unrecorded conversation, and so is classed with printed defamation. In any case, the term defamation generally includes both libel and slander. Words, pictures, cartoons, photo captions and headlines can all give rise to a claim for defamation.

The various states define libel somewhat differently, but largely to the same effect. In Illinois, for example, libel is defined by the courts as "the publication of anything injurious to the good name or reputation of another, or which tends to bring him into disrepute." In New York, a libelous statement is one that tends to expose a person to hatred, contempt or aversion or to induce an evil or unsavory opinion of the person in the minds of a substantial number of people in the community.

In Texas, libel is defined by statute as anything that "tends to injure a living person's reputation and thereby expose the person to public hatred, contempt or ridicule, or financial injury or to impeach any person's honesty, integrity, virtue, or reputation or to publish the natural defects of anyone and thereby expose the person to public hatred, ridicule, or financial injury."

• Liability for republication: the 'conduit' fallacy

A common misconception is that one who directly quotes a statement containing libelous allegations is immune from suit so long as the quoted statement was actually made, accurately transcribed and clearly attributed to the original speaker. This is not so. In fact, the common law principle is just the opposite — a republisher of a libel is generally considered just as responsible for the libel as the original speaker. That you were simply an accurate conduit for the statement of another is no defense to a libel claim.

In many circumstances, therefore, a newspaper can be called to task for republishing a libelous statement made by someone quoted in a story. This rule can lead to harsh results and therefore exceptions exist. For example, reporting the fact that a plaintiff has filed a libel suit against a defendant could, in certain circumstances, lead to a claim against a newspaper for repeating the libel alleged in the complaint. In most states, a "fair report privilege" shields the publisher of an accurate and impartial report of the contents of legal papers filed in court to avoid this result.

Many states also recognize that newspapers under the pressure of daily deadlines often rely on the research of other reputable news organizations in republishing news items originally appearing elsewhere. In such cases, reliance on a reputable newspaper or news agency often is recognized as a defense to a libel claim. Of course, this so-called "wire service defense" may not be available if the republisher had or should have had substantial reason to question the accuracy or good faith of the original story.

The fair report privilege and the wire service defense are exceptions to the basic rule. When the press reports that X has leveled accusations against Y, the press may be held to account not only for the truth of the fact that the accusations were made, but also for the steps taken to verify the truth of the accusations. Therefore, when accusations are made against a person, it generally is prudent to investigate their truth as well as to obtain balancing comment with some relation to the original charges. Irrelevant countercharges can lead to problems with the person who made the first accusation.

In short, always bear in mind that a newspaper can be held responsible in defamation for republishing the libelous statement made by another, even when the quote is correct.

• The five things a successful libel plaintiff must prove

Although the terminology may differ from state to state, a libel plaintiff suing a reporter or a news organization will have to prove five things in order to prevail on a claim for defamation:

1. A defamatory statement was made.
2. The defamatory statement is a matter of fact, not opinion.
3. The defamatory statement is false.

4. The defamatory statement is about ("of and concerning") the plaintiff.

5. The defamatory statement was published with the requisite degree of "fault."

By developing an understanding of the legal elements of a claim for libel, reporters and editors can fashion guideposts that will assist them in practicing their craft in a way that avoids wrongfully injuring the reputation of the subjects of their stories – and thereby to reducing the legal risk to the publications for which they write.

1. A defamatory statement was made

It may seem self-evident that a libel claim cannot exist unless a defamatory statement was made, but subjects of news stories (and their lawyers) often bring claims for libel without being able to demonstrate that what was written about them is capable of conveying a defamatory meaning. Put differently, not every negative news report is defamatory.

Generally, statements accusing someone of being a criminal, an adulterer, insane or infected with a loathsome disease are considered automatically "capable of defamatory meaning," as are statements that injure someone's professional reputation (such as that they are corrupt or incompetent). However, to determine whether any particular statement is susceptible of defamatory meaning, reference must be made, first, to the definition of libel adopted in the relevant state, and second, to the full context in which the challenged statement appeared when it was published.

For example, a New York court found that a statement identifying an attorney as a "flashy entertainment lawyer" was not, without more, defamatory, although a statement that a lawyer was an "ambulance chaser" with an interest only in "slam dunk" cases would be. The reasoning is that the first statement would not necessarily damage a lawyer's reputation, while the latter would. Likewise, in New York, allegations of drunkenness, use of "political clout" to gain governmental benefit, membership in the "Mafia," communist affiliation or that someone has cancer may or may not be defamatory, depending on the circumstances of the case.

In Illinois, courts make determinations about defamatory meaning on a case-by-case basis, though in Illinois, most statements will not be considered defamatory unless they charge a person with commission of a crime, adultery/fornication, or incompetence or lack of integrity in their business or profession. Under this approach, the statement that plaintiff left his children home at night and lost his job because of drinking was held to be defamatory as an accusation of child neglect and inability to discharge the duties of his job due to alcoholism. Similarly, reporting that an alderman had disclosed confidential information was held to be defamatory as indicating that the official lacked the integrity to properly discharge the duties of his office.

In Texas, a statement may be false, abusive and unpleasant without being defamatory. For example, a Texas court held that describing someone as resembling a "hard boiled egg," referring to baldness and pudginess, was not defamatory. Likewise, describing a political candidate as a "radical," "backed and financed by big-shot labor bosses" was not considered defamatory in Texas. On the other hand, an insinuation that a person is connected with gambling and prostitution was found to be defamatory. The assertion that a person who had made an allegation against another of child molestation had fabricated and since recanted the allegation was defamatory when no recantation had, in fact, been made.

While each potentially defamatory statement must be assessed in its own context, particular caution is in order where the statement involves allegations of crime or similar wrongdoing, incompetence or unprofessionalism, or infidelity.

2. The defamatory statement is a matter of fact, not opinion

To be actionable as libel, a defamatory statement must be provably false (or carry a provably false implication). Stated differently, only factual statements that are capable of being proven true or false can form the basis of a libel claim. "Opinions" that don't include or imply provably false facts cannot be the basis of a libel claim. Similarly, epithets, satire, parody and hyperbole that are incapable of being proven true or false are protected forms of expression.

The Supreme Court, in *Gertz v. Robert Welch Inc.* (1974), recognized a constitutional dimension to the prohibition of libel claims based on opinion, stating that "there is no such thing as a false idea." In a later case, *Milkovich v. Lorain Journal Co.* (1990), the Supreme Court denied that there is a distinct constitutional "opinion privilege," but held that any claim for libel must be based on a statement of fact that is provably false, thus shielding purely subjective opinions from liability. Under this approach, a statement is not protected "opinion" merely because it contains qualifying language such as "I think" or "I believe," if what follows contains an assertion of fact that can be proven true or false (e.g., "I believe he murdered his wife.").

Some examples of actual cases can provide a better sense of the distinction between an actionable false fact and a protected opinion:

In Virginia, "pure expressions of opinion" cannot be the basis of a claim for defamation. Under this standard, the statement "I wouldn't trust him as far as I could throw him" and the caption "Director of Butt-Licking" were held to be nonactionable opinion. The Virginia Supreme Court has found words charging that an architect lacked experience and charged excessive fees, or accusing a charitable foundation with failing to spend a "reasonable portion" of its income on program services, also to be protected opinions rather than to be verifiable facts.

In New York, the test for distinguishing a fact from an opinion asks whether: (1) the statement has a precise core of meaning on which a consensus of understanding exists; (2) the statement is verifiable; (3) the textual context of the statement would cause an average reader to infer a factual meaning; and (4) the broader social context signals usage as either fact or opinion. The first two factors focus on the meaning of the words used, the latter two factors consider whether the content, tone and apparent purpose of the statement should signal to the reader that the statement reflects the author's opinion.

Under these principles, calling a doctor a "rotten apple," for example, is incapable of being proved true or false and is therefore protected as an expression of opinion. Similarly, a statement that someone lacked "talent, ambition, initiative" is a nonactionable expression of opinion, since there is no provable, common understanding of what quantum of talent or ambition constitutes a "lack." In one New York case, a letter to the editor published in a scientific journal submitted by the International Primate Protection League and which warned that a multinational corporation's plans for establishing facilities to conduct hepatitis research using chimpanzees could spread hepatitis to the rest of the chimpanzee population was, given its overall context, protected as opinion.

Even when a fact is implicit in an opinion, the common law often protects the statement from liability. In many states, a statement of opinion based on true facts that are themselves accurately set forth is not actionable. Where the facts underlying the opinion are reported inaccurately, however, and would adversely affect the conclusion drawn by the average reader concerning the opinion expressed, the publication may give rise to a claim for libel. For example, the statement, "I believe he murdered his wife because he was found with a bottle of the same kind of poison that killed her," likely would not be actionable even if the plaintiff could prove he did not murder his wife *if* it is true that he was found with a bottle of the same kind of poison that killed her. The true facts on which the (erroneous) opinion was based were disclosed to the readers. If there was no bottle of poison, however, the suggestion that he was a murderer would certainly be actionable. If an opinion suggests or appears to rely on an undisclosed fact, however, a libel claim may still be brought upon the unstated, implied facts if they are both false and defamatory.

The statement that a sports commentator was a "liar" without reference to specific facts, under this approach, was considered to be protected opinion. Taken in the total context of an article, the statement that the plaintiff was a "neo-Nazi" was protected as opinion. Likewise, a statement calling a plaintiff a "commie," suggesting that he does not understand the subject he teaches and that he is "not traveling with a full set of luggage," was also protected as opinion. Statements accusing doctors of being "cancer con-artists," of practicing "medical quackery," and of promoting "snake oil remedies," were also protected. A newspaper column and editorial characterizing a nudist pageant as "pornography" and as "immoral" were also protected.

A court in California held that three questions should be considered to distinguish opinion from fact: (1) does the statement use figurative or hyperbolic language that would negate the impression that the statement is serious? (2) does the general tenor of the statement negate the impression that the statement is serious? (3) can the statement be proved true or false?

Under this test, a commentator's statement that a product "didn't work" was not an opinion because, despite the humorous tenor of the comment, it did not use figurative or hyperbolic language, it could reasonably be understood as asserting an objective fact and the fact could be proven true or false. Likewise, a statement made in a newspaper interview that plaintiff was an "extortionist" was not protected as opinion.

The common thread to these variations is that opinions offered in a context presenting the facts on which they are based will generally not be actionable. On the other hand, opinions that imply the existence of undisclosed, defamatory facts (i.e., if you knew what I know) are more likely to be actionable. In addition, a statement that is capable of being proven true or false, regardless of whether it is expressed as an opinion, an exaggeration or hyperbole, may be actionable.

3. The defamatory statement is false

In almost all libel cases involving news organizations, the plaintiff has the burden of proving that the defamatory statement is false. (The states are divided on whether a purely private individual has to prove falsity when the defamatory statement does not involve a matter of public concern.) Nonetheless, as a practical matter, a libel defendant's best defense is often to prove that the statement is true. While this may sound like six-of-one-half-dozen-of-the-other, there is considerable significance to placing on the plaintiff the legal burden of proving falsity: Where a jury feels it cannot decide whether a statement is true or false because the evidence is mixed, it is required to rule against the plaintiff — ties go to the defendant.

In almost all states, the question is not whether the challenged statement is literally and absolutely true, in every jot and title, but whether the statement as published is "substantially true." That is, a court will consider whether the gist or sting of the defamatory statement is accurate, or whether the published statement would produce a different effect in the mind of a reader than would the absolutely true version.

For example, most courts will dismiss a libel claim brought by a person charged with second degree burglary, if a newspaper mistakenly reported that he had been charged with first-degree burglary: The gist of the story (that the man is an accused burglar) is true, and most readers would not form a better opinion of the man had they been correctly informed that it was only second degree burglary with which he had been charged. But, where a newspaper mistakenly reports that the accused burglar has been charged with murder (or that a person thus far only accused of murder has been convicted of it), a court might well conclude that the "sting" of the statement is not substantially accurate, and that readers would think less of the person based on the false statement than they would have had the published report been accurate.

4. The defamatory statement is about the plaintiff

Since the law of libel protects the reputation of an individual or a business entity, only the individual or entity whose reputation has been injured is entitled to complain. Thus, a libel plaintiff must prove that the defamatory statement was "of and concerning" the plaintiff. It often is obvious whether a statement is about a particular person (for example, because it gives his or her full name, place of residence and age). But even where no name is used, a libel claim may be brought if some readers would reasonably understand the statement to be about the plaintiff. For example, the statement referring to "the woman who cooks lunch at the diner," when there is only one woman who cooks at that diner, will be considered "of and concerning" the female cook.

In a recent Illinois case, a news report on the commencement of a murder trial referred to the defendant as "suburban car dealer John Doe." While "John Doe" was indeed on trial for murder, he was not a suburban car dealer. His brother, "Joe Doe," was a suburban car dealer, but was not on trial for murder. The court concluded that reasonable readers could have understood the report to be about Joe (despite the fact that Joe's name was never mentioned, while John's was correctly used), and that Joe therefore would have the opportunity to show the statement was understood to be "of and concerning" him.

A few words about "group libel." Where a statement impugns a group of persons, but no individual is specifically identified, no member of the group may sue for libel if the group is large. For example, the statement, in a large city, that "all cab drivers cheat their customers out of money," does not allow any cab driver to sue for libel as a result, no matter how many fares the plaintiff cab driver may have lost because of the published statement. But, beware of publishing the same statement in a newspaper in a town with only a handful of cab drivers, where a court might well conclude the readers would reasonably think the statement was specifically referring to each of the town's four cab drivers, despite the absence of their names in the statement. Some courts have questioned whether the First Amendment permits claims for group libel under any circumstances, because the Supreme Court has said that the requirement that the statement be "of and concerning" the plaintiff is constitutionally required.

Finally, a word about the dead: It is mostly correct that you cannot defame the dead. Again, because libel protects personal reputation, and one has no practical need for a good personal reputation in this world after one has departed it, most states do not permit a person's survivors to bring a claim for statements made after the person's death.

5. The defamatory statement was published with the requisite degree of fault

For almost 200 years, libel in this country was a tort of strict liability. It did not matter whether the defendant was at fault or had acted in some improper way. The mere fact that a libel was printed was sufficient to establish liability

New York Times v. Sullivan changed everything. In that case the Supreme Court first recognized the constitutional requirement that a public official must demonstrate not only that an error was made, but also a high degree of fault by the publisher in order to prevail on a libel claim. This additional burden was required under the First Amendment, the court said, in order to provide the "breathing room" for the exercise of free speech that is essential to public discussion by citizens on matters concerning their self-government.

The court considered the *Sullivan* case "against the background of a profound national commitment to the principle that debate on public issues should be uninhibited, robust and wide-open, and that it may well include vehement, caustic and sometimes unpleasantly sharp attacks on government and public officials."

The ruling in *Sullivan* with respect to libel claims by public officials was extended three years later to libel claims by public figures, in *The Associated Press v. Walker*. The court reversed a $500,000 libel judgment won by former Maj. Gen. Edwin A. Walker in a Texas state court against the AP, after it had reported that Walker "assumed command" of rioters at the University of Mississippi and "led a charge of students against federal marshals" when James H. Meredith was admitted to the university in September 1962. Walker alleged those statements to be false.

In ruling for the AP, the Supreme Court found: "Under any reasoning, Gen. Walker was a public man in whose public conduct society and the press had a legitimate and substantial interest." It therefore held that Walker, too, was required to prove fault by the publisher even though he was not a public official.

The rulings in *Sullivan* and *Walker* cases were landmark decisions for freedom of the press and speech. They established safeguards not previously defined, but they did not provide news organizations with absolute immunity against libel suits by officials who are criticized. Rather, they stand for the principle that, to encourage public debate on matters of public concern, when a newspaper publishes information about a public official and publishes it without actual malice, it should be spared a damage suit even if some of the information turns out to be wrong.

The *Walker* decision made an additional important distinction concerning the context in which an article is prepared. In a companion case consolidated before the Supreme Court, Wallace Butts, former athletic director of the University of Georgia, had obtained a libel verdict against Curtis Publishing Co. His suit was based on an article in the Saturday Evening Post accusing Butts of giving his football team's strategy secrets to an opposing coach prior to a game between the two schools.

The Supreme Court found that Butts was a public figure, but said there was a substantial difference between the two cases. Unlike the AP report on the actions of Walker, "the Butts story was in no sense 'hot news' and the editors of the magazine recognized the need for a thorough investigation of the serious charges. Elementary precautions were, nevertheless, ignored."

Chief Justice Earl Warren, in a concurring opinion, referred to "slipshod and sketchy investigatory techniques employed to check the veracity of the source" in the Butts case. He said the evidence disclosed "reckless disregard for the truth."

The differing outcomes against The Associated Press and the Saturday Evening Post should be noted carefully. Although both involved public figures who were required to establish "actual malice," the evidence required to make this showing differed in the context of a "hot news" report from investigative reporting.

By 1974, in *Gertz v. Robert Welch, Inc.*, the Supreme Court had extended the requirement that a libel plaintiff show some fault on the part of the defendant to include all defamation claims against news organizations, although not all types of plaintiffs must show the highest degree of fault. The level of "fault" that a plaintiff must prove will vary depending on who the plaintiff is.

• Fault required for public officials and public figures

If the plaintiff is a public official or public figure, the plaintiff must establish by clear and convincing evidence that the publication was made with "actual malice," an unfortunate choice of phrase by the Supreme Court for a concept that might better have been called "constitutional fault," since the standard has little to do with whether a reporter harbored spite or ill will against the plaintiff.

The court has explained that "actual malice" means publication with knowledge that a statement is false, or in reckless disregard for whether it is true or false. The concept of "knowing falsity" is easy to understand. "Reckless disregard" has required further elaboration by the courts, which have described it as publication of a statement "with a high degree of awareness of its probable falsity." Put differently, a reporter may act with reckless disregard for truth if he or she publishes despite holding serious doubts about the truth of the published statement.

The test for actual malice thus looks to the subjective state of mind of the reporter/publisher at the time of publication. It inquires into whether the reporter or publisher believed the statement was false or whether they proceeded to publish despite recognizing that there was a good chance that the statement was false. Because most reporters and publishers are not in the business of publishing news reports unless they have good grounds to believe them to be true, generally speaking, it is difficult for a plaintiff to show that a newspaper published a story with actual malice.

As one Illinois court phrased it, actual malice is shown only when a reporter's investigation "has revealed either insufficient information to support the allegations in good faith or information which creates substantial doubt as to the truth of published allegations."

Thus, as interpreted by most states, "actual malice" cannot be proven simply by showing that a reporter made mistakes (either by getting facts wrong or by failing to talk to one or more key sources), or that the reporter disliked the plaintiff, or that the newspaper frequently published items critical of the plaintiff. Rather, the test focuses on whether the reporter in fact disbelieved, or strongly doubted the truth of, the published statement. In some cases, plaintiffs may establish actual malice if they can show that a reporter willfully turned a blind eye to the truth and, if acting in good faith, would have known that the statement was false.

• Fault required for private individuals

Under the First Amendment, even private individuals must show some degree of fault before they can recover for a libel by a news organization in a report on a matter of public concern. States are free to set the standard of care that must be met in reporting on private individuals, so long as they require at least a showing of negligence.

Most states have decided to adopt the minimum standard and require a private libel plaintiff to show only that a reporter was negligent. That means the plaintiff must show that the reporter's conduct was less careful than one would expect of a reasonable journalist in similar circumstances. In Texas and California, for example, the question in a private figure libel case is whether the defendant should have known, through the exercise of reasonable care, that a statement was false.

The courts have looked at a number of factors to evaluate whether "negligence" exists. The considerations include:

—Did the reporter follow the standards of investigation and reporting ordinarily adhered to by responsible publishers? In many libel cases plaintiffs will use "expert" witnesses to testify about what are the "acceptable journalistic practices."

—Did the reporter follow his or her own normal procedures? Any time that you do something differently from what you usually do in reporting a story — particularly if the change involves exercising less care, rather than more care — you'd better have a good explanation for why that was done.

—Did the reporter have any reason to doubt the accuracy of a source, or any advance warning that the story might not be right? Was it possible to find out the truth? This — like many of the factors the courts consider — is a matter of common sense. If you have received information that just doesn't ring true to you, and it is something that is easily checked, check it out before you run with the story!

—How *much* did the reporter do to check out the facts? Did the reporter take steps to confirm the information received, or simply run with the story without checking it out?

—Who are your sources of information? Are they reliable, and objective — or known "flakes" or people with a clear ax to grind? Are they anonymous sources? How many independent sources do you have (and how do they know the information they are giving you)?

Some courts set different fault levels for private figures depending on whether the publication at issue involved a matter of "public concern" or of "private concern." New York, for example, has held that if the plaintiff is a private individual involved in a matter of legitimate public concern, the plaintiff must establish by a preponderance of the evidence that the publication was made in a "grossly irresponsible" manner without due regard for the standards of information gathering and dissemination ordinarily followed by responsible parties involving similar matters. In cases involving matters of private concern, New York, too, applies a negligence standard, although New York courts typically defer to the press in determining what constitutes a matter of "public concern" (and thus the vast majority of New York private figure cases apply the "gross irresponsibility" standard).

Finally, a handful of states apply the actual malice standard to all libel cases, regardless of the plaintiff's status. These states include Alaska, Colorado, Indiana and New Jersey.

• Who is who?

Needless to say, being able to determine whether the subject of a news story is a public official or figure or a private figure bears directly on the amount of legal risk posed by the story.

While it is clear that not every government employee will be considered a public official for purposes of what they must prove in a libel case, the Supreme Court has yet to lay down definitive standards. Thus, the definition varies somewhat from state to state.

In New York, public officials are those who are elected or appointed to office and who appear to have substantial responsibility for control over public and governmental affairs. Judges, police officers, state troopers and corrections officers have all been held to be public officials under this standard. Similarly, in California, a public official is one who has, or appears to the public to have, substantial responsibility for or control over the conduct of governmental affairs. In California, people found to be public officers have included a police officer, an assistant public defender and an assistant district attorney.

Texas, in contrast, looks to the following criteria are relevant to determine whether a libel plaintiff is a public official: (1) the public interest in the public position held by the plaintiff; (2) the authority possessed by the plaintiff to act on behalf of a government entity; (3) the amount of governmental funds controlled by the plaintiff; (4) the number of employees the official supervises; (5) the amount of contact between the plaintiff and the public, and (6) the extent to which the plaintiff acts in a representative capacity for the governmental entity or has any direct dealings with the government.

Under this standard, (1) a county sheriff; (2) a Child Protective Services specialist with authority to investigate charges of child abuse, remove children from their homes and place them in foster care; (3) an undercover narcotics agent employed by the state's law enforcement agency; (4) a ranking officer in charge of a narcotics squad of four men; (5) an individual who was a high school athletic director, head football coach and teacher; (6) an assistant regional administrator of a branch office of the Securities and Exchange Commission, and (7) a part-time city attorney have all been found to be public officials.

But under the same Texas test, the following people were found not to be public officials: (1) a high school teacher; (2) a prominent member of two private organizations affiliated with a state university; (3) a former special counsel for a court of inquiry into county fund management; (4) a court reporter, and (5) an appointed justice of the peace (where the article appeared in a city where plaintiff was not justice of the peace and did not refer to plaintiff's official capacity).

While, at least at higher ranks, it is relatively easy to identify public officials, both reporters and the courts have confronted substantial difficulty in the area of public figures, particularly in separating those who are merely socially or professionally prominent from those who, because of their influence over public matters, are properly considered public figures for libel purposes.

For example, the 1976 case of *Time v. Firestone* stemmed from Time magazine's account of the divorce of Russell and Mary Alice Firestone. The magazine said she had been divorced on grounds of "extreme cruelty and adultery." The court made no finding of adultery. She sued. The former Mrs. Firestone was a prominent social figure in Palm Beach, Florida, and held press conferences in the course of the divorce proceedings. Yet, the Supreme Court said she was not a public figure because "she did not assume any role of special prominence in the affairs of society, other than perhaps Palm Beach society, and she did not thrust herself to the forefront of any particular public controversy in order to influence resolution of the issues involved in it."

Similarly, Sen. William Proxmire of Wisconsin was sued for $8 million by Ronald Hutchinson, a research scientist who had received several public grants, including one for $50,000. Proxmire gave Hutchinson a "Golden Fleece" award, saying Hutchinson "has made a fortune from his monkeys and in the process made a monkey of the American taxpayer." Hutchinson sued. The Supreme Court held in 1979 that, despite the receipt of substantial public funds, Hutchinson was not a public figure because he held no particular sway over the resolution of matters of public concern.

Note also the case of Ilya Wolston, who pleaded guilty in 1957 to criminal contempt for failing to appear before a grand jury investigating espionage. A book published in 1974 referred to these events. Wolston alleged that he had been libeled. In ruling on *Wolston v. Reader's Digest*, the Supreme Court said that he was not a public figure. The court said people convicted of crimes do not automatically become public figures. Wolston, the court said, was thrust into the public spotlight unwillingly, long after the events of public concern had ended. (But, the Supreme Court also has said, in a different context, that allegations of criminal activity by public officials, no matter how far in the past the conduct may have occurred, is always relevant to their fitness for public office.)

At bottom, although the Supreme Court has yet to definitively resolve the issue, the point appears to be that public figures are those who seek the limelight, who inject themselves into public debate, and who seek to influence public opinion. A person who has widespread influence over public opinion on many matters may be deemed a "general purpose public figure" and required to prove actual malice no matter the subject of a particular allegedly defamatory statement. Oprah Winfrey is an example of someone who likely would be deemed a general purpose public figure.

A person who seeks to influence public opinion in only one area (such as, for example, by leading a campaign to enact animal rights legislation), however, may be deemed a "limited purpose public figure" and required to prove actual malice only with respect to allegedly defamatory statements about his or her animal rights activities. Limited purpose public figures have included: a prominent attorney; religious groups; a belly dancer; and a "stripper for God," among others.

Texas courts generally ask three questions in order to determine whether someone is a limited purpose public figure: (1) is the controversy truly a public controversy? (i.e., (a) are people talking about the controversy and (b) are people other than those immediately involved in the controversy likely to feel the impact of its resolution?); (2) does the plaintiff have more than a trivial or tangential role in the controversy?; (3) is the alleged defamation relevant to the plaintiff's participation in the controversy? Under this standard, an abortion protester on a public street in the vicinity of an abortion clinic was considered a limited purpose public figure, as was a zoologist who appeared on television shows and gave interviews on his controversial work.

On the other hand, a public school teacher whose participation in public controversy did not exceed that which she was required to do by school district regulations (except that she responded to media inquiries), was not a public figure in California. Similarly, a corporation which conducted a closeout sale for a landmark department store was not a public figure simply because it was doing business with a party to a controversy.

A note on corporations: In many states, the same standards that determine whether an individual is a public figure apply to corporations. Some states, however, conclude that corporations are always public figures, while others apply a narrower standard. For example, a British corporation that did not deal in consumer goods and had not received significant past publicity was a private figure for the purposes of a Texas libel claim.

In addition, a few lower courts have embraced the concept of an "involuntary public figure," in which an otherwise private person becomes a public figure by virtue of his or her having become drawn into a significant public controversy.

While this area of the law is freighted with subtleties to which lawyers and judges devote considerable energy, the practical bottom line is that, while public officials and public figures always bear a high burden of proof in making out a libel claim, where a news story concerns a private individual, whether involved in a matter of public concern or not, his or her burden is likely to be lower, perhaps much lower, if the story is wrong. Accordingly, there are more legal risks to publishing reports about private individuals (especially where the matter is not of legitimate public concern).

• Defenses commonly available to news organizations

Where a news story is written in such a way that a plaintiff might be able to prove all five of the elements of a libel, the law nevertheless affords defenses to news organizations in certain circumstances. Among the most prominent are the "fair comment privilege," the "fair and accurate report privilege," and the "neutral report privilege." They are referred to as privileges because, where properly invoked, a news organization is "privileged" to print what otherwise would be an actionable libel.

1. Fair comment

The fair comment (sometimes, "fair criticism") privilege long predates the opinion doctrine and continues, in most states, to exist as an independent matter of state law. The right of fair comment has been summarized as follows: "Everyone has a right to comment on matters of public interest and concern, provided they do so fairly and with an honest purpose. Such comments or criticism are not libelous, however severe in their terms, unless they are written maliciously. Thus it has been held that books, prints, pictures and statuary publicly exhibited, and the architecture of public buildings, and actors and exhibitors are all the legitimate subjects of newspapers' criticism, and such criticism fairly and honestly made is not libelous, however strong the terms of censure may be." (*Hoeppner v. Dunkirk Pr. Co.*, 1930.)

Some states, such as Texas, have recognized the fair comment privilege as a matter of statutory law. The Texas statute protects reasonable and fair comment or criticism of the official acts of public officials and of other matters of public concern when published for general information.

Not all states recognize this privilege, and the specifics of its application vary among the states that do recognize it. But where an otherwise potentially libelous story is important to the public interest, careful consideration of whether this privilege might protect publication of the report may be appropriate.

2. Fair and accurate report

Under this privilege, a fair and accurate report of a public proceeding (such as a city council hearing) or document (such as a pleading filed in court) generally cannot be the basis of a libel suit.

Pursuant to the Texas fair report statute, for example, the privilege applies to "a fair, true and impartial account" of: (a) judicial proceedings; (b) an official proceeding to administer the law; (c) all executive and legislative proceedings; and (d) the proceedings of public meetings dealing with public purposes. New York and several other states likewise have created the privilege by statute along similar lines; in some states, the privilege is a product of judge-made law.

In order to qualify for the privilege in the states that recognize it, the account must be both substantially accurate and fair. This does not mean the newspaper is required to publish a verbatim account of an official proceeding or the full text of a government document, but any abridgement or synopsis must be substantially accurate and fairly portrayed. Where it applies, the privilege relieves a news organization of responsibility for determining the underlying truth of the statements made by the participants in these contexts, precisely because the very fact that the comments were made in an official proceeding is newsworthy regardless of whether the statements are actually true.

It bears emphasis, however, this privilege is limited to statements made in the contexts defined under state law, and it behooves practitioners to learn the particulars of the privilege in the states in which they practice journalism.

Statements made by government officials outside of official proceedings (e.g., statements by police or a prosecutor or an attorney on the courthouse steps), or in documents that have not been officially made part of the government record (e.g., a draft pleading provided by a lawyer that has not yet been filed with the court) may or may not qualify as privileged, depending on what state you are in and on the circumstances in which the statements are made. Some states only extend the privilege to such out of court statements if made by specified top officials. At least one New York trial court, however, has applied this fair report privilege to a news report based on information provided "off the record" by police sources.

In New York and some other states, court rules provide that the papers filed in matrimonial actions are sealed and thus not open to inspection by the general public. It is not clear whether the fair report privilege will attach to publication of the contents of such papers, which by court rule, or order of the judge, are to be kept confidential.

In one case where this very situation arose, the vice president of a company filed a libel suit in New York alleging that he was fired because a newspaper published his wife's charges of infidelity set forth in divorce proceedings. The newspaper responded that its report was a true and fair account of court proceedings. The New York Court of Appeals rejected that argument on grounds that the law makes details of marital cases secret because spatting spouses frequently make unfounded charges.

The lesson of this case is that information gleaned from "confidential" court documents might not be covered under the fair report privilege. In such a case, the paper will be put to the test of proving that it made a reasonable effort to determine the truth of the allegations before publishing them.

There are other "traps" to be aware of when relying on this privilege. For example, statements made on the floor of convention sessions or from speakers' platforms organized by private organizations may not be privileged under the fair report privilege. Strictly speaking, conventions of private organizations are not "public and official proceedings" even though they may be forums for discussions of public questions.

Similarly, while statements made by a governor in the course of executive proceedings have absolute privilege for the speaker (even if false or defamatory), the press' privilege to report all such statements is not always absolute. For example, after a civil rights march, George Wallace, then governor of Alabama, appeared on a television show and said some of the marchers were members of communist and communist-front organizations. He gave some names, which newspapers carried. Some libel suits resulted.

3. Neutral reportage

Once viewed as a promising development in the law likely to spread across most states, the advancement of the neutral report privilege has not proceeded as once anticipated. Many states have declined to consider whether the privilege should exist, while others have rejected it outright (most recently, in Pennsylvania in 2005). Where recognized, the neutral report privilege protects a fair, true and impartial account of newsworthy statements, regardless of whether the reporter knows or believes those statements to be true, if the statements have been made by prominent and typically responsible persons or organizations. The rationale is that some statements are newsworthy, and should receive public attention just because of who has made them.

Thus, for example, a news report concerning a statement by Michael Jordan concerning corruption in basketball, or by the NAACP regarding discrimination committed by a business, likely would be privileged as a neutral report, even if it should later turn out that Jordan or the NAACP were mistaken, since the mere leveling of charges by such prominent sources typically is of public concern.

Significantly, the privilege, where it exists, does not apply when the author of an article goes beyond reporting the fact the statements made and espouses or adopts the charges as the author's own.

California is one of the few states to recognize the neutral report privilege. There, the privilege is available when the plaintiff is a public figure, the defamatory statement is made by one who is a party to a public controversy and the publication is accurate and neutral. One California court applying the privilege found that a newspaper's account of an accusation that a police officer had improperly obtained a false confession to a crime from a person later released as innocent was not actionable where the newspaper also printed the officer's denial of the charge.

In some states, courts appear to have applied the principle without naming the privilege as such. In one 1997 case in Texas, the court held that a story that accurately reported that parents of school children had accused a school teacher of physically threatening and verbally abusing their children was substantially true regardless of whether the parents' allegations themselves were accurate. Similarly, in Illinois, a federal appeals court in 2004 held that several stories that accurately reported that a charitable organization was the target of a federal investigation into terrorism funding were not actionable because the fact that the organization was under investigation was true, regardless of whether it was actually guilty of funding terrorism.

New York state courts do not recognize a privilege for neutral reportage, though a federal court in New York has actually found a neutral reportage privilege grounded in the U.S. Constitution. As the federal court described the neutral report privilege in that case, "when a responsible, prominent organization ... makes serious charges against a public figure, the First Amendment protects the accurate and disinterested reporting of those charges, regardless of the reporter's private views regarding their validity." (*Edwards v. National Audubon Society*, 1977.)

• Summary of practical points

Although every AP story is expected to be accurate and fair, stories that involve negative reports about individuals or companies warrant particular attention. When evaluating such a story, it usually is prudent to ask these questions:

1. Are any statements in the story capable of defamatory meaning? In this regard pay close attention to the use of certain "red flag" words that may sound more negative (and thereby more defamatory) than if a different, but similar, word had been chosen. Words such as "fraud," "crony," "linked," "suspicious" and "contaminated" may suggest or imply bad conduct or have criminal connotations (like: "connected" to the Mafia or organized crime). Careful editing can ensure that the facts get reported without the use of "buzz words" that may trigger a libel claim.

—Remember that the fact that police are questioning someone about a crime does not necessarily justify the label suspect. Witnesses are obviously also questioned about a crime.

2. Are those statements ones of fact (capable of being proven true or false), or protected as opinion, or simply rhetorical hyperbole that no reasonable reader would understand as a statement of fact?

3. Could someone reading the report reasonably understand it to be about a specific person, whether or not the person is actually named? Could readers understand it to be about more than one person – the person we intend, but also someone else?

—Remember to be careful of descriptive phrases that may give rise to cases of mistaken identity. A report that "an elderly janitor for a local school" was arrested could lead to suits from every elderly janitor in the school district.

4. Could you prove that the statements in question are true (and do so without violating promises to any confidential sources)?

5. If it turns out that you have the facts wrong, would a jury think you did not do something that any reasonable journalist would have done to get it right?

6. Assuming there is some possibility that the first five questions could be answered in the plaintiff's favor, is there a privilege that nevertheless justifies proceeding to publish? For example, is the report a fair and accurate report of an official government proceeding or document?

—If a privilege applies, remember that the privilege does not remove the need for careful reporting and the use of editorial judgment. In many cases, courts have held that it is up to the jury to decide whether a particular publication was a fair and accurate report or whether there was "actual malice."

Headlines, photos and captions must be as accurate and objective as news stories. Remember that each of these elements of a story can also give rise to claims of libel.

• Corrections and retraction demands

A correction acknowledges an error in a story and sets the record straight. Published studies have shown that lawsuits against the press can sometimes be avoided if requests for corrections or clarifications are dealt with seriously, promptly and fairly. Anyone making a retraction demand should be dealt with courteously, and the request should be communicated promptly to the appropriate editor.

Do not be too hasty in drafting a correction, however. It is important to ensure that the correction is actually warranted, that it corrects all aspects of the story that may need correction, and that the correction itself is accurate. Some states have "retraction statutes" that limit the damages a plaintiff can recover or provide other benefits if an error is corrected when brought to the attention of the publisher. You should be aware of any legal requirement in your state setting a time within which a correction must appear.

Transmitting a corrective does not necessarily safeguard the AP against legal action. In fact, transmission of a corrective may itself have legal consequences because it formally acknowledges an error. Because of potential legal implications, a news manager or supervisor at a regional hub or vertical needs to approve all correctives and clarifications, before they are transmitted. Consult with the Standards Center in New York, or the News Center manager in off hours, if the issue involves libel, defamation or other legal issue, or a complicated member issue.

Any time that a kill or corrective is filed, it is crucial to ensure that it is transmitted on all wires that transmitted that original report. In addition, the bureau chief or news editor must prepare and maintain a file containing:

1. Wire copy of the original story and of the kill or corrective that was sent.

2. Wire copy of the substitute story, corrective or clarification filed.

3. A copy of any source material used by the writer or editor in preparation of the story, including member clip, reporter's notes and the like.

In addition, the bureau chief or the news editor, in consultation with the staff members involved, should prepare a statement on the circumstances. If legal action is a possibility, this explanation should not be prepared without prior consultation with the Standards Center or a senior news manager.

The statement should include relevant details, such as any contact with outsiders on the matter. The letter should be a factual report of what happened. It is not the place for extraneous comments about staff members or bureau procedures. Nor is it the place for apologies, nor any legal or factual speculation or conclusions.

Do not make any response to any letter or other communication in connection with any case where legal action seems possible, especially if a lawyer is involved, without first seeking advice from AP's lawyers in New York.

• Document preservation and discovery

A 1979 Supreme Court ruling, *Herbert v. Lando*, has had a significant impact on what materials a libel plaintiff can compel a news organization to disclose. The case ruled that retired Army Lt. Col. Anthony Herbert, a Vietnam veteran, had the right to inquire into the editing process of a CBS "60 Minutes" segment, produced by Barry Lando, which provoked his suit. Herbert had claimed the right to do this so that he could establish actual malice.

The decision formalized and called attention to something that was at least implicit in *New York Times v. Sullivan*: that a plaintiff had the right to try to prove the press was reckless or even knew that what it was printing was a lie. How else could this be done except through inquiry about a reporter's or editor's state of mind?

Despite an admonition in *Herbert v. Lando* that lower courts should carefully monitor (and, if necessary, reign in) discovery in libel cases, reporters and publications involved in libel suits are often forced to expend significant time and resources on discovery concerning their newsgathering, writing and editing activities.

Different reporters follow different practices about retaining their notes. There are potential litigation advantages and disadvantages from following a policy of either keeping notes for a number of years or disposing of notes as soon as they are no longer needed for reporting. The best practice is the one that best advances a reporter's journalistic goals. Whatever practice you follow, however, should be followed uniformly. A difficult issue is presented in litigation if a reporter generally keeps notes, but just doesn't happen to have the notes for a disputed story. Similarly, a reporter who never keeps notes, but happens to save them for a story that ends in litigation, can send a message that the story posed some unique concerns. Adopt a policy and follow it consistently.

Of course, once a lawsuit arrives, no documents should be destroyed, regardless of your usual practice. At that point any notes and drafts are potential evidence and their destruction, with knowledge of the lawsuit, may be illegal.

• Motions practice

If litigation arises, lawyers for a reporter will often seek to dispose of the claims without the necessity of a trial. A number of issues, such as whether a story is "of and concerning" the plaintiff or conveys the defamatory meaning alleged, can often be decided by a judge as a matter of law before any litigation discovery begins.

Courts also can impose "summary judgment" dismissing a case at any point when the evidence developed by the parties demonstrates that the plaintiff's claims are legally defective. A judge may not enter summary judgment if it rests on any facts in dispute. Only the jury may decide disputed issues of fact.

In a 1986 decision, *Anderson v. Liberty Lobby*, the Supreme Court held that summary judgment should be granted in libel actions against public officials and public figures unless the plaintiff can prove actual malice with "convincing clarity" or by "clear and convincing evidence." This rule further facilitates the dismissal of unmeritorious claims without the expense and burden of proceeding to trial.

• Trials and damages

The huge jury verdicts that often result in libel cases have caused much concern among legal commentators and the press. A number of remedies have been proposed, including statutory caps on both compensatory and punitive damages. A 1996 non-press Supreme Court case, holding that some excessive damage verdicts might violate the Constitution, holds out some possible promise of relief.

The Supreme Court addressed libel damages in *Gertz v. Robert Welch, Inc.* (1974), and held that in private figure cases, where "actual malice" has not been proven, any award of damages must be supported by competent evidence, represent compensation only for actual damages, must not be "presumed," and must not be punitive. "Actual damages," however, may include compensation for injury to reputation and standing in the community, personal humiliation, and mental anguish and suffering -- all items to which a jury assigns a dollar value. In cases where a plaintiff has proved "actual malice," he or she may also recover "presumed" and "punitive" damages.

While the First Amendment imposes severe restrictions on libel claims, and court rules encourage the dismissal of meritless cases at the earliest point, litigation can be a long, expensive, and disruptive process. The key to avoiding the distraction of litigation is always to remember AP's credo: Get it fast, but get it right.

• Invasion of privacy

The roots of the right of privacy are often traced to an article titled "The Right to Privacy" that appeared in the Harvard Law Review in 1890, and was co-authored by Louis D. Brandeis, who later became a Supreme Court justice. The article asserted that the press of the day was "overstepping in every direction the obvious bounds of propriety and decency," and urged courts to recognize a distinct cause of action that would protect the individual's "right of privacy." As a Supreme Court justice, Brandeis later wrote:

"The makers of our Constitution recognized the significance of man's spiritual nature, of his feelings and of his intellect. They knew that only a part of the pain, pleasure and satisfactions of life are to be found in material things. They sought to protect Americans in their beliefs, their thoughts, their emotions and their sensations. They conferred, as against the government, the right to be let alone — the most comprehensive of rights and the right most valued by civilized men." (*Olmstead v. United States*, Brandeis, J. dissenting.)

Over the following decades, legal commentators have vigorously debated the scope and nature of a cause of action for privacy, and identified four distinct forms of the "right of privacy:" (1) misappropriation of someone's name or likeness for a commercial purpose; (2) public disclosure of private facts; (3) unreasonable intrusion upon seclusion, and (4) false light in the public eye. In recent times, these causes of action have taken on significance to the press as plaintiffs have attempted to avoid the heavy burdens of proof placed on the libel plaintiff by alleging an invasion of a form of the right of privacy, instead.

The four distinct "branches" of the privacy tort each seek to protect a different aspect on individual's privacy. The "intrusion" tort primarily seeks to protect against physical intrusions into a person's solitude or private affairs. The tort does not require publications of information for recovery, and it is discussed previously as a newsgathering tort. The other three branches of privacy all require publication of some information in order for the plaintiff to have a claim.

States vary widely both in terms of their acceptance of any of these right to privacy claims and in terms of the rules governing any such claims. Of the four forms of the "privacy" cause of action, New York only recognizes the claim for misappropriation of name or likeness for commercial purposes. Texas recognizes claims for intrusion upon seclusion, public disclosure of private facts and misappropriation of name or likeness for commercial purposes. The California state constitution expressly incorporates a right of privacy and California courts recognize all four forms of the right of privacy cause of action. Illinois courts also recognize all four privacy torts, except there is some disagreement among them regarding whether to recognize the tort of intrusion upon seclusion, with some districts recognizing the cause of action, and others rejecting it.

The right of privacy creates liability for the publication of facts that are true, and thus raises particular concerns under the First Amendment. In a number of contexts the Supreme Court has struck down rulings imposing liability for reporting information that was both true and newsworthy, but it has consistently declined to hold that the First Amendment always bars such liability altogether.

It can generally be said that when people become involved in a news event, voluntarily or involuntarily, they forfeit aspects of the right to privacy. A person somehow involved in a matter of legitimate public interest, even if not a bona fide spot news event, normally can be written about with safety. However, the same cannot be said about a story or picture that dredges up the sordid details of a person's past and has no current newsworthiness.

Paul P. Ashley, then president of the Washington State Bar Association, summarized the privacy concern for reporters at a meeting of the Associated Press Managing Editors association:

"The essence of the wrong will be found in crudity, in ruthless exploitation of the woes or other personal affairs of private individuals who have done nothing noteworthy and have not by design or misadventure been involved in an event which tosses them into an arena subject to public gaze."

• Publication of private facts

When most people speak of an "invasion of privacy," they have in mind the public disclosure of highly embarrassing private facts. In those states where such a claim is recognized, the elements of a cause of action generally include: (1) "publicity" given to private information, (2) that a reasonable person would find highly offensive, and (3) which is not of any legitimate public interest.

In some states the lack of "legitimate public interest" or lack of "newsworthiness" is an element of the tort, meaning it is a plaintiff's burden to prove. In others, this element is an affirmative defense and the defendant must show how the information was indeed a matter of legitimate public concern. In all cases, newsworthiness is a complete defense to the tort. The First Amendment bars a claim for the true and accurate disclosure of a private fact so long as the information is newsworthy.

The first element of the tort requires "publicity" given to private information. This requires some element of widespread disclosure to the general public, not simply a communication to a single person or small group of people. Conversely, facts that are already known to the general public can not be the basis of a public disclosure claim, while facts known only to a small group can be.

For example, a California court allowed a privacy claim to be based upon the publication of a photograph of a Little League team in a national magazine to illustrate a story about the team's coach who had sexually abused some of the athletes. Although the photograph had been given to all the members of the team, the identities of the minors shown in the photograph were not known to a broader national audience. The court said their identities could therefore be considered "private" in the context of the story about sex abuse. Some courts have similarly ruled that a person who is recognizable in a picture of a crowd in a public place is not entitled to the right of privacy, but if the camera singled him out for no news-connected reason, then his privacy might be invaded.

The second element of the tort requires that the disclosure be "highly offensive" to a reasonable person. This factor goes to the embarrassing nature of the information itself. Reporting someone's age, for example, would not be highly offensive to a reasonable person, even if that information were not widely known. Reporting, over their objection, that someone was a victim of sexual abuse or suffered from an incurable disease might be.

Finally, no claim will lie if the information is newsworthy, or of legitimate public concern. Courts generally will defer to reporters and editors to determine what is "newsworthy," but the line is not always clear. Even in the context of a report on a plainly newsworthy topic, the disclosure of a highly embarrassing private fact may give rise to a claim for invasion of privacy if the facts are not logically related to the matter of public concern. For example, disclosure of the intimate sexual practices of a celebrity might support a claim for invasion of privacy if it were unrelated to any newsworthy report and amounted to prying into someone's life for its own sake.

Some examples can help to demonstrate the nature of this branch of the privacy tort:

—In a case against a Chicago newspaper, an Illinois trial court held that a mother had stated a cause of action for invasion of privacy where she alleged that she told the newspaper reporter that she did not want to make any public statement about her son's death and where the reporter nevertheless remained in the private hospital room with the mother, recorded her grief-stricken last words to her son and subsequently published a picture of the son's dead body and the mother's "last words" to her son.

—The unsavory incidents of the past of a former prostitute, who had been tried for murder, acquitted, married and lived a respectable life, were featured in a motion picture. She sued for invasion of privacy by public disclosure of private facts. The court ruled that the use of her name in the picture and the statement in advertisements that the story was taken from true incidents in her life violated her right to pursue and obtain happiness.

—Another example of spot news interest: A child was injured in an auto accident in Alabama. A newspaper took a picture of the scene before the child was removed and ran it. That was spot news. Twenty months later a magazine used the picture to illustrate an article. The magazine was sued for public disclosure of private facts and lost the case, the court ruling that 20 months after the accident the child was no longer "in the news."

—In another case, a newspaper photographer in search of a picture to illustrate a hot weather story took a picture of a woman sitting on her front porch. She wore a house dress, her hair in curlers, her feet in thong sandals. The picture was taken from a car parked across the street from the woman's home. She sued, charging invasion of privacy by intrusion upon seclusion and public disclosure of private facts. A court, denying the newspaper's motion for dismissal of the suit, said the scene photographed "was not a particularly newsworthy incident," and the limits of decency were exceeded by "surreptitious" taking and publishing of pictures "in an embarrassing pose."

• False light invasion of privacy

A claim for false light basically complains about publicity that places the plaintiff in a false light in the public eye. In those states that recognize this tort, the publicity must be of a kind that would be highly offensive to a reasonable person, and the defendant generally must have acted with the same level of fault that would be required if the plaintiff had filed a libel claim.

One form in which a claim for false light occasionally arises occurs where an opinion or utterance is falsely attributed to the plaintiff. In another version of the claim, the plaintiff's picture is used to illustrate an article to which he has no reasonable connection, as where the picture of an honest taxi driver is used to illustrate an article about the cheating propensities of cab drivers.

The Supreme Court of the United States ruled in 1967 that the constitutional guarantees of freedom of the press are applicable to claims for invasion-of-privacy by false light involving reports of newsworthy matters. *Time, Inc. v. Hill* (1967). The ruling arose out of a reversal by the Supreme Court of a decision of a New York court that an article with photos in Life magazine reviewing a play, "The Desperate Hours," violated the privacy of a couple who had been held hostage in a real-life incident. In illustrating the article, Life posed the actors in the house where the real family had been held captive.

The family alleged violation of privacy by false light in the public eye, saying the article gave readers the false impression that the play was a true account of their experiences. Life said the article was "basically truthful."

The court said:

"We create grave risk of serious impairment of the indispensable service of a free press in a free society if we saddle the press with the impossible burden of verifying to a certainty the facts associated in a news article with a person's name, picture or portrait, particularly as related to non-defamatory matter."

The court added, however, that these constitutional guarantees do not extend to "knowing or reckless falsehood." A newspaper still may be liable for invasion of privacy if the facts of a story are changed deliberately or recklessly, or "fictionalized." As with The New York Times and The Associated Press decisions in the field of libel, "The Desperate Hours" case does not confer a license for defamatory statements or for reckless disregard of the truth.

An Illinois court allowed a "false light" claim to proceed where a news report allegedly broadcast the plaintiff's comments (which were covertly recorded) out of context. More recently, federal appeals court concluded that Gennifer Flowers could maintain a false light claim against James Carville for publishing facts suggesting she had lied about the nature of her relationship with President Clinton. The court said the false light claim could compensate for emotional injury that would not be covered by a claim for defamation.

• Misappropriation

The final form of invasion of privacy recognized by the courts is misappropriation of the name or likeness of a living person for purposes of trade or advertising without that person's consent. In recent years, some states have included voice as well as name or likeness. This tort is intended to allow people to control the commercial use and exploitation of their own identities. The First Amendment provides for at least some exceptions to such a right — as where a candidate for public office includes his opponent's name and likeness in campaign advertisements.

The misappropriation tort is not generally a concern to reporters because it applies to the *commercial* exploitation of a person's name and likeness. It does not bar editorial uses and provides no remedy when a person's name or image (questions of copyright aside) is used in a news report. This branch of privacy is of little concern outside of the advertising department of a news organization.

• Publishing on the Internet and Social Media

Content published on the Internet in blogs, chat rooms, discussion groups, social media sites and the like is generally subject to the same rules and standards for libel, privacy and other legal actions as any print publication.

AP has adopted Social Media Guidelines that are intended to be followed by its employees. Those Guidelines require, among other things, that AP employees always "identify themselves as being from the AP if they are using [social networking site] accounts for work in any way." And, "if you or your department covers a subject . . . you have a special obligation to be even-handed in your tweets." The Guidelines also restrict AP employees from "declaring their views on contentious public issues in any public forum and must not take part in demonstrations in support of causes or movements. This includes 'liking' and 'following' pages and groups that are associated with these causes or movements." This means that AP employees should not "friend" or "like" political candidates or causes without a journalistic reason for doing so. (To keep track of tweets by newsmakers, a Twitter list will allow you to receive postings without joining the person's official list of followers. Reporters covering a specific politician may also "friend" the politician if essential to their reporting duties.) AP employees are also cautioned to avoid retweeting in a way that makes it look like they are expressing a personal opinion on the issues of the day. "A retweet with no comment can easily be seen as sign of approval of what you're relaying."

Because of the difficulty in verifying the authenticity of material posted on social media sites, it is important not simply to lift quotes, photos or video from social networking sites and attribute them to the domain or feed where the information was found. Before photos, videos or other online content is used, it is important to both verify its authenticity and ensure that any necessary rights for the reuse are obtained. (See discussion of Copyright, below].

• *Material Posted To Your Site(s) by Others*

Monitor any site you operate and remove material that violates the terms of use or is inconsistent with your journalistic standards. The AP's Social Media Guidelines encourage AP staffers to engage in dialogue with those who benefit from or critique AP content: "Any substantive criticism of our content should be taken seriously, however it may be phrased."

Postings to AP's, or your personal websites, Twitter accounts, Facebook wall, or other online platform by third parties who do so anonymously or using a pseudonym could result in legal actions seeking to identify the source of those comments. Courts have offered protection to some anonymous posters, and have generally required a showing of legitimate need before ordering disclosure of an anonymous poster's identity. If you receive such a subpoena or other legal document seeking information to identify the source of an anonymous or pseudonymous posting, please follow the policies and practices for handling subpoenas discussed above.

Copyright infringement

Copyright is the right of an author to control the reproduction and use of any creative expression that has been fixed in tangible form, such as on paper or computer disk. The right of Congress to pass laws protecting copyright is itself protected in the Constitution, and the First Amendment is therefore no defense to a valid claim for copyright infringement under the Copyright Act.

The types of creative expression eligible for copyright protection include literary, graphic, photographic, audiovisual, electronic and musical works. In this context, "tangible forms" range from film to videotape to material posted on the Internet. Personal letters or diaries may be protected by copyright even though they may not have been published and may not contain a copyright notice. Probably of greatest concern to reporters and editors are the copyrights in photographs used to illustrate a news report.

A copyright comes into existence the moment an original work of expression is captured in a tangible form. No government approval or filing is required for a work to be protected by copyright. Upon creation of the work, ownership of the copyright in that work is vested in the "author" of a work — the person to whom the work owes its origin.

The owner will generally be the author of the work, or the photographer in the case of an image. Under certain circumstances, however, someone other than the person who actually created the work may be deemed to be the work's "author" and thereby own the copyright. Under the work made for hire doctrine, copyright ownership of a particular work vests with the employer of the author when the work is created by an employee who is acting within the scope of his or her employment.

The owner of a copyright is given the exclusive right to reproduce, distribute, display and prepare "derivative works" of the copyright material. These rights exist for the life of the author plus 70 years. In the case of a "work for hire" owned by a corporation, the right exists for 95 years from the first publication or 120 years from creation, whichever is shorter.

• Limitations on copyright

Not all uses of copyright material constitute infringement. The most important limitation on the reach of copyright law for journalists is that ideas and facts are never protected by a copyright. What is protected by the copyright law is the manner of expression. The copyright pertains only to the literary, musical, graphic or artistic form in which an author expresses intellectual concepts.

For example, an author's analysis or interpretation of events, the way the material is structured and the specific facts marshaled, the choice of particular words and the emphasis given to specific developments, may all be protected by copyright. The essence of a claim for copyright infringement lies not in taking a general theme or in covering specific events, but in appropriating particular expression through similarities of treatment, details, scenes, events and characterizations.

This printed page illustrates the distinction between protected expression and nonprotected ideas and facts. Despite the copyright protecting this page, a subsequent author is free to report any of the facts it contains. The subsequent author may not, however, employ the same or essentially the same combination of words, structure, and tone, which constitute the expression of those facts.

A second limitation of the reach of copyright is the doctrine of "fair use." This doctrine permits, in certain circumstances, the use of copyright material without its author's permission. Courts will invoke "fair use" when a rigid application of the copyright law would stifle the very creativity the law is designed to foster.

To determine whether a particular use is "fair" and hence permitted, courts are required to evaluate and balance such factors as: (1) the purpose of the use; (2) the nature of the copyright work that is being used; (3) the amount and substantiality of the portion used in relation to the copyright work as a whole; and (4) the effect of the use upon the potential value of the copyright work. In addition, courts generally consider how "transformative" the use is. Uses that can be said to have transformed portions of the original work into something entirely new by "altering the first [work] with new expression, meaning or message" would factor in to a fair use finding. (See Campbell v. Acuff-Rose Music Inc.) Uses that merely supplant the work by presenting it essentially as it was in the original version tend not to be fair.

News reporting, criticism, and comment are favored purposes under the fair-use doctrine, but "scooping" a copyright holder's first use of previously unpublished material is not. Note, though, that "purpose" is only one of the fair-use factors. Thus, a use for a proper purpose may nevertheless constitute an infringement if other factors weigh against that use's being fair.

Here are some general guidelines to keep in mind when dealing with material written by others:

—Fair use is more likely to be found if the copyright work is informational rather than fictional.

—Documents written by the federal government are not protected by copyright, but documents written by state and local governments may be.

—The greater the amount of the copyright work used, the less likely that a court will characterize the use as fair. The use of an entire copyright work is almost never fair. Size alone, however, is not decisive; courts have found uses not to be fair when the portion used was small but so important that it went to the heart of the copyright work.

—Uses that decrease any potential market for the copyright work tend not to be fair. For instance, if a literary critic reproduces all five lines of a five-line poem, the potential market for the poem will be diminished because any reader of the critic's piece can also obtain a copy of the poem for free.

It is always possible to obtain permission from the copyright holder. Reporters and editors having questions about whether their use in a news story or column of copyright material is a fair use should review these factors. No mathematical formula can yield the answer.

It bears emphasis that the First Amendment provides no greater right to use copyright materials than those provided by the copyright law. If a use is not "fair" within the meaning of copyright law, it will be no defense to claim the use of the copyright material was newsworthy and therefore protected by the First Amendment. Moreover, proper attribution alone cannot transform an infringing use into a fair one.

In using copyright material in a news story or column, writers should make sure that no more of a copyright work than is necessary for a proper purpose is used, and that the work is not used in a way that impairs its value. Photographers in particular pose copyright issues. Any use of a photograph without permission of the owner of the copyright is likely to raise legal issues.

PROCEDURES FOR HANDLING KILLS, DISREGARDS, CLARIFICATIONS AND CORRECTIVES

This chapter summarizes how to make critical corrections to stories that have already been sent, and how to remove them completely or temporarily from the news report if needed. We use KILLS, CORRECTIVES and CLARIFICATIONS in these cases. The rules for the use of these items are more complex than for ordinary in-cycle corrections.

Managers of regional hubs and verticals approve correctives and clarifications for issues that originate in their areas. The Standards Center in New York or New York managers designated to handle correctives must approve any KILL and any CORRECTIVE or CLARIFICATION that involves a legal issue, such as libel or defamation. The New York Photo Desk must be consulted for photo problems.

In many cases, the story involved may have been transmitted over more than one service. Any corrective action must be taken on all services where the story was sent.

1. KILLS and DISREGARDS

KILLS AND DISREGARDS are used to permanently remove from the wire material that is still "live" — usually, copy that has been transmitted in the current 24-hour cycle. For material transmitted in a previous cycle, use a CORRECTIVE or CLARIFICATION.

KILLS replace the erroneous story on websites and advise AP members not to use stories at all in their publication or broadcasts. They may be used when the entire basis of the story is found to be wrong, and on stories with particularly damaging errors or that are potentially libelous. A KILL informs a member that the story, or part of a story, must not be used.

DISREGARDS have a similar effect, but are used in less serious cases - for instance, when an old story is retransmitted inadvertently or material is sent on a service where it is not supposed to appear.

2. FORMATS FOR KILLS and DISREGARDS

Workbench and ELVIS templates and the formats below should be used. For broadcast services, follow broadcast style.

Datelines on kills should be the same as on the original stories. Disregards and kills should carry the same category selections as the original story.

KILLS

A KILL should say succinctly what was wrong with the original story - for example, "Smith was charged with robbery, not murder." Do not make any legal conclusions in the KILL - e.g., "the story is potentially libelous" — when transmitting the KILL.

The form for a KILL:

Slug: BC-US--Smith Charged, KILL
Headline: STORY REMOVED: Smith Charged
Ext. Headline: STORY REMOVED: Smith Charged
Eds. Note: BULLETIN KILL. Do NOT use BC-US--Smith Charged. A kill is mandatory.
Dateline: NEW YORK

The Associated Press has withdrawn its story about charges being filed against Joe Smith. Smith was charged with robbery, not murder.

If a substitute story is sent, mark it as the next lead-writethru to the previous story. Include a nonpublishable editor's note advising that it replaces an earlier story that was KILLED.

The form is:

Slug: BC-US--Smith Charged, 4th Ld-Writethru
Headline: Smith charged with robbery in Philadelphia incident
Ext. Headline: Smith charged with robbery; Philadelphia police may also levy other charges in incident
Eds. Note: CORRECTS previous version, which was KILLED, to show that Smith was charged last year with armed robbery but was not convicted.

Use this format for killing an APNewsAlert:

Slug: BC-US--APNewsAlert, KILL
Headline: STORY REMOVED: BC-US--APNewsAlert
Ext. Headline: STORY REMOVED: BC-US--APNewsAlert
Eds. Note: BULLETIN KILL. Do NOT use BC-US--APNewsAlert. A kill is mandatory.
Dateline: NEW YORK

The Associated Press has withdrawn its APNewsAlert about a bankruptcy filing by XYZ Corp. The company has not filed for bankruptcy.
The AP

DISREGARDS

The form for a DISREGARD is:

Slug: BC-US--Practical Joke, DISREGARD
Editors:
Disregard BC-Practical Joke. The story was sent Tuesday and was inadvertently repeated today.
The AP

3. CORRECTIVES and CLARIFICATIONS

A CORRECTIVE is a publishable story that acknowledges an error in a story and sets the record straight. Regional hubs and verticals approve correctives and clarifications. Advise the Standards Center or other news manager in New York if the corrective involves a legal issue or other complication.

Do not be hasty in transmitting a CORRECTIVE. It is important to ensure that the correction is actually warranted, that it corrects all aspects of the story that may need correction and that the correction itself is accurate.

Transmission of a CORRECTIVE does not necessarily safeguard the AP against legal action. In fact, transmission of a CORRECTIVE may itself have legal consequences because it formally acknowledges an error.

You should be aware of any legal requirement in your region setting a time within which a correction must appear.

CORRECTIVES and CLARIFICATIONS should identify the previous incorrect story by keyword and date. They should carry the dateline and category code of the original story. Use Workbench templates and the formats below. For broadcast services, follow broadcast style.

CORRECTIVES and CLARIFICATIONS should carry headlines. The headlines should begin with the word Correction or Clarification, followed by a colon. In most cases, the slug and the word story will follow.

Slug: BC-US--Church Expenses, CORRECTIVE
Headline: Correction: Church Expenses story
Ext. Headline: Correction: Church Expenses story

or

Slug: BC-US--Church Expenses, CLARIFICATION
Headline: Clarification: Church Expenses story
Ext. Headline: Clarification: Church Expenses story

Note the slug of the story, *Church Expenses*, is uppercase, while *story* is down.

Occasionally, you will want to use something other than the slug after the word Correction or Clarification, to help online readers know what the content is. For example, the slug on a Benton Harbor riots story was *Crash Death-Disturbance*. An appropriate corrective headline in that case might be:

Slug: BC-US--Michigan Crash Death-Disturbance, CORRECTIVE
Headline: Correction: Michigan Riots story
Ext. Headline: Correction: Michigan Riots story

The format for a corrective:

Slug: BC-US--Fed-Indictments, CORRECTIVE
Headline: Correction: Fed-Indictments story
Ext. Headline: Correction: Fed-Indictments story
Eds. note: Eds: Editors who used BC-Fed-Indictments, sent Oct. 22 and datelined in New York, are asked to use the following story.
Dateline: NEW YORK
In an Oct. 22 story about federal indictments of city officials, The Associated Press reported erroneously the first name of one of those indicted. The correct name is Joseph Arnold, not John Arnold.

For correctives on stories that don't carry a dateline, use: **By The Associated Press**.

The proper form for a CORRECTIVE story often will be the straightforward statement that a previous AP report contained an error. However, where the AP did not originate the error, the CORRECTIVE should make that clear. For instance, "In a March 22 story about an embezzlement case, The Associated Press, quoting state police, erroneously identified the man charged. His correct name is Robert Smith, not Reginald Smith." When the original story cited a member as a source, consult with the member. We will usually cite the member in the corrective. If the original story used member material as a source but did not attribute it to the member, we sometimes handle the corrective as if the AP itself made the error. Consult local or New York news managers if necessary.

CLARIFICATIONS

A clarification is a publishable story used to clarify or expand upon a previous story which, while factually correct, may be unfair or subject to misinterpretation.

A clarification must NOT be used as a substitute for a kill or a corrective. The clarification is used to provide background or detail in the interest of clarity or fairness. It is not used to correct factual errors in copy.

The format:

Slug:	**BC-US--Airfares, CLARIFICATION**
Headline:	**Clarification: Airfares story**
Ext. Headline:	**Clarification: Airfares story**
Eds. note:	**Eds: Editors who used BC-Airfares of May 8 may wish to use the following, which explains that not all fares on domestic flights are subject to change.**
Dateline:	**WASHINGTON**

In a story May 8, The Associated Press reported that fares on domestic flights will increase beginning in April. The story should have specified that fares will increase for flights in the continental United States, but not for flights to Hawaii and Alaska.

For clarifications on stories without datelines, in the byline box use: **By The Associated Press**

4. Sending KILLS, CORRECTIVES AND CLARIFICATIONS

Every KILL must be sent to the same services as the original story. The news editor in charge of the hub, bureau or vertical where the problem arose should ensure that distribution of corrective or clarification is complete. If it involves a legal or membership issue, coordinate with the Standards Center or the designated news manager in New York, confirming transmission to all services to which the original item was sent.

The text news desks, Broadcast News Center, AP Digital, Graphics and Photos are responsible for ensuring that these items are sent wherever necessary in their services.

5. Report Requirements

Any time that a kill or corrective is filed, the bureau chief or news editor must maintain a file for the period of the statute of limitations for defamation claims in your state or country, plus three months. The file must contain:

1. Wire copy of the original story and the KILL and substitute story that were sent. Include material transmitted on broadcast

2. Wire copy of the original story and CORRECTIVE or CLARIFICATION filed.

3. A copy of any source material used by the writer or editor in preparation of the story, including member clip, handout and the like.

In the case of a KILL, or a CORRECTIVE or CLARIFICATION with potential ramifications, include a factual statement by the bureau chief or the news editor, in consultation with staff members involved, on the circumstances. If legal action is a possibility, the explanation should be prepared in consultation with the Standards Center or the general counsel.

The statement should cite relevant details, such as any contact with outsiders on the matter. Do not include extraneous comments about staff members or bureau procedures. It is not the place for apologies, or any legal or factual speculation or conclusions. Do not respond to any letter or other communication in connection with any case where legal action seems possible, especially if a lawyer is involved, without prior consultation with the Standards Center.

4. Procedures for handling CORRECTIVES, CLARIFICATIONS and KILLS with legal or other ramifications.

New York must approve all such items. Message the relevant information to the Standards Center. If it's a legal issue such as libel or defamation, or other sensitive matter such as a member issue, message the relevant information to the Standards Center or, at night or weekends, the News Center manager on duty. Say what was wrong and who contacted AP about it. Explain the source of the error. (If the matter is sensitive, phone an explanation.)

Include a proposed, fully formatted CORRECTIVE, CLARIFICATION OR KILL for each service the story moved on, using the format in "Templates" in Reporters Workbench or Elvis. Attach the original story to your message.

Immediately after transmitting any CORRECTIVE, CLARIFICATION or KILL, record in the Correctives Database, along with the required explanations. You can access the database via staff-only links in Inside AP.

SOCIAL MEDIA GUIDELINES

Why this section?
Journalists everywhere have looked to The Associated Press Stylebook for advice about how to gather and disseminate news since the guide was first published in 1953. During that time, methods of newsgathering and delivery have changed drastically – quickening the process and allowing people to learn more about the world around them than ever before.

Social networks have changed that even more quickly over the past decade, establishing an enormous, real-time database of people and thoughts. As daily life plays out all over the world, Facebook, Twitter and other networks constantly note what hundreds of millions of people care to share. Profiles can include everything from detailed biographical information to pinpoint snapshots of major life events, and users exchange thoughts, observations and content with one another.

A 2011 Nielsen study said Americans are spending nearly a quarter of their time on the Internet using social networks and blogs – nearly nine times the amount of time spent on news websites.

Social media presents unprecedented opportunities and challenges to journalists. Examples in this section will show ways social media can enhance beat reporting, simplify finding sources for stories and give journalists a direct connection with people who care about the news they cover. But fluency in social media takes time and effort, and challenges journalists to use the networks in a way that doesn't undermine their credibility.

Social networks don't replace other tools of reporting, but their strong footing in daily life proves that they demand our mastery – like typing, driving or using a smartphone. If we as journalists can't comfortably navigate the most popular areas of the Internet, why should our audience trust us with news at all?

While the speed of technological change may be intimidating and the popularity of individual networks may ebb and flow, this guide hopes to present a foundation that is relevant today but can similarly apply to tomorrow's digital landscape.

While AP journalists have been governed by the AP Stylebook for decades, the so-called "journalist's bible" is the offspring of something even more timeless: our cooperative's **News Values and Principles**. Accuracy, speed and honesty have been paramount for more than 165 years as the AP has grown to become the world's essential global news network.

Our social media section extends from those same **News Values and Principles**, challenging journalists to approach social networks with similar conviction.

What does the term social media mean?
The term refers to tools that allow the sharing of information and creation of communities through online and mobile networks of people.

What are some examples of social media?
There are many different manifestations of social media — and new ones are being developed all the time. Some of the most common types:

* Social networking sites like Facebook, Google Plus and LinkedIn form communities around common interests and share content, like news stories, videos, photos and general updates on what's going on in users' lives.

* Blogs, which are generally written by a single person or specified group of people, but where comment fields often allow for a broader discussion among readers.

* Microblogging sites, like Twitter, where a user can send short bits of information to those who choose to follow that user and findable by the broader Twitter community.

* Wikis, where content is collectively created by those who choose to participate in the process.

* Content-sharing services, like YouTube (for video) and Flickr (for photos and video), where anyone can upload content for easy sharing and discussion with others on the Web.

* Online forums, where participants can share ideas, debate topics and get help with everything from how to roast a turkey to how to take apart a laptop.

* Check-in services, like Foursquare, where users form communities and find out when fellow users have checked themselves into certain locations, events or activities.

* All sorts of other sites, from dating services to collaborative essay-writing projects.

How do journalists use social media in their work?

It varies from journalist to journalist, but these are some common uses:

* To track down sources — in particular, people who witnessed a news event or were directly affected by it.

* To gather user-generated content, like photos or videos, that a news provider may want to acquire and distribute/publish as part of its news report.

* To look for news tips or discussion trends that might lead to or form a story.

* To produce short-format original content, such as blog items.

* To find new sources and keep up with existing ones.

* To interact with news consumers directly to inform their reporting and to promote their work.

* To share links that provide an additional entry point to existing content.

* To get a preliminary sense of how members of the public — or at least social media users — are reacting to an event.

How, as a journalist, should I balance my public, professional presence with my personal privacy?

There are no one-size-fits-all answers to how journalists should manage their social media accounts with respect to their personal privacy. But journalists should consider various factors, including their newsroom's conduct and ethics policy, and approach social networks with clarity regarding their personal feelings and professional needs. At the AP, our social policies are built atop the foundation of our **News Values and Principles**. Some things to consider:

* Not all social networks, including Facebook, allow users to create more than one profile.

* Posts or messages that are intended to be personal can easily be shared, just like emails can be forwarded and conversations recorded. Journalists should never violate their newsroom's conduct or ethics policy under the assumption that their posts are personal, not professional. Social networks bring into clear focus that journalists are considered journalists by the public 24/7.

* Those reluctant to share at all on social media should think about whether they share parts of themselves outside of social media – and when and how. Are you comfortable enough with a source to share small talk about last night's baseball game or some new music? Perhaps sharing some of that during social media interactions with others won't stray too far from what you're comfortable with. There may be subjects that are off-limits for you — that's OK, too.

* Social credibility: When approaching sources on the street, a journalist often gains credibility by presenting a business card or identifying him or herself. On social networks, credibility is gained through consistency and by building connections through interaction and sharing.

How, in all formats, do you vet sources found through social media?

The general rule of thumb is that you should apply the same principles used in vetting a source found any other way. But there can be additional challenges, since it can be difficult to verify the identity of sources found online.

Most importantly, you should never simply lift quotes, photos or video from social networking sites and attribute them to the name on the profile or feed you found them under. Most social media sites offer a way to send a message to a user — use this to establish direct contact, over email or phone, so you can explain what you're working on and get more detailed information about the source.

If a source claims to be an official from a company, organization or government agency, call the place of business to confirm identity, just as you would if a source called on the phone. And if the source provides factual information that's central to a story, always pursue at least one additional source for confirmation.

If you come across photos, videos or other multimedia content that you would like to use in your news report, you'll need to verify the authenticity of the piece of content. You'll then need to determine who controls the copyright of the material and get permission from that person/organization to use it.

Use particular caution if you find a social networking page or feed that appears to belong to a person who is central to a story, especially if you can't get confirmation from that person. Phony accounts are rampant in the social media world, so examine the details to determine whether the page could have just as easily been created by somebody else.

How should social media not be used?

Social networks should never be used as a reporting shortcut when another method, like picking up a phone or knocking on a door, would yield more reliable or comprehensive information. For example, if a key question in a story is only partly or indirectly answered by a tweet sent by a government official, don't settle for that — reach out to the official to find out more. (Though the tweet might also be reported.)

KEY TERMS AND DEFINITIONS

aggregator A website or feed that amasses content from other sources and assembles it in a form digestible to its users.

API Abbreviation for *application programming interface*. A programming format/interface that a website or a piece of software uses to allow other websites or software to interact with it. For example, an API in eBay's website lets auction listings appear on other sites.

app Short for application. A program that runs inside another service. Many cellphones allow *applications* to be downloaded to expand their functions. *App* is acceptable on first reference. Explain the term in the body of the story.

avatar A version of yourself that you put forward in an online or video game setting. Sometimes bears a strong resemblance to the user; at other times, it is used to act out fantasies of a wished-for identity.

blog A website where short entries are usually (but not always) presented in reverse chronological order, with the newest entry first. Can be news, commentary, photos, video or any combination of the above and other items. An update to a blog is a *blog post* or *blog entry*. Blogs can also be distributed outside the website context via RSS feed.

Bluetooth A standard for short-range wireless transmissions, such as in headsets, that enable hands-free use of cellphones.

check in (v.), **check-in** (n. and adj.) When using a location-based social networking tool such as Four-square, the act of sharing a location via a mobile device.

click-thrus A way of measuring how many people click a link online to see its destination site. Click-thrus are often used to set advertising rates.

cloud The collection of data and use of related computing services via remote servers accessed through the Internet.

crowdsourcing The practice of asking a large collection of individuals online to help gather information or produce ideas. Twitter is one common platform used for crowd-sourcing. A blogger or journalist might crowdsource ideas for his or her writing, or a company might crowdsource a commercial from amateur video submissions.

curate The practice of selecting, packaging and presenting content to the public online in a more personal and hand-picked way, as opposed to automated news feeds. Often used in conjunction with social media.

direct message A personal message sent via Twitter to one of your followers. DMs differ from mentions and @ replies in that they can only be seen by the sender and recipient.

download To get information from another server or computer.

e-book The electronic, nonpaper version of a book or publication, sold digitally and commonly consumed on an *e-book reader* or *e-reader*, such as Amazon's Kindle.

emoticon A typographical cartoon or symbol generally used to indicate mood or appearance, as :-) and often looked at sideways. Also known as *smileys*.

end user (n.), **end-user** (adj.) A phrase commonly referred to by technology developers when imagining the audience for an application, software or hardware. *End-user experience.*

e-reader Or *e-book reader*. Devices such as Amazon's Kindle, Barnes & Noble's Nook and Sony's Reader used to display electronic books and other digital publications. Other devices, including laptops and Apple's iPad, have e-reader software that can perform similar functions.

Facebook The world's most popular social media service. Users communicate with friends and other users via private and public messages. Posted profiles, photos, lists of personal interests and privacy settings are key elements.

feed A stream of constantly updated material.

Foursquare A location-based social network. Users check in at certain places or businesses, collect rewards for visits and track friends who use the service.

friend, follow, like Acceptable as both nouns and verbs. Actions by which users connect to other users on social networks. Friend and like (formerly fan) are typically used on Facebook, while Twitter users follow and have followers.

geolocation The association of your virtual location with your physical location. Many social networks have enabled *geolocation* features (Facebook Places is one example), and some are built completely around *geolocation* (Foursquare).

geotagging The act of adding geographical metadata to pieces of media or social media updates. A *geotagged* photo would indicate the latitude and longitude of the location the photo was taken. A *geotagged* tweet would also indicate latitude and longitude, or a more general location, for example, Carolina Beach, N.C.

Google, Googling, Googled

Google is a trademark for a Web search engine. *Google*, *Googling* and *Googled* are used informally as a verb for searching for information on the Internet. Always capitalized.

Google Plus A social network owned by Google in which users can share text updates, videos, photos or other content, and organize fellow users into circles based on relationships or other factors. One popular feature of Google Plus is hangouts, where users can chat with others using webcams.

handle A self-selected, public-facing username on a social network, particularly Twitter. May be used interchangeably with *username*.

hashtag The use of a number sign (#) in a tweet to convey the subject a user is writing about so that it can be indexed and accessed in other users' feeds. If someone is writing about the Super Bowl, for example, the use of *#superbowl* could be an appropriate hashtag. No space is used between the hashtag and the accompanying search term.

IM Abbreviation for *instant message*; sometimes used as a verb: *IMing, IMed*. Acceptable on second reference for instant messaging. See **text messaging/instant messaging**.

Internet TV A television set that can be connected directly to the Internet and displays Web content without going through a computer.

iPad A trademark for a brand of tablet. Use *IPad* when the word starts a sentence or headline. See **tablet**.

iPhone Apple Inc.'s smartphone. Use *IPhone* when the word starts a sentence or headline.

keywords Terms used to define an online search or embed in a file so that it becomes searchable.

LinkedIn A social media site used mainly for professional networking. Users create contact networks for information exchanges, job searches and business opportunities.

link shortener A tool that allows users to shorten a longer URL to make it easier to share. Bit.ly and TinyURL are two link shorteners.

live-blog Snippets of information about a particular event that are posted online in real time, usually in reverse chronological order, with the newest entry first. Can be used as a noun or verb.

mashup A combination of two or more pieces of content, such as photos or video, used to create something new. For example, a video that blends audio from a song with footage from several movies to build a new storyline.

mention On Twitter, an @ mention tags an account in a tweet someone else is publishing. It often appears in place of the actual name. Example: *I refer to the @APStylebook as I edit stories.*

metadata Data about data. Examples of metadata include descriptors indicating when information was created, by whom and in what format. Do not use in a story without an explanation of what information is being revealed in a given set of metadata: *Investigators determined that Johnson wrote the document by analyzing its metadata, which indicated that it had been saved on his computer.*

microsite A tightly focused group of Web pages typically dedicated to a single topic, product or service.

modified tweet A tweet amended before forwarding uses the abbreviation MT.

reply On Twitter, an @ reply is a common technique to speak to other people directly. A tweet that begins with @username can be seen in Twitter feeds by people that follow both parties, though it can still be viewed on an individual's profile page. Example: *@APStylebook I have a style question that I need help with.*

retweet The practice, on Twitter, of forwarding a message or link from someone else to your followers. Users can either formally retweet to make the forwarded message appear exactly as written by the original user or use the informal convention of "RT @username:" to share the tweet and edit or add comment. Spelled out in all references, though common usage on Twitter abbreviates to RT. If you amend the tweet before forwarding, use the abbreviation MT for "modified tweet."

For AP staffers, retweets, like tweets, should not be written in a way that looks like an expression of personal opinion on the issues of the day. However, AP staffers can judiciously retweet opinionated material by making clear it is being reported, much like a quote in a story. Colons and quote marks help make the distinction.

Original tweet example: *@jonescampaign: smith's policies would destroy our schools*

Example amended for AP retweet:

Jones campaign now denouncing Smith on education: RT @jonescampaign: smith's policies would destroy our schools

RSS An abbreviation for *Really Simple Syndication*. A protocol for subscribing to and distributing feeds that notify people of new entries on news sites, blogs, podcasts or other online information sources. Also *RSS feed. RSS* is acceptable in all references.

scraping, mirroring The method of copying video, photo or audio content from an account and reposting it to a different one.

search engine optimization Any of a number of methods, both informal and algorithmic, used to ensure that online content shows up in search engines such as Google, thus increasing traffic to the content. *SEO* is acceptable on second reference.

smartphone An advanced mobile device, such as an iPhone, that can be used to check email, browse the Web and download applications.

social media Online tools that people use to connect with one another, including social networks.

social media optimization Any of a number of methods, mostly informal, used to ensure that online content is shared on social networks, thus increasing click-through

traffic to the originating website. *SMO* is acceptable on second reference.

social networks Online networks such as Facebook or Twitter where people share personal and professional information and content, and connect with friends and colleagues.

status A short string of words used on social networks to alert followers to a user's recent activities or point them to something of interest.

streaming A method of processing and delivering media in real time over the Internet. Videos on YouTube are an example of streaming content, as are many on-demand services like Netflix and Hulu.

subscribe A method of keeping track of public updates from Facebook users without necessarily adding them as a friend. The feature must be enabled by a user to allow users to subscribe to his or her updates.

tablet A touch-screen device, such as an iPad or Kindle Fire, that can be connected to the Internet via Wi-Fi or cellular data networks.

tag To identify someone or something in a post or piece of content. Photos are often tagged to identify people and objects in them.

text messaging, instant messaging Increasingly, terms and symbols used in text and instant messaging are showing up in quotations and regular written exchanges. The following are a selection of the most popular symbols, terms and abbreviations used in texting and IMing. Many are also used in social media updates.

2 Shorthand for *to* or *too*, as in *I have something 4 U 2.*

4 Shorthand for *for*.

BFF *Best friend forever*. Often used sarcastically.

BRB *Be right back*.

C Shorthand for *see*, as in *C U later*. Also used in lowercase.

capitalization Normal conventions of capitalization are often ignored in IM and text messages because the use of the shift key slows down letter entry.

G2G *Got to go*.

IDK *I don't know*.

IMO/IMHO *In my opinion, in my humble opinion*.

LOL *Laugh out loud* or *laughing out loud*. Use to indicate that the sender has found something funny. See also **ROFL**.

NSFW *Not safe for work*. Used to alert recipients that upcoming material or attachments may be objectionable in an office environment. Often used to warn recipients of impending coarse or pornographic images being sent.

POS *Parent over shoulder*. Used by teenagers and children to indicate, in an IM conversation, that a parent is approaching.

R Shorthand for *are*, as in, *R U kidding?* Also used in lowercase.

removal of punctuation, characters It is acceptable in instant-message and texting conventions to remove punctuation and characters, most often vowels, to save time typing or thumbing in letters. Thus, a word like *remember* could become *rmbr* or *American Idol* could be shortened to *Idol*.

ROFL *Rolling on the floor laughing*. One step beyond *LOL*.

thx Shorthand for *thanks*. Also *tnx*.

U Shorthand for *you*.

Y Shorthand for *why*.

trending Used to indicate that a particular topic is getting a lot of attention on a social network, search engine or website. Often used as a verb. Do not use without context and explanation, including describing the location of users where the topic is trending. *The topic of the Oscars is trending worldwide on Twitter today.*

Tumblr A blogging platform.

tweet A public message of up to 140 characters on Twitter. Also usable as a verb: to tweet.

Twitter A message-distribution system that allows users to post continual updates of up to 140 characters detailing their activities for followers or providing links to other content. The verb is to tweet, tweeted. A Twitter message is known as a tweet.

unfollow To remove an account from the list of accounts that populate a feed, usually on Twitter. Note that *unfollowing* on Twitter is a one-way action: I may unfollow you, but you may continue to follow me.

unfriend To remove someone from a list of friends, usually on Facebook.

user interface The features of a device, program or website that enable control by a human. *UI* is acceptable on second reference. Also called user experience or *UX*.

VoIP *Voice over Internet Protocol*. A method of transmitting sound as data over the Internet, allowing for inexpensive phone conversations. *VoIP* is acceptable on second reference.

website A location on the *World Wide Web* that maintains one or more pages at a specific address. Also, *webcam*, *webcast* and *webmaster*. But as a short form and in terms with separate words, *the Web, Web* *page* and *Web feed*. See **Web** in main section of Stylebook.

widget A small module with a specific purpose that appears on a website, desktop or other interface and allows access to content or functions.

wiki Software that allows a group of users to add, delete, edit and share information on an intranet or Internet website.

Wikipedia An online encyclopedia whose entries are created and edited by its users, regardless of a person's expertise. May contain useful links but should not be used as a primary source of information.

YouTube A video-serving network owned by Google that allows users to upload their own videos for access by anyone with a network connection.

THE BASICS

Each social network has unique characteristics, but a few basic rules generally apply to most sites:

HANDLE/USERNAME: When deciding on a username, choose something clear cut and easy to remember. First name, last name is always a good option. AP may be used for its staffers, though it is not required.

PHOTO: Upload a professional-looking photo of yourself and use it on all networks. People won't take you seriously without one.

BIO: Write a bio that accurately describes who you are. Feel free to include a personal tidbit or two, but remember that you are always representing the AP. You may want to include your email address so people can easily get in touch with you privately.

GOALS: Define some goals about how often you post or tweet and strike a balance among personal and professional posts, responses, links to stories, retweets or reposts.

BUILD CREDIBILITY: It comes through posting regularly. Show you're active, engaged and committed to the tool. You can't parachute in and expect to instantly have people's trust.

ENCOURAGE RETWEETS: On Twitter, tweets are a maximum of 140 characters but should be shorter if you want people to be able to easily retweet you without losing links or part of your message. Informal retweets also encourage users to keep their handles short. *"RT @johndoe:"* is 12 characters with spaces, which leaves 128 characters for the tweet.

CONNECT AND INTERACT: Seek out people who have the same interests as you and pay attention when they post.

BE YOURSELF: No one wants to interact with a robot. You can control how much of you to share, but you need to make it clear that you're human. Use colorful, persuasive language, insert some personality and use humor. Entice users to click your links.

SHARE WHAT YOU SEE: Journalists have a front row seat to history. Use that vantage point to engage with people. *"There's a difference between opinion and observation."* — Lou Ferrara, AP managing editor

USING LISTS TO STAY ORGANIZED AND PROTECT YOUR PRIVACY

Twitter

Twitter lists are a powerful, convenient way to organize and find new people. When you view a list you've created, you'll only see updates from the users you chose for that list. If you're using a third-party program like TweetDeck or HootSuite, you can organize lists into different columns, so you don't have to search through one long feed to find certain types of tweets. This can make things much easier if you're organizing information from lots of users. Lists can be public or private, allowing you to track users discreetly without directly following them or even share feeds of entire groups of people with the Twitterverse.

On **Twitter**, click the "Lists" drop-down and hit "Create a list." Name it and decide if you want it to be public or private. (You can always change from public to private and vice versa.) Make sure you choose public only if you don't mind anyone browsing your list and possibly following it. If you keep your list private, only you will be able to access it.

Once you've created lists, classify people you follow each time you add them. To add someone to a list that already exists, click on the small icon that looks like a picture of a person near their profile, then click "add to list," then add them to the appropriate list.

For reporters, private lists are an easy way to see tweets by newsmakers, regardless of whether you actually follow them. You may want to start organizing a private list by adding sources you already know. For a statehouse reporter, that could include lawmakers and their staffs, party officials, legislative research staffers, the governor and his/her key staffers, lobbyists, other reporters and bloggers. For a crime reporter: prosecutors (local, state, federal, tribal), defense lawyers, court staff (clerks, bailiffs, court administrators), other reporters or incarcerated criminals (don't laugh — they're on social networks). If you are sharing a list with colleagues you should come back to it regularly to ensure it is always up-to-date. Browsing through lists others have created is a smart way to find other people who might be relevant to you.

Twitter's help section (http://support.twitter.com) is a great resource for managing your account, finding and following people and creating lists.

Facebook

With Facebook, it's easy to keep friends separate from work contacts by putting people in lists. For example, you can allow people listed as family and friends to post comments on your wall, comment about photos posted by you or tagged by other people and even see your friends. But you can restrict access to your work list, so they see very little about you. Here are detailed directions from Facebook on how to do this: http://on.fb.me/uKtoYz and http://on.fb.me/ss4Wsx.

See **Social Media Guidelines for AP Employees**.

SEARCH FOR PEOPLE – AND THEIR PHOTOS AND VIDEOS

A plane crash. A hurricane. A shooting. These events and more can happen at all hours of the day in all parts of the world. But regardless of where and when news develops, it will likely be shared using social networks. Journalists should be able to quickly use social media search engines to find people, photos and video related to news. Even routine stories can benefit from real people found through social media.

Information and eyewitness content mined from social networks are essential to competing on big stories. Quick, smart reaction to breaking news can be key to finding people or securing exclusive photos and video. It can also help save time and resources. And often, it's the only way to reach people.

To get strong results from a social network search, be thoughtful about your search terms and refine them as you gauge your results. People who aren't journalists don't always think like journalists, so simplify your language and try to think of what they might say.

For example, if you're seeking user-generated content from passengers trapped on a cruise ship — as Associated Press reporters were in November 2010 — try to think of what tourists, their friends and families might say. Most social networks support the use of Boolean search operators to refine searches using quotes, "and," "or," "not" and other rules, so you might try a combination of words: "Carnival," "Splendor" "cruise," "stuck," "vacation," "port," "aboard," "sick" or "miserable."

While the ship was still stuck at sea and well out of cellphone range, a Facebook search yielded someone with a cousin onboard.

Toni Sweet
OMG! My cousins Vicky & Fernando (Monday) are on that cruise ship Splendor that had a fire in the engine room & is drifting afloat!! Tu boats have to bring them back to Long Beach in the next few days. Please say a quick prayer for all the passangers safe return!!!

Share · November 9, 2010 at 12:47am via mobile ·

An AP staffer sent her a message:

Carson Walker   November 9, 2010
cruise ship

Hi Toni. My name is Carson Walker and I'm an editor with The Associated Press and am wondering if you'd like to share your story about the people you know on the ship. If so, you may call me at 602-417-   .
Thanks much for considering.

That led to a phone interview, resulting in AP's first quotes from someone directly involved:

Toni Sweet, of San Pedro, Calif., was frustrated when she couldn't reach her cousin, Vicky Alvarez, aboard the ship.

"We know everything is fine, but we're just worried," Sweet said. "She was nervous about going on a cruise ship even before this happened and now with this, I don't think she'll ever go again."

Without having access to the ship's passenger list, social media was the best — and only — way to reach out to people who might know someone onboard and add a human element to the story.

The **Facebook** search page (https://www.facebook.com/search) makes it easy to filter by "People" or keywords under "Public Posts" (located in the left column). When you find someone, message them privately or comment on the post that you're contacting them about (while logged in), identify yourself and give the person a way to reach you through phone or email.

You can do people and keyword searches on **Twitter** (http://www.twitter.com) and save them. When you find someone, hit "Reply" (while logged into Twitter) and write something like:

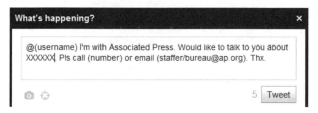

You may also follow people and ask them to follow you, so they can direct message you and make contact privately. Stakes in each situation will vary, but feel free to err on the side of private direct messages if the topic or your discovery seems competitive. Don't forget: Other media outlets can follow your tweets for tips and clues to what you're pursuing and can find what you write when you reply to someone.

Most days, it's pretty easy to find a reporter on a social network post something like: *"Are you or do you know anyone who's affected by Event X? If so, please msg me, I may want to talk with you for my story."*

That method can sometimes yield results, especially if a reporter has a specialized, tuned-in audience of people willing to either share the request or offer themselves up as sources without hesitation. But it's somewhat limiting.

Think about it: If you were on assignment doing a story about voters on Election Day (and were prohibited from using social media), would you simply walk outside your office and shout: "Hey, has anyone voted today?" Probably not. More likely, you'd head to a local polling place, watch voters walk in and out and try to speak with them there.

Finding people through social media requires the same detective-like mentality reporters use when they're wielding nothing more than a notepad and pencil.

Advanced searches allow you to narrow results by location, weed out posts by people simply passing along news links of a story you're working on, and quickly pinpoint relevant, real-world people with the ability to give firsthand contributions to your story.

In August 2010, a chemical similar to bleach seeped into the pool at the MGM Grand hotel-casino on the Las Vegas Strip. Authorities evacuated roughly

1,500 guests from the pool, sent more than two dozen to the hospital and treated about 100 people for breathing problems as a result.

As the AP reported on the story, its reporter decided to try to search for people at the pool in hopes of elevating the story beyond a brief. But with the casino a 20-minute drive away, and the likelihood of being restricted on the private property, he turned to **Twitter Advanced Search** (http://search.twitter.com/advanced):

Advanced **Search**

Words	
All of these words	MGM pool
This exact phrase	
Any of these words	
None of these words	http
These hashtags	
Written in	Any Language ⬍

People	
From these accounts	
To these accounts	
Mentioning these accounts	

Places	
Near this place	Las Vegas, NV
Within this distance	10 ⬍ ⦿ miles ○ kilometers

Other	
Select:	☐ Positive :) ☐ Negative :(☐ Question ? ☐ Include retweets

Search

Inputting "MGM pool" under "All of these words" was an obvious way to start. While patrons of the pool could have used many terms to describe what was happening, "MGM" and "pool" were likely to be there. Had we gotten more irrelevant results, we might have added more terms like "evacuate," "leak," "firemen" or "breathe."

Adding "http" under "None of these words" kept most links out of the results. Under "Near this place," we restricted the search to within 10 miles of Las Vegas, to avoid people in other parts of the country who were talking about the story but weren't at the pool.

The search yielded several results, including this tweet from Bryce Baril:

 brycebaril That was annoying. **MGM** Grand closed the **pool** for an undisclosed reason and firemen with breathers stormed in. Rumor is Cl gas leak.
Twitter - Aug 27, 2010

The reporter immediately responded with this tweet:

 oskargarcia @brycebaril Hi Bryce, I'm an AP reporter doing a story about the pool evacuation. Can you give me a call at 702-382-   or follow me to DM?
Twitter - Aug 27, 2010 - Full conversation

Baril immediately replied:

brycebaril @oskargarcia can't reply to your DM if you don't follow back
Twitter - Aug 27, 2010

If you're asking people to respond to you via social networks, be sure your settings and actions on the network don't prevent others from getting ahold of you directly. On Twitter, this meant the reporter needed to follow Baril to receive a direct message. He did, and Baril sent this direct message:

brycebaril
Aug 27, 2010, 3:45pm
My wife and I were there, enjoying our tenth anniversary. I have a crappy photo of the firemen on my wife's phone.

That led to a phone conversation, during which the reporter thoroughly questioned Baril to get as much detail as possible but also to verify and judge the believability of his story. If things didn't add up, the reporter would have skipped using him in the story. The conversation led to this passage:

Bryce Baril, 32, of Seattle, said he and his wife were preparing to go into the pool when a woman announced over the intercom that he and others needed to go to another pool. A few minutes later, she told everyone to leave all the pools, he said.

"We got up to the exit and in comes the hazmat or the fire department, breathing through their masks," Baril said. "We never smelled anything but we were supposedly right where it was."

The couple was in Vegas to celebrate their 10th wedding anniversary.

The entire Twitter exchange took about 15 minutes, allowing the quote to get to the wire faster than it would have taken had the reporter driven to the casino, parked and hoped to get lucky while restricted by casino officials about where to go on the property. The keys were using the right search terms, establishing one-on-one contact and thoroughly talking with sources and attributing their comments.

General tips:

—Put keywords and a hashtag (the number # symbol followed by a keyword, which is used to convey the subject a user is addressing) in the top boxes. You can use "and" and "or" in the searches and also choose among several languages.

—Under "None of these words" put "http" (to eliminate people who are passing along story links). You can also focus your search here. For example, with the cruise ship story, "church" was added to this box to eliminate tweets about "church carnivals," since it was a "Carnival" cruise ship. If you are searching for people posting photos or video, then filter those results that do include "http."

—The "People" search area lets you look for specific user accounts.

—Under "Places," put the city, ZIP code or landmark and set the number of miles/kilometers out you want to search. Start nearby and expand, depending on how many results you get.

—Once you run a search, you can tweak the criteria by clicking "Refine results" on top.

—There's also a save option on top.

Video Searches

Besides Twitter, Facebook and other networks, there are some good sites to specifically search for mobile video.

On **YouTube** (http://youtube.com), put your keyword(s) in the search box

| london riots | Search |

Search results for **london riots**

About **15,000 results**

Filter ▼

Sort by	Filter		
Relevance	uploaded today	channel	HD (high definition)
Upload date	uploaded this week	playlist	CC (closed caption)
View count	uploaded this mo...	movie	longer than 20 min
Rating		show	partner video
		3D	creative commons

and click "Filter" to choose an upload date:

Display your results in chronological order and refresh the page frequently to see new postings. Make sure you find the earliest example of a video to make sure you are chasing original content. Consider the words someone uploading video may use, as well as the city and specific streets or landmarks they may refer to.

To contact prospects regarding access to their video, all you need is a Google or YouTube login. To contact the person who posted the video, click on his or her username and you'll be taken to a new screen that includes a "Send Message" link:

On **Vimeo** (http://vimeo.com), pull up the newest videos of a keyword search by choosing the drop-down box that comes up under "Show me:"

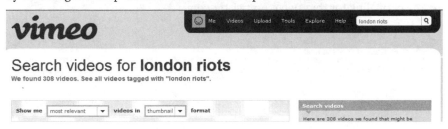

Photo Searches

Several sites are available to search for photos posted to Twitter or other sites:

—**Photobucket** (www.photobucket.com) is now the photo service that is officially linked to Twitter.

—**Twlpho** (http://twlpho.net) pulls images from twitpic.com, img.ly and yfrog.com, or you can search those sites individually.

—**Flickr** (http://www.flickr.com) is another great site to search. To contact someone, you first need a Yahoo or Flickr account. When you find an image, click on the username of the person who posted it, which will take you to his or her photostream. Click on the small envelope and contact him or her.

—Google's **Picasa** (http://picasa.google.com/) also draws a lot of user-generated content.

—**Inkstagram** (http://inkstagram.com) allows Web browsing of photos posted to the popular Instagram iPhone app.

In April 2011, a Southwest Airlines passenger took a cellphone image of a hole in the cabin of a Boeing 737 as it made an emergency descent from 36,000 feet to Yuma, Ariz. The flight from Phoenix to Sacramento, Calif., was diverted due to rapid decompression in the plane caused by a "fuselage rupture."

Tom Stathis, AP's regional photo editor for the West region in Phoenix, and a photo editor in San Francisco both quickly spotted the image on Twitter and contacted the passenger, who granted permission to the AP for its distribution. Outside of knowing someone onboard the plane, social media was the only way to connect with passengers to quickly obtain a photo of the hole.

Old Tweets

Trying to find old tweets, so you can capture an image of them, delete them or simply have a look? It's not as easy to find them as you'd think. Scrolling down through your feed is tedious, and will only go back so far. And a Twitter search will only get you a week or two of tweets. (As will most other search engines that find tweets.)

Topsy (http://topsy.com/advanced-search) is a fairly simple Twitter search engine, and it goes way back in time. Like other third-party Twitter searches, it's not entirely reliable — as in, you might not find all the tweets you're looking for.

But it often works. You can refine searches by keywords, a time range, the user who sent it and language. You can click on the timestamp on a search result to get the permalink for that tweet on twitter.com.

USER-GENERATED CONTENT

User-generated content, or UGC , is the term commonly used in the news industry for content with news or editorial value that has been produced by non-journalists. Sometimes this is also referred to as citizen journalism, when members of the public capture news events on their own devices either by chance or by purposely pursuing a story. User-generated content may be found via social networks but could equally be given to a reporter on the scene of a news event. It is essential to hold UGC to the same standards as all other information taken in and reported by the AP.

There are a number of challenges that face journalists handling UGC, most notably the issue of verification. Most broadly, do we know exactly what we are seeing, and how we have determined this? We should seek to tell the story surrounding each piece of video and audio and every photo we acquire with the level of accuracy people expect from the AP. This means tapping into our considerable knowledge base, drawing on the expertise of AP staff around the world.

Securing access to content can often be a challenge, especially in a breaking news situation when video or photos have been re-posted to social networks. You must always strive to seek the original source of the media you are seeking to acquire. Once that content owner has been identified, ask for permission to use the material, following all the established protocols the AP has in place.

When publishing UGC, you should make every effort to give due credit to the person who has created that content. Use the person's name if he or she is happy for you to do so, or a username (from a social network or platform) if it is applicable or the preference of the individual.

DIGITAL SECURITY FOR JOURNALISTS

It's impossible to be a productive journalist without extensive use of digital communication and production tools. But journalists are not always aware of how to keep their online accounts and private material secure.

Strong security is a combination of good technology and meticulous habits. It might sound attractive to employ the best possible security on all files and every communication channel, but this isn't practical because security always has a cost in terms of time, money or inconvenience. But you can secure your data against some types of unauthorized access.

Here are some basic techniques that will make your data more secure and help you to understand what is not protected. Probably, many of them will already be familiar to you. They may seem simplistic, but most security compromises are the result of lapses in good habits, not high-tech hacking.

1) Use secure passwords. If your passwords are easy to break, nothing else matters.

It is possible to log into an astonishing number of systems with the passwords "123456," "password" and "qwerty." Needless to say, these are terrible choices. But words in the dictionary are also no good because automated password crackers can make thousands of guesses per second. Passwords with letters replaced by numbers (such as zero for "o," three for "e" and one for "l") are also easily guessed by computer. The best passwords are actually passphrases, short sentences that are personally relevant and therefore memorable. If that's too long to type, you can make an acronym from the first letter of each word in your passphrase.

Particularly protect your email password. Most online services will email you a new password in case you forget yours, so if someone has control of your email, they pretty much have control of all of your accounts. Make sure your email password is well chosen and different from all other passwords. Change it immediately if you suspect someone has compromised your account. In fact you should change your important passwords several times a year to put a time limit on the damage that a stolen password can do.

Social networking and instant messenger passwords are also frequently compromised. Be sure to use a different password for each account. Otherwise, an attacker could gain control of all of your accounts simultaneously – and then change all the passwords, leaving you with few public channels to contest the identity theft!

Ideally, each place you log in should use a different password. No one can remember dozens of different passwords, but you can use a program like 1Password to securely store a completely random and un-guessable password for each service. The downside is that you must have your personal password database with you at all times, your master password exposes everything at once if it is compromised, and if you lose your master password you lose all of your access simultaneously.

2) Some computers and networks are more secure than others.

Sending an email at the office to a colleague is very secure if your organization runs its own mail servers (rather than using cloud-based email), because the message only travels across the internal network, not the Internet. But an email sent over WiFi at a coffee shop can be intercepted by anyone nearby, if they have the right software on their laptop.

In general, different networks have different levels of security. A computer attached directly to the public Internet is quite vulnerable, whereas a computer on an internal network, talking only to other internal servers, is quite insulated from the outside world.

VPN software creates a "virtual private network" that connects a remote computer to an internal network over an encrypted channel. It is quite secure — as long as you trust the computer you are running it on and don't forget to log out.

Other people's computers might have viruses, key-logging software or other malware installed. Avoid doing sensitive work on machines you can't vouch for. Especially try to avoid typing your passwords on a public computer or other system that might have key-logging software installed. If you must log in from an un-trusted machine, change your password later from a secure computer.

3) Be suspicious of people sending you links with generic descriptions, and always read the URL before you log in.

"Phishing" is the practice of tricking someone into revealing their password, and it's the most common method of gaining unauthorized access. There are many different ways to phish, but all of them are based on sending you a message with a link in it.

The original phishing scams involved an email or other message asking you to re-enter your password for "security purposes" that contained a link to a fake login screen that looks like a legitimate bank or social networking site. It's very easy to create a copy of a website at a fake address, and most people won't notice that the URL is wrong before happily typing in their passwords. For example, if the login screen looks like Twitter, the URL displayed in your browser must start with "twitter.com." Other addresses such as "itwitter.com" are scams. Be very wary of messages with links that take you to a login screen of any sort, and get into the habit of reading the URL before typing in your password.

Other phishing schemes are even more insidious because they exploit security flaws to steal passwords stored in your browser without ever asking you to log in. These attacks still come in the form of links, usually accompanied by very generic messages such as "check out this picture of you" or "did you see this site?" Be very suspicious of such generic links even if they come from a trusted source — your friends' accounts may have been compromised, and if you click the bad link, your account may be compromised too. Also, keep your Web browser up to date, including automatically downloaded updates to minimize your vulnerability to these types of attacks.

There have been hundreds of phishing scams, and there are sure to be more variants in the future. The only protection is to understand how these scams operate, read URLs before logging in and be wary of generic links delivered by email, Twitter, Facebook or any other messaging system.

4) Different communications tools have different levels of security.

Email has the weakest security of any communication method. It's transmitted unencrypted, so it's no more secure than sending a post card. Emails can be intercepted by any network operator between the source and destination, viewed by the administrators of the mail servers at either end or snooped by someone on the same public wireless network. Instant messages are often vulnerable in the same way.

All Web traffic is similarly transmitted without encryption, except for sites that can be accessed using "https" instead of "http," which is normally indicated by a little "lock" icon in the browser. When a website offers both, a URL starting with https is greatly preferable because https connections are encrypted, which makes it harder for eavesdroppers to record your password or other sensitive information. Standard mobile phones are difficult to intercept over the air, but of course the telecommunications company has full access to the connection, as well as your location (even when no calls are made). This may or may not be a problem depending on who wants to listen.

Skype connections are encrypted so that they cannot be intercepted en route by telecommunications companies or anyone else. Skype can be more secure than regular telephone calls in many situations, but it depends on who wants to eavesdrop and that person's relationship to Skype. Skype could still decrypt recorded conversations if it wants to — or if it is compromised or compelled by a third party. Other digital-telephony services have similar security profiles.

Email encrypted using the popular encryption program PGP can be very secure, but PGP is quite difficult to set up and use correctly — and can be compromised after the fact if a private key leaks.

The best solution for truly private communication is the OTR ("off the record") instant messaging system. OTR is built into many IM programs, including the popular Adium application. It is quite secure, even against state-level attackers and about as simple as secure communication gets. But it still demands good habits.

OTR will not hide whom you are communicating with, only what you are saying. Similarly, it's easy to pretend to be someone else over IM. The first time you connect, use another channel simultaneously (such as the phone) to ensure that the person on the other end is really who you think it is. Finally, no amount of communication security will help if someone later reads the chat logs stored on your computer. With Microsoft Office Communicator, chat logs are in the "Conversation History" folder in Outlook. You need to find where such logs are for OTR or other instant messaging programs.

5) Think about what data is stored and where. Caution on cloud computing.

How many copies of that sensitive chat log, photograph or private message are floating around on your laptop? Are there any on other computers? Did you give a copy to someone who might store it insecurely? Are there any copies in the cloud?

Many communications programs make automatic copies. There could be a sensitive email in a saved folder, or an online service might be saving your chat logs (as gchat does by default). Your organization may already have data retention policies or guidance on best practices. If your organization doesn't, consult with your own attorney about types of data to keep while reporting.

It's also important to know where your data are stored. Cloud computing can solve many problems, but whenever you store sensitive information on someone else's computer you are depending on them to keep it safe. In essence, you are betting on their competence and will to resist your attackers. Even if a cloud computing provider is honest and smart, do you know what they will do when served with a subpoena? It's best to consult with an attorney before placing sensitive material on a cloud.

This applies especially to online email and social networking service providers, most of whom routinely turn their user's data over to law enforcement agencies if asked. In many circumstances, this happens without any sort of warrant or other judicial oversight, or even notification to the user that their privacy has been compromised. This includes major vendors such a Facebook, Google and Yahoo, and applies in many countries including the United States.

Further, many governments operate massive Internet surveillance operations, so anything transmitted unencrypted must be assumed to be in the hands of one state agency or another.

6) Consider what might happen if your equipment falls into the wrong hands.

Communication security is important, but many people neglect physical security. A laptop can be lost or stolen, or someone might wander into the office while you are at lunch or even sneak into your hotel room. Computers and other electronics are also routinely seized by authorities of all stripes, including law enforcement and international customs. Encrypt your hard drive if you have sensitive material on your computer, and be careful to track all copies of critical files including those on thumb drives or other media. The same precautions apply to camera memory cards, phones containing images or video, etc.

7) If a security breach might cause serious harm, you need expert advice.

Tools such as OTR instant messaging and the Tor anonymity network can be enormously powerful and offer the possibility of truly secure communication, but they require considerable thought and care to use correctly. Encryption systems come in many flavors, but even the most sophisticated software is useless if you forget to log out at the right time. And digital security is just one part of operational security - it takes more than technology to keep secrets.

This little guide is no substitute for specialized training, technology and procedures. If the stakes are high, you need to consult an expert.

CONCLUSION

The explosion in the use of social media worldwide means journalists can't dismiss the medium as a fad. It's powerful enough to provide user-generated content from the front lines of political revolutions, yet simple enough to connect with real people for a feature story being written under deadline.

A few things to remember:

—You control how much you share and can protect your privacy.

—You have to give to social media to get anything from it.

—Basic ethics still apply, so think twice before you post and always verify information you find before passing it along to others or using it in a published report. The journalistic standards you hold yourself to don't change just because the tools change.

—Approach social media like a new challenge: learn the basics, use those skills during non-breaking-news situations so they're second nature and then share tips and tricks with colleagues.

SOCIAL MEDIA GUIDELINES FOR AP EMPLOYEES

Many news organizations have established social media guidelines for their employees. Below are the guidelines the AP has established for its own staff. AP's guidelines are regularly updated.

AP's Social Media Guidelines are based on our **Statement of News Values and Principles**. The guidelines below apply these long-tested principles to the social media space. The Social Media Guidelines are designed to advance the AP's brand and staffers' personal brands on social networks. They encourage staffers to be active participants in social networks while upholding our fundamental value that staffers should not express personal opinions on controversial issues of the day.

ACCOUNTS
All AP journalists are encouraged to have accounts on social networking sites. These sites are now an integral part of everyday life for millions of people around the world. They have become an essential tool for AP reporters to gather news and share links to our published work. We recommend having one account per network that you use both personally and professionally.

Many AP journalists have had great success with this strategy.

Employees must identify themselves as being from AP if they are using their accounts for work in any way. You don't have to include AP in your Twitter or other usernames, and you should use a personal image (not an AP logo) for the profile photo. But you should identify yourself in your profile as an AP staffer. Posting AP proprietary or confidential material is prohibited. Employees may not include political affiliations in their profiles and should not make any postings that express political views.

OPINION
AP staffers must be aware that opinions they express may damage the AP's reputation as an unbiased source of news. AP employees must refrain from declaring their views on contentious public issues in any public forum and must not take part in organized action in support of causes or movements. (See guidelines below on "liking" and following pages and groups that are associated with causes or movements.)

Sometimes AP staffers ask if they're free to comment in social media on matters like sports and entertainment. The answer is yes, but there are some important things to keep in mind:

First, trash-talking about anyone (including a team, company or celebrity) reflects badly on staffers and the AP. Assume your tweet will be seen by the target of your comment. The person or organization you're deriding may be one that an AP colleague is trying to develop as a source.

Second, if you or your department covers a subject — or you supervise people who do — you have a special obligation to be even-handed in your tweets. Whenever possible, link to AP copy, where we have the space to represent all points of view.

PRIVACY

Employees should be mindful that any opinions or personal information they disclose about themselves or colleagues may be linked to the AP's name. That's true even if staffers restrict their pages to viewing only by friends.

We recommend customizing your privacy settings on Facebook to determine what you share and with whom. However, as multitudes of people have learned all too well, virtually nothing is truly private on the Internet.

Posting on a social network is not just like uttering a comment to your friends in person. It's all too easy for someone to copy material out of restricted pages and redirect it elsewhere for wider viewing.

RETWEETING

Retweets, like tweets, should not be written in a way that looks like you're expressing a personal opinion on the issues of the day. A retweet with no comment of your own can easily be seen as a sign of approval of what you're relaying.

Examples:
RT @jonescampaign: smith's policies would destroy our schools

RT @dailyeuropean: at last, a euro plan that works bit.ly/xxxxx

These kinds of unadorned retweets must be avoided. Similarly, you shouldn't simply hit Twitter's "retweet" button on tweets like these.

However, we judiciously retweet opinionated material if we make clear we're simply reporting it, much as we would quote it in a story. Introductory words, colons and quote marks help make the distinction:

Examples:
Jones campaign now denouncing Smith on education: RT @jonescampaign: smith's policies would destroy our schools

Big European paper praises euro plan: RT @dailyeuropean: "at last, a euro plan that works" bit.ly/xxxxx.

These cautions apply even if you say on your Twitter profile that retweets do not constitute endorsements.

FRIENDING/FOLLOWING

It is acceptable to extend and accept Facebook friend requests from sources if necessary for reporting purposes. However, friending and "liking" political candidates or causes may create a perception among people unfamiliar with the protocol of social networks that AP staffers are advocates. Therefore, staffers should avoid friending and liking unless they have a true reporting reason for it. If we do friend or "like," we should avoid interacting with newsmakers on their public pages — for instance, commenting on their posts.

If reporters need to friend a newsmaker who is using a personal profile on Facebook, they should limit the newsmaker's access to their own personal information, using Facebook's lists and privacy settings. To keep track of tweets by newsmakers, we recommend using a Twitter list, which allows you to receive postings without joining the person's official list of followers. Again, the issue is possible perceptions by people who don't fully understand Twitter that we are supporters of the person.

AP managers should not issue friend requests to subordinates. It's fine if employees want to initiate the friend process with their bosses.

PUBLISHING

AP staff are encouraged to link to AP content in all formats. They can also link to content from other media organizations, except if the material spreads rumors or unconfirmed information not fit for AP's news services. Be mindful of competitive and corporate issues as you post links.

Staffers should link to content that has been published on an AP or subscriber platform, rather than directly uploading or copying and pasting the material.

Don't break news on social networks that we haven't published in AP's news services. If you have a piece of information, a photo, video or audio that is compelling, exclusive and/or urgent enough to be considered breaking news, you should make it available to AP services before you consider putting it out on social media. There may be occasional exceptions to this rule, but they must be prearranged with your manager and approved by a Nerve Center manager.

If material you have gathered meets our standards for quality and accuracy, but for a variety of reasons isn't sent to our subscribers, it is acceptable to share it on social networks. This includes material we commonly refer to as "cutting room floor" content — material that doesn't make it into our services because of space and time limits.

We rely on you to use your news judgment to determine if a piece of content is urgent enough that it should be filed first to our news services. If you have any hesitation about a tweet or post, you should consult with your manager, regional desk or the Nerve Center before sending it.

SOURCING

It can be difficult to verify the identity of sources found on social networks. Sources discovered there should be vetted in the same way as a source found by any other means. If a source you encounter on a social network claims to be an official from a company, organization or government agency, call the place of business to confirm the identity, just as you would if a source called on the phone.

You must never simply lift quotes, photos or video from social networking sites and attribute them to the name on the profile or feed where you found the material. Most social media sites offer a way to send a message to a user; use this to establish direct contact, over email or by phone, so you can explain what you're working on and get more detailed information about the source.

Use particular caution if you find a social networking page or feed that appears to belong to a person who is central to a story, especially if you can't get confirmation from that person. Fake accounts are rampant in the social media world and can appear online within minutes of a new name appearing in the news. Examine the details to determine whether the page could have just as easily been created by somebody else.

Many athletes, celebrities and politicians have verified Twitter accounts, meaning that Twitter has determined that the account really does belong to that person. However, even Twitter's verification process has been fooled, meaning we should still do our own checking with the newsmaker. Also, before you quote from newsmaker's tweets, confirm who is managing the account. Is it the famous person? His or her handlers? A combination? Knowing the source of the information will help you determine just how newsworthy the tweet is and how to characterize it.

To include photos, videos or other multimedia content from social networks in our news report, we must determine who controls the copyright to the material and get permission from that person or organization to use it. Any exceptions must be discussed with the Nerve Center and Legal.

INTERACTING WITH USERS

AP is strongly in favor of engaging with those who consume our content. Most feedback we receive is constructive. It often leads us to terrific information and imagery. But there's another side. People may accuse us of bias in our writing or photography. They may make denigrating comments about our writers and photographers.

Any substantive criticism of our content should be taken seriously, however it may be phrased.

AP's News Values and Principles say, "Staffers must notify supervisory editors as soon as possible of errors or potential errors, whether in their work or that of a colleague." Beyond that, responses to our audience can largely be guided by the nature of the comments that come in.

A thoughtful note from a reader or viewer that leads to a correction by us deserves an email or tweet of thanks (try to avoid repeating the original error). If someone offers a businesslike criticism of a story or image but has their facts wrong, it's good to reply, time permitting, to clarify the facts.

However, abusive, bigoted, obscene and/or racist comments posted to an AP-managed platform should be flagged to the Nerve Center immediately.

Other things to keep in mind:

I) Any response we make to a reader or viewer could go public. Email and direct Facebook and Twitter messages may feel like private communications, but may easily find their way to blogs and political pressure groups, attorneys and others. In the case of a story or image that stirs significant controversy, the editor is likely the best person to reply, rather than the person who created the content. The Standards Center can also reply, saying it looked into the complaint and here's what we found. This is particularly true if the response requires an explanation of AP policies or otherwise goes beyond the immediate content in question.

II) Any incoming message that raises the possibility of legal action should be reviewed by an AP attorney before a response is made.

III) We should not get into protracted back-and-forth exchanges with angry people that become less constructive with each new round. Particularly insulting or abusive comments directed to any individual staffer should be reported immediately to a manager. If such comments are posted online, contact the Nerve Center and we will work to get them removed, even from non-AP platforms. Of course, any comments that are truly threatening to individuals should be brought to the immediate attention of AP Global Security (Contact: Danny Spriggs at dspriggs@ap.org).

INTERACTING WITH AP ACCOUNTS

Staff are welcome to retweet and share material posted by official AP-branded accounts on social networking sites (e.g. @AP, @AP_Stylebook, etc.). We ask that AP staff refrain from liking or commenting on official AP-branded Facebook posts. These accounts are official, public-facing channels of communication, and we want to reserve the comments and the interactions for the public, not for journalists to talk among themselves in a public-facing spot. It can be off-putting and alienating for an average Facebook user to click on a post and see conversations between colleagues or virtual insider pats on the back.

DELETING TWEETS

Twitter.com allows us to delete tweets we've sent. Deletion, however, removes the tweet only from Twitter.com and perhaps some other Twitter clients. Tweets of ours that have been retweeted or reposted elsewhere will still remain publicly visible. If you believe a tweet should be deleted, contact a Nerve Center manager to discuss the situation.

CORRECTIONS

Erroneous tweets or other social media posts need to be corrected as quickly and transparently as errors in any other AP service. This applies to AP-related tweets or posts on personal accounts as well.

The thing to do is to tweet or post that we made a mistake and explain exactly what was wrong.

Example:
Correction: U.S. Embassy in Nigeria says bombings could happen this week at luxury hotels in Abuja (previously we incorrectly said Lagos): apne.ws/uxr9ph

Serious errors need to be brought to the attention of a Nerve Center manager and the appropriate regional or vertical desk.

SPORT IDENTIFICATION CODES

ARC — Archery
ATH — Athletics (Track & Field)
BAD — Badminton
BBA — Baseball-American League
BBC — Baseball-College
BBM — Baseball-Minor Leagues
BBN — Baseball-National League
BBO — Baseball-Other
BBH — Baseball-High School
BBI — Baseball-International
BBW — Baseball-Women's
BBY — Baseball-Youth
BIA — Biathlon
BKC — Basketball-College
BKH — Basketball-High School
BKL — Basketball-Women's Pro (WNBA)
BKN — Basketball-NBA
BKO — Basketball-Other
BKW — Basketball-Women's College
BOB — Bobsled
BOX — Boxing
BVL — Beach Volleyball
CAN — Canoeing
CAR — Auto Racing
CRI — Cricket
CUR — Curling
CYC — Cycling
DIV — Diving
EQU — Equestrian
FEN — Fencing
FIG — Figure Skating
FHK — Field Hockey
FBC — (American) Football-College
FBH — (American) Football-High School
FBN — (American) Football-NFL
FBO — (American) Football-Other
GLF — Golf
GYM — Gymnastics
HNB — Handball
HKC — (Ice) Hockey-College
HKN — (Ice) Hockey-NHL
HKO — (Ice) Hockey-Other

JUD — Judo
LUG — Luge
MMA — Mixed Martial Arts
PEN — Modern Pentathlon
MOT — Motorcycling
OLY — Olympics (with a specific sport code added where applicable)
RAC — (Horse) Racing
ROW — Rowing
RGL — Rugby League
RGU — Rugby Union
SAI — Sailing
SHO — Shooting
SKE — Skeleton
SKI — Skiing
SPD — Speed Skating
SBD — Snowboarding
SOC — Soccer
SOF — Softball
SQA — Squash
SUM — Sumo Wrestling
SWM — Swimming
TAE — Taekwondo
TEN — Tennis
TRI — Triathlon
TTN — Table Tennis
VOL — Volleyball
WPO — Water Polo
WEI — Weightlifting
WRE — Wrestling

SPORTS GUIDELINES AND STYLE

A

abbreviations It is not necessary to spell out the most common abbreviations on first reference: *NFL, AFC, NFC, NBA, NHL, NCAA, PGA, LPGA, USGA, NASCAR.*

Achilles tendon No apostrophe for the tendon connecting the back of the heel to the calf muscles. But it's *Achilles' heel*, with an apostrophe, for a vulnerable spot.

-added Follow this form in sports stories: *The $500,000-added sweepstakes.*

air ball

All-America, All-American The Associated Press recognizes only one All-America football and basketball team each year. In football, only Walter Camp's selections through 1924, and the AP selections after that, are recognized. Do not call anyone not listed on either the Camp or AP roster an *All-America* selection.

Similarly do not call anyone who was not an AP selection an *All-America basketball player*. The first All-America basketball team was chosen in 1948.

Use *All-American* when referring specifically to an individual: *All-American Michael Jordan*, or *He is an All-American.*

Use *All-America* when referring to the team: *All-America team*, or *All-America selection.*

archery Scoring is usually in

points. Use a basic summary. Example:

(After 3 of 4 Distances)
1. Darrell Pace, Cincinnati, 914 points.
2. Richard McKinney, Muncie, Ind. 880.

AstroTurf A trademark for a type of artificial grass.

athlete's foot, athlete's heart

athletic club Abbreviate as *AC* with the name of a club, but only in sports summaries: *Illinois AC.* See **volleyball** for an example of such a summary.

athletic director Use the singular *athletic* unless otherwise in a formal title.

athletic teams Capitalize teams, associations and recognized nicknames: *Red Sox, the Big Ten, the A's, the Colts.*

auto racing Follow the forms below for all major auto races:

LINEUP
NASCAR-Sprint Cup-Daytona 500 Lineup
By The Associated Press
After Thursday qualifying; race Sunday
At Daytona International Speedway
Daytona Beach, Fla.
Lap length: 2.5 miles
(Car number in parentheses)
1. (99) Carl Edwards, Ford, 194.738.
2. (16) Greg Biffle, Ford, 194.087.
3. (14) Tony Stewart, Chevrolet, 193.607.

RESULTS
NASCAR Sprint Cup-Daytona 500 Results
By The Associated Press
Monday
At Daytona International Speedway
Daytona Beach, Fla.
Lap length: 2.5 miles
(Start position in parentheses)
1. (4) Matt Kenseth, Ford, 202 laps, 100.9 rating, 47

points, $1,589,387.

2. (5) Dale Earnhardt Jr., Chevrolet, 202, 99.5, 42, $1,102,175.

3. (2) Greg Biffle, Ford, 202, 126.2, 42, $804,163.

For cars not finishing the race, include reason:

41. (17) Robby Gordon, Dodge, engine, 25, 30.5, 3, $268,150.

42. (8) Jimmie Johnson, Chevrolet, accident, 1, 28.3, 2, $327,149.

43. (25) David Ragan, Ford, accident, 1, 25.9, 1, $267,637.

After the final driver, add:

Race Statistics

Average Speed of Race Winner: 140.256 mph.

Time of Race: 3 hours, 36 minutes, 2 seconds.

Margin of Victory: 0.210 seconds.

Caution Flags: 10 for 42 laps.

Lead Changes: 25 among 13 drivers.

Lap Leaders: G.Biffle 1-9; R.Smith 10-11; G.Biffle 12-14; P.Menard 15-16; D.Hamlin 17-40; J.Burton 41-57; J.Gordon 58; T.Stewart 59-60; J.Burton 61-67; G.Biffle 68-76; M.Truex Jr. 77-81; G.Biffle 82; T.Labonte 83-85; G.Biffle 86-99; M.Truex Jr. 100-101; D.Hamlin 102-129; G.Biffle 130; M.Martin 131-132; G.Biffle 133-138; D.Hamlin 139-143; J.Logano 144-145; M.Kenseth 146-157; G.Biffle 158; D.Blaney 159-164; M.Kenseth 165-202.

Leaders Summary (Driver, Times Led, Laps Led): D.Hamlin, 3 times for 57 laps; M.Kenseth, 2 times for 50 laps; G.Biffle, 8 times for 44 laps; J.Burton, 2 times for 24 laps; M.Truex Jr., 2 times for 7 laps; D.Blaney, 1 time for 6 laps; T.Labonte, 1 time for 3 laps; P.Menard, 1 time for 2 laps; J.Logano, 1 time for 2 laps; M.Martin, 1 time for 2 laps; T.Stewart, 1 time for 2 laps; R.Smith, 1 time for 2 laps; J.Gordon, 1 time for 1 lap.

Top 12 in Points: 1. M.Kenseth, 47; 2. D.Earnhardt Jr., 42; 3. G.Biffle, 42; 4. D.Hamlin, 42; 5. J.Burton, 40; 6. P.Menard, 39; 7. K.Harvick, 37; 8. C.Edwards, 36; 9. J.Logano, 36; 10. M.Martin, 35; 11. C.Bowyer, 33; 12. M.Truex Jr., 33.

B

backboard, backcourt, backfield, backhand, backspin, backstop, backstretch, backstroke Some are exceptions to Webster's New World, made for consistency in handling sports stories.

badminton Games are won by the first player to score 21 points, unless it is necessary to continue until one player has a two-point spread. Most matches go to the first winner of two games.

Use a match summary.

ball carrier

ballclub, ballgame, ballpark, ballplayer

baseball The spellings for some frequently used words and phrases, some of which are exceptions to Webster's New World College Dictionary:

backstop	outfielder
ballclub	passed ball
ballpark	pinch hit (v.)
ballplayer	pinch-hit (n., adj.)
baseline	pinch hitter (n.)
bullpen	pitchout
center field	play off (v.)
center-field (adj.)	playoff (n., adj.
center fielder	put out (v.) putout (n.)
designated hitter	RBI (s.), RBIs (pl.)
doubleheader	right field
double play	right-field (adj.)
fair ball	rundown (n.)
fastball	sacrifice
first baseman	sacrifice fly
foul line	sacrifice hit
foul tip	shoestring catch
ground-rule double	shortstop
home plate	shut out (v.)
home run	shutout (n., adj.)
left-hander	slugger
left field	squeeze play
left-field (adj.)	strike
line drive	strike zone
line up (v.)	Texas leaguer
lineup (n.)	triple play
major league(s) (n.)	twinight doubleheader
major league (adj.)	wild pitch
major leaguer (n.)	

NUMBERS: Some sample uses of numbers: *first inning, seventh-inning stretch, 10th inning, first base, second base, third base, first home run, 10th home run, first place, one RBI, 10 RBIs. The pitcher's record is now 6-5. The final score was 1-0.*

LEAGUES: Use *American League, National League, American League West, National League East,* or *AL West* and *AL East,* etc. On second reference: *the league, the pennant in the West, the league's West Division,* etc.

Note: No hyphen in *major league, minor league, big league* (n. or adj.)

BOX SCORES: A sample follows. The visiting team always is listed on the left, the home team on the right.

Only one position, the first he played in the game, is listed for any player.

BC-BBN--BOX-Atl-SD

BRAVES 8, PADRES 3

ATLANTA					SAN DIEGO				
	ab	r	h	bi		ab	r	h	bi
Ogllen ss	5	1	1	1	QVeras 2b	4	1	0	0
Lckhrt 2b	5	2	2	0	SFinley cf	4	0	1	0
ChJnes 3b	4	2	2	1	Gwynn rf	4	1	1	1
Glrrga 1b	2	1	1	4	Cminiti 3b	3	0	1	0
Klesko lf	4	0	1	1	Leyritz 1b	3	1	2	2
Rocker p	0	0	0	0	Joyner 1b	1	0	1	0
Perez p	0	0	0	0	CHrndz c	4	0	1	0
Seanez p	0	0	0	0	RRivra lf	3	0	1	0
Lgtnbr p	0	0	0	0	MaSwy ph	1	0	0	0
JLopez c	4	1	1	1	Gomez ss	3	0	0	0
AJones cf	4	1	2	0	Miceli p	0	0	0	0
Tucker rf	2	0	1	0	Bhrngr p	0	0	0	0
GerWm rf	2	0	1	0	Lngstn p	0	0	0	0
Neagle p	2	0	0	0	GMyrs ph	0	0	0	0
DeMrtz p	0	0	0	0	JHmtn p	2	0	0	0
Clbrnn ph	1	0	0	0	RayMys p	0	0	0	0
DBtsta lf	1	0	0	0	Sheets ss	1	0	0	0
VnWal ph	1	0	0	0					
Totals	**36**	**8**	**12**	**8**		**34**	**3**	**8**	**3**

Atlanta	000 101 600 - 8
San Diego	000 200 000 - 2

DP_Atlanta 1, San Diego 2. LOB_Atlanta 4, San Diego 7. 2B_ChJones (1), Gwynn (1), RRivera (2). 3B_Lockhart (1). HR_Galarraga (1), JLopez (1), Leyritz (1).

	IP	H	R	ER	BB	SO
Atlanta						
Neagle	5 2-3	7	3	3	1	7
DeMrtz W, 1-0	1-3	0	0	0	0	0
Rocker	1 1-3	0	0	0	0	3
Perez	0	1	0	0	1	0
Seanez	2-3	0	0	0	0	0
Ligtenberg	1	0	0	0	1	2
San Diego						
JHamilton L, 0-1	6	7	4	4	2	5
RaMyers	2-3	2	3	3	1	0
Miceli	1-3	1	1	1	0	1
Boehringer	1	2	0	0	0	0
Langston	1	0	0	0	0	0

Perez pitched to 2 batters in the 8th, JHamilton pitched to 2 batters in the 7th.

Umpires_Home, Bonin; First, Davis; Second, Rippley; Third, Tata; Left, Poncino; Right, Hallion.

T_2:58. A_65,042 (59,772).

Example of an expanded box score:

BC-BBA--EXP-BOX-Ana-Tex

Rangers 3, Angels 2

Anaheim	AB	R	H	BI	BB	SO	Avg.
Erstad cf	4	0	3	2	0	0	.750
Gil ss	3	0	0	0	0	0	.000
a-OPalmeiro ph	1	0	0	0	0	0	.000
Nieves ss	0	0	0	0	0	0	.000
Salmon rf	4	0	1	0	0	1	.250
Glaus 3b	4	0	1	0	0	1	.250
GAnderson lf	3	0	1	0	1	0	.333
GHill dh	4	0	0	0	0	1	.000
BMolina c	4	1	1	0	0	1	.250
Spiezio 1b	3	1	1	0	0	1	.333
Eckstein 2b	3	0	1	0	0	0	.333
Totals	**33**	**2**	**9**	**2**	**1**	**5**	

Texas	AB	R	H	BI	BB	SO	Avg.
Greer lf	3	0	0	1	0	1	.143
Velarde 2b	4	0	1	0	0	1	.250
ARodriguez ss	4	0	1	0	0	3	.375
RPalmeiro 1b	2	0	0	0	2	0	.167
IRodriguez c	4	1	2	0	0	0	.250
Galarraga dh	3	1	1	1	0	0	.167
Caminiti 3b	2	0	1	0	1	0	.500
Curtis cf	2	1	1	0	0	0	.500
Mateo rf	3	0	1	0	0	1	.429
^Totals	27	3	8	2	3	6	

Anaheim	001 000 010_2 9 2
Texas	020 000 10X_3 8 0

a-grounded into double play for Gil in the 8th.

LOB_Anaheim 5, Texas 5. 2B_Erstad 2 (2), Glaus (1), BMolina (1), Spiezio (1), Velarde (1), IRodriguez (1), Galarraga (1). RBIs_Erstad 2 (2), Greer (1), Galarraga (1). SB_ARodriguez (1). SF_Greer. GIDP_OPalmeiro, GHill 2, IRodriguez, Curtis, Mateo.

Runners left in scoring position_Anaheim 4 (Salmon, Glaus, BMolina 2); Texas 3 (Greer, RPalmeiro, Caminiti). Runners moved up_Gil 2, Eckstein.

DP_Anaheim 3 (Gil, Eckstein and Spiezio), (Gil, Eckstein and Spiezio), (Eckstein, Gil and Spiezio); Texas 3 (ARodriguez, Velarde and RPalmeiro), (Velarde, ARodriguez and RPalmeiro), (Caminiti, IRodriguez and RPalmeiro).

	IP	H	R	ER	BB	SO	NP	ERA
Anaheim								
Schoeneweis L, 0-1	7	8	3	3	3	5	108	3.86
Weber	1	0	0	0	0	1	13	0.00
Texas								
Rogers W, 1-0	7 1-3	7	2	2	0	5	96	2.45
JRZimmermn H, 4	2-3	0	0	0	0	0	2	0.00
Crabtree S, 1	1	2	0	0	1	0	12	0.00

Inherited runners-scored_JRZimmermn 2-0.

IBB_off Crabtree (GAnderson) 1. HBP_by Schoeneweis (Curtis).

Umpires_Home, Rippley; First, Winters; Second, Barrett, Ted; Third, Marquez.

T_2:31. A_49,512 (49,115).

LINESCORE: When a bare linescore summary is required, use this form:

| Philadelphia | 010 200 000 - 3 4 1 |
| San Diego | 000 200 000 - 2 9 1 |

K. Gross, Tekulve (8) and Virgil; Dravecky, Lefferts (3) and Kennedy. W - KGross, 4-6. LDravecky, 4-3. Sv - Tekulve (3). HRs - Philadelphia, Virgil 2 (8).

LEAGUE STANDINGS:
The form:

All Times EDT

NATIONAL LEAGUE

	EAST			
	W	L	Pct.	GB
Pittsburgh	92	69	.571	-
Philadelphia	85	75	.531	61/2
	WEST			
	W	L	Pct.	GB
Cincinnati	108	54	.667	-
Los Angeles	88	74	.543	20

(Night games not included)

Monday's Results

Chicago 7, St. Louis 5

Atlanta at New York, rain.

Tuesday's Games

Cincinnati (Gullett 14-2 and Nolan 4-4) at New York (Seaver 12-3 and Matlack 6-1) 2, 6 p.m.

Wednesday's Games

Cincinnati at New York

Chicago at St.Louis, night

Only games scheduled.

In subheads for results and future games, spell out day of the week as: *Tuesday's Games*, instead of *Today's Games*.

basic summary This format for summarizing sports events lists winners in the order of their finish. The figure showing the place finish is followed by an athlete's full name, his affiliation or hometown, and his time, distance, points or whatever performance factor is applicable to the sport.

If a contest involves several types of events, the paragraph begins with the name of the event.

A typical example:

60-yard dash – 1, Steve Williams, Florida TC, 6.0. 2, Hasley Crawford, Philadelphia Pioneer, 6.1. 3, Mike McFarland, Chicago TC, 6.2. 4

100 – 1, Steve Williams, Florida TC, 10.1. 2

Additional examples are provided in the entries for many of the sports that are reported in this format.

Most basic summaries are a single paragraph per event, as shown. In some competitions with large fields, however, the basic summary is supplied under a dateline with each winner listed in a single paragraph. See the **auto racing** and **bowling** entries for examples.

For international events in which U.S. competitors are not among the leaders, add them in a separate paragraph as follows:

Also: 14, Dick Green, New York, 6.8.

In events where points, rather than time or distance, are recorded as performances, mention the word points on the first usage only:

1. Jim Benson, Springfield, N.J., 150 points. 2. Jerry Green, Canada, 149.

basketball The spellings of some frequently used words and phrases:

alley-oop	halftime
backboard	hook shot
backcourt	jump ball
baseline	jump shot
fast break	layup
field goal	man-to-man
foul line	midcourt
foul shot	pivotman
free throw	play off (v.)
free-throw line	playoff (n., adj.)
frontcourt	tip off (v.)
full-court press	tipoff (n., adj.)
goaltending	up-tempo
half-court pass	zone

NUMBERS: Some sample uses of numbers: *in the first quarter, a second-quarter lead, nine field goals, a 3-pointer, 10 field goals, the 6-foot-5 forward, the 6-10 center. He is 6 feet 10 inches tall.*

LEAGUE: *National Basketball Association* or *NBA.*

For subdivisions: *the Atlantic Division of the Eastern Conference, the Pacific Division of the Western Conference,* etc. On second reference: *the NBA East, the division, the conference,* etc.

BOX SCORE: A sample follows. The visiting team always is listed first.

In listing the players, begin with the five starters — two forwards, center, two guards — and follow with all substitutes who played.

Figures after each player's last name denote field goals made and attempted, free throws made and attempted and total points.

Example:

Hornets-Bulls, Box

NEW ORLEANS (95)

Ariza 7-12 0-0 16, Ayon 2-6 1-2 5, Kaman 7-18 3-4 17, Vasquez 4-10 4-4 12, Belinelli 3-7 0-0 6, Jones 4-10 2-2 10, Aminu 0-4 2-2 2, Jack 4-9 0-0 10, Henry 3-10 6-7 12, Thomas 2-3 1-1 5. Totals 36-89 19-22 95.

CHICAGO (99)

Deng 6-16 1-2 14, Boozer 7-14 0-0 14, Noah 7-12 1-3 15, Rose 11-24 9-11 32, Hamilton 2-5 1-1 5, Brewer 3-6 0-0 6, Gibson 2-4 1-2 5, Watson 0-2 0-0 0, Korver 2-6 0-0 5, Asik 1-1 1-1 3. Totals 41-90 14-20 99.

New Orleans 26•24•20•25_95

Chicago 30•17•29•23_99

3-Point Goals_New Orleans 4-9 (Jack 2-2, Ariza 2-2, Henry 0-1, Vasquez 0-1, Belinelli 0-3), Chicago 3-18 (Korver 1-5, Deng 1-5, Rose 1-5, Brewer 0-1, Hamilton 0-1, Watson 0-1). Fouled Out_None. Rebounds_New Orleans 55 (Kaman 11), Chicago 56 (Noah 16). Assists_New Orleans 22 (Kaman 5), Chicago 25 (Rose 9). Total Fouls_New Orleans 18, Chicago 16. Technicals_Boozer, Noah. A_21,919 (20,917).

STANDINGS: The format for professional standings:

Eastern Conference

Atlantic Division

	W	L	Pct.	GB
Boston	43	22	.662	–
Philadelphia	40	30	.571	5 1/2

In college boxes, the score by periods is omitted because the games are divided only into halves.

No. 19 CONNECTICUT 74, No. 8 SYRACUSE 66

CONNECTICUT (15-5)

Villanueva 9-13 3-7 21, Boone 2-4 3-5 7, Brown 0-2 5-6 5, Williams 3-11 1-2 9, Gay 6-13 4-4 18, Armstrong 2-2 2-2 6, Kellogg 0-0 0-0 0, Anderson 1-4 2-3 4, Nelson 1-1 2-3 4. Totals 24-50 22-32 74.

SYRACUSE (21-3)

Warrick 6-13 4-7 16, Pace 7-9 0-0 14, Forth 0-1 0-0 0, McNamara 4-18 0-0 9, McCroskey 2-5 0-0 4, Watkins 2-2 0-0 4, Edelin 3-8 1-2 7, Roberts 4-10 4-5 12. Totals 28-66 9-14 66.

Halftime_Connecticut 37-36. 3-Point Goals_Connecticut 4-14 (Gay 2-5, Williams 2-5, Brown 0-2, Anderson 0-2), Syracuse 1-9 (McNamara 1-9). Fouled Out_Roberts. Rebounds_Connecticut 36 (Villanueva 10), Syracuse 34 (Warrick 7). Assists_Connecticut 14 (Williams 6), Syracuse 17 (Edelin, McNamara 6). Total Fouls_Connecticut 15, Syracuse 24. A_27,651.

The format for college conference standings:

	Conference			All Games		
	W	L	Pct.	W	L	Pct.
Missouri	12	2	.857	24	4	.857

betting odds Use figures and a hyphen: *The odds were 5-4, he won despite 3-2 odds against him.*

The word *to* seldom is necessary, but when it appears it should be hyphenated in all constructions: *3-to-2 odds, odds of 3-to-2, the odds were 3-to-2.*

bettor A person who bets.

billiards Scoring is in points. Use a match summary. Example:

Minnesota Fats, St. Paul, Minn., def. Pool Hall Duke, 150-141.

bobsledding, luge Scoring is in minutes, seconds and tenths of a second. Extend to hundredths if available.

Identify events as *two-man, four-man, men's luge, women's luge.*

Use a basic summary. Example:

Women

1. Kaillie Humphries and Jennifer Ciochetti, Canada, 3 minutes, 48.57 seconds (57.10- 57.07-57.22-57.18).

2. Sandra Kiriasis and Petra Lammert, Germany, 3:48.90 (57.30-57.28-57.21-57.11).

3. Elana Meyers and Katie Eberling, United States, 3:49.57 (57.22-57.45-57.41-57.49).

bowl games Capitalize them: *Cotton Bowl, Orange Bowl, Rose Bowl,* etc.

bowling Scoring systems use both total points and won-lost records.

Use the basic summary format in paragraph form. Note that a comma is used in giving pinfalls of more than 999.

Examples:

ST. LOUIS (AP) – Second-round leaders and their total pinfalls in the $100,000 Professional Bowlers Association tournament:

1. Bill Spigner, Hamden, Conn., 2,820.

2. Gary Dickinson, Fort Worth, Texas, 2,759.

ALAMEDA, Calif. (AP) – The 24 match play finalists with

their won-lost records and total pinfall Thursday night after four rounds – 26 games – of the $65,000 Alameda Open bowling tournament:

1. Jay Robinson, Los Angeles, 5-3, 5,937.
2. Butch Soper, Huntington Beach, Calif., 3-5, 5,932.

boxing The four major sanctioning bodies for professional boxing are the World Boxing Association, the World Boxing Council, the World Boxing Organization and the International Boxing Federation.

Weight classes and titles by organization:

105 pounds – Mini Flyweight, WBF, IBF, WBO; Strawweight, WBC

108 pounds – Light Flyweight, WBA, WBC; Junior Flyweight, IBF, WBO

112 pounds – Flyweight, WBA, WBC, IBF, WBO

115 pounds – Super Flyweight, WBA, WBC; Junior Bantamweight, IBF, WBO

118 pounds – Bantamweight, WBA, WBC, IBF, WBO

122 pounds – Super Bantamweight, WBA, WBC; Junior Featherweight, IBF, WBO

126 pounds – Featherweight, WBA, WBC, IBF, WBO

130 pounds – Super Featherweight, WBA, WBC; Junior Lightweight, IBF, WBO

135 pounds – Lightweight, WBA, WBC, IBF, WBO

140 pounds – Super Lightweight, WBA, WBC; Junior Welterweight, IBF, WBO

147 pounds – Welterweight, WBA, WBC, WBO, IBF

154 pounds – Super Welterweight, WBA, WBC; Junior Middleweight, IBF, WBO

160 pounds – Middleweight, WBA, WBC, IBF, WBO

168 pounds – Super Middleweight, WBA, WBC, IBF, WBO

175 pounds – Light Heavyweight, WBA, WBC, IBF, WBO

190 pounds – Cruiserweight, WBA, WBC, IBF, WBO

More than 200 pounds – Heavyweight, WBA, WBC, IBF, WBO

Some other terms:

kidney punch A punch to an opponent's kidney when the puncher has only one hand free. It is illegal. If the puncher has both hands free, it is legal.

knock out (v.) **knockout** (n. and adj.) A fighter is knocked out if he takes a 10-count.

If a match ends early because one fighter is unable to continue, say that the winner stopped the loser. In most boxing jurisdictions there is no such thing as a technical knockout.

outpointed Not *outdecisioned*.

rabbit punch A punch behind an opponent's neck. It is illegal.

SUMMARIES: Use a match summary.

Some examples, with the fighters weights after their names and the number of rounds at the end.

Randy Jackson, 152, New York, outpointed Chuck James, 154, Philadelphia, 10.

Muhammad Ali, 220, Chicago, knocked out Pierre Coopman, 202, Belgium, 5.

George Foreman, 217, Hayward, Calif., stopped Joe Frazier, 214, Philadelphia, 2.

TALE OF THE TAPE:
An example:
SAN JUAN, Puerto Rico (AP) – The tale of the tape for the Jean Pierre Coopman-Muhammad Ali world heavyweight championship fight Friday night:

	Coopman	Ali
Age	29	34
Weight	202	220
Height	6-0	6-3
Reach	75	80
Chest Normal	43	44
Chest Expanded	45 1/2	46
Biceps	15	15
Forearm	13	13 1/2
Waist	34 1/2	34
Thigh	25 1/2	26
Calf	15	17
Neck	17	17 1/2
Wrist	7 1/2	8
Fist	12 1/2	13
Ankle	9	9 1/2

box office (n.) **box-office** (adj.)

bullfight, bullfighter, bull-fighting

bullpen One word, for the place where pitchers warm up.

C

Canada goose Not Canadian goose.

canoeing Scoring is in minutes, seconds and tenths of a second. Extend to hundredths if available.

Use a basic summary. Example:

Canoeing, Men
Kayak Singles, 500 meters
Heat 1 – Rudiger Helm, Germany, 1:56.06. 2. Zoltan Sztanity, Hungary, 1:57.12.
Also: 6. Henry Krawczyk, New York, 2 04.64.
First Repechage – 1, Ladislay Soucek, Czech Republic, 1:53.20. 2. Hans Eich, Germany, 1:54.23.

coach Lowercase as a job description, not a formal title. Capitalize only when used as a term of address. *Coach told me* or *Coach Taylor told me*, but *coach John Calhoun will miss the rest of the season.*

collective nouns Nouns that denote a unit take singular verbs and pronouns: *class, committee, crowd, family, group, herd, jury, orchestra, team.*

However, team names such as *the Jazz, the Magic, the Avalanche* and *the Thunder* take plural verbs.

Many singular names take singular verbs: *Boston is favored in the playoffs. The Cardinal is in the NCAA tournament.*

colt A male horse 4 years and under.

conferences Major college basketball and football conferences are listed on the following pages.

cross-country Note hyphen, which is an exception to the practices of U.S. and international governing bodies for the sport.

Scoring for this track event is in minutes, seconds and tenths of a second. Extended to hundredths if available.

National AAU Championship
Cross-Country
Frank Shorter, Miami, 5:25.67; 2. Tom Coster, Los Angeles, 5:30.72

Adapt the basic summary to paragraph form under a dateline for a field of more than 10 competitors.

See **auto racing** and **bowling** for examples.

cycling Use the basic summary format.

D

decathlon Summaries include time or distance performance, points earned in that event and the cumulative total of points earned in previous events.

Contestants are listed in the order of their overall point totals. First name and hometown (or nation) are included only on the first and last events on the first day of competition; on the last day, first names are included only in the first event and in the summary denoting final placings.

Use the basic summary format. Include all entrants in summaries of each of the 10 events.

An example for individual events:

Decathlon
(Group A)
100 – 1. Fred Dixon, Los Angeles, 10.8 seconds, 854 points. 2. Bruce Jenner, San Jose State, 11:09, 783.
Long jump – 1. Dixon, 24-7 (7.34m), 889, 1,743. 2. Jenner, 23-6 (7.17m), 855, 1,638.
Decathlon final – 1. Bruce Jenner, San Jose State, 8,524 points. 2. Fred Dixon, Los Angeles, 8,277.

discus The disc thrown in track and field events.

Major College Basketball Conferences

AMERICA EAST CONFERENCE – Albany (NY); Binghamton; Boston University; Hartford; Maine; New Hampshire; Stony Brook; UMBC (Maryland-Baltimore County); Vermont.

ATLANTIC 10 CONFERENCE – Charlotte; Dayton; Duquesne; Fordham; George Washington; La Salle; Massachusetts; Rhode Island; Richmond; St. Bonaventure; Saint Joseph's; Saint Louis; Temple; Xavier.

ATLANTIC COAST CONFERENCE – Boston College; Clemson; Duke; Florida State; Georgia Tech; Maryland; Miami; North Carolina; NC State; Virginia; Virginia Tech; Wake Forest.

ATLANTIC SUN CONFERENCE – Belmont; East Tennessee State; Florida Gulf Coast; Jacksonville; Kennesaw State; Lipscomb; Mercer; North Florida; S.C. Upstate; Stetson.

BIG 12 CONFERENCE – Baylor; Iowa State; Kansas; Kansas State; Missouri; Oklahoma; Oklahoma State; Texas; Texas A&M; Texas Tech.

BIG EAST CONFERENCE – Cincinnati; Connecticut; DePaul; Georgetown; Louisville; Marquette; Notre Dame; Pittsburgh; Providence; Rutgers; St. John's; Seton Hall; South Florida; Syracuse; Villanova; West Virginia.

BIG SKY CONFERENCE – Eastern Washington; Idaho State; Montana; Montana State; Northern Arizona; Northern Colorado; Portland State; Sacramento State; Weber State.

BIG SOUTH CONFERENCE – Campbell; Charleston Southern; Coastal Carolina; Gardner-Webb; High Point; Liberty; Presbyterian; Radford; UNC-Asheville; VMI; Winthrop.

BIG TEN CONFERENCE – Illinois; Indiana; Iowa; Michigan; Michigan State; Minnesota; Nebraska; Northwestern; Ohio State; Penn State; Purdue; Wisconsin.

BIG WEST CONFERENCE – Cal Poly; Cal State Fullerton; CS Northridge; Long Beach State; Pacific; UC Davis; UC Irvine; UC Riverside; UC Santa Barbara.

COLONIAL ATHLETIC ASSOCIATION – Delaware; Drexel; George Mason; Georgia State; Hofstra; James Madison; Northeastern; Old Dominion; Towson; UNC-Wilmington; Virginia Commonwealth; William & Mary.

CONFERENCE USA – East Carolina; Houston; Marshall; Memphis; Rice; SMU; Southern Mississippi; Tulane; Tulsa; UAB (Alabama-Birmingham); UCF (Central Florida); UTEP.

GREAT WEST – Chicago State; Houston Baptist; NJIT; North Dakota; Texas-Pan American; Utah Valley State.

HORIZON LEAGUE – Butler; Cleveland State; Detroit; Green Bay; Illinois-Chicago; Loyola of Chicago; Milwaukee; Valparaiso; Wright State; Youngstown State.

IVY LEAGUE – Brown; Columbia; Cornell; Dartmouth; Harvard; Pennsylvania; Princeton; Yale.

METRO ATLANTIC ATHLETIC CONFERENCE – Canisius; Fairfield; Iona; Loyola (Md.); Manhattan; Marist; Niagara; Rider; St. Peter's; Siena.

MID-AMERICAN CONFERENCE – East Division: Akron; Bowling Green; Buffalo; Kent State; Miami (Ohio); Ohio. West Division: Ball State; Central Michigan; Eastern Michigan; Northern Illinois; Toledo; Western Michigan.

MID-EASTERN ATHLETIC CONFERENCE – Bethune-Cookman; Coppin State; Delaware State; Florida A&M; Hampton; Howard; Maryland-Eastern Shore; Morgan State; Norfolk State; N.C. A&T; N.C. Central; Savannah State; S.C. State.

MISSOURI VALLEY CONFERENCE – Bradley; Creighton; Drake; Evansville; Illinois State; Indiana State; Missouri State; Northern Iowa; Southern Illinois; Wichita State.

MOUNTAIN WEST CONFERENCE – Air Force; Boise State; Colorado State; UNLV; New Mexico; San Diego State; TCU; Wyoming.

NORTHEAST CONFERENCE – Bryant; CCSU (Central Connecticut State); Fairleigh Dickinson; LIU (Long Island University); Monmouth (N.J.); Mount St. Mary's (Md.); Quinnipiac; Robert Morris; Sacred Heart; St. Francis (NY); St. Francis (Pa.); Wagner.

OHIO VALLEY CONFERENCE – Austin Peay; Eastern Illinois; Eastern Kentucky; Jacksonville State; Morehead State; Murray State; SIU-Edwardsville; Southeast Missouri State; Tennessee State; Tennessee Tech; UT-Martin.

PACIFIC-12 CONFERENCE – Arizona; Arizona State; California; Colorado; Oregon; Oregon State; Southern California; Stanford; UCLA; Utah; Washington; Washington State.

PATRIOT LEAGUE – American; Army; Bucknell; Colgate; Holy Cross; Lafayette; Lehigh; Navy.

SOUTHEASTERN CONFERENCE – Eastern Division: Florida; Georgia; Kentucky; South Carolina; Tennessee; Vanderbilt. Western Division: Alabama; Arkansas; Auburn; LSU; Mississippi; Mississippi State.

SOUTHERN CONFERENCE – North Division: Appalachian State; Chattanooga; Elon; Samford; UNC Greensboro; Western Carolina. South Division: College of Charleston; Davidson; Furman; Georgia Southern; The Citadel; Wofford.

SOUTHLAND CONFERENCE – East Division: Central Arkansas; Lamar; McNeese State; Nicholls State; Northwestern State; Southeastern Louisiana. West Division: Sam Houston State; Stephen F. Austin; Texas A&M-Corpus Christi; Texas State; Texas-Arlington; UTSA (Texas-San Antonio).

SOUTHWESTERN ATHLETIC CONFERENCE – Alabama A&M; Alabama State; Alcorn State; Arkansas-Pine Bluff; Grambling State; Jackson State; MVSU (Mississippi Valley State); Prairie View; Southern University; Texas Southern.

SUMMIT LEAGUE – IPFW (Indiana-Purdue-Fort Wayne); IUPUI (Indiana-Purdue-Indianapolis); North Dakota State; Oakland; Oral Roberts; South Dakota; South Dakota State; Southern Utah; UMKC (Missouri-Kansas City); Western Illinois.

SUN BELT CONFERENCE – East Division: FAU (Florida Atlantic); FIU (Florida International); Middle Tennessee; South Alabama; Troy; Western Kentucky. West Division: Arkansas State; Denver; Louisiana-Lafayette; Louisiana-Monroe; North Texas; UALR (Arkansas-Little Rock).

WEST COAST CONFERENCE – BYU; Gonzaga; Loyola Marymount; Pepperdine; Portland; Saint Mary's (Cal.); San Diego; San Francisco; Santa Clara.

WESTERN ATHLETIC CONFERENCE – Fresno State; Hawaii; Idaho; Louisiana Tech; Nevada; New Mexico State; San Jose State; Utah State.

INDEPENDENTS – CS Bakersfield; Longwood; Seattle.

Major College Football Conferences

ATLANTIC COAST CONFERENCE – Atlantic Division (Boston College; Clemson; Florida State; Maryland; NC State; Wake Forest). Coastal Division (Duke; Georgia Tech; Miami; North Carolina; Virginia; Virginia Tech).

BIG 12 CONFERENCE – Baylor; Iowa State; Kansas; Kansas State; Oklahoma; Oklahoma State; Texas; TCU; Texas Tech.

BIG EAST CONFERENCE – Cincinnati; Connecticut; Louisville; Pittsburgh; Rutgers; South Florida; Syracuse; West Virginia.

BIG TEN CONFERENCE – Legends Division (Iowa; Michigan; Michigan State; Minnesota; Nebraska; Northwestern). Leaders Division (Illinois; Indiana; Ohio State; Penn State; Purdue; Wisconsin).

CONFERENCE USA – East Division (East Carolina; Marshall; Memphis; Southern Mississippi; UAB; UCF). West Division (Houston; Rice; SMU; Tulane; Tulsa; UTEP).

MID-AMERICAN CONFERENCE – East Division (Akron; Bowling Green; Buffalo; Kent State; Miami (Ohio); Ohio; Temple). West Division (Ball State; Central Michigan; Eastern Michigan; Northern Illinois; Toledo; Western Michigan).

MOUNTAIN WEST CONFERENCE – Air Force; Boise State; Colorado State; Fresno State; Hawaii; Nevada; New Mexico; San Diego State; UNLV; Wyoming.

PACIFIC-12 CONFERENCE – North Division (California; Oregon; Oregon State; Stanford; Washington; Washington State). South Division (Arizona; Arizona State; Colorado; Southern California; UCLA; Utah).

SOUTHEASTERN CONFERENCE – East Division (Florida; Georgia; Kentucky; Missouri; South Carolina; Tennessee; Vanderbilt). West Divsion (Alabama; Arkansas; Auburn; LSU; Mississippi; Mississippi State; Texas A&M).

SUN BELT CONFERENCE – Arkansas State; Florida Atlantic; Florida International; Louisiana-Lafayette; Louisiana-Monroe; Middle Tennessee; North Texas; Troy; Western Kentucky.

WESTERN ATHLETIC CONFERENCE – Idaho; Louisiana Tech; New Mexico State; San Jose State; Texas State; UTSA (Texas-San Antonio); Utah State.

INDEPENDENTS – Army; BYU; Navy; Notre Dame.

Football Championship Subdivision

BIG SKY CONFERENCE – Cal Poly; Eastern Washington; Idaho State; Montana; Montana State; Northern Arizona; Northern Colorado; Portland State; Sacramento State; UC Davis; Weber State.

BIG SOUTH CONFERENCE – Charleston Southern; Coastal Carolina; Gardner-Webb; Liberty; Presbyterian; Stony Brook; VMI.

GREAT WEST CONFERENCE – North Dakota; Southern Utah.

IVY LEAGUE – Brown; Columbia; Cornell; Dartmouth; Harvard; Pennsylvania; Princeton; Yale.

MID-EASTERN ATHLETIC CONFERENCE – Bethune-Cookman; Delaware State; Florida A&M; Hampton; Howard; Morgan State; Norfolk State; North Carolina A&T; South Carolina State.

MISSOURI VALLEY CONFERENCE – Illinois State; Indiana State; Missouri State; Northern Iowa; North Dakota State; South Dakota; South Dakota State; Southern Illinois; Western Illinois; Youngstwon State.

NORTHEAST CONFERENCE – Albany (NY); Bryant; Central Connecticut State; Duquesne; Monmouth (NJ); Robert Morris; Sacred Heart; St. Francis (Pa.); Wagner.

OHIO VALLEY CONFERENCE – Austin Peay; Eastern Illinois; Eastern Kentucky; Jacksonville State; Murray State; Southeast Missouri State; Tennessee-Martin; Tennessee State; Tennessee Tech.

PATRIOT LEAGUE – Bucknell; Colgate; Fordham; Georgetown (DC); Holy Cross; Lafayette; Lehigh.

PIONEER LEAGUE – Butler; Campbell; Davidson; Dayton; Drake; Jacksonville; Marist; Morehead State; San Diego; Valparaiso.

SOUTHERN CONFERENCE – Appalachian State; Chattanooga; Elon; Furman; Georgia Southern; Samford; The Citadel; Western Carolina; Wofford.

SOUTHLAND CONFERENCE – Central Arkansas; McNeese State; Nicholls State; Northwestern State; Sam Houston State; Southeastern Louisiana; Stephen F. Austin.

SOUTHWESTERN ATHLETIC CONFERENCE – East Division (Alabama A&M; Alabama State; Alcorn State; Jackson State; MVSU). West Division (Arkansas-Pine Bluff; Grambling State; Prairie View; Southern U.; Texas Southern).

INDEPENDENTS – Georgia State; Lamar; N.C. Central; Savannah State; South Alabama.

diving Use a basic summary.

E

ERA Acceptable in all references to baseball's *earned run average*.

F

FBS Abbreviation for *Football Bowl Subdivision*. The higher level of NCAA Division I football. Formerly known as the I-A Division. *FBS* is used on second reference.

FBS (Football Bowl Subdivision) conferences: Atlantic Coast, Big 12, Big East, Big Ten, Conference USA, Mid-American, Mountain West, Pacific-12, Southeastern, Sun Belt, Western Athletic, Independents (Army, Navy, Notre Dame)

FCS Abbreviation for *Football Championship Subdivision*. The lower level of NCAA Division I football. Formerly known as the I-AA Division. *FCS* is used on second reference.

FCS (Football Championship Subdivision) conferences: Big Sky, Big South, Colonial Athletic Association, Great West, Ivy League, Mid-Eastern Athletic, Missouri Valley, Northeast, Ohio Valley, Patriot League, Pioneer League, Southern, Southland, Southwestern Athletic, Independents (North Carolina Central, Old Dominion, Savannah St.)

fencing Identify epee, foil and saber classes as: *men's individual foil, women's team foil*, etc.

Use match summary for early rounds of major events, for lesser dual meets and for tournaments.

Use basic summary for final results of major championships.

For major events, where competitors meet in a round-robin and are divided into pools, use this form:

Epee, first round (four qualify for semi-finals) Pool 1 – Joe Smith, Springfield, Mass., 4-1. Enrique Lopez, Chile, 3-2.

figure skating Use a basic summary. Example:

World Figure Skating Championships Results
By The Associated Press
Wednesday
At Moscow
Men
Short Program
1. Patrick Chan, Canada, 93.02 points.
2. Nobunari Oda, Japan, 81.81.
3. Daisuke Takahashi, Japan, 80.25.
Free Skating
1. Patrick Chan, Canada, 187.96 points.
2. Takahiko Kozuka, Japan, 180.79.
3. Artur Gachinski, Russia, 163.52.
Overall Standings
1. Patrick Chan, Canada, 280.98 points.
2. Takahiko Kozuka, Japan, 248.41.
3. Artur Gachinski, Russia, 241.86.

football The spellings of some frequently used words and phrases:

ball carrier	lineman
ballclub	line of scrimmage
blitz (n., v.)	out of bounds (adv.)
end line	out-of-bounds (adj.)
end zone	pitchout (n.)
fair catch	place kick
field goal	place-kicker
fourth-and-1 (adj.)	play off (v.)
fullback	playoff (n., adj.)
goal line	quarterback
goal-line stand	runback (n.)
halfback	running back
halftime	split end
handoff	tailback
kick off (v.)	tight end
kickoff (n., adj.)	touchback
left guard	touchdown
linebacker	wide receiver

NUMBERS: Use figures for yardage: *The 5-yard line, the 10-yard line, a 5-yard pass play, he plunged in from the 2, he ran 6 yards, a 7-yard gain; a fourth-and-2 play.*

Some other uses of numbers: *The final score was 21-14. The team won its fourth game in 10 starts. The team record is 4-5-1.*

LEAGUE: *National Football League*, or *NFL*.

STATISTICS: All football games, whether using the one- or two-point conversion, use the same summary style.

The visiting team always is listed first.

Field goals are measured from the point where the ball was kicked — not the line of scrimmage. The goal posts are 10 yards behind the goal lines. Include that distance.

Abbreviate team names to four letters or fewer on the scoring and statistical lines as illustrated.

The passing line shows, in order: completions-attempts-interceptions.

A sample agate package:

Jets-Giants Stats

N.Y. Jets	7	10	7	0_24
N.Y. Giants	0	7	14	14_35

First Quarter
NYJ_Rhodes 11 fumble return (Nugent kick), 8:36.
Second Quarter
NYG_Ward 8 run (Tynes kick), 10:54.
NYJ_B.Smith 16 pass from Pennington (Nugent kick), :33.
NYJ_FG Nugent 47, :00.
Third Quarter
NYG_Jacobs 19 run (Tynes kick), 11:17.
NYJ_L.Washington 98 kickoff return (Nugent kick), 11:03.
NYG_Shockey 13 pass from Manning (Tynes kick), :33.
Fourth Quarter
NYG_Burress 53 pass from Manning (Tynes kick), 7:52.
NYG_Ross 43 interception return (Tynes kick), 3:15.
A_78,809

	NYJ	NYG
First downs	16	21
Total Net Yards	277	374
Rushes-yards	22-55	39-188
Passing	222	186
Punt Returns	2-20	2-16
Kickoff Returns	5-200	3-62
Interceptions Ret.	1-1	3-68
Comp-Att-Int	21-36-3	13-25-1
Sacked-Yards Lost	1-7	0-0
Punts	4-45.3	5-46.8
Fumbles-Lost	0-0	1-1
Penalties-Yards	6-40	3-37
Time of Possession	26:15	33:45

INDIVIDUAL STATISTICS
RUSHING_N.Y. Jets, T.Jones 13-36, L.Washington 9-13, Pennington 2-6, B.Smith 1-0. N.Y. Giants, Jacobs 20-100, Ward 13-56, Manning 4-17, Droughns 2-15.

PASSING_N.Y. Jets, Pennington 21-36-3-229. N.Y. Giants, Manning 13-25-1-186.
RECEIVING_N.Y. Jets, Coles 8-89, Cotchery 4-31, Baker 3-52, B.Smith 3-44, T.Jones 2-14, L.Washington 1-(minus 1). N.Y. Giants, Burress 5-124, Ward 3-8, Shockey 2-33, Moss 1-10, Matthews 1-6, Hedgecock 1-5.
MISSED FIELD GOAL_N.Y. Jets, Nugent 42 (WL).

The rushing and receiving paragraph for individual leaders shows attempts and yardage gained. The passing paragraph shows completions, attempts, interceptions and total yards gained.

STANDINGS: The form for **professional standings**:

American Conference
East

	W	L	T	Pct.	PF	PA
y-New England	12	3	0	.800	464	321
N.Y. Jets	8	7	0	.533	360	344
Buffalo	6	9	0	.400	351	385
y-clinched division						

The form for college **conference standings**:

Atlantic Coast Conference
Atlantic Division

	Conference				All games			
	W	L	PF	PA	W	L	PF	PA
Wake Forest	6	2	175	145	11	2	289	191
Boston College	5	3	189	133	9	3	313	180

In college conference standings, limit team names to nine letters or fewer. Abbreviate as necessary.

fractions Put a full space between the whole number and the fraction.

G

game plan

golf Some frequently used terms and some definitions:
birdie, birdies One stroke under par.
bogey, bogeys One stroke over par. The past tense is *bogeyed*.

caddie
eagle Two strokes under par.
fairway
green fee A fee paid to play on a golf course. Not *greens fee*. *Green* refers to all parts of a golf course, not just the putting green.
hole-in-one
Masters, Masters Tournament No possessive. Use *the Masters* on second reference.
tee, tee off

NUMBERS: Some sample uses of numbers:

Use figures for handicaps: *He has a 3 handicap; a 3-handicap golfer, a handicap of 3 strokes; a 3-stroke handicap.*

Use figures for par listings: *He had a par 5 to finish 2-up for the round, a par-4 hole; a 7-under-par 64, the par-3 seventh hole.*

Use figures for club ratings: *a 5-iron, a 7-iron shot, a 4-wood.*

Miscellaneous: *the first hole, a nine-hole course, the 10th hole, the back nine, the final 18, the third round. He won 3 and 2.*

ASSOCIATIONS: *Professional Golfers' Association of America* (note the apostrophe) or *PGA.* Headquarters is in Palm Beach Gardens, Fla. Members teach golf at golf shops and teaching facilities across the country.

The *PGA Tour* is a separate organization made up of competing professional golfers. Use *tour* (lowercase) on second reference.

The PGA conducts the PGA Championship, the Senior PGA Championship, and the Ryder Cup as well as other golf championships not associated with the PGA Tour.

The *United States Golf Association* or *USGA* is headquartered in Far Hills, N.J. It conducts the United States' national championships. These include the U.S. Open, the U.S. Women's Open, the U.S. Senior Open, 10 national amateur championships and the State Team Championships.

SUMMARIES — Stroke (Medal) Play: List scores in ascending order. Ties are listed in the order in which they were played. Use a dash before the final figure, hyphens between others.

On the first day, use the player's score for the first nine holes, a hyphen, the player's score for the second nine holes, a dash and the player's total for the day:

First round:

| Lorena Ochoa | 35-34 – 69 |
| Se Ri Pak | 36-33 – 69 |

On subsequent days, give the player's scores for each day, then the total for all rounds completed:

Second round:

| Rory McIlroy | 66-69 – 135 |
| Tiger Woods | 65-71 – 136 |

Final round, professional tournaments, including prize money:

Final Round:

(FedExCup points in parentheses)

J.B. Holmes (4,500), $1,080,000 68-65-66-70 – 269
Phil Mickelson (2,700), $648,000 68-68-67-67 – 270

Use hometowns only on national championship amateur tournaments. For tournaments including both amateurs and professionals, indicate amateurs with an "a-" before the name:

a-Stacey Lewis, The Woodlands, Texas 70-69 – 139

The form for cards:

Par out	444 343 544-35
Watson out	454 333 435-34
Nicklaus out	434 243 544-33
Par in	434 443 454-35 – 70
Watson in	434 342 443-31 – 65
Nicklaus in	433 443 453-33 – 66

SUMMARIES — Match Play: In the first example that follows, "and 2" means that the 17th and 18th hole were skipped because Rose had a three-hole lead with two to play. In the second, the match went 18 holes. In the third, a 19th and 20th hole were played because the golfers were tied after 18.

Justin Rose def. Charles Howell III, 3 and 2.

Paul Casey def. Shaun Micheel, 2 up.

Nick O'Hern def. Tiger Woods, 20 holes.

Grey Cup The Canadian Football League's championship game.

Gulfstream Park The racetrack.

gymnastics Scoring is by points. Identify events by name: Men: *floor exercise, vault, pommel horse, still rings, horizontal bar* (or *high bar*), *parallel bars*. Women: *floor exercise, vault, balance beam, uneven bars*.

Use a basic summary. Example:

Parallel Bars _ 1. Joe Smith, Houston, 9.675 points. 2. Ed Jones, Albany, N.Y., 9.54. 3. Andy Brown, Los Angeles, 9.4

H

handball Games are won by the first player to score 21 points or, in the case of a tie breaker, 11 points. Most matches go to the first winner of two games.

Use a match summary. Example:

Bob Richards, Yale, def. Paul Johnson, Dartmouth, 21-18, 21-19.

Tom Brenna, Massachusetts, def. Bill Stevens, Michigan, 21-19, 17-21, 21-20.

hit and run (v.) **hit-and-run** (n. and adj.) *The coach told him to hit and run. He scored on a hit-and-run.*

hockey The spellings of some frequently used words:

blue line	play off (v.)
crease	playoff (n., adj.)
face off (v.)	power play
faceoff (n., adj.)	power-play goal
goalie	red line
goal line	short-handed
goal post	slap shot
goaltender	two-on-one break
penalty box	

The term *hat trick* is jargon for scoring three goals in a game. Use it sparingly.

LEAGUE: *National Hockey League*

or *NHL*.

For NHL subdivisions: *the Central Division of the Western Conference, the division, the conference*, etc.

SUMMARIES: The visiting team always is listed first in the score by periods.

Note that each goal is numbered according to its sequence in the game.

The figure after the name of a scoring player shows his total goals for the season.

Names in parentheses are players credited with an assist on a goal.

The final figure in the listing of each goal is the number of minutes elapsed in the period when the goal was scored.

Senators-Flyers, Sums

Ottawa	**1 1 1_3**
Philadelphia	**3 1 1_5**

First Period_1, Ottawa, Neil 8 (Simpson, Havlat), 4:07. 2, Philadelphia, Lapointe 4 (Somik, Slaney), 10:41. 3, Philadelphia, Recchi 25 (LeClair, Handzus), 11:11. 4, Philadelphia, Markov 6 (Handzus, LeClair), 16:10. Penalty_Amonte, Phi (ob.-holding), 5:17.

Second Period_5, Philadelphia, Johnsson 9 (Zhamnov, Slaney), 5:22 (pp). 6, Ottawa, Chara 15 (Spezza, Schaefer), 14:32 (pp). Penalties_Fisher, Ott (tripping), 3:57; Simpson, Ott (holding), 6:06; Somik, Phi (slashing), 13:08; Fisher, Ott (highsticking), 17:07.

Third Period_7, Philadelphia, Zhamnov 10 (Gagne, Amonte), 6:54. 8, Ottawa, Bondra 23 (Alfredsson, Schaefer), 19:47 (pp). Penalties_Alfredsson, Ott (rough) 9:03; Zhamnov, Phi (roughing), 9:03; Smolinski, Ott (roughing), 12:18; Sharp, Phi (roughing), 12:18; Simpson, Ott (slashing), 14:21; Philadelphia bench, served by Sharp (too many men), 15:57; Van Allen, Ott, major-double game misconduct (fighting), 18:15; Ray, Ott, major (fighting), 18:15; Lalime, Ott, minor-major-game misconduct (leaving the crease, fighting), 18:15; Simpson, Ott, major-game misconduct (fighting), 18:15 Brashear, Phi, double minor-double major-misconduct-game misconduct; (instigator, roughing, fighting), 18:15; Radivojevic, Phi, major-double game misconduct (fighting), 18:15; Esche, Phi, minor-major-double game misconduct (leaving the crease, fighting), 18:15; Markov, Phi, major-game misconduct (fighting), 18:15; Chara, Ott, minor-major-misconduct-game misconduct (instigator, fighting), 18:18; Neil, Ott, major (fighting), 18:18; Somik, Phi, major (fighting) 18:18; Timander, Phi, major (fighting), 18:18.

Shots on goal_Ottawa 7-9-10_26. Philadelphia 13-11-6_30.

Power-play Opportunities_Ottawa 2 of 6; Philadelphia 1 of 4.

Goalies_Ottawa, Lalime 22-19-7 (30 shots-25 saves), Prusek (18:15 third, 0-0). Philadelphia, Esche 18-7-5 (22-20), Burke (18:15 third, 4-3).

A_19,539 (19,519). T_2:39.

Referees_Marc Joannette, Dan Marouelli. Linesmen_ Jonny Murray, Tim Nowak.

STANDINGS: The form:

Eastern Conference
Atlantic Division

	GP	W	L	OT	Pts.	GF	GA
Philadelphia	71	47	10	14	108	314	184
NY Islanders	71	45	17	9	99	310	192

home-field (adj.), **home field** (n.)

horse races Capitalize their formal names: *Kentucky Derby, Preakness, Belmont Stakes*, etc.

horse racing Some frequently used terms and their definitions:

broodmare A female horse used for breeding.

bug boy An apprentice jockey, so-called because of the asterisk beside the individual's name in a program. It means that the jockey's mount gets a weight allowance.

colt A male thoroughbred horse 4 years old and under, or a standardbred 3 years of age.

entry Two or more horses owned by same owner running as a single betting interest. In some states two or more horses trained by same person but having different owners also are coupled in betting.

filly A female horse under the age of 5.

furlong One-eighth of a mile. Race distances are given in furlongs up through seven furlongs (spell out the number), after that in miles, as in *one-mile, 1/1-16 miles*.

gelding A castrated male horse.

graded stakes A thoroughbred race that derives its name from the stake, or entry fee, that owners must pay. There are three levels, assigned by the American Graded Stakes Committee. *Grade 1* is the highest level, the most prestigious, based partly on purse but also on such considerations as previous winners and race history. The other levels

are *Grade 2* and *Grade 3*. Do not use Roman numerals. *Grade 2*, not *Grade II*.

half-mile pole The pole on a racetrack that marks one-half mile from the finish. All distances are measured from the finish line, meaning that when a horse reaches the quarter pole, he is one-quarter mile from the finish.

horse A male horse over 4 years old.

long shot (two words)

mare A female horse 5 years and older.

mutuel field Not *mutual field*. Two or more horses, long shots, that have different owners and trainers. They are coupled as a single betting interest to give the field not more than 12 wagering interests. There cannot be more than 12 betting interests in a race. The bettor wins if either horse finishes in the money.

stallion A male horse used for breeding.

horses' names Capitalize. See **animals** in main section.

I

IC4A Abbreviation for *Intercollegiate Association of Amateur Athletes of America*. In general, spell out on first reference. A phrase such as *IC4A tournament* may be used on first reference, however, to avoid a cumbersome lead. If this is done, provide the full name later in the story.

indoor (adj.) **indoors** (adv.) *He plays indoor tennis. He went indoors.*

J

judo Use the basic summary format by weight divisions for major tournaments; use the match summary for dual and lesser meets.

K

Kentucky Derby *The Derby* on second reference. An exception to normal second-reference practice. Plural is *Derbys* — an exception to Webster's New World College Dictionary.

See **capitalization** in main section.

knuckleball One word is an exception to Webster's New World College Dictionary.

L

lacrosse Scoring in goals, worth one point each.

The playing field is 110 yards long. The goals are 80 yards apart, with 15 yards of playing area behind each goal.

A match consists of four 15-minute periods. Overtimes of varying lengths may be played to break a tie.

Adapt the summary format in **hockey**.

Ladies Professional Golf Association No apostrophe after *Ladies*. Use *LPGA Tour* in all references.

left hand (n.) **left-handed** (adj.) **left-hander** (n.)

M

marathon Use the formats illustrated in the **cross-country** and **track and field** entries.

match summary This format for summarizing sports events applies to individual contests such as tennis, match play golf, etc.

Give a competitor's name, followed either by a hometown or by a college or club affiliation. For competitors from outside the United States, a country name alone is sufficient in summaries sent for domestic use.

Rafael Nadal, Spain, def. Jarkko Nieminen, Finland, 7-5, 6-3, 6-1.

Serena Williams, United States, def. Nicole Vaidisova, Czech Republic, 6-3, 6-4.

metric system See main section.

minicamp

mixed martial arts Generic term for bouts featuring boxing, wrestling, taekwondo, judo and other disciplines. Do not use *ultimate fighting* as a synonym. It is a registered trademark for events sanctioned by Ultimate Fighting Championship. See **Ultimate Fighting**.

motor sports Two words unless different in the official name of an event.

motorboat racing Scoring may be posted in miles per hour, points or laps, depending on the competition.

In general, use the basic summary format. For some major events, adapt the basic summary to paragraph form under a dateline. See **auto racing** for an example.

motorcycle racing Follow the formats shown under **auto racing**.

N

NASCAR Acceptable in all references for National Association for Stock Car Auto Racing.

NCAA Acceptable in all references for National Collegiate Athletic Association.

nonconference No hyphen.

numerals See the main section on general use and entries on **betting odds** and **scores**.

O

offseason No hyphen.

Olympics Capitalize all references to the international athletic contests: *the Olympics, the Winter Olympics, the Olympic Games, an Olympic-size pool.*

Lowercase *the games* in second reference.

Sports in the 2012 Summer Olympics in London, July 27-Aug. 12: archery, badminton, basketball, beach volleyball, boxing, canoe/kayak, cycling, diving, equestrian, fencing, soccer, gymnastics, handball, field hockey, judo, modern pentathlon, rowing, sailing, shooting, swimming, synchronized swimming, table tennis, taekwondo, tennis, track and field, triathlon, volleyball, water polo, weightlifting, wrestling.

Sports in the 2014 Winter Olympics in Sochi, Russia, Feb. 7-23: biathlon, bobsled, curling, hockey, luge, figure skating, speedskating, short-track speedskating, Alpine skiing, cross-country skiing, Nordic combined, freestyle skiing, ski jumping, skeleton, snowboarding.

Sports in the 2016 Summer Olympics in Rio de Janeiro, Aug. 5-21: archery, badminton, basketball, beach volleyball, boxing, canoe/kayak, cycling, diving, equestrian,

fencing, soccer, golf, gymnastics, handball, field hockey, judo, modern pentathlon, rowing, rugby, sailing, shooting, swimming, synchronized swimming, table tennis, taekwondo, tennis, track and field, triathlon, volleyball, water polo, weightlifting, wrestling.

Sports in the 2018 Winter Olympics in Pyeonchang, South Korea, Feb. 9-25: biathlon, bobsled, curling, hockey, luge, figure skating, speedskating, short-track speedskating, Alpine skiing, cross-country skiing, Nordic combined, freestyle skiing, ski jumping, skeleton, snowboarding.

P

pingpong A synonym for *table tennis.*

The trademark name is *Ping-Pong.*

play off (v.) **playoff playoffs** (n., adj.)

postgame, pregame

postseason, preseason No hyphen.

R

racket Not *racquet,* for the light bat used in tennis and badminton.

racquetball Amateur games are played to 15 points in a best-of-three match. Professional matches are played to 11 points, unless it is necessary to continue until one player has a two-point spread. Most matches go to the winner of three of five games.

Use a match summary.

record Avoid the redundant *new record.*

right hand (n.) **right-handed** (adj.) **right-hander** (n.)

rodeo Use the basic summary format by classes, listing points.

rowing Scoring is in minutes, seconds and tenths of a second. Extend to hundredths if available.

Use a basic summary. An example, for a major event where qualifying heats are required:

Single Sculls Heats (first two in each heat qualify for Monday's quarterfinals, losers go to repechage Friday): Heat 1 – 1, Peter Smith, Australia, 4:24.7. 2. Etc. Heat 2 – 1, John Jones, Canada, 4:26.3. 72

runner-up, runners-up

S

scores Use figures exclusively, placing a hyphen between the totals of the winning and losing teams: *The Reds defeated the Red Sox 4-3, the Giants scored a 12-6 football victory over the Cardinals, the golfer had a 5 on the first hole but finished with a 2-under-par score.*

Use a comma in this format: *Boston 6, Baltimore 5.*

See individual listings for each sport for further details.

short-handed

skiing Identify events as: *men's downhill, women's slalom,* cross-country (note hyphen), etc. In ski jumping, note style where two jumps and points are posted.

Use a basic summary. Example:

90-meter special jumping – 1, Karl Schnabel, Austria, 320 and 318 feet, 234.8 points. 2, Toni Innauer, Austria, 377-299, 232.9. 3, Etc. Also; 27, Bob Smith, Hanover, N.H., 312-280, 201. 29

ski, skis, skier, skied, skiing
Also: *ski jump, ski jumping.*

soccer The spellings of some frequently used words and phrases:
    AFC Asian Football Confederation.
    Bundesliga German League first division.
    CAF Confederation Africaine de Football. Refer to it as the governing body of African soccer rather than spelling out French acronym.
    Champions League
    coach Also known as *manager* on British teams and *technical director* on some Latin American teams.
    CONCACAF The Confederation of North, Central American and Caribbean Association Football.
    Conference National Fifth-highest division of English soccer.
    Conference North, Conference South Sixth-highest division of English soccer.
    CONMEBOL Confederacion Sudamerica de Futbol. Refer to it as South America's governing body rather than spelling out Spanish acronym.
    Copa America South American national team championship. Use the Spanish name, not *America Cup.*
    Copa Libertadores South American club championship. Use the Spanish name, not *Liberators Cup.*
    defender Do not use *defenseman.*
    Eredivisie Netherlands first division.
    FA Cup Acceptable on first reference for The Football Association Cup.
    FIFA Federation International de Football Association. *FIFA* acceptable on first reference. Refer to it as the international soccer governing body rather than spelling out French acronym.
    forward or **striker**
    friendly An exhibition game.
    goalkeeper *Goalie* is acceptable.

Do not use *goaltender*.

La Liga Spanish first division.

League Championship Second-highest division of English soccer.

League Cup The No. 2 cup competition in England. Do not refer to as *Carling Cup*.

League One Third-highest division of English soccer.

League Two Fourth-highest division of English soccer.

Ligue 1 French first division.

midfielder

MLS Major League Soccer. *MLS* acceptable on first reference.

OFC Oceania Football Confederation.

offside

penalty area Sometimes referred to as *penalty box*. Do not refer to solely as *box* on U.S. wires.

Premier League Top league in England. Also the name of the top league in Scotland. Note that England, Scotland, Wales and Northern Ireland have separate national teams. Do not refer to *Premiership* or *Barclay's Premier League*.

Serie A Italian League first division.

sideline *Touchline* for international wires.

UEFA Union of European Football Associations.

World Cup Not *World Cup Finals*.

In summaries and key lines for international wires, the home team is listed first; on U.S. wires, the visiting team is listed first.

SUMMARY:
At Saint-Denis, France
Italy 0 2 – 2
France 2 0 – 2
(France won 4-3 on penalty kicks)
First half – 1, France, Zidane 4 (Djorkaeff), 12th minute. 2, France, Deschamps (penalty kick), 45th minute.
Second half – 3, Italy, own goal, 88th minute. 4, Italy, R. Baggio 6 (D. Baggio), 90th minute.
First overtime – None.
Second overtime – None.
Penalty kicks – France 4 (Zidane G, Lizarazu NG, Trezeguet G, Henry G, Blanc G); Italy 3 (Baggio G, Albertini NG, Costacurta G, Vieri G, Di Biagio NG).
Yellow Cards – Italy, Del Piero, 26th minute; Bergomi, 28th; Rostacurta, 113th. France, Guivarc'h, 53rd minute; Deschamps, 63rd.
Referee – Dallas (Scotland). Linesmen – Grigorescu (Romania),
Warren (England)
A –77,000
Lineups
Italy – Gianluca Pagliuca; Giuseppe Bergomi, Fabio Cannavaro, Alessandro Costacurta, Paolo Maldini; Francesco Moriero, Dino Baggio (Demetrio Albertini, 52nd), Luigi Di Biagio, Gianluca Pessotto (Angelo Di Livio, 90th); Christian Vieri, Alessandro Del Piero (Roberto Baggio, 67th).
France – Fabien Barthez; Lilian Thuram, Laurent Blanc, Marcel Desailly, Bixente Lizarazu; Didier Deschamps, Emmanuel Petit, Zinedine Zidane, Christian Karembeu (Thierry Henry, 65th); Stephane Guivarc'h (David Trezeguet, 65th), Youri Djorkaeff.

Lineup order is goalkeepers, defenders, midfielders, forwards.

Separate the different positions with semicolons and the players within a position with commas.

STANDINGS:

Scores and standings move in separate files.

Schedule on world wires has times GMT instead of EST or EDT.

Schedule lists home teams first.

Sunday, Jan. 31
Bari vs. Lazio of Rome, 0130
Cagliari vs. Juventus of Turin, 0130
Fiorentina vs. Vicenza, 0130

Standings for international leagues have a different style: *GP* (games played), *W* (wins), *D* (draws), *L* (losses), *GF* (goals for), *GA* (goals against) and *Pts* (points). Standings for Major League Soccer follow the same style as National Football League: *W* (wins), *L* (losses), *T* (ties), *Pts* (points), *GF* (goals for) and *GA* (goals against).

Spanish Soccer At A Glance

By The Associated Press
La Liga

Team	GP	W	D	L	GF	GA	Pts
Real Madrid	25	8	2	5	54	21	56
Barcelona	25	16	6	3	49	17	54
Villarreal	25	14	4	7	43	35	46

Major League Soccer

By The Associated Press

EASTERN CONFERENCE

	W	L	T	Pts	GF	GA
D.C. United	16	7	7	55	56	34
New England	14	8	8	50	51	43
New York	12	11	7	43	47	45

speedskating Scoring is in minutes, seconds and tenths of a second. Extend to hundredths if available.

Use a basic summary.

sports editor Capitalize as a formal title before a name. See **titles** in main section.

sports sponsorship If the sponsor's name is part of the event name, such as Buick Open, use the name in the title. If there is a previously established name commonly accepted for the event — *Orange Bowl, Sugar Bowl* — use that name even if there currently is a corporate sponsor. *Orange Bowl*, not *Discover Orange Bowl.* However, mention the sponsor somewhere in the story or in a self-contained paragraph after a 3-em dash at the bottom of the story.

sports writer Two words. An exception to Webster's New World College Dictionary.

stadium, stadiums Capitalize only when part of a proper name: *Yankee Stadium.*

swimming Scoring is in minutes, if appropriate, seconds and tenths of a second. Extend to hundredths if available.

Most events are measured in metric units.

Identify events as *men's 4x100 relay, women's 100 backstroke*, etc.

See **track and field** for the style on relay teams and events where a record is broken

Use a basic summary. Examples, where qualifying heats are required:

100 Butterfly

Final

1, Michael Phelps, United States, 50.77. 2, Ian Crocker, United States, 50.82. 3, Albert Subirats, Venezuela, 51.82.

T

table tennis See **pingpong**.

tennis The scoring units are points, games, sets and matches.

A player wins a point if his opponent fails to return the ball, hits it into the net or hits it out of bounds. A player also wins a point if his opponent is serving and fails to put the ball in play after two attempts, a *double fault.*

A player must win four points to win a game. In tennis scoring, both players begin at *love*, or zero, and advance to 15, 30, 40 and game. (The numbers 15, 30 and 40 have no point value as such — they are simply tennis terminology for 1 *point*, 2 *points* and 3 *points*.) The server's score always is called out first. If a game is tied at 40-all, or *deuce*, play continues until one player has a two-point margin.

A set is won if a player wins six games before his opponent has won five. If a set becomes tied at five games apiece, it goes to the first player to win seven games. If two players who were tied at five games apiece also tie at six games apiece, they may play a tiebreaker — a game that goes to the first player to win seven points. A player must win a tiebreaker by at least two points. In some cases, the rules call for a player to win by two games without a tiebreaker.

A match may be either a best-of-three contest that goes to the first player or team to win two sets, or a best-of-five contest that goes to the first player or team to win three sets.

Set scores would be reported this way: *Chris Evert Lloyd defeated Sue Barker 6-0, 3-6, 6-4.* Indicate tiebreakers in parentheses after the set score, using only the lower number: *7-6, (9)*

SUMMARIES: Winners always are listed first in agate summaries. An example:

Singles
Fourth Round
Roger Federer (1), Switzerland, def. Tomas Berdych (13), Czech Republic, 6-4, 7-6 (7), 6-3.

Doubles
Second Round
Eric Butorac, United States, and Kevin Ullyett, Zimbabwe, def. Juan Pablo Brzezicki and Agustin Calleri, Argentina, walkover.

Mixed Doubles
Second Round
Yan Zi, China, and Mark Knowles, Bahamas, def. Vladimira Uhlirova, Czech Republic, and Simon Aspelin, Sweden, 6-7 (4), 6-1, 10-5 tiebreak.

track and field Scoring is in distance, time or height, depending on the event.

Most events are measured in metric units. For those meets that include feet, make sure the measurement is clearly stated, as in *men's 100-meter, women's 880-yard run*, etc.

For time events, spell out *minutes* and *seconds* on first reference, as in *3 minutes, 26.1 seconds.* Subsequent times in stories and all times in agate require a colon and decimal point: *3:26.1.* For a marathon, it would be *2 hours, 11 minutes, 5.01 seconds* on first reference then the form *2:11:5.01* for later listings.

In running events, the first event should be spelled out, as in *men's 100-meter.* Later references can be condensed to phrases such as *the 200, the 400*, etc.

For hurdle and relay events, the progression can be: *100-meter hurdles, 400 hurdles*, etc.

For field events — those that do not involve running — use these forms: *26 1/2* for *26 feet, one-half inch*; *25-10 1/2* for *25 feet, 10 1/2 inches*, etc.

In general, use a basic summary. For the style when a record is broken, note the mile event in the example below. For the style in listing relay teams, note *4x400 meter relay.*

60-yard dash – 1, Steve Williams, Florida TC, 6.0 2, Hasley Crawford, Philadelphia Pioneer, 6.2 3, Mike McFarland, Chicago TC. 6.2 3.

100 – 1, Steve Williams, Florida TC 10.1.

Mile – 1, Filbert Bayi, Tanzania, 3:55.1, meet record, old record 3:59, Jim Beatty, Los Angeles TC. Feb. 27, 1963; 2. Paul Cummings, Beverly Hills TC. 3:56.1; 3

Women's 880 – 1, Johanna Forman, Falmouth TC. 2:07.9.

4x400 relay – 1, St. John's, (Jon Kennedy, Doug Johnson, Gary Gordon, Ordner Emanuel), 3:21.9. 2. Brown, 3:23.5. 3. Fordham, 3:24.1.

Team scoring – Chicago TC 32. Philadelphia Pioneer 29

Where qualifying heats are required:

Men's 100-meter heats (first two in each heat qualify for Friday's semifinals): Heat 1 – 1, Steve Williams, Florida TC. 10.1.

U

Ultimate Fighting A registered trademark. Use the generic term *mixed martial arts* for bouts featuring boxing, wrestling, taekwondo, judo and other disciplines. *Ultimate Fighting Championship* is acceptable for events sanctioned by that group.

USGA Acceptable in all references for the *United States Golf Association.*

V

volleyball In all international, U.S. college and USA Volleyball games, each of the first four sets is won by the first team to score 25

points. If the match is tied in sets after the first four sets, a deciding fifth set will be played to 15 points. In all five sets, teams must win by two points without a cap on points.
Use a match summary. Example:
U.S.-Women def. Korea 21-25, 25-16, 29-27, 16-25, 15-12.

volley, volleys

W

water polo Scoring is by goals. List team scores. Example:
World Water Polo Championship
First Round
United States 7, Canada 1
Britain 5, France 3

water skiing Scoring is in points. Use a basic summary. Example:
World Water Skiing Championships
Men
Overall – 1, George Jones, Canada, 1,987 points. 2, Phil Brown, Britain, 1,756.
Slalom – 1, George Jones, Canada, 73 buoys (two rounds).

water sports

weight In agate listings, use abbreviations for some sports, such as *lbs.* for pounds and *kg.* for kilograms.

weightlifting Use a basic summary. Example:
ATHENS, Greece (AP) _ Final results Saturday of the weightlifting event from the Summer Olympics:
^Men
^85kg
1. George Asanidze, Georgia, (2, 177.50-391; 3, 205.00-452), 382.50 kg.-843 lbs.
2. Andrei Rybakou, Belarus, (1, 180.00-397; 8, 200.00-441), 380.00-838.

wild-card (adj.) wild card (n.)

World Series Or *the Series* on second reference. A rare exception to the general principles under **capitalization**.

wrestling Identify events by weight division.

Y

yachting Use a basic summary, identifying events by classes.

yard Equal to 3 feet.
The metric equivalent is approximately 0.91 meter.
To convert to meters, multiply by 0.91 (5 yards x 0.91 = 4.55 meters).
See **foot**; **meter**; and **distances**.

yard lines Use figures to indicate the dividing lines on a football field and distance traveled: *40-yard line, he plunged in from the 2, he ran 6 yards, a 7-yard gain.*

yearling An animal 1 year old or in its second year. The birthdays of all horses arbitrarily are set at Jan. 1. On that date, any foal born in the preceding year is considered 1 year old.

FOOD GUIDELINES

Common Culinary Conversions
1 tablespoon = 3 teaspoons
2 tablespoons = 1 fluid ounce
1 cup = 16 tablespoons = 8 fluid ounces
1 pint = 2 cups = 16 fluid ounces
1 quart = 4 cups = 32 fluid ounces
1 pound = 16 ounces
1 stick butter = ½ cup = 8 tablespoons = 4 ounces

AP Recipe Style
Recipe guidelines. Always use figures. See **fractions**.

Break out recipes in list and instruction format. Do not write as regular text. Use figures for all quantities in recipes. Do not use abbreviations. Spell out *teaspoon, tablespoon*, etc.

Following is the format for recipes:
- The title of the recipe is capitalized.
- Start to finish time goes below the title, noting estimate for active time in parentheses, if hands-off cooking time is significantly longer than active prep time.
- The number of servings appears next.
- List ingredients in the order used and spell out all measurements. When appropriate, unusual ingredients can be clarified within the list, *ghee (clarified butter)*.
- Use numerals for all measurements, times and oven settings. Exception: When two numbers follow one another, write out the first for clarity, *two 12-ounce cans*.
- Instructions for making the recipe follow, and should be written in short, easy-to-digest paragraphs.
- When an oven is used, *Heat the oven to 350 F*, should be the first line of the method (unless the oven is not used until more than 30 minutes after the start of the recipe).
- Begin sentences with equipment and technique, rather than ingredients. *In a medium saucepan over low heat, whisk together the butter and sugar.*
- Nutrition information, if available, follows the method.
- The source of the recipe appears at the bottom in parentheses:
(*Recipe from John Smith's "Book of Recipes," Recipe Publishers, 2007.*)
(*Recipe from January 2007 issue of Gourmet.*)
(*Recipe from epicurious.com.*)
(*Recipe from the January issue of Gourmet, as listed at epicurious.com.*)
(*Recipe from AP Food Editor J.M. Hirsch*)
(*Recipe adapted from John Smith's "Book of Recipes," Recipe Publishers, 2007*)

PIZZA WITH RAINBOW CHARD, GOAT CHEESE AND EGG
Start to finish: 30 minutes
Servings: 4
1 tablespoon olive oil
1 bunch rainbow chard, chopped
1 medium yellow onion, diced
1/4 teaspoon red pepper flakes
2 cloves garlic, minced
20-ounce ball prepared pizza dough, room temperature
4 ounces (about 8 slices) prosciutto, finely chopped
8-ounce log chevre (fresh goat cheese)
4 large eggs
Heat the oven to 400 F. Lightly spritz 2 baking sheets with cooking spray.

In a large skillet over medium-high, heat the oil. Add the chard, onion, red pepper flakes and garlic. Saute until the chard is wilted, about 8 minutes. Set aside.

Divide the dough into 4 pieces. On a lightly floured surface, roll out each to the size of a dinner plate. Place 2 rounds of dough on each baking sheet. Top each piece of dough with a quarter of the greens, spreading them evenly.

Top the greens with the prosciutto, then crumble goat cheese over each pizza.

Bake for 12 minutes, or until the crust is lightly puffed, but not browned. Crack an egg into the center of each pizza, then bake for another 12 minutes, or until the whites are cooked but the yolks are still runny. Serve immediately.

Nutrition information per serving (values are rounded to the nearest whole number): 651 calories; 254 calories from fat; 28 g fat (11 g saturated; 0 g trans fats); 228 mg cholesterol; 70 g carbohydrate; 36 g protein; 4 g fiber; 1,668 mg sodium.

(Recipe from AP Food Editor J.M. Hirsch)

See the **food** entry in the main section for guidelines on when to capitalize the names of foods.

A

absinthe A bitter green liqueur made from wormwood.

adobo sauce A spicy red sauce made from chilies, herbs and vinegar that is common to Mexican cooking.

agave A honey-like syrup made from succulent plants.

aioli A garlic mayonnaise, an emulsification of olive oil, egg yolks and lemon juice.

a la carte A restaurant menu in which each item is individually priced.

a la king A chopped meat dish, often chicken or turkey, served in a cream sauce.

a la mode In the U.S., a dessert served with ice cream, often pies or cakes.

al dente Italian for *to the tooth*, refers to pasta cooked until tender, but slightly firm.

Alfredo A creamy Italian sauce made with butter and Parmesan cheese, *fettuccine Alfredo*.

alfresco A meal eaten outside.

all-purpose flour Preferred term for *white wheat flour*.

amuse-bouche French, a bite-sized dish served at restaurants before the meal, usually free.

andouille sausage

angel hair pasta A thin, spaghetti-like pasta.

Angus Angus cattle comprises two breeds of hornless cattle from the original Scottish Aberdeen stock, Black Angus and Red Angus. Black is the predominant color. Black Angus is the most popular breed for beef in the U.S.

antipasto Italian for *hors d'oeuvre* or *appetizer*.

apples Most varieties are capitalized, including *Cortland, Golden Delicious, Granny Smith, Honeycrisp* and *McIntosh*. An exception: *crabapple*.

arborio rice A short-grain, starchy Italian variety of white rice, used in risotto.

artisanal Foods and drinks produced in small batches often using traditional techniques and local ingredients.

Asiago cheese A sharp, aged cow's milk cheese from Italy's Veneto region.

B

baba ghanoush A Middle Eastern dish of pureed roasted eggplant with tahini, lemon juice and garlic.

baby back ribs

baked Alaska A cake topped with ice cream and meringue that is briefly baked.

baker's dozen 13, not 12.

baking sheet Preferred to cookie sheet.

baklava A Middle Eastern pastry of layered phyllo dough, honey and chopped nuts.

bananas Foster A dessert of sautéed bananas served with rum and vanilla ice cream. Created during the 1950s at Brennan's Restaurant in New Orleans. Named for a customer.

barbecue The verb refers to the cooking of foods (usually meat) over flame or hot coals. As a noun, can be both the meat cooked in this manner or the fire pit (grill). Not *barbeque* or *Bar-B-Q*.

basmati rice A long-grain aromatic rice.

bearnaise sauce A French sauce made from reduced wine, vinegar, tarragon, shallots, egg yolks and butter.

Beaujolais A fruity wine from France. *Beaujolais Nouveau* is a young version.

beef Wellington A fillet of beef wrapped and roasted in pastry.

Bellini A cocktail made from sparkling wine and peach juice.

bialy, bialys A Jewish-American yeast roll that is large, round and chewy, topped with onions.

bibb lettuce A variety of butter lettuce.

Bing cherries A variety of sweet cherries.

bisque A rich, thick soup often made from seafood and cream.

black-eyed pea A small beige bean with a black dot.

Black Forest cake A German layered chocolate cake with cherries and whipped cream.

blanch To briefly cook by submerging in boiling water, then cooling in cold water.

blind bake To bake the crust of a pie before filling it.

bloody mary A cocktail of tomato juice, vodka, Worcestershire sauce and Tabasco sauce.

bok choy A leafy vegetable, also called *pak choi* or *Chinese white cabbage*.

bologna The lunch meat.

Bolognese A thick Italian meat sauce made from beef or veal and vegetables, often served over pasta, also called *ragu*.

bonbon A filled chocolate candy.

Bordeaux Red or white wines made in France's Bordeaux region.

borscht A Russian or Polish soup made from beets.

Boston brown bread A steamed bread made from rye and wheat flours, cornmeal and molasses.

Boston cream pie Not a pie, two layers of spongecake with custard filling, usually dusted with powdered sugar or chocolate glaze.

Boston lettuce

bourbon An American whiskey named for Kentucky's Bourbon County.

bow tie pasta Also called *farfalle*.

brandy A spirit distilled from wine or fermented fruit.

Brazil nut

bread-and-butter pickles

breadbox

breadcrumb

breadstick

brie A soft, mold-ripened cow's milk cheese.

brioche A rich French yeast bread made with butter and eggs.

broccoli

broccoli raab

Broccolini A trademark for a broccoli hybrid.

Brussels sprouts

bulgur wheat A wheat that has been steamed, dried and crushed.

bulkie roll Bulkie roll, also called kaiser roll, Vienna roll or a hard roll, is popular in the United States and Canada. It is typically a crusty round roll, often sprinkled with poppy or sesame seeds, made by folding corners of a square inward so their points meet. Often used as a bun for sandwiches. *Bulkie roll* is used in New England.

Bundt pan A trademark for a fluted cake pan.

Burgundy Red or white wines, typically dry, produce in France's Burgundy region.

burrito, burritos A Mexican dish in which a flour tortilla is wrapped around meat, vegetables, cheese or a combination of ingredients, then heated.

busboy

buttercream A variety of frosting.

butterfat The fatty part of milk, from which butter is made.

C

cabernet sauvignon A grape variety used to produce many of the top red wines in California and Bordeaux. The wines tend to be full-bodied, fruity and boldly flavored.

Caesar salad A salad of greens, cheese, croutons and anchovies.

calamari Italian for *squid*.

California roll An American variety of rolled sushi (called *maki*), now popular worldwide. Generally contains avocado, crab and vegetables.

Calvados A French brandy made from apple cider.

Camembert A soft, creamy, partly ripened cheese.

Canadian bacon A lean smoked pork, called *back bacon* in Canada.

canape, canapes Hors d'oeuvres made from small pieces of bread or crackers topped with cheese, meat or vegetables.

cannellini A white bean common in Italian dishes.

cannelloni A large tubular pasta, often stuffed and baked.

cannoli A tube-shaped Italian pastry fried and filled with sweetened ricotta cheese and other fillings.

cantaloupe

cappuccino An espresso topped with the foam from steamed milk.

carnaroli rice An Italian variety of rice similar to arborio, often used in risotto.

cast-iron (adj.) **cast iron** (n.) A *cast-iron pot*, but the pot is made from *cast iron*.

catfish

cava A Spanish sparkling wine.

challah Jewish braided bread.

Champagne A sparkling wine from the Champagne region of France. If made elsewhere, call it *sparkling wine*.

chardonnay A grape variety used in white wines such as Champagne and white Burgundy. Chardonnays tend to be dry with buttery, creamy notes.

cheddar

cheesecloth

cheesemaker

chevre A soft goat cheese.

Chianti A bold, dry red wine made in the Chianti region of Italy.

chicken cordon bleu

chicken-fried steak

chicken Kiev A dish in which boneless, flattened chicken breasts are rolled, breaded and fried.

chili, chilies

china The tableware.

chipotle A dried, smoked jalapeno pepper, often packed in adobo sauce.

chocolate Bittersweet, dark, milk, semisweet, white.

chopsticks

Cobb salad Made famous by Hollywood's Brown Derby Restaurant in the 1920s. It typically consists of finely chopped chicken or turkey, bacon, hard-cooked eggs, tomatoes, avocado, scallions, watercress, cheddar cheese and lettuce tossed with a vinaigrette dressing and topped with a large portion of crumbled Roquefort or other blue cheese.

Coca-Cola, Coke, Coca-Cola Co.

coffeecake

cognac A variety of French brandy.

Cointreau A sweet, orange-flavored liqueur.

colander *Strainer* is preferred.

colby cheese A cow's milk cheese similar to cheddar.

cooking spray Use for nonstick cooking spray.

corkscrew

corn dog

corn flour

corn on the cob

cornbread

cornflakes

cornmeal

cornstarch

couscous A North African dish made from crushed semolina.

cow's milk cheese

crabcake

crabmeat

creme brulee A custard served topped with a crust of caramelized sugar.

creme fraiche A thickened cream similar in texture to Greek-style yogurt.

Crisco A trademark for a brand of vegetable shortening.

cupful, cupfuls

Crock-Pot A brand name, not to be used unless referencing that brand, otherwise *slow cooker*.

D

Danish pastry A flaky pastry, usually filled with fruit or cheese.

deep-fry, deep-fried *Deep-fried pickles*.

Dijon mustard

dimensions Pan dimensions are expressed as: *a 9-by-12-inch square pan*.

dolmades Stuffed grape leaves.

double boiler A pair of saucepans, one filled with water and heated, the other set above it for gentle cooking.

doughnut

draft beer Not draught.

Drambuie A trademark for a brand of Scottish liqueur.

dredge A cooking technique in which food is lightly coated with flour or another ingredient before frying.

drive-thru

Dr Pepper No period after *Dr*

dry-roasted

dulce de leche A caramel-like blend of cooked milk and sugar.

Dungeness crab A Pacific coast crab found from Alaska to Mexico.

Dutch oven A large, lidded heavy pot.

E

edamame Soybeans, often served steamed in the pod.

eggs Benedict A poached egg served with ham over an English muffin with hollandaise sauce. In eggs Florentine, spinach is substituted for the ham.

enchilada, enchiladas A Mexican dish in which a soft corn tortilla is wrapped around meat or other fillings. Served hot and topped with salsa and cheese.

endive A bitter green. Two most common varieties are Belgian, which resembles small, oval cabbages, and curly, which has frilly, loose leaves.

English muffin

entree

escargot French for *snail*. Generally refers to the dish of cooked snails served with melted butter.

escarole A variety of endive with a mild flavor.

espresso The coffee is *espresso*, not *expresso*.

extra-virgin olive oil

F

fair trade

fajita, fajitas A Mexican dish in which warm flour tortillas are wrapped around strips of marinated and grilled steak.

falafel A Middle Eastern fritter made from ground chickpeas.

farmers market No apostrophe.

farmstead Generally used to describe a cheese produced solely from the milk of one farm.

fettuccine A wide, flat pasta. Often confused with *linguine*, which is narrower.

filet mignon An extremely tender boneless cut of beef from the tenderloin. Usually cut 1 to 2 inches thick and cooked by searing briefly on the stove and finished in the oven or under a broiler.

Filet-O-Fish The fish sandwich served at McDonald's.

fillet As a noun, a boneless cut of fish or meat. As a verb, to cut or prepare as a fillet.

five-spice powder A Chinese spice blend.

flatbread

flaxseed

Fluffernutter A trademarked name for a sandwich made with peanut butter and Marshmallow Fluff.

focaccia A flat Italian yeast bread drizzled with olive oil and salt, sometimes rosemary.

foie gras The fatty liver of a force-fed goose or duck, often made into pate.

foil Use for *tin foil* or *aluminum foil*.

fontina cheese Also called fontina Val d'Aosta after the Italian valley from which it comes. It is a semi-firm and creamy cow's milk cheese. It has a mild, nutty flavor. The cheese is also made in Denmark, France and the United States.

foodie Slang for a person with a strong interest in good food.

fra diavolo An Italian dish with a spicy tomato sauce.

frankfurter

free-range (adj.)

French bread

French dressing

french fries Lowercase *french* because it refers to the style of cut, not the nation.

French toast

frisee A small, bitter salad green.

fruitcake

G

ganache A rich filling or icing made from chocolate and heavy cream.

garbanzo bean *Chickpea* is preferred.

gelato An Italian ice cream made from whole milk. Generally denser than American ice cream.

General Tso's chicken

ghee A clarified butter used in Indian cooking.

ginger Distinguish ground (dry) or fresh, as both have become common ingredients.

gingerbread

gingersnap cookie

gluten A protein found in wheat and some other grains; lends structure to bread and other baked goods. Also, *gluten-free*.

Gorgonzola cheese An Italian blue cheese.

Gouda A Dutch cow's milk cheese.

gourmand, gourmet A *gourmand* is a person who likes good food and tends to eat to excess; a *glutton*. A *gourmet* is a person who likes fine food and is an excellent judge of food and drink.

graham crackers Crackers made from a finely ground whole-wheat flour named for Sylvester Graham, a U.S. dietary reformer.

grand cru wines Wines produced from a specialized group of high-end French vineyards.

Grape-Nuts

grits Ground hominy, eaten as a porridge. The word normally takes plural verbs and pronouns.

Gruyere cheese A rich Swiss cheese.

H

half-and-half A blend of equal parts cream and milk.

hard-boil (v.) **hard-boiled** (adj.)

havarti cheese A semisoft Danish cheese.

hazelnut Preferred to *filbert*.

heatproof

herbes de Provence An herb blend from southern France.

Hereford A breed of hardy red-coated beef cattle of English origin with white faces and markings. Also raised in North and South America, Australia and New Zealand.

hibachi

hoisin sauce A dark, savory Chinese sauce.

hollandaise A creamy sauce made from butter, egg yolks and lemon juice.

hors d'oeuvre, hors d'oeuvres

horseradish

hot dog

hot plate

hot sauce A generic term for hot pepper-based sauces, such as *Tabasco*.

huitlacoche Also called *corn smut*. A fungus that grows on corn. Considered a delicacy of Mexican cuisine, it has a smoky-sweet flavor.

hummus

I

India pale ale

Irish coffee A coffee blended with Irish whiskey and topped with whipped cream.

J

Jamaica rum Not *Jamaican rum*.

Jarlsberg cheese A buttery cheese from Norway.

jasmine rice An aromatic rice from Thailand, similar to basmati.

Jell-O

jellyroll

jigger Also called a shot or shot glass, about 1 ½ fluid ounces.

johnnycake Dating to the early 1700s, the johnnycake is a flat griddlecake made of cornmeal, salt and either boiling water or cold milk. Today's johnnycakes often have eggs, oil or melted butter and baking powder.

K

kaiser roll A large round roll with a hard crust.

Kalamata olive A black Greek olive.

ketchup Not catchup or catsup.

Key lime

kielbasa A smoked Polish sausage.

kimchee Korean pickled vegetables.

Kobe beef An exclusive grade of beef from cattle raised in Kobe, Japan. The cattle are massaged with sake and fed a special diet that includes beer, resulting in a very tender and full-flavored beef. Extremely expensive.

Kool-Aid

kosher food Food that has been produced or prepared according to Jewish dietary laws.

kosher salt A coarse, additive-free salt. 1 ¼ teaspoons kosher salt = 1 teaspoon table salt.

L

ladyfinger A finger-shaped cookie. Can be spongy or crisp.

lager A beer aged at a low temperature after brewing.

latte An espresso mixed with steamed milk.

lemon grass A Thai herb.

liqueur A sweetened, flavored spirit.

locavore The preferred term for a person who strives to eat locally produced foods.

London broil A boneless beef steak that is marinated, broiled, then served thinly sliced.

low-fat

M

M&M's

Madeira A fortified wine.

manchego cheese A Spanish sheep's milk cheese.

mandarin orange

mandoline A vegetable slicer.

Manhattan cocktail A classic cocktail made from rye whiskey or bourbon.

Manhattan clam chowder A tomato-based soup of clams and salt pork. **New England clam chowder** is cream- or milk-based.

maraschino cherries

Marsala An Italian fortified wine.

Marshmallow Fluff A trademark. Use *marshmallow spread*

unless specifically referring to the *Marshmallow Fluff* brand.

mascarpone cheese A thick spreadable cream from Italy, similar to clotted cream.

matzo Unleavened Jewish bread.

McDonald's Corp.

meatball

meatloaf

medium-rare

melon baller

meringue A dessert made from egg whites and sugar beaten until stiff, then usually baked.

merlot A grape variety and a wine. The wines are similar to cabernet sauvignon, but milder.

mesclun A popular salad greens mix.

Meyer lemon

milkshake

mise en place A French term for having ingredients prepared before making a recipe.

molecular gastronomy An often deconstructive approach to cooking in which science and laboratory approaches and equipment are used in the kitchen.

Monterey Jack cheese A mild semisoft cheese, also called jack cheese.

Muenster cheese A mild semisoft cheese.

mushrooms Generally not

capitalized, as in *button*, *chanterelle*, *cremini*, *morel*, *porcini*, *portobello* and *shiitake*.

mustard Use for the condiment. Use *dry mustard* for powdered form.

N

naan An Indian flatbread.

napoleon A dessert made with crisp layers of puff pastry spread with pastry creme and either glazed with a thin icing or dusted with powdered sugar.

navel orange A seedless orange so named because it has a small depression, like a navel.

Neufchatel cheese A soft cow's milk cheese, similar to cream cheese.

nonstick

O

omelet

onions *Spanish onion*, also called *yellow onion*; *red onion*, also called *Italian onion*; *Vidalia onion*.

open-faced sandwich

orecchiette A small, disk-like pasta.

Oreo A trademark for a brand of chocolate sandwich cookie held together by a white filling.

ovenproof

P

pad thai A Thai noodle dish.

palate, palette A *palate* refers to the roof of the mouth and the sense of taste (*to have a sophisticated palate*), *palette* is the term for an artist's paint board.

pan-fry

parboil To partially cook in boiling water.

panko Coarse Japanese-style breadcrumbs.

Parmesan A hard, sharp cow's milk cheese style after Italy's Parmigiano-Reggiano.

Parmigiano-Reggiano An Italian Parmesan cheese, only used with cheese made in specific regions of Italy.

parsley Common varieties are *flat-leaf* (Italian) and *curly-leaf*.

pasteurize

pears In general, capitalize most varieties, including *Anjou*, *Asian* (also called *apple pear*), *Bosc* and *Bartlett*.

pecorino An Italian sheep's milk cheese.

pepitas Hulled pumpkin seeds popular in Mexico.

Peppadew A brand name for jarred red pepper from South Africa.

pepper jack cheese

Pepsi, Pepsi-Cola, PepsiCo Inc.

petit four, petits fours Bite-sized cakes.

Philly cheesesteak Also called *Philadelphia cheesesteak* or *cheesesteak*.

phyllo A paper-thin pastry dough common to Mediterranean cooking.

piccata A classic Italian dish using very thin, flattened slices of meat, such as veal or chicken, sautéed and served in a sauce of pan-drippings, lemon, butter and white wine. Capers, chopped Italian parsley, shallots and garlic are common additions.

Pilsner A pale lager.

pine nut Term is preferred to *pignoli*.

pinot grigio A light, dry white wine that originated in Italy.

pinot noir A grape and wine. The wines tend to be spicy and complex.

pitmaster

Pizza Hut

plonk A slang term for low-quality wine.

po'boy No space, classic New Orleans sandwich.

pomegranate

Popsicle A trademark for a brand of flavored ice on a stick.

port A sweet, fortified Portuguese wine.

porterhouse A beef steak cut from the loin.

pot sticker A small Asian-style dumpling.

potatoes Varieties are written *fingerling, new, red bliss, russet, Yukon Gold.*

potluck

potpie

pound cake

precooked

prix fixe A menu for which a set price is charged for all courses of the meal.

prosciutto A salt-cured Italian ham, served thinly sliced.

prosecco An Italian sparkling wine.

provolone A tangy cow's milk cheese, originally from Italy.

Pyrex A trademark for a brand of oven glassware.

Q

quinoa A high-protein seed originally from the Andes. It is cooked similar to rice and resembles couscous. It has a nutty flavor and a lightly crunchy texture.

R

ranch dressing A creamy salad dressing containing buttermilk.

ratatouille A popular vegetable dish from France's Provence region.

refried beans

restaurateur

Reuben sandwich The classic corned beef sandwich.

rib-eye steak

rickey Usually a cocktail with lime juice, soda water and liquor. Also a nonalcoholic drink, often made of seltzer water, lime juice and flavored syrups.

riesling A white wine that can range from quite sweet to dry.

rocky road ice cream

romaine lettuce

Roquefort cheese A strong blue cheese from France.

root beer

roux (singular and plural) A cooked blend of fat and flour, usually used to thicken sauces.

ruby red grapefruit

Russian dressing A mayonnaise- and chili sauce-based dressing.

S

salade nicoise

salmon Types are *king, coho* and *sockeye.*

saltine cracker

sandwich

sashimi A Japanese dish of thinly sliced raw seafood.

saute, sauteed, sauteing To cook with fat on the stovetop.

saute pan A wide, shallow pan with straight sides.

sauvignon blanc A grape and a wine. Wines are white and tend to be dry.

savoy cabbage

scallions The preferred term for *green onions.*

scotch Capitalize *Scotch* and use the spelling *whisky* only when the two words are used together.

Scotch whisky A type of whiskey distilled in Scotland from malted barley. The malt is dried over a peat fire.

seasonings In recipes, note whether herbs are fresh or dried: *1 teaspoon fresh oregano* or *1/2 teaspoon dried thyme.* For spices and other seasonings, when appropriate note whether *ground* or *whole*: *1 teaspoon ground black pepper* or *1 teaspoon whole cardamom pods.*

seltzer water Carbonated water. Differs from *soda water* (also called *club soda*), which contains sodium bicarbonate.

serrano chili A small, hot chili.

serrano ham Dry-cured Spanish ham.

7-Eleven Trademark for stores operated and licensed by 7-Eleven Inc., a subsidiary of Seven-Eleven Japan Co. Ltd.

7UP Trademark for a brand of soft drink.

shepherd's pie A baked dish that consists of layers of ground meat and mashed potatoes.

sherbet A frozen dessert similar to ice cream but made from sweetened fruit juice and water.

sherry A Spanish fortified wine.

shiraz A grape and a red wine, known as syrah in France. The wine tends to be bold and spicy.

Sichuan The preferred spelling, *Sichuan* peppercorns (not Szechwan).

skillet A long-handled shallow pan with gently sloping sides. Also called a *frying pan*, though *skillet* is preferred.

sloppy Joes

slow cooker

Smithfield Ham A trademark for a ham dry-cured, smoked and aged in Smithfield, Va.

s'more A campfire dessert of toasted marshmallow and chocolate between graham crackers.

sous vide A method of cooking in which food is vacuum sealed in plastic bags, then slowly cooked at low temperatures.

Spam

spareribs

spongecake

springform pan A baking pan with removable sides.

Sriracha sauce A Thai hot chili sauce.

stand mixer The preferred term for a stationary kitchen mixer. Use *electric mixer* for a hand-held mixer.

Stilton An English blue cheese.

stir-fry (n. and v.)

stockpot

sun-dried tomatoes

sugar Common varieties include *brown*, *granulated* (*white*), *powdered* (preferred to *confectioner's*), *superfine* and *turbinado* (a raw sugar). In recipes, if only granulated sugar is called for, *sugar* can be used alone.

sushi A Japanese dish of cooked, seasoned and cooled rice served topped or wrapped around seafood, vegetables or egg.

sweet-and-sour sauce

Swiss chard

Swiss cheese

T

Tabasco A trademark for a hot pepper sauce.

tabbouleh A Middle Eastern salad made from bulgur, vegetables, herbs, olive oil and lemon juice.

tacos

tahini

takeout

tamale, tamales A Mexican dish, usually wrapped and cooked in corn husks.

tapas The small plates of food usually served in bars in Spain.

tapenade A spread of black olives, capers and anchovies from France's Provence region.

T-bone steak

temperatures In recipes written as 450 F or 232 C.

Tex-Mex Characterized by elements of Texas and Mexico, such as *Tex-Mex cooking*.

Thai chilies, Thai chili sauce

Thai red curry paste

thermos

Thousand Island dressing

Toll House cookie

tomatoes Varieties are capitalized, as in *Brandywine*.

tonic water A carbonated water flavored with sugar and quinine.

triple sec A generic name for a clear orange liqueur.

tureen A large, deep serving dish with a lid, usually used for soups and stews. *Terrine* refers to a pate, as well as the dish it is made in.

Turkish delight A soft, gelatinous candy popular in the Middle East.

tzatziki A Greek yogurt sauce.

U

umami A Japanese term roughly translated as *savory*, the suspected fifth taste (in addition to sweet, salty, sour and bitter).

V

vinaigrette A blend of oil and vinegar, usually used as salad dressing.

vitamin Lowercase *vitamin C*.

W

wagyu Wagyu refers to several beef breeds of cattle, such as Japanese Black, Japanese Brown, Japanese Polled and Japanese Shorthorn, which are genetically bred to produce intense marbling. Wagyu beef is very expensive. Wagyu is also known as Kobe-style beef, although only beef raised in the Kobe prefecture of Japan can be called Kobe, a branded name. See **Kobe beef**.

Waldorf salad

waxed paper

wheat germ

wheatgrass

whiskey, whiskeys Use the spelling *whisky* only in conjunction with *Scotch*.

whole wheat (n.) **whole-wheat** (adj.) *Whole-wheat bread.*

whole-grain (adj.) *Whole-grain bread, whole-grain mustard.*

whoopie pie

wineglass

winemaker

wines Wine names for grape varietals, such as *chardonnay* and *shiraz*, are not capitalized. Wines named for regions, such as *Champagne* or *Chianti*, are capitalized.

wonton

Worcestershire sauce A condiment originally made by the English in India.

Y

yogurt

York peppermint patties

Z

zest As a noun, the thin, colorful outer skin of citrus, not the white pith beneath it. As a verb, to remove the thin outer skin of citrus, usually with a grater or zester.

zip-close bag Not *Ziploc* (a brand name).

FASHION GUIDELINES

A

A-line Skirt that is narrow at the waist, then flares out along a straight line to the hem like a triangle or an A.

Alaia, Azzedine (1940 -) Tunisian-born designer who enjoys an almost cult-like status among fashionistas with his skintight dresses that were a symbol of the 1990s supermodel era.

anorak Hooded jacket, often a pullover silhouette.

applique Decoration fastened to a larger piece of material.

argyle Geometric pattern on knitted garments of colored diamonds on plain background.

Armani, Giorgio (1934 -) Italian-born designer who started his label in 1975, making his mark with tailored suits. He also forged an early relationship with Hollywood, both on screen and on red carpets.

atelier A designer's workshop or studio.

B

babydoll

back-to-school clothing

Balenciaga, Cristobal (1895 - 1972) Spanish-born designer moved to Paris during the Spanish Civil War, where he solidified his reputa-

tion as a fine couturier. The house's current creative chief is Nicolas Ghesquiere.

ballgown

Barneys New York New York-based department store. No apostrophe.

batik Method of making colored designs on textiles using wax to resist the dye. Originated in Indonesia.

bespoke Custom-made item.

bias cut Fabric cut on an approximately 45-degree angle to create a clingy, draped effect. French designer Madeleine Vionnet introduced it in the 1920s.

Bloomingdale's Upscale U.S. department stores, owned by Macy's Inc. Flagship store is at 59th Street and Lexington Avenue in Manhattan.

boatneck, bateau Neckline named for its similarity in shape to a skimmer boat. It has a narrow opening that extends almost shoulder to shoulder.

bodysuit

boho Style that draws on bohemian influences.

boucle Curly yarn that gives fabric a tufted or knotted texture.

bra Acceptable in all references for *brassiere*.

brogue Lace-up shoe with perforations in the leather.

brooch

buffalo check Checkered pattern with bold, well-defined squares.

bustier Formfitting, corset-style garment shaped around the bustline and bodice that cinches the waist. Originally worn as an underpinning, it has been adapted to street clothes and, particularly, eveningwear.

button-down

C

camisole, cami Thin-strapped, sleeveless top for women.

capelet Short cape.

chambray Lightweight fabric woven with colored and white yarns.

Chanel Gabrielle Bonheur "Coco" Chanel (1883 – 1971) French designer, one of most famous names in modern fashion. Her skirt suits, with collarless jackets and braided chain hardware, are often imitated. German designer Karl Lagerfeld has been at helm of company since 1983.

citrine Lemon-colored.

cloche Close-fitting hat. Takes its name from French for bell.

closed-toe shoes

collections

colorblocking Garments with geometric chunks of bright colors, fashion staples since French designer Yves Saint Laurent's 1965 collection inspired by Dutch painter Piet Mondrian.

compliment, complement
Complement is a noun and a verb denoting completeness or the process of supplementing something: *The ship has a complement of 200 sailors and 20 officers. The tie complements his suit.*
Compliment is a noun or a verb that denotes praise or the expression of courtesy: *The captain complimented the sailors. She was flattered by the compliments on her project.*

couture, couturier *Couture* refers to the design and manufacture of fashionable clothing, usually custom made. *Couturier* is someone who makes and sells couture clothes. See **haute couture**.

cowl Draped, loose neckline with a cascading effect; also used as back of dress.

crinoline Stiff cloth used as a lining for stiffening garments.

culottes

D

de la Renta, Oscar (1932 -) Dominican-born fashion designer. After stints in Europe with the houses of Balenciaga and Lanvin, he opened his own label in New York in 1965. His specialties are elaborate eveningwear and dressed-up daywear with a refined uptown aesthetic.

decolletage, decollete A low neckline on a dress or top.

deconstructed Look implies edginess with exposed seams, fraying fabric edges and distressed finishes.

Dior, Christian (1905 – 1957)

French designer who dominated post-World War II fashion with his hourglass-shaped New Look, which debuted in 1947. Pierre Cardin and Yves Saint Laurent both served as his assistants before starting their own houses.

Dolce & Gabbana Italian fashion house started by designers Domenico Dolce and Stefano Gabbana. Note ampersand in name.

dolman sleeve Sleeve that is wide at the armhole and narrows toward the wrist, often creates the effect of a dropped shoulder.

d'Orsay Shoe style resembling pumps, but with high vamp on the front of the foot and cutout sides, exposing arch of foot.

double-breasted

double-faced

duchesse Soft, heavy type of satin.

dyeing Refers to changing colors.

E

Elbaz, Alber (1961 -) Moroccan-born Israeli designer who took over creative duties for the Parisian house Lanvin in 2001.

Elizabethan Characteristic of the time when Queen Elizabeth I ruled England in the 16th century. Her ornate neck ruffs, cloaks and jewels helped shape the royal look.

empire waist Waistline hits above the natural waist, sometimes right under the bust. Popular for babydoll tops, evening gowns and maternity clothes.

epaulet Fabric tab that sits on the shoulder, often found on military uniforms and military-inspired fashion.

F

faille Soft fabric with ribbed texture.

Fair Isle sweater Multi-colored geometric design in woolen sweaters, originating in the Shetland Islands, off Scotland.

fascinator Headpiece often anchored by a flower or feather, often called a *cocktail hat*.

fashion-forward label

fashion week Capitalize in an official name, such as *New York Fashion Week* or *London Fashion Week*.

Ferragamo, Salvatore (1898 - 1960) Italian shoe designer. Family-owned company, which now includes larger collections of clothing and accessories, continues to operate under his name.

fishnet Fabric often used in lingerie or hosiery, with an open-mesh weave resembling a fishing net.

flair, flare *Flair* is conspicuous talent or style. *Flare* is a curving or spreading outward, as in a skirt.

flannel Soft, brushed-finish fabric, typically made of cotton or wool.

formfitting

G

Gap Inc. U.S. clothing retailer. Do not use *The Gap*.

gauchos Mid-calf length pants with wide legs fashioned after South American cowboys.

gazar Silk organza.

Gres, Madame Germaine Emilie Krebs (1903-1993) Parisian couturier who used the name *Madame Gres*. She was considered master of the bias cut and credited with adapting the modern goddess gown. Gres was based on an anagram of her artist husband's first name, Serge. He signed his work Gres.

Gibson Girl Illustrator Charles Dana Gibson depicted in his work in the late 1800s and early 1900s the ideal fashionable young American woman.

girlie Connotes young, feminine, flirty.

Goth A dark, medieval-inspired style that also borrows elements from Victoriana, mourning clothes and the punk music scene.

gray

guipure lace Typically sturdy bobbin lace – as opposed to a needle lace – connected by its own pattern instead of sitting on a net background.

H

Halston Roy Halston Frowick (1932 – 1990) American designer who started as a milliner, famously designing Jacqueline Kennedy's pillbox hat on Inauguration Day in 1961. Halston's clothing, though, is more closely associated with the disco era, especially his jersey dresses.

haute couture French term refers to one-of-a-kind clothing produced by design houses that meet criteria established by French Ministry of Industry. A protected appellation. Used informally to mean fancy, expensive fashion.

headscarf, headscarves

henley Pullover shirt that is collarless, split with a short row of vertical buttons.

high-waisted

hoodie Short for hooded sweatshirt.

houndstooth Large dog-tooth pattern.

I

ikat Printed fabric based on a weaving technique originated in Uzbekistan; pattern created from tie-dyed thread.

indigo Blue dye originally derived from plants in the pea family, often used to color denim. Used to describe deep blue colors with purple overtones.

inverted pleats Pleats are folds of fabric. This style is a stacked box pleat on the inside of a garment so it lies flatter.

J

jabot Ruffled, sometimes-detachable collar on front of a shirt or blouse.

Jacobs, Marc (1963 -) New York-born designer has his own collections and is creative director for French fashion house Louis Vuitton. He is considered an industry showman, staging elaborate runway productions.

Jacquard Fabric with woven pattern, sometimes an elaborate one. In 1801, Joseph Marie Jacquard invented the loom that could control the pattern sequence using punch cards.

K

Karan, Donna (1948 -) New York-born designer who first served as head designer of Anne Klein before launching her own label in 1984. She routinely cites working women and her hometown as her inspirations.

keyhole Peek-a-boo opening used on neckline, front or back of garment. Oblong shape like a keyhole.

kimono Japanese wrap-style robe with wide sleeves and tied with a wide sash, or *obi*.

Klein, Calvin (1942 -) New York-born designer who made as much of a splash with his provocative advertising as his sexy, minimal styles. In 2003, he gave up his role in the company he co-founded in 1968 after a corporate sale to Phillips-Van Heusen Corp.

knife pleat Fold in fabric that creates a fan-like effect. Knife pleats are basic pleating technique.

L

Lagerfeld, Karl (1933 or 1938 -) German-born designer who moved to Paris in his teens. He is best known as the longtime creative director at Chanel but also designs for Fendi and under his own name. Also a photographer, he often shoots his own ad campaigns.

Lauren, Ralph (1939 -) New York-born designer known for polo pony logo and elegant sportswear. He has created a huge public company that has expanded to categories that range from home goods to uniforms for the U.S. Olympic teams.

Le Smoking Menswear-inspired outfit for women created by French designer Yves Saint Laurent. Tuxedo silhouette marked the beginning of an era of sexy, androgynous clothes.

luxe Luxury.

LVMH Moet Hennessy Louis Vuitton SA. Leading luxury goods conglomerate based in Paris. Parent company of fashion houses Louis Vuitton, Celine, Donna Karan, Givenchy, Marc Jacobs, Fendi and Christian Dior.

Lycra Unless referring to the trademark fiber or fabric, use a generic term such as *spandex* or *elastic* or *stretch fabric*.

M

Macy's Inc. Top U.S. department store chain, with about 850 stores under the Macy's and Bloomingdale's names. Macy's flagship store in Manhattan's Herald Square is the world's largest. The Macy's Thanksgiving Day Parade began in 1924. Formerly Federated Department Stores.

madras Lightweight cotton cloth, usually striped or plaid, originating in India.

maillot One-piece swimming suit or bodysuit.

makeup

mannequin

McQueen, Alexander (1969-2010) British designer who was considered one of the industry's most creative and skillful designers. After his 2010 suicide, his label was taken over by assistant Sarah Burton.

menswear Not men's wear.

miniskirt

monokini Topless swimsuit introduced by Austrian designer Rudi Gernreich in 1964. Term has evolved to describe one-piece swimsuits with deep cutouts.

mousseline Semi-opaque fabric.

N

negligee Light, filmy dressing gown.

Nehru jacket Fitted, single-breasted jacket with standup Mandarin or band collar. Named after late Indian Prime Minister Jawaharlal Nehru.

Neiman Marcus Inc. Dallas-based high-fashion retail stores.

New Look 1947 silhouette by French designer Christian Dior, with a nipped waist and full skirt that ushered in a different post-World War II style.

notched lapel Flap on front of a jacket that is common to business suits and tuxedos.

nude Avoid as a description of a color. Use more specific terms, such as *champagne* and *sand*.

nylon Not a trademark.

O

ombre Effect created by dip dyeing fabric with various gradations. Sometimes called *degrade*. Color appears lighter in some spots and darker in others. It can be done with more than one color, but shading a single color is more common.

opera gloves Over-the-elbow gloves, known in French as mousquetaire gloves, inspired by the gauntlets worn by musketeers in the 19th century.

organza Sheer and delicate, yet stiff, fabric.

Orlon Trademark for a form of acrylic fiber, similar to nylon.

overlay Outer layer of a garment.

P

paillette Flat sequin.

palette Color range.

pantsuit

passe

peacoat Double-breasted, hip-length coat with slash pockets and notched lapels, often made of heavy wool.

peplum Flounce of fabric that juts out just above the hips, typically on a fitted fabric or dress.

plait Braiding of hair.

pleat Fold in fabric.

plus-size clothing But *plus size* when used alone.

polka dot (n.) **polka-dot** (adj.)

pompom Ornamental ball or tuft on clothing; also crepe paper ball waved by cheerleaders.

portrait collar Open neckline that is wider than it is deep. It provides both a frame and blank space around the face, drawing the eye upward.

pouf, poufy, pouffed Any part of a garment with excess, gathered fabric.

Prada, Miuccia (1949 -) Italian designer whose usually minimalist designs largely set broader fashion trends. Prada, the brand, was founded in 1913 by her grandfather, Mario, as a leather company.

Proenza Schouler American designers Jack McCollough and Lazaro Hernandez founded their company — named after their mothers' maiden names — in 2002, after selling their final project for Parsons School of Design to Barneys New York.

pret-a-porter line Designer clothing sold ready-to-wear.

Q

Quant, Mary (1934 -) British designer whose miniskirts – a silhouette some credit her with inventing – epitomized Swinging London in the 1960s.

queens Elizabethan and Victorian refer to Britain's Queen Elizabeth I, who ruled in the 16th century, and Queen Victoria, 19th-century ruler. Elizabeth's ornate neck ruffs, cloaks and jewels helped shape the royal look. Queen Victoria moved from oversized crinoline-cage garments with high collars to a sleeker, elongated shape with a lower neckline.

quilting Sewing technique, initially used for bedding, now part of popular fashion. Quilted garments have three layers, two pieces of fabric as well as insular batting, sewn together with visible, often artful, stitching.

R

rayon Not a trademark.

riding pants Pants with roomy hips and tight-fitting legs started for equestrians. Modern fashion has interpreted them with an exaggerated shape. Also *jodhpurs*.

Reard, Louis (1897-1984) French creator of the bikini was, by trade, an auto engineer.

Rodarte California-based clothing company founded by sisters Kate and Laura Mulleavy.

ruching Detail of gathered fabric, often at a seam and, in particular, on the sides of the bodice.

S

Saint Laurent, Yves (1936 – 2008) Algerian-born designer who popularized many silhouettes that have since become fashion classics, including menswear for women, trapeze dresses, safari jackets and peasant skirts. He opened his own house in Paris in 1962 after years as Christian Dior's assistant and then hand-picked successor.

Saks Fifth Avenue Inc. Upscale retail store owned by Saks Inc. Flagship store is on Fifth Avenue in Manhattan. No apostrophe.

Savile Row Shopping street in London known for its bespoke tailoring.

serape Shawl or blanket worn as a cloak in Latin America.

shapewear Undergarments that mold the body's appearance; the 2000s brought a surge in popularity with improved shaping fabrics.

sheath Dress silhouette that is long and lean with a nipped waist, usually without a waistband, to create an hourglass shape.

shirtdress

sizes Use figures: *a size 8 dress,* *size 40 long, 10 1/2B shoes, a 34 1/2 sleeve.*

soigne Elegant, well-groomed.

soiree Party or gathering in the evening.

spandex See **Lycra**.

spectator Style of two-tone shoes. Men's are typically wing-tips and women's are pumps with wing tip-style perforation and details.

super-skinny

supermodel

sweatpants, sweatshirt, sweatsuit These are exceptions to Webster's New World College Dictionary.

T

tie-dye

Tiffany & Co. New York-based jewelry stores. No apostrophe.

trapeze Short dress style with narrow shoulders and a bodice that flares out in a trapezoid shape.

trenchcoat

T-shirt Acceptable to use *tee* on subsequent references.

tulip skirt Skirt shape that mimics an upside-down tulip; waist and hemline are similar widths.

tulle Fine net material used to make veils and dresses.

twin set Pairing of cardigan and crewneck sweaters.

U

underlay Underneath layer of a garment, often under a sheer fabric.

unitard Tight-fitting body stocking covering legs, torso and usually arms.

utilitarian Inspired by practical clothing. Cargo pants, ripstop nylon and hoodies have become fashionable details.

V

valise Small travel case with handles.

Velcro Trademark for a nylon material that can be pressed together or pulled apart for easy fastening and unfastening. Use a generic term such as *fabric fastener*.

Versace Fashion house based in Milan, Italy, known for super sexy styles. Founded in 1978 by Gianni Versace; his younger sister Donatella took over as creative director when he was murdered in 1997.

Victorian Characteristic of the reign of England's Queen Victoria from 1837 to 1901. Victoria moved from oversized crinoline-cage garments with high collars to a sleeker, elongated shape with a lower neckline.

vintage Term to describe clothes from another era. Antique clothes need to be more than 100 years old; vintage clothes are generally assumed to be newer but older than the most recent decade.

W

wash and wear Clothes that can be cleaned with soap and water, dried and worn without ironing.

-wear *Activewear, daywear, eveningwear, eyewear, headwear, menswear, outerwear, sportswear, swimwear, womenswear.*

windbreaker

Wintour, Anna (1949 -) British-born editor-in-chief of American Vogue magazine since 1988. Widely considered the most powerful person in fashion, making or breaking trends and careers.

womenswear Not *women's wear*.

wool

Wu, Jason (1982 -) Taiwanese-born, New York-based designer launched his first collection in 2006. Rose to stardom when first lady Michelle Obama wore a one-shoulder white gown designed by him to 2009 presidential inaugural balls.

Y

Yamamoto, Yohji (1943 -) Japanese designer whose signature style is skewed proportions. He was introduced to the mainstream via his Y-3 collaboration with German sportswear maker Adidas AG.

yoke Line across the shoulders or hips that creates a more fitted shape.

Z

zebra print Print that mimics the black-and-white stripes of a zebra. Zebra, cheetah and leopard prints became trends in the 1960s and are now considered classics.

zigzag

zoot suit Exaggerated style of long jackets and full, high-waisted pants worn mostly by young black and Latino men in the 1940s.

BUSINESS GUIDELINES

Our market is the individual reader of business news. We must write in a lively, clear and accessible style that provides explanation and content. We do not talk down to readers and we must avoid insider jargon while laying out complex issues in an understandable, straightforward manner. No story we write is too small or routine to meet this standard: Each has meaning for someone, because they own a stock, are buying some consumer product, have a job or some other connection to the news we are providing.

AP business journalists must not simply be careful with numbers; they have to quickly grasp what those numbers mean, in a cash flow statement, a pension fund report or a worker's paycheck. Only then can they turn those numbers into real stories, not just about companies or profits but about people's lives.

When stories break, or when you set out to break a story yourself, you need experts or insiders who can help you. And you need to know where you can find all the facts you need: in SEC filings, court documents, lists of shareholders and creditors, company histories, etc.

COVERING CORPORATE EARNINGS REPORTS

Federal law requires all corporations whose stock is publicly traded to report revenues and profits or losses each three months in an income statement. This is what business is all about, whether a corporation made money or lost it, and why. These statements are usually released on the major public relations wire services during an earnings "season," a three- or four-week period that begins roughly two weeks after the end of each quarter.

To prepare for an earnings story, first read the AP earnings stories from the previous couple of quarters, then check to see if there have been recent corporate developments at the company. Management changes at the top? Lawsuits or regulatory actions? Major contracts won or lost? Takeovers or divestitures announced? In short, you need to be up to date about issues the company is facing. That will help you better understand how the company makes or doesn't make money and why.

Our goal is to send to members and Web customers a fast file of at least 150 words, or about four paragraphs, within 15 minutes of the earnings release. The standard style for a slug is BC-Earns-Company Name.

The lead should tell the reader what the company does and give the increase or decline of net income, either in percentage or absolute terms, along with the reason. Profits are synonymous with income and earnings. The story should also include the company's revenues, which is sometimes called sales.

Comparisons of profits or losses and revenues/sales should be made with the same period a year earlier, expressed both as a total and as earnings-per-share, which is simply the profit divided by the number of shares of stock outstanding. Company statements often express this figure as *primary* or *basic* and *fully diluted*. AP uses *fully diluted* as a more meaningful figure.

Use active verbs — *rose, fell* and the like — not passive constructions like *were up/down*. And to calculate the percentage change in profits, use the year-over-year change in net income, not the earnings-per-share numbers. The number of shares outstanding can, and often does, change year to year, which doesn't make it a clear apples-to-apples comparison.

For subsequent versions, include the year-to-date figures for all of the above. The only quarter when this isn't done is the first quarter. Also include comments on the corporation's performance from the chief executive or outside analysts, and any background that puts the performance in perspective.

Be alert to announcements of job cuts — which, if significant, may share or even take over the lead from the earnings results — as well as warnings of a reduction of future earnings or upward revisions of earnings forecasts. You can usually find these quickly by doing a keyword search for "outlook" or "quarter."

Why we lead with net income

Net income truly is the bottom line and the benchmark for companies' performance over time. It's what they are required to report to the SEC in accordance with generally accepted accounting principles, and it gives us a standard reporting format that brings a consistency to our news report.

In the rare cases where companies don't provide the net income number in their news release, we need to press their representatives for those numbers. And if they are not immediately available, we need to be as transparent as possible in explaining to readers why we are providing pro forma or some other adjusted or non-GAAP representation of the company's results instead of the net income figures, which were not disclosed.

Wall Street analysts have been much more concerned in recent years with operating earnings per share, which are calculated by excluding one-time "extraordinary" gains or charges, and revenue totals. Operating earnings may exclude the costs of a big reorganization, such as severance payments to laid-off workers or penalties for breaking leases on factories that are closed. If a company has no extraordinary events, operating earnings and net earnings can be identical.

In the days and weeks before earnings reports, analysts issue EPS predictions, and these predictions are compiled into a "consensus" figure by research companies such as FactSet.

On the day of the report, investors compare the consensus prediction for operating earnings per share with the actual number and the stock price often moves up or down based on whether the company falls short of, meets or exceeds expectations. When AP says in a story "Company X's performance beat Wall Street analysts' predictions," this is the number we're referring to. In most stories, that means that after we lead with net income, we explain how the adjusted number was calculated and immediately compare the adjusted earnings per share to the consensus FactSet forecast.

It's worth noting that the consensus analyst forecast for earnings and revenues in a quarter often reflect the guidance provided by companies about what they expect their earnings and sales will be. That's why it's important to not only review what the analysts' consensus forecast is, but to determine whether a company has made a public forecast. When earnings or revenue disappoint, it's a much more powerful statement for us to say the company's earnings fell short of its own forecast, as well as analysts' expectations — assuming those facts are obtainable.

"Operating earnings" is sometimes confused with "earnings from continuing operations." Continuing operations is a subset of operations. It refers to business units that existed in the past and will exist in the future. It excludes "discontinued operations" which represent businesses that have been sold or shut down in the past year. Companies often downplay earnings of these operations since they are no longer relevant to future profits.

Importance of the conference call

Stocks often move within seconds of an unexpected pronouncement by the CEO or CFO on the analyst conference call after the earnings are released. It could come from their response to a question about a big contract, the reason for a revised sales or earnings forecast, or any number of other reasons. That's information we obviously will want in a quick write-thru of the story. But even if there are no dramatic announcements, it's important to listen to the call to gain a more complete understanding of how the company is positioning itself going forward. And it may provide a colorful key quote from a top company executive.

Make the company come to life

Earnings are the report cards for top corporate executives. The results, more often than not, are a consequence of decisions they made — acquisitions they engineered, factories they convinced their boards of directors to build or shutter, advertising campaigns they signed off on. Using real people to help frame companies' results isn't a call for us to lionize CEOs; it's a reminder that companies are made up of people who win or lose based on decisions they make.

How to assemble a wrap story

When two or more companies in the same industry report earnings on the same day, we often want an earnings wrap story after the separate earnings stories are out and updated with details from the conference calls. These should read like a seamless narrative with one or more thematic elements holding them together. And in almost every case, a wrap should have a forward-looking element that gives readers a sense of whether the good or bad earnings are likely to get better or worse in future quarters, and why.

The basis for the thematic element may come from one or more of the conference calls that company executives hold after releasing earnings. Or there may be cases where your reporting will take you in a different direction in identifying the unifying theme. Talk to money managers who own the stock, competitors and others who you think can provide insight into what is going on. There also may be cases where the earnings are so divergent that the theme could be that the industry appears to be in disarray. But in all cases, our aim should be to convey to readers who is winning, who is losing and why. That often means that the wrap story may have a more complete explanation of how specific decisions made by executives impacted the earnings.

It also isn't necessary to repeat in the wrap version every number that is in the separate earnings stories. Instead, you should use a common sense approach that asks the question: Is this number necessary to convey the main points we are trying to make? Sales and net income for each company almost always will be needed in the wrap. And they don't have to be lengthy expositions; if you can tell the tale in 400 or 500 words, all the better.

INTERNATIONAL BUREAUS

Currency Conversions

Currency conversions are necessary in stories that use foreign currency to make clear for readers how a number translates into dollars. But conversions should be used sparingly and preferably not in the lead unless it's a significant part of a story. A conversion is generally needed only the first time a currency is mentioned. The reader can make the necessary conversions after that.

Do not convert amounts that are not current because exchange rates change over time.

When conversions are needed, use the $ sign to report U.S. dollar amounts and the € sign for euros. Examples:

LONDON (AP) — BT Group PLC, Britain's largest phone company, on Thursday reported quarterly earnings rose 18 percent but said it would slash 6,000 more jobs by March to keep costs down and maintain its profits.

Net profit for the three months to Sept. 30 was 400 million pounds ($595 million), compared with 339 million pounds a year earlier, when profits were hit by a 232 million-pound one-time restructuring charge. Restructuring charges this year were 72 percent lower at just 65 million pounds.

PARIS (AP) — Airbus parent company EADS said Friday it rebounded to a profit in the third quarter thanks to lower costs for restructuring and fewer delays to aircraft programs. But it warned that continued setbacks in production of its military transporter will make achieving its full-year target challenging.

European Aeronautic Defence & Space Co. NV made a net profit of €679 million ($850 million) in the July-September period, compared with a €776 million loss a year ago.

For all other currencies, following the amount, spell out the name of the currency followed in parentheses by the equivalent in U.S. dollars. *Japan approved a 1.8 trillion yen ($18 billion) extra budget to partially finance an economic stimulus package.*

When dealing with a dollar currency of a country other than the United States, use the following abbreviations before the amount on second and subsequent references:

AU$ Australian dollars
CA$ Canadian dollars
SG$ Singapore dollars
NZ$ New Zealand dollars
HK$ Hong Kong dollars
NT$ New Taiwan dollars
ZW$ Zimbabwe dollars

Treasurer Wayne Swan approved a 16 billion Australian dollar ($10.74 billion) deal. Swan said AU$8 billion would be reserved for capital expenditure.

Different Accounting Rules

In some countries, companies don't report every quarter. The reports may come out every six months or even annually. Many foreign companies don't report "net earnings" or "earnings per share." Some report "earnings before taxes." If that's all they report, call them to see if they will give you net earnings. If they won't, use whatever number seems closest.

For the companies that report only half-year and full-year results, add a line saying, "The company did not break out quarterly results," so it's clear why we're not using them. Similarly, when reporting sales results for French companies, note that they often report sales a week or two before profits.

Foreign companies that sell shares in the United States (called American depositary receipts) often issue a separate earnings statement using American accounting standards. Use this when you can.

BANKRUPTCY

Bankruptcy categories – personal and business

Federal courts have exclusive jurisdiction over bankruptcy cases, and each of the 94 federal judicial districts handles bankruptcy matters. The primary purposes of the federal bankruptcy laws are to give an honest debtor a "fresh start" in life by relieving the debtor of most debts, and to repay creditors in an orderly manner to the extent that the debtor has property available for payment. Bankruptcies can also be **voluntary** or **involuntary**.

Chapter 7 of the Bankruptcy Code is available to both individual and business debtors. Its purpose is to achieve a fair distribution to creditors of the debtor's available non-exempt property. It provides a fresh financial start for individuals, although not all debt is wiped away; debts for certain taxes, fraudulently incurred credit card debt, family support obligations — including child support and alimony — and most student loans must still be repaid. And the new bankruptcy law that took effect in October 2005 limits Chapter 7 as an option for many Americans: Those deemed by a **"means test"** to have at least $100 a month left over after paying certain debts and expenses will have to file a 5-year repayment plan under the more restrictive Chapter 13 instead. **When a company files for Chapter 7, it usually leads to liquidation.** But a company in Chapter 7 proceedings can continue to operate under the direction of a court trustee until the matter is settled, and if it can settle with creditors in the interim, it may not have to be liquidated.

Chapter 11 of the Bankruptcy Code is available for both business and consumer debtors. Its purpose is to rehabilitate a business as a going concern or reorganize an individual's finances through a **court-approved reorganization plan**. When we refer to such a filing, we should say the company is **seeking Chapter 11 protection**. This action frees a company from the threat of creditors' lawsuits while it reorganizes its finances. The debtor's reorganization plan must be accepted by a majority of its creditors. Unless the court rules otherwise, the debtor remains in control of the business and its assets.

Chapter 12 of the Bankruptcy Code is designed to give special debt relief to a family farmer with regular income from farming.

Chapter 13 of the Bankruptcy Code is likely to be required for an increasing percentage of individuals seeking to wipe the slate clean. As mentioned above, those deemed by a "means test" to have at least $100 a month left over after paying certain debts and expenses will have to file a 5-year repayment plan under Chapter 13 that allows **unsecured creditors to recover part or all of what they are owed**. Supporters believe the changes will help rein in consumers who pile up credit card debt only to wipe it out with a Chapter 7 filing. Opponents say the law will hurt those who incur debt unexpectedly such as with health problems or lost jobs.

Chapter 15 of the Bankruptcy Code is a new section added in the 2005 reforms that deals with foreign bankruptcies. It is a way for companies with U.S. assets that are organized or nominally headquartered overseas to file bankruptcy in that foreign jurisdiction and in the U.S. as well, and have the U.S. court recognize the foreign bankruptcy as the primary one. The chapter is based on a model law developed by the United Nations in 1997. It has thus far been relatively uncommon, but **may be used more in the future, particularly by hedge funds that are organized overseas but operate in the U.S.**

How to prepare if a big corporate bankruptcy filing seems imminent

Burdensome debt and the refusal of lenders to extend new loans are the common denominators for most companies seeking bankruptcy court protection. Those tend not to crop up suddenly, which means you should be able to judge the likelihood that one of your companies may be filing. That's why we encourage all reporters to set up **SEC filing**

alerts for your key companies using their own user name and password on the 10kWizard service. Bankruptcy should be one of the keywords you choose because outside auditors often force companies to tip their hands by flagging to investors the possibility of a bankruptcy filing. One expression you'll want to add to your company alert setup is **"going concern."** That's the term companies use when they note that their outside auditor is questioning their ability to remain in business.

Beyond that, you need to have a good understanding of the **balance sheet** and the **income statement** of the major companies you cover to answer these questions: How much debt do they have and how much of it must be repaid or refinanced in this quarter or the quarters to come? Have they demonstrated an inability to raise fresh cash through the sale of stock or debt financing? Has cash flow gone negative?

After a company seeks Chapter 11 protection, **holders of the company's debt** are often the best source of information about the status of bankruptcy negotiations since they often stand to gain control of the company in the reorganization process.

Few companies will be chatty about bankruptcy filings ahead of time, but it's still a good idea to plant the seed with company spokesmen that you want to be alerted as soon as a filing is made, that you want to know in which court it will come (more and more of the big ones seem to be ending up in the Southern District of New York in Manhattan), and that you would like a full set of documents if possible.

Another question to ask is: What will happen to the company's employees? When a company seeks bankruptcy protection, it often pushes for job cuts, pay cuts and reductions in benefits. If any workers are represented by unions, those unions will likely fight those cuts. A company seeking Chapter 11 protection will sometimes try to use bankruptcy court to achieve concessions if it can't reach an agreement on its own with unions. So stay in contact with union representatives to keep up with out-of-court negotiations, and check docket reports on Pacer for requests for permission to impose wage concessions, to reject union contracts or anything similar.

Also, companies seeking bankruptcy protection often turn over their pension plans to the Pension Benefit Guaranty Corporation, the federal pension insurance agency (http://www.pbgc.gov). But eliminating pension plans altogether is also common — UAL Corp.'s United Airlines, US Airways Group Inc., TWA and Pan Am, among others, all canceled their pension plans in bankruptcy.

And a reminder on tracking a company's stock after it files for bankruptcy: Companies are usually **delisted** by the New York Stock Exchange and the Nasdaq stock market after they seek bankruptcy court protection. That means they usually begin trading on the over-the-counter market known as the **Pink Sheets**. The **letter Q** at the end of a ticker signifies that it is a bankrupt company and **PK** means it trades on the pink sheets. (Example: Delphi Corp. went from DPH on the New York Stock Exchange to DPHIQ.PK – four letters required in the ticker symbol for bankrupt companies – on the Pink Sheets.)

Is it a reorganization or a liquidation?
Knowing the answer to this question is key to how we describe the filing in our story. If it's a Chapter 11 filing and the company hopes to stay in business, don't say "Company XX filed for bankruptcy on DATE TK ..." Instead, we should say "Company XX **sought bankruptcy court protection** on DATE TK ..."

If a company closes its doors, says it's unable to raise new cash and is **going out of business** via a Chapter 7 filing, spell that out in the lead.

Secured and unsecured creditors

When you borrow money to buy a car, the lender is a **secured creditor**; they get to reclaim the car if you stop making payments. Similarly, companies usually have to pledge some kind of **collateral** when they sell bonds or otherwise borrow money. There can be several levels or rankings of security pledged for various categories of a company's debt. For our purposes, we need to know who stands first, second and so on in line for repayment if a company files for bankruptcy because their claims and desires often conflict with what management wants to happen.

In a bankruptcy reorganization, secured lenders and debt holders obviously want to be repaid 100 cents on the dollar. Management often is against that idea, because they need whatever money they still have to continue operating the company. What often happens is that after extensive negotiations (and big lawyer bills) secured debt holders agree to **exchange their securities for new shares of stock** (i.e., equity) in the post-bankruptcy company, which emerges as a consequence with a much-reduced debt load.

So what happens to **existing shareholders**? In most cases, **their shares become worthless**. But every so often, secured debt holders' claims can be satisfied in a way that leaves some residual equity value in the company. But even then, existing shareholders' ownership stake in the company is often **severely diluted** by the issuance of new shares to former debt holders. That's why the stocks of company's seeking bankruptcy protection often continue to trade at a few dollars a share. It's mostly a fool's game, but something we need to be able to explain as part of our reporting and writing.

Prepackaged bankruptcies and DIP financing

Companies heading toward bankruptcy sometimes start negotiations with major secured creditors on what is known as a **prepackaged bankruptcy** filing. If they can reach agreement on key details before the bankruptcy court supervision begins, it can speed the company's eventual reorganization and exit from bankruptcy. Known as an out-of-court restructuring plan, it is filed simultaneously with a Chapter 11 petition. But such plans require the approval of at least two-thirds in amount and more than one-half in the number of allowed claims held by creditors.

One study makes the case that the pre-packaged bankruptcy approach is taken most often by companies that had a higher ratio of operating income to total debt in the years before financial stress set in, and when long-term debt represents a larger percentage of total debt (which makes sense because there typically would be fewer debt holders to negotiate with).

These pre-packaged plans, as well as regular Chapter 11 reorganizations, often are accompanied by what is known as **debtor-in-possession financing**. This is a term for new money extended by a lender in Chapter 11 cases. Investopedia.com describes DIP financing as being unique from other financing methods in that it usually has priority over existing debt, equity and other claims.

Why should we care about DIP financing? It's a profitable line of business for banks like JPMorgan Chase. And companies' ability to obtain it often is a critical factor in whether they continue to operate or have to shut down.

Emerging from bankruptcy

When the reorganization is completed and a company emerges from bankruptcy, we should be able to spell out how much of the company debt has been wiped away. If debt holders swap their holdings for shares of the reorganized company, spell that out and explain what role they will play. And did the company attract new equity holders as part of the reorganization?

MERGERS AND ACQUISITIONS

Is it a merger or a takeover?

Few business combinations are truly a merger of equals, so we need to be precise and sparing in the use of the word "merger." It is **not a synonym for an acquisition or takeover**, which should be the preferred descriptive used in most of our stories. But how do we first decide whether or not it's a merger, and if the answer is not, what are the rules that should guide us in concluding who's buying whom?

The AP M&A Checklist:

1. Is one of the companies' stock being used as the currency? If the answer is yes, that's usually a good sign that company is the acquirer and it is not a merger.

2. What is the message from the exchange ratio in stock transactions? Typically when shareholders of Company A are offered new shares in a combined company at a 1-for-1 ratio, and Company B shares are exchanged at something less or more (i.e., each Company B will be exchanged for 0.47 percent of a share of the new company), it's an indication that Company A's stock is being used as the basis for the transaction. But it also could be a sign that the companies' boards have agreed to a merger that uses a formula to compensate for the differing market value (total number of shares multiplied by the closing stock price the day before the announcement) of the two companies to come up with an exchange ratio for stock in the new company.

3. What is the message from the stock movements after the announcement? Shares of companies being acquired typically rise and shares of the acquirer often fall after the announcement. Not always, of course, but that's usually the case because most bidders **pay a premium**, or an above-market price, for the shares of the company being acquired, and investors often are worried about the amount of debt the acquirer is taking on to complete the transaction.

4. Whose cash is being used to fund the cash portion of a transaction? If the announcement says Company A's cash will be used or that its existing lines of credit will be tapped to pay for Company B's shares, that's a pretty strong indication that Company A is the acquirer.

5. Which company's executives are filling most of the top management roles? The key distinction usually is who gets the CEO slot. But if one of the two CEOs is named to head the company for a limited period (say two years or less) before his fellow CEO takes over, that's a good sign of a political compromise to paper over the fact that the second CEO's company is going to be in charge long term.

6. Which company will end up with the majority of the seats on the new board of directors? This is often a key tie breaker. It's a good indication of which outfit is going to be in charge if one ends up with 60 percent of the board and the other gets 40 percent. Also, make sure to get not only the short-term makeup of the board of the combined company, but also whether there were any deals cut for some members to retire in short order.

7. Whose name will be on the big sign outside the headquarters? Usually an obvious tell, but not always. First Union clearly was the acquirer of Wachovia a couple of years ago, but the board members decided for their own reasons to use the Wachovia name when the two North Carolina banks combined operations. It may have been a deal killer for some Wachovia board members if their name didn't survive, or it may have simply been a marketing decision by First Union's brass that the name Wachovia had a better chance of standing out in the crowded banking space long term. Wachovia, incidentally, was acquired by Wells Fargo in 2008.

8. Where will the company be headquartered? Since CEOs typically do the negotiating and they typically aren't anxious to move, this can be an informative tell.

How to value the transaction.

Our basic rule is to **exclude the debt** of the acquired company when calculating the value of a takeover. If Company A has agreed to pay $50 a share in cash for all of the stock of Company B, you would multiply $50 times the fully diluted number of shares outstanding of Company B to come up with transaction's total value. Companies often include the debt in their news release trumpeting their daring takeovers, which places a higher total value on the transaction. In cases like that, if they spell out the debt total, back it out and fashion a lead something like this:

Company A, the world's largest TK, agreed Monday to pay $XX million to acquire Company B, whose product line XXX will do XXXX. The transaction, valued at $50 per share, or a X.X premium to Friday's closing price, includes the assumption of $XXX million of Company B's debt.

Unfortunately, news releases sometimes only provide the per-share number for the transaction. So in addition to calling the company to get the key numbers we need to value the transaction, we should backstop by reviewing the latest 10-Q filing of the acquired company on the GSI service to get the number of fully diluted shares outstanding so we can do the math ourselves. In some cases, companies only give the per-share number because they don't want to call attention to the fact that there are an enormous number of options of the acquired company that can be exercised as part of transaction.

When stock is the currency used in the transaction, or is part of a stock and cash offer, the valuation equation changes. If Company A offers 1 share of its stock for each share of Company B, for the fast file you would multiply the previous day's closing price of Company A by the number of fully diluted shares outstanding of Company B. When there is a cash component per share, or if the exchange ratio is greater or lesser than 1-for-1, the math gets a little more complicated, but it's also straight forward. First calculate the value of the stock portion (If Company A is offering 0.47 of a share of its stock that was trading at $50 yesterday, the stock portion is worth 50 x .47, or $23.50.) Then add whatever will be paid in cash per share (say $10) to give a total value of $33.50 per Company B share and multiply that times the total number of shares of Company B outstanding.

Any time stock of the acquirer is used as a currency in a takeover, the value of the transaction obviously can change throughout the day based on the stock movement of the acquirer. But for our purposes, on the day the takeover is announced, we should stay with our initial valuation (based on the closing price of the acquirer a day earlier) until the markets close.

Then we should redo the math based on that day's closing value of the acquirer's stock
— and make it clear to readers in the AMer why the total has changed from what they
have been reading throughout the day.

What needs to be in the APNewsNow

Lead with the **full name of the buyer** and include a descriptive size and scope, **explain
the terms** and **value of the deal** as simply as possible (all cash? cash and stock? all stock?)
while adding the name of the company to be acquired, and **provide a reason why** the deal
is happening — or, if the release is mum on that point, a description of what the combined company will look like or the capabilities it will have (making it the world's biggest
maker of fish tacos).

If there are **job cuts** or other major corporate developments, including a warning that
future earnings will be lower because of **earnings dilution**, aim to get those in the fast file.
Dilution occurs when a stock-based transaction increases the number of shares of the
acquirer without a near-term corresponding increase in earnings per share.

Specify where the two companies are **headquartered**. Also include **stock price history**
and **premarket trading**, if it is available, for both the acquirer and the acquiree. And if it
is easily obtainable, specify what the **premium** that the acquiring company is offering and
whether it is a **hostile bid**.

As the urgent series continues, include any pertinent details about potential antitrust
issues, contingencies like the need for board approval, government approval, shareholder
approval, court approval, break-up fees, **due diligence** (the review by the acquirer of
a target company's internal books and operations), and **nondisclosure/confidentiality
agreements**.

Also specify the **stage of the transaction** — letter of intent, definitive agreement, closing, etc. And if not added already, provide details about how the acquirer will finance the
takeover, what the seller's plans are for the proceeds it will be receiving, the projected effect on future sales/earnings, other details on how the companies will change as a result
of the deal (layoffs, management changes, etc.), and when the deal is expected to close.

Add historical perspective. A news story showed a good example: In early 2003, Over-
ture bought Altavista from CMGI for $140 million in cash and stock. That didn't look like
much of a deal until they added the needed perspective that CMGI bought Altavista from
Compaq only four years earlier for $2.3 billion.

What is the stock reaction telling us?

If Company A offers $50 in cash for Company B and the share price of Company B
rises to $55 or $60, that's a pretty strong indication that arbitrageurs are betting at least
one **competing bid** will emerge. Alternatively, if Company B's shares trade way below $50,
we need to find out why investors are skittish about the deal closing.

It also should be standard practice to keep track of the stock prices of both the acquirer and the target in the days and weeks after the initial announcement. Depending
on how they perform, you may want to write additional stories about whether investors
are betting the deal is on track or in trouble. And when stock is used as part or all of the
currency for a proposed takeover, it's a good idea to build the formula into a spreadsheet
and track it daily to see whether the spread between the market price is narrowing or
widening from the offer's valuation.

Arbs make and lose millions on these bets, so be careful when you interview them
about these deals — and make sure to explain what they have at stake if we quote them
either speaking in support of or objecting to the transaction.

Assessing the deal's chances for success

Besides the market implications about whether a deal will close or not, we should also from the first day be sharpening our analysis about whether the proposal makes business sense. There are several ways to approach this. Are the promised cost cuts doable, and what will they cause in human terms (jobs lost) and the effects on local economies? Will it deliver the higher profits the acquirer is promising? Will it position the acquirer's stock for future market gains? We should be asking these questions as part of our first-day coverage and come back as often as needed for deals both pending and completed.

BROADCAST GUIDELINES

"Barack Obama has been elected president of the United States."
"Osama bin Laden is dead."
"The Dow Jones industrial average has reached 13,000."

These sentences illustrate AP's broadcast news writing style. They are easily understood, but intelligent; conversational, but not stiff. Many broadcast stories can be effectively told using such straightforward writing and this simple structure:

Lead —> Backup —> Details —> Background

For example:

A huge wildfire in eastern Arizona is expected to spread to New Mexico. Both wind and dry lightning are forecast over the next two days.
Arizona fire officials say more than 1,000 firefighters are working the blaze. There have been no serious injuries, but hundreds of people have been evacuated, and 11 buildings have been destroyed.
The fire has burned more than 350 square miles. It's the third-largest wildfire in Arizona's history.

Lead. The first sentence in this story reports the essential facts that are the news:
A huge wildfire [*the subject of the story*] in eastern Arizona [*location*] is expected to spread to New Mexico [*the story's latest development*].
Backup. The second sentence "backs up" the lead:
Both wind and dry lightning are forecast over the next two days [*answers the implied question "Why is the fire expected to spread?*].
Details. These next sentences report additional important facts — mainly, the extent to which people are injured or at risk.
Arizona fire officials [*the story's sources*] say more than 1,000 firefighters are working the blaze [*these lives are potentially at risk*]. There have been no serious injuries, but hundreds of people have been evacuated [*impact of the fire on people*], and 11 buildings have been destroyed [*impact on property*].
Background. The story ends by putting the fire into current and historical perspective:
The fire has burned more than 350 square miles. It's the third-largest wildfire in Arizona's history.

The fire story follows principles used by AP's broadcast writers:

1. Lead with the news. The story first reports its latest newsworthy development. If the latest development had been evacuations, the lead would have been: "Hundreds of people are being evacuated because of a huge wildfire in eastern Arizona."
2. In leads, use forms of the present or future verb tenses. "The fire is expected to spread," not "The fire was expected to spread today." But don't write in

the simple present tense "headline" style: "Twelve buildings are destroyed in a wildfire." Present perfect tense sounds more natural: "A wildfire has destroyed 12 buildings."

3. Keep leads short and to the point. It's easy for listeners and viewers to miss details. Use the lead to introduce a story, and save details for subsequent sentences.

4. Favor the active voice. "Firefighters are working the blaze," not "the blaze is being worked by firefighters."

5. Attribute at the beginning of sentences. "Fire officials say...," not "...said fire officials."

6. Identify newsmakers before naming them. Write: "Fire information officer Ed Toby," not "Ed Toby, the fire information officer, says..." (Unless a name is essential to the story, it can generally be left out.)

7. Omit needless words. "It's the third largest fire in Arizona's history," not "This particular blaze is the third-largest in the history of the state of Arizona."

8. Prefer the simple to the complex. "Fire" or "blaze" but not "conflagration."

9. Don't strain for synonyms. "Arizona," not "the state." Someone who hears "...in the state's history" might not have heard the rest of the story.

10. Use direct quotes only when a paraphrase doesn't work better. In most cases, it does. "There have been no serious injuries," not, "Toby says, 'Two people reported bruises and five others pulled muscles carrying heavy suitcases while being evacuated, but otherwise no one was hurt.'"

11. Simplify numbers. "More than 350 square miles," not "352.67 square miles."

12. Use a variety of sentence lengths, but keep most of them short. The sentences in the fire story are 8, 9, 12, 13, 13 and 19 words long – and that's counting every word, including "a."

A radio story on the fire could include recorded sound of a newsmaker talking:

(*Reporter*) A huge wildfire in eastern Arizona is expected to spread to New Mexico. Both wind and dry lightning are forecast over the next two days.
Arizona fire officials say more than 1,000 firefighters are working the blaze. Fire information officer Ed Toby says still more may be needed:

(*Newsmaker*) *"We already have firefighters from New York, Colorado and Texas helping us. We might bring some more in from California."*

(*Reporter*) There have been no serious injuries, but hundreds of people have been evacuated, and 11 buildings have been destroyed.
The fire has burned more than 350 square miles. It's the third-largest wildfire in Arizona's history.

Always identify newsmakers before their voices are heard. Give a general sense of the subject of the upcoming sound bite, but don't "parrot." Write: "Toby says still more may be needed," not "Toby says firefighters from New York, Colorado and Texas are already helping."

A television story might incorporate not only sound and video, but also locator maps and graphics:

(*Reporter reading over animated map showing fire's location*) A huge wildfire in eastern Arizona is expected to spread to New Mexico. (*Over video of fire*) Both wind and dry lightning are forecast over the next two days.

(*Over video of firefighters working*) Arizona fire officials say more than 1,000 firefighters are working the blaze. Still more may be needed:

(*On-screen identification, seen over shot of newsmaker talking*)
Ed Toby
Fire Information Officer

"*We already have firefighters from New York, Colorado and Texas helping us. We might bring some more in from California.*"

(*Reporter reading over shots of people evacuating; then shots of destroyed buildings*) There have been no serious injuries, but hundreds of people have been evacuated, and 11 buildings have been destroyed.

(*Reporter on-camera, with fire burning in distance*) The fire has burned more than 350 square miles. It's the third-largest wildfire in Arizona's history.

A grasp of these basic concepts will help you go on to create more complicated stories, whether for wires, radio, TV or new media.

actuality In radio, the sound of a newsmaker talking. Generally, an actuality should be 10 to 20 seconds long. Don't use an actuality just to have newsmaker sound in a story. Use an actuality only if it makes sense, can be clearly understood and contributes something of substance to the story, such as the newsmaker's point of view or the unique way the newsmaker said something. If you, as a reporter or an anchor, can say something more effectively than the newsmaker, write the story without actuality.

b-roll In a video story, the supporting shots, scenes and interviews used to provide context and continuity for the main story. B-roll can be file or stock tape containing background or historical information. It is sometimes provided by sources outside the news organization, as when newsmakers provide personal videos.

cut In radio, a piece of audio, whether the sound of a newsmaker talking, a reporter's narrative or natural sound.

fade In radio, a gradual increase (fade-up) or decrease (fade-down) in sound. In video, a gradual increase (fade-in) or decrease (fade-out) in the appearance of video and, usually, in the volume of accompanying sound.

fast file Video segment with in and out points, but no additional edited-in content.

first person In a video piece, a newsmaker's description of a news event or subject matter, presented as one long sound bite.

incue, inq, in-point The first two or three seconds of sound signaling the start of a segment of audio or video. An incue can consist of any manmade or natural sound, including words, music or ambient noise.

live shot Broadcast report delivered in real time from the scene of a news event or a studio or newsroom.

lockout Words used by a reporter to end a radio story. A common format is name and location: *Sagar Meghani, Washington.* See **sigout**.

LSR Live Special Report. Short or long-form live program covering breaking news or a special event. Reports may be anchored from a studio or an outside location.

MOS Man on the street. Sound of randomly chosen people, traditionally walking on a city sidewalk, commenting on a news event. Also known as *vox pops*, shortened form of *vox populi* or *voice of the people*.

natural sound or **NATS** Nonverbal sound of a news event. Natural sound can include ambient sound, such as trucks rumbling or background cheers. It can also be the dominant sound of a news event, such as a band playing or a chainsaw cutting up debris from a storm. For AP Radio, a piece of natural sound should run 30 to 40 seconds, with fades at the beginning and end. Generally, the fade-up is fast (about four seconds) and the fade-down is slow (about eight seconds). If you're writing natural sound into a story for AP, begin with sound up and let it play long enough for the audience to recognize it, then fade down low enough to talk over it.

nonlinear editing Digital audio and video systems that allow editors to easily locate and pull sound bites and video sequences from master recordings while leaving the masters intact.

outcue, outq, out-point The final two or three seconds of sound signaling the end of a segment of audio or video. An outcue can consist of any manmade or natural sound, including words, music and/or ambient noise.

package For video, an umbrella term for fully edited stories with sound, fonts and possibly on-camera appearances by reporters. For audio, an umbrella term for fully edited stories with a reporter's voice and possibly newsmaker actuality. An audio package often includes a wrap or voicer and several individual sound bites. See **wrap** and **voicer**.

Q-and-A In radio, a sound bite of a correspondent taken from a question-and-answer session with another colleague. Q-and-A cuts run from 10 to 20 seconds and provide the reporter with a format in which a brief aspect of the story is reported. The rules of balance, objectivity and attribution all apply. A reporter should never express views or draw conclusions. There is no lockout. Reporters and their locations are identified in the anchors' lead-ins. In AP's online video products, Q-and-A pieces show a reporter or newsmaker answering questions posed in writing displayed on a graphic.

raw edit or **rough cut** Video and sound loosely edited together without voice track, reporter presence or font. This allows broadcast customers to have their own newspeople narrate a video package and gives them editing flexibility.

rough cut See **raw edit**.

scener In radio, a report from the actual scene of an event, with the sound of the event in the background. Whether live or taped, a scener must be done while the sounds in the background actually are taking place. The idea is to use words and background sound to create a picture of what's happening in the listener's mind. If you play back tape of an event behind your voice in a studio, that is not a scener – it's a voicer. AP Radio sceners run 35 seconds maximum.

sigout Words used to end a video story. A common format is name and location: *Haven Daley, San Francisco*. See **lockout**.

sound bite Snippet of sound of someone talking.

standup A portion of a video story in which a reporter faces the camera and addresses the audience directly. When a standup appears at the end of a story, it contains a sigout. When a standup appears between two pieces of video in the same story, it is referred to as a bridge. A hand-held standup is when a reporter holds a camera at arm's length and focuses on his or her own face. This allows the reporter to react to and narrate from the scene of a breaking news story.

UGC User-generated content. Information in the form of text, photos, video or audio supplied by users of a product which then becomes part of that product. Websites and, increasingly, TV news broadcasts, often contain UGC.

voice-over or **VO** Sound of a reporter's voice narrating a story as videotape plays. In radio, reporters may also speak over a music or natural sound track.

voice track or **track** Narration of an audio or video piece. In video, it may occur along with a voice-over or standup.

voicer Self contained radio correspondent report. All the listener hears from beginning to end is the sound of a reporter talking. AP Radio voicers run no more than 35 seconds and end in a lockout: *Sandy Kozel, Washington*. Many voicers are done in-studio. Compare to scener, which has no lockout and must be created at the scene of a news event, with natural sound in the background. See **scener**.

vox pops See **MOS**.

wall-to-wall coverage Continuous broadcast reporting, with few or no interruptions, of a single news story. Generally reserved for transcendent stories, such as the 9/11 terrorist attacks, the outbreak of war or the results of a U.S. presidential election.

wrap A radio voice report that includes both the correspondent and a newsmaker actuality. AP Radio wrap runs no more than 40 seconds and ends in a lockout: *Jerry Bodlander, Capitol Hill*. The newsmaker actuality generally should be no shorter than 10 seconds and no longer than 15 seconds.

PHOTO CAPTIONS

Nearly all AP captions follow a simple formula:

* The first sentence of the caption should follow this structure: the first clause should describe who is in the photograph and what is going on within the photo in the present tense followed by the city and state where the image was made, following AP style for the city and state as appropriate. Captions must give attribution for action not seen (e.g., the scene of accident where more than 10 died, according to police). The last portion of the first sentence should be the date, including the day of the week if the photograph was made within the past two weeks, and preceded by a comma. (e.g., Tuesday, Jan. 29, 2008). These three elements are MANDATORY and no caption is complete without all of them. Names should always be listed in order, left to right, unless it is impossible for the caption to read normally otherwise. With multiple people identified within the caption, enough representations to placement are necessary so there is no confusion as to each subject's identity.

* The second sentence of the caption is used to give context to the news event or describes why the photo is significant. While a second sentence can be illuminating, it also has the potential to create problems and is often where errors can be found. A photo caption's second sentence should be carefully crafted to include information from the text wire story when appropriate or additional relevant observations from the photographer on scene. There may be some instances when a second sentence is not needed. Many sports photos taken during a game or match, for example, do not require a second sentence; nor do photos from some ongoing news events. Most daily pictures of the president do not need a second sentence either.

* Whenever possible, try to keep captions to no more than two concise sentences, while including the relevant information. Try to anticipate what information the reader will need.

THIS IS AN EXAMPLE OF THE STANDARD AP CAPTION:

Democratic presidential hopeful U.S. Sen. Barack Obama, D-Ill., delivers his policy on Iraq speech, Wednesday, Sept. 12, 2007, in Clinton, Iowa. Obama called for the immediate withdrawal of all U.S. combat brigades from Iraq, with the pullout being completed by the end of next year. (AP Photo/Charlie Neibergall)

FOR HANDOUT PHOTOS (provided or released by governments, armies, companies or other official sources):

In this image released by the Milk Processor Education Program, actress Glenn Close is shown in the latest ad for the National Milk Mustache got milk? Campaign. (AP Photo/Milk Processor Education Program)

The caption should begin with *In this photo released by*, followed by the name of the providing body.

The name of the releasing body is then repeated in the photo credit: The name of the releasing person or organization should be translated according to AP style, where applicable.

ALL handout images from ANY source MUST, as a final step, be examined carefully in Photoshop by at least two editors on the handling regional photo desk. If there is any doubt about the integrity of a handout image, it should not be transmitted.

DO NOT use DESCRIPTIVE OVERLINES such as:

1. SAFE AT SECOND-For a baseball play at second base, or PRESIDENT AD-DRESSES WOMEN-For a presidential speech to a women's group. Regular captions have NO overlines.

INSTRUCTIVE OVERLINES will be used in the following cases:

1. For FILE PHOTOS the word FILE will be the OVERLINE.

Example: FILE — Johnny Depp is shown in London, in this Jan. 10, 2008, file photo. Depp won the Golden Globe for Best Actor in a Musical or Comedy for his role in "Sweeney Todd: The Demon Barber of Fleet Street", announced, Sunday, Jan. 13, 2008, in Los Angeles. (AP Photo/ Alastair Grant, File)

2. For ADVANCES the OVERLINE is the word ADVANCE and the RE-LEASE DATE. Do not use story slugs or writer's name in the OVERLINE.

Example: ADVANCE FOR WEEKEND MAY 15-16 - Sean Smith, a fish culturist at Vermont's new fish hatchery in Grand Isle, Vt., one of the Lake Champlain islands, moves young rainbow trout on May 4, 1993, to a new tank. (AP Photo/ Toby Talbot)

3. For EMBARGOED photos the OVERLINE should be the word EMBAR-GOED with the RELEASE TIME and DATE. Also, add HFR (Hold for Release) in the SUPPLEMENTAL CATEGORY field of the NAA/IPTC header for embargoed photos for same day release.

Example: EMBARGOED UNTIL 1 P.M. EST, SUNDAY, DEC. 10, 2006 -This undated handout photo provided by the Census of Marine Life shows a Kiwahirsuta, the Yeti crab, a new species found near Easter Island. (AP Photo/Ifremer, A. Fifis)

If the date when the photo was made is unknown, state "date of photo unknown" in the body of the caption and in the INSTRUCTIONS field of the NAA/IPTC header.

The SIGNOFF for an AP staffer or stringer is, in parentheses, AP Photo followed by a slash and the name of the photographer. Don't use str or stf. Example: (AP Photo/Rick Bowmer). If the name of the photographer is not known or needs to be withheld, the signoff is: (AP Photo).

MEMBER PHOTO SIGNOFF: (AP Photo/USA Today, Anne Ryan).

HANDOUT PHOTO SIGNOFF: (AP Photo/General Motors). If photographer is known: (AP Photo/General Motors, John Smith).

POOL PHOTO SIGNOFF: (AP Photo/Bill Waugh, Pool). For pool photos, do not name the newspaper or agency that shot for the pool in the caption signoff. However, put the name of the organization that shot the pool in the Source field, after the word POOL, for example, POOL AP. The BYLINE TITLE field of the NAA/IPTC header should contain the word POOL. The Instructions field should also say POOL PHOTO.

FILE PHOTO SIGNOFF: (AP Photo/Lenny Ignelzi, File). If the name of the photographer who shot the file photo is not known the signoff should be: (AP Photo/File)

TV FRAMEGRAB PHOTO SIGNOFF: (AP Photo/CNN)

HANDOUT PHOTOS: The use of handout photos requires the release of the copyright holder when known. The AP has created three categories of Handout photos with corresponding abbreviations:

The three byline titles are:
HOPD – Public Domain **HOEP** – Editorial Publicity **HONS** – Hand Out, One Time Use

HOPD
Public domain handouts take in photos from NASA, the White House, Department of Defense, NOAA, etc. When it is determined that a photo being edited fits this category, then it should be given the HOPD byline title in the appropriate metadata field, and corresponding HOPD language added to the special instructions field. The language for HOPD will read as follows:
AP provides access to this publicly distributed handout photo provided by [source goes here].

HOEP
Editorial publicity photos are of a promotional type given to the AP by companies often to accompany stories about new products in industries like the airlines, automotive and entertainment. The language for the HOEP group will read as follows:
AP provides access to this publicly distributed handout photo provided by [source goes here] for editorial purposes only.

HONS
Hand Out, one-time use photos are the photos images obtained for approved, story specific use only - often family handouts. The language for the HONS group will read as follows:
AP provides access to this handout photo to be used solely to illustrate news reporting or commentary on the facts or events depicted in this image.

CAPTION CORRECTIONS, ADDITIONS, ELIMINATIONS

An AP captions **CORRECTION** is moved when a simple and nonlibelous error occurs in a caption. Examples would be a misspelled name or wrong hometown, sports score or date. The procedure AP uses to file a caption correction is to point out the information that is being corrected in an overline at the start of the caption and to write a corrected caption in publishable form following. The word **CORRECTION** is added to the **OBJECT NAME** field in the NAA/IPTC header. The same procedure is followed for an AP caption **ADDITION**.

An AP caption **ADDITION** is moved when the original caption is incomplete but otherwise accurate. An AP caption **ADDITION** may add the name of someone in the photo or other important background information.

An AP caption **ELIMINATION** is issued when there are questions about a photo's copyright ownership, issues with a photo's integrity or authenticity, or when a photo's caption misrepresents the photo in some way. When this occurs, an AP caption **ELIMINATION** form is moved alerting members and subscribers, illustrating the image with a circle and line through the image.

TEXT WIRE FORMATS

PHOTO ADVISORIES — For routine notifications to members on major stories.

Slug: BC-PHOTO ADVISORY-School Siege
EDITORS:
Photos on the Arizona school siege will move within 30 minutes.
The AP

CAPTION CORRECTIONS — For significant corrections that should be pointed out on text wires, e.g., misidentification or other serious error.

Slug: BC-CAPTION CORRECTION-Blind Cyclist
EDITORS:
A correction, NY107, has moved on photo services to AP Photo BUF108 of Oct. 24, 2000, Blind Cyclist, from Buffalo, N.Y. The cyclist had been riding for 5 miles, not 50 miles.
The AP

PHOTO ELIMINATIONS — For major factual errors, poor taste or other circumstance that would require removing a photo from the report and archives.

Slug: BC-PHOTO ELIMINATION-Blind Cyclist
EDITORS:
AP Photo BUF108 of Oct. 24, 2000, Blind Cyclist, from Buffalo, N.Y., has been eliminated. The bicycle rider is not blind. Ensure that the photo is eliminated from your archives and is not published. The photo will not be retransmitted.
The AP

CAPTION ELIMINATIONS — For captions on otherwise acceptable photos that misrepresent the photo or present problems with bad taste or sensitivity.
Slug: BC-CAPTION ELIMINATION-CEO Resigns
EDITORS:
The caption on AP Photo BUF112, CEO Resigns, from Buffalo, N.Y., has been eliminated. Smith did not resign during his speech. The photo will be re-transmitted with a corrected caption.
The AP

PHOTO KILLS — For photos that present potential legal problems.
Slug: BC-PHOTO KILL-School Standoff
EDITORS:
AP Photo GLE122 of Oct. 24, 2000, School Standoff, from Glendale, Ariz., has been killed. The person in the photo is not under arrest. A kill is mandatory. Make certain the photo is not published. The photo will not be retransmitted. (Or: The photo will be retransmitted with a corrected caption.)
The AP

PHOTO CORRECTIVES — These are publishable stories designed to aid members that might have published a photo that was killed. In addition to the Corrective itself, we need to move an advisory. Use both formats below, as separate items.
Slug: BC-School Standoff, PHOTO CORRECTIVE
EDITORS:
Members who used AP Photo GLE122 of Oct. 24, 2000, School Standoff, from Glendale, Ariz., showing police and a handcuffed man outside a school, are asked to use the following story.]
GLENDALE, Ariz. (AP) _ The Associated Press reported erroneously in a photo caption Oct. 24 that John Doe, shown in the accompanying photograph, had been arrested. Doe had not been arrested.

Slug: BC-PHOTO CORRECTIVE-School Standoff, Advisory
EDITORS:
Please note a0444, BC-School Standoff, PHOTO CORRECTIVE, which corrects an error in the caption on AP Photo GLE122 of Oct. 24, 2000, School Standoff, from Glendale, Ariz.
The AP

PHOTO WITHHOLDS — Used to temporarily remove a photo that may or may not be incorrect, but which we are in the process of checking.
Slug: BC-PHOTO WITHHOLD-Iraq
EDITORS: Withhold AP Photo BAG123, transmitted Tuesday. The photo shows a U.S. Army soldier comforting a dying child wounded Monday in a car bomb blast in Mosul, Iraq. The U.S. Army, which initially said the photo was taken by the Army, has since said it was taken by an embedded photographer. The military asks that the picture not be used further in print or online until the photographer can be contacted to determine the availability of the photo.
The AP

NAA/IPTC HEADER FIELDS

Byline: The Byline field lists the name of the person who made the photo.

Byline Title: The Byline Title field lists the title of the person who made the photo, or in the case of HO, indicates the photo is a handout from a third party. This typically comes from a controlled list, with acceptable values of STF, STR, FRE, HO, CTR, MBR, MBO, POOL and SUB.

Caption: The Caption field is the text that accompanies the photo, containing the information of who, what, where, when and if necessary, why to assist in describing the photograph.

Caption Writer: The Caption Writer field lists the initials of all the people who wrote or edited the caption, header fields or image file. This includes toning and pixel editing.

Category: The Category field lists codes that aid in a more detailed search. (See category definitions in this section.)

City: The City field lists where the photo was originally made. For file photos, do not use the transmission point's city.

Country: The Country field lists the ISO Alpha-3 code where the photo was originally made. For file photos, do not put the transmission point's country.

Create Date Time: The Create Date Time field is the date the photo was originally made. For file photos, use the date the photo was originally made, if known. Vague dates (using zeros where exact dates are unknown) can be used in this field.

Credit: The Credit field is the name of the service transmitting the photo.

Headline: The Headline field primarily contains the names of those represented within the image delimited by a comma. The use of the Headline field for people's names is slated for future change.

Instructions: The Instructions field lists special notations that apply uniquely to a photo, such as if the photo is from files, a correction or, advance. This field may also contain restrictions on the use or outs.

Object Name: The Object Name field lists the story slug associated with a photo. For photos without a story, Associated Press photographers or photo editors will make up a logical slug to aid in a search. If a related story moves on DataStream, the photo should be retransmitted with the appropriate OBJECT NAME to match the story. This field should not contain punctuation marks, such as apostrophes, ampersands, currency symbols, asterisks, and most others. Exceptions to this are the underscore (_) and the hyphen (-).

Source: The Source field lists who is the original provider of a photo, typically the owner of the image. Such as: AP, an AP member, pool photo provider or handout photo provider.

State: The State field lists the state where the photo was originally made. Use U.S. postal code abbreviations. For file photos, do not use the transmission point's state.

Supp Categories: The Supplemental Categories field lists codes that aid in a more detailed search for a photo. (See supplemental categories definitions in this section.)

Trans Reference: The Trans Reference field lists a call letter/number combination associated with a photo. It may include an originating transmit point's call letters and picture number from that point's sequence of offerings for a given day. Example: NY105. Most likely it will contain the postal state code from where the image was transmitted, combined with two character initials of the person transmitting the image. This should NOT include an extension for the file type, such as .JPG.

SUPPLEMENTAL CATEGORIES

GENERAL:

ADV   Advance
APN   APNewsfeatures
ENT   Entertainment, celebrities (don't use the word people)
FEA   Feature pictures of a non-news nature
FILE   File photo
HFR   Hold for Release (embargoed photos for same day release)
MAP   Map or graphic
NAT   National Geographic package
OBIT   Obituary
PM   Internal filing code used to batch-move photos at beginning of daily cycle.
SPF   Special Features package
SPCL   Special
WEA   Weather

NEWS EVENTS:

CVN   National political conventions
ELN   For election cycles only
XGR   State legislatures

SPORTS: (See full list in Sports Guidelines.)

ATH   Athletics (Track & Field)
BAD   Badminton
BBA   Professional Baseball (American League)
BBC   College Baseball Men
BBH   High School Baseball
BBI   International Baseball
BBM   Minor League Baseball
BBN   Professional Baseball (National League)
BBO   Professional Baseball (Other)
BBW   Baseball Women
BBY   Youth Baseball (Little League)
BIA   Biathalon
BKC   College Basketball Men
BKH   High School Basketball
BKL   Basketball-Women's Pro (WNBA)
BKN   NBA Basketball
BKO   Basketball (Other)
BKW   Basketball-Women's College
BOB   Bobsleding
BOX   Boxing
CAR   Auto Racing
CER   Olympic Ceremony

CRI	Cricket
CYC	Bicycle Racing
DIV	Diving
EQU	Equestrian
FBC	College football
FBH	High School Football
FBN	NFL Football
FBO	Football (other)
FIG	Figure Skating
GLF	Golf
GYM	Gymnastics
HKC	College Hockey
HKN	NHL Hockey
HKO	Hockey (Other)
JUD	Judo
JUM	Ski Jumping
LUG	Luge
OLY	Olympics
RAC	Racing (animals)
RUG	Rugby
SHO	Skeet Shooting
SKI	Alpine skiing
SOC	Soccer
SOF	Softball
SPE	Speed Skating
SWM	Swimming
SYN	Synchronized Swimming
TEN	Tennis
TTN	Table Tennis
VBB	Beach Volleyball
VBL	Volleyball
WRE	Wrestling
WTL	Weightlifting
WTP	Water Polo
YAT	Yachting

AP Caption and NAA/IPTC Header
Quick Reference Guide

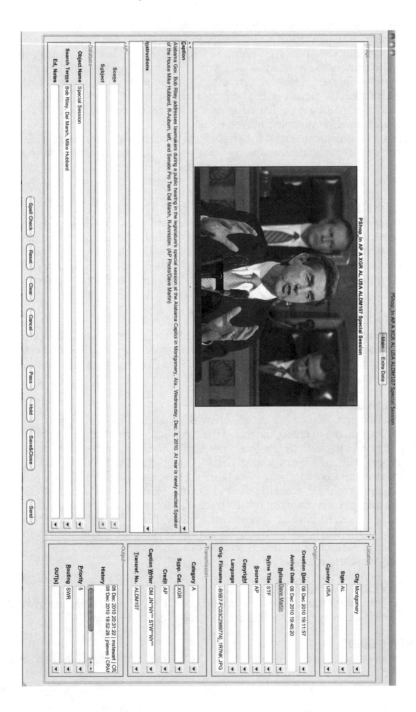

INTERACTIVES/GRAPHICS

Graphics and interactive projects are produced for breaking news and enterprise across all platforms, addressing complex issues with multilayered news stories that combine photos, graphics, video, illustration, animation, text and audio. The content is designed to align with the myriad ways people are consuming news online. Interactives are often continuously updated with fresh content through the news cycle. The interactives are presented in Flash and HTML. The graphics are published as Adobe Illustrator or PDF files. JPEGs of all graphics are also available for Web use.

As a visual enhancement of the traditional news experience, interactive stories provide insight on topics ranging from politics to natural disasters, sports to fashion, allowing users to sort through databases or media that might contain maps, charts, audio galleries or panoramas.

GRAPHICS

Infographics are produced for newspapers, websites and mobile devices. They are created in whole number sizes such as 1 column (112 pt) x 3 inches. The most common AP graphics are charts, maps and tables.

Weather maps and market graphics are published daily. All fonts are Arial to conform to Web standards. Graphics are transmitted and appear online as JPEGs.

GRAPHICSBANK

The GraphicsBank service produces static graphics, images and animation for broadcast customers. A database of more than 90,000 graphics are available, including information graphics, maps, logos, flags, headshots of leaders, celebrities and sports figures.

MOTION GRAPHICS

Animated graphics are produced for video, known as motion graphics, which layer various media to create narrative threads that provide depth, background or put the news in context. Designers construct highly advanced 2-D and 3-D animations, utilizing illustration, animation, photos and video to distill large concepts into an easy-to-digest visual form. These explainers might show what was happening to the reactors at the Fukushima plant in Japan after the devastating earthquake and tsunami or illustrate a process like reversing the flow of the Chicago river. In a breaking news situation, video explainers often focus on one angle of the story. In the case of a natural disaster, these animated graphics can explain how an earthquake, hurricane or tornado occurs, and incorporate historical facts and statistics.

DELIVERY INFORMATION

Interactives are transmitted via embed code. Graphics for print use are published to AP Exchange and AP Images as Adobe Illustrator and PDF files.

STYLE GUIDE

In many cases, style is amended to fit the format, and exceptions are often made for visual style over text style.

COLOR MODELS

RGB (Red/Green/Blue) is the color model for all devices generated by light sources — computers, televisions, digital cameras, mobile/tablet devices, etc. The wide range of colors are generated with varying degrees of the combinations of Red, Green and Blue. Black is generated when Red, Green and Blue have zero value; White is created when the three base colors have the maximum value.

HEX (Hexadecimal, aka Web Safe RGB) is the primary RGB naming convention used in code and the interactive color palette. The values are 0-1-2-3-4-5-6-7-8-9-A-B-C-D-E-F. The first two digits indicate the color for Red, the second two for Green and the third two for Blue. 000000 equals black, FFFFFF equals white.

CMYK (Cyan/Magenta/Yellow/Black) is the color model for ink-printed products. It has fewer color options than RGB. Because newsprint is so thin, it is best to use the fewest number of inks when possible. Too much ink can cause bleeding and blurriness.

NUMBERS

NUMERICAL ALIGNMENT: Numbers in vertical columns should be aligned on the decimal. Columns where all numbers have no decimals may be center-aligned. Avoid aligning numbers flush-left.

MULTIPLE DECIMAL PLACES:
• Numbers compared with one another should have the same number of decimal places.
• Do not add additional decimal points to rounded numbers. 3 million does not necessarily equal 3.0 million, as it could be anything from 2.51 million to 3.49 million.
• Rounding to one decimal place is preferred when the data has numerous decimal places: 1.2345 –> 1.2.
• Two decimal places may be used to help differentiate the numbers: 1.25 vs. 1.34.
• Three decimal places should only be used in statistics where it is the norm: i.e. a baseball batting average of .340.
• Zero has no decimal places; it should be always be listed as "0" (not "0.00").
• Numbers that round to zero should be clarified: 0.0004 does not equal zero. It should be noted as "Less than 0.1" or <0.01, where the number of decimal places listed matches the other numbers in the visualization.
• The numeral "0" should always appear before the decimal in numbers less than zero: 0.55 (not .55)

PUNCTUATION

Special characters are used for punctuation in interactives and graphics. Common symbols and how to type them using a Mac keyboard:
- Hyphen ("-" or minus sign)
– En-dash (option-hyphen)
— Em-dash (option-shift-hyphen)
_ Underscore (shift-hyphen)

• Bullet (option-8)
... Ellipsis (option-semicolon or three periods)
* Asterisk (shift-8)
Quotation marks and apostrophes
" Open quote (option-[)
" Close quote (option-shift-[)
' Apostrophe facing right (option-])
' Apostrophe facing left (option-shift-])
Lists should be used to help readers decipher blocks of text. The punctuation that appears before list items should be a clear visual guide.

HYPHEN (-) Don't use a hyphen to begin a list. It is too small and should only be used to combine words. (Examples: small-business owner, well-known person, Italian-American).

UNDERSCORE (_), EN-DASH (–) and EM-DASH (—) Underscores are sometimes seen in AP copy when dashes should be used instead. Always replace those underscores with an en-dash. Spaces are needed both before and/or after the en-dash.

BULLETS (•) When creating lists in interactives, begin with a bullet. This is an exception to text style requiring that lists begin with dashes.

ASTERISKS Used when the explanation can be abbreviated or it applies to specific elements. The asterisk appears to the right of the noted content with no space. The explanation appears as a footnote at the bottom or in the bottom right or left of the interactive/graphic with the asterisk at the beginning, followed by a space before the content. For multiple categories, up to three asterisks may be used:
Word or phrase referenced*
* Category one
** Category two
*** Category three
Quotation marks (" ") and apostrophes (' ')

SMART QUOTES (CURLY QUOTES) are preferred in content displayed to the viewer.

STRAIGHT QUOTES should be used to abbreviate feet (single) and inches (double): Five feet, five inches = 5'5"

STATE NAMES
• In maps, spell out if space permits. Otherwise, AP Stylebook abbreviations are preferred, or, when space is restricted in graphical content, postal abbreviations may be used.
• Use postal abbreviations for tabular content.

TEXT
Interactives and graphics are visual formats that include text to help the viewer navigate the visual story. Language should be edited down to be as short and concise as possible. Complete sentences are not always required.

HEADLINES

Headlines and subheadings are active narrative summaries that express the news to readers and consumers, published within editorial content.

• Lengthwise, they should aim to be as brief as possible.

• Avoid labels, category headers and duplicating the headline of other AP formats such as text and video.

SUBHEADS

• Subheads in the body of the graphic or interactive should be descriptions of the underlying content.

• Use Sentence case (capitalize first letter) and single quotation marks.

WIDOWS

Words that dangle after text blocks are called "widows." Edit text or modify the spacing as needed to eliminate them.

FOOTNOTES begin with "NOTE:" (all caps followed by a colon) followed by a statement in sentence case that may be a phrase with no period or a complete sentence. Keep footnotes as short as possible.

TIME

DAYS OF THE WEEK:

• In graphics, all-caps is preferred in charts and category headers: SUN, MON, etc.

• For narrow charts, such as for mobile devices, use S, M, T, W, T, F, S (first letter, capitalized; all seven days must be listed and in sequence).

MONTHS:

• Tabular abbreviation: In graphics, all-caps is preferred in charts and category headers: JAN, FEB, etc.

• For narrow charts, such as for mobile devices, use J, F, M, A, M, J, J, A, S, O, N, D (first letter, capitalized; months must be listed in sequence, showing a minimum of six months; may continue into multiple years as long as years are also labeled)

YEARS:

• For narrow charts, such as for mobile devices: An apostrophe followed by the last two numerals: 1999 becomes '99, 2009 becomes '09. Make sure that the apostrophe is facing left, curled away from the numbers

EDITING MARKS

ATLANTA (AP)—The organization
said Thursday. It was the first
indent for paragraph

paragraph

the last attempts.
With this the president tried
no paragraph

the Jones Smith company is not
transpose

over a period of sixty or more years
use figures

there were 9 in the group.
spell it out

Ada, Oklahoma is the hometown
abbreviate

The Ga man was the guest of
don't abbreviate

prince edward said it was his
uppercase

as a result This will be
lowercase

the accuser pointed to them
remove space

In these times it is necessary
insert space

the order for the later devices
retain

The ruling a fine example
insert word

according to the this source
delete

BF By DONALD AMES
boldface, center

J.R. Thomas
flush right

J.R. Thomas
flush left

insert comma

insert apostrophe

insert quotation marks

insert period

hyphen

dash

BIBLIOGRAPHY

Following are reference books and websites used in the preparation of The Associated Press Stylebook. They are the accepted reference sources for material not covered by the Stylebook.

First reference for spelling, style, usage and foreign geographic names:
Webster's New World College Dictionary, Fourth Edition, Wiley, Hoboken, N.J.

Other references for spelling, style, usage and foreign geographic names:
The American Heritage Dictionary of the English Language, Fifth Edition, Houghton Mifflin Company, Boston (and) New York
http://www.ahdictionary.com/
Concise Oxford English Dictionary, Eleventh Edition, Oxford University Press, Oxford
Webster's Third New International Dictionary of the English Language, unabridged, Merriam-Webster, Springfield, Mass.
National Geographic Atlas of the World, 8th Edition. National Geographic Society, Washington, D.C.
http://www.nationalgeographic.com/index.html

For aircraft names:
Jane's All the World's Aircraft; Coulsdon: Jane's Information Group, Surrey, U.K.

For military ships:
Jane's Fighting Ships; Coulsdon: Jane's Information Group, Surrey, U.K.

For nonmilitary ships:
Lloyd's Register of Shipping — Lloyd's Register, London

For railroads:
Official Railway Guide – Freight Service; Commonwealth Business Media Inc., East Windsor, N.J.

For federal government questions:
Congressional Directory; U.S. Government Printing Office, Washington, D.C.
This link allows searching of the directory for the 104th Congress (1995-1996) through the 112th Congress (2011-2012).
http://www.gpo.gov/fdsys/browse/collection.action?collectionCode=CDIR

For foreign government questions:
Political Handbook of the World; CQ Press, Washington, D.C.

For a company's formal name:
Consult the national stock exchanges: the New York Stock Exchange, http://www.nyse.com, or Nasdaq, http://www.nasdaq.com. AP staffers may also refer to an alphabetical list of all company names, with stock ticker abbreviations, at http://biz.ap.org.

For business information:
Capital IQ, a division of Standard & Poor's.

For religion questions:
Handbook of Denominations in the United States, 12th Edition; Abingdon Press, Nashville, Tenn., and New York.

World Christian Encyclopedia; Second Edition; Oxford University Press, New York, N.Y. http://worldchristiandatabase.org

Yearbook of American and Canadian Churches; Abingdon Press, Nashville, Tennessee, and New York, for the National Council of Churches of Christ in the U.S.A., N.Y.

For medical questions:
Centers for Disease Control and Prevention: http://www.cdc.gov/

The Merck Manuals Online Medical Library: http://www.merck.com/mmpe/index.html

U.S. National Library of Medicine and the National Institutes of Health, MedlinePlus: http://www.nlm.nih.gov/medlineplus/

Other references and writing guides consulted in the preparation of the AP Stylebook:

Bernstein, Theodore M. *The Careful Writer: A Modern Guide to English Usage.* Free Press, 1965.

Bernstein, Theodore M. *More Language That Needs Watching.* Channel Press, 1962.

Bernstein, Theodore M. *Watch Your Language.* Atheneum, 1958.

Cappon, Rene J. *The Word.* The Associated Press, 1982; second edition, 1991.

Follett, Wilson (edited and completed by Jacques Barzun). *Modern American Usage.* Hill & Wang, 1966.

Fowler, H.W. *A Dictionary of Modern English Usage.* Oxford University Press, 1965.

Fowler, H.W. and R.W. Burchfield. *Fowler's Modern English Usage.* Oxford University Press, 2004.

The Chicago Manual of Style, 15th Edition. University of Chicago Press, 2003.

Morris, William and Morris, Mary. *Harper Dictionary of Contemporary Usage.* Harper & Row, 1975; second edition, 1985.

Newton, Harry, *Newton's Telecom Dictionary*, 23rd Edition. Flatiron Books, 2007.

Shaw, Harry. *Dictionary of Problem Words & Expressions.* McGraw-Hill Book Co., 1975.

Skillin, Marjorie E. and Gay, Robert M. *Words into Type.* Prentice-Hall Inc., 1974.

Strunk, William Jr. and White, E.B. *The Elements of Style*, second edition. The Macmillan Co., 1972. New edition: 4th edition. Longman 1999.

Also consulted were the stylebooks of The Boston Globe, Dow Jones News-wires, The Kansas City Star, Los Angeles Times, The Miami Herald, Milwaukee Journal Sentinel, Newsday, The New York Times, The Wall Street Journal, The Washington Post, The (Wilmington, Del.) News Journal, the National Association of Hispanic Journalists and the U.S. Government Printing Office.

AP's New Look

The Associated Press unveiled its new visual identity along with an updated logo this year. A revitalization 30 years in the making, the new design boasts a fresh take customized for today's digital era.

The identity system greatly expands the range of colors and designs available for use in AP products and services. The new logo draws on the legacy of the old one, with the familiar stencil pattern, but the logotype is now black and underscored with a bold red line.

The new branding allows us to unite all of the work we do under a single comprehensive look and feel. The new logo stands behind our commitment to being the definitive source for news. It reiterates that when you see AP news, you know that you can trust us.

The AP Stylebook also features AP's new visual identity system, which was developed to visually capture our brand promise—a guarantee of accuracy, trust, service, resourcefulness and courage on the part of our journalists and all AP staff in gathering, delivering and supporting the news. The logo itself has been updated to modern design standards so it can more easily be formatted into print, Web and mobile devices.

Order the AP Stylebook

Do you want more copies of the AP Stylebook? How about getting the newest edition?

Or maybe you want to subscribe to the AP Stylebook Online? It's a fully searchable electronic style guide that is updated throughout the year and allows you to enter your own local style notes.

You can do all of that at **http://www.apstylebook.com.**

Order Form

Quantity	Item	Info	Remove	Unit Price	Total
	choose a product	❶	✪	0.00	$0.00
	choose a product	❶	✪	0.00	$0.00
	choose a product	❶	✪	0.00	$0.00
	choose a product	❶	✪	0.00	$0.00
	choose a product	❶	✪	0.00	$0.00
	choose a product	❶	✪	0.00	$0.00
	choose a product	❶	✪	0.00	$0.00
				Subtotal	$0.00
				Tax	$0.00
				Shipping	$0.00
				Total Due	**$0.00**

On our secure website, you can place an order and pay by credit card.

You can also place your order and create a PDF invoice to mail in a check, if you prefer, to:
The Associated Press
P.O. Box 415458
Boston, MA 02241-5458

Product and rate details for the spiral-bound Stylebook, the Web-based Stylebook Online, Stylebook Mobile and AP StyleGuard are available on **http://www.apstylebook.com.**

Stylebook offers customer support

Whether you have a question about when you can get the next edition of the spiral-bound Stylebook, how to reset your Stylebook Online password or how to pay for an order by check, AP Stylebook can help.

We have answers to many of the most common questions listed on our self-service website: **http://www.apstylebook.com/help**.

You can browse by topic to find what you need or search the help center to get an answer.

If you don't find the answer to your question, we offer a toll-free number to call and a form to request help via email, so you can get a personal response however it's most convenient for you.

We value your business. We want to make it easy for you to get answers any time of day or night.

Home > Help

AP Stylebook Help and Customer Service

Find answers to your questions by selecting a topic below. You can then choose a category and find your specific question and answer.

Help Center Topics

AP Stylebook product information
Learn about the printed Stylebook, Web-based Stylebook Online and Stylebook Mobile for iPhone and BlackBerry.

Sales support
Get information about placing an order, about how to check the status of an existing order, get a copy of your invoice, view tracking info and more.

Website technical support
Get help with your AP Stylebook Online subscription, including technical requirements for use of the APStylebook.com website.

AP Stylebook editorial queries
Get information about the content of AP Stylebook.

Media requests and marketing opportunities
Contact AP with media requests and marketing opportunities.

Search the help center
Find answers to commonly asked questions.

AP Stylebook Online

The AP Stylebook Online is a fully searchable version of the AP Stylebook, complete with interactive features, links and customization options.

This Web-based reference guide includes all the content you love about the Stylebook—A-Z guide to usage, spelling and punctuation, with guides to social media, broadcast, food, fashion, sports and business – and heightens your experience with additional online-only features:

• Submit questions via "Ask the Editor" and search thousands of previously answered questions in the archive

• Look up phonetic spellings of hundreds of words and hear audio files, as well, in our Pronunciation Guide

• Get comprehensive profiles of publicly traded companies, provided by Capital IQ

Stylebook Online is updated throughout the year as AP's editors add or change style guidance. Users can get email updates whenever a change is made, and check the new entries and recent changes section online.

It's the tool that you simply cannot go without. Rates are based on the number of users and for many organizations, it can prove more affordable than hard-copy books.

Learn more at **http://www.apstylebook.com/web.**

AP StyleGuard

AP StyleGuard, powered by Equiom Linguistic Labs, is a powerful yet easy solution that integrates with Microsoft Word and provides automatic checking of your documents for AP style.

Using defined structure and rules similar to Word's spelling and grammar checking, AP StyleGuard helps ensure the consistency of your writing style. It saves you the time of manually referring to the AP Stylebook and offers recommendations on items you might not have realized are covered by AP style.

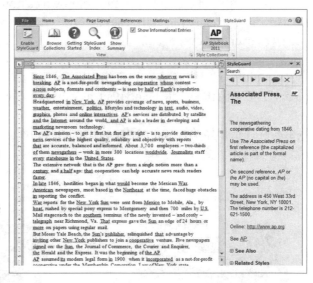

AP StyleGuard helps you stay on top of all of the current spelling, grammar, punctuation and usage guidelines from the journalist's bible.

StyleGuard includes the latest AP Stylebook guidance, with rules updated throughout the year to keep your writing covered by the newest additions and changes responding to news events and the evolution of the language.

StyleGuard operates on Windows XP and higher and on Microsoft Office 2007 and higher; no additional hardware or software is needed. Internet connection is optional. StyleGuard launched as a PC product with a Mac-compatible version following in summer 2012.

Learn more at **http://apstylebook.com/styleguard**.

AP Stylebook Mobile

With Stylebook Mobile, you never have to go anywhere without your AP style guidance. Your Stylebook can be where you are at all times.

Stylebook Mobile applications feature searchable listings for the main, sports, business, punctuation, social media, broadcast, food and fashion sections, along with the ability to add your own custom entries and notes on AP listings. You can even mark your favorite entries to easily find the ones you go to over and over again.

This definitive guide to journalistic writing is available for iPhone, also compatible with iPod Touch and iPad, as well as for BlackBerry.

Learn more at **http://www.apstylebook.com/mobile.**

AP Mobile

How important is visibility to you?

In today's digital era, news lives at the fingertips of mobile users. In the three years since it launched, AP Mobile has surged as one of the leading news applications, and the only mobile product that provides up-to-date local, national and global news from trusted sources across the country.

Completely redesigned, the latest version of AP Mobile is now available for iPad, iPhone and iPod Touch and a new layout makes navigation easier and brings more compelling AP content to your device. Also, enjoy the new customization feature that allows you to personalize your news feed by selecting categories that mean the most to you.

Let AP Mobile be your first choice for accurate global and local news every day.

Get more information and download the AP Mobile app at
http://www.getapmobile.com.

ABOUT THE AP

Since 1846, The Associated Press has been on the scene wherever news is breaking. AP is a not-for-profit newsgathering cooperative whose content – across subjects, formats and continents – is seen by half of Earth's population every day.

Headquartered in New York, AP provides coverage of news, sports, business, weather, entertainment, politics, lifestyles and technology in text, audio, video, graphics, photos and online interactives. AP's services are distributed by satellite and the Internet around the world, and AP is also a leader in developing and marketing newsroom technology.

The AP's mission – to get it first but first get it right – is to provide distinctive news services of the highest quality, reliability and objectivity with reports that are accurate, balanced and informed. About 3,700 employees – two-thirds of them newsgathers – work in more 300 locations worldwide. Journalists staff every statehouse in the United States.

The extensive network that is the AP grew from a single notion more than a century and a half ago: that cooperation can help accurate news reach readers faster.

In late 1846, hostilities began in what would become the Mexican War. American newspapers, most based in the Northeast at the time, faced huge obstacles in reporting the conflict.

War reports for the New York Sun were sent from Mexico to Mobile, Ala., by boat, rushed by special pony express to Montgomery and then 700 miles by U.S. Mail stagecoach to the southern terminus of the newly invented – and costly – telegraph near Richmond, Va. That express gave the Sun an edge of 24 hours or more on papers using regular mail.

But Moses Yale Beach, the Sun's publisher, relinquished that advantage by inviting other New York publishers to join a cooperative venture. Five newspapers signed on: the Sun, the Journal of Commerce, the Courier and Enquirer, the Herald and the Express. It was the beginning of the AP.

AP assumed its modern legal form in 1900 when it incorporated as a not-for-profit cooperative under the Membership Corporation Law of New York state. Today, the AP membership elects the board of directors, the cooperative's governing body.

AP staffers are governed by a comprehensive ethics statement, available for viewing at http://www.ap.org/company/news-values.

The Associated Press is the essential global news network, delivering fast, unbiased news globally to all media platforms and formats. AP today is the largest and most trusted source of independent news and information.

HEADQUARTERS
The Associated Press
450 West 33rd St.
New York, NY 10001
212-621-1500

Monday 10 a.m. - 10:30a.

Mond April 2 →

Monday
2:00 - 2:30 w/
Karl

---

update:

10 AM ET
(9a.m CT)

2:00 - 5:00 Et
(1:00 - 4:00 Ct)   — cut do 2:00
                               2:30

300 →

put
Wednsdy →